In recognition of their deep appreciation
for education and of their love and support,
we dedicate this book to our parents.

D1530476

INTERNATIONAL ECONOMICS
PAYMENTS, EXCHANGE RATES, AND MACRO POLICY
THIRD EDITION

DENNIS R. APPLEYARD
DAVIDSON COLLEGE

ALFRED J. FIELD, JR.
UNIVERSITY OF NORTH CAROLINA
AT CHAPEL HILL

Boston   Burr Ridge, IL   Dubuque, IA   Madison, WI   New York   San Francisco   St. Louis
Bangkok   Bogotá   Caracas   Lisbon   London   Madrid
Mexico City   Milan   New Delhi   Seoul   Sydney   Taipei   Toronto

Schroth

Irwin/McGraw-Hill

A Division of The **McGraw·Hill** *Companies*

International Economics: Payments, Exchange Rates, and Macro Policy

Copyright © 1998 by The McGraw-Hill Companies, Inc. 1995 and 1992 by Richard D. Irwin, Inc. All rights reserved. Printed in the United States of America. Except as permitted under the United States Copyright Act of 1976, no part of this publication may be reproduced or distributed in any form or by any means, or stored in a data base or retrieval system, without the prior written permission of the publisher.

This book is printed on acid-free paper.

domestic   1 2 3 4 5 6 7 8 9 0 VH VH 9 0 0 9 8 7 6

ISBN 0-07-109322-2

Editorial Director: *Mike Junior*
Publisher: *Gary Burke*
Sponsoring editor: *Paul Shensa*
Developmental editor: *Marilea Fried*
Marketing manager: *Nelson Black*
Project manager: *Robert A. Preskill*
Production supervisor: *Tanya Nigh*
Interior and cover designer: *Juan Vargas*
Cover photo: *Jim Barber/theStockRep, Inc.*
Compositor and Imaging: *Carlisle Communications, Ltd.*
Typeface: *10/12 Times Roman*
Printer: *Von Hoffman Press*

Library of Congress Cataloging-in-Publication Data

Appleyard, Dennis R.
    International economics : payments, exchange rates, and macro
policy / Dennis R. Appleyard, Alfred J. Field. — 3rd ed.
        p.   cm.
    Includes index.
    ISBN 0-07-109322-2
    1. Balance of payments.   2. Foreign exchange rates.
3. International finance.   I. Field, Alfred J.   II. Title.
HG3882.A67   1997
332′.042—dc21   97-36817
                                                                   CIP

http://www.mhhe.com

HG
3882
A67
1998

PREFACE

We have been teaching international economics since the late 1960s, mostly at the University of North Carolina at Chapel Hill, and have been very pleased with the strong student interest in the area over the years. This interest reflects the growing internationalization of economic activity and the recognition that no intelligent citizenry can focus only on its own country's economy when viewing and interpreting economic events. Especially in the United States, international economic events used to be confined to the business and financial sections of newspapers and newsmagazines, and seldom appeared in radio and television newscasts. Happily, this relative neglect has disappeared, particularly since the breakdown of the Bretton Woods system in 1971 and the occurrence of the first OPEC "oil shock" in 1973–1974. Concerned individuals, including of course college students, now can hardly avoid a passing acquaintance with such newsworthy events as the long-standing Japanese trade surpluses, the ongoing controversies associated with the implementation of the North American Free Trade Agreement and the Uruguay Round's trade liberalizing measures, monetary union in Europe, intellectual piracy by China and accompanying issues regarding U.S. most-favored-nation treatment for that country, continuing problems of exchange rate instability (such as in Mexico), and the difficulties of the transition to market economies in the countries of Central and Eastern Europe and the former republics of the Soviet Union.

Our motivation for writing this book was that we were not satisfied with the clarity and the coverage of existing texts. We found that the level of analysis was often either too advanced (thereby posing difficulties for noneconomics majors) or too elementary (thereby failing to stimulate economics majors). In addition, the quality of treatment of the two main subdivisions of international economics—international trade theory and policy and international monetary theory and policy—was often inconsistent. A very good treatment of trade was matched with a weaker treatment of international monetary economics or vice-versa. Further, we felt that it would be helpful to bring out more fully the insights of the Classical economists, as well as the insights associated with several of the newer trade theories and contemporary policy approaches. In addition, it seemed necessary to pay more attention to both the trade and monetary problems of the developing countries and the problems of economic integration among nations. In short, we wanted to write a text that was comprehensive and uniformly clear and, most importantly, that could help students move beyond recognition and toward an understanding of current and future international events.

We have been very flattered by the favorable response to the first and second editions of our book. In this third edition we have built upon the well-received features to develop a text that is even more attuned to our objectives. Because of the positive response to the coverage of international trade, no fundamental changes have been made in that material. However, we have importantly added material on the controversy regarding the possible link between expanded trade and growing income inequality in industrial countries and on the political economy of trade policy. The major change in this edition is a more thorough development of the international monetary material. In particular, we have added a chapter that provides extensive descriptive detail on various international asset markets (for bank deposits and lending, bonds, and stocks) and on the multitude of international financial instruments available for conducting asset transfers and managing the risk associated with such transfers. We have also divided the second edition's very long single chapter on balance-of-payments adjustment into separate chapters on the price (elasticities) and income approaches. As in the first two editions, we have maintained our reliance on the IS-LM-BP framework for analyzing macroeconomic policy, because we believe that the framework is effective in facilitating student understanding and since that material was favorably received by users of the first two editions. However, in this new edition we continue to incorporate key aspects of the monetary and portfolio approaches into the IS-LM-BP model, thus adding to the richness of the overall framework.

In addition, throughout the text, we have updated information and continue to include features to make the book student-friendly. As in the previous edition, chapter introductions contain a "roadmap" to indicate more thoroughly the topics of the chapter and to motivate student interest, and we have expanded the set of end-of-chapter questions in almost every chapter. Further, effective case studies from the first and second editions have been retained and updated, and a number of new cases have been introduced. As previously, we have attempted to keep the book at manageable length by deleting outdated and extraneous material.

As many instructors know, the rapidly expanding body of knowledge in international economics is making it increasingly difficult to cover both international trade and international monetary economics in a one-semester course. Consequently, growing numbers of colleges and universities are offering the subject in two semesters. Thus, a major innovation with the second edition that has been retained with the third edition is that this text is available not only in its entirety but also as two distinct parts (splits). Instructors in one-semester courses dealing with trade issues may wish to consider using the split, *International Economics: Trade Theory and Policy,* rather than the entire *International Economics* book. Similarly, for those teaching the monetary material by itself in a semester course, the split, *International Economics: Payments, Exchange Rates, and Macro Policy,* is available.

DESCRIPTION OF TEXT

Our book follows the traditional division of international economics into the trade and monetary sides of the subject. Although the primary audience for the book will be students in upper-level economics courses, we feel that the material can effectively reach a broad, diversified group of students—including those in political science, international studies, history, and business who may have fewer economics courses in their background. Having taught international economics ourselves in specific non-majors' sections and Master's of Business Administration sections as well as in the traditional economics department setting, we are confident that the material is accessible to both noneconomics and economics students. This broad audience will be assisted in its learning through the fact that we have included separate, extensive review chapters of microeconomic (Chapter 5 in both the entire book and the trade split) and macroeconomic (Chapter 25 in the entire book and Chapter 7 in the monetary split) tools.

International Economics presents international trade theory and policy first. For the trade section the numbering of all chapters is identical to that of the trade split, *International Economics: Trade Theory and Policy.* (The introductory material of Chapter 1 is identical in all three books.) Chapters 2–4 present the Classical model of trade, including a treatment of pre-Classical Mercantilism. A unique feature is the **devotion of an entire chapter to extensions of the Classical model** to include more than two countries, more than two goods, money wages and prices, exchange rates, and transportation costs. The analysis is brought forward through the modern Dornbusch-Fischer-Samuelson model including, in this new edition, a treatment of the impact of productivity improvements in one country on the trading partner and expanded discussion of the demand side of the model. Chapter 5 then presents an **extensive review of microeconomic tools** used in international trade, and can be thought of as a "short course" in intermediate micro. Chapters 6–9 present the workhorse neoclassical and Heckscher-Ohlin trade theory, including an examination of the assumptions of the model. Chapter 6 focuses on the traditional production possibilities-indifference curve exposition. We are unabashed fans of the offer curve because of the nice general equilibrium properties of the device and because of its usefulness in analyzing trade policy and in interpreting economic events, and Chapter 7 extensively develops this concept. Chapter 8 explores Heckscher-Ohlin in a theoretical context, and Chapter 9 is **unique in its focus on testing the factor endowments approach,** including empirical work on the trade-income inequality debate in the context of Heckscher-Ohlin.

Continuing with theory, Chapters 10–12 treat extensions of the traditional material. Chapter 10 **discusses various post-Heckscher-Ohlin trade theories** that relax standard assumptions such as international factor immobility, homogeneous products, constant returns to scale, and perfect competition. An important focus here is upon imperfect competition and intra-industry trade. In this edition, a brief treatment of the relationship between geography and trade has also been introduced. Chapter 11 explores the comparative statics of economic growth and the relative importance of trade, and new material has been added on endogenous growth models and on the effects of growth on the offer curve. Chapter 12 examines causes and consequences of international factor movements, including both capital movements and labor flows. In this edition, we have also brought in material on the economic impact of immigration, focusing on the United States.

Chapters 13–18 are devoted to trade policy. Chapter 13 is **exclusively devoted to presentation of the various instruments of trade policy.** Chapter 14 then explores the welfare effects of the instruments, including discussion of such effects in a "small country" as well as a "large country" setting. Chapters 15–16 subsequently work systematically through various arguments for protection. This **two-chapter treatment of the arguments for protection** (one for traditional arguments and one for newer approaches) is more extensive than in many competing texts. In this edition, Chapter 17 begins with a discussion of the political economy of trade policy, followed by a review of various trade policy actions involving the United States. Chapter 18—unlike the treatment in some texts—is a distinct, **separate chapter on economic integration** ("disintegration" in the case of Central and Eastern Europe and the former Soviet Union). We have updated the discussion of the transition economies, the European Union, and the North American Free Trade Agreement. Material has also been added on Mercosur, the proposed Free Trade for the Americas, Chile's trade agreements, and APEC. The trade part of the book concludes with Chapter 19, which provides an overview of how international trade influences growth and change in the developing countries.

The international monetary material begins with Chapter 20, which introduces balance-of-payments accounting (Chapter 2 in the monetary split, *International Economics: Payments, Exchange Rates, and Macro Policy*). In contrast to many texts, **balance-of-payments accounting is discussed prior to the foreign exchange market,** which is considered in Chapter 21 (Chapter 3 in the monetary split). We think this sequence makes more sense than the reverse, since the demand and supply curves of foreign exchange reflect the debit and credit items, respectively, in the balance of payments. A differentiating feature of the presentation of the foreign exchange market is the **extensive development of various exchange rate measures,** e.g., nominal, real, and effective exchange rates. Chapter 22 (Chapter 4 in the monetary split) then describes characteristics of "real-world" international financial markets in detail, and discusses a (we hope not too-bewildering) variety of international financial derivative instruments. Chapter 23

(Chapter 5 in the monetary split) presents in considerable detail **the monetary and portfolio balance (or asset market) approaches to the balance of payments and to exchange rate determination.** This chapter concludes with an examination of the phenomenon of **exchange-rate overshooting.** In Chapters 24 and 25 (Chapters 6 and 7 in the monetary split), our attention turns to the more traditional price and income adjustment mechanisms. Chapter 25 is in effect a **review of basic Keynesian macroeconomic analysis.**

Chapters 26–28 (Chapters 8–10 in the monetary split) are concerned with macroeconomic policy under different exchange rate regimes. As noted earlier, we continue to **utilize the IS-LM-BP, Mundell-Fleming approach** in this edition, rather than to employ exclusively the asset market approach. The value of the IS-LM-BP model is that it can embrace both the current and the capital accounts in an understandable and perhaps familiar framework for many undergraduates. This model is presented in Chapter 26 in a manner that does not require previous acquaintance with it, but does constitute review material for most students who have previously taken an intermediate macroeconomic theory course. The chapter concludes with an analysis of monetary and fiscal policy in a fixed exchange rate environment. These policies are then examined in a flexible exchange rate environment in Chapter 27, and the analysis is broadened to the **aggregate demand-aggregate supply framework** in Chapter 28.

The concluding chapters, Chapters 29 and 30 (Chapters 11 and 12 in the monetary split), focus on particular topics of global concern. Chapter 29 considers various issues related to the choice between fixed and flexible exchange rates. Chapter 30 then traces the historical development of the international monetary system from Bretton Woods onward, examines **proposals for reform** such as target zone proposals and, in this edition, contains new material on EMU, the proposed Tobin tax on short-term capital flows, and the G-7. This final chapter concludes with an overview of the external debt problems of developing countries.

Because of the length and comprehensiveness of the *International Economics* text, it is not wise to attempt to cover all of it in a one-semester course. For such a course, we recommend that material be selected from Chapters 1–3, 5–8, 10, 13–15, 20–21, 23–27, and 30. If more emphasis on international trade is desired, additional material from Chapters 16–18 can be included. For more emphasis on international monetary economics, we suggest the addition of selected material from Chapters 22, 28, and 29. For a two-semester course, the entire *International Economics* book can be covered (or the two splits). Whatever the course, occasional outside reading assignments from academic journals, current popular periodicals, and a readings book can further help to bring the material to life. The "References for Further Reading" section at the end of the book, which is organized by chapter, can hopefully give some guidance. If library resources are limited, the text contains summaries of some noteworthy contributions both in the main body and in Case Studies.

PEDAGOGICAL DEVICES

To assist the student in learning the material, we have included a variety of pedagogical devices. We like to think of course that the major device in this edition is again clear exposition. Although every author stresses clarity of exposition as a strong point, we continued to be pleased that many reviewers praised this feature. Beyond this general feature, more specific devices are:

Boxes

Boxes that are analytical in nature (24 in total) further explore some difficult concepts or relationships for the interested student. We also have retained several biographical Boxes in this edition. These short sketches of well-known economists add a personal dimension to the work being studied, and they discuss not only the professional interests and concerns of the individuals but also some of their less well-known "human" characteristics.

Case Studies   There are 71 Case Studies contained in *International Economics*. These Case Studies serve to illuminate concepts and analyses under discussion, and they give the student an opportunity to see the relevance of the material to events going on in practice. The cases also provide a break from the sometimes heavy dose of theory which permeates this (and virtually any other) international economics text.

Concept Checks   These are short "stopping points" at various intervals within chapters (about two per chapter). The Concept Checks pose questions that are designed to see if basic points made in the text have been grasped by the student.

End-of-Chapter Questions and Problems   These are standard fare in all texts. The questions and problems are broader and more comprehensive than the questions contained in the Concept Checks.

Lists of Key Terms   The major terms in each chapter are boldfaced in the chapters themselves and then are brought together at the end of the chapter in list form. A review of each list can serve as a quick review of the chapter.

References for Further Reading   These lists occur at the end of the book, organized by chapter. We have provided bibliographic sources that we have found useful in our own work as well as entries that are relatively accessible and offer further theoretical and empirical exploration opportunities for interested students.

Instructor's Manual   This companion publication offers instructors assistance in preparing for and teaching the course. We have included suggestions for presenting the material as well as answers to the end-of-chapter questions and problems. In addition, sample examination questions are provided, including some of the hundreds of multiple-choice questions and problems that we have used for examining our own students.

Student Workbook   This book offers a companion student workbook as a guide for grasping the text's material and for applying international economics concepts in practice. The workbook has been prepared by Steven L. Cobb of the University of North Texas. Professor Cobb is an insightful and dedicated teacher whom we both were lucky enough to have had as a graduate student in our courses at the University of North Carolina at Chapel Hill.

ACKNOWLEDGMENTS

Our major intellectual debts are to the many professors who taught us economics, but particularly to Robert Stern of the University of Michigan and Erik Thorbecke of Cornell University. We also have found conversations and seminars over the years with our faculty colleagues at the University of North Carolina at Chapel Hill to have been extremely helpful. We particularly wish to thank Stanley Black, Patrick Conway, William A. Darity, Jr., Richard Froyen, and James Ingram. Thanks also to colleagues at Davidson College (where Appleyard has been located since 1990), especially Peter Hess, Clark Ross, and Vikram Kumar, and to the many students at Chapel Hill and Davidson who were guinea pigs for the material. We also express our appreciation to Cynthia Harris for assistance with this edition's Case Studies, and to Barbara Carmack for her cheerful and very extensive help with the mechanics of manuscript preparation. Assistance in manuscript preparation was also provided by Patrick Foy, Dawson Granade, and Nathan Ohler.

We are also indebted to the entire staff at Irwin/McGraw-Hill, especially Natalie Durbin, Marilea Fried, Susan Goffried, Gary Nelson, Robert Preskill, and Wendi

Sweetland. We thank them for their cooperation, patience, encouragement, and guidance in the development of this third edition.

In addition, we are grateful to the following reviewers; their thoughtful, prescriptive comments have helped guide the development of these three editions.

Eric Bond	Pennsylvania State University
Harry Bowen	University of California/Irvine
Drusilla Brown	Tufts University
Charles Chittle	Bowling Green State University
Joseph Daniels	Marquette University
Alan Deardorff	University of Michigan
Mary Epps	University of Virginia
Jim Gerber	San Diego State University
Norman Gharrity	Ohio Wesleyan University
Stephen Haynes	University of Oregon
Pershing Hill	University of Alaska
William Kaempfer	University of Colorado
Patrick Kehoe	University of Pennsylvania
Frank Kelly	Indiana University-Purdue University Indianapolis
David Kemme	Wichita State University
Thomas Love	North Central College
Thomas McGahagan	University of Pittsburgh at Johnstown
Joseph McKinney	Baylor University
John Pomery	Purdue University
James Rakowski	University of Notre Dame
James Rauch	University of California-San Diego
W. Charles Sawyer	University of Southern Mississippi
Don Schilling	University of Missouri
John N. Smithin	York University
Jeffrey Steagall	University of North Florida
Edward Tower	Duke University

These reviewers greatly improved the quality of the material, and a special commendation goes to David Cushman of the University of Saskatchewan for his detailed and insightful suggestions for this third edition. Dan Friel of NationsBank and Joe Ross of Goldman Sachs also provided useful information for this edition. We also wish to thank David Ball (North Carolina State University), Guzin Erlat (Middle East Technical University-Ankara), Art Goldsmith (Washington and Lee University) and Michael Jones (Bowdoin College) for their helpful comments on earlier editions. Of course, any remaining shortcomings or errors are the responsibility of the authors (who each blame the other).

Finally, a special note of thanks to our families, especially Gwen and Betts, for their understanding, support, and forbearance throughout the time-absorbing process required to complete all three editions.

Dennis R. Appleyard
Alfred J. Field, Jr.

CONTENTS IN BRIEF

CONTENTS

PART II

MACROECONOMIC POLICY IN THE OPEN ECONOMY   191

PART III

ISSUES IN WORLD MONETARY ARRANGEMENTS 263

THE WORLD OF INTERNATIONAL ECONOMICS

INTRODUCTION

Welcome to the study of international economics. No doubt you have become increasingly aware of the importance of international transactions in daily economic life. When people say that "the world is getting smaller every day," they are referring not only to the increased speed and ease of transportation and communications but also to the increased use of international markets to buy and sell goods, services, and financial assets. This is not a new phenomenon, of course: in ancient times international trade was important for the Egyptians, the Greeks, the Romans, the Phoenicians, and later for Spain, Portugal, Holland, and Britain. It can be said that all the great nations of the past that were influential world leaders were also important world traders. Nevertheless, the importance of international trade and finance to the economic health and overall standard of living of a country has never been as clear as it is today.

Signs of these international transactions are all around us. The clothes we wear come from production sources all over the world: the United States to the Pacific Rim to Europe to Central and South America. The automobiles we drive are produced not only in the United States but also in Canada, Mexico, Japan, Germany, France, Italy, England, Sweden, and other countries. The same can be said for the food we eat, the shoes we wear, the appliances we use, and the many different services we consume. Further, products manufactured in the United States often use important parts produced in other countries. At the same time, many U.S. imports are manufactured with important U.S.-made components.

This increased internationalization of economic life is made even more complicated by foreign-owned assets. More and more companies in many countries are owned partially or totally by foreigners. In recent years foreigners have been purchasing U.S. government bonds in record numbers, facilitating the financing of the large U.S. government deficit. The overall heightened presence of foreign goods, foreign producers, and foreign-owned assets causes many to question the impact and desirability of all international transactions. It is our hope that after reading this text you will be better able to understand how international trade and payments affect our country and that you will know how to evaluate the implications of government policies that are undertaken to influence the level and direction of international transactions.

You will be studying one of the oldest branches of economics. People have been concerned about the goods and services crossing their borders for as long as nation-states or city-states have existed. Some of the earliest economic data relate to international trade, and early economic thinking often centered on the implications of international trade for the well-being of a politically defined area. Although similar to regional economics in many respects, international economics has traditionally been treated as a special branch of the discipline. This is not terribly surprising when one considers that economic transactions between politically distinct areas are often associated with many differences that influence the nature of exchanges between them rather than transactions within them. For example, the degree of factor mobility between countries often differs from that within countries. Countries can have different forms of government, different currencies, different types of economic systems, different resource endowments, different cultures, different institutions, and different arrays of products.

The study of international economics, like all branches of economics, concerns decision making with respect to the use of scarce resources to meet desired economic objectives. It examines how international transactions influence such things as social welfare, income distribution, employment, growth, and price stability, and the possible ways public policy can affect the outcomes. In the study of international trade, we ask, for example: What determines the basis for trade? What are the effects of trade? What determines the value and the volume of trade? What factors impede trade flows? What is the impact of public policy that attempts to alter the pattern of trade? In the study of international monetary economics we address questions such as: What is meant by a country's balance of payments? How are exchange rates determined? How does trade affect the economy at the macro level? Why does financial capital flow rapidly and sizably across country borders? How do international transactions affect the use of monetary and fiscal policy to pursue domestic targets?

THE NATURE OF MERCHANDISE TRADE

Before delving further into the subject matter of international economics, however, it is useful to take a brief look at some of the characteristics of world trade today. The value of world merchandise exports reached an all-time high of over $5.1 trillion in 1996, a 3.7 percent increase over the value of exports in 1995 and a 4.0 percent increase in physical volume. The growth in value represented an increase of $180 billion. This is even more

TABLE 1   **Growth in World Production and Trade, 1963–1996 (average annual percentage change in volume)**

	1963–1973	*1970–1979*	*1980–1985*	*1985–1990*	*1990–1994*	*1995*	*1996*
Production							
All commodities	6.0%	4.0%	1.5%	3.0%	0.5%	3.7%	4.0%
Agriculture	2.5	2.0	2.5	2.0	1.0	NA	NA
Mining	5.5	2.5	−2.5	3.0	1.5	NA	NA
Manufacturing	7.5	4.5	2.5	3.0	0.0	NA	NA
Exports							
All commodities	9.0%	5.0%	2.0%	6.0%	5.0%	8.5%	4.0%
Agriculture	14.0	4.5	1.0	2.0	4.5	NA	NA
Mining	7.5	1.5	−2.5	5.0	4.0	NA	NA
Manufacturing	11.5	7.0	4.5	6.5	5.5	NA	NA

NA = not available.

Sources: General Agreement on Tariffs and Trade (GATT), *International Trade 1985–86* (Geneva: GATT, 1986), p. 13; GATT, *International Trade 1988–89,* I (Geneva: GATT, 1989) p. 8; World Trade Organization, press release of April 4, 1997, obtained from www.wto.org.; International Monetary Fund, *World Economic Outlook,* May 1997 (Washington, DC: IMF, 1997), p. 5 (for 1995 and 1996 world production).

dramatic when one realizes that the value of goods exported worldwide was less than $2 trillion in 1985. Throughout the past three decades, international trade volume has, on average, outgrown production (see Table 1). Trade has grown particularly rapidly in several countries called "most dynamic traders" by the World Trade Organization (see Table 2).

The Geographical Composition of Trade

In terms of major economic areas, the industrialized countries dominate world trade, accounting for about 70 percent of world trade in recent years. Details of trade on a regional basis are provided in Table 3. The relative importance of the European Union and the United States, Canada, and Japan is evident in terms of both imports and exports. Asia accounts for over 55 percent of the developing countries' imports and exports.

To obtain an idea of the geographical structure of trade, look at Table 4, which provides information on the destination of merchandise exports from several regions. The first row, for example, indicates that 36.9 percent of the exports of countries of North America went to other North American countries, 14.1 percent of North American exports went to Latin America, 18.9 percent to Western Europe, and so forth. From this table it is clear that the major markets for all regions' exports are in North America, Western Europe, and Asia. This is true for these three areas themselves, especially for Western Europe, which sends 68.1 percent of its exports to itself. In addition, the table makes it evident that the countries in the regions of Latin America, Central and Eastern Europe and the former Soviet Union, Africa, and the Middle East trade relatively little with themselves.

At the individual country level (see Table 5), the relative importance of Europe, North America, Japan, and East Asia is again quite evident. The largest world trader is the United States, followed by Germany. Japan, France, the United Kingdom, and Italy are the next largest and, with the United States and Germany, account for 45 percent of world trade. Also noteworthy has been the spectacular growth in the trade of Hong Kong, the

TABLE 2   **Countries with Rapid Trade Growth in the 1990s**

Exporting Country	Average Annual Growth Rate of Dollar Value of Exports, 1990–1996*	Importing Country	Average Annual Growth Rate of Dollar Value of Imports, 1990–1996*
Malaysia	18%	Argentina	34%
Philippines	17	Poland	22
China	16	Malaysia	18
Thailand	16	Philippines	18
Singapore	15	China	17
Mexico	15	Brazil	17
Ireland	13	Colombia	16
Kuwait	12	United Arab Emirates	15
Korea, Republic of	12	Chile	15
Indonesia	12	Mexico	14
Argentina	12	Singapore	14
India	11	Korea, Republic of	14
Spain	11	Thailand	13
		Indonesia	12
		Turkey	11
		Israel	11
		Taiwan	11

*Countries with at least $10 billion of exports or imports and a growth rate of exports or imports at least 1.5 times the average annual world growth rate of 7 percent from 1990–1996.

Source: World Trade Organization, press release of April 4, 1997, obtained from www.wto.org.

TABLE 3   **Exports and Imports by Region, 1996 (billions of dollars and percentage of world totals)**

	Exports*		Imports†	
	Value ($, billions, f.o.b.)	*Percentage Share*	*Value ($, billions, c.i.f.)*	*Percentage Share*
North America‡	$ 826	16.2%	$ 995	19.0%
Latin America	250	4.9	272	5.2
Western Europe	2,271	44.5	2,212	42.2
(European Union)§	(2,103)	(41.2)	(2,031)	(38.8)
Transition economies	171	3.4	172	3.3
(Central and Eastern Europe)	(81)	(1.6)	(109)	(2.1)
Africa	113	2.2	127	2.4
Middle East	160	3.1	146	2.8
Asia	1,310	25.7	1,315	25.1
(Japan)	(413)	(8.1)	(350)	(6.7)
Total	$ 5,100	100.0%	$ 5,240	100.0%

Note: Components may not sum to totals because of rounding.
*Exports are recorded f.o.b. (free on board).
†Imports are recorded c.i.f. (cost, insurance, and freight).
‡Canada and the United States.
§Austria, Belgium, Denmark, Finland, France, Germany, Greece, Ireland, Italy, Luxembourg, the Netherlands, Portugal, Spain, Sweden, United Kingdom.
Source: World Trade Organization, press release of April 4, 1997, obtained from www.wto.org.

TABLE 4   **Geographical Destination of Exports, 1994**

	North America	*Latin America*	*Western Europe*	*Central and Eastern Europe and former U.S.S.R.*	*Africa*	*Middle East*	*Asia*	*Total*
North America	36.9%	14.1%	18.9%	0.8%	1.5%	2.6%	25.2%	100.0%
Latin America	48.4	20.2	17.8	0.8	1.2	1.0	9.4	100.0
Western Europe	8.2	2.5	68.1	4.2	2.8	3.0	9.5	100.0
Central and Eastern Europe and former U.S.S.R.	5.2	1.7	59.5	15.9	1.6	1.8	13.7	100.0
Africa	14.6	2.2	52.7	1.1	9.7	1.4	12.1	100.0
Middle East	13.0	2.8	23.2	1.5	1.9	9.1	45.6	100.0
Asia	25.9	2.5	16.3	1.0	1.3	2.5	48.5	100.0

Note: Destination components may not add to 100.0% because of incomplete coverage.
Source: World Trade Organization, *International Trade 1995: Trends and Statistics* (Geneva: WTO, 1995), p. 39.

Republic of Korea (South Korea), Taiwan, China, and Singapore, which have now moved into the top 15 world traders. This remarkable achievement is evident in the comparison of growth rates of trade value shown in Table 6. Finally, the 10 largest countries are the source of almost 60 percent of world trade. World trade thus tends to be concentrated among relatively few major traders, with the remaining 180-plus countries accounting for slightly over 40 percent.

TABLE 5   **Leading-Country Merchandise Exporters and Importers, 1996 (billions of dollars and percentage share of world totals)**

	Exports			Imports		
Country	Value ($, billions, f.o.b.)	Percentage Share	Country	Value ($, billions, c.i.f.)	Percentage Share	
1. United States	$ 624.8	11.9%	United States	$ 817.8	15.2%	
2. Germany	521.2	9.9	Germany	456.3	8.5	
3. Japan	412.6	7.9	Japan	349.6	6.5	
4. France	290.3	5.5	United Kingdom	278.6	5.2	
5. United Kingdom	259.1	4.9	France	275.3	5.1	
6. Italy	250.7	4.8	Italy	207.0	3.8	
7. Canada	201.2	3.8	Hong Kong	202.0	3.7	
			(retained imports)	(48.5)	(0.9)	
8. Netherlands	197.1	3.8	Canada	175.0	3.2	
9. Hong Kong	180.9	3.4	Netherlands	174.1	3.2	
(domestic exports)	(27.4)	(0.5)				
10. Belgium-Luxembourg	166.7	3.2	Belgium-Luxembourg	154.6	2.9	
11. China	151.1	2.9	Korea, Republic of	150.3	2.8	
12. Korea, Republic of	129.8	2.5	China	138.8	2.6	
13. Singapore	125.1	2.4	Singapore	131.5	2.4	
(domestic exports)	(73.6)	(1.4)	(retained imports)	(79.9)	(1.5)	
14. Taiwan	116.0	2.2	Spain	121.9	2.3	
15. Spain	102.1	1.9	Taiwan	102.5	1.9	
16. Mexico	95.9	1.8	Mexico	90.3	1.7	
17. Sweden	84.2	1.6	Malaysia	78.6	1.5	
18. Switzerland	80.0	1.5	Switzerland	78.5	1.5	
19. Malaysia	78.4	1.5	Thailand	68.3	1.3	
20. Russian Federation*	70.4	1.3	Austria	66.0	1.2	
21. Australia	59.9	1.1	Sweden	65.8	1.2	
22. Austria	58.0	1.1	Australia	65.5	1.2	
23. Saudi Arabia	56.3	1.1	Brazil	57.5	1.1	
24. Thailand	54.8	1.0	Russian Federation*	44.4	0.8	
25. Ireland	50.0	1.0	Denmark	43.2	0.8	
Total	$4,416.6	84.1%		$4,393.4	81.5%	
World†	$5,254.0	100.0%		$5,390.0	100.0%	

Note: Components may not sum to totals because of rounding.

*The Russian Federation figures exclude trade with the Baltic countries and the Commonwealth of Independent States (CIS). If included, Russian exports and imports would be $89.6 billion and $64.3 billion, respectively.

†The World figures include significant reexports and imports for reexport and thus differ from the totals in Table 3.

Source: World Trade Organization, press release of Aprill 4, 1997, obtained from www.wto.org.

The Commodity Composition of Trade

Turning to the commodity composition of world trade (Table 7), trade in manufactures accounts for almost 75 percent of international trade, with the remaining amount consisting of primary products. Among the primary goods, trade in food products is the largest (9.3 percent) followed by trade in fuels (7.6 percent). Trade in raw materials, ores, and metals accounts for 5.7 percent. In the manufacturing category, machinery and transport equipment account for 38.8 percent of world trade. Automotive products is a major subcategory, absorbing 9.6 percent of world trade. Other important categories of manufactures include trade in chemicals (9.3 percent) and in textiles, clothing, and miscellaneous consumer goods (15.6 percent).

TABLE 6   **Growth of Merchandise Trade for Selected Countries, 1970–1994 (average annual percentage change)**

Exports (f.o.b.)				Imports (c.i.f.)		
1970–1987	1987–1994	1994		1970–1987	1987–1994	1994
26.8%	10.6%	16.8%	Korea, Republic of	19.5%	14.0%	22.1%
23.5	8.2	9.7	Taiwan	20.1	13.7	10.9
19.0	17.6	11.9	Hong Kong[a]	18.0	18.5	17.4
18.7	19.0	30.8	Singapore[a]	16.4	17.8	20.5
18.3	8.6	18.0	Turkey	16.8	7.2	−20.9
18.2	17.4	31.9	China	18.9	15.1	11.3
17.9	21.4	21.9	Thailand	14.5	22.7	18.0
17.2	12.9	8.8	Indonesia	16.5	13.9	12.9
17.2	11.7	16.7	Mexico	10.2	23.8	22.3
16.9	12.1[c]	17.3	Ireland	13.3	10.5[c]	14.4
16.9	13.5[c]	15.9	Spain	14.7	15.2[c]	11.9
15.7	7.3	9.6	Japan	13.0	9.0	13.9
15.6	11.8	22.5	Tunisia	14.5	11.7	5.9
15.0	10.4	14.2	Israel	12.0	8.4	11.7
14.9	9.8	28.0	Ecuador	12.6	7.1	42.2
14.9	18.5	24.7	Malaysia	13.8	24.7	30.5
14.8	8.5	10.1	Pakistan	13.0	6.2	−6.4
14.3	14.5[c]	13.5	Portugal	13.5	16.2[c]	9.9
14.2	7.5	12.9	Brazil	10.9	11.7	29.8
14.2	7.5	12.5	Austria	14.0	7.8	13.9
14.0	2.4	16.0	Iceland	14.6	−1.1	9.1
14.0	7.8[c]	7.2	Greece	11.3	12.0[c]	6.1
13.8	7.7	−6.3	Saudi Arabia	22.0	4.7	−10.1
13.8	6.4	11.2	Switzerland	13.0	4.3	11.7
13.7	7.1	8.9	Norway	11.2	2.7	14.0
13.7	8.8[c]	12.0	Italy	13.3	8.4[c]	13.1
13.6	5.8	26.5	Finland	12.6	2.4	28.7
13.5	7.7[d]	NA	Germany, Fed. Rep. (former)	12.7	8.7[d]	NA
13.4	2.0[e]	14.7	U.S.S.R. (former)[b]	13.0	−8.4[e]	8.1
13.2	9.7[c]	11.6	France	13.2	8.6[c]	12.5
13.0	8.6[c]	11.5	Netherlands	12.0	8.1[c]	11.8
12.9	−5.5[e]	11.9	Bulgaria	13.8	−1.4[e]	−4.8
12.7	9.8[c]	10.7	Denmark	10.9	6.6[c]	14.9
12.4	1.6	20.2	Hungary	12.0	5.7	16.2
12.4	8.2[c]	16.1	Belgium-Luxembourg	12.4	8.5[c]	17.9
11.9	−0.6	16.4	Yugoslavia (former)	9.1	0.8	19.4
11.9	7.7[c]	12.9	United Kingdom	12.2	7.5[c]	10.1
11.7	4.7	22.9	Sweden	10.9	3.5	21.2
11.5	9.8	19.8	Colombia	10.1	15.2	21.0
11.1	2.5	19.6	Czechoslovakia (former)[b]	11.4	3.3	19.0
11.1	7.8[f]	NA	German Dem. Rep. (former)	10.6	−11.2[f]	NA
11.0	7.8	15.6	New Zealand	10.9	7.3	23.6
10.9	10.5	10.3	United States	14.5	7.2	14.2
10.9	7.7	13.9	Canada	11.6	7.6	11.5
10.7	2.8	−10.1	Nigeria	9.6	5.3	−25.0
10.7	12.0	16.2	India	12.9	7.0	17.6
10.6	8.6	11.3	Australia	10.9	9.0	17.2
10.6	5.1	0.6	Morocco	11.1	7.9	6.3
10.4	13.1	20.3	Philippines	10.6	17.8	20.1
10.1	7.0	16.3	Uruguay	9.9	13.5	19.3
13.0	7.7	12.9	World	13.2	7.7	12.8

NA = not applicable.
[a]Includes reexports and imports for reexport.
[b]Imports are f.o.b.
[c]1987–1992 due to changes in European Union data collection methods as of 1993.
[d]1987–1989.
[e]1990–1994.
[f]1987–1990.

Sources: General Agreement on Tariffs and Trade, *International Trade 1987–1988*, Vol. 1: *Preliminary* (Geneva: GATT, 1988), p. 21; World Trade Organization, *International Trade 1995: Trends and Statistics* (Geneva: WTO, 1995), pp. 138–43.

TABLE 7   **The Commodity Composition of World Trade, 1994 and 1980**

Category	Value of Exports ($, billions)	Percentage of World Exports 1994	1980
Food	$ 379	9.3%	11.0%
Raw materials	108	2.6	3.7
Ores and other minerals	48	1.2	2.1
Fuels	311	7.6	23.0
Nonferrous metals	78	1.9	2.5
Total primary products	$ 923	22.6%	42.4%
Iron and steel	$ 118	2.9%	3.8%
Chemicals	379	9.3	7.0
Other semimanufactures	317	7.8	6.7
Machinery and transport equipment	1,586	38.8	25.8
Office and telecom equipment	(469)	(11.5)	(4.2)
Automotive products	(394)	(9.6)	(6.5)
Other machinery	(723)	(17.7)	(15.2)
Textiles	129	3.1	2.7
Clothing	140	3.4	2.0
Other consumer goods	373	9.1	5.8
Total manufactures	$3,042	74.3%	53.9%
Total exports	$4,090	100.0%	100.0%

Note: Details may not add to totals because of incomplete classification and rounding.
Source: World Trade Organization, *International Trade 1995: Trends and Statistics* (Geneva: WTO, 1995), p. 77.

TABLE 8   **Growth Rates of Export Prices (dollar unit-values)**

	1980–1985	1985–1990	1990–1994	1994
Total merchandise	−3.0%	6.0%	−0.5%	3.0%
Agricultural products	−3.0	7.5	−0.5	5.5
Mining products	−2.5	−2.0	−6.0	−3.5
Manufactures	−3.0	8.0	0.5	3.5

Source: General Agreement on Tariffs and Trade, *International Trade 1985–86* (Geneva: GATT, 1986), p. 164; World Trade Organization, *International Trade 1995: Trends and Statistics* (Geneva: WTO, 1995), p. 25.

What is especially notable is the current importance of trade in manufactures and the declining importance of primary products. Comparison of the last column of Table 7 with the next-to-last column illustrates the relatively sluggish growth of primary products in world trade compared with the growth in manufactured goods. For example, food products accounted for 11.0 percent of world exports in 1980 but only 9.3 percent in 1994; fuels, which constituted 23.0 percent in 1980, fell dramatically in importance to 7.6 percent in 1994; and the share of primary products in total dropped from 42.4 percent in 1980 to 22.6 percent in 1994. Of additional note is the steady decline of the prices of mining products (see Table 8). These developments are of particular relevance to the developing countries, whose trade has traditionally been concentrated in primary goods. Specialization in commodity groups that are growing relatively more slowly makes it difficult for them to obtain the gains from growth in world trade accruing to countries exporting manufactured products. The demand for primary products not only tends to be less responsive to income growth but is also more likely to demonstrate greater price

TABLE 9   **U.S. Merchandise Trade by Area and Country, 1996 (millions of dollars)**

	Exports	*Imports*	*Balance*
Total	$611,669	$799,343	$–187,674
Western Europe	137,207	161,268	–24,061
EU	124,785	146,054	–21,269
Belgium-Luxembourg	12,685	9,501	3,184
France	14,442	18,625	–4,183
Germany	23,005	38,820	–15,815
Italy	8,627	18,203	–9,576
Netherlands	16,476	7,476	9,000
United Kingdom	30,238	28,753	1,485
Other	19,312	24,676	–5,364
Other Western Europe	12,422	15,214	–2,792
Canada	133,993	159,215	–25,222
Japan	65,980	115,194	–49,214
Australia	11,703	3,887	7,816
Eastern Europe	7,354	6,978	376
Latin America and other Western hemisphere	109,074	122,910	–13,836
Brazil	12,343	8,761	3,582
Mexico	56,998	73,793	–16,795
Venezuela	4,665	12,904	–8,239
Asia (excluding Japan)	135,382	211,071	–75,689
China	11,941	51,494	–39,553
Hong Kong	13,891	9,857	4,034
Korea, Republic of	25,632	22,631	3,001
Singapore	16,247	20,336	–4,089
Taiwan	17,522	29,907	–12,385
Africa	10,653	18,550	–7,897
(OPEC members)	(15,690)	(29,337)	(–13,647)

Source: U.S. Department of Commerce, *Survey of Current Business,* April 1997, pp. 44–45. Data are preliminary.

fluctuations. This has been the case in recent years as primary goods prices have shown greater price variation as well as a decline relative to the prices of manufactures.

U.S. International Trade

To complete our discussion of the current nature of merchandise trade, we take a closer look at the geographic and commodity characteristics of recent U.S. international trade (see Tables 9 and 10). Geographically, Canada is the most important trading partner for the United States, both in exports and imports. NAFTA partners (Canada and Mexico) are the largest multicountry unit, followed by the EU. The third-largest individual trading partner country of the United States, behind Canada and Japan, is Mexico, followed by China, Germany, the United Kingdom, Korea, and Taiwan. Of note is the fact that a major portion (47 percent) of the trade deficit of the United States in 1996 could be traced to Japan and China.

Turning to the commodity composition of U.S. trade, agricultural products (foods, feeds, and beverages) are an important source of exports and generate a trade surplus. The capital goods category is the largest single export category and produces the largest trade surplus for the United States. Industrial supplies, dominated by chemicals and metal/nonmetallic products, is also an important export category for the United States, although imports are now larger than exports in the entire category. Sizable net imports occur in consumer goods, autos, and energy products. The largest import category is also capital goods followed closely by industrial supplies and materials. Currently, energy products

TABLE 10   **The Commodity Composition of U.S. Trade, 1996 (millions of dollars)**

	Exports	*Imports*	*Balance*
Total	$611,669	$799,343	$−187,674
Foods, feeds, and beverages	55,493	35,704	19,789
Industrial supplies and materials	147,660	204,383	−56,723
Energy products	15,401	75,297	
Chemicals, excluding medicinals	42,386	26,881	
Metals and nonmetallic products	33,368	47,736	
Iron and steel products	5,438	17,210	
Nonferrous metals	15,433	21,651	
Capital goods, except automotive	252,918	228,959	23,959
Machinery, except consumer-type	219,990	214,392	
Electric generating machinery, electric apparatus, and parts	24,039	24,773	
Oil drilling, mining, and construction machinery	12,646	5,642	
Computers, peripherals, and parts	43,700	61,511	
Semiconductors	35,688	36,713	
Telecommunications equipment	20,339	14,345	
Civilian aircraft, engines, and parts	30,846	12,627	
Automotive vehicles, engines, and parts	64,460	130,085	−65,625
Consumer goods (nonfood), except automotive	70,160	171,118	−100,958
Nondurable goods, manufactured	34,096	80,789	
Durable goods, manufactured	33,168	81,595	
Unspecified	20,978	29,094	−8,116

Source: U.S. Department of Commerce, *Survey of Current Business,* April 1997, pp. 46–47. Data are preliminary.

account for around 10 percent of total imports. It is not surprising that the United States is a major importer of several primary products, such as petroleum, and also of products that traditionally rely relatively heavily on labor in production such as textiles and apparel. What is of particular interest is the increasing importance of capital goods, consumer durables, and automobiles in U.S. imports and the continued size of U.S. exports of agricultural products. Not surprisingly, the countries in East Asia account for much of the growing U.S. imports of consumer goods in general.

WORLD TRADE IN SERVICES

The discussion of world trade has to this point focused on merchandise trade and has ignored the rapidly growing trade in services, estimated to be $1.2 trillion in 1996 (over one-fifth of the total trade in goods and services). The rising importance of services in international trade should not be unexpected since the service category now accounts for the largest share of income and employment in many industrial countries including the United States. More specifically, services account for 72 percent of gross domestic product (GDP) in the United States, 56 percent in Canada, 70 percent in the Netherlands, 66 percent in the United Kingdom, 61 percent in Germany, 71 percent in France, and 60 percent in Japan.[1] In this context, services generally include the following categories in the International Standard Industrial Classification (ISIC) system: wholesale and retail trade,

[1]World Bank, *World Development Report 1990* (Oxford: Oxford University Press, 1990), p. 183; World Bank, *World Development Report 1995* (Oxford: Oxford University Press, 1995), p. 167; World Bank, *World Development Report 1997* (Oxford: Oxford University Press, 1997), p. 237.

restaurants and hotels, transport, storage, communications, financial services, insurance, real estate, business services, personal services, community services, social services, and government services.

International trade in services broadly consists of commercial services, investment income, and government services, with the first two categories accounting for the bulk of services. Discussions of trade in "services" generally refer to trade in commercial services. During the 1970s this category grew more slowly in value than did merchandise trade. However, during the 1980s, exports of commercial services outgrew merchandise exports, and the relative importance of commercial services is roughly the same today as it was in the early 1970s. A word of caution is in order, however: The nature of trade in "services" is such that it is extremely difficult to obtain accurate estimates of the value of these transactions. This results from the fact that there is no agreed definition of what constitutes a traded service, and the ways in which these transactions are measured are less precise than is the case for merchandise trade. Estimates are obtained by examining foreign exchange records and/or through surveys of establishments. Since many service transactions are not observable (hence, they are sometimes referred to as the "invisibles" in international trade), the usual customs records or data are not available for valuing these transactions. Thus, it is likely that the value of trade in commercial services is underestimated. However, there may also be instances when firms may choose to overvalue trade in services, and reported figures must be viewed with some caution.

In terms of the geographical nature of trade in services, this trade is also concentrated among the industrial countries (see Table 11). The principal world traders in merchandise are also the principal traders in services, although in slightly different order. Although there has been little change among the major traders in services, notable increases in both exports and imports of services have been made by countries such as Thailand, Taiwan, Singapore, and South Korea.

The nature of trade in services is such that until recently they have been virtually ignored in trade negotiations and trade agreements. However, because of their increasing importance, there has been a growing concern for the need to establish some general guidelines for international transactions in services. Consequently, discussions regarding the nature of the service trade and various country restrictions that may influence it were included in the last completed round of trade negotiations (the Uruguay Round) conducted under the auspices of the General Agreement on Tariffs and Trade (GATT), which became the World Trade Organization in 1995. Clearly, with the rapid advances that have already been made in communications, it is likely that trade in services will continue to grow. It is important that guidelines for trade in services be established so that country restrictions on trade in services and information flows do not impede their movement and the benefits which occur because of them.

THE CHANGING DEGREE OF ECONOMIC INTERDEPENDENCE

It is important not only to recognize the large absolute level of international trade but also to recognize that the relative importance of trade has been growing for nearly every country and for all countries as a group. The relative size of trade is often measured by comparing the size of a country's exports with its gross domestic product (GDP). Increases in the export/GDP ratio indicate that a higher percentage of the output of final goods and services produced within a country's borders is being sold abroad. Such increases indicate a greater international interdependence and a more complex interna-

TABLE 11   **Leading Exporters and Importers of Commercial Services (billions of dollars and percentages)**

	Exports					Imports				
Rank		1995				Rank		1995		
1970	1995	Value ($, billions)	Percentage Share			1970	1995	Value ($, billions)	Percentage Share	
1	1	$ 189.5	16.2%	United States		2	1	$ 130.3	10.7%	Germany
3	2	96.0	8.2	France		1	2	128.3	10.5	United States
4	3	79.5	6.8	Germany		5	3	121.6	10.0	Japan
2	4	69.4	5.9	United Kingdom		4	4	76.9	6.3	France
5	5	64.7	5.5	Italy		6	5	62.9	5.2	Italy
6	6	63.9	5.4	Japan		3	6	57.8	4.7	United Kingdom
6	7	47.2	4.0	Netherlands		8	7	45.3	3.7	Netherlands
8	8	39.6	3.4	Spain		9	8	33.7	2.8	Belgium-Luxembourg
NA	9	36.1	3.1	Hong Kong		7	9	29.3	2.4	Canada
10	10	35.3	3.0	Belgium-Luxembourg		32	10	27.5	2.3	Korea, Republic of
15	11	31.5	2.7	Austria		NA	11	24.6	2.0	China
22	12	29.3	2.5	Singapore		NA	12	23.8	2.0	Taiwan
12	13	26.1	2.2	Switzerland		18	13	23.1	1.9	Austria
27	14	25.1	2.1	Korea, Republic of		16	14	21.6	1.8	Spain
9	15	21.2	1.8	Canada		NA	15	21.2	1.7	Hong Kong
NA	16	18.4	1.6	China		NA	16	20.2	1.7	Russian Federation
26	17	15.6	1.3	Taiwan		NA	17	18.6	1.5	Thailand
14	18	15.2	1.3	Sweden		11	18	17.2	1.4	Australia
17	19	15.1	1.3	Australia		10	19	17.1	1.4	Sweden
33	20	14.7	1.2	Thailand		40	20	16.5	1.4	Singapore
NA	21	14.5	1.2	Turkey		13	21	15.9	1.3	Norway
16	22	14.3	1.2	Denmark		15	22	15.4	1.3	Switzerland
11	23	14.2	1.2	Norway		17	23	14.0	1.1	Denmark
NA	24	11.6	1.0	Russian Federation		NA	24	13.2	1.1	Indonesia
20	25	9.5	0.8	Greece		NA	25	13.2	1.1	Brazil
	Total	$ 997.5	85.3%					$ 989.2	81.1%	
	World	$1,170.0	100.0%					$1,220.0	100.0%	

NA = not available.

Sources: General Agreement on Tariffs and Trade, *International Trade 1988–89,* I (Geneva: GATT, 1989), p. 34; World Trade Organization, press release of April 4, 1997, obtained from www.wto.org.

tional trade network encompassing not only final consumption goods but also capital goods, intermediate goods, primary goods, and commercial services. The recent increase in international interdependence is evident in the various export/GDP ratios for selected countries for 1970 and 1995 shown in Table 12.

Although the degree of dependence on exports varies considerably among countries, the relative importance of exports has increased in almost all individual cases and for every country grouping where data are available. This means not only that individual countries are experiencing the economic benefits that accompany the international exchange of goods and services but also that their own economic prosperity is dependent upon economic prosperity in the world as a whole. It also means that competition for markets is greater and that countries must be able to facilitate changes in their structure of production consistent with changes in relative production costs throughout the world. Thus, while increased interdependence has many inherent benefits, it also brings with it greater adjustment requirements and greater needs for policy coordination among trading

TABLE 12   **International Interdependence for Selected Countries and Groups of Countries, 1970 and 1995 (exports of goods and nonfactor services as a percentage of GDP)**

	1970	1995
Industrialized countries:		
Australia	14%	20%
Belgium	52	74
Canada	23	37
France	16	23
Germany	NA	23
Italy	16	26
Japan	11	9
Netherlands	42	53
United Kingdom	23	28
United States	6	11
Developing countries:		
Argentina	9	9
Chile	15	29
China	3	21
Czech Republic	NA	52
India	4	12
Iran	24	(1994) 30
Kenya	30	33
Korea, Republic of	14	33
Mexico	6	25
Nigeria	8	(1994) 22
Russian Federation	NA	22
Singapore	102	(1994) 177
Low- and middle-income countries:		
Sub-Saharan Africa	21	28
East Asia and Pacific	7	29
South Asia	5	14
Europe and Central Asia	NA	NA
Middle East and North Africa	29	NA
Latin America and Caribbean	13	17

NA = not available.

Source: World Bank, *World Development Report 1993* (Oxford: Oxford University Press, 1993), pp. 254–55; World Bank, *World Development Report 1996* (Oxford: Oxford University Press, 1996), pp. 212–13. World Bank, *World Development Report 1997* (Oxford: Oxford University Press, 1997), pp. 238–39.

partners. Both of these are often more difficult to achieve in practice than one might imagine, since even though a country as a whole may benefit from relative increases in international trade, individual parties or sectors may end up facing significant adjustment costs.

Even though the United States is less dependent on exports than most of the industrialized countries, the relative importance of exports has almost tripled since 1960, when the export/GDP ratio was around 4 percent. Thus, the United States, like most of the countries of the world, is increasingly and inexorably linked to the world economy. This link will, in all likelihood, grow stronger as countries seek the economic benefits that accompany increased economic and political integration. Such movements have been evident in recent years as Europe has pursued greater economic and monetary union and the North American Free Trade Agreement was implemented by Canada, Mexico, and the United States.

SUMMARY

International trade has played a critical role in the ability of countries to grow, develop, and be economically powerful throughout history. International transactions are becoming increasingly important in recent years as countries seek to obtain the many benefits that accompany increased exchange of goods, services, and factors. The relative increase in the importance of international trade makes it increasingly imperative that we all understand the basic factors that underlie the successful exchange of goods and services and the economic impact of various policy measures that may be proposed to influence the nature of international trade. This is true at both the micro level of trade in individual goods and services and the macro level of government budget deficits, money, exchange rates, interest rates, and possible controls on foreign investment. It is our hope that you will find the economic analysis of international transactions helpful in improving your understanding of this increasingly important type of economic activity.

 APPENDIX   A GENERAL REFERENCE LIST IN INTERNATIONAL ECONOMICS

The various books, articles, and data sources cited throughout this text will be useful for those of you who wish to examine specific issues in greater depth. Students who are interested in pursuing international economic problems on their own, however, will find it useful to consult the following general references:

Specialized Journals
Finance and Development (World Bank/IMF)
International Economic Journal
The International Economic Review
International Monetary Fund Staff Papers
The International Trade Journal
Journal of Common Market Studies
The Journal of International Economics
Journal of International Money and Finance
Review of International Economics
The World Economy

General Journals
American Economic Review
American Journal of Agricultural Economics
Brookings Papers on Economic Activity
Canadian Journal of Economics
Challenge: The Magazine of Economic Affairs
The Economic Journal
Journal of Economic Literature
Journal of Economic Perspectives
Journal of Finance
Journal of Political Economy
Kyklos
Quarterly Journal of Economics
Review of Economics and Statistics

Sources of International Data
Balance of Payments Statistics Yearbook (IMF)

Bank for International Settlements Annual Report
Direction of Trade Statistics (IMF, quarterly and
    annual yearbook)
Federal Reserve Bulletin
International Financial Statistics (IMF, monthly
    and annual yearbook)
OECD Main Economic Indicators
Survey of Current Business (U.S. Department
    of Commerce)
UN International Trade Statistics Yearbook
UN Monthly Bulletin of Statistics
US Economic Report of the President
World Development Report (World Bank)
World Economic Outlook (IMF)

General Current Information
The Asian Wall Street Journal
The Economist
IMF Survey
The International Herald Tribune
The Los Angeles Times
The New York Times
The Wall Street Journal
The Washington Post

Internet Sources
www.imf.org
www.worldbank.org
www.wto.org

PART I

FUNDAMENTALS OF INTERNATIONAL MONETARY ECONOMICS

> So much of barbarism, however, still remains in the transactions of most civilized nations, that almost all independent countries choose to assert their nationality by having, to their own inconvenience and that of their neighbours, a peculiar currency of their own.
>
> John Stuart Mill, 1848

The study of international economics encompasses not only micro issues related to the exchange of goods and services between countries but also macro issues regarding the interaction of international transactions with aggregate variables such as income, money, and prices. To assess the broader macro implications of international trade, it is necessary to understand the basic underpinnings of international monetary economics and the ways international trade and financial flows affect and are affected by the overall economy.

It is not uncommon for people to feel somewhat mystified by the entire process by which exchange rates are set, currencies move between countries, and the day-to-day activities of foreign exchange dealers and international bankers and investors take place. Even seasoned international travelers continue to be amazed that exchange rates are virtually the same in London, Paris, and New York and that it really is easy to buy, sell, travel, or invest internationally even though different countries and currencies are involved. In reality, many of the fundamental macro-money aspects are not that difficult to grasp and involve merely routine transactions, except that they are between countries. Nevertheless, these international transactions influence money, prices, and national income and can affect economic policy.

This Part introduces you to some of the basic principles of international monetary economics in order to provide a background for examining the policy dimensions of this activity. The upcoming chapter, "The Balance-of-Payments Accounts," will focus on how the international activity of a country is recorded and will explain how this information can be interpreted. The chapter, "The Foreign Exchange Market," provides an introduction to the foreign exchange markets and explains how they function on a daily basis to facilitate the exchange of goods, services, and investment. The foreign exchange market has been altered in recent years by the introduction of many new financial instruments. A sampling of this array of instruments is provided in the succeeding chapter, "International Financial Markets and Instruments: An Introduction." The analysis is extended into a more general framework in the chapter "The Monetary and Portfolio Balance Approaches to External Balance," which covers those approaches to the determination of the balance of payments and exchange rates. The last two chapters in this Part focus on how changes in exchange rates and the current account of the balance of payments lead to and are influenced by price and income adjustments in a country.

> The study of the elasticities of supply and demand is, thus, the core of the theory of foreign exchange rates.
>
> Fritz Machlup, 1939

CHAPTER 2

THE BALANCE-OF-PAYMENTS ACCOUNTS

INTRODUCTION

To carry out the many transactions involved in international trade, money is obviously necessary, but international transactions are also complicated by the fact that different countries use different currencies. A purely domestic transaction, such as the purchase of a chair made in North Carolina by a resident of South Carolina, involves no need to convert one currency into another. The buyer's "South Carolina dollar" is identical to the "North Carolina dollar" desired by the chair manufacturer—they are the same currency unit, the U.S. dollar. But the transaction is complicated when the North Carolina furniture maker sells the chair to a French citizen. The seller wishes to receive U.S. dollars, since that is the currency unit in which the firm's workers, suppliers, and shareholders are paid, while the French consumer wishes to complete the transaction with French francs. Because each country participating in *international* trade generally possesses its own *national* currency unit, a foreign exchange market is needed to convert one currency into another. In a broad view, the foreign exchange market is thus the mechanism that brings together buyers and sellers of different currencies. The nature and operations of the foreign exchange market and the determination of the equilibrium exchange rate are dealt with in the following three chapters.

This chapter will focus on how foreign economic transactions are recorded for any specific country. The international transactions of a country encompass payments outward from the country for its imports, gifts, and investments abroad and payments inward for exports, gifts, and investments by foreigners. In recording these transactions, a country is keeping its **balance-of-payments accounts.** These accounts attempt to maintain a systematic record of all economic transactions between the home country and the rest of the world for a specific time period, usually a year. You will learn the placement of various types of transactions in the accounts, how to interpret a country's balance-of-payments statement, and the meaning of different balances in the accounts such as the "balance of trade" and the "current account balance" that are frequently reported in the media. In addition, we will discuss the meaning of a related term, the *net international investment position* of a country. The stage will then have been set for understanding the foreign exchange market and the determination of exchange rates in later chapters. However, as a prelude, we first examine briefly the recent growth in international trade and payments activity.

RECENT GROWTH OF TRADE AND CAPITAL MOVEMENTS

The international transactions that are recorded in a country's balance-of-payments statement reflect summarily the size of that country's activity with the rest of the world taking place in any given year. An important part of that activity is trade in goods and services; extensive data on trade flows were provided in Chapter 1, "The World of International Economics," but Table 1 gives an overall look at the rapid growth of trade in goods since 1973. (Services data are less reliable and available for this span of years.) This growth in value of world exports (which conceptually equal world imports) has in monetary terms been at an annual average rate of 9.9 percent during this 23-year period. Although there was a slowdown of trade between 1980 and 1985 because of world recession and because trade is measured in dollars (the large rise in the value of the dollar between 1980 and 1985 meant that greater trade measured in other currencies translated into fewer dollars), the general upward trend from 1973 to 1996 is undeniable.

However, international transactions have increasingly involved more than just trade in goods and services. Individuals, corporations, financial institutions, and governments now hold international assets to a considerably greater degree than previously. These assets range from bank deposits held overseas by domestic citizens and corporations to foreign bonds, stocks, and physical facilities (e.g., factory buildings in other countries).

Table 2 provides some indicators of the increasing asset interdependence among countries in recent years. Row (1) portrays the increase in holdings by banks and other depository institutions of liabilities (checking and savings accounts, certificates of deposit, etc.) to foreign citizens, institutions, corporations, and governments. The 14.1 percent average annual rate of increase in these liabilities (assets for the foreign holders of them) from $746 billion in 1976 to $8 trillion in 1994 reflects how money and financial markets are becoming increasingly international in scope. The next two rows give other dimensions of international capital flows. Foreign direct investment flows include activities such as the purchase of a controlling interest in foreign firms and the establishment of new plants overseas. Row (2) indicates that this activity rose from an annual average of $40 billion in 1976–1980 to $234 billion in 1994, an increase of almost 500 percent. Finally, row (3) illustrates the general growth in the size of gross stock and bond transactions across country lines (inflows and outflows) of several industrial countries, expressed as a percentage of gross domestic product (GDP). For example, the volume of these transactions for the United States in 1975 was 4 percent of GDP (or about $65 billion since GDP was $1,631 billion), but it had risen to 135 percent by 1995 (about $9.8 trillion). This was an *annual* average rate of increase in the dollar volume of such transactions from 1975 to 1995 of over 28 percent.

TABLE 1   **World Exports, Selected Years, 1973–1996**

Year	Value of World Exports ($, billions)
1973	$ 582
1980	2,036
1985	1,947
1990	3,485
1996	5,100

Sources: 1973—General Agreement on Tariffs and Trade, *International Trade 88–89,* vol. 2 (Geneva, 1989), table A3; 1980, 1985, 1990—General Agreement on Tariffs and Trade, *International Trade 90–91,* vol. 2 (Geneva, 1992), p. 77; 1996—World Trade Organization, press release of April 4, 1997, obtained from "www.wto.org".

The dramatic increase in the amount of monetary activity can also be gleaned from the international reserves held by countries' central banks. With the recent large growth in the value of international trade in goods and assets/liabilities, the size of both the payments outward from countries and the payments inward to countries has grown rapidly. When growth occurs in the value of transactions, it is possible that the size of imbalances (differences between the payments outward and payments inward by private citizens and institutions) will also grow. International reserves constitute government-held, internationally acceptable assets that can be used to settle the balance-of-payments deficits that occur when outflows exceed inflows. In the past, gold was a widely held international reserve asset; at the present time, widely used currencies such as the U.S. dollar, the Japanese yen, and the German deutsche mark constitute the vast majority of international reserves. Table 3 illustrates the rapid growth of international reserves as countries have become more economically and financially interdependent. An average annual growth of almost 10 percent has occurred despite the fact that exchange rates have become considerably more flexible since 1973, and, as we shall develop in later chapters, increased exchange rate flexibility should, other things being equal, reduce the need for international reserves.

TABLE 2   **Indicators of Increasing Financial Interdependence**

	1976	1980	1985	1990	1994
(1) Foreign liabilities of depository institutions ($, billions)	$746	$1,901	$3,057	$7,137	$8,047
	1976–1980	1981–1985	1986–1990	1993	1994*
(2) Total outflows of foreign direct investment, annual average ($, billions)	$ 40	$ 43	$ 168	$ 199	$ 234
(3) Cross-border transactions in bonds and equities, as percentage of GDP	1975	1980	1985	1990	1995
Canada	3%	10%	27%	64%	194%
France	NA	5	21	54	180
Germany	5	7	33	57	172
Italy	1	1	4	27	253
Japan	2	8	62	119	65
United States	4	9	35	89	135

NA— not available.
*The 1994 direct investment figure is preliminary.

Sources: Foreign liabilities of depository institutions—International Monetary Fund, *International Financial Statistics Yearbook 1991* (Washington, DC: IMF, 1991), p. 72; *International Financial Statistics Yearbook 1993* (Washington, DC: IMF, 1993), p. 60; *International Financial Statistics,* May 1997, p. 42; foreign direct investment—Bank for International Settlements, *65th Annual Report* (Basle, Switzerland: BIS, June 12, 1995), p. 66; cross-border transactions in bonds and equities—Bank for International Settlements, *67th Annual Report* (Basle, Switzerland: BIS, June 9, 1997), p. 79.

TABLE 3   **World International Reserves, Selected Years, 1973–1996**

Year-End	International Reserves ($, billions)
1973	$ 184.2
1980	452.4
1985	481.3
1990	954.0
1996	1,609.1

Sources: International Monetary Fund, *International Financial Statistics Yearbook 1996* (Washington, DC: IMF, 1996), pp. 13, 70, 71; International Monetary Fund, *International Financial Statistics,* May 1997, pp. 4, 37.

In overview, the world economy has seen a very rapid growth in international transactions of both a real and a monetary sort over the last two decades. The remainder of this chapter will focus on how these transactions are recorded in the balance-of-payments accounts and in the international investment statement of a country.

CREDITS AND DEBITS IN BALANCE-OF-PAYMENTS ACCOUNTING

In keeping track of a year's international transactions for a country, the balance-of-payments accountant employs a variety of procedures. We do not need to worry about all the details because we are seeking only a working knowledge of the accounts for the purpose of interpreting and understanding broad economic trends, events, and policies. Nevertheless, it is essential to understand the classification system of credits and debits. As a general working rule, **credit items in the balance-of-payments accounts** reflect transactions that give rise to payments inward to the home country. The major items are exports, foreign investment inflows to the home country, and receipts of interest and dividends by the home country from earlier investments abroad. By convention, credit items (which give rise to a payments inflow) are recorded with a *plus* sign. **Debit items in the balance-of-payments accounts** reflect transactions that give rise to payments outward from the home country. The major items are imports, investments made in foreign countries by domestic nationals, and payments of interest and dividends by the home country on earlier investments made in it by foreign investors. By convention, debit items (which lead to a payments outflow) are recorded with a *minus* sign.

Our presentation of credit and debit items generally uses the analytic framework followed by the International Monetary Fund in its annual assemblage of balance-of-payments statistics for its 181 member countries and certain terminology employed by the U.S. Department of Commerce in its presentation of U.S. data. Items are grouped into the four major categories discussed below.[1]

Category I: Current account. Credit items (+ sign) consist of exports of goods and services, income (such as interest and dividends) received from investments abroad, and a "unilateral transfer" item representing gifts received from abroad. Debit items (− sign) are imports of goods and services, income paid to other countries' residents from foreign investments in the home country, and "unilateral transfers" representing gifts sent abroad.

Category II: Direct investment and other long-term capital flows. This category and the next two constitute the *capital account* in a country's balance of payments. Category II is concerned with changes in holdings of long-term real physical assets and financial assets, where "long-term" refers to assets with a maturity of one year or longer. If there is an increase in long-term assets in the home country held by foreign citizens, corporations, and governments (capital inflow to the home country), a credit entry (+ sign) is made; if a sale of these holdings by foreigners causes a decrease, a debit entry (− sign) is made (capital outflow from the home country). Alternatively, if domestic citizens, corporations, and governments increase their holdings of long-term assets abroad, a debit entry is made (capital outflow from the home country); if a sale of these assets decreases holdings abroad by the home country, a credit entry is made (capital inflow to the home country as the sale proceeds are brought home). An easy way to remember this treatment is to note that credits represent a *net increase in holdings of assets in the home country by the foreign country* and debits represent a *net increase in holdings of assets in foreign countries by the home country.*

. . . .

[1]For a somewhat similar approach, see James C. Ingram, *International Economies,* 2nd ed. (New York: Wiley, 1986), chap. 3.

Category III: Short-term nonofficial capital flows. This category records transactions in short-term assets (maturity of less than one year). The transactions are basically private; that is, they are carried out by parties other than central banks or monetary authorities. As in category II, an increase in foreign holdings of these assets in the home country is a credit item and a decrease is a debit item. Alternatively, if the home country's private sector increases its holdings of these assets in foreign countries, the entry is a debit; a decrease is a credit.

Category IV: Changes in reserve assets of official monetary authorities (central banks). If foreign central banks acquire assets (e.g., bank accounts) in the home country, this is a credit item; a decrease is a debit. On the other hand, if the home country's central bank acquires international reserve assets or assets of other countries (e.g., foreign bank deposits), this is treated as a debit item in balance-of-payments accounting; a sale of or decrease in such assets is a credit.

SAMPLE ENTRIES IN THE BALANCE-OF-PAYMENTS ACCOUNTS

To obtain a better grasp of balance-of-payments (BOP) accounting, it is helpful to use hypothetical transactions. In this example and in all discussions of the balance of payments, it is crucial to recognize that the principle of **double-entry bookkeeping** is employed. This means that any transaction involves two sides to the transaction, so the monetary amount is recorded *twice*—once as a debit and once as a credit. It follows that the *sum* of all the debits must be equal to the *sum* of all the credits; that is, the *total* BOP account statement must always be in balance. (Remember that the debits are recorded with a minus sign and the credits with a plus sign. The "equality" of the sums really means equality of the absolute values of the debits and the credits.)

Let us now turn to our hypothetical examples. We designate the home country as country A (e.g., United States) and treat all foreign countries as one country—country B (e.g., Britain). We will describe seven different transactions and indicate at each step the manner in which the transaction is recorded.

Transaction 1. *Exporters of country A send $6,000 of goods to country B, receiving in exchange a short-term bank deposit (e.g., checking account deposit) of $6,000 in country B.* In this transaction, the balance-of-payments accountant records the two sides of the transaction as follows:

Credit: Category I, Exports of goods, +$6,000
Debit: Category III, Increase in short-term private assets abroad, −$6,000

The credit entry is obvious. This particular debit entry occurs because country A's exporters now have checking account deposits in country B. These deposits are classified as short-term assets.

Transaction 2. Suppose that *country A's consumers purchase $12,000 of goods from country B firms and that payment is made by citizens of country A by transferring $12,000 to the bank accounts of country B firms in country A (e.g., in New York).* For this transaction, the entries made by the balance-of-payments accountant are:

Debit: Category I, Imports of goods, −$12,000
Credit: Category III, Increase in foreign short-term private assets in country A, +$12,000

We list the debit entry first, using the practice in these examples of first recording the initial part of the transaction or the initiating entry, followed by the "financing" part of the transaction. Imports have gone up in this instance, but remember that imports constitute debit items; thus, a minus sign is affixed to the entry. In paying for the imports, home country citizens have increased the bank accounts of country B firms in country A; this entry for the financing of the imports has a positive sign.

Transaction 3. Residents of country A send $1,000 of goods to country B's citizens as a gift. This is a special type of entry in the balance-of-payments accounts, and it differs from our previous entries because no purchase or sale is involved. Nevertheless, there has been economic interaction with foreigners, so it must be recorded somewhere. In this case, since goods have been sent from the home country, the credit entry is "exports." However, since double-entry bookkeeping is involved, a debit entry is mandated even though no "payment" has taken place. The balance-of-payments accountant "creates" a debit entry in this instance, much like a "goodwill" or "contributions" entry in an individual firm's balance sheet when there is no payment entry because a gift has been made. The entries for "transaction" 3 are:

> *Credit:*   Category I, Exports of goods, +$1,000
> *Debit:*   Category I, Unilateral transfers made, −$1,000

Transaction 4. Country A firms provide $2,000 of shipping services to country B firms. Country B firms pay for these services by transferring some of their checking account deposits in country A banks to the accounts of country A shipping firms in country A banks. The transaction is recorded as:

> *Credit:*   Category I, Exports of services, +$2,000
> *Debit:*   Category III, Decrease in foreign short-term private assets in country A, −$2,000

The debit entry is explained by the fact that the foreign firms have reduced their bank accounts in home country banks and thus have fewer assets in country A.

Transaction 5. A country B firm sends $2,500 of dividends to its country A stockholders. Payment is made by the country B firm writing checks on its bank account in a country A bank. This transaction is recorded as follows:

> *Credit:*   Category I, Investment income receipts from abroad, +$2,500
> *Debit:*   Category III, Decrease in foreign short-term private assets in country A, −$2,500

The debit entry occurs because the foreign firm now has reduced assets in the home country.

Transaction 6. A citizen of country A purchases a $5,000 long-term corporate bond issued by a country B company. Payment is made by the A citizen by deducting this amount from his or her bank account in country A and transferring the funds to the country A bank account of the country B firm. This transaction is an exchange of assets, and no goods are involved. The bookkeeping entries recognize that a long-term financial asset (the bond) is acquired by the home country citizen in exchange for a short-term asset (the checking account deposit).

> *Debit:*   Category II, Increase in long-term assets abroad, −$5,000
> *Credit:*   Category III, Increase in foreign short-term private assets in country A, +$5,000

Transaction 7. This transaction previews the operation of a foreign exchange market when a country's central bank participates in the market. Suppose that commercial banks (which are regarded as "private citizens") in country B wish to decrease their A-currency balances (e.g., U.S. dollars) in country A banks by converting some of them into their own country's currency (e.g., British pounds). This desire to shift out of dollars may reflect, for example, the anticipation by the commercial banks of a lower future value of the dollar. One method of reducing dollar holdings is to sell them (for pounds) to the Bank of England, and the Bank of England is willing to buy dollars if it is committed, as in a system of fixed exchange rates, to keep the dollar from falling in value against other currencies. Transaction 7 consists of *the sale of $800 to country B's central bank by B's commercial banks. The foreign central bank's dollar accounts in country A banks are increased, and the foreign commercial banks have reduced their dollar balances in country A banks.* This exchange of dollar account holdings in country A banks can and does occur if country A is the United States, since foreign commercial banks as well as central banks maintain balances in New York banks. The balance-of-payments accountant for country A records this change in ownership of dollar assets as follows:

Debit: Category III, Decrease in foreign short-term private assets in country A, −$800
Credit: Category IV, Increase in foreign short-term official assets in country A, +$800

There is no change in the total foreign holdings of dollar assets, but the distribution of such holdings has been altered between the foreign private and public sectors.

ASSEMBLING A BALANCE-OF-PAYMENTS SUMMARY STATEMENT

We can now turn to the construction of country A's balance-of-payments statement. In the real world, there are millions of transactions in any given year for a country such as the United States. But let us suppose that the seven transactions we worked through constitute the entire set of international transactions in a given year, and from these we build the BOP statement.

We first list in T-account form in Table 4 the debit and credit items enumerated in the previous section. The parenthetical numbers in the left-hand column indicate the transaction numbers. From these entries, we now assemble the BOP summary statement in Table 5 and work through this statement.

Looking first at exports and imports of goods, country A has imported $5,000 more of goods than it has exported ($7,000 of exports, $12,000 of imports). Adding the (+) exports of goods and the (−) imports of goods (or the subtraction of imports of goods from exports of goods) yields the **balance of trade,** or **merchandise trade; balance.** When this balance is positive, the result is referred to as a **balance-of-trade surplus** or **merchandise trade surplus;** when negative, the result is a **balance-of-trade deficit** or

TABLE 4   **International Transactions, Country A**

	Debits (−)		*Credits (+)*	
(1)	Increase in short-term private assets abroad	−$ 6,000	Exports of goods	+$ 6,000
(2)	Imports of goods	− 12,000	Increase in foreign short-term private assets in country A	+ 12,000
(3)	Unilateral transfers made	− 1,000	Exports of goods	+ 1,000
(4)	Decrease in foreign short-term private assets in country A	− 2,000	Exports of services	+ 2,000
(5)	Decrease in foreign short-term private assets in country A	− 2,500	Investment income receipts from abroad	+ 2,500
(6)	Increase in long-term assets abroad	− 5,000	Increase in foreign short-term private assets in country A	+ 5,000
(7)	Decrease in foreign short-term private assets in country A	− 800	Increase in foreign short-term official assets in country A	+ 800
		−$29,300		+$29,300

TABLE 5   **Balance-of-Payments Summary Statement, Country A**

Category

I.	Exports of goods (+$6,000 + $1,000)	+$ 7,000
	Imports of goods	− 12,000
	Balance of trade (merchandise trade balance)	−$ 5,000
	Exports of services	+ 2,000
	Imports of services	− 0
	Balance on goods and services	−$ 3,000
	Investment income receipts from abroad	+ 2,500
	Investment income payments abroad	− 0
	Balance on goods, services, and investment income	−$ 500
	Unilateral transfers received	+ 0
	Unilateral transfers made	− 1,000
	Balance on current account (current account balance)	−$ 1,500
II.	Net increase (+) in foreign long-term assets in country A	+ 0
	Net increase (−) in long-term assets abroad	− 5,000
	Balance on current account and long-term capital (basic balance)	−$ 6,500
III.	Net increase (+) in foreign short-term private assets in country A (+$12,000 + $5,000 − $2,000 − $2,500 − $800)	+ 11,700
	Net increase (−) in short-term private assets abroad	− 6,000
	Official reserve transactions balance (overall balance)	−$ 800
IV.	Net increase (+) in foreign short-term official assets in country A	+ 800
	Net increase (−) in official reserve assets or official assets abroad	− 0
		$ 0

merchandise trade deficit. By convention, a surplus is often referred to as a **favorable trade balance** and a deficit is referred to as an **unfavorable trade balance**—terms carried over from the period of Mercantilism in the sixteenth–eighteenth centuries. The balance of trade or merchandise trade balance is usually quoted in newspapers and on the national television and radio news reports, and the figure is released on a monthly basis. However, you should note that it is a very incomplete measure of the balance of payments, since it omits many other items.

The merchandise trade balance is but one of several balances that can be identified in a balance-of-payments statement. To get to other balances and a broader picture of the international transactions of a country, we must add in other items from the transactions in Table 4. The next step is to add services to the merchandise trade balance. Since country A exported $2,000 of services and imported none, the services account has a surplus of $2,000 that is set against the balance-of-trade deficit of $5,000. The resulting **balance on goods and services** of −$3,000 gives the net flow of payments associated with goods *and* services transactions with other countries during the time period. Beginning in January 1994, this balance has been published monthly in the United States, although other balances below are available only on a quarterly basis.

Continuing with category I items, we now enter investment income receipts and payments. When the investment income receipt of +$2,500 is entered (there were no investment income payments to foreign countries in our examples), we arrive at another balance—the **balance on goods, services, and investment income** of −$500. (In official U.S. accounts, this is called the balance on goods, services, and income.)

The next item to be included in our balance-of-payments summary consists of unilateral transfers. When transfers of −$1,000 are added to the balance on goods and services and investment income, we arrive at the **current account balance** or **balance on current account** of −$1,500.

The current account balance is important because it essentially reflects sources and uses of national income. Exports of goods and services generate income when they are produced, and gifts and investment income received from abroad are also a source of income in the current time period. On the other hand, the home country's citizens and government use current income to purchase imports of goods and services and to make gifts and investment income payments abroad.

Another way to view the current account balance is to relate it to aggregate income and expenditure. Remember the basic macroeconomic identity:

$$Y = C + I + G + (X - M) \tag{1}$$

where Y = aggregate income, C = consumption spending, I = investment spending on plant, equipment, and so forth, G = government spending on goods and services, X = exports, and M = imports. In reality, X consists of all the credit items in the current account, not only exports, because they all generate income. Further, M consists of all current account debit items, which are uses of current income, not just imports. Now rearrange the identity:

$$Y - (C + I + G) = (X - M) \tag{2}$$

This rearrangement indicates that the current account balance is simply the difference between income of the country and $(C + I + G)$, and $(C + I + G)$ constitutes spending by the country's residents during the time period. If a country has a current account deficit [$(X - M)$ is negative], it means that $(C + I + G)$ is greater than Y and the country is spending more than its income and living beyond its means. This has been the case in the United States since 1982. Of course, if a country has a current account surplus [$(X - M)$ is positive], the country is spending less than its income; this has been the case with Japan since 1981.

This relationship of the current account balance to macroeconomics can be carried further. Besides expression [1], income can also be written as

$$Y = C + S + T \tag{3}$$

meaning that income can be used only for the purposes of consumption (including imports and transfers abroad), saving, and paying taxes. If we then utilize expressions [1] and [3] by remembering that they both show equalities of variables with Y, we obtain

$$C + I + G + (X - M) = C + S + T$$

or

$$(X - M) = S + (T - G) - I \tag{4}$$

If S is private saving and $(T - G)$ is government saving (which can be negative), then the current account balance is also the difference between a country's saving and the country's investment. Thus, a current account deficit [$(X - M)$ is negative] means that the country is *saving less than it invests* (i.e., the country is not "saving enough"). This is another implication of the U.S. current account deficit since 1982. Of course, a current account surplus [$(X - M)$ is positive] indicates that the country is saving more than it invests. (See Box 1.)

✖ BOX 1   CURRENT ACCOUNT DEFICITS*

As noted in the text, a current account deficit for a country means that the country is spending more than its income or, alternatively, is saving too little relative to its investment. However, it should not be assumed that a current account deficit (CAD) is necessarily a "bad thing" and that a country should focus its attention on adopting policies to obtain balance or a current account surplus. In actuality, there are times when a current account deficit can be viewed in a positive manner. For example, a CAD could reflect the positive development that the country is recovering from a recession more rapidly than are its trading partners. With the rapid recovery the higher incomes are leading to the purchase of more imports, while exports are not being boosted by any significant rise in incomes abroad. Or the home country may be an attractive source of foreign investment because of expected high returns due to favorable business conditions, technological change, or overall increases in productivity. The investment inflows produce a capital account surplus, which, as we will see must be associated with a current account deficit. Yet another source of a capital account surplus could be the liquidation of foreign production facilities and the subsequent transfer of capital to a domestic production site. Finally, net financial capital inflows associated with a CAD tend to put downward pressure on home country interest rates, stimulating investment, growth, and employment.

From a long-term perspective, developing countries may require a net capital inflow (and therefore a CAD) to assist them in their early efforts at industrialization. Even as their growth picks up and they become less reliant on foreign capital, the interest and/or dividend payments on the accumulated foreign capital stock can result in a current account deficit. Ultimately, however, if repayment is needed on some or all of the initial foreign investment, the developing country will experience a current account surplus and a capital account deficit. This transition from a debtor (capital-importing) nation to a creditor (capital-exporting) nation has been regarded by some economists as part of a natural sequence in the development process.

*For a useful discussion of many of these points, see "Schools Brief: In Defence of Deficits," *The Economist,* Dec. 16, 1995, pp. 68–69.

We now turn to categories II, III, and IV in the BOP statement in Table 5. A main point to note is that, since the current account items have added up to −$1,500, the sum of these capital account items by themselves *must* be +$1,500. Why? Because the sum of the total credits (with a plus sign) and total debits (with a minus sign) of all the items in the balance-of-payments must be *zero* due to the nature of double-entry bookkeeping. Hence, when someone speaks of a "balance-of-payments deficit," that person cannot be speaking of *all* the items in the balance of payments because all of the items must sum to zero. The loosely used term "balance-of-payments deficit" therefore refers only to some *part* of the balance-of-payments statement, not to the entire statement. This part could be only the balance of trade, or the balance on goods and services, or the current account balance, for example. The term *balance-of-payments deficit* is deficient because it lacks precision in indicating which items in the account are being discussed, and the term is clearly nonsensical if it refers to all of the items in the balance of payments.

Now return to our sample entries by adding category II, the long-term capital account. Since there was a long-term capital outflow of $5,000 and no long-term capital inflows, the value of category II by itself is −$5,000. When this is added to the current account figure of −$1,500, we have a new balance (of −$6,500), known as the **balance on current account and long-term capital.** This cumbersome term is often shortened to the term **basic balance** to emphasize the point that the first two categories of the balance-of-payments statement reflect basic long-term forces in the economy of a country. The current account balance reflects such influences on the balance of payments as national income and its growth, spending habits, and international competitiveness; in addition, the long-term capital flows reflect the judgments of long-term investors on the relative profitability of investing overseas rather than in the home country. These decisions presumably embrace a long-term view on the economic future of particular industries and countries. Long-term relationships influencing the balance of payments must be distinguished from shorter-term forces such as sudden changes in interest rates or anticipated exchange rate movements. Shorter-term forces are most likely reflected by short-term capital movements in category III.

We now turn to category III, which covers flows of short-term private assets. This category has a high proportion of entries in the real world, because the items in it reflect "financing" items for transactions in categories I and II and short-term capital transactions initiated on their own. There has been a net increase in foreign short-term private assets (credit item) in country A of $11,700 (= $12,000 + $5,000 − $2,000 − $2,500 − $800), and a debit item of an increase in short-term private assets abroad of −$6,000. Thus, category III by itself has a value of + $5,700 (= $11,700 − $6,000).

Finally, the cumulative balance after considering categories I to III (the current account, long-term capital flows, and short-term private capital flows) is −$800. This balance is the one that is generally meant when economists use the broad term "balance-of-payments deficit (or surplus)." A more precise phrasing is the "balance after considering goods, services, investment income, unilateral transfers, long-term capital flows, and short-term private capital flows." For simplicity, however, the balance is called the **official reserve transactions balance** or **overall balance,** which reflects the net effect of all transactions with other countries during the time period considered but excluding government short-term capital transactions ("official reserve transactions"). Since categories I to III have a sum of −$800, then category IV must by itself have a value of +$800; government activity was necessary to cover or "settle" the net balance of the previous transactions. This $800 is essentially a measure of the amount of participation or intervention by the official monetary authorities in the foreign exchange market, the B central bank purchases of dollars in our example. In this context, economists sometimes use the phrases "autonomous items in the balance of payments" and "accommodating items in the balance of payments." The term **autonomous items in the balance of payments** refers to international economic transactions that take place in the pursuit of ordinary economic goals such as profit maximization by firms and utility maximization by individuals. These transactions are undertaken independently of the state of the country's balance of payments and are reflected in categories I to III in the BOP statement. The term **accommodating items in the balance of payments** refers to transactions that occur because of other activity in the balance of payments, i.e., the government items in category IV.

We have now used all the entries in the sample transactions in country A's balance of payments, and it should come as no surprise that the net result of all the entries is a balance of $0. Categories I to IV as a whole must sum to zero since each transaction in each category has been entered twice—once as a credit entry and once as a debit entry. Further, the current account balance (category I) *must* be equal but opposite in sign to the balance of the three capital accounts (categories II, III, IV) by themselves. This also is obviously a result of double-entry bookkeeping. Thus, our current account balance in the example (−$1,500) matches the sum of categories II to IV by themselves:

Category II	−$5,000
Category III	+ 5,700
Category IV	+ 800
Capital account balance	+$1,500

This **capital account balance** constitutes an additional measure of "balance" in the balance of payments that has received substantial attention in the United States.

In assembling the balance-of-payments statement, we have thus identified seven different measures of balance. These balances have different monetary values, and it is imperative when you hear or read about a country's "balance of payments" to understand which one is being discussed. The balances in our numerical example were:

Balance of trade (merchandise trade balance)	−$5,000
Balance on goods and services	− 3,000
Balance on goods, services, and investment income	− 500
Current account balance (balance on current account)	− 1,500
Balance on current account and long-term capital (basic balance)	− 6,500
Official reserve transactions balance (overall balance)	− 800
Capital account balance	+ 1,500

In practice, the decision of which balance to emphasize reflects the particular items that the analyst has in mind for reasons of policy or academic interest. There is no one true measure of a country's balance; the different balances reflect concentration on different items in the balance of payments. For example, the balance of trade may be the focus in studying international competitiveness in goods alone. The current account balance may be the focus in examining a country's national income-spending relationship. Further, the official reserve transactions balance may be the focus if interest centers on the amount of official government intervention in foreign exchange markets. Regardless of the focus, the assembling of the complete BOP statement is necessary if we are to analyze and interpret the international economic transactions of a country with the rest of the world during any particular time period.

CONCEPT CHECK

1. What does a balance-of-payments statement portray? Why is the BOP always in balance?
2. What is the difference between the current account balance and the balance of trade?

3. What rule do accountants follow in recording transactions in the balance of payments? In what manner would an export of wheat be recorded? A purchase of a foreign stock?

BALANCE-OF-PAYMENTS SUMMARY STATEMENT FOR THE UNITED STATES

Having worked extensively through the recording of sample transactions and the process of assembling a balance-of-payments summary statement for a hypothetical country, we now present the U.S. balance-of-payments statement for 1996 (Table 6).

The first point to note about this table is that it does not quite conform to the presentation discussed above. For approximately the last 25 years, the United States has not presented the capital account items in the category II (long-term capital account) and category III (short-term private capital account) format. Category IV (short-term official capital account) is also not listed per se but can be derived.[2] This change in presentation means that of the various balances, only the merchandise trade balance; the balance on goods and services; the balance on goods, services, and investment income; and the current account balance are listed in government publications. Prior to the change, official measures of the basic balance and the official reserve transactions balance were also given. (The capital account balance has never been officially listed.) The official reserve transactions balance and the capital account balance can still be derived from the figures,

---

[2]The reasons for this change in official presentation involve the movement from relatively fixed exchange rates to floating exchange rates in 1973 and need not concern us at this point.

TABLE 6   **U.S. International Transactions, 1996 (in billions of dollars)**

Exports of goods	+$611.7
Imports of goods	− 799.3
Merchandise trade balance	−$187.7
Exports of services	+ 223.9
Imports of services	− 150.4
Balance on goods and services	−$114.2
Income receipts on U.S. assets abroad	+ 196.9
Income payments on foreign assets in the United States	− 205.3
Balance on goods, services, and income	−$122.6
Unilateral transfers, net	− 42.5
(Government −$18.9)	
(Private −$23.6)	
Current account balance	−$165.1
U.S. official reserve assets, net (increase, −)	+$ 6.7
U.S. government assets abroad, other than official reserve assets, net (increase, −)	−$ 0.7
U.S. private assets abroad, net (increase, −)	−$312.8
Foreign official assets in the United States, net (increase, +)	+$122.8
Other foreign assets in the United States, net (increase, +)	+$402.3
Statistical discrepancy	−$ 53.1

Notes: (*a*) Data are preliminary. (*b*) Components may not sum to totals due to rounding.
Source: U.S. Department of Commerce, *Survey of Current Business,* April 1997, p. 43.

but the basic balance cannot. Despite the lack of conformity of official U.S. data to our conceptual presentation, we can still discuss them in reasonable concordance with that framework.

At the top of Table 6, you will notice that the United States had a large merchandise trade deficit of $187.7 billion in 1996. Except for 1973 and 1975, the United States has had a merchandise trade deficit every year since 1971, when the traditional U.S. merchandise surplus that had existed since the end of World War II ceased.

The merchandise trade deficit was somewhat offset by a surplus on services trade in 1996. The services surplus was $73.5 billion (exports of services of $223.9 billion minus imports of services of $150.4 billion). Important items in services are tourist expenditures and receipts, royalties and license fees, charges for telecommunications, banking, insurance, and so forth. Investment income receipts from U.S. assets abroad ($196.9 billion) and investment income payments on foreign assets in the United States ($205.3 billion) resulted in a negative figure of $8.4 billion. Only since 1994 have investment income outflows exceeded investment income inflows in the entire post-World War II period. The balance on goods and services (−$114.2 billion) and the balance on goods, services, and investment income (−$122.6 billion) both showed smaller deficits in 1996 than did the merchandise trade balance.

Moving next in Table 6 to unilateral transfers, the net result in 1996 was a debit (or net outflow) of $42.5 billion. When this deficit is coupled with the deficit on goods, services, and investment income, the result was a U.S. current account deficit of $165.1 billion.

How is it economically possible for the current account balance to be negative? The answer of course is that the balance-of-payments accounts must have an equal and off-setting capital account surplus, that is, a net inflow of funds from abroad. Let us now look at the capital accounts for the United States in 1996 to examine this net capital inflow.

Although the U.S. official balance-of-payments accounts no longer list capital-flow items systematically in the framework of categories II, III, and IV, we can glean the combined long-term capital account and short-term private capital account from the data in the table. Consider first the two headings "U.S. government assets abroad, other than official reserve assets" and "U.S. private assets abroad." These government assets transactions are those that do not involve the short-term, liquid assets of our category IV. The U.S. private assets category contains both long-term and short-term asset purchases and sales, including long-term direct investments, U.S. transactions in foreign securities of various maturities, and short-term claims on foreigners by U.S. banks and nonbanking firms. The two broad headings essentially represent the debit amount of "increase in U.S. assets abroad" (capital outflows), both long-term and short-term together, of the nonofficial type of categories II and III. The result in 1996 was a net debit amount of −$0.7 −$312.8 = −$313.5 billion.

Consider next "Other foreign assets in the United States," which indicates the change in assets in the United States held by foreigners, but it too is a consolidation of long-term as well as private short-term capital flows. There was a substantial U.S. net credit amount of $402.3 billion in 1996.

Finally, look at the remaining two capital account items, "U.S. official reserve assets" and "Foreign official assets in the United States." These items correspond to our category IV (short-term official capital account). The "U.S. official reserve assets" entry has a *minus* sign if there is a net increase in reserve assets (since the increase is a debit item) and a plus sign if there is a net decrease. In 1996, there was a decrease of $6.7 billion. "Foreign official assets in the United States" indicates the change in holdings of assets in the United States by foreign central banks (+ if an increase, − if a decrease). The substantial credit (+) entry for 1996 indicates that foreign monetary authorities increased their holdings of U.S. assets by $122.8 billion. When category IV as a whole is thus considered, we obtain a figure of +$129.5 billion = +$6.7 billion +$122.8 billion. Therefore, because of double-entry bookkeeping, *the sum of categories I through III for the United States must have been −$129.5 billion. Thus, the official reserve transactions balance for the United States in 1996 was a deficit of $129.5 billion.*[3]

Looking back over Table 6 as a whole, remember that the current account balance was −$165.1 billion (a current account deficit of $165.1 billion). Since double-entry book-keeping means that the capital accounts should add up to $165.1 billion, let's check this result. The capital account items and their net debit or credit values that we have identified are as follows:

U.S. government assets abroad, other than official reserve assets, net	−$ 0.7
U.S. private assets abroad, net	− 312.8
Other foreign assets in the United States, net	+ 402.3
U.S. official reserve assets, net	+ 6.7
Foreign official assets in the United States, net	+ 122.8
	+$218.3

What is wrong here? Why do the capital account items add up to +$218.3 billion rather than +$165.1 billion? The reason is that U.S. authorities use incomplete data in compiling the balance-of-payments statement. The accountants are unable to get enough information to make all the double entries in the double-entry bookkeeping framework. Data on trade are collected from customs information as goods enter and leave the United States, but data on the financing of trade and on capital flows are gathered independently from

---

[3]We are ignoring one small detailed procedure that would make the deficit slightly smaller.

commercial banks and other institutions. Some transactions escape the recording and accounting framework altogether; this certainly applies to smuggling and money laundering, but it also applies to legal transactions. Further, the timing of the current account items and related flows in the capital account does not always exactly coincide with the same calendar year. Thus, the accountant creates a special category, **statistical discrepancy** or **net errors and omissions,** to deal with the fact that the sum of the debits and credits actually recorded is not zero in practice. In Table 6, you will note that the statistical discrepancy entry has a value of −$53.1 billion. (This item is often thought to consist primarily of unrecorded short-term capital flows, but unrecorded exports may also be involved—see Ott 1988.) When the −$53.1 billion is combined with the capital account figure of +$218.3 billion, we arrive at +$165.2 billion, a figure that matches the current account balance of −$165.1 billion (difference due to rounding).

This completes our discussion of balance-of-payments accounting, perhaps in too detailed a fashion for your tastes(!). (For one of the authors, BOP accounting is his second favorite thing—the first is root canal work.) However, we think that a grasp of the fundamental concepts of the various balances and classifications is important for understanding international payments, the foreign exchange market, and macroeconomic policy decisions. While we have presented actual U.S. data for the BOP, the concepts and classifications apply to all countries. For a look at data on a controversial balance-of-payments experience, see Case Study 1, which discusses the Japanese trade and current account balances.

INTERNATIONAL INVESTMENT POSITION OF THE UNITED STATES

We conclude this chapter by looking at another kind of statement that portrays the international economic relationships of a country, using the United States as our example. This statement indicates the **international investment position of a country,** or sometimes, if presented with the opposite sign, the **international indebtedness position of a country.**

A country's international investment position is related to the capital accounts in its balance-of-payments statement, but it differs in an important way. The capital account in a balance-of-payments statement shows the *flows* of capital during the year being examined. In the economist's terminology, the balance of payments is a *flow concept,* meaning that it portrays some type of economic activity during a particular time period. Flow concepts are the kind most frequently encountered in economic analysis, and familiar examples are national income during a year, investment expenditure by firms during a year, or sales of a good during a particular month. On the other hand, the international investment position is a stock concept rather than a flow concept. A *stock concept* examines the value of a particular economic variable at a point in time. Thus, the capital stock of a country at the end of a year, the number of automobiles in existence at the end of a given month, and the year-end size of the money supply are stock concepts. While the capital account in the balance of payments shows the size of capital flows during a year, the international investment position shows the *cumulative* size of a country's foreign assets and liabilities at a given point in time (usually defined as at the end of a particular year). The flows of capital during the year will change the size of the cumulative stock, and the end-of-the-year international investment position reflects this flow and all previous flows. The statement of the end-of-the-year international investment position allows the observer to compare the size of the country's foreign assets with the size of its foreign liabilities (i.e., the total assets of foreign countries in this country). If the assets exceed the liabilities, the country is a **net creditor country;** if the liabilities exceed the assets, the country is said to be a **net debtor country.**

A matter of considerable controversy in recent years has been Japan's continuing large merchandise trade surpluses. U.S. policymakers and potential exporters to Japan have complained bitterly that these large surpluses indicate the "closed" nature of the Japanese economy and that formal and informal barriers to imports of an "unfair" sort are widely prevalent. Figure 1 shows the trade and current account balances of Japan from 1974 to 1995. The trade balance was virtually zero in 1974 (although positive prior to that time). It improved to over $20 billion by 1978 and then returned to near-balance in 1979–1980. However, the trade balance then began a dramatic rise to an all-time high of $144.4 billion in 1994. The current account balance has occasionally been negative and has always been less positive than the trade balance over the period, reflecting Japan's position as a net importer of services, such as transportation, and larger travel expenditures overseas than travel expenditures by foreigners in Japan. (Remember, the merchandise trade balance does not include services.) Interestingly, the official reserve transactions balance or overall balance (not shown in Figure 1) has been *negative* or in deficit in about one-third of the years and has averaged

only +$4.2 billion annually. Large current account surpluses in conjunction with near-balance in the official reserve transactions balance indicate large private capital outflows from Japan and relatively little Japanese central bank activity in exchange markets.

It should be noted in addition that the Japanese surplus with the United States *bilaterally* has been over $40 billion annually since 1985 and was $67 billion in 1994 and $60 billion in 1995. This bilateral surplus has been of particular concern to the United States, and U.S. policymakers have urged Japan to grow more rapidly because higher incomes would lead to more Japanese purchases of U.S. goods. U.S.-Japanese discussions have been held to reach precise agreement on the steps to take to reduce the Japanese surplus and on specific "targets" for surplus reduction. However, in 1995, Japan imported over $75 billion of goods from the United States, far above Japan's imports from any other country (China was second at $36 billion). Japan also has continuing bilateral deficits with some countries (e.g., Australia, China, and Indonesia). In addition, because of its total reliance on imported oil, Japan has had deficits of over $20 billion annually since 1989 with petroleum-exporting countries.

FIGURE 1   **Trade and Current Account Balances of Japan, 1974–1995**

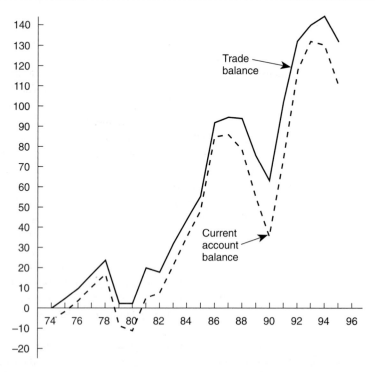

Sources: The following International Monetary Fund publications: *Balance of Payments Statistics Yearbook 1996* (Washington, DC: IMF, 1996), p. 393; *Direction of Trade Statistics Yearbook 1996* (Washington, DC: IMF, 1996), pp. 267–69; *International Financial Statistics Yearbook 1993* (Washington, DC: IMF, 1993), p. 440; *International Financial Statistics Yearbook 1996* (Washington, DC: IMF, 1996), pp. 460–61; and *International Financial Statistics,* May 1997, p. 388. Also, U.S. Department of Commerce, *Survey of Current Business,* July 1996, p. 78. ✿

TABLE 7   **International Investment Position of the United States, December 31, 1995
(in billions of dollars)**

A. U.S. Assets Abroad

U.S. official reserve assets		$ 176.1
U.S. government assets abroad other than official reserve assets		81.5
U.S. private assets abroad		2,674.3
Direct investment abroad*	$ 880.1	
Foreign bonds	310.7	
Foreign corporate stocks	411.1	
U.S. claims on foreigners reported by U.S. banks and nonbanks	1,072.4	
Total U.S. assets abroad		$2,931.9

B. Foreign Assets in the United States

Foreign official assets in the United States		$ 677.9
Other foreign assets in the United States		3,068.0
Foreign direct investment*	$ 638.5	
U.S. Treasury securities	388.9	
Corporate and other bonds	533.2	
Corporate stocks	465.4	
U.S. liabilities to foreigners reported by U.S. banks and nonbanks	1,041.9	
Total foreign assets in the United States		$3,745.9
Net International Investment Position of the United States = Total U.S.		–$ 814.0
assets abroad minus Total foreign assets in the United States = $2,931.9 minus $3,745.9		

*Direct investment is valued at current cost.
Notes: (*a*) Data are preliminary.
    (*b*) Components may not sum to totals due to rounding.
Source: U.S. Department of Commerce, *Survey of Current Business,* July 1996, p. 42.

Given this background, Table 7 shows the statement of the U.S. international investment position at the end of 1995. Part A, "U.S. assets abroad," indicates the claims of U.S. citizens and government on foreigners. (Some of the assets such as stock certificates may be physically held in the United States.) The first item, "U.S. official reserve assets," represents the stock of international reserve assets held by the U.S. government as contrasted with the flows of these assets during a given year which are indicated in a U.S. BOP statement. The second item, "U.S. government assets abroad other than official reserve assets," includes primarily U.S. government loans to other countries and funds paid by the United States as membership subscriptions to international organizations such as the International Monetary Fund and the World Bank. The category of "U.S. private assets abroad" embraces a variety of items, with the largest two entries being U.S. direct investment abroad and U.S. claims reported by U.S. banks (over 70 percent of the $1,072.4 billion figure for claims by banks and nonbanks). The bank claims item reflects deposits made in foreign financial institutions by U.S. banks and individual depositors. The most rapidly growing item in the private assets category in recent years in percentage terms was U.S. private holdings of foreign corporate stocks (from $18.9 billion in 1980 to $411.1 billion in 1995, an increase of over 2,000 percent). The total value of foreign assets held by U.S. citizens and government at the end of 1995 was $2,931.1 billion or $2.9 trillion.

Part B of Table 7 reflects foreign holdings of assets in the United States. The "foreign official assets in the United States" entry indicates the cumulative buildup of holdings by foreign central banks of financial instruments such as U.S. Treasury securities and commercial bank deposits. The 285 percent increase in these foreign official asset holdings in recent years (from $176.1 billion in 1980 to $677.9 billion in 1995) was

✸ CASE STUDY 2   TRENDS IN THE U.S. INTERNATIONAL INVESTMENT POSITION

The international investment position of the United States deteriorated markedly after 1980. From the 1980 level of +$392.5 billion, the figure turned negative by 1987 and then reached Table 7's −$814.0 billion at the end of 1995. The position over the 1977–1995 period is shown graphically in Figure 2. Remembering that the net international investment position shows the total stock of U.S. assets abroad minus the total stock of foreign assets in the United States, a decrease in the position reflects net capital flows inward to the United States (a capital account surplus/current account deficit). The dramatic decline in the U.S. position since 1980 therefore can be regarded as a reflection of the U.S. current account deficits. In turn, since the current account deficits reflected greater spending than income by the United States (or inadequate saving to finance investment), another way to view the decrease in the U.S. international investment position is that foreign citizens, institutions, and governments have been financing the excess spending through a capital inflow to the United States.

A noteworthy departure from the pattern of the total net international investment position is the behavior of the net *direct* investment position. This category involves acquisition and start-up of new factories and real production facilities. Throughout the entire 1977–1995 period, the stock of U.S.-owned direct investment assets overseas has been greater than the stock of foreign-owned direct investment assets in the United States. The stock of foreign direct investments in the United States

increased dramatically from 1977 to 1995 (rising from $57 billion to $639 billion), but U.S. direct investments overseas rose from $253 billion to $880 billion, thus maintaining the positive *net* position shown in Figure 2. As of 1991, the U.S. Department of Commerce began valuing direct investment assets here and abroad at current replacement cost (used in this Case Study), a method that replaced that of valuing assets at their original cost. The previous method resulted in a smaller net direct investment position for the United States because the country's direct investment facilities abroad were of older vintage than foreign direct investment assets in the United States. Under original-cost valuation, the value of these older assets had not been adjusted upward with inflation.*

Finally, the net international investment position, when negative, implies that a country is a *net debtor* as referred to in the text. However, do not confuse the U.S. net debtor position with the popular term *national debt* (over $5 trillion) that has been prominent in the news and was made especially prominent in 1992 by Ross Perot. That term is basically a misnomer because it refers to the debt of the U.S. federal government only, most of which (over 80 percent) is owed to U.S. (not foreign) citizens and institutions, and is an asset for the bondholders. When assessing relative claims of the United States versus claims of other nations on the United States, the net international investment position is a much more appropriate measure than the federal government's debt.

*The U.S. Commerce Department also now publishes a series of calculations using market valuation of the assets rather than current replacement cost, but the market valuation series has greater measurement problems.

Sources: Data from U.S. Department of Commerce, *Survey of Current Business,* June 1992, p. 49, and July 1996, p. 44.

(Continued)

dwarfed by the huge increase in private holdings of U.S. assets reflected in the "other foreign assets in the United States" category. The figure for this category was $367.7 billion in 1980, and its increase to $3,068.0 billion by the end of 1995 represented a 734 percent increase from 1980 to 1995. As the United States has been running large current account deficits, the counterpart has been this inflow of foreign funds to finance these deficits. The cumulative amount of foreign direct investments (at current cost) in the United States, for example, stood at $125.9 billion in 1980 but increased to $638.5 billion by the end of 1995. Foreign private ownership of U.S. Treasury securities during the 1980–1995 period increased from $16.1 billion to $388.9 billion; private foreign holdings of U.S. corporate and other bonds increased from $9.5 billion to $533.2 billion (an increase of *5,513 percent!*); and private foreign holdings of U.S. corporate stocks increased from $64.6 billion to $465.4 billion. At the end of 1995, total foreign holdings (government plus private) of U.S. assets were $3,745.9 billion, or $3.7 trillion.

FIGURE 2   **Net International and Direct Investment Positions of the United States, 1977–1995**

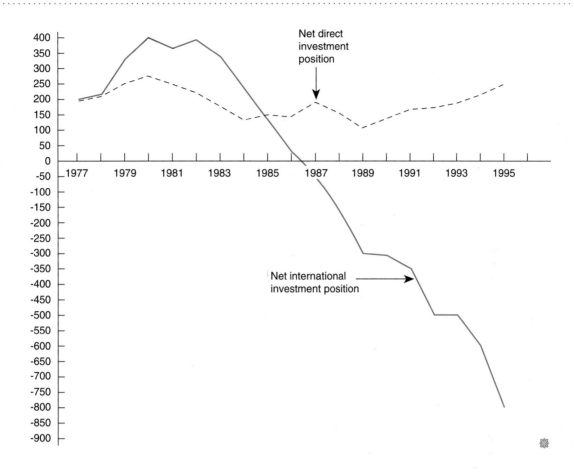

The commonly cited figure for a country's net international investment position is simply the difference between the country's assets abroad and the foreign assets in the country. This figure for the United States for 1995 is indicated at the bottom of Table 7, *minus* $814.0 billion. No country in the world has such a large negative net international investment position (that is, net international indebtedness position).

There are certainly disadvantages to such a position for the United States. For example, interest and dividends will have to be paid to overseas debt holders and stockholders in the future (as well as perhaps debt principal), which eventually involves a transfer of goods and real income abroad. (There is also worry that a "too large" amount of assets held by foreign individuals, firms, and governments can threaten a loss of national sovereignty.) However, the cumulative capital inflows, if productively used, will have generated the income with which to make these future payments. In addition, some economists think that the inflow of foreign funds may have kept U.S. interest rates lower than they would have been otherwise. Beyond consideration of the net debtor position itself, however, a very important point is that the huge $2.9 trillion of U.S. assets abroad and the huge $3.7 trillion of foreign-held assets in the United States are a striking indication of the increased mobility of capital and the increased interdependence of countries in the modern world.

It should be noted that the current net debtor position for the United States is a recent phenomenon. Case Study 2 reviews the U.S. experience since 1977.

CONCEPT CHECK

1. How would you characterize the current U.S. balance-of-payments situation? How does it relate to the claim that the United States has been engaging in trade as though it had possession of an international credit card?
2. Why is the current account balance not exactly offset in practice by the capital ac-

count balance? What recording brings the BOP into balance?
3. What does it mean to say that the United States is a debtor country? How long has this been the case?

SUMMARY

A balance-of-payments statement summarizes a country's economic transactions with all other countries during a particular time period, usually a year. In accordance with various accounting conventions, the statement indicates debits and credits in goods and services and investment income flows, unilateral transfers, long-term capital flows, short-term private capital flows, and short-term capital flows associated with activity by the country's monetary authorities. The statement is broadly divided into the current account and the capital account. A current account imbalance must be matched by an equal (but of opposite sign) capital account imbalance; for example, the large current account deficits of the United States

in recent years have been matched by large capital account surpluses. The most widely cited "balances" in a balance-of-payments statement are the merchandise trade balance and the current account balance. These and other balances (especially the official reserve transactions balance when central banks participate in the foreign exchange market) are useful for interpreting economic events and for guiding the decisions of policymakers. Finally, a country's statement of its net international investment position portrays the total assets of the country abroad and the total foreign assets in the home country. This statement indicates whether a country is a net debtor or a net creditor vis-à-vis foreign countries at a given point in time.

KEY TERMS

accommodating items in the balance of payments
autonomous items in the balance of payments
balance-of-payments accounts
balance of trade (or merchandise trade balance)
balance-of-trade deficit (or merchandise trade deficit)
balance-of-trade surplus (or merchandise trade surplus)

balance on current account and long-term capital (or basic balance)
balance on goods and services
balance on goods, services, and investment income
capital account balance
credit items in the balance-of-payments accounts
current account balance (or balance on current account)
debit items in the balance-of-payments accounts

double-entry bookkeeping
favorable trade balance
international investment position of a country (or international indebtedness position of a country)
net creditor country
net debtor country
official reserve transactions balance (or overall balance)
statistical discrepancy (or net errors and omissions)
unfavorable trade balance

QUESTIONS AND PROBLEMS

1. Explain how the following items would be entered into the U.S. balance of payments (the initiating entry):
   A disaster relief shipment of wheat to Bangladesh
   Imports of textile machinery
   Opening a $500 bank account in Zurich
   A $1,000,000 Japanese purchase of U.S. government bonds
   Hotel expenses in Geneva

The purchase of a BMW automobile
Interest earned on a bank account in London
The Union Carbide purchase of a French chemical plant
Sales of lumber to Japan
The shipment of Fords to the United States from a Mexican production plant; and the profits from that same plant

2. What is the difference between the capital account and the current account?

3. What is meant by the "net international investment position" of the United States? What would happen to this net position if the United States experienced a current account surplus? Why?

4. Why has Japan's current account surplus been smaller than its trade surplus in recent years? Explain why Japan's official reserve transactions balance has been close to zero.

5. Since the capital account balance must exactly offset the current account balance, why do government accountants bother to record the capital account?

6. Explain why a current account deficit indicates that a country is using more goods and services than it is producing.

7. "Direct foreign investment affects both the capital account and the current account over time." Agree? Disagree? Explain.

8. Suppose that two events occur simultaneously: (i) A firm in country A exports $1,000 of goods to country B and receives a $1,000 bank deposit in country B in exchange; and (ii) a country A immigrant gives $500 to a relative in country B in the form of a $500 buildup of the relative's bank account in country A.

   What is the impact of these two events on country A's (*a*) merchandise trade balance, (*b*) current account balance, and (*c*) official reserve transactions balance?

9. Japanese officials have maintained that a key step for reducing the U.S. current account deficit is *not* that foreign markets should become more open to U.S. exports but, rather, that the U.S. government should reduce its budget deficit. Is there validity to this point? If so, why? If not, why not?

THE FOREIGN EXCHANGE MARKET

INTRODUCTION

In the previous chapter, we examined how a country's transactions with the rest of the world are recorded for a specified period of time. An important point of this discussion was that any deficit or surplus in the current account is offset exactly by a net surplus or deficit in the capital accounts that reflects the change in the net asset position abroad. The movement of financial assets and goods and services reflected in the balance of payments takes place between many different countries, each with its own domestic currency. Economic interaction can only occur in this instance if there is a specific link between currencies so that the value of a given transaction can be determined by both parties in their own respective currencies. This important link is the foreign exchange rate. This chapter examines how this link is established in the foreign exchange market and underlying economic factors that influence it. The principal components of the market are analyzed and various measures of the exchange rate discussed. Finally, you will be made aware of how the foreign exchange market and the financial markets are intertwined and of the formal relationship that exists between the foreign exchange rate and the interest rate.

THE FOREIGN EXCHANGE RATE AND THE MARKET FOR FOREIGN EXCHANGE

The **foreign exchange rate** is simply the price of one currency in terms of another (for example, U.S.\$/U.K.£ or, alternatively, U.K.£/U.S.\$). Not surprisingly, this price can be viewed as the result of the interaction of the forces of supply and demand for the foreign currency in any particular period of time. Although this price is fixed under some monetary system arrangements, if a country is to avoid continual BOP surpluses or deficits, the fixed exchange rate must be approximately that which would result from market determination of the exchange rate. We will therefore proceed to examine the foreign exchange rate assuming that it is the result of the normal market interaction of supply and demand. This market simultaneously determines hundreds of different exchange rates daily and facilitates the hundreds of thousands of international transactions that take place. The worldwide network of markets and institutions that handle the exchange of foreign currencies is known as the **foreign exchange market.** Within the foreign exchange market, current transactions for immediate delivery are carried out in the spot market and contracts to buy or sell currencies for future delivery are carried out in forward and futures markets. The nature of these specific markets and the manner in which they function will be discussed in greater detail later in the chapter.

Demand Side

Individuals participate in the foreign exchange market for a number of reasons. On the demand side, one of the principal reasons people desire foreign currency is to purchase goods and services from another country or to send a gift or investment income payments abroad. For example, the desire to purchase a foreign automobile or to travel abroad produces a demand for the currency of the country in which these goods or services are produced. A second important reason to acquire foreign currency is to purchase financial assets in a particular country. The desire to open a foreign bank account, purchase foreign stocks or bonds, or acquire direct ownership of real capital would all fall into this category. A third reason that individuals demand foreign exchange is to avoid losses or make profits that could arise through changes in the foreign exchange rate. Individuals who believe that the foreign currency is going to become more valuable in the future may wish to acquire that currency today at a low price in hopes of selling it tomorrow at a high price and thus make a quick profit. Such risk-taking activity is referred to as **speculation** in a foreign currency. Other individuals who have to pay for an imported item in the future may wish to acquire the needed foreign currency today, rather than risk the possibility that the foreign currency will become more valuable in the future and would increase the cost of the item in local currency. Activity undertaken to avoid the risk associated with changes in the exchange rate is referred to as **hedging.** The total demand for a foreign currency at any one point in time thus reflects these three underlying demands: the demand for foreign goods and services (and transfers and investment income payments abroad), the demand for foreign investment, and the demand based on risk-taking or risk-avoidance activity. It should be clear that the demands on the part of a country's citizens correspond to debit items in the balance-of-payments accounting framework covered in the previous chapter.

Supply Side

Participants on the supply side operate for similar reasons (reflecting credit items in the balance of payments). Foreign currency supply to the home country results firstly from foreigners purchasing home exports of goods and services or making unilateral transfers or investment income payments to the home country. For example, U.S. exports of wheat and soybeans are a source of supply of foreign exchange. A second source arises from foreign investment in the home country. Foreign purchases of U.S. government bonds, European purchases of U.S. stocks and placement of bank deposits in the United States, and Japanese joint ventures in U.S. automobile or electronics plants are all examples of financial activity that provides a supply of foreign exchange to the United States. Finally, foreign speculation and hedging activities can provide yet a third source of supply. The total supply of foreign exchange in any time period consists of these three sources.

Before moving on to more technical aspects of the foreign exchange market, let us take a moment to discuss in a general way how it operates (see Figure 1). The foreign exchange market here is presented from the U.S. perspective and, like any normal market, contains a downward-sloped demand curve and an upward-sloped supply curve. The price on the vertical axis is stated in terms of the domestic currency price of foreign currency, for example, $\$_{US}/\text{franc}_{Swiss}$, and the horizontal axis measures the units of Swiss francs supplied and demanded at various prices (exchange rates). The intersection of the supply and demand curves determines simultaneously the equilibrium exchange rate e_{eq} and the equilibrium quantity (Q_{eq}) of Swiss francs supplied and demanded during a given period of time. An increase in the demand for Swiss francs on the part of the United States will cause the demand curve to shift out to D'_{Sfr} and the exchange rate to increase to e'. Note that the increase in the exchange rate means that it is taking *more U.S. currency to buy each Swiss franc.* When this occurs, the U.S. dollar is said to be *depreciating* against the Swiss franc. In similar fashion, an increase in the supply of Swiss

FIGURE 1   **The Basic Foreign Exchange Market**

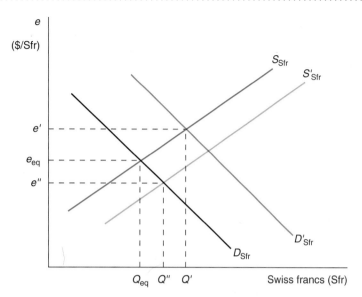

The equilibrium rate of exchange, e_{eq}, is determined by the interaction of the supply and demand for a particular foreign currency (in this case the Swiss franc). An increase in domestic demand for the foreign currency is represented by a rightward shift in the demand curve to D'_{Sfr}, which causes the equilibrium exchange rate to increase to e'. Since it now takes more units of domestic currency to buy a unit of foreign exchange, the domestic currency (the \$) has depreciated. In a similar fashion, an increase in the supply of foreign exchange to S'_{Sfr} leads to an appreciation of the \$, that is, to a lower equilibrium exchange rate e''.

francs (to S'_{Sfr}) causes the supply curve to shift to the right and the exchange rate to fall to e''. In this case, the dollar cost of the Swiss franc is decreasing and the dollar is said to be *appreciating*. It is important to fix this terminology in your mind. **Home currency depreciation** or **foreign currency appreciation** takes place when there is an increase in the home currency price of the foreign currency (or, alternatively, a decrease in the foreign currency price of the home currency). The home currency is thus becoming relatively less valuable. **Home currency appreciation** or **foreign currency depreciation** takes place when there is a decrease in the home currency price of foreign currency (or an increase in the foreign currency price of home currency). In this instance, the home currency is becoming relatively more valuable. Changes in the exchange rate take place in response to changes in the supply and demand for foreign exchange at any given point in time.

The link between the balance of payments and the foreign exchange market can readily be shown using supply and demand. For purposes of this discussion, consider the supply and demand for foreign exchange as consisting of two components, one related to current account transactions and the other linked to the financial flows including the speculative and hedging activities (capital account transactions). In Figure 2, the demand and the supply of foreign exchange are each broken down in terms of these two components. Ignoring unilateral transfers, $D_{G\&S}$ and $S_{G\&S}$ portray the demand and supply of foreign exchange associated with the domestic and foreign demands for foreign and domestic goods and services, respectively. The demand and supply of foreign exchange associated with financial transactions are then added to each of the curves, creating a total demand and a total supply of foreign exchange. If the financial desire for foreign

FIGURE 2   **The Foreign Exchange Market and the Balance of Payments**

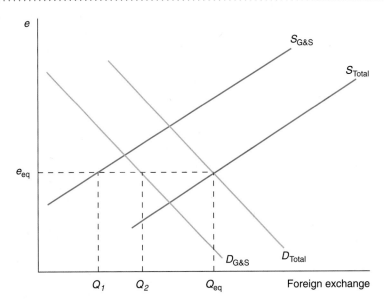

The demand and supply of foreign exchange are broken down into the transactions linked to the flows of goods and services (ignoring unilateral transfers), that is, the current account ($D_{G\&S}$, $S_{G\&S}$), and the transactions linked to financial transactions, that is, the capital account. Since the two must sum to D_{Total} and S_{Total}, desired financial transactions are the difference between the "Total" curves and the "G&S" curves. The equilibrium exchange rate e_{eq} will be determined by the interaction of D_{Total} and S_{Total}. In the above case, e_{eq} is below that which would equate demand and supply in the current account, $D_{G\&S}$ and $S_{G\&S}$, leading to a current account deficit ($Q_2 - Q_1$). However, at e_{eq} the supply of foreign exchange resulting from financial transactions, ($Q_{eq} - Q_1$), is greater than the demand for financial transactions ($Q_{eq} - Q_2$) by the amount ($Q_2 - Q_1$). The surplus in the capital account thus exactly offsets the deficit in the current account at the equilibrium rate of exchange.

exchange is assumed to take place primarily for reasons such as expected profits, expected rates of return, and so forth (that is, for reasons independent of the exchange rate), the total curves are drawn a fixed distance from the $D_{G\&S}$ and the $S_{G\&S}$ curves. If the exchange rate influences these financial flows, then the relationship between the goods and services curves and the total curves is more complex. For ease of discussion, however, we proceed with the curves as drawn in Figure 2.

The equilibrium exchange rate is now seen to be determined by the intersection of the D_{Total} and the S_{Total} curves. This is not necessarily going to be the same exchange rate that would equilibrate $D_{G\&S}$ and $S_{G\&S}$. This would only be the case if the current account was exactly in balance at the equilibrium rate, e_{eq}. In Figure 2, the equilibrium rate is below that which would balance the current account. Consequently, at e_{eq} there is an excess demand ($Q_2 - Q_1$) for foreign currency for trade in goods and services (the current account) and an offsetting excess supply ($Q_2 - Q_1$) in foreign exchange in the financial (capital) account. The supply of foreign exchange arising from financial transactions ($Q_{eq} - Q_1$) exceeds the demand for foreign exchange for financial transactions ($Q_{eq} - Q_2$) by ($Q_2 - Q_1$), the amount of the current account deficit. Thus, one again sees that a deficit in the current account will be exactly offset by an equivalent surplus in the capital account at the market clearing exchange rate. Similarly, any surplus in the current account will be exactly offset by an equivalent deficit in the capital account at the equilibrium exchange rate.

THE SPOT MARKET

Having discussed the general nature of the foreign exchange market, we now turn to a more rigorous examination of this market. We begin by looking at the operation of the daily or current market, referred to as the **spot market,** and then examine the market for foreign exchange for future delivery (the forward market).

Principal Actors

As was indicated in the previous section, the motivations for demanding or selling foreign exchange are based in the transactions related to the current and capital accounts. These actions involve individuals and institutions of all kinds at the retail level and the banking system at the wholesale level. The major participants in the foreign exchange market are the large commercial banks, although multinational corporations whose day-to-day operations involve different currencies, large nonbank financial institutions such as insurance companies, and various government agencies including central banks such as the U.S. Federal Reserve and the German Bundesbank also play important roles. Not surprisingly, the large commercial banks play the central role since the buying and selling of currencies most often involves the debiting and crediting of various bank accounts at home or abroad. In fact, most foreign currency transactions take place through the debiting and crediting of bank accounts with no physical transfer of currencies across country borders. Consequently, the bulk of currency transactions takes place in the wholesale market in which these banks trade with each other, the **interbank market.** In this market a large percentage of these interbank transactions is conducted by foreign exchange brokers who receive a small commission for arranging trades between sellers and buyers. The buying and selling of foreign exchange by the commercial banks in the interbank market that is not done through foreign exchange brokers, but directly with other banks, is called *interbank trading*. While bank currency transactions are done to meet their various retail customers' needs (corporations and individuals alike), banks also enter the foreign exchange market to alter their own portfolios of currency assets.

The Role of Arbitrage

As was indicated earlier, the foreign exchange market consists of many different markets and institutions. Yet, at any given point in time, all markets tend to generate the same exchange rate for a given currency regardless of geographical location. The uniqueness of the foreign exchange rate regardless of geographical location occurs because of **arbitrage.** As you recall, arbitrage refers to the process by which an individual purchases a product (in this case foreign exchange) in a low-priced market for resale in a high-priced market for the purpose of making a profit. In the process, the price is driven up in the low-priced market and down in the high-priced market. This activity will continue until the prices in the two markets are equalized, or until they differ only by the transaction costs involved. Because one is buying and selling currency simultaneously, there is no risk in this activity and hence there are always many potential arbitragers in the market. In addition, because of the speed of communications and the efficiency of transactions in foreign exchange, the spot market quotations for a given currency are remarkably similar worldwide, and any profit spread on a given currency is quickly arbitraged away.

In a world of many different currencies, there is also a possibility for arbitrage if exchange rates are not consistent between currencies. This point can be most easily seen in a three-currency example. Suppose the dollar/sterling rate is $1.40/£, and the dollar/French franc rate is $0.20/ff. In this case, the franc/sterling rate must be 7ff/£ for the three rates to be consistent and for there to be no basis for arbitrage [($1.40/£)/($0.20/ff) = 7ff/£]. Suppose that the dollar/sterling rate increases to $1.60/£. This rate is inconsistent with the $0.20/ff and the 7ff/£ rate, and there is a clear profit to be made by simultaneously buying and selling all three currencies. For example, one could take $1.40 and acquire 7ff, use the 7ff to buy 1 pound sterling, and immediately exchange the £1 for $1.60, thereby making a quick $0.20 profit. This is a situation of multicurrency arbitrage, in this case called **triangular arbitrage** since it involves an inconsistency between three different currencies. The triangular arbitrage produces **cross-rate equality,** meaning that all three exchange rates are internally consistent. Arbitragers are constantly watching the foreign exchange market for any inconsistencies, and they immediately buy and sell foreign exchange to take advantage of such a situation. In the above example, the arbitrage process should tend to drive up the dollar-franc price, drive up the franc-sterling price, and drive down the dollar-sterling price. These adjustments would take place until a new consistent equilibrium emerged—for example, $1.56/£, $0.21/ff, and 7.43ff/£. (You should verify for yourself that there is no possibility for profitable arbitrage at these new prices.) The arbitrage process is thus relied upon not only to maintain a similar individual currency value in different foreign exchange markets but also to make certain that all the cross rates between currencies are consistent.

Different Measures of the Spot Rate

The discussion of the foreign exchange market to this point has focused on some of the more important conceptual factors underlying current or "on the spot" exchanges of currency between two countries. While this spot rate is certainly useful, it does not provide information about what the spot rate should be, given the nature and structure of the two countries; it does not provide any information on the change in overall strength of the domestic currency with respect to all of the home country's trading partners; and it does not give any indication of the real cost of acquiring foreign goods and services in a world of changing prices. To obtain information about the latter two factors, we must turn to alternative measures, measures which are often cited in the international sections of major news publications.

Let us look first at the problem of assessing the relative strength or weakness of a currency when a country has numerous trading partners, each with its own exchange rate. Since different exchange rates are similar to different commodities, one cannot simply add them together and take a simple mean. Just as in assessing economywide price changes, one is forced to construct an index wherein each commodity (currency) can be appropriately weighted by its importance in a given country's international trade. To avoid the aggregation problem associated with adding up different currencies, each exchange rate is indexed to a given base year. The base year is assigned a value of 1, and all other observations for any given year are valued relative to it, that is, $eI_i = e_i/e_{i,base}$, where eI_i = exchange rate index for currency i, e_i = actual exchange rate for currency i, and $e_{i,base}$ = exchange rate for currency i in the base year. While one cannot add up the exchange rates, the indexes of individual exchange rate movements can be aggregated to arrive at a conclusion as to whether the home currency has appreciated or depreciated against the other currencies as a group. If all the currencies were equally important, then merely adding up all of the index values for a given year and dividing by the number of currencies involved would produce a correct assessment of the exchange rate movements relative to the base year. Since the base year would have a value of 1, a conclusion could be made regarding the overall change in average strength of the home currency.

Since all exchange rates are not equally important, however, a scheme has to be devised to weight each exchange rate index value in an appropriate manner. The weight most commonly employed is the value of imports from and exports to a given partner country i divided by total imports and total exports of the home country, that is, $w_i = (M_i + X_i)/(M_{total} + X_{total})$, where $\Sigma_i w_i = 1$ and the Σ_i symbol indicates summation of the

TABLE 1   **Effective Exchange Rate Calculation (U.S. trade in billions of dollars)**

(1)	(2)	(3)	(4)	(5)	(6)
	Exchange Rate		eI_i 1995	**U.S. Trade, 1995**	
Country	e_{1990}	e_{1995}		**Exports and Imports**	w_i
France	\$.184/ff	\$.200/ff	1.087	31.4	.042
Germany	\$.619/DM	\$.698/DM	1.128	58.6	.079
Italy	\$.0008/L	\$.0006/L	.750	25.0	.034
United Kingdom	\$1.785/£	\$1.579/£	.885	54.8	.074
Canada	\$.857/\$$_C$	\$.729/\$$_C$	.851	275.7	.372
Japan	\$.0069/¥	\$.0106/¥	1.536	186.6	.252
Mexico	\$.356/p	\$.156/p	.438	108.5	.147
Total				740.6	1.000

$$EER_{US\text{-}1995} = (1.087)(.042) + (1.128)(.079) + (.750)(.034) + (.885)(.074) + (.851)(.372) +$$
$$(1.536)(.252) + (.438)(.147)$$
$$= 0.994$$

weights over the currencies of all i countries. The measure of average relative strength of a given currency, called the **effective exchange rate (EER),**[1] is

$$EER = \Sigma_i \, eI_i \, w_i$$

To see how an EER is calculated, consider the information in Table 1 for the United States and selected major trading partners for 1990 and 1995. (The data for exchange rates and trade come from the IMF's *International Financial Statistics* and the U.S. Department of Commerce's *Survey of Current Business,* respectively.) The levels of trade (column 5) and the associated trade weights (column 6) are shown, as are the annual average exchange rates (columns 2 and 3) and the associated exchange rate indexes, eI_i, for 1995 (column 4—based on 1990 = 100). The EER for 1995 can be calculated using the information (columns 4 and 6) in the table. The fact that the EER is less than 1 indicates that, with respect to this group of countries, the dollar was, on average, slightly stronger in 1995 compared to 1990, since the average price of foreign exchange declined from 1.0 in 1990 to 0.994 in 1995. In other words, the index of the price of the *dollar* in 1995 rose to (1.0/0.994) = 1.006, with 1990 = 1.0. The EER result reflects the fact that the dollar depreciated strongly against the Japanese yen, important in U.S. trade, while the dollar appreciated against the Italian lira, the Canadian dollar, the British pound, and, especially, the Mexican peso. The dollar depreciated against the French franc and the German mark. The impact of these various changes on the EER for the United States depended, of course, on the trade weights employed in the analysis. In this instance, trade weights based on 1995, the end year of the period, were used. Beginning-year trade weights or an average of the two years could also have been chosen. If the trade structure had changed significantly over the period, the choice of the trade year and the corresponding trade weights could significantly affect the EER.

Another issue relates to the problem of interpreting changes in the exchange rate when prices are not constant. When the prices of goods and services are changing in either the home country or the partner country (or both), one does not know the change in the *relative* price of foreign goods and services by simply looking at changes in the spot

- -

[1]An effective exchange rate (labeled "U.S. dollar: J. P. Morgan index against 19 currencies") appears daily in *The Wall Street Journal* on the first page of Section C, "Money and Investing."

exchange rate and failing to take the new level of prices within both countries into account. For example, if the dollar depreciates by 10 percent against the pound sterling, but U.K. prices fall relative to U.S. prices by 10 percent, the relative price of U.K. goods and services to U.S. buyers remains the same. In this case, we would not expect the quantity demanded of U.S. imports from the United Kingdom to decline even though the dollar had depreciated. For this reason, a **real exchange rate (RER)** is often calculated, where the RER embodies the changes in prices in the two countries in the calculation. In a U.S.-U.K. situation, the RER would be calculated as follows, where PI refers to price index:

$$RER_{\$/\pounds\ 1995} = e_{1995}\frac{PI^{UK}_{1995}}{PI^{US}_{1995}}$$

For example, if the U.K. price index in 1995 was 118.2 and the U.S. price index was 116.6 (with 1990 = 100 in both cases), then the RER $_{\$/\pounds\ 1995}$ = ($1.57/£) (118.2/116.6), which equals $1.601/£. The fact that the RER is higher than the 1995 nominal rate of $1.579/£ reflects the slightly greater increase in prices that took place in the United Kingdom relative to the United States from 1990 to 1995. Since the actual exchange rate was $1.785/£ in 1990, we conclude that the dollar appreciated in real terms against the pound sterling from 1990 to 1995 (from $1.785/£ to $1.601/£), or that the pound depreciated in real terms against the dollar. Since changes in prices are more the rule than the exception, it is important to examine the RER as well as the nominal rates when analyzing the foreign exchange market. For a comparison of several nominal and real exchange rates, see Figure 3.

A third exchange rate concept, the **real effective exchange rate (REER),** calculates an effective exchange rate based on real exchange rates instead of nominal rates. In this case, the exchange rate index is calculated using real rates, which are then weighted by the appropriate trade weights. The consumer price index (CPI) for each of the seven countries used in calculating the EER (see Table 1) is given in Table 2 for 1995 (1990 = 100), along with the resulting real exchange rates for 1995. (The CPIs are taken from the IMF's *International Financial Statistics*.) Using the last column of Table 2 and the trade weights found in column 6 of Table 1, the REER is calculated as follows:

$$REER = \Sigma_i \ (RER\ index)_i\ (w_i)$$
$$= (1.038)(.042) + (1.150)(.079) + (.875)(.034) +$$
$$(.897)(.074) + (.816)(.372) + (1.406)(.252) +$$
$$(.843)(.147)$$
$$= 1.012.$$

The REER of 1.012 indicates that, in terms of the dollar, foreign exchange was on average 1.2 percent more expensive in real terms in 1995 than in 1990. In other words, the dollar depreciated in real terms by about 1 percent. This depreciation according to the REER contrasts with the EER result of 0.994, a nominal dollar *appreciation* of about ½ percent (although both changes are rather small). A possible reason for the differing EER and REER results is that, from 1990 to 1995, the dollar price of the Mexican peso in real terms fell about 16 percent (to an RER index of 0.843), while the nominal price of the peso (see Table 1) fell considerably more (by 56 percent—from $0.356 per peso to $0.156 per peso). If this Mexican "peso crisis" situation, which was associated with massive withdrawals of international funds from Mexico, is plausibly considered as very unusual, then Mexico might well be dropped from the sample of countries used for calculating the EER and the REER. If this is done and the weights assigned to the remaining countries are increased appropriately, the EER becomes 1.042 and the REER becomes 1.090—

FIGURE 3   **Selected Nominal and Real Exchange Rates, 1978–1996**

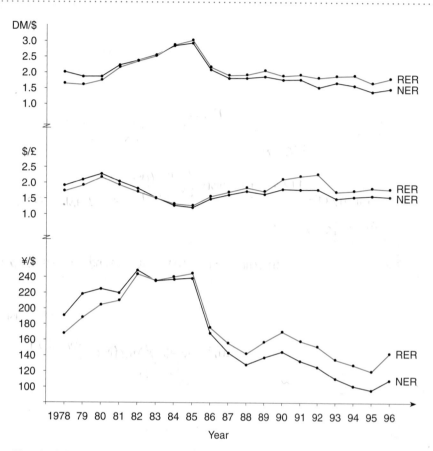

Note: The price indexes used in these calculations are based on 1982–1984 = 100.

Source: *Economic Report of the President,* February 1994 (Washington, DC: U.S. Government Printing Office, 1994), pp. 392, 394; *Economic Report of the President,* February 1997 (Washington, DC: U.S. Government Printing Office, 1997), pp. 420, 422. Any differences from Tables 1 and 2 reflect the different data source.

TABLE 2   **Real Effective Exchange Rate Calculation**

Country	CPI, 1990	CPI, 1995	RER, 1995	e, 1990	RER Index (1990 = 100)
France	100	111.6	$.191/ff	$.184/ff	1.038
Germany	100	119.0	$.712/DM	$.619/DM	1.150
Italy	100	127.8	$.0007/L	$.0008/L	.875
United Kingdom	100	118.2	$1.601/£	$1.785/£	.897
Canada	100	111.8	$.699/$$_C$	$.857/$$_C$	.816
Japan	100	107.0	$.0097/¥	$.0069/¥	1.406
Mexico	100	224.5	$.300/p	$.356/p	.843
United States	100	116.6			

meaning that the dollar depreciated more in real terms than in nominal terms. Hence, conclusions regarding the EER and the REER are indeed sensitive to the countries included in the calculations.

The fourth measure of the spot rate is concerned with identifying the true equilibrium rate that would lead to the current account (and hence the capital account) being in balance. An approach commonly used to estimate the underlying true equilibrium rate is the **purchasing power parity (PPP)** approach and it exists in two versions, an absolute PPP version and a relative PPP version.

The PPP approach rests on the postulate that any given commodity tends to have the same price worldwide when measured in the same currency. This is sometimes referred to as the **law of one price,** which many believe operates if markets are working well both nationally and internationally. Under these conditions, arbitrage will quickly erase any price differences between different geographical locations. In the presence of transportation and handling costs, arbitrage will not cause prices to equalize between different geographical locations, but it is felt by proponents of the law of one price that this will not distort the general one-price concept. If goods and services do in fact seem to follow the law of one price, then, it is argued, the absolute level of the exchange rate should be that level that causes traded goods and services to have the same price in all countries when measured in the same currency. This is referred to as **absolute purchasing power parity.** For example, if a bushel of wheat costs $4.50 in the United States and £3 in the United Kingdom, then the exchange rate should be equal to $4.50 per bushel divided by £3 per bushel, or $1.50/£. If we generalize over many goods, the absolute PPP estimate of the equilibrium exchange rate would be

$$PPP_{absolute} = \text{Price level}_{US}/\text{Price level}_{UK}$$

when the price levels are expressed in dollars and pounds, respectively. (For examination of PPP in the context of a single tasty commodity, see Case Study 1.)

Not surprisingly, the absolute version of PPP does not seem to be borne out empirically. Factors such as transportation costs and trade barriers, which keep prices from equalizing across different markets, combined with the difference in the composition and relative importance of various goods, explain in part why the absolute version does not seem to hold. In short, every country's measure of the price level reflects a set of goods and services unique to that country and not directly comparable to the goods and services of other countries. For these reasons, a weaker version of PPP is often used that relates the *change* in the exchange rate to *changes* in price levels in the two countries. This is referred to as **relative purchasing power parity** (PPP_{rel}).

In the PPP_{rel} version, if prices in the home country are rising faster than prices in the partner country, the home currency will depreciate. If prices in the home country are rising slower than prices in the partner country, the home currency will appreciate. Given an initial base period exchange rate, the equilibrium rate (PPP_{rel} rate) at some later date will reflect the relative rates of price change in the two countries. More specifically, the PPP_{rel} rate (stated in terms of units of domestic currency per unit of foreign currency) should equal the initial period exchange rate multiplied by the ratio of the price index in the home country to the price index in the partner country. For example, the PPP_{rel} for a U.S.-U.K. situation for 1995, with 1990 as the base year, would be calculated as

$$1995\ PPP_{rel}^{\$/£} = [e_{1990}^{\$/£}]\,[PI_{1995}^{US}/PI_{1995}^{UK}]\,.$$

Returning to the data used in Table 2,

$$1995\ PPP_{rel}^{\$/£} = [\$1.785/£]\,[116.6/118.2]$$
$$= \$1.761/£$$

✺ CASE STUDY 1   THE BIG MAC INDEX

For the past decade *The Economist* has annually evaluated the relative position of major currencies of the world by using its now well-known Big Mac Index (BMI—not to be confused with BMW!). The BMI is nothing more than an absolute PPP measure of the "true equilibrium value" of a particular currency based upon *one* commodity, a McDonald's Big Mac. The basic idea here is that a particular commodity should cost the same in a given currency wherever it is found in the world—if the prevailing exchange rate is the true underlying rate. Thus, the estimate of the PPP exchange rate (units of foreign currency/U.S. dollar) for a given currency is simply the value of the ratio of the Big Mac price in local currency divided by the U.S. dollar price. A currency is then determined to be undervalued or overvalued depending upon whether the Big Mac price ratio is greater than the current spot rate (undervalued) or less than the current spot rate (overvalued). For example, the recent price of a Big Mac in Canada was C$2.88, while the U.S. price was $2.42. The implied PPP exchange rate (C$/US$) was thus C$1.19/US$1 (= C$2.88/US$2.42). Since the actual spot exchange rate at that time was C$1.39/US$1, the BMI suggests that the Canadian dollar was undervalued by 14 percent [= (1.39 − 1.19)/1.39]. Several examples from the most recent BMI are given below for you to chew on.

The BMI has proved to be surprisingly consistent with other more sophisticated PPP measures over the years in spite of its many limitations. In fact, the 1996 BMI turned out to be a useful predictor for the exchange rate movements of eight of twelve currencies of large industrial economies. In addition, the directions of movement of six of the seven currencies whose value changed by more than 10 percent were correctly indicated by the BMI. This success came about in spite of the fact that the BMI assumes that there are no barriers to trade, including transportation costs. In addition, no provision is made for different tax structures, relative costs of nontraded inputs, or different market structures and profit margins. (Thus, for example, the current relevance of the BMI was seriously threatened with the unexpected February 1997 announcement by McDonald's that the U.S. price of the Big Mac was to be slashed by 65 percent.)

Although it was originally developed for fun, the BMI has triggered not only annual interest and amusement but also several pieces of serious academic work. It now appears that many who initially turned up their noses at the BMI and asked "Where's the beef?" are now intrigued with the possibility that there might actually be something useful there to sink their teeth into.

	Big Mac Prices, Local Currency	The Hamburger Standard		Overvaluation (+) or Undervaluation (−) of Local Currency
		Implied PPP	*Actual Spot Rate, 4/7/97*	
United States	$2.42	—	—	—
Belgium	Bfr 109	Bfr 45.0/$1	Bfr 35.3/$1	+28%
Brazil	Real 2.97	Real 1.23/$1	Real 1.06/$1	+16
France	Ffr 17.5	Ffr 7.23/$1	Ffr 5.76/$1	+26
Hong Kong	HK$9.90	HK$4.09/$1	HK$7.75/$1	−47
Mexico	Peso 14.90	Peso 6.16/$1	Peso 7.90/$1	−22
Switzerland	Sfr 5.90	Sfr 2.44/$1	Sfr 1.47/$1	+66

Sources: "Big MacCurrencies," *The Economist,* Apr. 9, 1994, p. 88; "Big MacCurrencies," *The Economist,* Apr. 15, 1995, p. 74; "McCurrencies: Where's the Beef?" *The Economist,* Apr. 27, 1996, p. 82; "Big MacCurrencies," *The Economist,* Apr. 12, 1997, p. 71.   ✺

Since the actual exchange rate (see Table 1) was $1.579/£ in 1995, PPP$_{rel}$ suggests that the dollar was actually overvalued relative to the pound sterling in 1995 (the pound was undervalued relative to the dollar), based on the rates of price increase in the two countries over the period from 1990 to 1995. This conclusion, of course, rests on the assumptions that the exchange rate in 1990 was an equilibrium market rate and that the two price indexes used accurately reflect the changes in prices of *traded* goods. Changes in both the structure of relative prices between traded and nontraded goods in the two countries and the composition of traded goods could cause serious estimation problems. Historically, estimated PPP exchange rates and nominal (the actual market) exchange rates have differed considerably in their movements. For two cases in point, see Case Study 2.

✦ CASE STUDY 2   SPOT AND PPP EXCHANGE RATES, MARK/DOLLAR AND YEN/DOLLAR, 1973–1996

The accompanying two figures illustrate the annual movements of the relative PPP rate and the spot rate for the value of the U.S. dollar in terms of German marks and Japanese yen from 1973 to 1996. According to these estimates, the dollar appears to have been slightly undervalued in terms of deutsche marks during 1977–1979, 1987, and 1995 and overvalued in the remainig years (especially 1980–1986). The dollar in terms of the yen appears to have been overvalued from 1973–1986 and perhaps slightly undervalued during most of the other years. These observations are of course subject to the various limitations associated with PPP calculations.

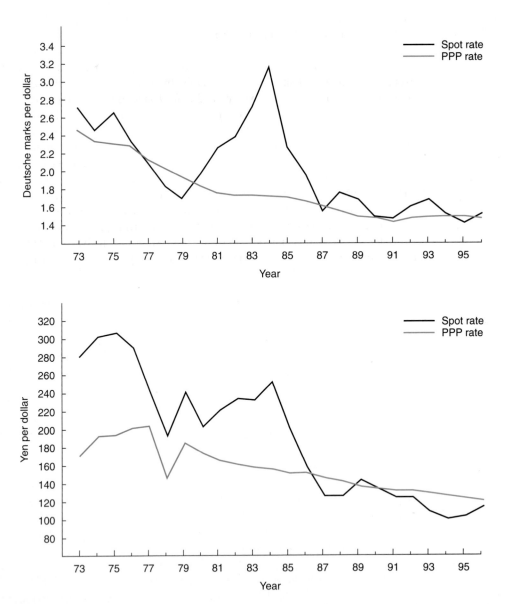

Sources: International Monetary Fund, *International Financial Statistics Yearbook 1996* (Washington, DC: IMF, 1996), pp. 376–79, 458–61, 788–89; International Monetary Fund, *International Financial Statistics,* May 1997, pp. 304, 306, 386, 388, 710.   ✦

CONCEPT CHECK

1. If the dollar/yen nominal exchange rate increases, has the dollar appreciated or depreciated? Why?
2. What is the difference between the nominal (actual) exchange rate and the real exchange rate?

3. If the deutsche mark/dollar actual exchange rate is below the relative PPP rate, why is the dollar said to be undervalued?

THE FORWARD MARKET

Our discussion of the foreign exchange market to this point has focused on the current or spot market for foreign exchange. Somewhere in the world foreign exchange is being bought or sold at every time of the day. Thus, exchange rates are subject to change at any moment. Although an individual can acquire relatively small amounts of foreign exchange at the going spot rate immediately, the most common exchange of currencies takes place two business days after the exchange contract has been struck. The two-day-later date, or **value date** when the transaction is completed, allows the bank accounts involved in the transaction sufficient time to clear. You can find daily quotations of the spot rate for the currencies of many countries in major news publications and can get current information by contacting many banks and financial exchange centers. A typical set of foreign exchange quotations, expressed in both domestic and foreign currency, appears in Table 3. Note that the quotations are for a specific time on the previous day and that they are the wholesale or interbank selling rates for $1 million or more. Retail customers pay a higher rate for foreign exchange; the difference between the two rates is the bank's charge for providing this service. Finally, commercial banks also make money in the foreign exchange markets by buying foreign exchange at a lower price than they sell it. For example, if you are traveling in England, you might pay $1.50/£ when you purchase pounds and receive only $1.48/£ when you sell back any unused pounds even though the exchange rate has not changed. The difference between the buying and selling price is the **retail spread** or the **retail trading margin.** These margins also exist at the wholesale level.

In many instances, however, transactions contracted at one point in time are not completed until a later date. For example, suppose that a U.S. automobile importer contracts to purchase 10 Rolls-Royce automobiles at a cost of £100,000 per automobile, which at the current exchange rate of $1.50/£ would cost $150,000 per automobile, for a total contract cost of $1,500,000. The delivery and payment date on the 10 automobiles is six months from the time the contract was signed. Since the contract is written in pounds sterling, the importer is faced with the possibility that the exchange rate may change within the six-month period. For example, the exchange rate might fall to $1.40/£, causing the dollar cost of the 10 cars to fall from $1.5 million to $1.4 million. On the other hand, the exchange rate could increase to, for example, $1.60/£. In either case, the cost of the autos changes by $100,000. The passage of time between when a contract is signed and the deal is finalized interjects an element of risk at the future point in time. If the contract above had been written in dollars instead of pounds sterling, the element of risk would have fallen on the U.K. exporter instead of the U.S. importer.

Since the contract in the above case is written in pounds sterling, the risk falls on the importer. If the U.S. buyer does nothing and waits until the delivery day to purchase the £1 million, he or she is taking what is referred to as an **uncovered,** or **open, position.** Suppose that the importer was risk-averse and wished to hedge against an unfavorable

TABLE 3 Spot and Forward Exchange Rates

Tuesday, May 6, 1997
EXCHANGE RATES

The New York foreign exchange selling rates below apply to trading among banks in amounts of $1 million and more, as quoted at 4 p.m. Eastern time by Dow Jones and other sources. Retail transactions provide fewer units of foreign currency per dollar.

Country	U.S. $ equiv. Tue	U.S. $ equiv. Mon	Currency per U.S. $ Tue	Currency per U.S. $ Mon
Argentina (Peso)	1.0014	1.0014	.9986	.9986
Australia (Dollar)	.7766	.7807	1.2877	1.2809
Austria (Schilling)	0.8240	.08200	12.136	12.195
Bahrain (Dinar)	2.6525	2.6525	.3770	.3770
Belgium (Franc)	.02814	.02798	35.540	35.739
Brazil (Real)	.9391	.9395	1.0648	1.0643
Britain (Pound)	1.6333	1.6223	.6123	.6164
1-month forward	1.6323	1.6213	.6127	.6168
3-months forward	1.6305	1.6195	.6133	.6175
6-months forward	1.6281	1.6169	.6142	.6185
Canada (Dollar)	.7255	.7245	1.3783	1.3803
1-month forward	.7272	.7405	1.3751	1.3504
3-months forward	.7301	.7290	1.3697	1.3717
6-months forward	.7343	.7332	1.3618	1.3639
Chile (Peso)	.002392	.002393	418.05	417.90
Colombia (Peso)	.0009290	.0009359	1076.39	1068.53
Czech. Rep. (Koruna)	.....	.....	.....	.....
Commercial rate	.03243	.03236	30.832	30.905
Denmark (Krone)	.1523	.1514	6.5680	6.6030
Ecuador (Sucre)	.....			
Floating rate	.0002589	.0002597	3862.50	3850.00
Finland (Markka)	.1928	.1913	5.1875	5.2265
France (Franc)	.1720	.1710	5.8155	5.8470
1-month forward	.1723	.1714	5.8040	5.8348
3-months forward	.1730	.1720	5.7808	5.8131
6-months forward	.1741	.1731	5.7452	5.7783
Germany (Mark)	.5802	.5772	1.7235	1.7325
1-month forward	.5815	.5785	1.7198	1.7286
3-months forward	.5841	.5810	1.7119	1.7212
6-months forward	.5882	.5850	1.7000	1.7093
Greece (Drachma)	.003650	.003632	273.98	275.33
Hong Kong (Dollar)	.1291	r.1291	7.7470	r7.7470
Hungary (Forint)	.005480	.005487	182.49	182.25
India (Rupee)	.02791	.02796	35.830	35.770
Indonesia (Rupiah)	.0004124	.0004122	2425.00	2426.00
Ireland (Punt)	1.5029	1.4901	.6654	.6711
Israel (Shekel)	.2938	.2933	3.4038	3.4100
Italy (Lira)	.0005858	.0005839	1707.00	1712.75
Japan (Yen)	.007976	.007903	125.38	126.54
1-month forward	.008011	.007939	124.82	125.96
3-months forward	.008086	.008010	123.67	124.85
6-months forward	.008196	.008122	122.01	123.12
Jordan (Dinar)	1.4094	1.4094	.7095	.7095
Kuwait (Dinar)	3.2862	3.2873	.3043	.3042
Lebanon (Pound)	.0006480	.0006480	1543.25	1543.25
Malaysia (Ringgit)	.3989	.3990	2.5070	2.5065
Malta (Lira)	2.6076	2.5974	.3835	.3850
Mexico (Peso)	.....	.....	.....	.....
Floating rate	.1266	.1265	7.8970	7.9050
Netherland (Guilder)	.5155	.5133	1.9397	1.9480
New Zealand (Dollar)	.6842	.6891	1.4616	1.4512
Norway (Krone)	.1401	.1396	7.1368	7.1608
Pakistan (Rupee)	.02513	.02513	39.790	39.790
Peru (new Sol)	.3770	.3774	2.6527	2.6497
Philippines (Peso)	.03793	.03793	26.365	26.365
Poland (Zloty)	.3165	.3160	3.1595	3.1645
Portugal (Escudo)	.005769	.005748	173.34	173.97
Russia (Ruble) (a)	.0001738	.0001737	5755.00	5758.00
Saudi Arabia (Riyal)	.2666	.2666	3.7504	3.7505
Singapore (Dollar)	.6918	.6918	1.4455	1.4455
Slovak Rep. (Koruna)	.03080	.03080	32.473	32.473
South Africa (Rand)	.2245	.2244	4.4545	4.4565
South Korea (Won)	.001117	.001119	894.95	893.50
Spain (Peseta)	.006865	.006849	145.66	146.01
Sweden (Krona)	.1280	.1263	7.8155	7.9163
Switzerland (Franc)	.6841	.6782	1.4617	1.4745
1-month forward	.6864	.6806	1.4568	1.4693
3-months forward	.6912	.6850	1.4467	1.4598
6-months forward	.6985	.6922	1.4317	1.4446
Taiwan (Dollar)	.03605	.03608	27.736	27.720
Thailand (Baht)	.03835	.03831	26.075	26.100
Turkey (Lira)	.00000734	.00000735	136280.00	136015.00
United Arab (Dirham)	.2723	.2723	3.6720	3.6720
Uruguay (New Peso)	.....			
Financial	.1082	.1083	9.2450	9.2350
Venezuela (Bolivar)	.002075	.002077	481.88	481.50
SDR	1.3674	1.3635	.7313	.7334
ECU	1.1315	1.1252	....	....

Special Drawing Rights (SDR) are based on exchange rates for the U.S., German, British, French, and Japanese currencies; data from International Monetary Fund. European Currency Unit (ECU) is based on a basket of community currencies. a-fixing. Moscow Interbank Currency Exchange. r-Revised. Friday's Hong Kong (dollar) was 7.7478.

Source: *The Wall Street Journal*, May 7, 1997, p. C13.

change in the exchange rate. What, if anything, can be done to reduce the risk of the pound appreciating against the dollar in the next six months? One alternative open to the importer is to acquire pounds sterling today at the rate of $1.50/£, invest them in England for the six-month interim period, then use the proceeds to meet the contract payment. This could of course involve transaction costs as well as the opportunity cost of any earnings differential if interest rates are higher in the United States than in the United Kingdom.

A second hedging option open to the importer is to contract today with a bank to acquire £1,000,000 on the delivery date for a specific number of dollars determined by the **forward exchange rate.** The forward rate differs from the spot rate in that the delivery date is more than two days in the future. With a forward contract, the foreign exchange agreement is made at the present time, but the actual exchange of currencies does not take place until the day the foreign currency is needed. In making this contract, the importer is guaranteed the contracted forward rate (for example, $1.51/£) for the million pounds even if the spot pound price should rise to $1.60 before the automobiles are delivered.

In this case the bank or broker is operating as an intermediary between those who are demanding pounds sterling for delivery in six months and those who desire to supply pounds sterling in six months. Possible suppliers in this market are U.S. exporters who are to receive pounds sterling on that day and wish to contract forward to hedge the risk of the pound depreciating against the dollar. Another potential supply source consists of individuals or institutions who are willing to speculate (that is, take an uncovered position) on the dollar-pound exchange rate in six months. These speculators hope to make an immediate profit on the delivery day due to the difference between the contracted forward rate and the current (spot) market rate on that day. If a speculator expects that the actual future spot rate will be higher than the current forward rate, the speculator will purchase foreign currency forward (take a **long position** in foreign exchange). If the expectation is realized, forward foreign exchange is acquired on the delivery date at the contracted price and then immediately resold at the spot price at that time for a profit. If it is expected that the actual future spot rate will be less than the current forward rate, the speculator will contract to sell foreign exchange forward, or take a **short position.**

The forward market thus consists of parties demanding or supplying a given currency at some future point in time for the purpose of either minimizing risk of loss due to adverse changes in the exchange rate (hedging) or making a profit (speculating). Obviously, expectations play an important role in this market, particularly on the part of those holding an uncovered position. The opportunity cost of hedging in this market consists of the difference between the contracted exchange rate and the rate that actually exists on the contracted delivery day. As a general rule, the more volatile the market in question, the greater the risk and hence the likely spread between the actual and the contracted rate. Compared to the first hedging option involving the acquisition of foreign currency at today's rate and short-term investment of the funds in the foreign country, however, hedging through the forward market is convenient and attractive to those unfamiliar with short-term investment opportunities in the foreign country in question. Information on the forward market is readily available to both hedgers and speculators. Daily quotations of forward rates on the previous day can also be found in major news publications (see Table 3).

In addition to the forward market, there are two additional possibilities for buying and selling foreign exchange in the future. These two alternatives include buying or selling foreign exchange (major currencies only) in the foreign currency futures market or buying an option on the futures market. Basically, a **futures contract** is similar to a forward contract; it is an agreement to buy or sell a specified quantity of a foreign currency for delivery at a future point in time at a given exchange rate. More specifically, however, it generally refers to a futures contract entered into through the Chicago Mercantile Exchange (CME). Although they are remarkably similar, the futures contract differs from the forward contract in several ways. In the futures market, the contractor is represented by a foreign exchange broker who negotiates a contract for a standard amount of foreign exchange at the best rate possible. Once signed, the CME stands behind the futures contract and guarantees that the currency will be delivered and paid for on schedule. In addition, a margin deposit is required—generally a fixed percentage of the contract value. The futures contract is, however, resalable up until the time of maturity, whereas the forward contract is not. A final difference is the fact that a futures contract is available only for four specific maturity dates (the third Wednesday of March, June, September, and December); in contrast, forward transactions are private deals for any type of contract the two parties agree upon (usually 30, 60, 90, or 180 days) from any beginning day. Although the futures market carries on activity similar to the forward market, it is argued that it is a useful element in the foreign exchange markets that adds an element of competition. In addition, since the futures market tends to be more highly centralized and standardized, it caters more to the smaller customer and the speculator than the forward market. The cost of using the futures market, however, appears to be higher than the cost of using the forward market.[2]

Another way to participate in the forward market is by participating in foreign currency options.[3] A **foreign currency option** is a contract that gives the holder the right to buy or sell a foreign currency at a specific exchange rate at some future point. Unlike the forward or futures contract, however, the holder is not obligated to exercise the option if he or she chooses not to. To participate in this market, one must either buy or sell an option contract.[4] The option buyer (holder) acquires the right to exchange foreign currency with the option seller (writer) for a fee or premium. This fee represents the maximum loss the buyer would experience should the option not be exercised. The completion of the option contract involves the actual exchange of the currencies.

There are basically two types of option contracts, puts and calls. The *call* option contract gives the holder the right to acquire foreign exchange for dollars at the contracted exchange rate, while the *put* option contract gives the holder the right to acquire dollars for foreign exchange at the contracted rate. Because options themselves are negotiable, there are four possible ways of participating in this market. One can buy a call option (acquiring the right to purchase foreign exchange), sell a call option (transferring the right to acquire foreign exchange), buy a put option (acquiring the right to purchase dollars), or sell a put option (transferring the right to purchase dollars). Each of these carries different risk and uncertainty. However, the most the option buyer can lose is the premium, while potential gains fluctuate with the spread between the contract exchange rate and the market rate. Symmetrically, the most the seller can gain is the premium, while potential loss will fluctuate with the spread between the contract rate and the market rate at the time the option is exercised. The buyer is thus paying the seller to undertake the risk associated with exchange rate movements. The premium is the amount that is necessary for the seller of the option to assume the risk associated with the change in the exchange rate. Option contracts have been available since 1982. Foreign currency options provide an additional means of managing the risk of foreign exchange movements, and they are of particular value to those who wish to hedge against future transactions that may or may not occur.

THE LINK BETWEEN THE FOREIGN EXCHANGE MARKETS AND THE FINANCIAL MARKETS

The foreign exchange market consists of the spot market, forward market, and futures/options markets. Although our discussion treated these markets individually, in practice the exchange rates in these different markets are determined simultaneously in conjunction with the interest rates in various countries. To grasp why this is so, it is necessary to

[2]This paragraph has drawn heavily on Norman S. Fieleke, "The Rise of the Foreign Currency Futures Market," Federal Reserve Bank of Boston, *New England Economic Review,* March/April 1985, pp. 38–47. This article is an excellent evaluation of the role of the futures market. Of particular interest is the observation (p. 47) that "[S]tandardization within the futures market is facilitated by the fact that the futures price and the spot price for a currency converge as the futures contract nears maturity, providing a link between the two prices that allows hedging to take place with relatively few maturity dates for futures contracts."

[3]This discussion is based on Brian Gendreau, "New Markets in Foreign Exchange," Federal Reserve Bank of Philadelphia, *Business Review,* July/August 1984, pp. 3–12.

[4]A "European option" is one that can be exercised only on the expiration date, while an "American option" is a contract that can be exercised anytime up to the expiration date.

first examine the reasons why commercial banks, individuals, and companies might choose to buy or sell foreign assets, that is, assets denominated in currencies other than the home currency. While trade in merchandise and services for many years received the bulk of the attention in analyzing the foreign exchange market, the recent growth in the volume of transactions in foreign currency assets is such that these transactions clearly dominate the market today. This is evident when one considers that by the early 1990s the stock of international bank lending had grown to $7.5 trillion a year, the level of options, futures, and so forth was $6.9 trillion a year, cross-border transactions in equities were $1.4 trillion a year, turnover in foreign exchange totaled more than $900 billion each day, and the global stock of direct foreign investment was estimated at over $1.7 trillion.[5]

The Basis for International Financial Flows

International financial flows include a wide variety of transactions. The various categories include such items as bank lending of foreign currency, bank lending of domestic currency to foreigners, foreign bonds, domestic bonds, foreign and domestic equities, direct foreign investment, financial services such as banking and insurance, and various spot and forward currency transactions. These various transactions can be further subdivided on the basis of maturity into long-term or capital assets (a maturity one year or longer) and short-term or money market assets (maturity of less than one year). Money market assets include short-term government securities, certificates of deposit (CDs), and short-term corporate debt, to name just a few. They are traded in highly competitive markets, tend to involve a fixed rate of interest, and are highly liquid (easily convertible into cash). Capital markets, on the other hand, include not only long term CDs and bonds but also stocks, real investment, and other forms of equity for which a less certain rate of return exists. (See the next chapter for further discussion of international financial instruments.)

The decision to invest internationally rests on the expected rate of return on the international asset compared to domestic alternatives. If the expected rate of return is greater abroad than at home, one would expect domestic residents to invest abroad. If the expected rate of return on home assets is higher than that on foreign assets, foreigners would be expected to invest in the home country. If there are no barriers to investment flows, funds should move from areas of low return to areas of high return until the expected returns are similar. However, it is not quite that simple since there is a major difference between the domestic investment and the foreign alternative. The total return on the foreign asset to a potential home country investor includes not only the specific return on the asset in question but also any return associated with appreciation of the foreign currency against the home currency during the time of the investment (or loss if the foreign currency depreciates against the home currency). Thus, an investment in the United Kingdom made by a U.S. resident that earned 8 percent per year would actually yield a 10 percent return if the value of the English pound increased from $1.50 to $1.53 (a 2 percent appreciation of the pound) over the year between the initial investment date and the time of reconversion back into dollars. On the other hand, if the value of the pound had fallen to $1.47, the U.S. investor would have realized only a 6 percent return on the U.K. investment. Depreciation of the currency in which the investment is denominated can thus offset, or more than offset, any apparent rate of return advantage of the foreign instrument.

The investor considers three elements when deciding whether to invest in the home country or in a foreign country: (1) the domestic interest rate or expected rate of return, (2) the foreign interest rate or expected rate of return, and (3) any expected changes in the exchange rate. In this situation, equilibrium in the financial markets does not necessarily lead to equality of interest rates or expected rates of asset yield between the two countries.

---

[5]"Fear of Finance: A Survey of the World Economy," *The Economist*, Sept. 19, 1992, p. 9.

To see why, let us examine the situation in which the investor would be indifferent between investing in the home country or in the foreign country, setting aside for the moment any consideration of differences in risk between the two investments. (We shall return to the issue of exchange rate risk and using the forward markets to insure oneself against it shortly.) Very simply, the investor would be indifferent between a domestic and a foreign investment whenever he or she expects to earn the same return on both after taking into account any expected change in the spot rate before the maturity date. Using the United States and the United Kingdom as an example, this parity condition for a 90-day investment of $1 would be stated as follows:

$$\$1(1 + i_{\text{NY}}) = [(\$1)/(e)] (1 + i_{\text{London}})[E(e)]$$
$$(1 + i_{\text{NY}})/(1 + i_{\text{London}}) = E(e)/e \qquad [1]$$

where the interest rates are for 90 days, e is the spot rate in $\$/£$, and $E(e)$ is the **expected spot rate** in 90 days. Under the above condition, a dollar invested in New York for 90 days will be worth the same amount as a dollar invested in London for 90 days (after converting the dollar to pounds sterling at the current spot rate and reconverting the principal plus interest back to dollars on the maturity date), given the interest rate in each of the two locations and the expectation regarding the 90-day spot rate. Thus, suppose that the annual interest rate in New York is 8 percent (= 90-day interest rate of 2 percent). Investing $1,000 in New York would produce an amount (principal plus interest) of $1,020 in 90 days. Suppose that the current spot rate is $1.60/£ and that the annual interest rate in London is 12 percent (= 90-day interest rate of 3 percent). Investing $1,000 in London would yield [$1,000/($1.60/£)] or £625 plus (£625)(.03) or £643.75 in 90 days. An expected 90-day spot rate of $1.5845 would make the two investments equivalent [($1.5845/£) · £643.75 = $1,020].

Returning to equation [1], this equilibrium condition is often stated in a more general manner. The right-hand side of the equation, $E(e)/e$, is equal to (1 + **expected percentage appreciation of the foreign currency** over the 90-day period).[6] Designating the expected percentage appreciation of the foreign currency as xa, $E(e)/e$ is equal to $(1 + xa)$ and equation [1] now becomes

$$(1 + i_{\text{NY}})/(1 + i_{\text{London}}) = (1 + xa), \text{ which equals}$$
$$(1 + i_{\text{NY}})/(1 + i_{\text{London}}) - 1 = xa, \text{ which can be written as}$$
$$(1 + i_{\text{NY}})/(1 + i_{\text{London}}) - (1 + i_{\text{London}})/(1 + i_{\text{London}}) = xa$$
$$(i_{\text{NY}} - i_{\text{London}})/(1 + i_{\text{London}}) = xa \qquad [2]$$

This condition states that equilibrium in the international financial markets occurs whenever the expected appreciation (depreciation) of the foreign currency is roughly equal to the difference between the higher (lower) domestic return and the lower (higher) foreign return. Precise equilibrium condition [2] is approximated by[7]

$$(i_{\text{NY}} - i_{\text{London}}) = xa \qquad [3]$$

. . . .

[6]Mathematically, $E(e)/e = [e + E(e) - e]/e = 1 + [E(e) - e]/e$. The second term is the percentage by which $E(e)$ is above e.

[7]This approximation is arrived at in the following way:

$$(1 + i_{\text{NY}}) = [E(e)/e](1 + i_{\text{London}})$$
$$(1 + i_{\text{NY}}) = (1 + xa)(1 + i_{\text{London}})$$
$$1 + i_{\text{NY}} = 1 + xa + i_{\text{London}} + (xa)(i_{\text{London}})$$

Assuming that $(xa) (i_{\text{London}})$ is of the second order of smalls, it is dropped from the expression. Subtracting 1 and i_{London} from both sides produces the final approximation,

$$i_{\text{NY}} - i_{\text{London}} = xa$$

Since the investor is bearing all the risk of changes in the exchange rate, this equilibrium condition is referred to as **uncovered interest parity (UIP).** Should this condition not hold, for example, $(i_{NY} - i_{London}) > xa$, investments in the United States are more attractive than those in the United Kingdom and investment funds would flow into the United States. If $(i_{NY} - i_{London}) < xa$, investment funds would be flowing to the United Kingdom.

It is important to note that a change in expectations about the future spot rate will lead to current investment flows, which force a change in the spot rate until the expected appreciation (depreciation) rate is again consistent with the difference in the two interest rates. Simply stated, the expected rate and the spot rate should move in tandem as long as the interest rate differential remains the same. Why does this take place? Assume that the financial markets are in equilibrium and that there is a sudden change in expectations regarding the dollar/pound exchange rate; for example, the U.S. interest rate is 6 percent, the U.K. interest rate is 5 percent, and the expected appreciation of the pound increases from 1 to 2 percent. This means that the expected return on U.K. investments is now higher (7 percent) than the expected return on equivalent U.S. domestic investments (6 percent) and investors would start investing in the United Kingdom. This activity increases the demand for pounds on the spot market, causing the price of pounds to increase (the dollar to depreciate against the pound). Investment in the United Kingdom, with the accompanying upward pressure on the dollar/pound spot exchange rate, continues until the expected rate of appreciation of the pound is again equal to the difference between the interest rates in the two countries. What has happened in the process is that the increase in the expected appreciation of the pound (or expected depreciation of the dollar), the rise in $E(e)$, has led to an appreciation of the pound in the spot market, a rise in e, until xa, which equals $[E(e)/e - 1]$, is again 1 percent. Expectations thus play an important role in exchange rate movements.

Of course, people do not have perfect foresight. Consequently, the actual return on the foreign investment in 90 days may not match what was expected when the investment decision was made. For example, foreign returns may be less certain because of unexpected changes in the exchange rate, possible limitations on the transfer of earnings back home, and so forth. The investor who is bearing the risk of changes in the foreign exchange rate and possible other factors may thus require an additional payment for undertaking the risk linked to these unanticipated developments. This additional financial factor is often called the **risk premium** (*RP*) and, expressed as a percentage, leads to a restatement of the previous equilibrium condition:

$$(i_{NY} - i_{London}) = xa - RP \qquad [4]$$

Thus, for example, if the risk premium is 2 percent and i_{NY} is 6 percent, then $(i_{London} + xa)$ must equal at least 8 percent because of the additional 2 percent risk premium in order for the New York investor to place funds in London. In equilibrium in this situation, the difference in the two interest rates reflects not only the expected appreciation of the foreign currency (xa) but also the additional return needed to cover the risk of the investment exposure overseas. A great deal of empirical work has focused on determining whether a risk premium exists when the investor is uncovered and how important it is to the foreign investment decision, but to estimate this factor is an extremely difficult exercise. If payments for undertaking foreign risk are an important factor, then not only changes in the expected exchange rate but also changes in the risk premium can contribute to sudden investment flows and to changes in the spot rate even when interest rates remain unchanged.

Covered Interest Parity and Financial Market Equilibrium

Up to now, our analysis has assumed that the risk of changes in the exchange rate is borne by the investor. Any risk associated with changes in the exchange rate can of course be hedged in the forward market if the investor does not want to go uncovered. Then the covered investment position includes the interest earned on the foreign investment plus the cost of the forward market hedge.

The link between the spot rate and the forward rate is often discussed in terms of premium and discount. When the exchange rate is stated in terms of domestic currency units per unit of foreign currency, the foreign currency is **at premium** whenever the forward rate is higher than the spot rate. If the forward rate is less than the spot rate, the foreign currency is **at discount.** It is common to define the link between the spot and forward rates in the following way:

$$p = [e_{fwd}/e] - 1$$

where e_{fwd} = the forward rate of the relevant period and where p, the percentage premium, is positive when the foreign currency is "at premium" and negative when the foreign currency is "at discount." To illustrate, suppose that the actual pound price is $1.608/£ in the 90-day forward market and $1.600/£ in the spot market. The 90-day forward pound is then at a 0.5 percent premium ($1.608/1.600 - 1 = 0.5$ percent).

The link between the foreign exchange market and the financial markets can readily be seen by examining two types of transactions that involve the spot rate, the forward rate, and interest rates. As you will recall, a several-month delay between the signing of an import-export contract for goods and services and the exercising of that contract interjects an element of risk into the transaction, since the exchange rate may change in the ensuing period of time. If the contract is written in the exporting country's currency, this risk falls on the importer, who has the choice of going uncovered (and absorbing the risk) or of hedging the risk. The risk may be hedged by buying the foreign currency in the spot market now and investing the proceeds abroad until the delivery date, or by using one of the forward markets. Presumably, the importer will choose the least expensive method. This will involve comparing the difference in the cost of the contract at the forward rate versus the current spot rate with the opportunity cost associated with acquiring foreign currency now and investing it abroad at an interest rate different from what the money is earning (costing) at home. Similarly, the forward rate will be considered by a short-term financial investor sending funds abroad in order to protect against a decline in the value of the foreign currency by the time the investment funds are returned home.

If the financial markets are working well, in equilibrium the risk-averse importer should be indifferent between hedging by using the short-term foreign investment and hedging by using the forward market, and the risk-averse short-term investor should be indifferent between the domestic and the foreign investments. The link between the spot market, forward markets, and the money markets that generates these equality conditions is achieved through **covered interest arbitrage.**

Consider now an investor determining whether to place funds at home (e.g., New York) or overseas (e.g., London). If the investor chooses to protect against the risk of spot rate fluctuations, that is, to cover, the forward market will be used. In this case the equilibrium condition is

$$\$1(1 + i_{NY}) = (\$1)(1/e)(1 + i_{London})(e_{fwd}) \qquad [5]$$
$$(1 + i_{NY})/(1 + i_{London}) = (e_{fwd})/(e) = p + 1$$
$$[(1 + i_{NY})/(1 + i_{London})] - 1 = p$$
$$[(1 + i_{NY})/(1 + i_{London})] - [(1 + i_{London})/(1 + i_{London})] = p$$
$$(i_{NY} - i_{London})/(1 + i_{London}) = p \qquad [6]$$

where e is the spot \$/£ rate, e_{fwd} is the \$/£ rate on 90-day forward currency, and p is the actual premium on 90-day forward pounds.

This condition can also be approximated, following the procedure of footnote 7, by the following:

$$i_{NY} - i_{London} = p \qquad\qquad\qquad [7]$$

In equilibrium, any difference in the interest rates between the two financial markets should be approximately offset by the foreign exchange premium. For example, if the $i_{NY\text{-}90} = 2.5$ percent and the $i_{London\text{-}90} = 2$ percent, the financial and exchange markets will be in equilibrium if the forward pound is contracted at a price which is 0.5 percent above the spot rate.[8] In this case the person who invests in London is receiving 2 percent on the short-term investment plus a 0.5 percent return due to the forward premium. The sum of these two returns is equal to 2.5 percent; that is, the return that would be received on a short-term investment in New York. It is clear that interest rates will not necessarily equalize between countries even if markets are functioning efficiently. In fact, one would not expect them to be equal as long as forward rates are different from spot rates.

Given the covered interest arbitrage condition, one can now predict the movement of financial investment between countries taking into account both the interest rates in the two countries and the foreign exchange markets. Whenever the interest rate differential ($i_{home} - i_{foreign}$) is greater than the premium (from the home country perspective), funds would flow into the home country. Whenever the interest rate differential is less than the forward premium, investment funds would flow out of the home country. In equilibrium, one would expect no net short-term financial movements based on interest rate considerations. It is important to note that this condition holds for both positive and negative interest rate differentials. If the domestic interest rate is less than the foreign rate, investment will still flow into the country as long as the negative premium (percent discount) is less than (a larger negative) the negative difference in interest rates. For example, if the annual interest rate in New York is 8 percent and the annual interest rate in London is 11 percent, funds would still flow into New York as long as the pound sterling is at discount (the dollar is at premium) by more than 3 percent, for example, 3.5 percent. In this instance, the British investor obtains the 8 percent rate of interest on the investment plus a 3.5 percent forward dollar premium and would prefer the investment in New York to that in London.

The equilibrium condition is presented in Figure 4. The interest rate differential between New York and London is plotted on the vertical axis and the forward premium on the pound on the horizontal axis. With the axes scaled in a similar manner, the points of equilibrium between the interest rate differential and the premium are on the 45° line that passes through the origin. This line is referred to as the **covered interest arbitrage parity** line **(CIAP).** The points located above the *CIAP* line indicate conditions of disequilibrium that will produce inflows of foreign financial investments into New York, while those points lying below the line indicate conditions when funds should flow from New York to London.

The discussion to this point has proceeded assuming that there are no transaction costs involved in the interest arbitrage activity. In fact, such financial transactions are not without cost. Since these costs are incurred, one would not expect *CIAP* to obtain. The equilibrium condition in this case needs to incorporate the transaction costs, so the approximate equilibrium condition becomes

$$i_{NY} - i_{London} = p \pm \text{transaction costs}$$

[8]It is critical that the interest rate and the premium be calculated over the same period. In this case of a 90-day forward rate, for example, the appropriate rate of interest could be approximated by $i_{annual}/4$; in the case of a 180-day forward premium, $i_{annual}/2$; and so forth.

FIGURE 4   **The Covered Interest Arbitrage Parity Line**

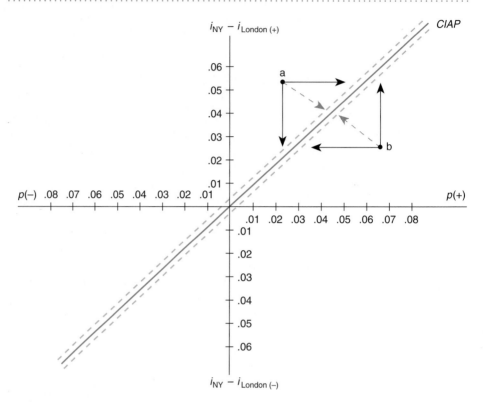

International financial markets are in equilibrium when any interest rate difference (e.g., $i_{NY} - i_{London}$) between two countries is virtually equal to the foreign exchange premium p when financial transactions are costless. The possible equilibrium points are thus found on straight line *CIAP*, which passes through the origin and bisects the 90° angle (assuming that the scale on both the vertical and horizontal axis is the same). However, since financial transactions are not costless, the interest rate difference and the forward premium can differ in equilibrium by the amount of the transaction cost. Market equilibrium will thus lie in the neighborhood of the *CIAP* line defined by the pair of dashed lines, whose distance from the *CIAP* line reflects some average transaction cost.

In Figure 4, the *CIAP* line is bounded on either side by two dashed lines. These lines are drawn equidistant on either side of the *CIAP* line at a rate of 0.25 percent, a commonly used rule of thumb for transaction costs. This is, at best, a general guideline, since costs vary considerably from transaction to transaction in response to many factors, including the size of the transaction. It is important to remember that transaction costs are incurred *both* in the financial transaction and in the acquisition and sale of foreign currency. Thus, it is not an inconsequential consideration. Robert Z. Aliber, a prominent international monetary specialist, has indicated that transaction costs are anywhere from 0.1 to 1 percent of the value of the transaction involved.[9]

It is also important to note that additional factors may contribute to the difference between interest rates in two countries. Capital market imperfections, differential costs in

....
[9]Cited in Francisco Rivera-Batiz and Luis Rivera-Batiz (1994), p. 112. Frank McCormick (1979, p. 416), also cited in Rivera-Batiz and Rivera-Batiz, p. 112, estimated that 20 to 30 percent of the difference between the interest rate on Treasury bills in the United States and that in the United Kingdom could be explained by transaction costs.

gathering information about alternative investments, and noncomparability of specific assets all can contribute to the existence of interest rate differentials between countries beyond that explained by covered interest arbitrage. There is also the possibility that the political risk associated with investment in a foreign country will be a factor. Political risk, as noted earlier, reflects the fact that a foreign government can intervene in the financial markets and/or expropriate or freeze the capital assets of foreigners. The returns to assets can clearly be affected by the imposition of exchange controls and changes in government regulation.

Another point to make at this juncture is that a diagram very similar to Figure 4 can be employed to illustrate the concept of uncovered interest parity (discussed in the previous section). All that needs to be done is to relabel the horizontal axis from the premium on forward exchange, p, to expected appreciation of the foreign currency, $\{xa$ or $[E(e) - e]/e$ or $[E(e)/e] - 1\}$. The 45° $CIAP$ line then becomes a 45° UIP (uncovered interest parity) line. Then, if investors are located at a point such as point b in Figure 4, the expected appreciation of the foreign currency exceeds the interest rate differential. That is, $xa > i_{NY} - i_{London}$ or $i_{London} + xa > i_{NY}$. There is an incentive to send funds to London, which necessitates a spot purchase of pounds. The e increases and $[E(e)/e] - 1$ falls. In addition, with funds leaving New York, i_{NY} may rise and i_{London} may fall with the inflow into London. As you can see from the $(i_{London} + xa > i_{NY})$ expression, this means that the two sides of the inequality are converging. With complete UIP, the process would stop at the 45° line. In practice, however, the UIP line will not quite be reached because of transaction costs.[10]

In view of Figure 4 and its conceptual modification to embrace UIP, a very important point is this: If $CIAP$ holds ($p = i_{NY} - i_{London}$) and UIP also holds $\{[E(e) - e]/e = xa = i_{NY} - i_{London}\}$, the result is that the premium in the forward market *equals* the expected rate of appreciation of the foreign currency. This is a situation of an **efficient foreign exchange market** in that the forward rate is a measure of the expected exchange rate and that there are no further unexploited opportunities to make a profit. We will return to the concept of market efficiency in later chapters.

Simultaneous Adjustment of the Foreign Exchange Markets and the Financial Markets

Although we have shown the conditions under which financial flows will take place and the direction of their movement, little has been said about how the markets involved respond and whether the flows themselves generate a movement toward equilibrium in the sense used in this discussion. Let's return to covered interest arbitrage and analyze the adjustment process in our continuing U.S.-U.K. example, and examine four markets: (*a*) the London money market, (*b*) the New York money market, (*c*) the dollar/pound spot market, and (*d*) the dollar/pound forward market for time *t*. These four markets are presented in Figure 5. We begin by assuming that the interest rate differential is greater than the forward premium and that short-term investment thus has an incentive to flow to New York from London. As English investors withdraw funds from the London money market to invest in New York, the supply of loanable funds in London declines [shifts to the left in panel (a)], exerting upward pressure on i_{London}. These funds are then brought to the foreign exchange spot market to be exchanged for U.S. dollars, which shows up as a rightward shift in the supply curve of pounds sterling [panel (c)]. This influx of pounds has the impact of putting downward pressure on the dollar/pound spot exchange rate (appreciating the dollar). Since these investors are risk-averse and wish to hedge against

[10]Note that xa would also differ from the forward premium if there is a risk premium associated with uncovered arbitrage. With the risk premium (and no transactions costs), $i_{NY} - i_{London} = xa - RP = p$ in equilibrium and therefore $xa = p + RP$.

FIGURE 5   International Financial and Exchange Rate Adjustments

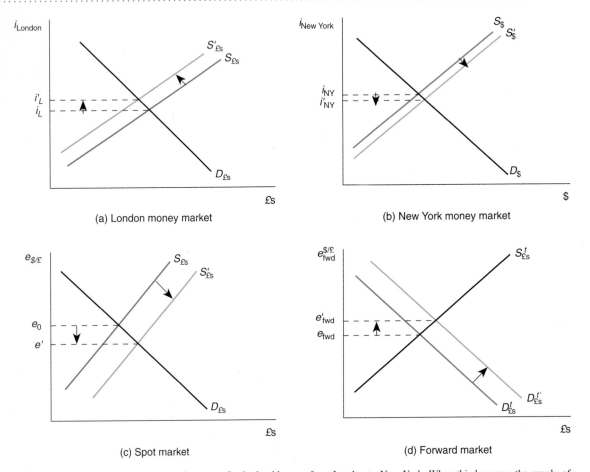

(a) London money market

(b) New York money market

(c) Spot market

(d) Forward market

Assuming that $i_{NY} - i_{London} > p \pm$ transaction costs, funds should move from London to New York. When this happens, the supply of loanable funds declines from $S_{£s}$ to $S'_{£s}$, putting upward pressure on the London interest rate (panel a). The conversion of pounds into dollars in the spot market (panel c) increases the supply of pounds, putting downward pressure on the spot rate (appreciating the dollar). Investors covering themselves against changes in the exchange rate then purchase pounds forward, increasing the demand in this market, putting upward pressure on the forward rate (panel d). Finally, when the funds are invested in New York, the supply of loanable funds increases there (panel b), placing downward pressure on i_{NY}. All of these price movements—the increase in i_{London}, the decrease in the spot rate, the increase in the forward rate, and the decline in i_{NY}—work to reduce the initial inequality. Market equilibrium attains in London and New York when the interest differential comes into line with the forward premium and transaction costs.

changes in the foreign exchange rate, they will at the same time purchase pounds sterling forward. This increases the demand for pounds (shifts the demand for pounds to the right) in the forward market [panel (d)] and puts upward pressure on the forward rate. Finally, as British investors make their desired investments in New York, there will be an increase in the supply of funds in the New York money market [a rightward shift of the supply curve in panel (b)] and a downward pressure on i_{NY}. Returning to our equilibrium condition, we note the nature of these adjustment pressures with arrows:

$$(i_{NY}\downarrow - i_{London}\uparrow)\downarrow \quad \text{and} \quad [e_{fwd}\uparrow/e\downarrow]\uparrow - 1 \rightarrow p\uparrow$$

Note that the movement of interest rates unambiguously makes the interest rate differential smaller. At the same time, the movement in the exchange rates unambiguously makes the forward premium larger.[11] Investment will continue to flow from London to New York until these movements of interest rates and exchange rates bring about a new equilibrium.

The nature of this adjustment process is shown back in Figure 4 by the arrows at point *a* and at point *b*. The adjustments from disequilibrium can take place through the foreign exchange markets (horizontal adjustments), the money markets (vertical adjustments), or some combination of the two. There has been considerable interest recently in how equilibrium is attained in the international short-term capital markets. If interest rates are the adjustment mechanism, then movements in *equilibrium* interest rates should be highly correlated between the countries with major financial markets; in other words, rises (falls) in interest rates in one country will be associated with rises (falls) in interest rates in other countries. If exchange rates are doing the adjusting, then one would expect little or no correlation between interest rate changes in the leading industrial countries. A study by Kasman and Pigott (1988) has indicated that for the United States, changes in the short-term interest rate are highly correlated with short-term interest rate changes in Canada but are poorly correlated with interest rate changes in other trading partners. Changes in long-term interest rates do not appear to be highly correlated either. These results suggest that much of the equilibrium adjustment is taking place through the foreign exchange markets. This may be due in part to the fact that money markets are large relative to the size of the forward market so that a change in the demand or supply of foreign exchange has little impact on interest rates. By the same token, short-run financial adjustments could be contributing to the volatility of the foreign exchange market.

Before leaving this discussion, it is important to point out several additional factors that make it difficult to observe the adjustment process and that can cause the simple equilibrium condition not to be met. The existence of varying transaction costs mentioned earlier is one of these factors. A second factor that obfuscates the issue is the difficulty in choosing a representative interest rate in the two countries that is sufficiently comparable. Contributing to this problem is the fact that the variance of the distribution of returns on alternative investments within the countries may be different due to such things as different liquidities, different credit risks, and different tax treatments across what outwardly appear to be similar types of investments. Finally, the operation of the equilibrating process in the money and foreign exchange markets may be hampered by government policies and other institutional imperfections that slow or even impede altogether the adjustment process. If governments attempt to hold interest rates constant by monetary policy, then the short-run international financial market adjustment will necessarily fall even more heavily on the foreign exchange markets.

CONCEPT CHECK

1. What is the difference between the forward market, the futures market, and the options market?

2. Does it ever make sense to invest abroad at a lower interest rate than at home? If so, when? Why?

3. What is the covered interest arbitrage parity line?

4. What is an uncovered interest parity line?

. . . .
[11]Note also that, with an efficient foreign exchange market, a larger forward premium would also be matched by a larger *xa* or expected appreciation of the pound in the situation of uncovered interest arbitrage.

SUMMARY

This chapter has focused on foreign exchange rates and the operation of the foreign exchange market. Attention was directed to the principal components of this market and how they influence the foreign exchange rate. The links between the spot market, the forward market, and interest rates were developed, and the market equilibrium condition between the money markets and the foreign exchange markets was established under uncovered and covered scenarios. Testing for the presence of uncovered parity is difficult in practice because of the problem of ascertaining expectations on exchange rates.

Although the covered interest arbitrage condition tends to hold empirically to some extent, it can be affected by such things as government policies in the participating countries, transaction costs, and the differing distribution of asset returns between countries. Some evidence seems to suggest that international financial adjustment takes place principally in the foreign exchange markets and not in the domestic money markets, adding further to exchange rate volatility under flexible exchange rates.

KEY TERMS

absolute purchasing power parity
arbitrage
at discount
at premium
covered interest arbitrage
covered interest arbitrage parity
  (CIAP)
cross-rate equality
effective exchange rate (EER)
efficient foreign exchange market
expected percentage appreciation
  of the foreign currency
expected spot rate
foreign currency option

foreign exchange market
foreign exchange rate
forward exchange rate
futures contract
hedging
home currency appreciation (or
  foreign currency depreciation)
home currency depreciation (or
  foreign currency appreciation)
interbank market
law of one price
long position
purchasing power parity (PPP)

real effective exchange rate
  (REER)
real exchange rate (RER)
relative purchasing power parity
retail spread (or retail trading
  margin)
risk premium
short position
speculation
spot market
triangular arbitrage
uncovered interest parity (UIP)
uncovered (or open) position
value date

QUESTIONS AND PROBLEMS

1. The United States presently has a current account deficit with Japan. What would happen to the dollar/yen spot exchange rate and the current account deficit if there were a decrease in Japanese investment in the United States? Incorporate the foreign exchange market into your answer.

2. Suppose that you observe the following exchange rates: $2/£; $.0075/¥; and £.005/¥. Is there cross-rate equality? If yes, why? If not, what would you expect to happen?

3. A dollar appreciation against the French franc is no guarantee that the dollar will "go further" than it previously did in acquiring French goods. Do you agree? Explain.

4. Explain the difference between the real exchange rate and the PPP exchange rate. What is the purpose of each?

5. Suppose the deutsche mark price of a dollar was 1.8175 DM/$ in 1980 and 1.7981 DM/$ in 1987. With 1980 = 100, if the price index for Germany was 121.11 in 1987 and that for the United States was 137.86 in 1987, was the

dollar overvalued or undervalued in 1987 according to PPP? Explain.

6. Suppose that i_{NY} = 2 percent, i_{London} = 6 percent, xa (expected appreciation of the pound) = *minus* 1 percent (i.e., the pound is expected to depreciate by 1 percent), and *RP* (risk premium for investing in London) is 2 percent. Assuming these numbers all apply to the same time period, explain why this is a disequilibrium situation and how uncovered interest parity is attained.

7. You observe that the German annual interest rate is 10.5 percent, the U.S. annual interest rate is 9.5 percent, the 90-day forward rate is $0.6652/DM, and the spot rate is $0.6686/DM. Assuming that transaction costs are 0.2 percent, are the financial markets in equilibrium?

8. Using the information in Question 7, assume that the interest rate in the United States increases to 9.8 percent. What financial adjustments would you expect to see?

9. On May 7, 1997, *The Wall Street Journal* reported the following (for May 6):

Prime interest rates: United States 8.50 percent; Switzerland 3.50 percent; Japan 1.625 percent

Spot rates: $0.6841 = 1 Swiss franc; 125.38 Japanese yen = $1

90-day forward rates: $0.6912 = 1 Swiss franc; 123.67 Japanese yen = $1

(*a*) In terms of the dollar, was the Swiss franc at a forward discount or a forward premium? By what percent? Looking at the prime rates of the United States and Switzerland, is your calculated percentage discount/premium reasonably consistent with covered interest parity? Why or why not?

(*b*) In terms of the Japanese yen, was the U.S. dollar at a forward discount or a forward premium? By what percent? Looking at the prime rates of Japan and the United States, is your calculated percentage discount/premium reasonably consistent with covered interest parity? Why or why not?

10. If you observe that the French franc in terms of the dollar is at a 1.2 percent 90-day forward premium, under what conditions could you therefore say that the French franc is expected to rise by 1.2 percent relative to the dollar in 90 days? Explain.

4

INTERNATIONAL FINANCIAL MARKETS AND INSTRUMENTS: AN INTRODUCTION

INTRODUCTION

The preceding two chapters have provided a look at the composition and recording techniques in a country's balance-of-payments accounts and at the broad forces at work in the foreign exchange markets. But in today's world, where the value of foreign exchange transactions involving international assets far exceeds the value of foreign exchange transactions involving goods and services, the nature of these assets needs a closer examination.

The actors in the international financial system have developed a huge and bewildering variety of different types of traded assets, with each asset designed to satisfy particular liquidity, risk, and return demands of financial investors and asset holders. In this chapter we survey different general types of assets that are exchanged internationally, and we provide information on their size, characteristics, and markets. We begin by looking at international bank deposits and then examine international bonds and stocks (equities). We then consider in some detail a number of specific financial instruments that belong to the broad category "financial derivatives." The intent of this chapter is to familiarize you in a general way with the range of financial instruments available for transferring wealth across country borders and to indicate the many possibilities that exist internationally for satisfying financial investors' particular preferences.

INTERNATIONAL BANK DEPOSITS AND LENDING

In its coverage of money and banking, your introductory economics course made the implicit assumption when examining banks' balance sheets that loans and deposits of the banks were entirely domestic in nature. In other words, deposits (which are assets of the depositors and liabilities of the banks) placed into banks (and other depository institutions) were presumed to come from domestic citizens. These deposits provided checking accounts with which the depositors could carry out economic transactions, and savings and time deposit accounts from which the depositors could earn interest and thus provide for future consumption. The deposits provided funds from which the banks could, after satisfying bank legal reserve requirements, make domestic loans (which are assets of the banks and liabilities of the borrowers). However, this simple, straightforward textbook treatment has become less and less realistic over the last several decades, as depositors now seek international outlets for their savings and banks increasingly seek international borrowers for their funds. In addition, the domestic banks themselves now often have many branches located in foreign countries.

TABLE 1   **Deposit Banks' Foreign Liabilities, December 31, 1994
(in billions of U.S. dollars)**

Industrial Countries			$5,942.3
United Kingdom		$1,274.0	
United States		941.3	
Japan		723.7	
France		592.6	
Luxembourg		386.8	
Switzerland		384.4	
Germany		378.8	
Belgium		263.3	
Italy		230.5	
Netherlands		187.0	
Developing countries			2,104.7
Asia		$1,094.0	
Hong Kong	531.8		
Singapore	381.3		
Western hemisphere		842.0	
Middle East		113.0	
Europe		36.5	
Africa		19.2	
All countries			$8,047.0

Source: International Monetary Fund, *International Financial Statistics,* June 1997, p. 42.

Table 1 illustrates why the narrow domestic focus is no longer very appropriate. The table shows estimates by the International Monetary Fund of the value of banks' foreign liabilities (i.e., bank deposits held by foreign individuals and institutions) at the end of 1994. (A brief look at the recent growth of these liabilities was provided in Table 2 of the chapter "The Balance-of-Payments Accounts.") For all countries, this figure was $8 *trillion* at the end of 1994, a figure almost twice the value of world merchandise trade in that year. As can also be seen, about 75 percent of these liabilities are in banks of industrial countries, with an additional $1.1 trillion located in Asia (mainly in Hong Kong and Singapore).[1]

Another prominent feature of these cross-border bank deposits is that the deposits themselves are denominated in different currencies. A bank in the United Kingdom, for example, which holds deposits of U.S. citizens and firms does not necessarily have those deposits denominated in British pounds. Indeed, the deposits can be denominated in dollars, German marks, Japanese yen, or other currencies. While evidence on the currency denomination of deposits is unfortunately difficult to obtain, Table 2 attempts to provide some meaningful estimates pertaining to currency composition.

This table shows the currency denomination of banks' international assets (claims). We are thus looking at the other side of the balance sheet as compared with the deposits (liabilities) of Table 1; nevertheless, deposits received in a given currency will be lent in that currency (and held in that currency if not lent), and, conceptually, banks' total

[1]The developing countries in the Western hemisphere are also important locations for bank foreign liabilities. The bulk of these Western hemisphere liabilities is located in banks in the Cayman Islands and the Bahamas, with $445.7 billion and $160.9 billion, respectively, in 1993. (No individual 1994 figures for these two countries were available at the time of this writing.) These banks are primarily "offshore" branches of U.S. banks, which take advantage of favorable regulatory and tax treatment.

TABLE 2   **Currency Composition of Banks' Cross-Border Claims, 1994 (in billions of U.S. dollars and percentages)**

Currency	Claims in Domestic Currency		Claims in Foreign Currency		Total Claims	
	Value	*Share*	*Value*	*Share*	*Value*	*Share*
U.S. dollar	$ 477.4	26.1%	$1,867.5	51.9%	$2,344.9	43.2%
German mark	257.5	14.1	576.0	16.0	833.5	15.4
Japanese yen	569.5	31.1	183.6	5.1	753.1	13.9
French franc	128.0	7.0	105.4	2.9	233.4	4.3
British pound	105.8	5.8	113.4	3.2	219.2	4.0
Swiss franc	95.3	5.2	119.1	3.3	214.4	4.0
Italian lira	49.4	2.7	121.1	3.4	170.5	3.1
European Currency Unit (ecu)			152.4	4.2	152.4	2.8
Other	146.1	8.0	356.9	9.9	503.0	9.3
All currencies	$1,828.9	100.0%	$3,595.6	100.0%	$5,424.5	100.0%

Note: Components may not sum to totals because of rounding.

Source: Bank for International Settlements, *65th Annual Report* (Basle, Switzerland: BIS, June 12, 1995), p. 169.

cross-border claims will therefore equal their total cross-border liabilities if all banks and all countries are accounted for in the data. However, the data in Table 2 pertain to a more restricted set of countries than do the data in Table 1—they consist of cross-border claims in banks of industrial countries that report to the Bank for International Settlements (BIS). The BIS is an institution located in Geneva, Switzerland, that sponsors conferences of central bankers on international monetary cooperation, acts as a clearinghouse for central bank settlements, and deals with various other international banking matters. While the Table 2 information thus has some differences from the data set of Table 1, Table 2's figures can be useful for indicating the extent to which different currencies play a role in the international banking system.

The banks' international claims in Table 2 are divided into two components: (1) cross-border claims denominated in domestic currency (e.g., a U.K. bank's foreign claim held and denominated in British pounds), and (2) cross-border claims denominated in foreign currency (e.g., a German bank's foreign claim held and denominated in British pounds). As the table shows, at the end of 1994 the U.S. dollar was by far the leading currency of denomination of these foreign assets, but dollar claims did not constitute a majority in total. This is a marked change from the situation during most of the post-World War II period. Immediately after the war and until 1958, major European currencies (except for the British pound) were not readily convertible into other currencies because of exchange controls; hence, the dollar (and to some extent the pound) dominated in foreign currency holdings. In recent years, and especially beginning in the 1980s, other currencies (particularly the deutsche mark and the yen) have assumed greater importance. In addition, a noteworthy item at the present time is the presence of the European Currency Unit (*ecu*) in the list of leading currencies. This currency unit is a composite unit of account employed by the European Monetary System that is a weighted average of the values of most European Union currencies.[2] (The European Monetary System is discussed in the last chapter in this book, "The International Monetary System: Past, Present, and Future.")

....

[2]The ecu is no country's domestic currency and hence does not appear in the first two columns of Table 2.

TABLE 3   **Gross and Net International Bank Lending, December 31, 1995
(in billions of dollars)**

Part A

(1) Total cross-border bank claims		$7,925.8
(2) Local claims in foreign currency		1,297.9
(3) *Gross international bank lending*		$9,223.6
(4) *Minus:* Interbank deposits		4,578.6
(5) *Net international bank lending*		$4,645.0

Part B

(6) Claims on inside-area countries		$7,987.4
(7) Claims on nonbanks	$2,326.3	
(8) International financing of banks' domestic lending	1,082.4	
(9) Interbank deposits	4,578.6	
(10) Claims on outside-area countries		994.3
(11) Unallocated claims by area		242.0
Gross international bank lending		$9,223.6

Note: Components may not sum to totals because of rounding.

Source: Bank for International Settlements, *66th Annual Report* (Basle, Switzerland: BIS, June 10, 1996), pp. 140–41.

Table 1 has portrayed the size of international bank deposits, and Table 2 has looked at a restricted set of bank claims. Of course, looked at from the vantage point of bank claims, these really represent **international bank lending,** on which we now focus our attention. Such lending, which constitutes a loan across country borders, can occur for many reasons. For example, domestic banks may lend funds to private firms abroad that wish to undertake real investment projects and that find the domestic banks' lending terms to be more favorable than bank lending terms in the firms' own countries. Or domestic banks may purchase foreign financial instruments (such as certificates of deposit offered by foreign banks) with excess reserves in order to earn a higher return than is available domestically on comparable instruments. Or foreign banks may borrow funds from domestic banks to obtain domestic currency working balances to meet various needs of their (the foreign banks') customers.

Table 3 provides a summary view of the cumulative stock of claims that has resulted from international bank lending as of the end of 1995. In Part A of the table, the first row gives the estimate by the BIS of "total cross-border bank claims." This figure is comparable to the "total claims" item in Table 2, but here the BIS figure refers to a broader set of countries.[3] These claims are loans made by banks to borrowers in other countries, and they are obviously part of international lending. Row (2) in Part A, "local claims in foreign currency," indicates loans by banks to domestic borrowers, but these loans have been made in *foreign* currency. Since the foreign currency was clearly obtained from foreign sources at some time in the past, it also reflects an international loan. The sum of these two items, row (3), represents the stock of **gross international bank lending**—$9,223.6 billion, or $9.2 *trillion,* at the end of 1995 (when valued in dollars using exchange rate conversions for the nondollar currency components).

However, an adjustment to this gross lending figure is necessary if we wish to determine the *net* stock of lending that has occurred over time. Simply put, if a U.S. bank

[3]Twenty-three countries in total: the Group of Ten countries (Belgium, Canada, France, Germany, Italy, Japan, Netherlands, Sweden, the United Kingdom, and the United States) plus Austria, the Bahamas, Bahrain, the Cayman Islands, Denmark, Finland, Hong Kong, Ireland, Luxembourg, Netherlands Antilles, Norway, Singapore, and Spain. Note also that Table 3 gives 1995 data, while Table 2 pertains to 1994.

lends $3 million to (that is, deposits $3 million in) a German bank and a German bank lends the equivalent of $2 million to (that is, deposits the equivalent of $2 million in) a U.S. bank, the net international flow of funds is only a $1 million outflow from the United States (whereas the gross flow is $5 million). Row (4) makes this type of adjustment by subtracting "interbank deposits." As is evident, this is a large figure—$4,578.6 billion. These interbank deposits occur, for example, because domestic (foreign) banks may maintain deposits in foreign (domestic) banks for the purposes of facilitating transactions with economic actors in the foreign (domestic) country, of earning favorable rates of return on particular certificates of deposit in the foreign (domestic) country, or of general portfolio diversification. In the case of portfolio diversification, risk is reduced by holding a wide variety of assets (by not "keeping all your eggs in one basket"), including foreign assets. When these interbank deposits are netted out, the stock of **net international bank lending** [row (5)] at the end of 1995 was $4,645.0 billion.

Part B of Table 3 arrays the international lending information in a different manner in order to focus on the broad types of borrowers of the funds. Row (6), "claims on inside-area countries," depicts the loans of the banks in the 23 countries reporting to the BIS (listed in footnote 3) to borrowers who were also located in those 23 countries—$7,987.4 billion, or 87 percent of the gross lending. Of this amount, $2,326.3 billion [row (7)], or 25 percent of the gross lending, consisted of loans to nonbanks (for example, commercial and industrial firms). Row (8) shows that $1,082.4 billion, 12 percent of the gross lending, was funds borrowed by domestic banks from abroad in order to finance loans to domestic borrowers. (For example, a U.S. bank uses its own funds as well as funds of a French bank to make a loan to a U.S. shopping center developer.) Next, row (9) lists the interbank deposits (50 percent of the gross lending), as given earlier in Part A. Finally, the remaining two rows of components show [in row (10)] loans of the banks in the 23 reporting countries to countries outside the 23 countries themselves, for which data on type of borrower are not available, and [in row (11)] loans for which the BIS was unable to determine the precise location of the borrowers.

It is useful to examine gross international bank lending in more detail. This lending (and the associated deposits that result from the lending), as discussed above in regard to Tables 2 and 3 and the BIS data, essentially consists of three components:

1. Domestic bank loans in domestic currency to nonresidents (that is, the "claims in domestic currency" item in Table 2). This component would be exemplified by a bank in France lending francs to a U.S. firm for the firm's purchase of French exports.

2. Domestic bank loans in foreign currency to nonresidents (that is, the "claims in foreign currency" item of Table 2). An example of this type of activity would be the lending of dollars by a bank in France to a U.S. firm so that the firm could undertake the purchase of oil supplies from a Saudi Arabian exporter who wishes to be paid in dollars (oil prices are in fact quoted in dollars).

3. Domestic bank loans in *foreign* currency to domestic residents (that is, the "local claims in foreign currency" item of Table 3; this item is not contained in Table 2 since the loans are not cross-border loans). This situation would be represented by a bank in France lending dollars to a French citizen for the purchase of a U.S. Treasury bond.

In the literature, component 1 above (loans in domestic currency to nonresidents) is generally referred to as **traditional foreign bank lending.**[4] This type of activity has a

[4]See Johnston (1982, pp. 1–2). However, unlike the BIS presentation which we follow, Johnston refers to international bank lending as comprising only components 1 and 3 rather than components 1, 2, and 3.

long history: banks are providing domestic currency to foreign citizens and firms for the financing of international trade. However, components 2 and 3 of the gross lending (loans in foreign currency to nonresidents and loans in foreign currency to domestic residents) are relatively new, becoming of large size only since the 1960s. These two situations reflect the use of a currency outside the country that issues the currency, and they have been dubbed as representing activity in the **Eurocurrency market.** Indeed, a *Eurocurrency deposit* is defined as a deposit in a financial institution that is denominated in a currency other than the currency of the country in which the financial institution is located. Originally, this market was called the **Eurodollar market** because the major deposits involved were dollar deposits located outside the United States, chiefly in Europe. With the rise in importance of other currencies in this market (see Table 2), "Eurodollar" is often broadened to "Eurocurrency" to include these other currencies. Of course, even the term *Eurocurrency* is inadequate because such deposits are now also located in financial centers outside Europe (particularly Singapore and Hong Kong).

We now look in more detail at the origin and the implications of the Eurodollar and Eurocurrency markets. We focus in particular on Eurodollars, since dollars constitute a larger fraction of Eurocurrency deposits than any other currency does and since the emergence of Eurodollars was the catalyst for the later use of other currencies in these markets.

There are a number of ways in which a Eurodollar or Eurocurrency deposit can arise. A typical case[5] would be a situation where a U.S. exporter sells goods to a British buyer and receives dollar payment. (Assume that the foreign exchange market transaction to get the dollars has been carried out by the British importer.) However, the U.S. exporter may wish to leave the dollars abroad in a London bank (London is in fact the largest center for Eurodollars in Europe) so that the dollars will be conveniently available for use, say, for foreign input purchases from British (or other European) firms. The London bank will keep this deposit as a *dollar* deposit, and it will be matched by a claim by the London bank on the U.S. bank in which the U.S. exporter has an account (and with which bank the London bank has a "correspondent" relationship). Like any bank deposit, this London deposit can now be loaned out by the British bank to customers who require dollars. Indeed, the amount of Eurodollar deposits can grow in multiple fashion because the British bank can initiate the multiple-deposit expansion process associated with fractional reserve banking. Thus, if the original deposit by the U.S. exporter is $1 million and the bank wants to lend 90 percent of it, the loan of this $900,000 (say, to a London importing company for the purchase of goods from a French firm that wishes to have dollars) could be redeposited in Europe and would form the basis for another $810,000 loan (if 90 percent of the $900,000 is again lent out). As you may remember from discussing bank deposit expansion in your principles course, this series of loans (if 90 percent is always "relent") can lead to a cumulative total of $10 million in Eurodollar deposits ($10 million = $1/0.10 \times$ the initial deposit of $1 million).[6] In this Eurodollar expansion process, the loans involved are usually loans of six months or less, and the banks making the loans are referred to as **Eurobanks,** even though the banks may be located outside Europe (such as in Singapore). In addition, the interest rate on the loans normally consists of a markup, the size of which depends on

[5]For further discussion, see Kaufman (1992, pp. 311–25).

[6]However, it should be noted that, in the multiple expansion process, if a deposit of Eurodollars is at any point borrowed by a *U.S.* bank, the process will stop because the deposit is no longer a Eurodollar deposit (since the funds will be located in the United States). See Kvasnicka (1986, pp. 175–76).

risk and market conditions, above the **London Interbank Offered Rate (LIBOR),** the rate at which Eurobanks lend among themselves.[7]

Historically, the Eurodollar market began to be of significance in the 1950s. (See Kaufman 1992, pp. 317–18, and Gibson 1989, pp. 10–15.) At that time, due to Cold War considerations, the Soviet Union shifted dollar deposits out of the United States and placed them in London banks. In addition, dollar deposits in London were enhanced when Great Britain, worried about its balance-of-payments deficits and hence about its ability to maintain the value of the pound under the pegged exchange rates of the period, imposed some controls on the use of the pound for import and capital-outflow transactions. The consequence of this British government action was that British banks, desiring to continue financing these transactions, increasingly conducted them in dollars. Further, dollars were becoming considerably more abundant in Britain and Europe because of the large (for the time) official reserve transactions deficits in the U.S. balance of payments. Another factor at work, especially in the late 1960s, was the existence of legal ceilings (Regulation Q of the Federal Reserve) on the interest rates that could be paid by U.S. banks on their time and savings deposits. With higher interest rates available in Europe, U.S. depositors chose to place their dollars there, and the Eurobanks were quite willing to receive them. An important reason for the ability of the Eurobanks to offer higher rates was that Eurodollars were not subject to any legal reserve requirements, unlike the situation with bank deposits in the United States. Thus, because Eurobanks could lend a larger fraction of any given deposit than could U.S. banks, the Eurobanks could earn higher returns from their deposits and could offer higher rates of interest to depositors in order to attract funds.

Two other factors that led to a rise in the Eurodollar (Eurocurrency) markets should be mentioned—one on the demand side and one on the supply side. On the demand side, there was a general monetary tightening in the United States toward the end of the 1960s because of inflationary pressures associated with the conduct of the Vietnam war. Due to this tightening, borrowers seeking dollars found them to be more expensive in New York and other American financial centers. This increasing difficulty in obtaining dollars from U.S. financial institutions particularly burdened foreign borrowers because two additional, restrictive policy steps had already been undertaken in the United States in the mid-1960s to reduce the worsening U.S. balance-of-payments problem by limiting capital outflows. These steps were the introduction by the Federal Reserve of voluntary foreign lending "guidelines" for banks (giving specific recommended percentage reductions for loans to particular geographic areas) and the imposition of the (nonvoluntary!) Interest Equalization Tax on loans taken out by foreigners from U.S. institutions and markets. This tax discouraged foreign borrowing because it amounted to an extra charge above the regular interest charge on the loans. Thus, due to these measures and the general monetary tightening, dollar loans from the United States were more difficult to obtain and pressure emerged for the buildup of dollar accounts abroad; rather than convert existing dollars abroad into their own currencies, foreign holders found it profitable to keep the deposits in dollar form overseas. In addition, some of the increased demand for Eurodollars came from U.S. banks themselves. Because money was tight in the United States, U.S. banks sought to get dollar funds from their overseas branches and from foreign banks. This demand for Eurodollars was facilitated by the fact that *lending* rates

---

[7]More precisely, LIBOR is the average of interbank rates offered for dollar deposits in London, based on the quotes of five major banks. These banks issue the quotes at 11 A.M. on each business day. LIBOR is listed every day in *The Wall Street Journal* and other financial publications.

in Europe tended to be lower than those in the United States, even as *deposit* rates in Europe were higher. This rate structure existed because Eurobanks were able to operate with lower margins between lending and deposit rates, in part because of the lack of reserve requirements on Eurodollars, than were U.S. banks. Other factors that we examine later in this chapter were also involved.

On the supply side, new dollar deposits abroad grew for several reasons. A very important factor in their growth was the first "oil shock," in 1973–1974, when the Organization of Petroleum Exporting Countries (OPEC), after maintaining a partial export embargo, startled the world with a virtual quadrupling of oil prices. With oil prices being quoted and oil transactions being conducted in dollars, there was a vast inflow of dollars (known as "petrodollars") to the OPEC countries, and many of these dollars were deposited in banks in London and in other European cities. Indeed, despite the dramatic fall in oil prices during the 1980s, petrodollar deposits have continued at high levels. For example, Herbert Kaufman (1992, p. 318) notes that, after the Iraqi invasion of Kuwait in 1990, the overthrown Kuwaiti government was still able to make a contribution to the financing of Operation Desert Storm because the Kuwaiti ruling family had perhaps $10 billion invested outside Kuwait, with a sizable amount in Eurobanks.

With this background on the nature of the Eurodollar and Eurocurrency markets, we now briefly consider the significance of these markets. The major consequence of the rise of these markets is that the mobility of financial capital across country borders has been greatly increased. This means that interest rates (and general credit conditions) are increasingly linked across countries although, due to such factors as differing risk, transaction costs and other factors to be discussed later, interest rates are not equalized. Nevertheless, because the majority of deposits in the Euromarkets are interbank deposits—deposits of one bank in another bank—and because banks are very sensitive to interest rate movements, the link is indeed strong despite the fact that interest rate equality is not achieved.

To elaborate, consider a hypothetical large U.S. bank. This bank is interested in attracting deposits and in earning interest from its subsequent loan of those deposits, and it is cognizant of conditions in both domestic and foreign money markets.[8] It compares the cost of obtaining an additional domestic deposit with the return from placing that deposit in the Eurodollar market (either with a different bank or with an overseas branch of its own bank). The cost of acquiring the new deposit involves the interest rate to be paid to the depositor as well as the forgone opportunity cost incurred by holding any required reserves against the deposit.[9] However, in recent years in the United States, the reserve requirement on nonpersonal (corporate) time deposits has been eliminated, so the cost on these deposits is basically only the interest cost. If this interest cost is less than the return in the Eurodollar market *and* if the return in that market is greater than the return on comparable domestic assets, then placing the funds in the Eurodollar market could be profitable. The outflow of funds from the United States would thereby perform an arbitrage function because the withdrawal of the funds from the U.S. money market would put upward pressure on U.S. interest rates and the inflow of funds to the Eurodollar market would put downward pressure on Eurodollar interest rates. The reverse pressures are set in operation when Eurodollar rates are less than domestic rates,

----

[8]See Kreicher (1982, pp. 11–13).

[9]Additional costs in the United States are (1) any premium that needs to be paid for the deposit insurance associated with the deposit and (2) any applicable state and local taxes. We neglect these items in our discussion for the moment.

for then the U.S. bank would borrow funds from the Euromarkets and lend them in the United States.[10]

Thus the Eurodollar and Eurocurrency markets have been a force for moving interest rates across countries toward each other, and these markets have hence played a major role in enhancing financial integration across international borders. In addition, precisely because the markets have been a force for international integration, the consequence is that any country's monetary policy with respect to interest rates is less independent than would otherwise be the case. An attempt to raise interest rates in one country will lead to an inflow of funds, which will dampen the rise in the initial tight-money country and put upward pressure on interest rates in the other countries. Hence, it is no longer possible (at least in developed countries) to conduct a completely independent monetary policy. This increasing integration of financial markets could have been accomplished without the rise of the Euromarkets per se, because the general relaxation of barriers to capital flows in recent decades would most likely have accomplished much the same result. Nevertheless, the rise of the Eurodollar and Eurocurrency markets hastened the process.

Finally, it is important to note that many observers worry that the surge in international bank lending in general and in Euromarket activity in particular *has fostered potential economic instability.* Because a central bank of a country does not have jurisdiction over deposits abroad, there is no effective control of the amount of money in existence that is denominated in the country's currency. Eurodollars, for example, can be borrowed by U.S. banks for use *in the United States,* with the result that an attempt by the Federal Reserve to implement restrictive monetary policy can be made more difficult. Or a foreign subsidiary of a U.S. multinational firm can borrow dollars from German or U.K. banks and use these dollars to increase spending on U.S. goods at the same time that the Federal Reserve is trying to reduce U.S. bank loans as part of an anti-inflationary stance. Further, deposits denominated in dollars, say, in France, are also not under effective control of the French central bank. The uncontrolled growth associated with those deposits could potentially lead to undesirable consequences for *France,* too, if France wished to adopt an anti-inflationary policy.

CONCEPT CHECK

1. What is a Eurodollar deposit? Is the dollar deposit of a French company in a New York bank a Eurodollar deposit? Why or why not?

2. What is the distinction between gross international bank lending and net international bank lending?

THE INTERNATIONAL BOND MARKET

Besides international bank lending, increasingly sizable activity has been taking place in the last several decades in the **international bond market.** The issuance of bonds by governments and corporations represents borrowing by the issuing entities, and the time period of the loan is generally longer than one year. Within the general bond category, a

---

[10]Incidentally, with the elimination of reserve requirements on U.S. banks' time deposits—and time deposits are the principal financial instruments involved in the Eurodollar market—it is less likely that the narrower spread between Eurobanks' lending and deposit rates (as opposed to that spread in U.S. banks) will remain so narrow. Remember that this spread was important in the emergence of the Eurodollar market; with that huge market in existence, however, the reduction of the difference in the spread will not reduce the size of the market. (The spread would actually have to become narrower for U.S. banks than for Eurobanks in order to do so.) In addition, we discuss later in this chapter other factors involving risk that work to maintain a narrower spread in Eurobanks than in U.S. banks.

distinction is often made between *notes,* which have a maturity of less than ten years, and *bonds,* which have a maturity of ten years or longer. We will generally use the term *bonds* to refer to both of these types of debt instruments.

Bonds have a *face value* or *maturity value* (for example, $1,000) which indicates the amount that will be paid back to the lender at the end of the life of the bond, and interest payments (or *coupon payments*) are usually made each year [for example, $60 per year or a 6 percent (= $60/$1,000) *coupon rate*].[11] In addition, the issuance of bonds often involves **bond underwriters,** which are banks and other financial institutions that conduct the sale of the bonds (for a fee) for the issuing entity. These underwriters purchase the bonds from the firms or governments, and the underwriters thus assume the risk that the bonds might not be sold. Further, in international bond markets, banks often join together to form a *loan syndicate* for marketing the bonds.

In considering the international bond market, a distinction is made between two situations (see Mendelson 1983, p. 5.1·3 and Magraw 1983, pp. 5.3·3–5.3·4):

1. The borrower in one country issues bonds in the market of another country (the host country) through a syndicate in the host country. The sale is mainly to residents of the host country, and the bonds are denominated in the currency of the host country. These transactions are said to be taking place in the **foreign bond markets.**

2. The borrower in one country issues bonds in the markets of many countries, with the help of a *multinational* loan syndicate, to residents of many countries. The bonds can be denominated in any of several different currencies (including the currency of the country of the issuer but also other currencies that are not necessarily of the countries in which the bonds are sold). These transactions are said to be taking place in the **Eurobond markets.**

The two types of markets—the foreign bond markets and the Eurobond markets— together constitute the aggregate international bond market. In actual practice, the distinction between foreign bonds and Eurobonds is somewhat blurred (for example, because one bank may underwrite an offering by itself and use neither a domestic syndicate nor a multinational syndicate). In either the foreign bond or the Eurobond markets, the issued securities themselves can pay a fixed interest rate or a variable (floating) interest rate (usually tied to LIBOR). In addition, some bonds are sold at a substantial discount below face value and issued as "zero-coupon" bonds. In this instance, there are no regular interest payments, and the total interest is received when the bond matures at its face value.

. . . .

[11]As you may remember from an earlier economics course, the market price of a bond does not have to equal the maturity value. In a simple, extreme example, suppose that an issuer of a bond is trying to sell the $1,000-face-value bond with the annual coupon payment of $60. If interest rates on competing assets are 10 percent, this issuer will not be able to sell the bond for $1,000 because the interest return to the buyer is only 6 percent. In order to induce a buyer to purchase the bond, the price would have to be lowered to $600. This is so because only at a $600 price will the actual interest rate or yield (= $60 coupon payment/$600 price) on this bond be equal to 10 percent, the yield that is obtainable on other assets in the market. Similarly, if market interest rates are 4 percent, the $1,000-face-value bond with a $60 coupon payment could be sold for $1,500 because then its yield would also be 4 percent (= $60/$1,500). The issuer would not be willing to sell it for any amount less than $1,500 as that would mean that the issuer would be paying a higher interest rate than is necessary for obtaining funds. Thus, an important feature of bond markets is that *interest rates and bond prices move inversely with each other.* In practice, the swings in bond prices when market interest rates change are not as wide as in this example for reasons that we need not go into, but the inverse relationship remains intact.

TABLE 4   **Stock of International Bonds, December 31, 1995 (in billions of U.S. dollars)**

Part A: Type of Instrument

International bonds (without Euronotes)	$2,209.6
Euronotes	593.8
	$2,803.3

Part B: Location of Issuers of Instruments

Developed countries		$2,149.7
Europe	$1,306.4	
United States	313.7	
Japan	238.4	
Canada	181.3	
Offshore centers		187.9
Other countries		156.9
International institutions		308.7
		$2,803.3

Part C: Currency Denomination of Instruments

U.S. dollar	$ 984.9
Japanese yen	496.8
German mark	319.7
Other currencies	1,001.9
	$2,803.3

Part D: Type of Issuer of Instruments

Commercial banks and other financial institutions	$1,038.6
Governments, state agencies, and international institutions	986.7
Corporations	778.1
	$2,803.3

Note: Components may not sum to totals because of rounding.

Source: Bank for International Settlements, *66th Annual Report* (Basle, Switzerland: BIS, June 10, 1996), p. 147.

Table 4 presents data on the size of the stock of international bonds (foreign bonds and Eurobonds) in existence at the end of 1995. Eurobonds with less than 10 years maturity at issuance, called **Euronotes,** are listed separately by the source for this table (the BIS) because these notes have been growing more rapidly than the rest of the international bonds. As can be seen from Part A of the table, the broad stock of international bonds (*including* the Euronotes) stood at $2.8 trillion at the end of 1995. The geographical locations of the issuers of the bonds are listed in Part B—about 75 percent are issued by borrowers located in developed countries (primarily in Europe). Bonds are also issued in *offshore centers,* such as the Cayman Islands, the Bahamas, and Netherlands Antilles. These centers are intermediary or "pass-through" locations for international funds:[12] because of tax or regulatory advantages, a branch of a U.S. bank in the Cayman Islands, for example, borrows from its parent bank in the United States in order to make loans to non-U.S. borrowers. The remaining issuers of the bonds in Table 4 are in developing countries or are multilateral institutions such as the World Bank and the International Monetary Fund. As is also evident from Table 4 (Part C), the U.S. dollar, the Japanese yen, and the German mark are the principal currencies of denomination of the bonds, but other currencies are used for more than one-third of the bonds. Finally, in Part D, we see

....
[12]See Eng and Lees (1983, p. 3.6·3).

the importance of commercial banks and other financial institutions in the underwriting and issuance of bonds. Significant in this item have been bank borrowing to finance mergers and acquisitions worldwide and, as globalization of asset markets proceeds, the relative shift of the composition of balance sheets toward international liabilities and away from domestic liabilities. At the same time, governments have also intensified their borrowing from international markets relative to domestic markets (BIS, June 10, 1996, p. 148).

The growth of the international bond markets began in much the same way as did the Eurodollar market. The imposition of the Interest Equalization Tax, or IET (see the discussion earlier in this chapter on the origin of Eurodollars), in mid-1963 is regarded as a main factor. (See Mendelsohn 1980, pp. 32–36.) This tax applied to the income from new and existing foreign securities (mainly European) held by U.S. citizens, and the consequence of its introduction was that the prices of such bonds fell in the United States in order to get Americans to purchase them. (Higher interest returns on the bonds were needed to cover the tax and to make the after-tax returns comparable with the returns on domestic bonds, and remember that higher interest rates on bonds mean lower prices on bonds.) When this tax restriction was followed in the mid-1960s by the "voluntary" lending restraints imposed on U.S. bank lending abroad and by suggested government guidelines for foreign direct investment by U.S. firms that aimed to reduce that investment, the consequence was that foreign borrowers moved away from the U.S. lending market and began issuing bonds in Europe. Foreign subsidiaries of U.S. firms abroad (which might previously have issued bonds in the United States) also issued bonds abroad. Hence, a stimulus was given to the growth of bond markets outside the United States. With the relaxation of capital controls in Europe that had been accomplished in the late 1950s and with the generally increasing economic integration taking place within the European Community, the new bond issues abroad were denominated in a variety of different currencies. By the mid-1970s, when the U.S. lending restraints and the IET were removed, the European markets had become sizable and the growth was irreversible.

There is no reason to think that, with the increasing mobility of capital across country borders, these markets will retrench; rather, they can fully be expected to continue growing. In recent years, additional stimuli have also been given to Eurobond issues. For example, in 1995, Japan took major steps to promote investment in foreign securities by its citizens and also removed restrictions on the sale of Euroyen bonds in Japan. Further, in 1995 Italy abolished restraints on the issuance of Eurolira bonds by foreign banks, and many developing countries have for the last several years been permitting greater issuance of foreign currency–denominated bonds by their firms. The developing countries, including the transition economies of Central and Eastern Europe and the former republics of the Soviet Union, have also been introducing liberalizing reforms in their capital markets in general (BIS, June 10, 1996, p. 152).

The economic implications of the Eurobond markets are much the same as those of the Eurocurrency markets. Financial capital is increasingly able to flow across international borders and thus to intensify the tendency for interest rates on similar assets to equalize. (See Case Study 1.) From an economic perspective, the growth of these markets therefore results in a more efficient allocation of financial capital. However, as was also true for the Eurocurrency markets, interest rates will not become exactly equal even on two identical assets (a domestic bond and a Eurobond)—and not just because of transaction costs and other factors previously mentioned. An additional factor preventing equality is exchange rate risk. If a German holder of a U.S. dollar–denominated bond (which may in fact have been issued by a French firm) judges that the dollar will fall during the life of the bond

✳ CASE STUDY 1 INTEREST RATES ACROSS COUNTRIES

As suggested in the text, increased mobility of financial capital should set forces at work to narrow interest rate differentials across countries. In theory, and with other things equal, we would thus expect interest rates on similar assets to be nearly identical. However, as noted in the text and as will also be discussed at length later in the chapter, rates may not equalize in practice because of risk elements in the markets and other reasons.

Nevertheless, with the increased integration of financial markets in recent years, we would not expect interest rates to diverge sharply from each other. In order to consider this conjecture with respect to bond markets, Table 5 gives data on government bond yields (average yields to maturity in annual percentage rates) for 13 developed countries and 7 developing countries in 1995. Column (1) lists nominal (market) interest rates for these assets; however, this column is not particularly meaning-

ful because no allowance has been made for inflation rates. As you may recall from an earlier economics course, the *real interest rate* is more useful for making economic decisions. The approximate real interest rate can be found by subtracting the inflation rate from the nominal interest rate, and such an adjustment is necessary, for example, because an investor earning a 10 percent nominal return on a one-year security is in fact earning only 2 percent in real, purchasing power terms if the inflation rate is 8 percent. Hence, column (2) of Table 5 indicates the 1995 inflation rate for the 20 countries, and column (3) lists the resulting real interest rates on bonds.

Column (3) suggests that, for the developed countries, there is a reasonable similarity in real interest rates, but they are obviously not identical. In addition to risk factors, the differences may also be partly explained by

TABLE 5 **Bond Yields in Developed and Developing Countries, 1995 (average yield to maturity in percent per annum)**

	(1) Nominal Yield*	(2) 1995 Inflation Rate†	(3) Real Yield
Developed countries:			
Austria	6.5%	2.3%	4.2%
Belgium	7.3	1.5	5.8
Canada	8.3	2.2	6.1
Denmark	7.6	2.1	5.5
France	7.6	1.8	5.8
Germany	6.5	1.8	4.7
Italy	12.2	5.2	7.0
Japan	2.5	−0.1	2.6
Netherlands	7.2	1.9	5.3
Spain	11.0	4.7	6.3
Switzerland	3.7	1.8	1.9
United Kingdom	8.3	3.4	4.9
United States	6.6	2.8	3.8
Developed country mean	7.3%	2.4%	4.9%
Developing countries:			
Jamaica	26.9%	29.5%	−2.6%
Korea, Republic of	12.4	4.5	7.9
Malawi	38.6	83.3	−44.7
Netherlands Antilles	8.0	2.8	5.2
Pakistan	13.0	12.3	0.7
South Africa	16.1	8.6	7.5
Venezuela	53.4	59.9	−6.5

*Nominal yields have been rounded to one decimal place to be consistent with the inflation data.

†Inflation rates are percentage changes in consumer price indexes.

Source: International Monetary Fund, *International Financial Statistics,* February 1997, pp. 65, 69, 71.

(Continued)

(CASE STUDY 1—CONTINUED)

different maturities of bonds in the various markets. Further, since changes in price levels are used to convert the nominal yields into real yields, these price-level changes would necessarily have to move in accordance with relative purchasing power parity (PPP) in order to make real yields equal. Nevertheless, the real bond yields in Table 5 differ by less than 1 percentage point from the mean in 7 of the 13 developed countries and by less than 1.5 percentage points in 10 of the 13 countries.* For the three developed countries that deviate more than 1.5 percentage points, Italy's positive deviation most likely embodies uncertainty regarding political stability and regarding the future of the lira in this relatively high-inflation country; Japan's negative divergence is consistent with the existence of Japan's controls on capital outflows; and Switzerland's negative deviation may be associated with the time-honored stability

of the country and with its reputation as a safe haven for financial investment.

Finally, the developing countries' real rates as a general rule differ substantially from those of the developed countries, as the developing countries are not very well integrated into the world financial system. This is especially true for the countries with *negative* real interest rates—these countries are not regarded as good places by foreign investors for placement of funds. However, it is noteworthy that the Netherlands Antilles, an offshore center for developed-country funds, has a real interest rate that is very close to the average real rate for the developed countries. This suggests that that country, because of its special offshore center circumstance, is closely tied to the financial markets of North America and Western Europe.

*For those of you who have had a statistics course, the variance of the group of real bond yields around the mean (that is, the sum of squared deviations from the mean ÷ 12 in this case) is 2.17 and the standard deviation is 1.47. For the *nominal* yields, the variance is 6.47 and the standard deviation is 2.54—clearly larger than that for the real bond yields.

(or during the period when the holder possesses the bond, which may not be its entire life), the owner will need to be receiving a higher yield than would be received if the bond were denominated in deutsche marks and if there is any risk that cannot be covered or hedged. In a bond setting, there is likely to be more uncovered risk than in markets for shorter-term assets, because hedging instruments are not as available for the longer-term bond assets. Further, the availability and the frequency of use of hedging techniques decrease as the time period of bonds themselves lengthens, leading to the necessity of even greater compensation for risk.

Another implication of the international bond market is, of course, that foreign exchange markets themselves will be more active than would be the case if these markets did not exist. Bondholders may choose to purchase bonds of a particular currency denomination because they envision that interest rates differ more than is justified by exchange rate expectations, and an exchange market transaction may thus be necessary to obtain the particular currency in order to make the purchase. Similarly, at the bond's maturity date, an exchange market transaction may be mandated if the bond seller has no special need for the currency at that time. Further, the original bond issuer may also need to make an exchange market transaction to pay off the bond at maturity. Hence, the exchange markets will be subject to greater buffeting than would otherwise have been the case.

Finally, the existence of the international bond markets (as with the Eurocurrency markets) can reduce the independence that exists for any given country's monetary authority. If the Bank of Canada wishes to drive down long-term interest rates to stimulate real investment, this attempt will be frustrated if Canadian bondholders switch to the purchase of foreign bonds where yields are now relatively higher (and bond prices are therefore relatively lower). This could result in a monetary outflow from Canada, possibly resulting in a worsened balance-of-payments position (under fixed exchange rates) and a depreciation of the Canadian dollar (under flexible exchange rates).

INTERNATIONAL STOCK MARKETS

Other assets that have become more widely traded across international borders in recent years are shares of common stocks (equities) of corporations. This type of asset differs from bonds in that the holding of stock by individuals and institutions (for example, insurance companies, pension funds) brings with it ownership of the company whose stock is held. Hence, in theory, there is an element of control involved with stocks that is absent from bonds. In practice, however, any one investor generally holds such a small relative amount of any given corporation's stock that effective control by that investor is precluded. Nevertheless, the financial features of stock differ in a way that makes the purchase decision more complicated than is the case with bonds and other debt instruments. An investor considering the acquisition of a company's stock is faced with making an uncertain projection of the company's future earnings, the variability of those earnings, the real factors lying behind demand for and supply of the company's product that may influence the firm's future courses of action, the ratio of the stock's price to the company's earnings per share, the dividend payout rate, and many other performance indicators. In the international context, expectations of the future exchange rate behavior of the foreign currency in which the stock is quoted relative to the home currency of the investor are also important, as well as the anticipated macroeconomic behavior of the country in which the stock is being sold. An individual investor in recent years has been increasingly able to shift the analysis of the selection of stock to mutual funds which bring together the financial resources of many buyers and which specialize in transactions in international stocks, but the fund managers themselves obviously still need to take account of all these influences.

Unfortunately, information on the size of stock purchases made across country borders is difficult to obtain. A general consensus among observers and participants in the market is that the volume of such equity transactions has been increasing with the spread of multinational companies, the increased mobility of capital in general, and the emergence and maturing of stock exchanges in many developing countries (see Case Study 2). While hard data are thus lacking, we present below various pieces of evidence that are consistent with the prevailing view of the increased international purchases of stocks.

Table 7 illustrates the growth of cross-border transactions in bonds and stocks *in total* from 1980 to 1995 (as was also shown in a previous chapter). While it would be desirable to have the breakdown into bonds and stocks provided separately, the source for this table (the BIS) does not do so. However, because bonds and equities are both important in international financial transactions, and therefore the possibility that the data are completely dominated by bonds is small, the table can be suggestive of trends in stock purchases. Notice that, in the United States for example, gross international financial transactions rose from 9 percent of U.S. GDP in 1980 to *135 percent* of U.S. GDP in 1995—a phenomenal increase. (Note: "Gross transactions" means that, for any given country, a summation is being made of all purchases of international bonds and stocks by that country's residents and all purchases of that country's bonds and stocks by foreign residents.) Every other country in the table (except for Japan) had an even higher ratio of cross-border transactions to GDP in 1995 than did the United States.

Table 8 provides additional information on cross-border transactions. Although this table pertains only to the United States, the figures focus on stock purchases exclusively rather than on bonds and stocks together. The value of these gross equity transactions (transactions in U.S. equities by foreign buyers plus transactions in foreign equities by U.S. buyers) rose from $93 billion in 1980 to $1,523 billion in 1994, a compound annual

❧ CASE STUDY 2   STOCK MARKET PERFORMANCE IN DEVELOPING COUNTRIES

Stock markets in developing countries have been increasing dramatically in recent years with respect to their size and participation by investors (including foreign investors). Much of this increased activity is associated with the general liberalization of the various economies that has featured, *inter alia,* reductions of tariff and nontariff barriers, relaxation of internal government controls on production and sale of goods, and privatization of former state enterprises. With this "freeing up" of the economies, however, market instability has increased, and turmoil has also emerged because of the removal of government provision of employment and income support. In addition, the prospects for increased income inequality have been enhanced with the arrival of the different and more risky environment.

Table 6 provides an indication of the potential gains and losses for financial investors in the face of the instability and yet the promise of the new, market-oriented regimes. The table lists the percentage changes in leading stock market price indexes during calendar year 1996 in 25 "emerging market economies." (Stock price index information for these markets is available each week on the last page of *The Economist.*) As can be seen, there were large stock appreciations in some former Soviet-bloc countries (Hungary, Poland, Russia) and also in liberalizing China, Venezuela, and Brazil. On the other hand, South Korea—an increasingly important player in world markets—experienced a large fall, associated with labor unrest and the uncertainty regarding the intentions and future evolution of North Korea. A decline also occurred (when expressed in dollar terms) in South Africa as the new Nelson Mandela–led government grappled with adjustment problems involved in the transition to majority rule, which instilled uncertainty in foreign investors that was reflected in a depreciation of the rand against the dollar. Chile and Thailand, which are liberalizing countries also becoming important on the international scene, were faced with internal political difficulties and saw movement downward in the values of the equities of their companies.

TABLE 6   Performance of Stock Price Indexes, Developing Countries, December 29, 1995–January 1, 1997

| Country | Percentage Change | | Country | Percentage Change | |
	In Local Currency	In Dollar Terms		In Local Currency	In Dollar Terms
Argentina	+25.1%	+25.1%	Malaysia	+24.4%	+25.1%
Brazil	+63.8	+53.2	Mexico	+20.4	+17.5
Chile	−14.6	−18.1	Philippines	+22.2	+21.7
China	+66.0	+66.5	Poland	+89.1	+62.4
Colombia	+11.6	+10.3	Portugal	+34.8	+30.6
Czech Republic	+26.7	+23.6	Russia	+170.5	+124.8
Greece	+2.1	−1.1	Singapore	−2.2	−1.3
Hong Kong	+33.5	+33.5	South Africa	+6.9	−16.7
Hungary	+170.4	+133.5	Taiwan	+34.4	+33.5
India	+4.8	+3.0	Thailand	−35.1	−36.3
Indonesia	+24.0	+20.5	Turkey	+143.8	+34.1
Israel	−4.0	−7.0	Venezuela	+231.3	+131.9
Korea, Republic of	−26.2	−32.4			

Source: *The Economist,* Jan. 4, 1997, p. 98.   ❧

growth rate of *22 percent.*[13] Thus, while we do not have reliable data at hand for countries other than the United States, Table 8 does suggest rapidly increasing activity on the international level across countries.

....
[13]If the data sources were the same for Tables 7 and 8 and if the estimates were consistent across the two tables, this would suggest a method for determining a division in Table 7 between bonds and equities. Since U.S. GDP was $6,936 billion in 1994 and (from Table 7) the bond and stock transactions in total were 131 percent of 1994 U.S. GDP, bonds and stocks together would have a 1994 value of $9,086 billion. Thus, since U.S. cross-border stock transactions in 1994 (from Table 8) were $1,523 billion, stocks were about 17 percent (= $1,523/$9,086) of the total. However, we are not certain enough of the comparability of the two tables to be conclusive with respect to this bond-stock division.

TABLE 7   **Cross-Border Transactions in Bonds and Equities**
(gross purchases and sales expressed as a percentage of GDP)

Country	1980	1985	1990	1994	1995
Canada	10%	27%	64%	212%	194%
France	5	21	54	201	180
Germany	7	33	57	159	172
Italy	1	4	27	207	253
Japan	8	62	119	60	65
United States	9	35	89	131	135

Source: Bank for International Settlements, *67th Annual Report* (Basle, Switzerland: BIS, June 9, 1997), p. 79.

TABLE 8   **Gross Cross-Border Equity Transactions in the United States, 1980–1994**
(in billions of dollars)

Year	Value of Transactions	Year	Value of Transactions
1980	$ 93	1988	$ 517
1981	94	1989	649
1982	96	1990	616
1983	165	1991	684
1984	155	1992	780
1985	205	1993	1,171
1986	378	1994	1,523
1987	671		

Note: Gross cross-border transactions are the value of transactions in U.S. equities by foreign buyers plus the value of transactions in foreign equities by U.S. buyers.
Source: Lowell Bryan and Diana Farrell, *Market Unbound: Unleashing Global Capitalism* (New York: Wiley, 1996), p. 34.

Because stock transactions of the cross-border type have been increasing rapidly, it is possible that movements of stock prices across countries will tend to become increasingly similar to each other. This co-movement might arise because of the general result that occurs when markets become less separated or segmented and arbitrage occurs between them. However, stock markets can differ in this co-movement respect from usual markets because of the central role of expectations in stock markets and the resulting potential volatility that can emerge from sudden swings in those expectations. If the prices of stocks in market A soar while those in market B languish, investors may shift from B to A and drive prices further up in A and down in B because of expectations that A will continue to rise and B will continue to stagnate. On the other hand, the soaring prices in market A might yield the result that investors will expect them to fall and thus will shift the composition of their portfolios toward stocks in market B. In this case, the prices in the two markets might converge and, with regular such behavior, might never have diverged to a great extent in the first place—any rise in one market would cause a switch to the other market, causing a rise there.

In addition, a force that may generate a common trend movement of stock price indexes across countries is the phenomenon of **international portfolio diversification** to reduce risk in investors' portfolios. (See Mayo 1997, pp. 803–11.) If the price changes are not highly correlated with each other across countries, there is an advantage to holding stocks in several countries because a rise (fall) in one market will not be closely matched with a rise (fall) in other markets. Since many investors are risk-averse, the

TABLE 9   **Stock Market Price Indexes, December 1993–March 1996**
(end of December 1994 = 100)

Country	December 1993	December 1994	December 1995	March 1996
Australia	114	100	115	116
Belgium	106	100	112	119
Canada	103	100	112	118
France	121	100	100	109
Germany	108	100	107	118
Italy	97	100	93	92
Japan	92	100	101	105
Netherlands	97	100	118	133
Spain	113	100	112	120
Sweden	95	100	118	129
Switzerland	108	100	123	135
United Kingdom	111	100	118	121
United States	102	100	134	141

Source: Bank for International Settlements, *66th Annual Report* (Basle, Switzerland: BIS, June 10, 1996), p. 76.

purchase of stock in several markets will reduce the likelihood of wide swings in total portfolio value. Indeed, mutual funds with global scope are doing precisely this type of diversified investing. But if portfolios become diversified across international markets and if some balance between the stocks across the various markets is maintained over time as portfolios grow, then the markets may well move in somewhat parallel fashion.

Table 9 presents data on the joint movement of stock price indexes in a recent relatively short period (December 1993 to March 1996). As can be seen, the indexes in most of the 13 countries fell from December 1993 to December 1994, rose from December 1994 to December 1995, and continued to rise from December 1995 to March 1996. Only Italy, Japan, the Netherlands, and Sweden showed a rise from December 1993 to December 1994; only Italy fell from December 1994 to December 1995 (France remained constant); and only Italy fell from December 1995 to March 1996. While other, common factors obviously also could have caused this parallel movement (such as world recovery from the recession of the early 1990s), and while the degree of movement differs among the countries, the data still are consistent with the fact that integration among the various markets has taken place.

This general co-movement of stock market price indexes is examined more carefully in Table 10. The table indicates the correlation coefficients between U.S. stock prices and stock prices in eight other countries during approximately six years before and about two years after the large fall, or "crash," in the U.S. stock market in October 1987.[14] A suggestion that emerges from the table is that diversification out of U.S. stocks after the crash generated an increased co-movement of the various market indexes, which would be consistent with closer integration of the markets and greater international portfolio diversification.[15]

[14]For those unfamiliar with correlation coefficients, a very general description is as follows: If two series move precisely together in direct (positive) fashion, the correlation coefficient between them is +1.0; if the series move in precisely inverse (negative) fashion, their correlation coefficient is −1.0; and if the two series move in an entirely unrelated manner, their correlation coefficient is zero.

[15]The rise in the correlation coefficients also suggests that there is less stability to be achieved in the investors' portfolios in the future through increased diversification than there was prior to October 1987. (See Mayo 1997, p. 807.)

TABLE 10   **Correlation Coefficients between U.S. and Selected Foreign Stock Price Indexes**

Country	June 1981 to September 1987	November 1987 to December 1989
Canada	+0.72	+0.92
France	+0.39	+0.79
Germany	+0.21	+0.71
Italy	+0.22	+0.56
Japan	+0.33	+0.15
Netherlands	+0.47	+0.42
Switzerland	+0.50	+0.74
United Kingdom	+0.51	+0.95

Source: Herbert B. Mayo, *Investments: An Introduction,* 5th ed. (Fort Worth, TX: Dryden, 1997), p. 809.

Before concluding this look at international equity markets, we take note of the emergence of a new investment vehicle for making such transactions across country borders. As indicated briefly earlier, **mutual funds** are becoming increasingly important for such purchases. (Mutual funds of this international type also have become prominent in bonds, but we concentrate here on stock funds.) These funds collect the savings of small individual investors as well as large institutional investors and place the pool of collected savings into portfolios of financial assets comprising equities of companies located in many different countries. From the standpoint of U.S. investors, there are four main types of such internationally focused mutual funds (Mayo 1997, pp. 810–11):

1. **Global funds** purchase packages of equities that contain stocks of corporations both in the United States and in other countries.[16]

2. **International funds** do not hold U.S. securities but purchase exclusively the stocks of companies located in other countries.

3. **Emerging market funds** hold a portfolio of stocks of companies in developing countries—for example, in Argentina, the Czech Republic, Indonesia, and Malaysia.

4. **Regional funds** focus on securities of companies in particular geographic areas or countries—for example, in Asia, Latin America, China, Germany, and Japan.

To participate in these funds, shares of the funds can be purchased in some cases on organized stock exchanges and in other cases (more prominent) directly from the mutual fund companies. Aside from the differing countries in which the various funds invest, there are other differing characteristics among them: *no-load* funds require no explicit charge for purchase or sale; *low-load* and *load* funds impose a charge for entering the portfolio; *redemption-charge* funds levy a fee upon exit; and *closed-end* funds are traded on regular stock exchanges and thus involve a broker's fee upon entry and exit. With mutual funds, the choice set for investors is indeed large. For example, in the United States, there were 990 different funds with an international orientation that were included in a 1997 survey by *U.S. News & World Report* (Feb. 3, 1997, p. 60).

Finally, with respect to stock markets, we close by emphasizing again that, as with international bonds and international bank lending, the increasing integration of these

. . . .

[16]Typically, 25 to 50 percent of the assets are U.S. stocks. See Kurt Badenhausen, "Leaving Home," *Financial World,* Feb. 18, 1997, p. 64.

markets serves to facilitate the flow of capital toward its best use. As financial investors respond to perceived profit opportunities beyond their own borders, they are transferring capital to destinations where it can earn a higher return. As financial capital flows for the purchase of the stock of a foreign company that is productive and profitable, this raises the book value of the company and encourages its expansion because of its more favorable balance sheet.[17] Encouragement of profitable, productive firms and discouragement of poorly managed, unproductive companies of course serve to improve the allocation of world resources. In the broad context of international monetary economics, however, the use of international stock transactions to improve capital allocation potentially comes at a price. This price, especially if the stock transactions involve speculative behavior due to unfounded rumors and "bandwagon" effects, is the increased volatility in world financial markets (and particularly in foreign exchange markets) that can occur.

Thus far, we have focused in this chapter on international bank deposits and lending, international bond markets, and stock market activity in an international context. In overview, these various asset markets have been growing dramatically in size and scope in recent years. International investors now have open to them financial opportunities previously unavailable, and the activity in these increasingly integrated markets has meant that countries are becoming linked ever more tightly together economically. The impacts of financial developments in one country spill over into other countries, and the new environment poses challenges as well as opportunities for economic actors.

CONCEPT CHECK

1. Distinguish participation by an investor in foreign bond markets from participation by that investor in Eurobond markets.

2. Why do bond prices and bond yields move inversely with each other?

3. Why would a financial investor wish to pursue international portfolio diversification?

FINANCIAL LINKAGES AND EUROCURRENCY DERIVATIVES

With this broad look at international banking, international bonds, and the international purchase of stocks as background, we now turn to a more detailed examination of particular financial instruments and financial strategies employed in the international asset and foreign exchange markets. As should be clear, the world of international finance is becoming increasingly complicated; at the same time, however, it is becoming increasingly fascinating. We hope that, after studying the material below, you will have a broader understanding of the instruments behind the forces and policies influencing economic activity in both individual countries and the world macroeconomy.

Basic International Financial Linkages: A Review

In the previous chapter, "The Foreign Exchange Market," we discussed the formal links between the foreign exchange markets and the financial markets. It was seen that the decision to invest at home or abroad depends on the expected rate of return of the foreign and domestic alternatives under consideration. If the expected rate of return on domestic

---

[17]Since most stock purchases are of previously issued stock and not of newly issued stock, the funds flowing in for a stock purchase are generally not flowing to the company per se. However, the company's net worth or capital value on its balance sheet increases as its stock rises in price, and the company is thus in a better position to, among other things, obtain loans or issue new stock for the financing of expansion of the firm.

assets is higher, the individual will invest at home. Conversely, if the expected rate of return is higher on the foreign asset, the individual would be expected to invest abroad. If there are no barriers to financial investment flows, then funds should move from areas of low rates of return to areas of high rates of return until the expected returns are similar, differing only by the transaction costs involved in moving between the two markets.

It is critical, as noted earlier, to remember that rates of return on foreign investments result both from the return on the financial asset in question and from changes in the exchange rate over the period of the investment. Thus the domestic investor must take into account (1) the expected rate of return on the domestic financial asset, (2) the expected rate of return on the foreign asset, and (3) any expected change in the exchange rate. The investor is thus indifferent between a foreign asset and a domestic asset only when he or she expects to earn the same return on each possibility after taking into account any gains or losses associated with expected changes in the exchange rate. This "parity" condition was stated more formally in the preceding chapter in the following manner:

$$(1 + i_{\text{home}})/(1 + i_{\text{foreign}}) = E(e)/e$$

where:

$$i_{\text{home}} = \text{domestic rate of interest}$$
$$i_{\text{foreign}} = \text{foreign rate of interest}$$
$$e = \text{spot foreign exchange rate in units of domestic currency per unit of foreign currency}$$
$$E(e) = \text{expected future exchange rate at the end of the investment period}$$

This is more commonly expressed in terms of the expected percentage appreciation of the foreign currency. If xa is used to represent the expected percentage appreciation of the foreign currency, then $E(e)/e$ is equal to $(1 + xa)$ and the above equation simplifies to

$$(i_{\text{home}} - i_{\text{foreign}})/(1 + i_{\text{foreign}}) = xa$$

which is often approximated by

$$(i_{\text{home}} - i_{\text{foreign}}) \cong xa$$

This condition states that equilibrium occurs in the financial market whenever any difference in the interest rates in the two countries is approximately offset by the expected change in the exchange rate. (Ignore for the moment any transaction costs.) Because of the lack of perfect foresight, the actual return on the foreign investment may not equal that which was expected because of unanticipated changes in the exchange rate. Such unanticipated changes can lead to the attachment of a risk premium if actors are risk-averse, and if the premium is expressed as a percentage, *RP*, the above equilibrium condition is modified to become

$$(i_{\text{home}} - i_{\text{foreign}}) \cong xa - RP$$

Adjusting further for transaction costs, *TR,* leads to the more complete equilibrium condition

$$(i_{\text{home}} - i_{\text{foreign}}) \cong xa - RP - TR$$

From this basic exercise it is clear that the investment decision over time now involves two sources of risk. The first is the aforementioned risk associated with changes in the exchange rate, which affect the overall rate of return on the investment. The second source of risk is the *interest rate risk* that arises if the financial transaction is not to be undertaken and completed for a period of time.

As we discussed in the previous chapter, the foreign exchange risk can be removed (hedged) by using the forward market. In this case, the basic equilibrium condition in the financial market can be expressed in the following manner:

$$(i_{\text{home}} - i_{\text{foreign}}) \cong p - TR$$

where p is the actual premium on the forward exchange rate, that is, $p = (e_{\text{fwd}}/e) - 1$. Thus, in equilibrium, any difference in the two interest rates must be approximately equal to the foreign exchange premium contracted in the forward market. These forward contracts can be purchased in the formal forward market, the futures market, or the options market. Therefore, as we pointed out in our discussion of the foreign exchange market, in the absence of capital controls or other market barriers, all credit markets (foreign and domestic) are linked to one another through arbitrage and currency expectations.

The financial activities of participants in the financial markets, including borrowing, lending, and the assignment of risk through hedging actions, ensure that the difference between interest rates in the two countries equals not only the forward premium (via forward contracts) but also the expected exchange rate change on the part of those who are bearing the risk of changes in the foreign exchange rate. As was demonstrated at the end of the previous chapter, if markets are efficient, the following should hold:

$$i_{\text{home}} - i_{\text{foreign}} \cong p = xa$$

However, to the extent that there is a risk associated with foreign exchange that cannot be avoided by combining foreign exchange holdings with other assets (i.e., a foreign exchange risk that cannot be diversified away), an additional risk premium, as noted earlier, would be required by those going uncovered; that is,

$$i_{\text{home}} - i_{\text{foreign}} \cong p = xa - RP$$

Whether or not such a risk premium exists is still a subject of considerable debate among financial researchers.

International Financial Linkages and the Eurodollar Market

How does the Eurodollar market enter into these financial considerations? The presence of the Eurodollar market in essence creates a second interest rate possibility in each currency. The financial investment now includes the following *six* financial variables, using the United States (home) and the United Kingdom (foreign) as the two country examples:

Interest rates:	U.S. interest rate
	U.K. interest rate
	Euro*dollar* interest rate (foreign-held dollar funds)
	Euro*sterling* interest rate (foreign-held British pounds)
Exchange rates:	Spot rate (dollars/pound)
	Forward exchange rate (dollars/pound)

Lenders and borrowers now have the alternatives of two different markets in which to operate, one at home and one abroad. The relationship between the rates in these markets would appear to be very straightforward. If all things were equal, Eurobanks should pay no less than the deposit rate in the United States. If they paid less, why would depositors place their funds abroad instead of at home? Similarly, Eurobanks cannot lend Eurodollars at a higher lending rate than that in the United States; and further, why should a Eurobank be willing to lend dollars at a rate lower than that in the United States? Thus, a priori, it appears as though the borrowing and lending rates in the United States should establish similar rates in the Eurodollar market.

❈ CASE STUDY 3   U.S. DOMESTIC AND EURODOLLAR DEPOSIT AND
LENDING RATES, 1989–1996

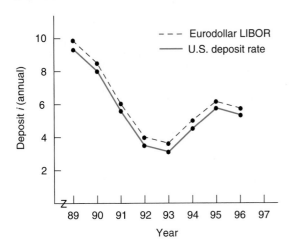

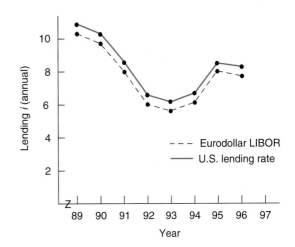

The graphs above illustrate the annual average bank deposit rate in the United States, the annual average London Eurodollar deposit rate, and the annual average U.S. lending rate as reported by the International Monetary Fund for the 1989–1996 period. An estimate was made of the annual average Eurodollar lending rate, since the IMF does not report that information. As can be seen from the left graph, U.S. and Euro-dollar deposit rates tracked each other very closely, although Eurodollar deposit rates were higher. If Eurodollar lending rates have continued their historical pattern, they would track U.S. ending rates but would be below them, as shown conceptually in the right graph.

Sources: International Monetary Fund, *International Financial Statistics,* February 1996, pp. 54, 57, 58, and February 1997, pp. 56, 60, 62. The annual average lending rates in the graphs above were estimated by applying the same annual margin difference as was indicated in the deposit data.   ❈

However, because of the different institutional settings, it can be argued that U.S. interest rates will likely bound the Eurodollar rates, that is, the domestic lending rate lies above the Eurocurrency lending rate and the domestic deposit rate lies below the Eurocurrency deposit rate. This historically appears to have been the case, as was indicated earlier in this chapter. Available data on recent deposit rates are consistent with this observation. (See Case Study 3.) The relatively lower Eurocurrency lending rate and relatively higher deposit rate can be explained from the standpoint of a foreign risk differential and an institutional cost differential. Turning first to the risk dimension, if potential lenders or borrowers perceive a relative difference in risk associated with the foreign deposit or loan, they will require a risk premium in the form of a lower lending rate or higher deposit rate. When U.S. borrowers or investors contract with a foreign bank, they become involved in a foreign jurisdiction. Thus the risk on the foreign deposits or loans is somewhat greater than the risk on similar transactions within the United States. The two dollar markets are thus separated by possible foreign government actions or restrictions that increase the risk of doing business abroad instead of at home. Legal restrictions or potential policy actions that might interfere with the movement of funds between, for example, a London bank and the United States can drive a wedge between U.S. domestic rates and Eurodollar rates in the United Kingdom. Government policies can impact directly through restrictions on capital outflows and foreign exchange controls which alter the nonresident convertibility of the dollar holdings abroad. In addition, there is always the slight possibility that the assets or liabilities of the Eurobanks can be seized by the authorities where they operate. Further, differences in liquidity or institutional structure related to such things as the number and size of financial dealers and the accessibility of adequate financial information can also influence the risk environment.

From the cost perspective, banks face additional costs when utilizing domestic deposits compared with Eurocurrency deposits. These additional costs arise whenever banks are not subject to the reserve requirements or deposit insurance assessments on Eurocurrency deposits that can be required on domestic deposits. It is obvious that the bank could earn more by being able to lend out a full deposit than by having to retain a certain percentage as a reserve requirement. In the presence of domestic reserve requirements, therefore, a U.S. domestic bank would pay a lower rate on domestic deposits than could be earned on Eurodollar deposits abroad. Generalizing, the deposit rates on Eurocurrency should exceed domestic deposit rates of the same given currency by an amount equal to the relative cost of central bank regulation.[18]

With this expanded view of the international financial market in perspective, let us again examine the nature of adjustments in the United States and the United Kingdom when there is a change in credit conditions in one of the countries, for example, the United States. This process is similar to that described in the chapter "The Foreign Exchange Market," except that there are now six markets involved instead of four. The six markets are (1) the U.S. money market, (2) the U.K. money market, (3) the Eurodollar market, (4) the Eurosterling market, (5) the spot market, and (6) the forward market. Suppose that the markets start out in equilibrium and the following interest rate parity equilibrium rates prevail:

Lending i_{NY}	= 7%	Lending i_{London}	= 8%
Lending $i_{Eurodollar\ London}$	= 6.5%	Lending $i_{Eurosterling\ NY}$	= 7.5%
Deposit i_{NY}	= 5%	Deposit i_{London}	= 6%
Deposit $i_{Eurodollar\ London}$	= 5.5%	Deposit $i_{Eurosterling\ NY}$	= 6.5%
Spot $e_{\$/£}$	= \$1.6912/£	90-day forward $e_{\$/£}$	= \$1.6869/£

It can be easily demonstrated that the covered interest arbitrage parity condition holds across all pairs of rates, after dividing the annual interest rate difference by 4 so that it approximates the 90-day forward period. For example:

$$i_{NY} - i_{London} \cong p$$
$$(.07 - .08)/4 \cong (\$1.6869 - \$1.6912)/\$1.6912$$
$$-.0025 \cong -.0025$$

. . . .

[18]An estimate of the higher rate on Eurocurrency deposits taking into account any reserve requirement and any applicable deposit insurance fees charged on domestic deposits is therefore

Eurocurrency deposit rate = effective cost of domestic deposit =
$(i_{domestic\ deposit} + \text{deposit insurance fees})/(1 - \text{reserve requirement})$

Hence, if the reserve requirement is 5 percent, $i_{domestic\ deposit}$ is 8 percent, and the deposit insurance fee is 0.083 (= 1/12) percent, then

Eurocurrency deposit rate = (.08 + .00083)/(1 − 0.05) = .08509, or 8.51%

This ignores any differential tax treatment or any difference in bank regulatory practices regarding the two types of deposits.

Suppose that the Federal Reserve moves to raise U.S. domestic interest rates by 1/2 percentage point. This will immediately make investments in New York more attractive to investors, and the markets will begin to adjust to a new equilibrium position taking into account the new interest rates in the United States. In all likelihood, the first adjustment to the rate changes in New York will take place in the Eurodollar rate abroad. In order for London banks to maintain their dollar deposits, the Eurodollar deposit rate will rise to 6 percent and the Eurodollar lending rate will be bid up to 7 percent, thus maintaining the same spread difference as existed prior to the increase in the U.S. rates. At the same time, as U.K. investors attempt to take advantage of the higher U.S. rates, they will increase their demand for dollars (supply of British pounds) causing the spot dollar rate to appreciate. Simultaneously, investors who wish to insure themselves against unforeseen changes in the exchange rate will buy pounds forward (increase the supply of dollars forward), leading to a depreciation of the dollar in the forward market, just as was the case in the adjustment process discussed in the previous chapter. If U.K. interest rates remain unchanged, all adjustment to market equilibrium will take place in the foreign exchange market. However, upward pressure will come to bear on U.K. interest rates and the Eurosterling rate. Increases in these rates will reduce the degree of change in the exchange rates to bring the markets into a new equilibrium position. With the new U.S. interest rates and U.K. rates/Eurosterling rates remaining unchanged, market equilibrium would again take place if, for example, the 90-day forward rate moved up (the dollar depreciated) to $1.688/£ and the spot rate moved down (the dollar appreciated) to $1.690/£. Of course, should interest rates in the United Kingdom (and the Eurosterling rates) start to increase, one would expect to see the forward rates begin to decline and the spot rates begin to increase.

These financial adjustments are demonstrated in the six graphs in Figure 1. The tighter money market in the United States causes domestic interest rates to rise [graph (a)]. This immediately leads to an increase in demand for Eurodollars, which drives up Eurodollar rates until they again differ from U.S. domestic rates by the risk-cost differential [graph (b)]. The higher interest rates in the United States lead to an increase in the U.K. demand for dollars (supply of pounds) for financial investment in the United States because of the higher return [graph (c)]. At the same time, these investors will be selling dollars forward to return to pounds at the end of the investment period [graph (f)]. The other markets that might eventually be involved in the financial adjustment process are the U.K. money market [graph (e)] and the Eurosterling market [graph (d)]. As funds move from the United Kingdom to the United States, upward pressure on U.K. domestic and Eurosterling interest rates will be experienced. Should the Bank of England choose not to intervene to hold U.K. interest rates constant and consequently the U.K. rates rise, there will be further readjustments in all six markets until equilibrium again attains.

Having observed how the foreign currency markets, the domestic financial markets, and the Eurodollar markets interact, we now turn to a discussion of how interest rate risk can be reduced or eliminated in international financial markets.

Hedging Eurodollar Interest Rate Risk

A number of new international financial markets have emerged in recent years to provide alternative instruments for spreading risk related to both foreign exchange and future interest rates. Having discussed in the previous chapter how foreign exchange forward, futures, and options markets provide a means for reducing or avoiding foreign exchange risk, we now briefly introduce several of the more important instruments or tools that are available in the international financial markets to hedge interest rate risk. These financial instruments belong to a category of financial tools referred to as **derivatives.** Derivatives are simply financial contracts whose value is linked to or derived from an underlying asset. Examples of the underlying assets include stocks, bonds, commodities, loans,

FIGURE 1   **International Financial Adjustment in the Money Markets, Foreign Exchange Markets, and Eurocurrency Markets**

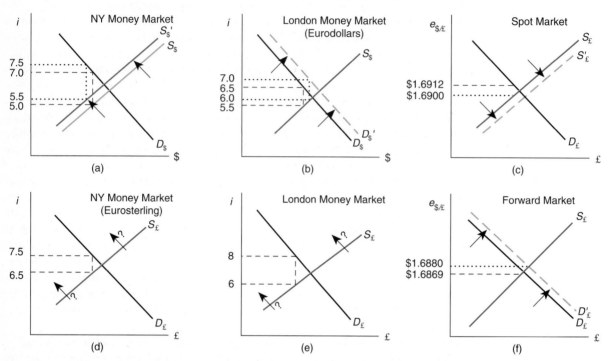

International financial adjustments in the presence of Eurocurrency markets are demonstrated in the above graphs. A tighter money market in the United States [leftward shift in the supply curve in graph (a)] causes domestic interest rates to rise. This leads to increased demand for Eurodollars [rightward shift of the demand curve in (b)], which drives up Eurodollar rates until they again differ from U.S. rates by the risk-cost differential. The higher U.S. interest rates lead to an increased U.K. supply of spot pounds [rightward shift of $S_£$ to $S'_£$ in (c)], which are hedged in the forward market [rightward shift of $D_£$ to $D'_£$ in (f)]. Further adjustments may occur in the U.K. money market and the Eurosterling market that would lead to higher interest rates in these markets [graphs (d) and (e)], although the result is uncertain because the Bank of England may intervene to offset upward pressure on interest rates in the London money market. [Note: In graphs (a), (b), (d), and (e), the upper rates reflect lending rates and the lower rates indicate deposit rates. The lending and deposit rates form a bracket around what would be the common equilibrium rate if lending and borrowing rates were equal.]

certificates of deposit (CDs), and foreign exchange. For many financial institutions, interest rate risk management is critical to their successful operation inasmuch as they often can anticipate future lending and future borrowing actions both at home and abroad and would prefer to reduce the risk of possible changes in the market interest rate prior to when the anticipated borrowing or lending occurs. Several of the more commonly used types of financial instruments or tools from which the manager can choose to hedge against unforeseen interest rate changes include (1) maturity mismatching, (2) future rate agreements, (3) Eurodollar interest rate swaps, (4) Eurodollar cross-currency interest rate swaps, (5) Eurodollar interest rate futures, (6) Eurodollar interest rate options, (7) options on swaps, and (8) equity financial derivatives. We will examine each one, and then conclude with a short discussion of the current size and importance of these transactions in the international financial arena.[19]

....

[19]For in-depth discussions of the Eurodollar derivative instruments introduced here, see the excellent presentations in Bryan and Farrell (1996), Burghardt, Belton, Lane, Luce, and McVey (1991), and Dufey and Giddy (1994). The Burghardt et al. volume also provides very thorough coverage of the legal features of these instruments.

Maturity mismatching

Maturity mismatching is one of the easiest and simplest ways for financial institutions to remove the risk of changes in the interest rate between now and some future time. It is carried out by acquiring two or more financial contracts whose maturities overlap. For example, suppose that a fund manager knows that her company will receive $100,000 in three months and needs to hold those funds for dollar payment of a financial obligation six months from now. Being concerned that the interest rate may fall prior to the receipt of the funds, the fund manager looks for a way to lock in the current deposit rate for the three-month period during which the $100,000 cash surplus will be held. She accomplishes this by borrowing $100,000 for three months and investing it in a fixed-rate instrument for six months, which will mature just at the time it is needed for the future expected payment. When the $100,000 is received at the end of three months, it is then used to pay back the initial three-month loan when it comes due, while the invested funds continue to earn a known fixed amount of interest until they are needed six months from now. The cost of fixing the future interest rate now is the difference between the deposit rate and the loan rate for the first three months, that is, the three-month overlap. In similar fashion, if one wished to lock in a lending rate for six months, beginning two months from now, this could be accomplished by borrowing the needed funds today for an eight-month period, placing the funds in a short-term fixed-rate deposit for two months, and at the end of two months using the funds to pay the anticipated financial commitment. Again, by overlapping the maturities of two financial instruments, the future lending rate is secured at a known interest rate, and the cost of the hedge is the difference between the two-month deposit rate and the eight-month loan rate for the two-month overlap.

Future rate agreements

A **future rate agreement** (FRA) is essentially a contract between two parties to lock in a given interest rate starting at some given point in the future for a given time period. This instrument originated in the early 1970s and is often referred to as a *forward-forward.* (It is also sometimes referred to simply as a *forward rate contract.*) The procedure was modified in the mid-1980s through the development of a cash-compensation process whereby compensation is paid for deviations of the market interest rate from the contracted rate rather than through the actual borrowing or lending of funds between the two contract participants. The process works as follows: The two contracting parties agree on a particular lending or borrowing rate at some future date for a specific amount and loan period. For example, Ms. Jones may wish to secure the interest rate on a $10,000 loan in three months for a period of nine months. After negotiating through a broker over the future rate, a contract will be signed between Jones and the seller of the contract (Mr. Brown) whereby a loan rate of 7.5 percent is locked in for the time period under consideration. This contract guarantees the interest rate for both parties but does not involve any commitments for the loan itself. In three months, when Ms. Jones needs the funds, she obtains a nine-month loan at the current market interest rate. If the market rate at the time of the loan is 7.8 percent, the other party in the FRA (Brown) pays her the difference between the market rate and the rate in the FRA, that is, 0.3 percent or 30 **basis points,**[20] for the specified $10,000 loan for nine months.[21] Should the market rate have

---

[20]A basis point is defined as one one-hundredth of a percent; that is, 1 percentage point contains 100 basis points.

[21]The actual amount paid by Brown (the seller) at the time of the loan is

$$\text{Cash} = (.078 - .075)(270/360)(\$10,000)/[1 + (.078)(270/360)]$$
$$= \$22.50/1.0585 = \$21.26$$

The interest rate differential (.003) is adjusted to reflect the nine-month period (270/360) as opposed to one year. The entire amount is then discounted for the nine-month period since Brown will be meeting the contract payment at the beginning of the loan period and not at the end when the interest is due. The payment is thus reduced by the interest that the contract payment will earn over the nine-month period of the loan.

fallen to 7.25 percent, Ms. Jones would reimburse Mr. Brown the difference, that is, 0.25 percent for the specified nine-month loan. Jones is thus hedged against any increase in the lending rate between now and the time of the actual undertaking of the loan. She is, however, locked out of receiving any benefits associated with a fall in the loan rate. Of course, if the market rate is the same as the contract rate, then no offsetting payments are made by either party and the contract terminates. In essence, Jones has contracted with Brown to exchange a floating or uncertain rate for a fixed rate over a specific time period. Indeed, an FRA is often defined as *a forward contract in which two parties agree to exchange a floating rate for a fixed rate for some future time period.* LIBOR is commonly used as the floating rate in these agreements.

Eurodollar interest rate swaps

A **Eurodollar interest rate swap** is similar to an FRA but involves several future periods. In this case parties agree to exchange interest rates of two different kinds for several periods in the future, each usually three or six months long. Again, one of the rates is generally the appropriate LIBOR rate, and the contract often involves the exchange of a fixed rate for a floating rate, as is the case in the one-period FRA. However, an interest rate swap can also involve an exchange of two floating interest rates where one is LIBOR and the second is another interest rate or an index of a package of rates, such as an index of Eurocommercial paper rates. The case in which both sides are contracting a floating rate is referred to as a *basis swap* or a *floating-floating swap.* An interest rate swap works as follows: Suppose Ms. Smith has a three-year Eurodollar-based loan at 8 percent and wishes that it were a variable-rate debt (perhaps because she expects interest rates to fall in the future) and Mr. Brown has a Eurodollar loan on which he is paying six-month LIBOR plus 30 basis points (0.3 percent) and wishes to have a fixed-rate debt. Under the agreed-upon swap arrangement, Smith agrees to pay Brown the six-month LIBOR plus 0.3 percent every six months and Brown in turn agrees to pay Smith the 8 percent (perhaps plus some additional amount, e.g., 50 basis points per annum). Smith has thus converted her fixed-rate commitment to a variable rate and Brown has converted his variable rate to a fixed rate. If interest rates decline, Smith will benefit by obtaining a cheaper loan. Brown feels relieved to have obtained a fixed rate more cheaply than obtaining a formal, new fixed-rate loan and refinancing, and he effectively has reduced his interest rate exposure. Should interest rates fall during the swap contract and threaten to rise again, Smith could phone a swaps trader and enter into a second swap arrangement to again fix the interest rate commitment but this time at the new, lower level.

Eurodollar cross-currency interest rate swaps

The **Eurodollar cross-currency interest rate swap** is a financial derivative that permits the holder of a floating interest rate investment or debt denominated in one currency to change it into a fixed-rate instrument in a second currency. It, of course, can also permit the holder of a fixed-rate debt in one currency to convert it to a floating-rate debt in a second currency. It thus links several segments of international capital markets. It has all the characteristics of a normal interest rate swap except that it is a combination of an interest rate swap and a currency hedge.

CONCEPT CHECK

1. How can maturity mismatching remove the risk associated with a future interest rate change?
2. Why would a borrower want to use a future rate contract? What opportunity is being lost by doing so?
3. What is the risk being avoided by the use of an interest rate swap? What additional risk is avoided with a cross-currency interest rate swap?

BOX 1   How to Read Eurodollar Interest Rate Futures Market Quotations

Quotes for Tuesday, February 25, 1997
EURODOLLAR (CME)–$1 million; pts of 100%

	Open	High	Low	Settle	Chg.	Yield Settle	Chg.	Open Interest
Mar	94.51	94.51	94.49	94.51	−.01	5.49	+.01	387,872
June	94.38	94.40	94.36	94.37	−.03	5.63	+.03	401,049
Sept	94.24	94.26	94.21	94.22	−.03	5.78	+.03	299,364
Dec	94.05	94.07	94.01	94.02	−.03	5.98	+.03	220,094
Mr98	93.96	93.97	93.90	93.91	−.03	6.09	+.03	187,687
.	.	.	.	.	.	.	.	.
.	.	.	.	.	.	.	.	.
Mr01	93.24	93.24	93.20	93.21	+.01	6.79	−.01	23,874
.	.	.	.	.	.	.	.	.
Mr04	92.71	92.72	92.70	92.70	+.01	7.30	−.01	2,036

Estimated volume: 286,615; volume Mon: 205,936.

Source: *The Wall Street Journal,* Feb. 26, 1997, p. C16.

These quotations pertain to the Chicago Mercantile Exchange (CME), and the face value of each three-month contract is $1 million. Each basis-point (.01 percent) change in the contract price is valued at $25 [= ($1,000,000)(.0001)/4]. The Eurodollar futures "Yield" is calculated on a 360-day basis. The price is equal to 100 − yield, or the yield is equal to 100 − the quoted price. Thus, with a settle price of 94.51, the yield is 5.49 percent (= 100 − 94.51). The prices listed are the various strike (contracting) prices for contracts expiring in the month indicated. On the actual expiration date, the third Wednesday of the expiration month, the futures yield converges to the cash market yield, that is, LIBOR. The "Open" price is the initial contract price of the day; the "High" and the "Low" indicate the ranges of price fluctuation during the day under consideration; and the

"Settle" price or closing price is the reference price used to make the daily adjustment of margin accounts. In the case of the CME, the settle price is equal to 100 − spot LIBOR, obtained by taking two surveys of London banks (one at closing and one 90 minutes earlier). "Chg." refers to the change from the previous day, and the change is given both for the settle price and the settle yield. "Open Interest" refers to the number of contracts open as of the previous day. Finally, "Estimated volume" refers to the number of contracts sold on that particular day. On this particular Tuesday, futures contracts were sold for up to seven years out, but the number of contracts steadily declined as the length of time to the expiration date increased. The yield required by the seller also increased steadily as the contract period moved further and further into the future.

Eurodollar interest rate futures

Just as in the foreign exchange market, there are **Eurodollar interest rate futures** in addition to interest rate forwards. Similar to currency futures, interest rate futures are contracts to deliver a certain amount of bank deposits at some future date at a specified interest rate or price. These may take the form of either Eurodollar time deposits or Eurodollar CDs of a major bank. They carry the locked-in interest rate that was agreed upon when the contract was signed, and the gain (loss) of the contract will depend upon whether the interest rate on the day the contract comes due is less (more) than the contracted rate, multiplied by the amount of the contract.

These contracts differ from a forward market transaction in several ways. They are transacted or traded on organized exchanges such as the Chicago Mercantile Exchange. Three-month futures interest contracts are sold in $1 million units and are traded in March, June, September, and December. (See Box 1 on how to read published market information on Eurodollar futures.) Unlike the case in the forward market, where forward gains or losses are settled on the maturity date, gains and losses are settled on a daily basis in the futures market. Participants are required to maintain a "margin" account, and the daily gains or losses are added or subtracted from this account depending on whether the current daily rate is below or above the contract rate. Thus, for every 1 basis point decline (increase) in the current interest rate compared with the final settlement rate on the previous day, $25 is added to (subtracted from) the holder's margin account for each forward interest contract.[22] The daily cash settlements are based on the daily final settlement price of three-month LIBOR obtained from 12 reference banks randomly selected during the last 90 minutes of trading (Dufey and Giddy 1994, p. 189).

The futures market is thus useful for lenders/depositors who wish to lock into a specific future interest rate in Eurocurrencies. If you know that you will have funds to invest in the future for a specific period of time, the futures market offers you the opportunity to avoid a fall in interest rates by fixing the interest rate now through buying a futures interest rate contract for Eurodollar delivery at the expected future time. At the specific future date, the futures contract is completed and the contract margin adjustment funds plus the anticipated investment funds are invested at the current market rate of interest. If interest rates have fallen by the time the investment is made and the futures contract is due, the holder of the futures contract will settle the margin account payments due on the contract and invest them along with the new funds at the then-current interest rate. At the end of the investment period she will earn approximately the same amount as the initial futures contract rate even though there was an actual decline in interest rates. The gain in the futures contract, which will be invested along with the newly acquired funds, will result in a rate of return similar to the initial rate in the futures contract even though the entire amount is earning a lower rate of market interest. This activity is referred to as a *long hedge.*

Similarly, potential borrowers in the future can guard against a rise in the borrowing rate by selling a futures contract for the period in the future during which they are going to be in need of borrowing funds (that is, a contract to acquire funds at a specific loan rate). This activity is referred to as a *short hedge.* If interest rates rise by the time that the loan is needed, the seller receives the funds associated with the daily margin adjustment, which can be used to reduce the amount of the necessary loan. The result is that the borrower has the necessary funds over the period needed at approximately the contracted rate because the lower amount of the required borrowing offsets the higher market interest rate. More simply, the gain from the futures contract offsets the increased cash borrowing costs. In fact, the borrower actually ends up paying a slightly lower rate than would have been the case if the same hedge had been made using the forward market.[23] It should be pointed out that the Eurodollar contract is unlikely to provide a perfect hedge since there is unlikely to be a perfect match between the hedging instrument and the financial instrument being hedged. The lack of a perfect hedge is often referred to as *basis risk.*

When it is desired to hedge against changes in the interest rate for periods longer than three months, it is possible to do so by acquiring a series of successive futures contracts. For example, if someone wished to fix his return for a one-year period starting in September, he would simply purchase a December futures contract, a March futures

---

[22]This occurs because each of the contracts is for $1 million for three months. Each 1-basis-point change thus leads to a payment equal to ($1,000,000) (.0001)/4 = $25. The minimum fluctuation in price is 1 basis point.

[23]Intuitively, this takes place because the rate adjustment payments are made throughout the period prior to the completion of the contract with a futures contract, whereas the payment reflecting the interest rate adjustment in a forward contract is made at the end, when the contract is fulfilled. In this case, "time is money," and the relatively lower cost of the hedge with the futures contract reflects this fact.

contract, a June futures contract, and a September futures contract. As the December contract came to an end, it would be replaced by (rolled over into) the March contract, and that would be rolled over into the June contract and that into the September contract. He would thus be protected against shifts in the overall level of interest rates. This collection of multiple short-term three-month futures contracts to hedge changes in interest rates for a longer period is referred to as a **Eurodollar strip.** Eurodollar futures can thus be used to hedge as much as seven years out (Dufey and Giddy 1994, p. 165). Another way to hedge a more distant future than is available directly in the futures markets is to acquire a shorter-term futures contract or strip and replace it with new contracts closer to the desired time period as each of the shorter contracts gains in liquidity. For example, one could acquire the strip discussed above, hold it for the first three-month period and roll it over into a new twelve-month strip, and keep doing this until the desired period is attained, say, three years from now. Such hedging with a short-term futures contract that is subsequently replaced with other contracts is referred to as a *stack.*

Finally, it has become common to combine interest rate hedges with currency hedges to provide interest rate protection in a particular currency. For example, a Eurobanker in France may be faced with needing to guarantee a French customer an interest rate for a future three-month loan in Dutch guilders. To do so, the banker would lock in the future Eurodollar interest rate with a Eurodollar futures contract, and then couple that with both a forward contract to buy Dutch guilders at the time the loan is made and a forward contract to sell Dutch guilders three months later, when the loan is repaid.

Eurodollar interest rate options

All of the hedging contracts discussed to this point essentially obligate the two parties to exchange something in the future. The **Eurodollar interest rate option,** on the other hand, gives one party the right, but not an obligation, to buy or sell a financial asset under a set of prescribed conditions, including the relevant interest rate. As is the case with currency options, there are two types of transactions, *puts* and *calls.* The buyer of a **Eurodollar call option** obtains the right to purchase a Eurodollar time deposit bearing a certain interest rate (for example, 8 percent) on a specific date. This option will cost the buyer an up-front price called the *option premium.* If the market interest rate is above 8 percent, then the holder of the call option can choose not to exercise the option, place her funds in an account paying the higher rate of interest, and simply lose the up-front premium. Should the market rate be below 8 percent, then the buyer of the call will exercise the option and acquire the financial instrument bearing the higher interest rate. The buyer of the call is thus insured against a fall in the interest rate (without giving up the option of depositing at a higher rate later), and the up-front premium is the cost of the insurance policy. The higher the likelihood that interest rates will fall, the greater the likelihood that the option will be exercised and the higher the up-front premium.

The investor who purchases a **Eurodollar put option** acquires the right to sell a Eurodollar time deposit (acquire Eurodollars) to the writer of the option contract for a specified interest rate at a future date. Again, should the spot rate on the date in question be above the contracted rate, the option will be exercised and the recipient of the Eurodollar funds will have been protected against a rise in the cost of borrowing. On the other hand, if the lending rate is less than the contract rate on the contract date, the purchaser of the put contract will simply choose not to exercise the contract and will obtain the necessary funds at the lower market rate. The premium on the put option is thus the cost of insuring that the borrower does not end up paying a higher borrowing rate. (See Box 2 for an explanation of published futures options quotations.)

In both the case of a put and that of a call, Eurodollar interest rate options contain an asymmetrical risk profile in that the purchaser can always choose not to exercise the

BOX 2   How to Read Eurodollar Interest Options Quotations

Eurodollar Interest Futures Options, Tuesday, February 25, 1997
EURODOLLAR (Chicago Mercantile Exchange)
Contracts for $1 million; pts. of 100%

Strike Price	Calls—Settle			Puts—Settle		
	Mar	Apr	May	Mar	Apr	May
9400	0.51	0.38	—	0.00	0.01	0.02
9425	0.26	0.16	0.18	0.00	0.04	0.06
9450	0.03	0.02	—	0.03	0.15	—
9475	0.00	0.00	—	0.24	—	—
9500	0.00	0.00	—	0.49	—	—
9525	0.00	0.00	—	0.74	—	—

Est. volume: 81,850   —:   no option offered
Min. vol.: 32,745 calls; 12,198 puts   0.00: no option traded
Open interest Mon: 1,008,058 calls; 1,194,961 puts

Source: *The Wall Street Journal,* Feb. 26, 1997, p. C16.

These quotations reflect options on $1 million Eurodollar deposits at the CME for Tuesday, February 26, 1997. The "Strike Price" is the exercise price and, as with futures, is quoted as 100 – yield. The strike prices (in basis points) are quoted in 1/4 percent intervals. Thus if you were interested in investing $4 million in Eurodollars in April (acquire Eurodollar deposits) and were willing to pay to guarantee that you receive 5¾ percent, you would buy four April call option contracts at the strike price of 9425 for which you would have to pay 16 basis points. Just as in futures, each basis point is worth $25, so the cost of the option contract would be 16 × $25, or $400, for each of the four contracts. You are now "long" by four call contracts and the option writer is "short" by four option contracts. At expiration, if the market rate is above 5¾ percent, you will simply choose not to exercise the options, and you will lose only the cost of the contracts. Similarly, if you wished to guarantee that you could borrow, say, 2 million Eurodollars in May at 5¾ percent, you would purchase two May put option contracts that would cost you 6 basis points, or $150, for each contract. Again, should the market rate of interest be below 5¾ percent on the expiration date, you would simply choose not to exercise the option, would acquire a loan at the lower market rate of interest, and would lose only the $150 cost of each option contract. The estimated daily volume of option contracts is given at the bottom of the table, along with the volume of puts and calls that were traded the previous day (Monday, February 24) and the number of option contracts that were open at the end of the Monday trading day.

option if it is not to his or her advantage. The writer of the option contract thus bears all the risk of an interest rate change and charges an option premium to compensate for that risk. In the forward, future, and swap arrangements discussed previously, both the writer and the buyer of the contract can potentially lose, depending on the nature of the interest rate change (symmetrical risk profile). The result of this risk difference implies that Eurodollar interest rate options are most appropriate when expectations regarding interest rate changes on a given instrument are nonsymmetrical. For example, if an investor in floating-rate securities wants to ensure only against a likely fall in the market rate, purchasing a Eurodollar call option effectively places a floor under the interest rate. Similarly, if the financial outlook suggests that interest rates may rise, the borrower wishing to protect herself against a rise in the lending rate can hedge by purchasing Eurodollar put options. In like manner, a financial lender with a fixed-cap mortgage in place could protect himself against a rise in the market rate above the interest rate cap by purchasing put contracts in Eurodollars. In similar fashion, lenders holding floating-rate notes guaranteeing never to pay less than some floor rate can protect themselves against falling rates by purchasing Eurodollar interest rate call options.

Caps, floors, and collars.   The standard options interest rate derivatives discussed above are similar to futures in that they are traded in the same financial centers in standardized three-month contracts in $1 million–face-value units, with expiration dates in March, June, September, and December. Option contracts for longer periods of time can be constructed by combining several individual option contracts, as was done with futures contracts. The multiperiod hedge over several interest rate periods is essentially a strip of put or call options which provides a cap or a floor, that is, limits, on a floating interest rate. More specifically, a *cap* is a contract in which the seller agrees to compensate the buyer whenever the interest rate in question exceeds the contracted "ceiling rate" throughout a medium- or long-term financial transaction. As is the case with the futures contract, the buyer of the cap pays a premium (generally up front) to the seller for the insurance against having to pay more than the contracted rate throughout the loan period. If, on the other hand, interest rates fall below the contracted rate, nothing takes place, since this is another example of an asymmetric risk contract. Take, for example, the hypothetical case of Small and Company. Small has arranged to borrow $10 million for two and a half years at an assumed six-month LIBOR of 7 percent. In order to guarantee that the company will not have to pay more than 7 percent in each of the four subsequent six-month periods, the financial officer purchases a cap, contracted at a 7 percent ceiling rate for which he pays a premium of, say, 0.3 percent (30 basis points) of the $10 million being financed up front. Should LIBOR rise above 7 percent in any of the subsequent loan periods, the seller of the cap will pay Small and Company the difference between the cost of the six-month loan at current LIBOR and the 7 percent ceiling rate in the cap. Should the interest rate fall to 6.8 percent, nothing takes place between the contracting parties because this contract covers only where the interest rate rises above 7 percent. Today it is not uncommon to see an initial floating-rate loan contract carry an interest rate provision in which the contracting parties agree that the loan rate will never exceed a certain level, whatever happens to LIBOR. A floating-rate contract with a built-in interest ceiling is referred to as a *cap-floater.*

Similarly, like a strip of Eurodollar call options, a *floor* is a contract that establishes an interest rate under which the financially contracted rate cannot fall for a series of future periods. For example, Ms. Jones has just contracted to lend $5 million to the Thompson Company for four years at six-month LIBOR, which at the time of the loan is at 7½ percent. In order to protect herself from earning less than 7½ percent should future LIBOR decline, Jones purchases a floor contract for a premium of 0.4 percent (40 basis points) of the initial loan amount, which fixes the floor at 7½ percent. Should LIBOR fall below 7½ percent in any of the seven future loan periods, the difference between market LIBOR and the contracted rate of 7½ percent will be paid by the seller of the floor. Jones is thus protected against earning anything less than 7½ percent. In both of these cases a floating-rate instrument has been modified into a fixed-rate instrument through use of the cap or floor contract. Finally, the simultaneous purchase of both a cap and a floor creates a *collar.* In this instance the borrower's rate cannot rise above a certain rate, but neither can it fall below a certain interest rate level. Caps, floors, and collars are similar to combinations of several short-term put and call options and can therefore be traded like other financial assets.

Options on swaps

Following on the success of caps, it did not take financial markets long to develop the **options on swaps** derivative. These instruments offer an enormous amount of flexibility in corporate finance transactions. Just as you would expect, these financial contracts give the buyer the option to enter into a future swap or the right to cancel a future swap. In the first case (sometimes referred to as a "swaption"), purchasing a call option gives the buyer the right to receive a fixed rate in a swap and pay a floating rate. Purchasing a put option gives the buyer the right to pay a fixed rate in the swap and receive a floating rate. In contracting for the option to cancel a swap, buying a call option (a callable swap) gives the side paying a fixed and receiving a floating rate the right to cancel. In purchasing a put option to cancel a swap (a putable swap), the buyer paying the floating rate and receiving the fixed rate has the right to cancel.

Equity financial derivatives

While commodity futures and options have existed for a long time and the derivative markets in currency and interest-bearing instruments have been exploding over the past 15 years, international equity derivatives have started to be utilized only recently. In many countries such as the United States the equity option has existed domestically for many years, but it is only recently that international options and swaps have become widespread. With an *equity swap,* an investor can swap the returns on a currently owned equity to another investor for a price. As financial markets have globalized, it is increasingly common to find investors in one country contracting with market insiders or agents in another country to buy and hold equities and pass on to the foreign investor any gains and losses associated with the equity package for an agent's fee. This derivative allows the international investor to participate in a foreign equity market without having to pay local market execution fees or having to be concerned about the risk of being unfamiliar with local insider trading practices. It also protects the identity of the foreign investor. Thus, as in the other derivative markets, the equity derivatives serve to assist the global investor in the management of risk.

CONCEPT CHECK

1. Why would a potential borrower be interested in an interest rate futures contract? Would this person sell or buy a futures contract? Briefly explain.
2. Suppose the settle price of an interest rate futures contract on the Chicago Mercantile Exchange is 93.62. What is the yield on this contract?
3. Suppose that, in March, you hold a call option for May on a Eurodollar time deposit at 6 percent. If the interest rate in May is 5 percent, would you exercise your option? Why or why not?

THE CURRENT EURODOLLAR DERIVATIVES MARKET

Futures have been traded on a wide variety of metals and agricultural commodities since the middle of the nineteenth century in the United States (and several centuries earlier in other parts of the world). However, in the past 15 years, there has been monumental growth in the global use of foreign currency, interest rate, and equity derivatives. Why has this development taken place? Very simply, the participants in the international financial markets have found that the use of financial derivatives could increase their returns and/or lower their risk exposure. They can literally unbundle and alter their exposure to the foreign exchange risk, interest rate risk, and price risk embodied in assets and liabilities. International investors can now trade away the risks they are not comfortable with in exchange for a risk exposure more suitable to their personal tastes and finances. Inasmuch as different people are exposed to different types of risk, have

FIGURE 2   **Interest Rate and Currency Swaps, 1980–1995**

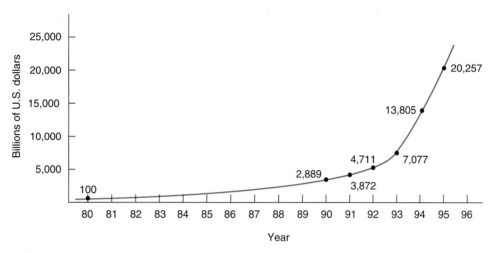

As can be seen in the graph, substantial growth occurred in the dollar value of interest rate and currency swaps in the 1980–1995 period. From 1980–1990, the annual average growth rate was 33.6 percent. From 1990–1995, the average annual growth rate was higher, moving up to 39 percent.

different skills in assessing risk, have widely differing capacity to absorb risk, and have different risk preferences, the evolution of these derivatives has worked to make the global financial markets more efficient. Nowhere has the growth in these instruments been more evident than in the interest rate and currency swaps. (See Figure 2 and Table 11.) Between 1980 and March 1995, the value of outstanding over-the-counter contracts in these instruments grew from approximately $100 billion to $20.3 trillion annually.[24] The notional global total value of outstanding over-the-counter derivatives contracts in March 1995 was estimated to be $40.7 trillion. Of that amount, more than 25 percent was booked in the United States. The global market value of outstanding over-the-counter derivatives was estimated to be around $1.7 trillion.

The data in Table 11, based on a recent survey conducted by 26 central banks and reported by the Federal Reserve Bank of New York, revealed the following: Among the financial derivatives, interest rate swaps currently account for two-thirds of the transactions and 45 percent of the total notional amount of all derivatives. Foreign exchange forwards and swaps are second, accounting for slightly over 20 percent of the notional total. The other two important categories are interest rate options (8.7 percent) and currency options (5.8 percent). Equity and commodity derivatives account for only about 2.2 percent. The survey also concluded that cross-border transactions in 1995 accounted for over one-half of exchange rate and interest rate contracts, a clear reflection of the global nature of activity in these markets. Further, the data indicated that financial activity was dispersed among many countries of the world and not restricted to two or three major players. For example, the combined turnover of the largest participants (the United Kingdom, the United States, and Japan) amounted to only 56 percent of the total. An additional indication of the global nature of these transactions was that many trades are entered into in one location and then booked in another country. There is clear evidence

....
[24]These figures are *notional values* or reference amounts that are based on gross face values of contracts. The *market value* is an estimate of the net value of the cash flows to be exchanged between the participants over the lifetime of the contract.

TABLE 11   **Outstanding Over-the-Counter Derivative Contracts***

Product Category	Global Totals		Contracts Booked in the United States	
	Amount (US$, billions)	Percentage†	Amount (US$, billions)	Percentage†
Panel A: Notional Amounts				
Foreign exchange forwards and swaps	8,742	72	1,264	47
Currency swaps	1,974	11	258	10
Currency options	2,375	16	1,114	42
Forward rate agreements	4,597	17	874	11
Interest rate swaps	18,283	69	5,558	68
Interest rate options	3,548	13	1,595	20
Equity forwards and swaps	52	9	8	22
Equity options	547	91	28	78
Commodity forwards and swaps	208	66	127	64
Commodity options	109	34	72	36
Total‡	40,714		11,044	
Panel B: Market Values				
Foreign exchange forwards and swaps	602	70	94	59
Currency swaps	345	22	32	20
Currency options	69	7	32	20
Forward rate agreements	18	3	2.4	1
Interest rate swaps	560	87	130	85
Interest rate options	60	9	20	13
Equity forwards and swaps	7	14	1	37
Equity options	43	86	1.5	63
Commodity forwards and swaps	21	78	10	70
Commodity options	6	22	4	30
Total‡	1,745		328	

*Figures are for the end of March 1995. Adjustments have been made for double-counting of trades between reporting dealers. The U.S. share in the global totals is smaller than the ratio of the two columns because of cross-border dealer trades.

†Percentage of each product within the corresponding product group.

‡The totals include "other foreign exchange" and "other interest rate" products, which were a very small proportion of all currency and interest rate products (in terms of both notional amounts and market values). The global totals of foreign exchange forwards and swaps do not include contracts booked in the United Kingdom because data were not collected.

Source: John Kambhu, Frank Keane, and Catherine Benadon, "Price Risk Intermediation in the Over-the-Counter Derivatives Markets: Interpretation of a Global Survey," Federal Reserve Bank of New York, *Economic Policy Review,* vol. 2, no. 1 (April 1996), p. 3. Global totals were compiled by the Bank for International Settlements; figures for contracts booked in the United States were compiled by the Federal Reserve Bank of New York.

of this in the fact that the United States accounts for a significantly higher share of the global over-the-counter contracts that are booked than it does for its share of global turnover in these derivatives.

Some of the recent growth in global finance can be attributed to new developments in the institutional aspects of lending. Individual bank lending to individual customers, which has been the banking norm for years, has been complemented recently by the development of the underwriting and syndication of financial credits and the subsequent trading of these credits in the financial markets, generally between banks. The syndication of the lending process occurs when a highly structured group of well-capitalized banks agree to provide a particular loan and then sell shares of the credits to a wider range of smaller and less well-informed banks. In the Eurodollar markets the loan may thus originate in one country, while the ultimate lenders or holders of the loan credits reside in other countries. Administratively, it is typical for the syndicate to appoint a manager or agent who interacts with the borrower, thus retaining in part the banking principal–lending-agent relationship. The formal syndication loan agreement can take the form of a **direct loan syndicate** or a **loan participation syndicate.** In the first case, the direct loan syndicate, participant banks sign a common loan agreement which serves as the lending instrument. The participating banks essentially are colenders in this form of syndication. In the second case, that of a participation syndicate, a lead bank usually executes the loan instrument with the borrower and then syndicates the loan by entering into participation agreements with other banks. In this case, the participating banks are not formal colenders. Syndicated loan arrangements protect the borrower from the undue influence of any one bank and, at the same time, protect a single bank from being excessively exposed to the credit risk associated with a particular borrower. This latter characteristic is of particular value to international lenders who wish to diversify risk such as that associated with lending to sovereign borrowers. Perhaps even more importantly, in the rapidly expanding world of global finance, traditional financial links are becoming less and less important. Syndication permits the managing or agent bank to obtain funds for a particular borrower faster, in larger amounts, and likely at a lower cost than does the traditional single-bank approach. Indeed, syndication is the most prevalent way of lending in foreign markets whenever the borrowing amounts are large and the lending period exceeds 12 months (Dufey and Giddy 1994, p. 250). Growth in the international financial markets has thus been fostered not only by the development of new financial derivative instruments but also by changes in the forms of institutional lending which have increased the efficiency of international finance.

SUMMARY

This chapter has provided a general profile of the markets and instruments that currently exist for facilitating financial capital flows among nations. International bank lending and international transactions in bonds and stocks are now of huge size and take place in financial centers worldwide. Within these markets, a wide variety of specific instruments, including many different kinds of derivatives, have emerged. These instruments enable international investors, particularly in Eurocurrency markets, to unbundle the various aspects of risk associated with the instruments in order to better distribute and hedge the risks. A key aspect of modern lending technology is the ability to separate the currency of denomination of a particular financial instrument from its respective jurisdiction. Thus, the characteristics of a Eurocurrency instrument can be separated or unbundled and repackaged in a manner that is more profitable and/or contains a risk profile that is more suitable to the individual investor. The wide array of instruments for dealing with the risk associated with exchange rates, interest rates, and equity prices clearly appears to be playing an important role in improving the efficiency of rapidly globalizing international financial markets.

KEY TERMS

basis points	Eurodollar interest rate option	international funds
bond underwriters	Eurodollar interest rate swap	international portfolio
derivatives	Eurodollar market	diversification
direct loan syndicate	Eurodollar put option	loan participation syndicate
emerging market funds	Eurodollar strip	London Interbank Offered Rate
Eurobanks	Euronotes	(LIBOR)
Eurobond markets	foreign bond markets	maturity mismatching
Eurocurrency market	future rate agreement	mutual funds
Eurodollar call option	global funds	net international bank lending
Eurodollar cross-currency interest	gross international bank lending	options on swaps
rate swap	international bank lending	regional funds
Eurodollar interest rate futures	international bond market	traditional foreign bank lending

QUESTIONS AND PROBLEMS

1. What factors have been primarily responsible for the growth of the Eurodollar market? Should growth in Eurodollars be of concern to the U.S. Federal Reserve? Why or why not?

2. You notice in *The Wall Street Journal* that the interest rate in the U.S. money markets is 7½ percent and the interest rate in London is 9 percent. Would you expect the pound to be at premium or discount? Why?

3. In addition to the interest rate information in Question 2 above, you also note that the deposit rate in the United States is 6½ percent and the lending rate is 8½ percent. Where would you expect the Eurodollar deposit and lending rates to be? Why? What would you expect to happen to any difference between the above pairs of interest rates if U.S. local tax rates on international financial activity were reduced? Why?

4. What would you estimate the Eurodollar deposit rate to be if the domestic U.S. dollar deposit rate is 6½ percent, the reserve requirement on time deposits is 2 percent, and the combined cost of taxes and deposit insurance amounts to 10 basis points (1/10 percent)?

5. Explain in terms understandable to a noneconomist why, for example, when interest rates rise sharply, the subsequent headline in the newspaper may say "Bond Prices Plunge in Active Trading."

6. Why can a country's *nominal* interest rate never be negative? Why can a country's *real* interest rate indeed be negative? If a country has a negative real rate, do you think that this suggests that the country is not well integrated into world financial markets? Explain.

7. Since futures contracts are short-term, three-month contracts for fixed value, how does one use the futures market to hedge against longer-term risk for larger amounts of Eurodollars?

8. Financial institutions have found themselves in short-run financial liquidity problems because of overexposure in the futures markets. Explain how this could happen if you took a "long position" in a foreign currency or a "long hedge" in a Eurodollar deposit or CD.

9. Briefly explain the benefits that accrue to each of the contracting parties in a Eurodollar interest rate swap. What is the difference between a normal swap and a basis swap? If a swap contract is signed and one of the parties wishes to return to his or her initial market position, for example, a floating rate, what, if anything, can be done?

10. Why are futures contracts defined as symmetrical contracts, while options, caps, and floors are described as asymmetrical contracts? How is the asymmetry dealt with in the latter type of contracts?

11. Explain how loan syndication has fostered international financial growth, particularly with regard to loans to governments (sovereign loans). What is the difference between a participation syndicate and a direct loan syndicate?

12. You wish to acquire a Eurodollar interest rate option for $6 million in March and want to lock in a deposit interest rate of 7½ percent. You look in the options market quotations under Mar and find the following information:

Strike Price	Calls–Settle	Puts–Settle
9200	0.50	0.05
9225	0.41	0.30
9250	0.54	0.15
9275	0.26	0.18

What will be the cost of using the options market to hedge the interest rate risk?

THE MONETARY AND PORTFOLIO BALANCE APPROACHES TO EXTERNAL BALANCE

INTRODUCTION

In this chapter, we examine two broad, aggregate approaches to the determination of a country's balance-of-payments (BOP) position and the exchange rate. These approaches emphasize the role of money and international asset exchanges as the primary forces at work in the foreign exchange markets, reflecting the much greater importance in recent years of financial transactions than trade flows in exchange market activity. More specifically, we study the monetary approach to the balance of payments and the exchange rate, which focuses on how a balance-of-payments deficit or surplus or a change in the spot exchange rate reflects an imbalance in a country's demand for and supply of money. Next, we examine some empirical work pertaining to the monetary approach. The second approach, called the portfolio balance approach (or the asset market approach), moves beyond money alone and postulates that changes in a country's balance-of-payments position or exchange rate reflect changes in the relative demands and supplies of domestic and foreign financial assets. We will also examine empirical work on this approach. The chapter ends with a consideration of the phenomenon of "overshooting" in exchange markets and how this phenomenon contributes to exchange rate instability. In overview, an important result of looking at the monetary and portfolio balance approaches is that you can gain insights as to how asset movements influence exchange rates and why exchange rates can demonstrate considerable volatility in the real world.

THE MONETARY APPROACH TO THE BALANCE OF PAYMENTS

The **monetary approach to the balance of payments** emphasizes that a country's balance of payments, while reflecting real factors such as income, tastes, or factor productivity, is essentially a monetary phenomenon. This means that the balance of payments should be analyzed in terms of a country's supply of and demand for money. In the international payments context, attention is principally focused on Category IV in the balance-of-payments accounting framework, the "official short-term capital account." If a country has a BOP deficit (that is, an official reserve transactions deficit), then there is an outflow of international reserve assets. As we shall see, an outflow of international reserves implies that the country's supply of money exceeds its demand for money. Similarly, an official reserve transactions surplus implies that the country's money supply is less than its demand. If we are concerned about forces causing a BOP deficit or surplus, we must focus on the supply of and demand for money.

107

The Supply of Money   A country's supply of money can be viewed through the following basic expression:

$$M_s = a(BR + C) = a\,(DR + IR) \tag{1}$$

where: M_s = money supply

BR = reserves of commercial banks (depository institutions) ⎤ central bank
C = currency held by the nonbank public   ⎦ liabilities
a = the money multiplier

DR = domestic reserves   ⎤ central bank assets
IR = international reserves   ⎦

The money supply has various definitions, but the monetary approach usually deals with either M1 or M2. M1 is traditionally defined as currency held by the nonbank public (that is, held outside financial institutions), traveler's checks, and all checkable deposits in financial institutions. M2 includes the components of M1 but principally adds savings and time deposits (except for very large time deposits—of $100,000 or more in the United States) and a few other items. (This distinction between M1 and M2 per se is not important for our development of the basic monetary approach.) The amount of deposits in turn is a function of the amount of reserves of commercial banks (and other depository institutions such as savings and loan associations and credit unions) and the **money multiplier.**

The money multiplier reflects the process of multiple expansion of bank deposits, which is usually discussed in introductory courses. For example, if the required reserve ratio against deposits is 10 percent, an initial deposit of $1,000 in a bank creates $900 of excess reserves since only 10 percent (or $100) is required to be held by the commercial bank. The $900 of excess reserves can be lent out, which, after being spent by the loan recipient, will be redeposited in another (or the same) bank, which will generate 0.90 times $900 of new excess reserves (or $810) in the second bank. This $810 can then be lent, which keeps the process going. In the end, the original $1,000 gets "multiplied" by the money multiplier of $1/r$, where r is the required reserve ratio. In this example, with r of 10 percent, the original $1,000 deposit can lead to $1,000 \cdot (1/r) = \$1,000 \cdot [1/0.10] = \$1,000 \cdot 10 = \$10,000$ of "money." The money multiplier in the example is thus $(1/r)$ or 10. However, this simple expression is unrealistic, as the money multiplier must be adjusted for such factors as leakages of deposits into currency, different required reserve ratios on savings and time deposits than on checkable deposits, and the holding of excess reserves by banks. (See any standard money and banking text for elaboration.) We are not interested in the mechanics, however, but in the fact that the a term in expression [1] reflects a general money multiplier process.

The sum of reserves held by banks plus currency outside banks ($BR + C$) is usually called the **monetary base.** This base originates on the liabilities side of the balance sheet of the central bank (the Federal Reserve in the United States). Currency is issued by the central bank, and part of the reserves of banks are held by the central bank (the other part is held as vault cash by the commercial banks). Thus, any increase in assets held by the central bank permits an increase in these liabilities and thereby permits an increase in the money supply. On the asset side of the central bank, the most important assets for our purposes are (1) loans and security holdings by the central bank, called domestic credit issued by the central bank or **domestic reserves,** and (2) **international reserves** held by the central bank, which consist of foreign exchange holdings and holdings of any other internationally acceptable asset.

It is important to understand the relationships between these assets (domestic and international reserves) and the money supply. Suppose that the central bank purchases

※ CASE STUDY 1   RELATIONSHIPS BETWEEN MONETARY CONCEPTS
IN THE UNITED STATES

The various monetary concepts discussed in the text can be illustrated by an example. Looking first at bank reserves and deposits, the average reserves of all depository institutions in the United States in February 1997 were $48.1 billion.* The amount of currency held by the nonbank public was $397.7 billion. Hence, the monetary base obtained by summing these two components was $445.8 billion. (In actual computation, the base was somewhat larger at $459.7 billion because of two minor technical adjustments.) Required reserve ratios against checkable deposits were 3 percent for the first $49.3 million of deposits in a bank and 10 percent for deposits above that level. The money supply (M1) was $1,066.2 billion. The money multiplier was thus $1,066.2 billion divided by the monetary base of $459.7 or 2.32.

Turning to the central bank, the Federal Reserve's balance sheet at the end of February 1997 is shown in summary form in Table 1. On the liabilities side of the balance sheet, we see that banks and other depository institutions held $18.9 billion on deposit at the Federal Reserve. The item "Federal Reserve notes" represents currency issued by the Fed. (The figure is larger than the nonbank currency figure of $397.7 billion because financial institutions maintain some currency on hand.) With respect to assets, the loans and securities figure of $405.2 represents domestic credit issued by the Fed or domestic reserves. The gold and SDR accounts represent holdings of these international assets. (These assets are discussed in the last chapter in this book.) Finally, the foreign currency holdings of $17.9 billion constituted another component of international reserves held by the Fed. (Note: In the United States, not all international reserves are held by the Federal Reserve—some are held by the Exchange Stabilization Fund of the U.S. Treasury.)

TABLE 1   **Balance Sheet, Federal Reserve Banks, February 28, 1997 (in billions of dollars)**

Assets		*Liabilities and Capital Accounts*	
Gold and SDR certificate accounts	$ 20.5	Federal Reserve notes	$417.6
Loans and securities	405.2	Deposits of depository institutions	18.9
Assets denominated in foreign currencies	17.9	Other deposits and liabilities	14.3
Other assets	16.6	Capital accounts	9.4
Total assets	$460.2	Total liabilities and capital accounts	$460.2

Source: Board of Governors of the Federal Reserve System, *Federal Reserve Bulletin,* May 1997, p. A10.

* All figures in this case study are taken from Board of Governors of the Federal Reserve System, *Federal Reserve Bulletin,* May 1997.   ※

government securities (increasing domestic assets or extending domestic credit) in open market operations. This will increase the reserves of commercial banks, lead to new loans, and thereby ultimately increase the money supply by a multiplied amount. In addition, suppose that the central bank purchases foreign exchange from an exporter; this acquisition of international reserves also increases the money supply because the exporter will deposit the central bank's check into a commercial bank or other depository institution and set in motion the multiple deposit expansion process. Thus, increases in central bank reserves permit a multiplied expansion of the money supply, and, analogously, decreases in these reserves will lead to a multiplied decrease in the money supply. (For a brief discussion of these concepts in practice, see Case Study 1.)

The Demand for Money

Consider now the demand for money. Remember that the term **demand for money** does not mean the demand for "income" or "wealth." Rather, it refers to the desire to hold wealth in the form of money balances (basically either currency or checking accounts, using the M1 definition of money) rather than in the form of stocks, bonds, and other financial instruments such as certificates of deposit. The demand for money (*L*) can be specified in the following general form:

$$L = f[Y, P, i, W, E(\dot{p}), O] \qquad [2]$$

where: *Y* = level of *real* income in the economy
P = price level
i = interest rate
W = level of real wealth
$E(\dot{p})$ = expected percentage change in the price level
O = all other variables that can influence the amount of money balances a country's citizens wish to hold

What are the predicted relationships between *Y, P, i, W,* and $E(\dot{p})$ (the independent variables) and *L*? We begin with the influence of the level of income. The relationship between *Y* and *L* is expected to be positive, reflecting the **transactions demand for money**. As your income rises, you will want to spend more on consumption. Thus, more money needs to be held in order to finance these additional transactions. A positive relationship is also expected between *P* and *L,* because a higher price level means that more money, that is, a larger cash balance, is required to purchase a given amount of goods and services.

The influence of the interest rate on the demand for money is negative. If the interest rate rises, a smaller proportion of wealth is held in the form of money balances (currency and checking accounts in financial institutions) and more in the form of other assets, which are now more attractive. (Currency, of course, does not pay interest. Many checking accounts also do not pay interest; those that do pay interest pay lower rates than certificates of deposit or bonds.) Similarly, a fall in the interest rate will induce people to hold more of their wealth in the form of money, because the opportunity cost of holding money balances has fallen.[1] This relationship of the interest rate to the demand for money is often called the "asset" demand for money. It reflects not only the opportunity cost phenomenon discussed above but also the fact that, in order to undertake risk, wealth holders must be compensated. When the interest rate rises, people move out of money balances and into more risky assets because the compensation for doing so has increased.

An additional reason hypothesized by economists for the negative influence of the interest rate on money demand involves the relationship between interest rates and bond prices. (For elaboration, consult money and banking or intermediate macroeconomics texts such as Froyen 1996, Chaps. 6 and 15.) As noted in the previous chapter, interest rates and bond prices are inversely related to each other. Briefly, since a bond usually pays a fixed money amount to the bondholder, say, $60 per year, the price of the bond in the bond markets determines the "yield" or interest rate that the holder of the bond is earning. This interest rate will be in line with other interest rates in the economy (because of asset market competition). To simplify, if the market price of the bond you hold is $600, then your receipt of $60 per year of interest is a 10 percent return (= $60/$600). However, if the bond price rises to $800, then your realized interest *rate* has fallen to 7.5 percent (= $60/$800). Similarly, if the price of the bond falls to $500, then the interest rate is 12 percent (= $60/$500).

[1]When we speak of "the interest rate," we are referring to a general average level of interest rates in the economy.

In the context of the demand for money, suppose that financial investors have some conception of a "normal" interest rate and that the current interest rate is at that level. (Of course, different investors may have different views of what is the "normal" rate.) If the interest rate now rises above that level, investors will expect that it will fall back toward that level eventually. Since the rise in the interest rate means that there has been a fall in bond prices, individuals are thus expecting bond prices to rise when the interest rate falls back toward "normal." With the expected rise in bond prices, bonds are now an attractive asset to hold in comparison to money not only because of the higher interest rate but also because of the expected capital gain from the higher bond prices. Hence, smaller money balances will be desired. In the other direction, a fall in the interest rate below the normal level leads to an expectation that the interest rate will rise back toward normal. In other words, there is an expectation that bond prices will fall. In this situation, investors prefer money to bonds if the expected capital loss from the falling bond prices is larger than the interest return. Hence, the interest rate–bond price relationship gives us another reason for an inverse relationship between the amount of money demanded and the interest rate.

The income level, price level, and the interest rate are thought to be the major influences upon the demand for money, but the remaining independent variables can also have an impact. With respect to W, real wealth, the influence on the demand for money is expected to be positive because, as a person's wealth rises, that person wants to hold more of all assets, including money. With respect to the expected inflation rate, $E(\dot{p})$, the hypothesized relationship is negative. If you expect prices to rise, you realize that this inflation will mean a decline in the real value of a constant *nominal* amount of money balances. In such a situation, there is an incentive to substitute away from holding money and toward holding nonmoney assets whose prices may rise with the inflation.

Finally, the O term is included to incorporate other influences on the demand for money. The O term reflects institutional features of the economy such as the frequency with which people receive paychecks. If you are paid weekly, your average money balances will be smaller than if you are paid on a monthly basis. Another institutional feature would be the importance of credit cards in the transactions network in the economy. The greater the relative importance of credit card transactions, the less money you need on hand on any given day. These institutional features are not thought to vary to any great extent, especially during relatively short time periods.

A frequently used and simple formulation of the demand for money hypothesizes that the general functional expression in [2] can be given the specific form of

$$L = kPY \qquad\qquad [3]$$

where P and Y are defined as above and k is a constant term embodying all other variables. This simple formulation will sometimes be used later in our discussion.

Monetary Equilibrium and the Balance of Payments

The money market is in equilibrium when the amount of money in existence (the money supply) is equal to the amount of cash balances that the public desires to hold (money demand). In the most general case, this means that equilibrium is determined by using expression [1], the supply-of-money expression, and expression [2], the demand-for-money expression:

$$M_s = L \qquad\qquad [4]$$

or

$$\underbrace{a(DR + IR) = a(BR + C)}_{M_s} = \underbrace{f[Y, P, i, W, E(\dot{p}), O]}_{L} \qquad\qquad [5]$$

Alternatively, we can write a simpler equation for monetary equilibrium by using expression [3] for money demand:

$$M_s = kPY \qquad\qquad [6]$$

This expression is often used and explicitly specifies that money demand depends primarily on the price level and the level of real income.

With this background, we now discuss the manner in which the monetary approach to the balance of payments uses the relationships between the supply of and demand for money in explaining BOP deficits and surpluses. *Suppose that the exchange rate is fixed.* Consider a situation where, from an initial equilibrium between money supply and money demand, the monetary authorities increase the supply of money by purchasing government securities on the open market (i.e., an increase in *DR*). Since the money market was originally in equilibrium, this expansionary policy leads, because of the subsequent increase in *BR* and/or *C,* to an excess supply of money. When M_s is greater than *L,* the cash balances people have on hand and in bank accounts exceed their desired cash balances. When this happens, people attempt to reduce their cash balances, an action that has several important effects on the BOP.

Current account

First, the presence of excess cash balances means that individuals will spend more money on goods and services. This bids up the prices of goods and services (that is, bids up *P*). Further, if the economy is not at full employment because of money wage rigidity or other rigidities, the level of real income (*Y*) rises. In addition, if part of any new real income is saved, the level of real wealth (*W*) in the economy increases. What is the consequence of these potential impacts, other things equal, on *P, Y,* and *W* on the current account in the balance of payments? A rise in *P* will lead to larger imports as home goods are now relatively more expensive compared to foreign goods; the rise in *P* will also make it more difficult to export to other countries. In addition, the increase in *Y* induces more spending, and some of this spending is on imports. Finally, increased wealth enables individuals to purchase more of all goods, some of which are imports and some of which are goods that might otherwise have been exported. Hence, the excess supply of money generates pressures leading to a current account deficit.

Private capital account

The presence of the excess cash balances also has an impact on the private capital account in the BOP. Since an alternative to holding cash balances is to hold other financial assets, some of the excess cash balances will be used to acquire such assets. This purchase of financial assets bids up their price and drives down the interest rate. At the same time, the purchase of financial assets will include the acquisition of some foreign financial assets since financial investors wish to hold a diversified portfolio. There will thus be a capital outflow to other countries, with the end result being a tendency for a deficit to occur in the private capital account.

Balance-of-payments deficit

Given these impacts on the current account and the private capital account, it is obvious that a country with an excess supply of money has a tendency to incur a balance-of-payments deficit. The total impact on the current and private capital accounts combined is a net debit position, so the official short-term capital account (Category IV) in the balance of payments must be in a net credit position to finance the official reserve transactions deficit (a decrease in *IR*). A way of summarizing these various reactions to the excess supply of money is to say that the excess supply causes individuals to switch to other assets than money, including physical assets (goods) as well as financial assets, and that some of these assets are foreign goods and financial assets. In turn, the acquisition of foreign goods and financial assets results in a balance-of-payments deficit. Clearly, a policy prescription for ending the BOP deficit emerges from this discussion: Eliminate the excess supply of money by halting the monetary expansion.

In the monetary approach to the balance of payments, however, a policy action may not be necessary to eliminate the excess supply of money. Consider the changes we have specified above: (a) Y is rising; (b) P is rising; (c) i is falling; and (d) W is rising. What do these four developments have in common? They all *increase the demand for money.* This point is important because it means that, even without policy action, the initial excess supply tends to be worked off because the demand for money will be rising. Further, the supply of money itself will be decreasing. This decrease occurs because the balance-of-payments deficit reduces the country's international reserves due to the excess demand for foreign exchange (to buy imports and foreign assets) at the fixed exchange rate. This reduction in reserves leads to a decrease in the money supply. The central bank might temporarily offset the decrease in the money supply (called "sterilization" of the money supply from the BOP deficit) by expansionary open market operations, but this would set the whole process in motion again and the central bank would ultimately run out of international reserves. Thus, the conclusion of the monetary approach is that an excess supply of money will set forces in motion that will automatically eliminate that excess supply. When the excess supply has disappeared, the balance of payments is back in equilibrium.

Expected inflation rate

One complicating factor not addressed thus far in our discussion of the adjustment process to the excess money supply is the role of the expected inflation rate, $E(\dot{p})$. If the monetary expansion by the authorities generates expectations that prices will increase, this will *reduce* the demand for money. This reduction in money demand will, by itself, enlarge the excess supply of money, in contrast to the other four determinants of the demand for money. Hence, other things equal, the presence of the inflationary expectations will add to the BOP deficit and will mean that the job to be performed by $Y, P, i,$ and W is greater. As these other determinants begin to work, however, the inflationary expectations should dampen unless the monetary authorities continue to pump new money into the economy.

Other comments

We have focused to this point on a broad formulation of the demand for money, wherein we have specified five particular determinants of that demand. More traditional in textbook formulations of the monetary approach is the simple demand-for-money equation of expression [3]. In that simple context, if there is always full employment (and Y is therefore fixed), the introduction of new money by the monetary authorities has only one impact if k is assumed to be constant: The level of prices (P) will rise. (Economists call this simplified approach the "crude quantity theory of money.") The result is a BOP deficit because of the inflation's impact upon the current account, and the BOP deficit will continue until the excess supply of money is dissipated and prices have stabilized again. This basic model is instructive for emphasizing the link between the money supply, money demand, the price level, and the balance of payments, but it obviously leaves out other factors that influence the demand for money.

It should be evident that the general adjustment process to an excess supply of money in the monetary approach works in reverse when there is an excess demand for money. If, beginning from an equilibrium position, the monetary authorities contract the money supply, an initial excess demand for money occurs. Individuals hold smaller cash balances than they desire. They restore their cash balances by reducing spending on goods and services, which implies that the demand for imports falls. Income also falls because of the reduced spending, as does the price level (assuming that prices are somewhat flexible downward). When prices fall, exports increase and imports decrease. Thus, the current account moves into surplus. In addition, cash balances can be increased by selling off holdings of financial assets, including some sales to foreign citizens. These sales lead to a surplus in the private capital account in the balance of payments. With the official reserve transactions balance thus being in surplus, international reserves will be flowing into the country and expanding the money supply. The excess demand for money and the BOP surplus will eventually be eliminated.

In overview of the monetary approach to the balance of payments under fixed exchange rates, we see that it contains an automatic adjustment mechanism to any disturbances to monetary equilibrium. If the process is allowed to run its course, disequilibria in the money market and BOP deficits and surpluses will not exist *in the long run.* Any imbalances in the balance of payments reflect an imbalance between the supply of and demand for money, and these imbalances can be interpreted as part of an adjustment process to a discrepancy between the desired stock of money and the actual stock of money.

CONCEPT CHECK

1. What happens to the size of the money multiplier if the required reserve ratio increases? Why?
2. Why, other things equal, do increases in real income, real wealth, and the price level increase the demand for money, while increases in the interest rate and the expected inflation rate decrease the demand for money?
3. Explain why an excess supply of money in a fixed exchange rate regime will lead to a deficit in the balance of payments.

THE MONETARY APPROACH TO THE EXCHANGE RATE

To this point in the monetary approach, the analysis has assumed that the exchange rate is fixed. With that assumption, attention was drawn to the possibility of a deficit or surplus in the balance of payments. We now turn to the **monetary approach to the exchange rate** when the exchange rate is free to vary. With a flexible exchange rate, BOP deficits and surpluses will be eliminated by changes in the rate, but we need to examine the exchange rate changes in the context of money supply and demand.

Suppose that we begin from a position of equilibrium where M_s equals L. Now assume that the monetary authorities increase the supply of money and thereby create an excess supply of money. Remember that with an excess supply of money, the cash balances of individuals exceed the cash balances desired in connection with existing prices, real income, interest rates, wealth, and price expectations. The result of this money supply increase is that more spending by individuals occurs on goods and services and on financial assets in order to get rid of the excess money supply. With the increase in spending, there are increased imports, a possible decrease in exports as some such goods are now purchased by home country citizens, and an increase in purchases of financial assets from foreign citizens. With a flexible exchange rate, these factors are all working to cause a *depreciation of the home currency.* Hence, whereas a money supply increase under a fixed exchange rate leads to a BOP deficit, the money supply increase under a flexible rate leads to an **incipient BOP deficit** (that is, there would be a BOP deficit if the exchange rate did not change) and therefore to a fall in the value of the home currency relative to other currencies. This depreciation is thus a signal that there is an excess supply of money in the economy.

As with a fixed exchange rate, the excess supply of money is only temporary if no further money supply increases by the authorities are introduced. This is because the depreciation itself causes Y (if the economy is below full employment) and P to rise (since foreign demand for exports and home demand for import-substitute goods is rising). The level of wealth will also rise when saving occurs out of any new real income. In addition, the interest rate will fall due to increased purchases of financial assets. These changes generate an increase in the demand for money, and, ultimately, the excess supply of money is absorbed by the growing money demand. (If we take a crude quantity-theory-of-money view, the only home variable that will be changing in the adjustment process will be P, but this change too will ultimately restore equilibrium between money supply and money demand.)

As in the fixed-rate analysis, a potentially disturbing factor is the existence of changing inflation expectations, $E(\dot{p})$. If the inflation resulting from the depreciation generates a rise in $E(\dot{p})$, this would decrease the demand for money and, other things equal, would *add to* the excess supply of money. Therefore, the increase in L generated by changes in Y, P, W, and i needs to be greater than it would be if these increased inflation expectations were absent.

It should be clear that an excess demand for money will generate just the opposite reactions. With an excess demand (due to, say, a contraction of the money supply), individuals find that their cash balances fall short of those desired. Hence, spending is reduced on goods and services, and financial assets are sold in order to acquire larger cash balances. There is then an **incipient BOP surplus** (that is, there would be a BOP surplus if the exchange rate did not change), and the result is an *appreciation of the home currency*. This appreciation also eventually comes to a halt because of the adjustment process. In overview, the monetary approach under a flexible rate parallels that of the fixed-rate case, except that the phrase "balance-of-payments deficit" is replaced by the phrase "depreciation of the home currency" and the phrase "balance-of-payments surplus" is replaced by the phrase "appreciation of the home currency."

A Two-Country Framework

It is instructive to extend the monetary approach with a flexible exchange rate to a two-country framework. A straightforward way to do this is to return to the simple money demand–money supply formulation in expression [6]. Assuming that the time period is long enough for full price adjustment and that absolute purchasing power parity holds (see the chapter "The Foreign Exchange Market") and defining the exchange rate e as the number of units of home currency per unit of foreign currency,

$$P_A = eP_B \qquad \text{or} \qquad e = P_A/P_B \qquad [7]$$

where P_A is the price level in country A (the home country), P_B is the price level in country B (the foreign country), and e is the exchange rate expressed in terms of number of units of A's currency per 1 unit of B's currency.

Now utilize expression [6]. For country A, we can write

$$M_{sA} = k_A P_A Y_A \qquad [8]$$

where: M_{sA} = money supply in country A

P_A = price level in country A

Y_A = real income in country A

k_A = a constant term embodying all other influences on
money demand in country A besides P_A and Y_A

A similar expression can be written for country B, where all letters refer to the same items as in [8] but the subscript B is employed:

$$M_{sB} = k_B P_B Y_B \qquad [9]$$

Now divide each side of the equality in [8] by the corresponding side of the equality in [9]:

$$\frac{M_{sA}}{M_{sB}} = \frac{k_A P_A Y_A}{k_B P_B Y_B} \qquad [10]$$

Since $(P_A/P_B) = e$ by [7], we can obtain

$$\frac{M_{sA}}{M_{sB}} = \frac{k_A Y_A}{k_B Y_B} \cdot e \qquad [11]$$

A final rearrangement leads to

$$e = \frac{k_B Y_B M_{sA}}{k_A Y_A M_{sB}} \qquad [12]$$

This last expression is instructive because it shows the impact of changes in both economies on the exchange rate.[2] For example, if the money supply in country A (M_{sA}) increases and everything else is held constant, then e will rise by the same percentage as does the money supply. This is a strict monetary approach interpretation where, for example, a 10 percent rise in the home money supply will lead to a 10 percent depreciation of the home currency. (Remember that a rise in e is a fall in the relative value of the home currency.) We can also see from [12] that a rise in M_{sB} will lead to a proportional fall in e (an appreciation of the home currency). Thus, the monetary approach puts crucial importance on changes in relative money supplies as determinants of changes in the exchange rate. If a country is "printing money" faster than its trading partners are, its currency will depreciate; if a country is more restrictive with respect to its monetary growth than its trading partners, its currency will appreciate.

Expression [12] can also be used to indicate the effects of income changes in either economy. Suppose that national income in country A (Y_A) increases. What impact will this have on e? As should be clear, e will fall when Y_A rises (which increases A's demand for money), meaning that the home currency appreciates. Similarly, a rise in Y_B will cause a depreciation of A's currency. Hence, the implication in the monetary approach is that the faster-growing country will see its currency appreciate.

A BRIEF LOOK AT EMPIRICAL WORK ON THE MONETARY APPROACH

There has been a considerable amount of empirical testing of relationships in the monetary approach model. We present in this section a brief discussion of a few of these tests.

---

[2]The relationships in [12] can also be examined through growth rates. Designating a percentage change by a · over a variable, expression [12] in terms of growth rates is

$$\dot{e} = (\dot{Y}_B - \dot{Y}_A) + (\dot{M}_{sA} - \dot{M}_{sB}) \qquad [12']$$

There are no k terms in [12'] because k_A and k_B are assumed to be constant.

The Monetary Approach under Fixed Exchange Rates

With respect to the monetary approach under fixed exchange rates, we very briefly summarize one representative test. Junichi Ujiie (1978) has done work on Japan for the fixed-rate period 1959–1972. His general testing equation is[3]

$$BOP = a + b\Delta D + c\Delta i^* + f\Delta Y \qquad [13]$$

The dependent variable is the balance-of-payments position.[4] If BOP is positive, there is an official reserve transactions surplus (or an inflow of international reserves) while a negative number constitutes a deficit (or an outflow of international reserves). On the right-hand side, a is a constant term, ΔD represents the change in domestic credit (which influences the monetary base), Δi^* indicates the change in *foreign* interest rates, and ΔY indicates the change in Japanese real income.[5]

What signs do we expect for the coefficients b, c, and f in the context of the monetary approach? (We ignore a, as it is not important for any conclusions.) A positive ΔD indicates that the money supply is rising, and, other things equal, there is thus an excess supply of money; hence we expect BOP to be moving into deficit and b to be negative. On the other hand, in terms of the monetary approach (Ujiie himself used a different interpretation), an exogenous rise in the foreign interest rate will mean a reduced demand for money overseas, generating a potential BOP deficit overseas and therefore a potential BOP surplus for Japan (the home country). This gives a positive sign for c. Finally, the monetary approach leads us to expect a positive sign for f, because a rise in Y will generate greater demand for money and therefore a rise in BOP.

After carrying out various tests, Ujiie's general conclusion was that the domestic credit variable clearly performed as expected (that is, b was always negative in a statistically significant sense). On the other hand, he could not make any firm statements as to the signs of c and f. Hence, this test is robust with respect to the influence of changes in domestic credit and thereby the money supply, but uncertainty exists regarding the relationships of foreign interest rates and domestic income to the balance of payments. It seems fair to say that, considering Ujiie's and others' work with respect to a fixed-rate system, the money supply does seem to have its predicted relationship with the BOP position. However, there is disagreement as to the influence of other included variables.

The Monetary Approach Under Flexible Exchange Rates

We now turn to brief summaries of two empirical studies of the monetary approach under a flexible exchange rate regime. The first study was done by Jacob Frenkel (1978), formerly economic counselor of the International Monetary Fund. The period examined is a favorite one chosen for studying the monetary approach—the German hyperinflation after World War I.[6] The technique used is a common one of employing natural logarithms of variables. While we need not dwell on the natural logarithm concept, a useful feature of such an approach is that the estimated coefficients of the independent variables are *elasticities*. Thus, a coefficient of 2.0 on an independent variable means that a 1 percent

---

[3]In the interest of simplicity, we are not listing all of Ujiie's independent variables.

[4]The *dependent* variable in a testing equation is the variable on the left-hand side, the variable being "explained." The *independent* variables, on the right-hand side of the equation, are variables thought to have a causal influence on the dependent variable. The terms such as b, c, and f above show the extent of influence and are called the *coefficients* of the independent variables.

[5]In his tests, Ujiie actually employed the concept of "permanent income" rather than current income, but this is immaterial for our purposes.

[6]Hyperinflation is a situation where prices are rising extremely rapidly, such as over 1,000 percent per year. In Germany during 1920–1923, the wholesale price index (1913 = 1.0) was 14.40 in December 1920 and 1,200,400,000,000 in December 1923. See Graham (1930, pp. 105–6).

rise in the value of the independent variable would be associated with a 2 percent rise in the value of the dependent variable.

The Frenkel testing equation for the behavior of the German exchange rate from February 1921 through August 1923 was

$$\log e = a + b \log M_s + c \log E(\dot{p}) \qquad [14]$$

where: e = exchange rate (units of German marks per one U.S. dollar)
   a = a constant term
   M_s = German money supply
   $E(\dot{p})$ = a measure of inflationary expectations in Germany[7]

If the monetary approach has validity, b would be positive. Indeed, if the exchange rate moves proportionately with the money supply, we can make a stronger statement—that b should be 1.0. The term c is also expected to be positive, since greater expected price rises lead individuals to reduce their demand for money. This would generate an excess supply of money and a depreciation of the currency. The term a has no expected sign a priori and is inconsequential for our purposes.

For the German hyperinflation period, Frenkel found b to be highly significant statistically, with a value of +0.975. Thus, the exchange rate depreciated virtually proportionately with the money supply. In addition, the c term was a highly significant +0.591. This result is also consistent with the monetary approach. The Frenkel test (among others) gives substantial support for the monetary approach to the exchange rate. In criticism, the point has often been raised that, in conditions of hyperinflation, prices dominate all other influences and the money supply dominates prices to the exclusion of all other factors. (Frenkel had also found a virtual identity of the movements of German price indexes with changes in the German money supply.) Thus, strong support for the monetary approach is almost inevitable. If more normal conditions rather than hyperinflation are selected, critics of the monetary approach doubt that such powerful results could be found.

A test for a nonhyperinflationary period has been conducted by Rudiger Dornbusch ("Exchange Rate Economics," 1980). (See Box 1.) Dornbusch considered the 1973–1979 period, during which there was sizable inflation by developed-country standards, but by no means was there an experience similar to that of Germany in the 1920s. In addition, there was substantial flexibility in the exchange rates of major industrialized countries.

Dornbusch estimated the following equation:

$$e = a + b\,(m_s - m_s^*) + c\,(y - y^*) + d\,(i - i^*)_S + f\,(i - i^*)_L \qquad [15]$$

This equation was estimated for five industrialized countries (Canada, France, Japan, the United Kingdom, the United States) as a group against West Germany, with the five countries being treated as the "home" country and West Germany as the "foreign" country. In this equation, e refers to the natural logarithm of the dollar-per-mark exchange rate.[8] The term a is again a constant term with no a priori expectation as to sign. The term m_s is the logarithm of the group's money supply, while m_s^* is the logarithm of the West German money supply. Similarly, y is the logarithm of real income in the group, while y^* is the logarithm of West German real income. The i and i^* terms refer to interest rates in the five countries and in West Germany, respectively. The subscript S refers to short-term interest rates and subscript L refers to long-term interest rates.

---

[7]We will not go into details on the inflationary expectations measure. Economists have devised several such measures and have quarreled continuously over them.

[8]More precisely, it is the logarithm of the weighted-average value of the five countries' currencies expressed in terms of dollars per mark.

※ **BOX 1**   RUDIGER DORNBUSCH (B. 1942)

Rudiger Dornbusch was born on June 8, 1942, in Krefeld, Germany. He did undergraduate work in Geneva before coming to the United States in 1966, whereupon he entered the University of Chicago and received his Ph.D. in 1971. He was an assistant professor at Chicago in 1971 and at the University of Rochester in 1972–1973 and an associate professor at the Massachusetts Institute of Technology from 1975 to 1977. He was rapidly promoted to full professor at MIT in 1977, and later he assumed his current chaired professor rank as Ford International Professor of Economics. He has held positions at Fundação Getúlio Vargas in Rio de Janeiro and at the Universidad del Pacífico in Lima, Peru.

Professor Dornbusch is an acknowledged expert on macroeconomics in an open economy context. His best-known work in that area is his "Expectations and Exchange Rate Dynamics" (*Journal of Political Economy,* December 1976, which is discussed later in this chapter. This paper is a classic pioneering piece on "overshooting" of exchange rates beyond their equilibrium level: it is cited on almost any occasion when overshooting is discussed, and it has been the source of a multitude of graduate examination questions. Also well known is his article "Devaluation, Money and Non-traded Goods" (*American Economic Review,* December 1973). This paper is a landmark for its incorporation of the nontraded sector into the analysis of exchange rate changes—a necessary incorporation since such changes affect all relative prices in the economy, not only the prices of traded goods. In addition, he has written a widely respected intermediate level textbook, *Open Economy Macroeconomics.*

Professor Dornbusch has also made his mark in other areas of economics, an achievement that is rare in this age of academic specialization. His paper (with Stanley Fischer and Paul A. Samuelson) on "Comparative Advantage, Trade, and Payments in a Ricardian Model with a Continuum of Goods" (*American Economic Review,* December 1977) is regarded as the classic work on the extension of the Ricardian international trade model to a multicommodity world. More recently, Professor Dornbusch has done considerable writing on the external debt of developing countries and liberalization, which has resulted in great demand for his consulting and advising services.

Besides his direct scholarly contributions and his policy advising, Professor Dornbusch has served as coeditor of the *Journal of International Economics,* associate editor of the *Quarterly Journal of Economics* and the *Journal of Finance,* and advisor to the Institute for International Economics in Washington, D.C. In addition, he has been honored as a Guggenheim Fellow and as a Fellow of the American Academy of Arts and Sciences. He was also a vice president of the American Economic Association in 1990.

Sources: Mark Blaug, ed., *Who's Who in Economics: A Biographical Dictionary of Major Economists 1700–1986,* 2nd ed. (Cambridge: MA: MIT Press, 1986), pp. 227–28; Rudiger Dornbusch, John H. Makin, and David Zlowe, eds., *Alternative Solutions to Developing-Country Debt Problems* (Washington, DC: American Enterprise Institute for Public Policy Research, 1989), p. xi; *Who's Who in America,* 47th ed., 1992–93 vol. 1 (New Providence, NJ: Marquis Who's Who, 1992), p. 896.

Consistent with the monetary approach, we expect *b, d,* and *f* to be positive. A faster rate of growth of money in the other countries relative to Germany [as reflected in an increase in the $(m_s - m_s^*)$ term] should result in an appreciation of the mark (that is, *e* should rise). Similarly, an exogenous increase in interest rates in the other countries relative to Germany [as reflected in an increase in the $(i - i^*)$ terms] should cause an appreciation of the mark.[9] On the other hand, a faster increase in real income in the other countries than in Germany [an increase in $(y - y^*)$] should increase the relative demand for money in the other countries (according to the monetary approach). This will lead to an appreciation of the other currencies and a depreciation of the mark. Hence, *c* is expected to be negative.

Dornbusch's results were hardly encouraging for the applicability of the monetary approach for explaining exchange rate movements. The *b* coefficient was actually *negative,*

[9]Remember that in the monetary approach, a rise in the domestic interest rate reduces the demand for money, leading to an excess supply of money. The excess money supply generates depreciation. In this test, an increase in *i* will lead to depreciation of the five countries' currencies, i.e., an appreciation of the mark.

though not statistically significant. The c coefficient had the expected sign but was also not statistically significant. Only the coefficients on the interest rates were of the expected sign and were also statistically significant. Dornbusch concluded that, at least from his testing, there is "little doubt that the monetary approach . . . is an unsatisfactory theory of exchange rate determination" (Dornbusch, "Exchange Rate Economics," 1980, p. 151).

Given the sharply contrasting conclusions of Dornbusch and Frenkel with respect to the monetary approach to the exchange rate, there is controversy over the validity of this approach. In a recent survey of relevant literature for the post-1973 period, when the exchange rates of major industrialized countries have been fluctuating, MacDonald and Taylor (1992, p. 11) offer the summary statement that the "monetary approach appears reasonably well supported for the period up to 1978" but that this is not true for studies using sample years after that time (into which they place the above Dornbusch study). In particular, Mark Taylor (1995, p. 29) has noted that the later estimating equations for exchange rates often contained incorrect signs. For example, estimates for the dollar/mark exchange rate yielded results that implied that an increase in the German money supply would cause the mark to *appreciate*. (See also Frankel 1982, 1993.) There has been controversy over this relationship, as some economists think the unexpected sign is the result of mis-specifications in the equations, especially with respect to wealth effects. For instance, if wealth is increasing (perhaps due to an increase in the money supply itself), individuals might wish to hold more mark-denominated assets. This could raise the value of the mark and more than offset the mark depreciation that would be expected under the monetary approach when the German money supply increased.

Finally, much empirical work has been done with respect to a building block of the monetary approach—purchasing power parity. Tests have been conducted for the recent floating-rate period with respect to both absolute PPP and relative PPP.[10] In their survey of empirical literature, MacDonald and Taylor (1992, p. 40) say that both absolute PPP and relative PPP have been "resoundingly rejected by the data." However, this conclusion is called into question by recent work carried out by Yin-Wong Cheung and Kon Lai (1993). They examined the period 1974–1989 with the United States as the home country and Canada, France, Germany, Switzerland, and the United Kingdom as foreign countries and found supportive evidence for (relative) PPP. In addition, Jeffrey Frankel and Andrew Rose (1996) found, in a study utilizing data from 150 countries and for 45 years, that convergence toward relative PPP occurs over time and that deviations from relative PPP erode at a rate of about 15 percent per year on average. Hence, there is dispute in the literature regarding not only the monetary approach in general as an explanation of exchange rate behavior but also the particular PPP feature of the approach.

CONCEPT CHECK

1. Assuming a flexible exchange rate, explain the impact of an exogenous reduction in a country's money supply upon the value of the country's currency.
2. In the monetary approach, other things equal, what will happen to the exchange rate between the currencies of countries A and B if there is greater income growth in country B than in country A? Explain.

---

[10]Remember that, with absolute PPP, for countries A and B, the exchange rate e (number of units of A's currency per unit of B's currency) equals the price level in A divided by the price level in B. With relative PPP, the percentage change in e moves directly proportionally with the ratio of the price index in A (relative to a base year) divided by the price index in B (relative to a base year).

THE PORTFOLIO BALANCE APPROACH TO THE BALANCE OF PAYMENTS AND THE EXCHANGE RATE

The **portfolio balance** or **asset market approach** to the balance of payments and the exchange rate extends the monetary approach to include other financial assets besides money. This literature has primarily developed since the mid-1970s, and there is an extremely large number of asset approach models in existence. We will provide only a general discussion of these models, all of which emphasize a few overriding characteristics:

1. Financial markets across countries are extremely well integrated. Thus, individuals hold a variety of financial assets, both domestic and foreign.

2. Though holding both domestic and foreign financial assets, individuals regard these assets as *imperfect substitutes.* In particular, additional risk is generally thought to be associated with the holding of foreign financial assets. Hence, there is a positive risk premium attached to foreign assets. This premium was discussed in the preceding two chapters.[11]

3. Asset holders, with the objective of maximizing the return on their asset portfolio as a whole, stand ready to switch out of one type of asset and into another whenever events occur that alter the expected returns on various assets. These adjustments in portfolios have implications for the balance of payments (under some fixity in the exchange rate) and for the exchange rate (when the exchange rate has some variability).

4. In addition, this literature recognizes the importance of investor expectations regarding future asset prices (including the price of foreign exchange, which can be free to vary). The most common procedure hypothesized for the formation of expectations is that of **rational expectations,** whereby forward-looking, utility-maximizing investors utilize all available relevant information and a knowledge of how the economy and the exchange markets work in order to form forecasts.

Asset Demands

As with the monetary approach, the portfolio balance approach specifies the factors that influence the demand for money, but it also specifies the factors that influence the demand for other financial assets. The general framework of the approach is that there are two countries (a home country and a foreign country), two moneys or currencies (domestic money and foreign money), and two non-money securities, usually classified as bonds (a home bond and a foreign bond). The domestic bond yields an interest return i_d, while the foreign bond yields an interest return i_f. In this framework we consider below the demand functions for the various assets by home country citizens. We designate demand for home money as L, demand for the home bond as B_d, and demand for the foreign bond as B_f. The typical home individual is assumed to be able to hold any of these three assets.[12]

Before proceeding with the demand functions, however, it is useful to discuss the relationship specified in portfolio balance models concerning interest rates in the two countries. Since the models assume mobile capital across countries, the uncovered interest parity relationship of the previous chapters is assumed to hold. With somewhat

[11]It is possible that the risk premium could be negative if foreign assets are deemed to carry less risk than domestic assets. We ignore this possibility in our discussion.

[12]We follow the bulk of the literature in assuming that home country citizens do *not* hold foreign currency. This is a simplification but it makes the analysis more manageable than would otherwise be the case.

imperfect substitution between domestic and foreign assets, a risk premium term (*RP*) is also included. Therefore,

$$i_d = i_f + xa - RP \qquad [16]$$

where *xa* is the expected percentage change in value of the foreign currency. A positive *xa* is an expected appreciation of the foreign currency and a negative *xa* is an expected depreciation of the foreign currency. (Alternatively, a positive *xa* is an expected depreciation of the home currency, and a negative *xa* is an expected appreciation of the home currency.) The more formal specific definition of *xa* is

$$xa = \frac{E(e) - e}{e} = \frac{E(e)}{e} - 1 \qquad [17]$$

where $E(e)$ is the expected future spot exchange rate (expected future home currency price of foreign currency). The risk premium *RP*, expressed as a positive percentage, is the extra percentage compensation needed to induce the home investor to hold the foreign asset. With *RP* positive, $(i_f + xa)$ will be greater than i_d in equilibrium.

Let us now specify the demand functions of a typical home country individual for the three assets of home money, home bonds, and foreign bonds (a parallel set of demand functions exists for foreign individuals). Starting first with the home individual's demand for domestic money, consider the general functional form in expression [18]. (Note: The general framework described here is an adaptation of that presented in a useful article by William Branson and Dale Henderson 1985.)

$$\overset{-\ -\ -\ +\ +\ +}{L = f(i_d,\ i_f,\ xa,\ Y_d, P_d, W_d)} \qquad [18]$$

where, in addition to the already-identified i_d, i_f, and *xa*,

Y_d = home country real income
P_d = home country price level
W_d = home country real wealth

Note that *RP* is not included separately in [18] because, with $i_d = i_f + xa - RP$ from [16], *RP* is a residual and its influence is already embodied in the i_d, i_f, and *xa* terms. In this expression, the plus or minus sign above each independent variable indicates the expected sign of the relationship between the independent variable and the demand for home money.

How do we explain the predicted signs of expression [18]? First, the negative sign for the i_d is clear from preceding discussions in this chapter. For similar reasons, a rise in i_f will induce the domestic citizen to stop holding as much domestic money and add to holdings of foreign bonds. The influence of *xa* works in the same manner as does i_f, for a rise in *xa* indicates that the expected return from holding the foreign bond (which is denominated in foreign currency) has risen. The signs on real income, the domestic price level, and home wealth are as discussed above in the monetary approach.

Next consider the demand for domestic bonds or securities by the domestic individual (B_d). We write the demand for the asset as a function of the same independent variables:

$$\overset{+\ -\ -\ -\ -\ +}{B_d = h(i_d,\ i_f,\ xa,\ Y_d,\ P_d,\ W_d)} \qquad [19]$$

These signs are consistent with the investor's motivations as discussed earlier. A rise in i_d will make domestic bonds more attractive because of their higher return. A rise in i_f

causes the individual to desire to hold the now higher-yielding foreign bonds instead of domestic bonds, so i_f has a negative sign. A rise in xa acts in the same fashion. The wealth variable behaves as previously indicated for home money demand, but the signs on Y_d and P_d are *negative* in the case of home bond demand. Why so? The reason is rooted in the transactions demand for money. *Ceteris paribus,* a rise in income causes an increase in the transactions demand for money; if total wealth is assumed not to change because of the *ceteris paribus* assumption, then the investor will have to give up some holdings of domestic bonds in order to acquire money. Similar reasoning produces a negative sign for the domestic price level.

The demand function for the third and final asset, the foreign bond (B_f), is expressed in domestic currency by multiplying B_f by e and is given as

$$eB_f = j\ (\overset{-}{i_d},\ \overset{+}{i_f},\ \overset{+}{xa},\ \overset{-}{Y_d},\ \overset{-}{P_d},\ \overset{+}{W_d}) \qquad [20]$$

In this demand function, the signs for Y_d, P_d, and W_d can be explained in similar fashion as for the demand for domestic bonds. The signs on the interest rates are reversed from those in the domestic bond situation—a rise in i_d causes the investor to shift out of foreign bonds and into domestic bonds, and a rise in i_f (and in xa) causes bondholders to prefer the foreign bond to the domestic bond.

Once these various demand functions are specified in the portfolio balance model, a key feature of such models is evident: All three assets are substitutes for each other, and therefore any change in any variable will set in motion a whole host of adjustments on the part of investors. Further, it should be noted again that we have only discussed one-half of the demand functions, because foreign citizens are also going to have demand functions for the two bonds and for foreign money. Clearly, a complicated model can emerge.

Portfolio Balance   Given the various demands for assets as indicated above, the asset model then specifies supply functions for each asset. As a simplification, we consider the supply of money in each country to be under the control of each country's respective monetary authority. If so, then money supplies are exogenous to the model, meaning that they are determined by outside factors.[13] The supplies of the two bonds are usually treated as exogenous as well. If the bonds are government securities, then fiscal policy can clearly affect the volume of such securities in existence. If the bonds are private securities, decisions on their issuance may also be assumed to be outside the model per se. These bond supplies, together with the money supply (see MacDonald and Taylor 1992, p. 9), define the wealth of the domestic country (W_d) in terms of its own currency as

$$W_d = M_s + B_h + eB_o \qquad [21]$$

where M_s is the money supply of the home country, B_h is the stock of home bonds (government and private) actually held by domestic residents, and B_o is the stock of foreign bonds actually held by domestic residents. The stock of foreign bonds is multiplied by the exchange rate e in order to put the value of those assets into domestic currency terms.

When the asset demands are put together with the asset supplies, financial equilibrium is attained. It is important to note that equilibrium in the financial sector implies that *all* the individual asset markets are in equilibrium simultaneously. Thus, in portfolio balance

---

[13]However, more complex models allow for an endogenous money supply. This means that the model itself will generate changes in a country's money supply; for example, under fixed exchange rates, a balance-of-payments deficit results in a reduction in the deficit country's money supply as holdings of international reserves by its central bank decline.

equilibrium, the amount of each asset desired to be held is equal to the amount that is actually held—home money demand (L) equals the home money supply (M_s), home demand for domestic bonds (B_d) equals the home bonds actually held by domestic residents (B_h), and home demand for foreign bonds (eB_f) equals the stock of foreign bonds actually held by domestic residents (eB_o). The attainment of this equilibrium results in the determination of the equilibrium price of each bond, the equilibrium interest rate in each country, and the *equilibrium exchange rate.* The exchange rate emerges from the model because, in moving to equilibrium, any switches from (to) domestic bonds and money to (from) foreign bonds involve new demands for (supplies of) foreign exchange.

Portfolio Adjustments

Given that investors have reached equilibrium, we now consider several exogenous actions in the economy that will set into motion various adjustments in the financial sector. The overview of these adjustments is that an autonomous disturbance causes asset holders to rearrange their portfolios. The previous equilibrium portfolio for each investor is no longer an equilibrium portfolio; in response, the investors buy and sell the various assets in order to attain their new desired portfolio, whereupon the investors reach a new equilibrium position.

1. Consider first the autonomous policy action of a *sale of government securities in the open market by the monetary authorities of the home country* (i.e., a contraction of the home money supply and an increase in the domestic bond supply). The immediate impact of this action is an increase in the home country interest rate (i_d). How do asset holders react? One response is that the rise in i_d causes domestic citizens to reduce their demand for home money. (See expression [18].) In addition, the demand for foreign bonds will fall (see expression [20]) because of the negative relationship between i_d and eB_f. This decreased demand for foreign bonds occurs on the part not only of domestic asset holders but also of foreign country asset holders (whose demand functions were not shown above). Further, as indicated by expression [19], the quantity of domestic bonds demanded will rise because of their higher yield. Finally, foreign country investors will also switch from holding their own currency to holding the home country bond. (We did not show the demand function of foreigners for their own currency, but it would parallel [18].) Thus adjustments take place in the markets for all four assets—the home and foreign currencies and the home and foreign bonds.

These adjustments continue until a new portfolio equilibrium is attained by all investors. Of interest are some of the implications of the adjustment process. For example, what is likely to happen to the foreign interest rate because of the rise in the domestic interest rate? It should be clear that i_f will rise. This will happen because the reduced demand for foreign bonds will drive down the price of foreign bonds and thus increase i_f.

In addition to the impact on i_f, of course, e will change if variability in the exchange rate is permitted. Hence, in terms of expression [17],

$$xa = \frac{E(e) - e}{e} = \frac{E(e)}{e} - 1$$

e will *fall* (the foreign currency depreciates) because there are fewer purchases of foreign exchange in order to acquire foreign bonds and because there are greater purchases of home currency by foreign citizens in order to acquire domestic bonds.[14] Therefore,

[14]Note that, in the portfolio balance model, a rise in i_d causes an appreciation of the home currency. (If the exchange rate were fixed, the result would be a balance-of-payments surplus.) In the other direction, a fall in i_d would cause a depreciation of the home currency (and a BOP deficit with fixed rates). The impact of the interest rate on the exchange rate (or the BOP) is thus opposite to the impact in the monetary approach.

holding the expected future exchange rate $E(e)$ constant, *xa rises* because e has fallen. In sum, the previous uncovered interest parity (UIP) of $i_d = i_f + xa - RP$ has been disturbed by a rise in i_d due to the contraction of the domestic money supply. With i_d now greater than $(i_f + xa - RP)$, portfolio adjustments lead to a new equilibrium through a rise in i_f *and* a rise in *xa,* that is, through a rise in the foreign interest rate as well as a rise in the expected future appreciation of the foreign currency.[15]

We will carry this case of a monetary policy action no further, but note that other, "second-round" effects will ensue after the adjustments already discussed. (For example, the rise in i_d may reduce home country real income.) Nevertheless, what we have said so far indicates the complexity and yet the potential usefulness of the comprehensive view of financial markets offered by the portfolio balance approach. The key point to be emphasized is that a contraction of the domestic money supply raises the home interest rate, the foreign interest rate, and the expected depreciation (perhaps) of the home currency, as well as causes an appreciation of the spot home currency.

2. As a second example of portfolio adjustments, consider a situation where, for whatever reason, home country citizens decide that greater home inflation is likely in the future. In other words, individuals in the home country now have *greater inflationary expectations.* With a flexible exchange rate and with some notion of PPP that is often embodied in these models, the expectation of a future price rise at home implies that the home currency will be expected to depreciate. In terms of our demand functions, *xa* rises. What is the outcome from the standpoint of the portfolio adjustment process?

First consider the demand for home money. As expression [18] indicates, home money demand will decrease (the sign of *xa* is negative). In addition, expression [19] shows us that the demand for domestic bonds also decreases. Both of these demands are reduced because investors are demanding more foreign bonds (see expression [20]) in anticipation of the increased yield when converted into home currency at a later date. Thus, the adjustments in the portfolio generate a depreciation of the home currency since there is an excess supply of money at home and an outflow of funds to purchase foreign bonds. Clearly, the expectation of a depreciation can cause a depreciation. A variety of additional effects could be considered, but the important result is that greater inflationary expectations have generated a depreciation of the home currency. (Under a fixed exchange rate, the result would be a BOP deficit.)

3. Next, consider *an increase in real income in the home country.* By looking at the signs of the Y_d variable in [18], [19], and [20], we see the primary impact immediately. With an increase in home income, investors want to hold more domestic money because of an increased transactions demand for money. This point is familiar from the monetary approach. However, the portfolio balance approach enables us to see more explicitly the behavior involved. With increased income, individuals attempt to increase their money holdings by selling both domestic and foreign bonds. (Real income has a negative sign in [19] and [20].) Further, the sale of the foreign bond "improves" the balance of payments under a fixed exchange rate system and leads to an *appreciation of the home currency* under a flexible rate system. This is a result consistent with the monetary approach's view that an increase in income leads to a BOP surplus under fixed rates and to currency appreciation with flexible rates. In the portfolio adjustment model, however, the process is more evident.

---

[15]We have also assumed that the risk premium (RP) remains unchanged. In addition, it should be noted that if the depreciation of the foreign currency (the fall in e) leads to a revision of the expected future exchange rate $E(e)$ itself toward a further depreciation of the foreign currency [a fall in $E(e)$], then, in expression [17], $E(e)$ and e will both be falling and the rise in *xa* will be less pronounced or could even be negative. In that case, the equilibrating job to be done for restoring uncovered interest parity by a rise in i_f in response to the rise in i_d will be even greater.

4. Now consider an increase in home bond supply, for example, through issuance of new corporate bonds to finance the purchase of physical assets. This rise in domestic bonds increases home country wealth (W_d). What is the implication for the exchange rate? With portfolio diversification, expressions [18], [19], and [20] tell us that home investors will want to hold more domestic money, more domestic bonds, *and* more foreign bonds. If the domestic money supply is unchanged, the increased supply of domestic bonds will lead to a fall in home bond prices and a rise in i_d. Other things equal, the rise in i_d will induce a capital inflow into the home country, and with a flexible exchange rate the capital inflow will lead to an appreciation of the home currency. However, the increased demand for foreign bonds associated with the domestic wealth increase alone will, *ceteris paribus,* lead to a depreciation of the home currency. Hence, without more information on the relative strength of these opposing effects, the direction of impact on the exchange rate of the increase in home bond supply is indeterminate. Nevertheless, if domestic bonds and foreign bonds are good substitutes for each other, the capital inflow from the relative rise in i_d is likely to yield a substantial increase in the purchase of domestic bonds relative to foreign bonds, offsetting any pure wealth effect on the demand for foreign bonds, and the home currency will on net appreciate. This result seems *prima facie* most likely in practice.

5. Now consider another change: an increase in home country wealth because of a home country current account surplus. First, why does a current account surplus increase the wealth of the country with the surplus? Because, under balance-of-payments accounting, a country that has a current account surplus *must* have a capital account deficit; that is, with a current account surplus, the home country acquires foreign assets due to the net inflow of foreign exchange on current account. This increase in wealth (W_d) will increase the home country's demand for money [by expression (18)], its demand for domestic bonds [by expression (19)], and its demand for foreign bonds (by expression [20]). The increased demand for money will work to increase i_d, while the increased demand for domestic bonds will decrease i_d; hence, the net impact on i_d is indeterminate without more information. In the foreign country (the country with the current account deficit), there is a reduction in wealth and hence in that country's demand for money and its own bonds. The impact on i_f is thus also indeterminate. With uncertainty as to the impact on interest rates, therefore, no firm prediction can be made regarding the impact on the exchange rate. If bond market impacts on interest rates dominate money market impacts on interest rates, then i_d would fall relative to i_f and the wealth transfer would lead to a depreciation of the home currency relative to the foreign currency.

6. Now consider one final change: an increase in the supply of foreign bonds because of a foreign government budget deficit (for elaboration, see Rivera-Batiz and Rivera-Batiz 1994, pp. 566–67). With an increase in the supply of already-risky foreign bonds, the risk premium in the UIP expression [16] will rise (and the right-hand side of the expression will thus fall). Other things equal, this would serve to *appreciate the home currency* (depreciate the foreign currency). In addition, if the foreign government budget deficit is associated with the expectation that foreign prices will rise, this too could cause a (purchasing power parity type of) depreciation of the foreign currency (appreciation of the home currency). Another useful way to think of the situation is that the increase in the supply of foreign currency-denominated bonds requires a reduction in their price in order to sell some of the new bonds to home country investors. Such a price reduction to home investors can be accomplished by reducing e, since e multiplied by the foreign currency price of the bonds gives the price to home country investors of those bonds. No matter how the mechanism is viewed, the portfolio balance model suggests that a government budget deficit financed by issuing new bonds will depreciate the currency of the country with the government budget deficit.

Finally, it should be noted that, in the six examples above and in the portfolio balance model generally, the existence of a BOP surplus or deficit, or of a home currency appreciation or depreciation, is only temporary. It occurs only while the adjustment process to the new equilibrium portfolios is taking place. Once the new desired portfolios have been attained, there is no longer any net flow out of or into foreign securities to or from domestic money or bonds, and the balance-of-payments imbalance or the exchange rate change ceases. A BOP deficit or surplus (and a depreciation or appreciation) will not exist once **asset stock equilibrium** (i.e., a simultaneous equilibrium of demands and supplies of all financial assets) has been achieved. Therefore, the presence of a continuing BOP imbalance or a continuing exchange rate change must mean that equilibrium in portfolio holdings has not been attained. The persistent disequilibrium occurs either from a slow adjustment process or from continuing exogenous changes.

EMPIRICAL WORK ON THE PORTFOLIO BALANCE MODEL

In this section, we briefly look at empirical studies regarding the portfolio balance or asset market approach. Relatively little work has been done on testing the portfolio balance or asset market model because of difficulties encountered in relating the theoretical models to real-world data. In particular, as noted in Taylor (1995, p. 30), questions arise as to which non-money assets to include and how to obtain uniform data across countries. Further, uncertainty exists as to how to quantify the risk premium that reflects the imperfect substitutability of domestic and foreign assets.

The first test we examine is that of Jeffrey Frankel (1984). While all such studies face the problem that there are inadequate data on the composition of portfolios, Frankel employed various assumptions to obtain estimates for the 1973–1979 period and then tested hypothesized relationships. The dependent variable in his testing equations is the home currency/dollar exchange rate. (The "home country" in his analysis consists of five developed countries—Canada, France, West Germany, Japan, and the United Kingdom; the "foreign country" is the United States.) The independent variables were (1) wealth in the home country, W_h; (2) wealth in the foreign country (the United States), W_{US}; (3) the supply of home currency–denominated assets on the world market, B_h; and (4) the supply of foreign currency– (dollar-) denominated assets on the world market, B_{US}. (Note: The B terms have a slightly different meaning than they did in our earlier discussion because they apply to the entire world market, not only to holdings by domestic citizens.)

In terms of the portfolio balance model, W_h is expected to have a negative sign because increased wealth in the home country (e.g., West Germany) appreciates the home currency (see example 4 in the previous section and assume that the substitution effect between domestic and foreign bonds dominates the pure wealth effect), and thus the mark/dollar rate will fall. An increase in U.S. real wealth for analogous reasons causes the mark/dollar rate to rise and produces a positive sign for W_{US}. An increase in the supply of mark-denominated bonds B_h (such as through a German government budget deficit) will increase the mark/dollar exchange rate—generating a positive sign. (This follows from the discussion in example 6 in the previous section.) Finally, for analogous reasons, a rise in the supply of foreign (U.S.) assets generates a negative sign for B_{US}. Table 2 presents the signs Frankel obtained for the 1973–1979 period. While not all of these signs were statistically significant in his test, it is clear that the results are not very satisfactory from the standpoint of the portfolio balance model. The "wrong sign" occurs in two countries for W_h and B_h (Germany and the United Kingdom) and in three countries for B_{US} (France, Germany, and the United Kingdom); and only Canada has the correct sign for W_{US}. Whether these

TABLE 2   **Signs of Regression Coefficients in Frankel Test of the Portfolio Balance Model (dependent variable: home currency per dollar exchange rate)**

Home Country	W_h (domestic wealth)	W_{US} (foreign wealth)	B_h (domestic assets)	B_{US} (foreign assets)
Canada	−	+	+	−
France	−	−	+	+
Germany, Fed. Rep. of	+	−	−	+
Japan	−	−	+	−
United Kingdom	+	−	−	+

Source: Jeffrey A. Frankel, "Tests of Monetary and Portfolio Balance Models of Exchange Rate Determination," in John F. O. Bilson and Richard C. Marston, eds., *Exchange Rate Theory and Practice* (Chicago: University of Chicago Press, 1984), p. 250.

poor results occur because of data problems and the testing method employed, failure of the theory, or foreign exchange market intervention is of course unknown.

Turning to other literature, increased attention has been focused (despite the difficulties) on isolating the risk premium in the uncovered interest parity equilibrium equation $i_d = i_f + xa - RP$. A study by Kathryn Dominguez and Jeffrey Frankel (1993) attempted to measure the risk premium through survey data on exchange rate expectations. The risk premium was then tested as to its relationship to exchange rate variations (of the dollar/mark and dollar/Swiss franc rates) and to the composition of wealth between domestic and foreign assets. Of importance for this chapter, there did seem to be an association between relative size of domestic to foreign assets in portfolios and the risk premium that is consistent with the portfolio balance model's assumption that home and foreign assets are imperfect substitutes. (See also Taylor 1995, pp. 30–31.)

Among other studies, some interesting work has been done by Richard Meese (1990) and by Meese and Kenneth Rogoff (1983). They attempted to ascertain whether standard asset market models can be of value in forecasting the exchange rate. (See the appendix to this chapter for more detail.) The procedure first was to obtain, from several years data, an equation with the exchange rate as the dependent variable, using independent variables suggested by the monetary and portfolio balance models. Meese and Rogoff then used this equation to forecast the exchange rate for later periods, and compared the forecast with the actual exchange rate that later did exist for those periods. The predictive success of the theoretical equation's forecast of the later spot rates was then compared with the success in predicting later spot rates (1) by using only the current period's forward rate for predicting next period's spot rate and (2) by predicting next period's spot rate as differing from this period's rate by only a random number (meaning the exchange rate is a "random walk").

Sadly for the theoretical equation, it performed less well (or more poorly) than did the random walk and the forward rate. This led Meese to conclude (1990, p. 132): "Economists do not yet understand the determinants of short- to medium-run movements in exchange rates." Other economists have disagreed with this view, and the issue continues to generate much theoretical and empirical investigation. Hence, although the portfolio balance (and monetary) models have suggested particular influences on the exchange rate, considerable work remains to be done to document these influences more convincingly. In view of the huge volume and rapid growth of international assets, as discussed in the previous chapter, this work is very important and necessary.

EXCHANGE RATE OVERSHOOTING

Many different asset market models exist in the literature, and we have barely scratched the surface in discussing their characteristics. However, one additional feature of a large number of these models is that (within a flexible exchange rate framework) they often involve **exchange rate overshooting.** "Overshooting" occurs when, in moving from one equilibrium to another, the exchange rate goes beyond the new equilibrium but then returns to it. We present below two treatments of this phenomenon.

The first explanation of overshooting draws upon the work of Rudiger Dornbusch (1976). However, we adopt some simplifications to keep the discussion consistent with previous material in this chapter. These simplifications mean that it is not truly the Dornbusch model in some respects. Nevertheless, the general conclusions are those of Dornbusch, and these conclusions have been very influential in the literature and in interpretations of real-world events. As will be seen, Dornbusch focuses on two key phenomena—short-run asset market behavior and long-run PPP behavior.

Turning first to the asset market, Dornbusch assumes that the home country is a "small country," which in this context means that the country has no effect on world interest rates. In addition, perfect capital mobility is assumed, meaning that home and foreign financial assets are perfect substitutes (and that there is no risk premium). These assumptions mean that an equation similar to our earlier uncovered interest parity expression [16] (without the risk premium) applies. Hence:

$$i_d = i_f + xa \qquad [22]$$

where i_d and xa have the same meaning as in [16]. The term i_f in this expression refers to the given *world* interest rate. Dornbusch assumes that, since perfect capital mobility exists, there is extremely rapid adjustment in the asset market. Hence, the asset market equilibrium relationship in expression [22] quickly reestablishes itself if disturbed.

Let's begin by reviewing asset/money market equilibrium. Consider how goods prices and exchange rate behavior are reflected in equation [22] and how equilibrium is restored following a disturbance. Suppose the home price level rises. A higher price level will lead to an increase in the transactions demand for money and, with an assumed fixed money supply, i_d will rise. Thus, for the moment, i_d is greater than $(i_f + xa)$. Because i_f is fixed by outside world conditions, the entire asset market adjustment in [22] must come through xa. Now recall from our earlier discussions that an increase in the transactions demand for money will lead to an appreciation of the exchange rate. This appreciation plays a crucial role in restoring asset market equilibrium. The home currency must appreciate enough so that investors begin to *expect* it to *depreciate* toward its original level. More precisely, because of the inflation the home currency must appreciate until its expected rate of depreciation, *xa,* is high enough to make the right-hand side of [22] equal to the now higher left-hand side. Thus, if i_d was originally 8 percent and i_f was also 8 percent, there was no expected depreciation of the home currency (or expected appreciation of the foreign currency). However, if the price rise and the resulting increased home demand for money raise i_d to 10 percent, xa must increase to 2 percent for equilibrium to be restored.

The equilibrium asset market schedule is shown in Figure 1 as line *AA.* The price level is represented on the vertical axis and the exchange rate on the horizontal axis. The previous paragraph has essentially explained the negative slope of this curve. Suppose that an initial equilibrium position is point *B,* with price level P_1 and exchange rate e_1. If there is a rise in the price level to P_2, a vertical movement to point *C* occurs. However, the higher prices and the accompanying increase in the demand for money set in motion

FIGURE 1   **Asset Market Equilibrium in the Dornbusch Model**

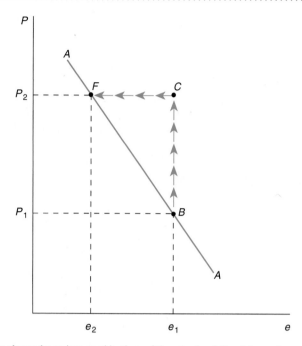

The AA schedule shows the various combinations of the price level P and the exchange rate e that satisfy the asset market equilibrium condition that $i_d = i_f + xa$. If, from an initial equilibrium position such as point B, the price level rises from P_1 to P_2, movement occurs to point C. This rise in prices increases the transactions demand for money, which, with a fixed money supply, increases domestic interest rate i_d. The increase in money demand causes the home currency to appreciate, indicated by the fall in e from e_1 to e_2. At new equilibrium point F, the equilibrium condition $i_d = i_f + xa$ is again satisfied. Since i_d has increased but the world interest rate i_f is fixed, equilibrium requires that xa increase by the amount by which i_d exceeds i_f. In other words, e must appreciate sufficiently to generate expectations of a future depreciation by the difference between the domestic interest rate and the world interest rate.

an appreciation of the home currency (a decrease in e). This appreciation continues until point F is reached, with exchange rate e_2. Although Figure 1 does not show xa directly, the expected depreciation associated with e_2 is such that the asset market is again in equilibrium. The line AA thus shows all combinations of P and e that yield equilibrium in the asset market.

Let us now turn to the PPP feature of the Dornbusch model and consider how P and e are related to each other in the goods market. In the *short run* in the goods market, there is no particular neatly specified relationship because goods prices are assumed to be "sticky"; that is, they adjust slowly to changing conditions. (In view of this price "stickiness," the Dornbusch model is often called a "fixed-price" monetary model as distinct from a "flexible-price" monetary model such as that used in the early part of this chapter.) This is in contrast to the asset market, where there is very quick adjustment from one equilibrium to another. However, in the *long run,* goods prices do adjust fully to the changed conditions in the economy. In the simple version of the Dornbusch model considered here, the economy is assumed to be at full employment and real income does not change. (A more complicated Dornbusch version drops this assumption.) In this situation, a depreciation of the home country currency will, *when goods prices eventually adjust,* cause a proportional change in the home price level. This PPP relationship is

FIGURE 2   **Adjustment to an Increase in the Money Supply in the Dornbusch Model**

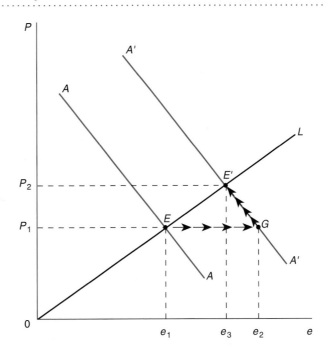

The ray $0L$ from the origin indicates the proportional relationship between changes in e and changes in P in the long run when goods prices adjust. The AA line is the asset market equilibrium schedule from Figure 1. Starting from long-run equilibrium point E, an increase in the money supply shifts AA to $A'A'$. With sticky goods prices, the exchange rate moves from e_1 to e_2. This depreciation of the home currency occurs until (the new, lower) i_d again equals $i_f + xa$ at point G. The term xa must become negative to restore equilibrium in the asset market, meaning that the home currency must depreciate until its expected appreciation matches the difference between the fixed i_f and i_d. As goods prices eventually begin to rise, movement occurs along $A'A'$ until the new long-run equilibrium position E' is reached. Exchange rate overshooting has occurred because the exchange rate change from e_1 to e_2 exceeds the long-run equilibrium rate change from e_1 to e_3.

depicted by the straight line from the origin, $0L$, in Figure 2. (Ignore the other features of the graph for the moment.) The line is upward-sloping because depreciation of the home currency creates excess demand for home goods. The excess demand arises because exports are now cheaper to foreign buyers and because import substitutes produced at home are now relatively less expensive to home consumers. This excess demand will eventually bid prices up in proportional fashion.

Given these relationships between P and e in the asset and goods markets, let us now address the phenomenon of overshooting. In Figure 2 the asset market schedule AA from Figure 1 and the goods market schedule $0L$ are put together. The initial equilibrium position is at E, where both markets are in equilibrium. The equilibrium exchange rate is e_1, and prices are in equilibrium at P_1. This is a long-run equilibrium position; therefore, e_1 is expected to persist. With e_1 expected to persist, $xa = 0$.

From this equilibrium position E, suppose that the monetary authorities now increase the money supply. The first impact of this action is a rightward shift in the AA schedule, to $A'A'$. This shift occurs because there is now an excess supply of money at the old equilibrium P and e. An elimination of this excess supply requires an increase in e and/or an increase in P, both of which increase the transactions demand for money and serve to absorb the excess supply. But, since goods prices are sticky and there is very rapid adjustment in the asset market, the adjustment occurs through the exchange rate and the next step is a horizontal movement from E to point G. This movement indicates a depreciation of the home currency (from e_1 to e_2). The depreciation occurs because the increased money supply has lowered domestic interest rates, and thus asset holders will shift their portfolios from home securities to foreign securities in order to earn a higher interest return. More importantly, asset holders expect a future depreciation of the home currency because of the money supply increase, and this will also cause home assets to be sold and foreign assets to be bought. The capital outflow resulting from these motivations will depreciate the home currency.

These adjustments take place quickly. The new equilibrium position *in the asset market* is found on the new asset equilibrium schedule $A'A'$ at point G. Since asset market equilibrium requires that $i_d = i_f + xa$, xa must be *negative* at point G because i_d has fallen while i_f is fixed. In other words, in the new asset equilibrium position, the home currency has depreciated so much that it is now *expected to appreciate*. (Remember that a negative xa is an expected depreciation of the foreign currency or an expected appreciation of the home currency.) This result occurs at e_2.

What happens after point G is attained? Recalling that the asset market maintains itself in equilibrium, upward movement takes place along the $A'A'$ schedule until E' is reached. This movement occurs because goods prices finally start to rise because of the excess demand for goods associated with the depreciated value of the home currency. As goods prices rise, the consequent increased transactions demand for money bids up the domestic interest rate, which results in an appreciation of the home currency until E' is attained. At long-run equilibrium position E', both the goods and asset markets are again in equilibrium. In comparison with original equilibrium E, expansionary monetary policy has raised prices (from P_1 to P_2) and has increased the exchange rate (depreciated the home currency) from e_1 to e_3.

There are two points to be emphasized. The most important one is that the exchange rate has indeed "overshot" its long-run equilibrium level. From e_1 it has risen to e_2 (depreciation of home currency) and then has fallen to e_3 (appreciation of home currency). Second, however, note that, in the adjustment from point G to point E', the home currency is appreciating at the same time that domestic prices are rising! This is hardly a result that conventional theory would lead us to expect. The Dornbusch model, in overview, has offered a mechanism that, in the opinion of many economists, has value in interpreting experiences in the post-1973 period, when most industrialized countries have had floating exchange rates.

Moving away from the Dornbusch model, with its incorporation of uncovered interest parity, overshooting can also occur in a framework that emphasizes covered interest parity and hence the forward market. (See Michael Melvin 1995, pp. 189–92.) To begin, recall from previous chapters that the covered interest parity condition between money markets is

$$i_d = i_f + (e_{fwd} - e)/e \qquad [23]$$

where i_d is the domestic interest rate, i_f is the foreign interest rate (no longer necessarily a fixed world rate), e_{fwd} is the forward rate for foreign currency, and e is the spot rate for foreign currency. In other words, covered interest parity occurs when the domestic interest rate is equal to the foreign interest rate plus the forward premium on the foreign currency. If i_f is greater than i_d, then the foreign currency will be at a forward discount [that is, a negative forward premium since $(e_{fwd} - e)/e$ will be negative]. If i_d exceeds i_f, interest arbitrage will yield a positive forward premium.

How does [23] relate to [16] without the risk premium (or to expression [22])? The modern literature on exchange rates utilizes the concept of "efficiency" in the exchange markets. Efficiency in this context exists when the *current forward rate equals the* expected future spot rate. The key to this equality can be seen as follows: Suppose that the expected price of the French franc in 90 days [the expected future spot rate, $E(e)$] is $0.18 per franc and the current forward rate on francs, e_{fwd}, is $0.16 per franc. In this situation, a speculator will buy francs on the forward market at $0.16 per franc at the present time since the speculator anticipates that, in 90 days, the francs can be sold for $0.18 per franc. Clearly this will put upward pressure on the current forward rate of the franc until an equilibrium is reached at which $E(e)$ equals e_{fwd} (ignoring transaction costs). Similarly, if the expected future spot rate is less than the current forward rate, speculators will sell the francs forward since they anticipate that francs can be bought in the future (to cover the forward sale obligation) at less than the forward price to be received. This sale of forward francs drive e_{fwd} down until it eventually is equal to $E(e)$. Speculative activity thus ensures that $E(e) = e_{fwd}$. If $E(e)$ is equal to e_{fwd} in practice—an extremely difficult hypothesis to test because of the empirical problem of ascertaining expectations—the exchange market is said to be an **efficient exchange market.** This term means that there are no unexploited profit opportunities.

The implications of this discussion for expression [23] are straightforward. That expression was

$$i_d = i_f + (e_{fwd} - e)/e$$

which can now be rewritten through substitution of $E(e)$ for e_{fwd} (since the two terms are equal to each other) as

$$i_d = i_f + [E(e) - e]/e$$

But $[E(e) - e]/e$ is simply the expected percentage change in the current e. Hence, $[E(e) - e]/e = xa$. Through further substitution we obtain

$$i_d = i_f + xa$$

which is expression [22] or expression [16] (without the risk premium), or uncovered interest parity. Thus, with an efficient market, covered and uncovered parity both hold, or, alternatively, the expected appreciation of the foreign currency is equal to the forward premium on the foreign currency.

Let us return now to overshooting, using [23]. Suppose that beginning at the equilibrium position of [23], the domestic monetary authorities now increase the home money supply. Assuming little slack in the economy, the increase in the money supply causes individuals to expect that the home price level will rise. Since the higher prices will produce the expectation of an incipient BOP deficit, this means that market participants expect e to rise along with the price level. But the new expected spot rate, $E(e)$, will generate (as we have just seen) a new forward rate equal to it, since $E(e)$ must be the same as e_{fwd}. The result is that, in [23], the term $[e_{fwd} - e]/e$ will increase.

But wait a minute! In expression [23], i_d is equal to $i_f + (e_{fwd} - e)/e$, but we have just increased the right-hand side at the same time that we have *decreased* the left-hand side. The left-hand side (i_d) decreased because the increased home money supply has depressed the domestic interest rate. How is covered interest parity able to be maintained? The answer is that the two sides of the equation are made equal again by a rise in e, the current exchange rate. In fact, e must rise by *more* than e_{fwd} in order to maintain interest arbitrage equilibrium. If this adjustment in e did not occur, $i_f + (e_{fwd} - e)/e$ would be greater than i_d and interest arbitragers would have an incentive to send funds overseas by purchasing spot foreign exchange and simultaneously selling forward foreign exchange. Thus, after the increase in the money supply, interest arbitragers bid up e sufficiently so that the equilibrium in [23] is reestablished.

In this analysis, Melvin, like Dornbusch, hypothesizes that the prices of goods adjust slowly relative to the speed of adjustment in the exchange markets. When the price level finally does start to rise after the reestablishment of equilibrium in expression [23], there is an excess demand for money in the home country (due to the higher price level), and i_d therefore begins to rise. When i_d rises, there is an inflow of funds, so the home currency begins to appreciate. When prices have eventually adjusted to their new equilibrium level, the system settles down. The domestic currency has ultimately depreciated from its original level (that is, e has risen) because of the increase in the money supply, but notice that the exchange rate adjustment (an overall depreciation) was accomplished by an initial larger depreciation that was then followed by an appreciation. Hence, the exchange rate overshot its new long-run equilibrium position, then returned to that position.

This concludes our discussion of the phenomenon of overshooting. Many models have been developed to explain this phenomenon, and they have emerged in response to exchange rate behavior among the industrialized countries since 1973. As well as emphasizing stock equilibrium positions and adjustments, differential speeds of adjustment in different markets, and expectations, this literature has incorporated other influences such as "speculative bubbles," the role of surprising "news," and policy "reaction functions" on the part of the monetary authorities. While we do not go further in our development of overshooting, it should be clear that the complexity of the real world means that exchange rates do not always move smoothly and directly from one long-run equilibrium position to another.

CONCEPT CHECK

1. Why can the existence of a risk premium mean that $(i_f + xa)$ can exceed i_d in equilibrium?
2. In the portfolio balance model, why does a rise in domestic wealth lead to an appreciation of the home currency?
3. What will happen to the value of a country's currency in the foreign exchange markets if

the country's citizens suddenly revise upward their expectations of the home inflation rate? Why?
4. In the Dornbusch overshooting model, how is it possible that a country's currency can be appreciating at the same time that its price level is rising relative to the price level in other countries?

SUMMARY

The monetary approach to the balance of payments interprets a country's BOP deficits or surpluses (with fixed exchange rates) and currency depreciations or appreciations (with flexible exchange rates) as the results of a disequilibrium between the country's supply of and demand for money. If there is an excess supply of money, then a BOP deficit (or home currency depreciation) will occur during the process of moving to equilibrium. Similarly, an excess demand for money generates a BOP surplus (or home currency appreciation). The approach enables the analyst to make predictions concerning the impact on the external sector of changes in such economic variables as price levels, levels of real income, and interest rates. Some empirical tests of the monetary approach have been successful.

The portfolio balance approach goes further than the monetary approach in that it incorporates expectations, other assets besides money, and a risk premium because home and foreign financial assets are imperfect substitutes. Investors hold an equilibrium portfolio of the various assets, and changes in

economic variables and conditions affect the composition and size of the desired portfolios. Recognizing that asset markets across industrialized countries are well (though not perfectly) integrated, the conclusion emerges that changes in absolute and relative demands and supplies of assets will have impacts on interest rates and exchange rates. A particular feature that has attracted widespread attention is the conclusion that exchange rate "overshooting" can occur.

In overview of the monetary and portfolio balance approaches, their objective is to explain the behavior of the external sector in an environment where countries are closely interrelated and where exchange rates change frequently and sizably (such as among major industrialized countries since 1973). They focus not on the current account but on the asset exchanges (capital account) that heavily influence exchange rates today (especially in the short run). With these approaches in mind, we turn next to other features of the exchange market, including considerations of the current account.

KEY TERMS

asset stock equilibrium
demand for money
domestic reserves
efficient exchange market
exchange rate overshooting
incipient BOP deficit

incipient BOP surplus
international reserves
monetary approach to the balance
    of payments
monetary approach to the
    exchange rate

monetary base
money multiplier
portfolio balance (asset market)
    approach
rational expectations
transactions demand for money

QUESTIONS AND PROBLEMS

1. Suppose that there is an increase in national income in a country. Under a fixed exchange rate system, according to the monetary approach, will the country's balance of payments move toward surplus or toward deficit? Why? How would you modify your explanation (though not your conclusion) if you were using the portfolio balance approach in a fixed exchange rate context?

2. "A higher price level will increase the demand for money, but expectations of a rise in the price level will reduce the demand for money." Is this statement true or false according to the monetary approach? Why?

3. In the simple framework where $M_s = kPY$, suppose that k increases because of a change in the institutions of payment (e.g., people get paid larger amounts on a less frequent basis). What effect will this institutional change have on the country's exchange rate in a flexible exchange rate system? Explain.

4. Why is relative purchasing power parity (PPP) more likely to hold in a hyperinflationary period than in a more "normal" period of price behavior?

5. Dornbusch has concluded that there is "little doubt that the monetary approach . . . is an unsatisfactory theory of exchange rate determination." Do you agree? Why or why not?

6. In the portfolio balance model, what impact, other things equal, will a foreign government's budget deficit financed by issuing bonds have on the home country's currency value and why? (Assume a flexible exchange rate.)

7. In the portfolio balance model, what impact will a rise in i_d have on the value of the domestic currency with a flexible exchange rate? Why? Why would this *not* be the result in the monetary approach?

8. "An increase in a country's money supply can result in a depreciation of the country's currency that 'overshoots' its long-run equilibrium level." Defend this statement.

9. What reasons can you suggest to support the standard assumption that asset markets adjust more rapidly to a disequilibrium situation than do goods markets?

10. Why is $i_f + xa$ equal to $i_f + (e_{fwd} - e)/e$ in an efficient exchange market (with no risk premium)?

11. In your view, what are the strengths of the portfolio balance or asset market approach as an explanation of exchange rate determination? What are the weaknesses of the approach?

⊠ **APPENDIX**   THE MEESE/ROGOFF FORECASTS OF EXCHANGE RATES

Richard Meese (1990) and Meese and Kenneth Rogoff (1983) have attempted to determine the forecasting value of a standard asset market model. In particular, the following general exchange rate equation was employed (see Meese 1990, p. 124):

$$e = a + b(m - m^*) + c(y - y^*) + d(i - i^*) + f(p - p^*) + g(tb - tb^*) \qquad [24]$$

where: e = exchange rate (units of home currency per unit of foreign currency)
$m\ (m^*)$ = home (foreign) money supply
$y\ (y^*)$ = home (foreign) country industrial production
$i\ (i^*)$ = home (foreign) interest rate
$p\ (p^*)$ = home (foreign) price level
$tb\ (tb^*)$ = home (foreign) country cumulated trade balances (This represents the notion that trade surpluses increase a country's wealth.)

All variables are expressed as natural logarithms except for $i, i^*, tb,$ and tb^*.

TABLE 3   **Root Mean Squared Errors of Exchange Rate Forecasts,
November 1976–June 1981**

Exchange Rate	Horizon (months)	Random Walk	Forward Rate	Model 1*	Model 2[†]
Mark/dollar	1	3.22	3.20	3.65	3.50
	6	8.71	9.03	12.03	9.95
	12	12.98	12.60	18.87	15.69
Yen/dollar	1	3.68	3.72	4.11	4.20
	6	11.58	11.93	13.94	11.94
	12	18.31	18.95	20.41	19.20

*Model 1 is equation [24] with $g = 0$.

[†]Model 2 uses all the variables in equation [24].

Source: Richard Meese, "Currency Fluctuations in the Post-Bretton Woods Era," *Journal of Economic Perspectives* 4, no. 1 (Winter 1990), p. 125.

In general, we know the predicted signs from our discussion in this chapter. In the portfolio balance approach, b should be positive (more rapid growth in the home money supply leads to a depreciation of the home currency), c should be negative (a relative rise in home income or industrial production appreciates the home currency), and d also should be negative (a relative rise in the home interest rate generates a capital inflow into the home country and an appreciation of the home currency). In addition, f should be positive (greater inflation at home depreciates the home currency). Finally, our earlier discussion suggests that the sign of g is indeterminate (a relative increase in home wealth because of a trade surplus has an uncertain impact on the exchange rate because of differing effects in the money and bond markets).

Meese and Rogoff (1983) initially estimated the coefficients with monthly data for the period March 1973 (when industrial countries' exchange rates began floating) through November 1976. They were not interested in the estimated coefficients per se, however, but rather in the forecasting ability of the equation with respect to exchange rates. To ascertain this forecasting ability, Meese and Rogoff used the estimated coefficients (a, b, c, d, f, g) with actual data on the independent variables from November 1976 through June 1981 to see if the equation did a decent job of predicting the actual exchange rates that did in fact exist during that 1976–1981 period. The errors of the portfolio balance equation's predicted exchange rates from the actual exchange rates were then compared to the errors of two alternatives: (1) a random walk—meaning that the predicted exchange rate next period simply differs from this period's rate by a random amount, which implies that the average expected change of the exchange rate is zero, and (2) the forward rate—meaning that the spot exchange rate next period is simply predicted to be the forward rate this period for next period's currency.

The results of this exercise were very disappointing from the perspective of the forecasting ability of the portfolio balance model. The criterion used to judge the success of prediction was a term called the *root mean squared error* (RMSE), which you need not worry about per se, but it is the average of the squared forecast errors for each prediction horizon. The lower the RMSE, the better the prediction. The results are given in Table 3 for the (natural logarithms of the) mark/dollar and yen/dollar exchange rates, with time horizons of 1, 6, and 12 months ahead.

To understand this table, consider the mark/dollar forecasts for 6 months ahead during each of the 56 months in the November 1976–June 1981 period. The table shows that a random walk forecast had an RMSE from the actual exchange rates of 8.71. (The absolute size of the RMSE is not important for our purposes, but only the relative size.) Using the forward rate produced an RMSE of 9.03. Using model (1), that is, equation [24] above without the trade balance terms, produced an RMSE of 12.03, and using all of equation [24] produced an RMSE of 9.95. Thus, for the six-month mark/dollar rate, a random walk was the best predictor (8.71), the forward rate was second-best (9.03), model 2 was third-best (9.95), and model 1 was the worst predictor (12.03). Indeed, for the mark/dollar rate and the yen/dollar rate, neither of the two asset market models was *ever* the best predictor (or even second-best). Of the six instances, the random walk was best in four cases and the forward rate in the remaining two cases. (Note, however, that forecasting ability is better for shorter time horizons—the RMSEs were uniformly lower for one-month predictions and uniformly higher for twelve-month predictions than for the six-month period.) Clearly, these results are hardly supportive of the asset market approach.

CHAPTER 6

PRICE ADJUSTMENTS AND BALANCE-OF-PAYMENTS DISEQUILIBRIUM

INTRODUCTION

Given the working knowledge we have of the basics of the foreign exchange market and the nature of asset adjustment in the capital account of the balance of payments, we next turn to an examination of the manner in which changes in the exchange rate trigger changes in the current account. We will first examine the nature of the response of traded goods and services to changes in the price of foreign exchange under a system of flexible exchange rates and the impact that these responses have on the current account balance. Particular attention will be paid to describing the market conditions which are necessary for current account imbalances to be corrected by changes in the exchange rate. In recent years, depreciation of a country's currency has not always been immediately accompanied by a reduction in its current account deficits, leaving the impression that the foreign exchange market may be unstable. We therefore examine this issue from both a short-run and a longer-run perspective under flexible exchange rates. The discussion of flexible-rate adjustment is followed by an analysis of the price adjustment process when the exchange rate is fixed or not allowed to move outside certain limits.

This chapter should enable you to better grasp how changes in the foreign sector trigger short-run and medium-term price adjustments. It will help you to understand the difficulties of carrying out economic policy in the open economy when changes in the exchange rate and prices must be taken into account. Economic policy itself is the focus of later chapters.

THE PRICE ADJUSTMENT PROCESS AND THE CURRENT ACCOUNT UNDER A FLEXIBLE-RATE SYSTEM

In this section we examine the manner in which changes in the exchange rate affect the movement of goods and services between countries, that is, the nature of the current account. In the chapter "The Foreign Exchange Market," that market was presented in terms of market components describing the current account and the capital account. The demand for foreign exchange needed to purchase goods and services with respect to different exchange rates was graphed in a "normal" downward-sloping manner, and the supply of foreign exchange earned from exports of goods and services at various exchange rates reflected the positive relationship associated with "normal" supply curves. In this normal market configuration, changes in the exchange rate triggered changes in expenditures between domestic and foreign goods consistent with well-known standard

139

market adjustments. For example, assuming a current account deficit, an increase in the exchange rate (depreciation of the home currency) causes foreign goods to become more expensive, leading consumers to reduce consumption of imports and increase consumption of domestic alternatives. At the same time, home exports become relatively cheaper to foreign buyers, causing them to switch expenditures from their own products to the cheaper imports. The **expenditure switching** reflected in both of these responses contributes to a reduction in the current account deficit. Underlying this adjustment is the assumption that consumers and producers respond quickly to changes in the exchange rate and that supply prices of traded goods do not change with the changes in expenditures in either country (infinitely elastic supply). In addition, any possible effects on income, the interest rate, the expected profit rate, or other factors are also ignored. The adjustment to changes in relative prices brought about by changes in the exchange rate is called the **elasticities approach** to adjustment in the foreign exchange market, or the **price adjustment mechanism** that follows upon changes in the exchange rate. However, since current account adjustments do not always appear to take place in the manner described above, it is important to take a closer look at this component of the foreign exchange market and its adjustments.

The Demand for Foreign Goods and Services and the Foreign Exchange Market

If we are to anticipate the impacts of changes in the foreign exchange rate on the current account balance more accurately, it is critical that we understand the basic forces underlying this market. To do this, we turn to the sources of demand and supply for a currency within the current account and examine the factors that influence them. As you recall from the chapters "The Balance-of-Payments Accounts" and "The Foreign Exchange Market," the current account–based demand for foreign currency results from the desire to purchase goods and services from another country and to make unilateral transfers. In a sense, the demand for foreign currency is a secondary or derived demand because the foreign currency is a means to acquiring something else.

Ignoring unilateral transfers, the demand for foreign currency in the current account is thus determined by the factors that drive the demand for real goods and services. The demand for real imports is influenced principally by the domestic price of any foreign good or service, the presence of any tariffs or subsidies, the price of domestic substitutes and/or complements, the level of domestic income, and tastes and preferences. The domestic price of the foreign good or service is of course the product of the price ex- pressed in foreign currency times the appropriate exchange rate (e.g., $P_{US\$} = P_{UK£} \times e_{\$/£}$). Since the demand for foreign currency by the home country is simply the supply of home currency to the foreign country, if one knows the demand for foreign exchange in each of two countries, the supply of foreign exchange to each country is also known.

To get a better feel for the nature of this unique relationship between a country's home demand for foreign currency (its consequent supply of domestic currency to the exchange market), consider the following hypothetical demands for foreign exchange in two countries, the United States and the United Kingdom (see Table 1). It is assumed that the demand for foreign exchange for acquiring goods and services responds to changes in the exchange rate because of its impact on the domestic price of foreign goods. The data in the table were constructed under the assumption that the supply prices of the traded goods are invariant with the quantity demanded [see column (3)]. In this example, the variation in the domestic price of the foreign good(s) is brought about by altering the exchange rate from $1.50/£ to $1.00/£ [column (1)]. When the U.K. pound becomes relatively cheaper (depreciates), the dollar price of the U.K. goods falls as shown in part (a) of Table 1. As this happens, the quantity demanded of the U.K. good rises due to normal income and substitution effects [column (5)]. Given the constant British price of the import good, the

TABLE 1   **The Demand for Imported Goods and Services and the Foreign Exchange Market**

(1)	(2)	(3)	(4)	(5)	(6)	(7)
(a) United States						
$e_{\$/£}$	$(e'_{£/\$})$	P_{UK}	(P_{US})	Q_{D-US}	$Q_{D£-US}$	$Q_{S\$-US}$
$1.50/£	(£0.67/$)	£10	($15.00)	100 units	£1,000	$1,500
$1.25/£	(£0.80/$)	£10	($12.50)	140 units	£1,400	$1,750
$1.00/£	(£1.00/$)	£10	($10.00)	180 units	£1,800	$1,800
(b) United Kingdom						
$(e'_{\$/£})$	$e_{£/\$}$	P_{US}	(P_{UK})	Q_{D-UK}	$Q_{D\$-UK}$	$Q_{S£-UK}$
($1.50/£)	£0.67/$	$20	(£13.33)	100 units	$2,000	£1,333
($1.25/£)	£0.80/$	$20	(£16.00)	80 units	$1,600	£1,280
($1.00/£)	£1.00/$	$20	(£20.00)	60 units	$1,200	£1,200

increase in U.S. quantity demanded of the U.K. good leads to an increase in the quantity demanded of pounds [column (6) of part (a)]. Hence, the quantity demanded of pounds varies inversely with the price of the pound, and a normal downward-sloping demand curve results. Changes in the exchange rate thus produce a movement along the demand curve for foreign exchange and a corresponding change in quantity demanded. The position of the demand curve, however, is determined by factors other than the exchange rate, and any change in these variables will cause the demand curve to shift. For example, an increase in income, an autonomous increase in domestic prices relative to foreign prices, and a shift in tastes and preferences toward the import good would all cause the demand curve for foreign exchange associated with goods and services to shift out.

Part (b) of Table 1 proceeds similarly with the U.K. demand for a U.S. good. The depreciation of the pound from $1.50/£ to $1.00/£ (i.e., the appreciation of the dollar from £0.67/$ to £1.00/$) causes the United Kingdom to reduce its quantity demanded of the U.S. good [column (5)]. The smaller quantity demanded of the U.S. good at the lower $/£ exchange rate results in a smaller quantity demanded of dollars [column (6)]. This demand for dollars is then converted into a supply of pounds in column (7) of part (b).

With the above information, we can now proceed to graph the foreign exchange market for the U.S. dollar and the U.K. pound. This will be done both from the U.S. perspective [Figure 1(a)] and from the U.K. perspective [Figure 1(b)]. The demand curve for pounds in the United States is found by plotting the quantity of pounds demanded against the various exchange rates from part (a) of Table 1. The supply of pounds available to the United States from the United Kingdom at the various exchange rates is found by plotting the first and last columns of part (b) for U.S. goods. The intersection of the two curves indicates the exchange rate that leaves the current account in balance. In this case, the equilibrium rate lies somewhere between $1.25 and $1.50 per pound.

A similar procedure is followed in presenting the foreign exchange market from the perspective of the United Kingdom. The demand for dollars [column (6) of Table 1, part (b)] is plotted against the appropriate exchange rate [column (2) of part (b)] to generate the expected downward-sloping curve. It is important to note that the price on the vertical axis is the inverse of the exchange rate in the earlier case, that is, £/$ rather than $/£. For the supply of dollars, we turn to the information on U.S. demand for U.K. products at different exchange rates. The quantity of dollars supplied from the United States [column (7) of Table 1, part (a)] at the various exchange rates is then plotted, and the intersection of the supply and demand curves again provides the equilibrium exchange rate. In this

FIGURE 1   **The Demand and Supply of Foreign Exchange Resulting from Trade in Goods and Services**

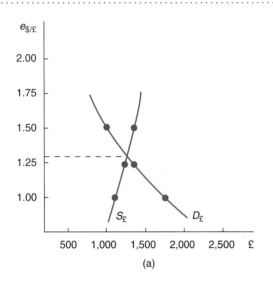

(a)

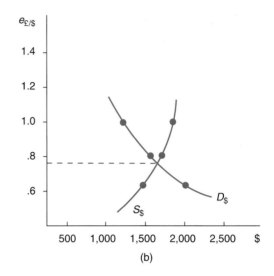

(b)

The market for foreign exchange that results from the demand for traded goods displayed in Table 1 is demonstrated in the two graphs. In panel (a), the market is presented from the vantage point of the United States. It shows the demand and supply of pounds that result from each country's demands for the other country's goods, at alternative dollar prices of the pound. In panel (b), the same demands are expressed in terms of the demand and the supply of dollars, at alternative pound prices of the dollar. The market equilibrium that results is the same, in that the $/£ price is the inverse of the £/$ exchange rate.

case, it lies somewhere between £0.67/$ and £0.80/$. (If we knew the equations for the demand curve and the supply curve we could solve for the exact equilibrium price.) It is important to note here that the equilibrium exchange rate is the same in both cases since the figures show two ways of viewing the same market. One price is the reciprocal of the other. If, for example, the equilibrium exchange rate is $1.38/£ from the U.S. perspective, it would be 1/($1.38/£) or £0.72/$ from the U.K. perspective. Thus, it makes no difference whether the foreign exchange market is presented in pounds or dollars, since the same equilibrium exchange rate results.

The market shown in Figure 1 is stable with respect to deviations of the exchange rate from equilibrium. Comparative-statics analysis also suggests that shifts in demand and supply will lead to new equilibria appropriate to the changing market condition. For example, an increase in U.S. income would increase the demand for foreign goods and, hence, the demand for foreign exchange. This would cause the demand curve for foreign exchange to shift to the right, creating a current account deficit and requiring an increase in the price of pounds (a depreciation of the dollar) to balance the current account [see Figure 2(a)]. A similar effect would result from an increase in the U.S. price level relative to the U.K. price level. However, in this instance both of the curves will shift. U.S. demand for pounds will rise as consumers shift from the now higher-priced U.S. products to British goods and services. At the same time, British demand for U.S. goods and services (and hence the supply of pounds) will fall as British consumers shift from the now more expensive U.S. goods and services to the relatively cheaper domestic products. The result again, of course, is the increase in the dollar cost of pounds [see Figure 2(b)] that is necessary to bring the current account into balance. Changes in expectations regarding future prices and exchange rates as well as changes in tastes and preferences would also be expected to shift the supply and demand curves for foreign exchange.

FIGURE 2   **Adjustment in the Foreign Exchange Market**

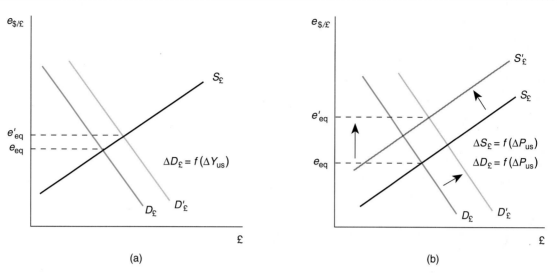

(a)   (b)

An increase in U.S. income increases the demand for U.K. goods and hence the demand for pounds as shown by the rightward shift in the demand curve in panel (a). This, of course, leads to a current account deficit at e_{eq}. Balance in the current account will be obtained only through depreciation of the dollar (i.e., a higher exchange rate). An increase in U.S. prices, on the other hand, leads to a shift in both the demand and the supply curve of pounds, as U.S. consumers demand more of the now cheaper U.K. imports and U.K. consumers reduce their demand for U.S. goods and services. The combined result of the reduced supply of pounds and the increased demand for pounds is an even greater current account deficit and hence an even larger depreciation of the dollar to again reach a current account balance, as indicated in panel (b).

It is important to reiterate here that the current account can be brought into balance in this "normal" market example if the dollar depreciates when the demand for pounds exceeds the supply of pounds and if the dollar appreciates when pound supply exceeds pound demand.

Market Stability and the Price Adjustment Mechanism

Up to this point, we have assumed that the foreign exchange market is characterized by normal downward-sloping demand curves and upward-sloping supply curves. This condition was important because it generated a market equilibrium that can be characterized as being stable with respect to price (exchange rate). **Market stability** occurs when the characteristics of supply and demand are such that any price deviation away from equilibrium sets in motion forces that move the market back toward equilibrium. With downward-sloping demand and upward-sloping supply curves, a price that is too low creates an excess demand, causing consumers to bid up the price until supply again equals demand and the excess demand is removed. Similarly, a price that is set too high creates an excess supply, causing producers to begin lowering price until supply again equals demand. Thus, the market is stable with respect to deviations of price away from equilibrium. Stability thus ensures that price increases (currency depreciation) will remove an excess demand for foreign exchange (current account deficit) and price decreases (currency appreciation) will remove an excess supply of foreign exchange (current account surplus).

If the price adjustment mechanism is to work, it is necessary that the demand and supply curves have the appropriate configuration. In Figure 3, three different market configurations are shown (for any good or service, not just for foreign exchange). In panel (a), the supply and demand curves produce an excess demand when price is too low and an excess supply when price is too high. The market is thus stable in the manner

FIGURE 3   **Market Stability**

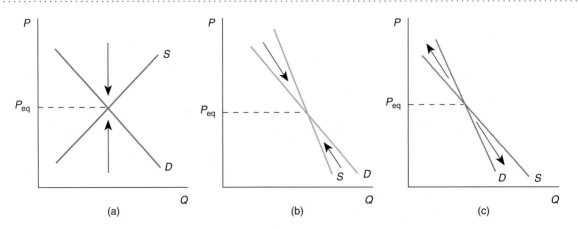

Panel (a) depicts a normal market with a downward-sloping demand curve and an upward-sloping supply curve. If price moves away from P_{eq}, forces of supply and demand are automatically set in motion to move price back to P_{eq}. Panel (b) demonstrates a market that is also stable with respect to price even though it has a downward-sloping supply curve. The fact that too low (high) a price still creates an excess demand (supply) means that market forces are automatically set in motion to return the market to equilibrium at P_{eq}. Panel (c), however, depicts an unstable market. If price is set too low (high), an excess supply (demand) occurs that leads to a further movement away from P_{eq}, not a movement back to equilibrium.

discussed above. In panel (b), the demand curve has the usual negative slope, but the supply curve is backward-sloping. However, the supply curve is steeper than the demand curve, with the result that there is still an excess demand when price is below the equilibrium price and an excess supply when price is above equilibrium. Thus, the market is also stable with respect to price. Finally, in panel (c) there is a third market configuration that is similar to (b) except that the backward-sloping supply curve is flatter than the demand curve. In this instance, a price below the equilibrium price leads to an excess supply, and a price above the equilibrium price leads to an excess demand. Since an excess demand leads to increases in price and an excess supply leads to decreases in price, any movement away from equilibrium sets in motion forces leading to further movements away from equilibrium, not movements back to equilibrium. Thus, this is an example of a market that is unstable with respect to price.

Returning to the foreign exchange market, can we expect that market to be "normal" as long as the demand for foreign goods and services is inversely related to price (that is, there is a downward-sloping demand curve)? To answer this question, consider the demand schedule in the United Kingdom for U.S. goods in Table 2. Note again that the price of U.K. imports rises [column (4)] to the British as the pound depreciates [columns

TABLE 2   **An Alternative U.K. Demand for Imported U.S. Goods**

UK'						
(1) $e'_{\$/£}$	*(2)* $e_{£/\$}$	*(3)* P_{US}	*(4)* (P_{UK})	*(5)* Q_{D-UK}	*(6)* $Q_{D\$-UK}$	*(7)* $Q_{S£-UK}$
($1.50/£)	£0.67/$	$20	(£13.33)	100 units	$2,000	£1,333
($1.25/£)	£0.80/$	$20	(£16.00)	85 units	$1,700	£1,360
($1.00/£)	£1.00/$	$20	(£20.00)	80 units	$1,600	£1,600

FIGURE 4   **The Foreign Exchange Market**

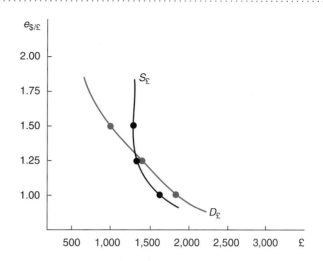

The alternative U.K. demand for imports of U.S. goods and services (see Table 2) produces a supply curve of pounds that is downward-sloping (or backward-sloping), not upward-sloping. However, since the demand curve is still flatter than the supply curve, the equilibrium remains stable with respect to changes in price (foreign exchange rate).

(1) and (2)] and that U.K. consumers behave in a "normal" fashion by demanding a smaller quantity of U.S. goods and hence fewer dollars [column (6)]. However, even though quantity demanded falls, British consumers end up supplying *more* pounds sterling for the imports they would be willing to buy [column (7)]. If we now reconstruct this portion of the foreign exchange market from the U.S. perspective using this new example (see Figure 4), we find that we have a market characterized by a backward-sloping supply curve of foreign exchange (pounds). However, since the supply curve is steeper than the demand curve, the market is still stable with respect to deviations in price. This example indicates that a backward-sloping supply curve of foreign exchange can occur even if foreign demand for imports is normal. Whether it produces a stable or an unstable market depends on the slopes of both the supply and the demand curves for foreign exchange. More about this later.

Explaining the backward-sloping supply curve of foreign exchange

Let us examine the circumstances that produced the backward-sloping supply curve of foreign exchange. If we return to the numerical examples in Tables 1 and 2 for the United Kingdom, note that the change in the exchange rate produced two effects. First, as the dollar became more expensive, more pounds sterling were required to buy each given unit of imports from the United States; at the same time, however, the number of units was falling because of the increase in price in terms of pounds. Whether the total quantity supplied of pounds increased or decreased with the change in the exchange rate depended on the relative size of these two effects.

The nature of this relationship can be measured by using the familiar concept of price elasticity of demand. As you recall from microeconomics, this elasticity is simply the ratio of the percentage change in quantity demanded to the percentage change in price. Since we are examining rather large changes in both price and quantity and not small marginal changes in the neighborhood of a given price and quantity, it is appropriate to use an arc elasticity measure rather than a point elasticity estimate. This is done by using the means of the two quantity and price points over which the change in quantity and price is being examined. The arc elasticity is then defined as follows:

$$\eta_{arc} = \frac{\Delta Q/[Q_1 + Q_2)/2]}{\Delta P/[(P_1 + P_2)/2]}$$

In the first numerical example in part (b) of Table 1, as the U.K. price increased from £13.33/unit to £16/unit [column (4)], the quantity demanded fell from 100 units to 80 units [column (5)]. The arc elasticity of demand for this change in price is equal to (80 − 100)/[(100 + 80)/2] divided by (16.00 − 13.33)/[(13.33 + 16.00)/2], which equals (−).222/.182 = (−) 1.22. Since the (absolute) value of the elasticity is greater than 1.0, demand is said to be elastic. If a similar calculation were carried out for the second change in the exchange rate (the increase in price from £16/unit to £20/unit), the arc elasticity is 1.29, which also is greater than 1.0 and hence elastic. The results confirm what we know about elastic demand. An increase in price leads to a decline in total expenditures since the percentage change in quantity demanded is greater than the percentage change in the price. Thus, whenever the partner country elasticity of demand for home country products is elastic, the supply curve of foreign exchange will be upward-sloping.

What happened in the case in Table 2 to make the supply curve of foreign exchange backward-sloping? A quick calculation of the elasticity of demand for imports sheds some light on this question. As price rose from £13.33 to £16/unit, the quantity demanded fell from 100 units to 85 units. The arc elasticity over this range is equal to (−).162/.182 or (−).89, which is less in absolute value than 1.0. Hence, demand for imports is inelastic in this range. After the price increase from £16 to £20/unit, quantity demanded fell from 85 units to 80 units. This indicates an elasticity of demand of (−).061/.222 = (−).275, which again is less in absolute value than 1.0 and is inelastic. The inelastic demand means that at the higher import price in pounds, U.K. consumers are willing to supply more pounds (see the last column of Table 2). The mystery of the backward-sloping supply curve of foreign exchange is now solved. If foreign demand for home goods is inelastic, the supply curve of foreign exchange is backward-sloping (that is, negatively sloped). If demand is elastic, the supply of foreign exchange will be upward-sloping.

The link between the demand curve for imported goods and services and the supply curve of foreign exchange

This link between the demand curve for imported goods and services and the supply curve of foreign exchange can now be discussed in a general way. Recall that with a linear demand curve, elasticity varies as we move from high prices to low prices. More specifically, at prices above the midpoint of the demand curve, demand is elastic; at prices below the midpoint, demand is inelastic; and at the midpoint, demand is unitary elastic. Since the U.S. price of the U.K. import good is being held constant, the change in price in our calculations is due entirely to changes in the exchange rate. In this case, the demand for dollars with respect to changes in the exchange rate has the same elasticity value as does the U.K. demand for imports with respect to U.K. domestic price of imports over the same range. Consider the U.K. demand curve for U.S. dollars in Figure 5(a). Corresponding to each range is a segment of the supply curve of pounds sterling to the United States [Figure 5(b)]. The elastic range of the U.K. demand curve for dollars corresponds to the upward-sloping portion of the supply curve of pounds. Since the price of foreign exchange from the U.S. perspective is the inverse of the price from the U.K. perspective ($/£ versus £/$), range *a* of high prices in the United Kingdom corresponds to low prices of foreign exchange in the United States. Consequently, as the foreign exchange rate falls in terms of £/$, it is rising in terms of $/£. Thus, as the exchange rate in £/$ is falling toward *b*, the point of unitary elasticity, it is rising toward *b* in $/£. At points below *b*, demand for dollars is inelastic and, hence, the supply of pounds sterling

FIGURE 5   **Elasticity of Demand and the Supply Curve of Foreign Exchange**

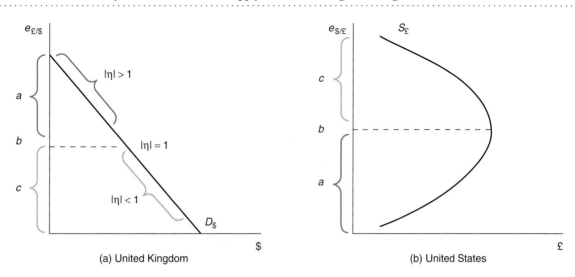

(a) United Kingdom   (b) United States

The elastic range of the foreign (U.K.) demand for home country (U.S.) goods and services exports in panel (a) generates an upward-sloping supply curve of pounds in panel (b). In like fashion, the inelastic segment of the U.K. demand curve for imports of goods and services from the United States generates a backward-sloping supply curve of pounds to the United States. Thus, a country facing an inelastic foreign demand for its exports will experience a backward-sloping supply curve of foreign exchange. An overall elastic demand for exports will, on the other hand, produce the normal upward-sloping supply curve of foreign exchange.

is backward-sloping (range c). While these ranges hold specifically only for linear demand curves, the general relationship between import demand elasticity and the supply of foreign exchange holds. Inelastic import demand produces a backward-sloping supply curve of foreign exchange to the partner country, and elastic demand produces a normal, upward-sloping supply curve.

Since a backward-sloping supply of foreign exchange will result whenever the partner demand for imports is inelastic, under what conditions will an unstable foreign exchange market result? In other words, will a depreciation of the home currency lead to a decrease in the excess demand for foreign exchange? If it does (does not), the exchange market is stable (unstable). Ignoring unilateral transfers and capital flows, the problem is to assess the change in the current account balance that results when there is a change in the exchange rate.[1] For a basic demonstration of the problem, consider the price and quantity adjustments in Figure 6. Panel (a) shows the demand and supply schedules for the home country's imports, assuming that the price of the partner's goods and services is constant. Panel (b) shows the demand and supply schedules for home country exports (partner country imports) again assuming a constant price of the goods and services. The prices in both cases are expressed in home currency ($). The initial prices are p_1 and p'_1, with corresponding quantities q_1 and q'_1. Assume that there is a depreciation of the dollar. When this happens, S_M shifts vertically upward to S'_M in panel (a), and D_X shifts to D'_X in panel (b). Since the domestic price of imports has gone up, the home country demands a smaller quantity. In the partner country, the *domestic* price of its imports has gone down

. . . .

[1]Since instability occurs whenever the demand curve is steeper than the (backward-sloping) supply curve, the condition for stability must necessarily take the characteristics of both curves into account. For a simple derivation of the stability condition, see Dennis R. Appleyard and Alfred J. Field, Jr., (1986).

FIGURE 6   **Market Effects of a Change in the Foreign Exchange Rate**

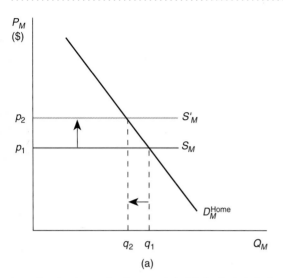
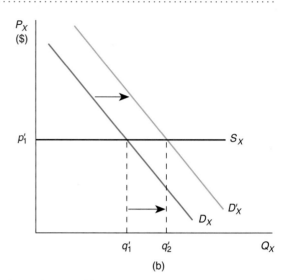

(a)   (b)

Assuming that the supply of exports is infinitely elastic in both countries (i.e., the supply curve of imports and the supply curve of exports in the home country are horizontal), a depreciation of the home currency leads to (1) an upward shift in the supply curve of imports from S_M to S'_M (due to the higher domestic price of imports in the home currency) and (2) a rightward shift in the demand for exports from D_X to D'_X (since the foreign currency price of home country exports has fallen relatively). The impact of the depreciation on the value of imports depends on the elasticity of the demand for imports. Given that import outlays before the depreciation were $p_1 q_1$ and after the depreciation are $p_2 q_2$, the depreciation reduces import outlays only if import demand is elastic. If demand is inelastic, the value of import outlays in dollar terms actually rises. The value of export receipts increases unambiguously since a larger quantity q'_2 than the original q'_1 is purchased at a constant-dollar price. The ultimate impact of depreciation on the current account balance thus depends on the sum of these two effects, and can be positive or negative depending on the elasticity of demand in each country for the other country's goods and services.

even though the home country export price has remained constant (since the partner country currency has appreciated), which causes its demand curve to shift to the right. This shift reflects the fact that foreigners are prepared to buy more home country goods and services at each dollar price.

Exchange market stability and the Marshall-Lerner condition

The ultimate impact on the current account balance depends on the changes in expenditures associated with the change in the exchange rate. If home country demand is elastic, then the current account balance unambiguously improves with depreciation, since the increase in domestic price of imports leads to a reduction in total expenditures on imports and the reduced price of exports to foreigners leads to an increase in their expenditures on home country exports. Similarly, the current account balance improves if home country demand is unit-elastic because total expenditures on imports will be unchanged and foreign expenditures on home country exports will increase. If domestic demand is inelastic, however, the impact of depreciation is ambiguous. In this instance, the increase in the price of foreign goods and services leads to an increase in total expenditures for imports, which may or may not be offset by the increased expenditures by the partner country on exports. As long as the increase in foreign expenditures more than offsets the increased domestic expenditures on imports, the current account balance will improve with depreciation and hence the foreign exchange market will be stable. If, however, the increase in domestic expenditures on imports is greater than the increase in expenditures on home country exports, the current account balance will worsen with depreciation and the foreign exchange market will be unstable.

As it turns out, the unstable result will not occur as long as the sum of the absolute values of the home country price elasticity of demand for imports, η_{Dm}, and the price

FIGURE 7   **Import Market Response to Changes in the Foreign Exchange Rate When Foreign Supply Is Not Infinitely Elastic**

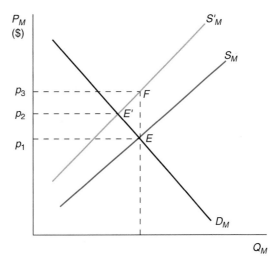

If foreign supply of traded goods is not infinitely elastic, the supply curve slopes upward to the right. Depreciation of the home currency will thus lead to an upward shift in the curve equal to the percentage change in the exchange rate. S'_M thus lies above S_M by a constant percentage of the price and not by a fixed amount (i.e., S'_M will diverge from S_M). The resulting change in the market price of imports will reflect both the elasticity of demand *and* the elasticity of supply of the traded goods and will be less than the percentage change in the exchange rate. This is demonstrated above where the new equilibrium price p_2 reflects a smaller increase in domestic price (relative to p_1) compared to the impact of the depreciation of the currency *EF*.

elasticity of demand for home country exports (partner country imports), η_{Dx}, is greater than 1.0 in the case of initial balanced trade, that is, $|\eta_{Dm}| + |\eta_{Dx}| > 1$. In the case of unbalanced trade (expressed in units of home currency), the condition becomes

$$\frac{X}{M} \cdot |\eta_{Dx}| + |\eta_{Dm}| > 1$$

where X and M refer to total expenditures on exports and imports, respectively. This general condition for exchange market stability is referred to as the **Marshall-Lerner condition.**[2]

In the situation just discussed, the supply curves of imports and exports were horizontal, or "infinitely elastic." If we examine the effect of the exchange rate change on the current account balance when supply curves take their normal shape, the analysis is more complicated than in the previous case. In Figure 7, depreciation of the dollar shifts the supply curve S_M vertically upward by the percentage of the depreciation to S'_M. Thus, for example, the price p_3 associated with point F is 10 percent higher than price p_1 (associated with the point E) if the depreciation of the dollar is 10 percent. Such a 10 percent vertical shift occurs everywhere along S_M. Price p_3 would in fact have been the new equilibrium price if the S_M schedule had been horizontal, as in Figure 6(a). However, in Figure 7, the final price p_2 is lower than p_3. The final change in import outlays due to

....
[2]For a mathematical derivation of this result, see the appendix at the end of this chapter. We are discussing the balance in terms of the home currency because BOP accounts are kept in the home currency. The balanced-trade result is the same if examined in terms of foreign currency, but the unbalanced condition is then

$$|\eta_{Dx}| + \frac{M}{X}|\eta_{Dm}| > 1$$

✸ CASE STUDY 1   ESTIMATES OF IMPORT AND EXPORT DEMAND ELASTICITIES

Jaime Marquez (1990) estimated demand elasticities in international trade for a number of countries. Using quarterly data extending from the first quarter of 1973 through the second quarter of 1985, he calculated both bilateral elasticities for trade between any two given trading partners and the implied multilateral elasticities of a given country with all trading partners. The multilateral price elasticity results that he accorded the most weight are listed in Table 3.

In the context of the Marshall-Lerner condition, these estimates suggest that stability obtains as a general rule. The sum of the absolute values of the import and export demand elasticities exceeds 1.0 in all cases except that of the United Kingdom. Further, since these are quarterly (short-run) estimates, it is clear that the long run is even more likely to exhibit stability, since long-run elasticities are generally thought to be higher than short-run elasticities.

TABLE 3   **Estimated Price Elasticities of Demand for Imports and Exports (quarterly, 1973:I–1985:II)**

Country or Unit	Import Price Elasticity	Export Price Elasticity	Sum of Import and Export Elasticities
Canada	−1.02	−0.83	−1.85
Germany	−0.60	−0.66	−1.26
Japan	−0.93	−0.93	−1.86
United Kingdom	−0.47	−0.44	−0.91
United States	−0.92	−0.99	−1.91
Other developed countries	−0.49	−0.83	−1.32
Developing countries	−0.81	−0.63	−1.44
OPEC	−1.14	−0.57	−1.71

Source: Jaime Marquez, "Bilateral Trade Elasticities," *Review of Economics and Statistics* 72, no. 1 (February 1990), pp. 75–76.   ✸

the depreciation thus involves looking at not only the elasticity of D_M but also the elasticity of S'_M. These elasticities in turn reflect the elasticities involved in the underlying conditions of consumption and production in both trading countries. We do not examine these underlying elasticities in this chapter, but clearly matters become more complex.

A similar analysis would apply to the export side. In a diagram for the export case (not shown), a depreciation of the home currency would shift D_X to the right along an *upward-sloping* S_X curve, and the export good's price would rise [whereas it does not in Figure 6(b)]. For market stability in cases of upward-sloping S_M and S_X curves, the Marshall-Lerner condition becomes more complicated. An extension for these cases is, however, beyond the scope of this text.[3]

Estimating the actual elasticities in international trade is a difficult job given the complex and changing nature of trade. Considerable controversy has existed over estimates of these elasticities, particularly with respect to the econometrics employed. Although some statistical results suggest that these elasticities are quite low, the current general consensus appears to be that market responses to price changes are sufficiently large to generate a stable foreign exchange market (see Case Study 1). In addition, since long-run elasticities are higher (in absolute value) than short-run elasticities, the time frame can be important. The short-run versus long-run nature of elasticities will be discussed in the next section.

. . . .

[3]In the case of upward-sloping supply curves, it can be shown through more advanced treatments (and can also be reasoned out through graphs) that the simple Marshall-Lerner condition is a sufficient condition but no longer a necessary condition for depreciation to improve the current account balance. In other words, the absolute demand elasticities can sum to < 1 and the balance can still improve.

CONCEPT CHECK

1. What is the difference between a stable market equilibrium and an unstable equilibrium? Will a downward-sloping supply curve always produce market instability? Why or why not?
2. What condition is required for stability in the foreign exchange market if both domestic

and foreign supplies of traded goods are infinitely elastic?
3. How does the analysis of foreign exchange market stability relate to the impact of depreciation on the current account balance?

The Price Adjustment Process: Short Run vs. Long Run

In the last section, we established that depreciating the currency would reduce current account deficits and appreciating the currency would reduce current account surpluses as long as the sum of the absolute values of the foreign and domestic elasticities of demand for imports was greater than 1.0 (the Marshall-Lerner condition for market stability). In this situation, the changes in the exchange rate bring about appropriate switches in expenditures between domestic and foreign goods. Assuming a current account deficit, an increase in the exchange rate (depreciation of the home currency) causes foreign goods to become more expensive, leading consumers to reduce consumption of imports and increase consumption of domestic alternatives. At the same time, home exports become relatively cheaper to foreign buyers, causing them to switch expenditures from their own products to the cheaper imports. It was generally assumed in this analysis that consumers and producers responded quickly and that supply prices did not change with the switch in expenditures in either country (infinitely elastic supply). Any possible effects on income, the interest rate, the expected profit rate, or other variables were also ignored. In this instance, the Marshall-Lerner condition is sufficient to bring about the desired change in expenditures.

As suggested earlier, short-run elasticities of supply and demand tend to be smaller (in absolute values) than long-run elasticities. On the demand side, consumers do not often adjust immediately to changes in relative prices. Since it may take time for consumers to alter consumption plans or product commitments, they may be slow to react to changes in the exchange rate. In many cases, contracts may already have been signed that commit importers to a certain volume of imports at the previous exchange rate. Under certain scenarios, the volume of imports may even rise if importers view the initial change in the exchange rate as the first of several rises and purchase more now to avoid an even higher domestic price in the future. It is not surprising, then, to see the quantity of imports demanded and hence (other things equal) the amount of foreign exchange needed remain relatively constant in the short run even though the domestic currency is depreciating (i.e., the short-run demand for foreign exchange is vertical). With the passage of time, the demand curve for foreign exchange will more closely approximate the long-run demand curve as more normal quantity responses occur.

On the supply side of foreign exchange, the supply of exports may not increase immediately in response to depreciation simply due to the decision-making lags involved. These lags include (*a*) a recognition lag with respect to the change in the exchange rate, (*b*) a decision-making lag, (*c*) a production/inventory replacement lag, and (*d*) a delivery lag. The supply of exports also may not rise if producers choose to raise the domestic price in response to the increased foreign demand and to increase short-term profit margins at the expense of increased sales. (See Case Study 2 for an indication of how traded goods prices have responded to changes in the exchange rate in the case of the United States.) If the quantity of exports does not rise in the short run with depreciation of the currency, then the short-run supply curve of foreign exchange will be backward-sloping as long as domestic prices remain constant or do not increase as fast as the exchange rate. However, with the passage of time, the supply curve will tend to take on the characteristics of the long-run response.

Continued on page 154

❈ CASE STUDY 2   U.S. AND FOREIGN EXPORTERS' PRICE/COST RATIOS, "PASS-THROUGH," AND THE EXCHANGE RATE

If exporters base their prices on costs and do not adjust prices for changes in the exchange rate, one would not likely observe price/cost ratios moving in sympathy with changes in the exchange rate. In such a situation, **complete exchange rate pass-through** is said to occur, meaning that the exchange rate change is allowed to register its full impact on the foreign consumer price of the good. If, on the other hand, exporters adjust sales prices to offset fully changes in the exchange rate to maintain a given sales quantity, then the exchange rate change is not allowed to have an impact on the foreign consumer price of the good. In this case, movements in the exchange rate will be correlated with movements in the price/cost ratio of exporters. More specifically, U.S. exporters would increase domestic prices when the dollar depreciates (thereby increasing their price/cost ratios) and decrease them when the dollar appreciates (decreasing price/cost ratios) in order to keep prices to foreign buyers relatively constant. In the case of foreign goods sold to the United States, without complete pass-through, foreign *export* prices to the United States would rise when the dollar appreciates (thereby increasing for-

eign price/cost ratios) and decline when the dollar depreciates (decreasing foreign price/cost ratios), thus keeping dollar *import* prices of U.S. imports relatively constant.

The chart below indicates that U.S. exporters' price/cost ratios did not appear to be correlated with movements in the exchange rate over the period in question (from 1975 to 1987). Foreign price/cost ratios did, however, appear to move in conjunction with changes in the exchange rate. The latter price adjustments certainly absorbed part of the effect of the exchange rate changes and inhibited the working of the price adjustment mechanism. (Some of the movements in the chart may of course merely reflect deficiencies in the proxy variables being used to measure the price/cost ratios.) While less than complete "pass-through" of the price effect of a change in the foreign exchange rate can also be expected for other reasons (for example, market supply and demand conditions in periods of reduced demand, barriers to trade, changes in the pattern of trade), the foreign price/cost ratio behavior provides a partial explanation of why U.S. imports may not respond as strongly as expected to changes in the value of the dollar.

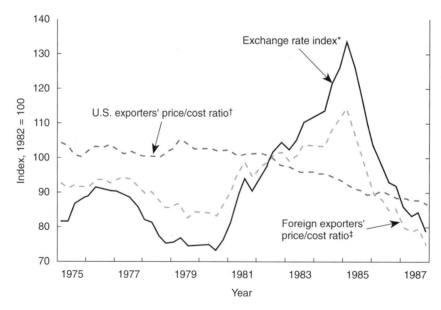

*Multilateral trade-weighted value of the dollar against the currencies of 10 industrialized countries.

†Ratio of the implicit price deflator for nonagricultural exports to the U.S. producer price index for finished goods.

‡Ratio of the implicit price deflator for nonpetroleum imports to a trade-weighted wholesale price index for eight industrial countries excluding the United States divided by the exchange rate index.

Note: Data for fourth quarter 1987 were preliminary.

Source: *Economic Report of the President*, February 1988 (Washington, DC: U.S. Government Printing Office, 1988), pp. 120–22.

✹ CASE STUDY 2 (CONTINUED)

Recent work by Jiawen Yang (1997) of George Washington University has confirmed that complete pass-through of exchange rate changes does not generally occur in the case of foreign exports to the United States. Yang used a sample of imports in 87 U.S. manufacturing industries to calculate the **elasticity of exchange rate pass-through** during the December 1980–December 1991 period. This elasticity on an industry basis is the percentage change in the import price index for a good (in dollars) divided by the percentage change in the (nominal effective) exchange rate. If there is complete pass-through of an exchange rate change into import prices, the elasticity would be equal to 1.0, meaning that the exchange rate change is fully reflected in the dollar price of the good to U.S. consumers. If there is no pass-through, it would be equal to zero, indicating that, despite the exchange rate change, the dollar price to U.S. consumers does not change. If the elasticity is between 0 and 1, there is **partial exchange rate pass-through.** In his estimates of short-run pass-through ("short-run" meaning the impact of an exchange rate change during one quarter on the import price in the succeeding quarter), Yang's estimates were that, in 77 of the 87 industries, the elasticities of pass-through were positive but less than 1.0. This partial pass-through was reflected in an average elasticity of 0.3185, with elasticities in the 77 industries ranging from 0.025 in hardwood veneer and plywood to 0.757 in printing trades machinery. In general, he found that the nonelectric machinery and instruments industries had greater pass-through than did other industries. His estimates for long-run elasticities (using a slightly smaller sample) were higher, with some of the nonelectric machinery industries approaching a value close to 1.0.

Of particular interest in the Yang study was his attempt to investigate the determinants of the relative degree of pass-through across industries. First, for example, he postulated that the elasticity of pass-through would be higher with greater product differentiation in an industry, because such product differentiation implies that consumers are loyal to a particular variety of a product and would not be as prone to switch away from that variety as its import price rose due to depreciation of the domestic currency. Using various proxy measures for the degree of product differentiation, his hypothesis was generally confirmed empirically. Second, Yang ex-

pected that pass-through would be smaller the greater the elasticity of marginal cost of production with respect to output in the supplying firms in the industry. The reasoning is that with a high response of marginal cost to output changes, an initial rise in product price because of attempted pass-through will reduce output of the foreign firm as consumers reduce purchases; however, the reduction in output will decrease marginal cost significantly (i.e., the firm moves back down a steep marginal cost curve). The decrease in marginal cost will then mean that the profit-maximizing firm will decrease product price, and the price reduction will offset some of the upward effect on price of the initial attempted pass-through. Hence, with a high elasticity of marginal cost with respect to output, product price will ultimately rise less than would otherwise have been the case, and a negative relation would exist between the degree of pass-through and the elasticity of marginal cost with respect to output. This result was also found in his empirical tests.

Third, Yang specified that the degree of pass-through could be affected by the market share of foreign firms in the domestic market—his hypothesis was that the degree of pass-through would be inversely related to a foreign firm's market share. Yang's reasoning was that a firm with a large market share will have a high markup over cost because the price elasticity of demand for its product is relatively low since there are few substitutes in consumption. This high markup allows the firm to absorb more of the exchange rate change rather than pass it along to consumers. However, Yang could find no significant relationship empirically between the degree of pass-through and foreign firms' market share in the U.S. market. Since a case could also be made that a large market share means that a firm has to worry less about losing customers when the firm increases its product price (which would imply a positive relationship between market share and degree of pass-through), Yang's insignificant empirical results do not seem surprising.

For the purposes of this chapter, the important result of this study is that Yang (like others) has suggested after careful study that pass-through of exchange rate changes does occur but it is less than complete (at least in the United States). His work has also given us insights on the degree of pass-through that we might expect in different industries.   ✹

FIGURE 8   Adjustment Time and the Foreign Exchange Market

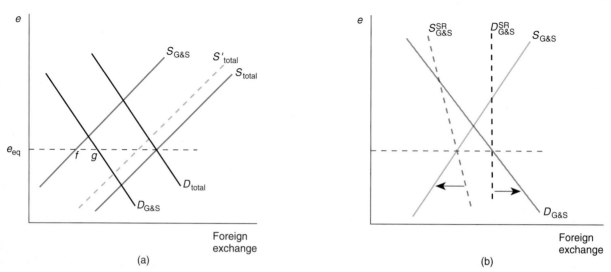

(a)   (b)

The equilibrium foreign exchange rate represented in panel (a) produces a deficit (*fg*) in the current account. A reduction in the supply of foreign exchange (to S'_{total}) would immediately depreciate the currency and reduce or possibly eliminate the current account deficit if the market responds in the short run in the manner depicted by supply and demand curves $S_{G\&S}$ and $D_{G\&S}$. However, in the short run, consumers and producers may be unable or unwilling to respond to the price signals given by the exchange rate change. The short run may thus be characterized by supply and demand curves of foreign exchange in the current account similar to those depicted by the dashed lines $S_{G\&S}^{SR}$ and $D_{G\&S}^{SR}$ in panel (b). In such an instance, depreciating the currency leads to a worsening of the current account deficit in the short run; that is, the gap between the two dashed curves gets wider with depreciation. Given enough time, consumers and producers respond in a manner consistent to that described by $S_{G\&S}$ and $D_{G\&S}$, and the depreciation leads, as expected, to a reduction in the current account deficit.

If the short-run responses of producers and consumers are similar to those described above, they can theoretically create certain problems with respect to the price adjustment mechanism. In Figure 8, panel (a), the normal long-run supply and demand for foreign exchange are shown with an equilibrium exchange rate that produces a current account deficit, although there is overall equilibrium in the balance of payments at rate e_{eq}. Suppose that there is now a reduction in the supply of foreign exchange, due, for example, to less foreign investment in the United States. This would immediately put upward pressure on the exchange rate, presumably leading to a reduction in the current account deficit.

However, suppose that short-run supply and demand curves for foreign exchange for goods and services have the shapes described above [as indicated by the dashed lines in Figure 8(b)]. With a vertical demand curve for foreign exchange and a backward-sloping supply curve, an increase in the exchange rate will lead to a larger current account deficit, not a smaller one. In the short run, this will cause the dollar to depreciate even further as demand for foreign currency continues to exceed supply. The current account deficit will continue to worsen in this case until sufficient time has passed for quantities supplied and demanded to adjust to the change in relative prices and for the longer-run supply and demand configurations to come about. As this adjustment takes place, the current account deficit will begin to decline and the market will seek a new long-run equilibrium consistent with the change in market conditions. This current account adjustment to changes in the exchange rate is often plotted against time, producing a graph like that shown in Figure 9. Due to the shape of the response curve, it is often referred to as the

FIGURE 9   **The J Curve**

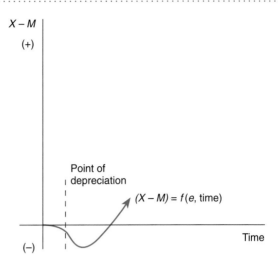

If consumers and producers do not respond immediately to changes in prices of traded goods and services resulting from shifts in the exchange rate, depreciation of the currency may actually lead to a worsening in the current account balance in the short run. If with the passage of time, however, the price effects do have an impact on both consumers and producers, the deficit will begin to narrow. The lagged adjustment response of the current account balance to depreciation of the currency traces out a locus that resembles the letter *J*. Hence, it is referred to as the J curve.

J curve. With the current account in deficit, a depreciation of the currency would presumably lead to a removal of the deficit. However, if consumers and producers are unresponsive in the short run, depreciation actually leads to a short-run worsening in the current account before it ultimately gets better. The longer both groups remain unresponsive to the change in the exchange rate, the deeper is the J curve response. Such an adjustment response is of concern to policymakers since it adds to the uncertainty already present in the market. As discussed in Case Study 3, some evidence appears to suggest that there is a lag between exchange rate changes and trade adjustment. If short-run market conditions do not meet the Marshall-Lerner condition for stability, the exchange rate can overshoot the new long-run equilibrium rate and then adjust back down as the longer-run responses become evident.

Thus, considering the J curve, changing the exchange rate eventually leads to the predicted current account impacts. In addition, other economywide indirect effects of an exchange rate change may have a bearing on the nature of the adjustment in the foreign sector. For example, depreciating the currency may stimulate income and employment as long as the export and import-competing goods sectors and their intermediate good suppliers are at less than full employment. However, depreciation in an economy with little or no excess capacity may do nothing more than stimulate domestic price increases, which offset the initial effects of depreciation and lead to little or no change in the current account. Depreciation may also stimulate investment in export and import-competing industries and shift it away from other domestic uses. If such structural changes are not consistent with the long-run comparative advantages in the country, they can actually decrease growth of output, income, and employment. In a similar fashion, appreciation will stimulate contraction in export goods and import-competing goods. As such, it will tend to have a deflationary effect on the economy. To the extent the deflationary effect

✤ CASE STUDY 3   LAGGED RESPONSE OF NET EXPORTS TO EXCHANGE RATE CHANGES

An analysis by the Council of Economic Advisers of the changes in real net exports (exports minus imports) and the effective exchange rate in the United States suggests that the lag in producer and consumer response in the 1970s and 1980s was about six quarters (one and a half years). This analysis was extended by the authors beyond 1987 in the chart below. The chart indicates that if the movement of current net exports is compared to the movement in the effective exchange rate six quarters earlier, the movements are very similar in nature (highly correlated). For example, a rise of the exchange rate line (a depreciation of the dollar, given the arrangement of

the left scale) is associated with a rise in real net exports (right scale), as we would expect. The two lines in terms of levels become more disparate after 1987, but the direction of change in each time period is still rather similar until after 1995. (Whether the post-1995 divergence represents a fundamental structural change can be ascertained only after more times passes.) This evidence generally supports the idea of time lags in the adjustment to changes in the exchange rate, and hence different short-run and long-run elasticities in the foreign exchange market.

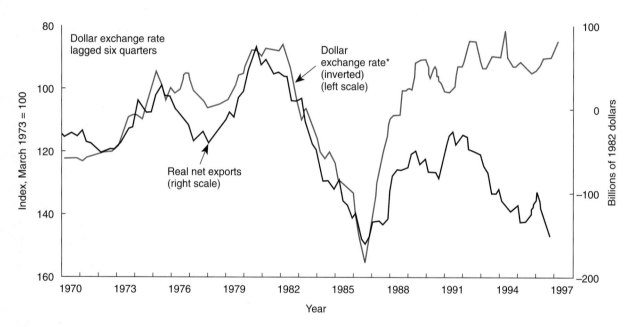

*Nominal multilateral trade-weighted value of the dollar against the currencies of 10 industrialized countries.

Sources: *Economic Report of the President,* February 1988 (Washington, DC: U.S. Government Printing Office, 1988), p. 27; post-1987 data compiled by the authors from various years' *Economic Report of the President.*   ✤

reduces income growth and hence imports, the indirect effects will again offset some of the direct effects of the appreciation. In cases where the indirect effects are further influenced by monetary or interest rate effects on investment, the short-run impact of changes in the exchange rate via the price adjustment mechanism becomes even less clear. In sum, while the price adjustment mechanism seems to function with certain regularity in long-run situations, the short-run effects are relatively more volatile and less certain.

THE PRICE ADJUSTMENT MECHANISM IN A FIXED EXCHANGE RATE SYSTEM

Gold Standard

Instead of letting the foreign exchange market determine the value of the exchange rate, countries often fix or peg the value of the domestic currency. In the case of a **gold standard** (as operated successfully in the world economy from 1880 to 1914), currencies are valued in gold, and all currencies that are pegged to gold are therefore automatically linked to each other. The price is maintained because the government stands ready to buy and sell gold to all customers at the pegged value. For example, if the dollar is fixed at $50 per ounce of gold and the pound sterling is fixed at £25 per ounce of gold, then the dollar/pound **mint par** exchange rate is $2/£. Should this rate or any of the related cross-rates get out of line, arbitrage will quickly bring them back in line.

Since the exchange rate is not allowed to change in this system, some other type of adjustment must be relied upon to make certain that the demand for foreign exchange is equal to the supply of foreign exchange. To ensure proper adjustment, the following **"rules of the game"** are assumed to hold under a gold standard:

1. There is no restraint on the buying and selling of gold within countries, and gold moves freely between countries.
2. The money supply is allowed to change in response to the change in gold holdings in a country.
3. Prices and wages are assumed to be flexible upward and downward.

The operation of a gold standard is straightforward. Consider the foreign exchange market in Figure 10(a) describing the dollar/pound exchange rate in a gold standard context. Assume that the market is initially in equilibrium at the pegged rate of $2/£. Now assume that the demand for pounds sterling rises due to an increase in income in the United States (shown by $D'_£$). With the increase in demand for pounds, there is now an excess demand at the pegged rate. The excess demand for pounds sterling will produce upward pressure on the exchange rate in order to remove the market disequilibrium. The fact that governments stand ready to buy and sell currency at the pegged rate means that there is automatically an upper and lower limit to the amount that the exchange rate can change. Buyers and sellers of foreign exchange know that they can always buy or sell the foreign currency at mint par by using gold as a medium of exchange. By buying gold domestically and then shipping it to the partner country, one can obtain the mint par rate of exchange. In fact, if the transaction costs and shipping costs associated with the movement of gold were zero, the exchange rates would never vary from the mint par value, since any difference in market value from the mint par value would quickly be arbitraged away. However, since the transaction/transport costs associated with the use of gold are not zero, the exchange rate can vary slightly as long as its movement away from mint par value does not exceed the amount of the costs associated with the exchange of gold.

To illustrate, assume that the cost of acquiring gold, shipping it to the partner country, and then exchanging it for the foreign currency is 2 percent of par value. In our example, this would mean that the cost would be $0.04 on either side of the mint par value of $2.00/£. As the exchange rate inches upward due to the increase in the demand for pounds, demanders will pay up to $2.04/£ but no more, since they can acquire all the pounds they wish at the rate of $2.04/£ by using gold as a medium of exchange. The supply of pounds sterling becomes perfectly elastic at this "break-even" price, since it is assumed that an unlimited amount of pounds can be acquired at this price ($2.04/£) by buying and exporting gold to England and acquiring pounds at the pegged value. Similarly, a shift in the supply curve to the left, which would raise the exchange rate

FIGURE 10   **The Foreign Exchange Market under a Gold Standard**

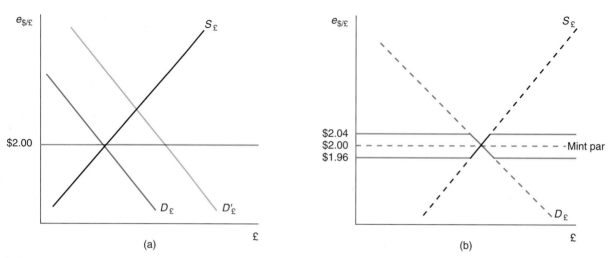

(a)   (b)

Under a fixed exchange rate system, an increase in the demand for foreign exchange to $D'_£$ in panel (a) will put upward pressure on the exchange rate and the home currency (the dollar) will begin to depreciate. However, assuming that the transaction/transport cost for acquiring and using gold to acquire pounds is 2 percent, a U.S. resident need never pay more than \$2.04/£ [as indicated by the upper solid lines in panel (b)]. Hence when e approaches this point, gold will be purchased and used to acquire the needed foreign exchange; that is, gold exports from the United States will take place. Similarly, the British need never pay more than \$1.96/£ [the lower solid lines in panel (b); \$2.00 minus the 2 percent transaction/transport cost]. At that price, they can acquire all the dollars they wish by first buying gold and then exchanging the gold for dollars; that is, gold would flow into the United States. The unrestricted acquisition and use of gold as an intermediary between the two currencies will thus maintain the market exchange rate within the band around the mint par value determined by transaction/transport costs.

above \$2.04/£, would cause domestic residents who desire pounds to use the gold mechanism to acquire them at \$2.04/£ instead of using the more costly foreign exchange market. Thus, the demand curve for foreign exchange becomes horizontal at \$2.04/£ as well. The upper break-even price at which the supply and demand for pounds become perfectly elastic is often referred to as the **gold export point.**

From the English perspective, a similar point exists at a price of \$1.96/£. The English never need pay a higher price for dollars or receive a lower price for pounds than \$1.96/£ (£0.51/\$) since that is the cost associated with acquiring gold in England, shipping it to the United States, and exchanging it for dollars at the pegged rate. Thus, if the exchange rate starts edging downward from \$2/£, it will never go beyond \$1.96/£ because at that point gold will start moving into the United States to be exchanged for dollars. From the U.S. standpoint, the demand for pounds sterling also becomes perfectly elastic at this point because if the exchange rate fell below this level, it would immediately be profitable to acquire pounds sterling with dollars, purchase gold with the pounds sterling, ship it to the United States, convert it to dollars, and make a profit. This floor on the exchange rate set by transaction/transport costs is referred to as the **gold import point,** since any excess supply of pounds at that price will be converted into gold and shipped to the United States to be exchanged for U.S. dollars. Thus, the actual exchange rate in the foreign exchange market is automatically maintained within this narrow band by the unrestricted movement of gold between trading countries, relying on nothing more than free-market arbitrage and the government's commitment to stand behind its currency at the pegged value. The foreign exchange market under a gold standard thus takes on the configuration described in Figure 10(b), with the ceiling and floor to the rate set by the gold import and export points.

The price adjustment mechanism and gold

If the exchange rate remains fixed within these narrow bounds, does this mean that there is no price adjustment mechanism to correct any structural imbalance leading to gold flows? While relative price changes via exchange rate changes basically cannot occur, an aggregate price adjustment takes place as the money supply responds to the gold flow. Assuming a link between money and prices through a quantity theory of money relationship ($M_s = k\,P\,Y$ from the preceding chapter), as gold leaves a country the money supply falls, leading to a fall in prices. Assuming in addition that the demand for tradeable goods is elastic, the fall in prices in the "deficit" country tends to reduce import outlays and increase export receipts. This effect is strengthened by the fact that the money supply and prices are increasing in the surplus country receiving the shipments of gold. Thus, the "price adjustment mechanism" that operates through the gold standard is an aggregate price effect operating through changes in the money supply resulting from the movement of gold. However, flexibility in wages and prices is obviously required for this mechanism to work. Price-wage rigidities in practice will thus be a hindrance to effective adjustment.

The change in the money supply can also lead to interest rate and income effects. Indeed, for many economists, the principal effect of changes in the money supply is on the level of interest rates and then indirectly on income and prices. From this perspective, a fall in the money supply will lead to an increase in interest rates, which will reduce investment, income, and hence aggregate demand in the economy. The fall in demand will lead to excess inventories and falling prices and wages. With the fall in prices comes an adjustment in the foreign exchange market similar to that discussed above. In addition, the increase in the interest rate will attract short-term capital from overseas (as appears to have been important in the actual gold standard period). An inflow of gold produces the opposite effects. Again, any price effect is an aggregate phenomenon, not a direct adjustment occurring only in the foreign sector.

The Price Adjustment Mechanism and the Pegged Rate System

Exchange rates can, of course, be pegged without any direct reference to gold. Under a **pegged rate system,** governments fix the price of their currency and stand ready to support the fixed price in the foreign exchange market (government intervention). If an increase in the demand for foreign currency threatens to drive the exchange rate up beyond some stated limit, the government must stand ready to supply a sufficient amount of foreign exchange to hold the exchange rate within the limits or band it has agreed to. Similarly, any increase in supply of foreign exchange that will drive the exchange rate below the lower limit must be offset by sufficient government purchases of the foreign currency. The central bank thus stands ready to intervene by buying foreign currency when the domestic currency is strong and by selling foreign currency when the domestic currency is weak, in order to maintain the pegged value.

This type of system differs from a gold standard in that the initiative comes from central banks buying and selling foreign currencies in the intervention process rather than from individuals buying and selling gold. This, of course, requires that governments that peg their currencies must have a sufficient supply of foreign exchange reserves to defend the value of their currency. The adjustment effects under a pegged system are similar to those of the gold standard. Upward pressure on the exchange rate brought about by an increase in the demand for foreign exchange will cause the central bank to supply the market with foreign exchange (sell foreign exchange for domestic currency). The purchase of domestic currency by the central bank will lead to a reduction in the money supply and to macroeconomic adjustments in interest rates, income, and prices. Symmetrically, a market increase in the supply of foreign exchange will lead to the purchase of foreign currency by the central bank with domestic currency, which will increase the money supply and stimulate expansionary macro effects on interest rates, income, and prices.

If any of these automatic adjustment effects are to take place under a fixed-rate system, whether a formal gold standard or a pegged system, the central bank must allow the actions being taken in the foreign exchange market to exercise their influence on the domestic money supply. Thus, not only does the central bank lose control of the money supply as a policy tool for other purposes, but shocks in the foreign sector result in a direct macro adjustment through changes in interest rates, income, and prices. Structural disequilibria in the foreign sector can thus become the "tail that wags the dog" since the problem can be solved only by an economywide adjustment under a fixed-rate system. This will be discussed in greater detail in following chapters.

CONCEPT CHECK

1. Explain why producers and consumers respond differently to price (exchange rate) changes in the short run relative to the long run.
2. What effect can lagged consumer-producer response to exchange rate changes have on the current account balance? On price adjustment in the foreign exchange markets?
3. How would a decrease in the demand for foreign exchange affect a country's supply of gold under a gold standard? Why?

SUMMARY

This chapter focused on issues related to price adjustments and balance-of-payments disequilibrium. The conditions underlying the demand and supply of foreign exchange were examined and the market stability conditions analyzed with respect to price adjustments. The link between the demand for traded goods and services and the elasticities that characterize the current account were developed, and the Marshall-Lerner condition for market stability was considered. Assuming market stability, the price adjustment mechanism under flexible exchange rates causes expenditure switching between foreign and domestic goods and services as relative prices change with changes in the exchange rate. This expenditure-switching occurs to the extent that exchange rate changes influence goods prices (i.e., to the extent that "pass-through" occurs). In the adjustment process under fixed-rate systems, any price adjustment takes place at the macro or aggregate level in response to changes in the money supply accompanying the gold or foreign exchange movements that are required to maintain the fixed rate. This macro adjustment process works best when "rules of the game" are followed.

KEY TERMS

complete exchange rate pass-through
elasticities approach
elasticity of exchange rate pass-through
expenditure switching
gold export point
gold import point
gold standard
J curve
market stability
Marshall-Lerner condition
mint par
partial exchange rate pass-through
pegged rate system
price adjustment mechanism
"rules of the game"

QUESTIONS AND PROBLEMS

1. "The existence of a downward- (or backward-) sloping supply curve of foreign exchange is a *sufficient* condition for the generation of an unstable equilibrium position in the foreign exchange market." Assess the validity of this statement.

2. "The existence of a downward- (or backward-) sloping supply curve of foreign exchange is a *necessary* condition for the generation of an unstable equilibrium position in the foreign exchange market." Assess the validity of this statement.

3. Suppose that both the supply curve of imports to country A and the supply curve of exports from country A are horizontal (as in Figure 6). Assume that at a predepreciation value of A's currency, country A sells 975 units of exports and purchases 810 units of imports. (You do not need to know the actual prices of imports and exports, but assume that trade is initially balanced.) Suppose now that there is a 10 percent depreciation of A's currency against foreign currencies and that because of the depreciation exports rise to 1,025 units and imports fall to 790 units. Would the simple Marshall-Lerner condition suggest that country A's current account balance has improved or deteriorated because of this depreciation of its currency? Explain carefully.

4. The U.S. dollar depreciated markedly against the yen in the early 1990s, and yet U.S. net imports from Japan continued to rise in the short run. How might this counterintuitive behavior be explained?

5. Do you as a consumer think that there is much of a time lag between when a price change of an imported good in your market basket occurs and when you react (if at all) to this price change? If so, why? If not, why not? If your reaction time is shared by all consumers of imports, what implication would there be for the impact of a change in currency values on the current account balance in the short run? Explain.

6. Sometimes the charge is made that a country (e.g., Japan) is arbitrarily enhancing its current account surplus by keeping its currency at "too low" a value, that is, that exchange market intervention by the central bank is keeping the country's currency depreciated below the free-market equilibrium value. How would such behavior influence the country's exports and imports? What assumption is being made regarding demand elasticities in making the charge of arbitrary enhancement of the surplus? Explain.

7. Suppose that under the gold standard the mint par of 1 ounce of gold is \$40 in the United States, £20 in the United Kingdom, and DM60 in Germany. Assume that the cost of transporting gold between any pair of countries is \$1 (or equivalent in £ or DM) per ounce.
    (a) Calculate (in \$/£) the gold export point from the United States to the United Kingdom and the gold import point to the United States from the United Kingdom.
    (b) Calculate (in DM/£) the gold export point from Germany to the United Kingdom and the gold import point to Germany from the United Kingdom.
    (c) Calculate (in DM/\$) the gold export point from Germany to the United States and the gold import point to Germany from the United States.

8. It has been argued that the appreciation of the yen against the dollar in the early 1990s did not have the anticipated effect on U.S. imports from Japan partly because the extent of pass-through was reduced by Japanese exporters during this period. Briefly explain what is meant by "pass-through" and how Japanese exporters would have been behaving if the allegation in the previous sentence were true.

◈ APPENDIX   DERIVATION OF THE MARSHALL-LERNER CONDITION

The requirements for stability in the foreign exchange market were discussed in the chapter, accompanied by a brief intuitive explanation. A more formal derivation of this important condition follows.

Given the following definitions:

P_x, P_m = domestic prices of exports and imports, respectively
Q_x, Q_m = quantities of exports and imports, respectively
V_x, V_m = value of exports and imports, respectively

the domestic trade balance, B, is defined as

$$B = V_x - V_m = Q_x P_x - Q_m P_m \qquad [1]$$

and the change in the trade balance, dB, is defined as

$$dB = P_x dQ_x + Q_x dP_x - P_m dQ_m - Q_m dP_m \qquad [2]$$

Assuming that the supply prices of traded goods and services do not change, that is, the supply curves are perfectly elastic over the range of quantity change, then the change in the prices of traded goods and services is attributable only to changes in the exchange rate. Since we are viewing the trade balance in terms of domestic currency in this example, dP_x is therefore equal to 0, whereas P_m

changes by the percentage increase in the exchange rate, k. Therefore, dP_m is equal to kP_m. [If the exchange rate increases (the domestic currency depreciates) by 10 percent, the domestic price of imports increases by 10 percent.] We utilize the following definitions of export and import demand elasticity:

$$\eta_x = (dQ_x/Q_x)/[d(P_x/e)/(P_x/e)] \tag{3}$$

$$\eta_m = (dQ_m/Q_m)/(dP_m/P_m) \tag{4}$$

where P_x/e is the price of domestic exports in foreign currency. Turning to equation [3], the elasticity definition is reworked to obtain an expression for dQ_x in terms of η_x:

$$\eta_x = (dQ_x/Q_x)/\{[(edP_x - P_x de)/e^2]/(P_x/e)\}$$
$$= [(dQ_x/Q_x)(P_x/e)]/[(edP_x - P_x de)/e^2]$$
$$= (dQ_x/Q_x)/[(dP_x/P_x) - de/e]$$

Since dP_x/P_x is assumed to be 0, then:

$$\eta_x = (dQ_x/Q_x)/(-de/e)$$

thus,

$$\eta_x = (dQ_x/Q_x)/(-k)$$

and

$$\eta_x(-k)Q_x = dQ_x \tag{5}$$

Using equation [4], one can rewrite dQ_m in terms of the import demand elasticity η_m, that is:

$$(\eta_m Q_m dP_m)/P_m = \eta_m Q_m k = dQ_m \tag{6}$$

For a depreciation to improve the trade balance, the increase in the value of exports must exceed any increase in the value of imports. If demand for imports is elastic, that is no problem, since the value of total imports falls with the increase in price of foreign goods and services. If, however, demand for imports is inelastic, then depreciation of the currency leads to an increased expenditure for imports. We now return to equation [2] and rewrite it in terms of the two demand elasticities using [5] and [6], taking note that if depreciation is to improve the balance, $dB > 0$:

$$dB = P_x \eta_x(-k)Q_x - P_m \eta_m k Q_m - Q_m k P_m > 0$$

or

$$P_x \eta_x k Q_x + P_m \eta_m k Q_m + Q_m k P_m < 0$$

thus,

$$P_x \eta_x Q_x + P_m \eta_m Q_m < -Q_m P_m$$

and

$$\eta_x(P_x Q_x/P_m Q_m) + \eta_m < -1 \tag{7}$$

or, stating the elasticities in absolute value terms,

$$|\eta_x|(P_x Q_x/P_m Q_m) + |\eta_m| > 1 \tag{8}$$

The expressions in [7] and [8] constitute the Marshall-Lerner condition. In the case of balanced trade, $P_x Q_x/P_m Q_m = 1$, and thus the sum of the absolute values of the two elasticities must be greater than 1 if depreciation is to improve the balance. This is the basic Marshall-Lerner condition. When trade is not balanced, the condition is modified as indicated in [7] and [8] when the value of trade is measured in domestic currency.

NATIONAL INCOME AND THE CURRENT ACCOUNT

INTRODUCTION

In this chapter we examine the manner in which the macroeconomy influences and is influenced by changes in exports and imports. Thus, we move away from price relationships linking the external and internal sectors of the economy to the interrelationships between the two sectors that involve real national income. To accomplish this task, we develop the macroeconomics of an open economy—an economy with foreign trade—in the context of Keynesian income analysis. The basics of Keynesian income analysis, named after the British economist John Maynard Keynes (see Box 1), were likely presented in your principles course. The traditional single-country focus is supplemented here by examining the real income response to exogenous factors when countries are linked through international trade. The last section of the chapter is a synthesis of price and income effects. The forthcoming terms and relationships should already be at least somewhat familiar to you, and, by the end of the chapter, you should feel more comfortable with your understanding of macroeconomic analysis that incorporates the effects of international trade.

THE CURRENT ACCOUNT AND NATIONAL INCOME

The Keynesian Income Model

In a **Keynesian income model,** the focus is on aggregate spending in the entire economy. Aggregate spending consists of the desired expenditures on the economy's goods and services. An assumption is made that prices are constant, so the focus is on real income movements and not on price changes. In addition, monetary considerations such as the interest rate are assumed to be nonchanging. It is also generally assumed that the economy is not at full employment, usually because of downward money wage rigidity. For example, because of institutional features such as unions or a desire by employers to keep the best workers from leaving due to wage decreases during slack times, the wage rate does not fall to clear the labor market during such periods.

In the simple open-economy Keynesian model, **desired aggregate expenditures** (E) during a time period consist of consumption spending by the economy's households on goods and services (C), investment spending by firms (I), government spending on goods and services (G), and export spending by foreign citizens on the country's products (X). In addition, since some of the domestic spending is on imports (M), these must be subtracted to obtain the demand for home goods and services. Hence, desired expenditures or aggregate demand can be written as

$$E = C + I + G + X - M \qquad [1]$$

✸ BOX 1   JOHN MAYNARD KEYNES (1883–1946)

John Maynard Keynes was born in Cambridge, England, on June 5, 1883. The son of an economist (John Neville Keynes), he attended Eton and then King's College, Cambridge, where he received a degree in mathematics in 1905. He then studied under the neoclassical economist Alfred Marshall, who pleaded with him to become an economist. Keynes entered the British Civil Service in the India Office, and his first book, *Indian Currency and Finance* (1913), assessed the Indian currency system as an example of a gold/pegged exchange rate system. He attained widespread fame in 1919 when he wrote *The Economic Consequences of the Peace.* This book, as well as later famous journal articles, castigated the Treaty of Versailles for the heavy burdens it placed on Germany in connection with reparations payments after World War I. Keynes's view was that the price adjustments required for Germany to earn the foreign exchange to make the payments (that is, the price changes needed to increase exports and decrease imports sufficiently that the current account surplus would match the required capital outflow associated with the payments) would be excessive. They would deteriorate Germany's terms of trade and welfare greatly, and the payments might never be accomplished because of their harshness.

Keynes then published the influential *A Treatise on Probability* in 1921. However, his most important academic contributions occurred in the 1930s—*A Treatise on Money* (1930) and, especially, *The General Theory of Employment, Interest and Money* (1936). *The General Theory* was a broadside attack on the apparatus of Classical economics with its view that the economy would settle automatically at the full-employment level of income. (The Classical view was very hard to sell to anyone during the Great Depression!) He emphasized the role of aggregate demand and the possibility of attaining national income equilibrium at less than full employment. The demand for money and its relationship to the interest rate also received revolutionary treatment and played a major role in his aggregate demand formulation. Keynesian analysis assigned a prominent role to fiscal policy in affecting national income and employment—which had been denied in the Classical model. Keynes also met with Franklin D. Roosevelt, who

was later to use public works expenditures as a measure for attempting to get out of the Depression. Although Keynes is reported not to have been impressed with FDR's economic knowledge, FDR wrote in a letter to Felix Frankfurter (later a long-time U.S. Supreme Court Justice), "I had a grand talk with K and liked him immensely" (quoted in Harrod 1951, p. 448).

Keynes's life was a whirlwind of activity. Aside from his roles as policy advisor to the British government and Cambridge don, he was a patron of the arts, a collector of rare books, editor of *The Economic Journal,* first bursar of King's College, and chairman of the board of the National Mutual Life Insurance Company. He also amassed a personal fortune through shrewd investments. In addition, Keynes was a member of the Bloomsbury circle, a group of artists, intellectuals, and writers that included Lytton Strachey and Virginia Woolf. Further, and most impressively to some, he married a premier Russian ballerina in 1925, giving rise to the ditty, "There ne'er was such union of beauty and brains, as when Lydia Lopokova wed John Maynard Keynes."

Keynes's final years were spent successfully negotiating a large war loan for Britain from the United States during World War II and hammering out the Bretton Woods agreement for the formation of the International Monetary Fund. With his usual persuasive powers, personal charm, and magnetism, he forcefully presented and fought for his proposals for the postwar international monetary system. In the end, the new Bretton Woods system (see the last chapter in this book) resembled more closely the American plan than the British plan, but he had been the dominant figure at the extended conference. John Maynard Keynes died on Easter Sunday, 1946.

Sources: R. F. Harrod, *The Life of John Maynard Keynes* (New York: Harcourt, Brace, 1951); Robert L. Heilbroner, *The Worldly Philosophers: The Lives, Times, and Ideas of the Great Economic Thinkers,* 3rd ed. (New York: Simon and Schuster, 1967), chap. 9; Don Patinkin, "John Maynard Keynes," in John Eatwell, Murray Milgate, and Peter Newman, eds., *The New Palgrave: A Dictionary of Economics,* Vol. 3. (London: Macmillan, 1987), pp. 19–41. ✸

What determines the amount of *C*? Keynes hypothesized that the most important determinant of a country's current consumption spending is the amount of current income (*Y*) in the economy. In general terms, then, consumption depends on or is a function of disposable income of households; that is,

$$C = f(Y_d) \qquad\qquad [2]$$

where disposable income (Y_d) is income in the economy (Y) minus taxes (T); that is,

$$Y_d = Y - T \qquad\qquad [3]$$

The general expression [2] is usually written in a more precise way:

$$C = a + bY_d \qquad\qquad [4]$$

This equation is a standard Keynesian **consumption function.** To put numerical content to it, suppose we specify

$$C = 100 + 0.80Y_d$$

This equation indicates that if disposable income is $600 (in billions, for example), then consumption spending is equal to $100 plus (0.80 × $600), or $100 plus $480, or $580. If disposable income rises to $700, then consumption spending is equal to $100 plus (0.80 × $700) = $100 + $560 = $660.

In this consumption function, the a term (or $100 in the example) is designated as **autonomous consumption spending,** meaning that this amount of consumption spending is determined by *other things besides income.* These "other things" can consist of the level of interest rates, the size of the population, attitudes toward thrift, the level of accumulated wealth, expectations of future income, and so forth. The part of consumption that does depend on current income is labeled bY_d, or $0.80Y_d$, and is known as **induced consumption spending.** Within the induced consumption component bY_d, a key feature is the term b, or 0.80 in our example. The b is known as the **marginal propensity to consume,** or **MPC.** The MPC is defined as the change in consumption divided by the change in disposable income, that is, the fraction of additional Y_d spent on consumption goods. Therefore, designating "change in" by Δ,

$$MPC = \Delta C/\Delta Y_d \qquad\qquad [5]$$

In addition to this consumption propensity, the **marginal propensity to save,** or **MPS,** is defined as the change in saving (S) divided by the change in disposable income, that is, the fraction of any additional Y_d allocated to saving:

$$MPS = \Delta S/\Delta Y_d \qquad\qquad [6]$$

Since any change in income can be allocated only to consumption and saving, it follows that

$$MPC + MPS = 1.0 \qquad\qquad [7]$$

In our sample consumption function, where MPC = 0.80, the MPS must equal 0.20.

Finally, the consumption function $C = a + bY_d$ immediately tells us the nature of the **saving function** for households in the economy. Remembering that by definition disposable income can be allocated only to consumption and saving, the saving function can be easily obtained:

$$\begin{aligned} Y_d &= C + S \\ &= a + bY_d + S \\ S &= Y_d - (a + bY_d) \\ &= -a + (1 - b)Y_d \end{aligned}$$

or

$$S = -a + sY_d \qquad\qquad [8]$$

where $s (= 1 - b)$ is the marginal propensity to save.

The consumption and saving functions are illustrated in Figure 1. Panel (a) portrays the consumption function for $C = 100 + 0.80Y_d$ and panel (b) shows the associated

FIGURE 1   **Consumption and Saving Functions**

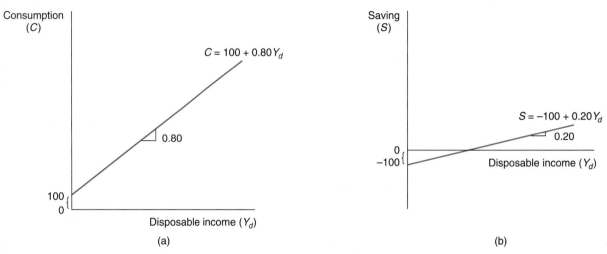

(a)   (b)

Panel (a) shows a typical Keynesian consumption function. The autonomous component (100) is consumption that is independent of disposable income. The induced component of consumption is 0.80 times the disposable income level, with 0.80 being the marginal propensity to consume (MPC). Since the MPC is constant in this example at 0.80, the consumption function is a straight line. Panel (b) shows the associated saving function by households. Since $Y_d = C + S$, therefore $S = Y_d - C = Y_d - (100 + 0.80Y_d) = -100 + 0.20Y_d$. This function is a straight line with a slope of 0.20, which is the marginal propensity to save (MPS).

saving function $S = -100 + 0.20Y_d$. Relating Figure 1(a) to the consumption function equation, the a term (or 100) is the height of the intercept on the vertical axis, while the slope of the consumption schedule is b, that is, the MPC (or 0.80). Since the MPC is constant, the slope is constant, meaning that the consumption function is a straight line. Similarly, the intercept in Figure 1(b) is *minus a* (or −100), and the slope is s, the MPS (or 0.20).

A further necessary step with respect to consumption, however, is to relate it to *national* income (Y) rather than to disposable income (Y_d), since the other components of aggregate spending are going to be related to Y. Remembering that $Y_d = Y - T$, we specify taxes (T) as[1]

$$T = tY \tag{9}$$

We assume that taxes depend only on income, with t as the marginal tax rate. Thus, for our numerical example, we specify

$$T = 0.25Y$$

This function is plotted in Figure 2, panel (a).

Next, with consumption equal to $a + b(Y - T)$, we can write C as a function of national income alone through the substitution of expressions [3] and [9] into expression [4]:

$$C = a + bY_d$$
$$= a + b(Y - T)$$
$$= a + b(Y - tY)$$
$$= a + (b - bt)Y$$

[1]Transfer payments can be regarded as negative taxes. A more complete representation of taxes and transfers would be to specify expression [9] as $T = \bar{T} + tY$, with $\bar{t}$ symbolizing taxes that are independent of income and, if negative, transfer payments. We omit this term in our discussion for simplicity.

FIGURE 2   **Taxes, Consumption, and Saving in Relation to National Income**

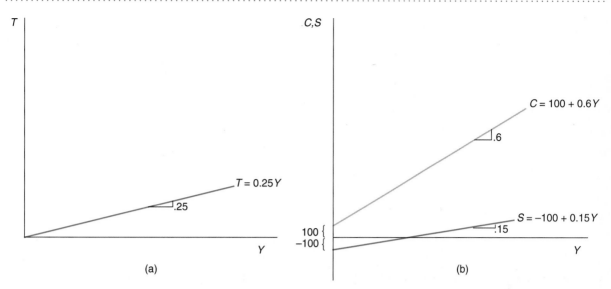

In panel (a), taxes (*T*) are equal to the marginal tax rate (*t* = 0.25) times the level of national income (*T*), a positive and proportional relationship. In panel (b), consumption and saving are expressed in relation to national income rather than in relation to disposable income. The slope of the consumption function is now the MPC minus the product of the MPC and the tax rate, or [0.8 − (0.8) (0.25)] = 0.6 in our example. The slope of the saving function is the MPS minus the product of the MPS and the tax rate, or [0.2 − (0.2) (0.25)] = 0.15.

or

$$C = a + b(1-t)Y \qquad [10]$$

In terms of our numerical example:

$$C = 100 + [0.8 - (0.8)(0.25)]Y$$
$$C = 100 + 0.6Y$$

Similarly, saving can also be related to national income rather than to disposable income:

$$S = -a + s(Y-T)$$
$$= -a + s(Y-tY)$$
$$= -a + (s-st)Y$$

or

$$S = -a + s(1-t)Y \qquad [11]$$

In terms of the numerical example:

$$S = -100 + [0.2 - (0.2)(0.25)]Y$$
$$= -100 + 0.15Y$$

The consumption and saving functions thus expressed in relation to national income are shown in Figure 2, panel (b).

We now turn to investment spending. Remember that investment decisions (in the sense of *real* investment spending on plant and equipment, residential construction, and changes in inventories, not in the sense of financial investment in stocks, bonds, etc.) are made by business firms and not by households. Thus there is no necessary direct link between consumption spending and investment spending. In this simple income model,

FIGURE 3 **Autonomous Investment, Government Spending, and Export Schedules**

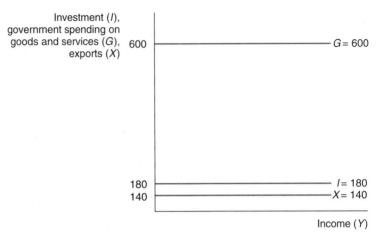

Investment, government spending on goods and services, and exports are all assumed to be autonomous or independent of current income in the simple Keynesian model (i.e., they depend on factors other than income). Thus, in our numerical example, $I = 180$, $G = 600$ and $X = 140$ no matter what the level of national income.

investment is usually assumed to be entirely autonomous or independent of current national income in the economy, meaning that investment spending is determined by factors other than income (e.g., interest rates, wage rates, and the expectations of firms concerning the future). When investment is assumed to be independent of current income, the investment equation is written as

$$I = \overline{I} \qquad [12]$$

where the bar means that investment is fixed at a given amount for all levels of income. Thus, the equation $I = 180$ would indicate that investment spending by firms is \$180 no matter what the level of income in the economy. The assumption that I is independent of income is clearly unrealistic in a strict sense. However, it may well be the case that interest rates, wage rates, technological change, and so forth, are more important for the investment decision than is the current level of national income. The graphical depiction of the autonomous investment function is given as the line $I = 180$ in Figure 3.

Government spending on goods and services in the simple Keynesian open-economy model (G) is also assumed to be independent of current income. This means that G is treated as being dependent on government priorities with respect to items such as national defense, highways, and education and on policy measures, and not on the level of national income. Clearly, this is also a simplification, but for our purposes, we write

$$G = \overline{G} \qquad [13]$$

Thus, in terms of our numerical example, let us assume that $G = 600$. This autonomous government spending on goods and services is represented by the $G = 600$ line in Figure 3.

Exports (X) in the simple open-economy income model are also specified as being autonomous or independent of the country's current level of national income. The export equation is thus

$$X = \overline{X} \qquad [14]$$

where $\overline{X}$ indicates the autonomous exports. To continue our numerical example, let us say that

$$X = 140$$

Exports are constant at \$140. This is also represented graphically in Figure 3. Home country exports are more likely to depend on other countries' incomes than upon home income, since domestic exports are dependent on the buying power of other countries as determined by their incomes. In addition, home exports depend on nonincome factors such as relative prices of domestic goods compared to foreign goods, the exchange rate (assumed to be fixed in the Keynesian model), innovation in home export industries, and foreign tastes and preferences. If any of these factors change so that more domestic exports are demanded, then the export function will shift vertically upward in parallel fashion; if other countries decreased their demand for the home country's goods, the export line would shift vertically downward in a parallel manner.

In the simple Keynesian macro model, imports (M) are generally made to depend on only one variable—the level of home country income. The relationship between imports and national income is expressed by the **import function.** Its general form is

$$M = f(Y) \qquad [15]$$

A specific form is

$$M = \overline{M} + mY \qquad [16]$$

$\overline{M}$ represents **autonomous imports,** the amount of spending on imports that is independent of income. This spending on imports depends on factors such as tastes and preferences for foreign goods as opposed to home goods, and relative prices of foreign goods compared to home goods. The term mY refers to **induced imports,** the spending on foreign goods that is dependent on the level of income. Thus, as the income of a country rises, more spending occurs on goods and services, and some of this additional spending is on imported goods and services. If imports consisted only of consumption goods and services, disposable income (Y_d) would appear in expression [16] rather than national income (Y). However, we assume here (and it is true in practice) that imports contain not only consumption goods and services but also inputs into the domestic production process (which depend on total income). Hence, and also for simplicity, we use Y in the import equation rather than Y_d. Continuing with our numerical example, suppose

$$M = 20 + 0.10Y$$

This equation states the value of autonomous imports as \$20 and the value of induced imports as 0.10 times the income level. The figure 0.10 (or the letter m in expression [16]) is the **marginal propensity to import,** or **MPM.** This concept is defined as the change in imports divided by the change in income:

$$MPM = \Delta M/\Delta Y \qquad [17]$$

Thus, if income rises by \$100 and the MPM is 0.10, consumers will spend an additional \$10 on imports. The MPM is to be distinguished from the **average propensity to import,** or **APM,** which is the total spending on imports divided by total income:

$$APM = M/Y \qquad [18]$$

Another term emerges from this analysis: the **income elasticity of demand for imports** or **YEM,** which is the percentage change in the demand for imports divided by the percentage change in income. The term has useful applications because it indicates the

Table 1 presents the average propensities to import for five major industrialized countries for 1973 to 1996. As can be seen, there has been a major increase in openness for the United States and a slight increase for Canada, especially recently. For the United Kingdom and Germany, there appears to have been little change in the APM over this period, and Germany's APM has been rather variable. Japan's average propensity to import may well have declined.

The calculation of marginal propensities to import is more difficult, since the problem is to isolate the impact of income changes alone on changes in imports from year to year, abstracting from other short-run changes in the economy. However, to get some broad, general idea of the MPM of each country over the period, we employ the income elasticities of demand for imports statistically estimated by Jaime Marquez for 1973 to 1985, assuming that these YEMs were also relevant in the 1986–1996 period. His YEMs for the five countries over the 1973–1985 period were the following: Canada, 1.84; Germany, 1.88; Japan, 0.35; United Kingdom, 2.51; United States, 1.94.* Remembering that YEM = MPM/APM and thus MPM = YEM × APM, we obtain

$$MPM_{Canada} = (1.84)(.263) = .484$$
$$MPM_{Germany} = (1.88)(.260) = .489$$
$$MPM_{Japan} = (0.35)(.105) = .037$$
$$MPM_{UK} = (2.51)(.270) = .678$$
$$MPM_{US} = (1.94)(.103) = .200$$

These results are obviously crude, and more careful work would need to be done to get firm MPM estimates. Nevertheless, a fair conclusion seems to be that, given the YEM, the resulting MPM, and the trend of the APM, Japan did not become relatively more open to products of other countries between 1973 and 1995.[†] Perhaps this will change in view of Japan's recent steps and commitments to become more receptive to imports.

* Jaime Marquez, "Bilateral Trade Elasticities," *Review of Economics and Statistics* 72, no. 1 (February 1990), p. 75.
[†]Some of the decline in Japan's APM from the mid-1970s (and early 1980s) into the 1990s was undoubtedly associated with the decline in world oil prices (since Japan is a heavy oil importer). Nevertheless, allowance for this factor would not seem to alter the general conclusion.

TABLE 1   **Average Propensities to Import, Selected Countries, 1973–1996**

Year	Canada	Germany	Japan	United Kingdom	United States
1973	.220	.202	.100	.255	.068
1974	.246	.236	.143	.324	.087
1975	.241	.232	.128	.272	.077
1976	.229	.248	.128	.293	.086
1977	.235	.247	.115	.290	.092
1978	.249	.236	.094	.269	.095
1979	.265	.259	.125	.274	.102
1980	.264	.287	.146	.249	.109
1981	.261	.303	.139	.237	.105
1982	.221	.301	.138	.243	.096
1983	.221	.289	.122	.255	.096
1984	.249	.303	.123	.285	.107
1985	.258	.312	.111	.277	.103
1986	.264	.273	.074	.263	.106
1987	.255	.264	.072	.264	.112
1988	.258	.270	.078	.265	.113
1989	.255	.289	.093	.277	.112
1990	.256	.294	.101	.269	.113
1991	.255	.255	.085	.245	.109
1992	.271	.238	.078	.251	.107
1993	.298	.217	.072	.266	.110
1994	.330	.221	.073	.273	.117
1995	.349	.220	.080	.291	.124
1996	.353	.233	NA	.299	.126
Average for period	.263	.260	.105	.270	.103

NA = not available.

Note: Figures are imports of goods and services in the GDP accounts divided by GDP.

Sources: Calculated from data in International Monetary Fund, *International Financial Statistics Yearbook 1994* (Washington, DC: IMF, 1994), p. 374; International Monetary Fund, *International Financial Statistics Yearbook 1996* (Washington, DC: IMF, 1996), pp. 260–61, 380–81, 460–61, 784–85, 790–91; International Monetary Fund, *International Financial Statistics,* June 1997, pp. 186, 308, 390, 710, 718. ✼

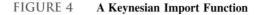

FIGURE 4   **A Keynesian Import Function**

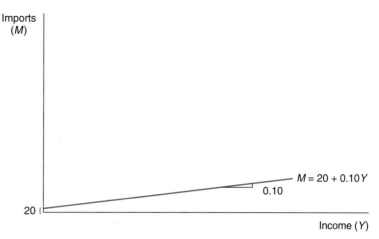

The autonomous component of imports (20) reflects imports purchased independently of income. The induced component of imports is 0.10 times the income level, with 0.10 indicating the marginal propensity to import (MPM). With a constant MPM, the import function is a straight line.

percentage growth in imports that will occur as a country's national income grows over time. It can be shown that the YEM is related in simple fashion to the APM and the MPM:

$$YEM = (\%\Delta M) \div (\%\Delta Y) \qquad\qquad [19]$$
$$= (\Delta M/M) \div (\Delta Y/Y)$$
$$= (\Delta M/\Delta Y) \div (M/Y)$$
$$= MPM \div APM$$

Thus, if a country's MPM exceeds its APM, imports relative to income will rise as the country's income grows (YEM is elastic). If the MPM is less than APM, the YEM is inelastic and imports will fall as a fraction of income as income rises. Finally, if MPM equals APM, the YEM is unit-elastic and imports as a fraction of national income stay the same as income rises. In the past several decades, trade as a fraction of national income in the United States has been rising, indicating that the MPM of the United States is larger than the APM. For examples of the APMs of selected countries (and a general idea of the associated MPMs), see Case Study 1.

The import function is shown in Figure 4, plotting the specific function given earlier, namely, $M = 20 + 0.10Y$. The intercept of the import function is located at the value of autonomous imports, $\overline{M}$. The slope of the (straight-line) import function is the MPM, or 0.10 in our example.

Determining the Equilibrium Level of National Income

The next step in the analysis involves the actual determination of the **equilibrium level of national income** in this type of model. The equilibrium income level is the level at which there is no tendency for the income level to rise or to fall (that is, the economy is "at rest"). This level of income occurs when desired spending exactly matches the production level of the economy. If such is the case, then there is no net tendency for economic activity to change. However, if spending exceeds production (which equals income), then firms have not produced enough output to meet demand and their inventories of goods will fall. Output will consequently rise in order to prevent this

FIGURE 5   **The Equilibrium Level of Income**

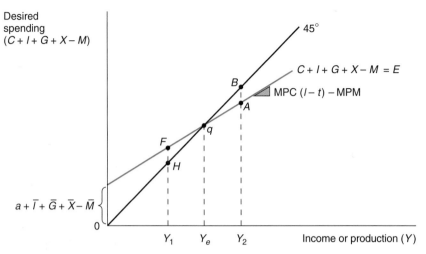

Total desired spending on domestic goods in relation to income is indicated by the $C + I + G + X - M$ line, with a slope of [MPC $(1 - t)$ − MPM]. Equilibrium income level $0Y_e$ occurs where desired spending equals production. At lower income level $0Y_1$, spending (= Y_1F) is greater than production (= $0Y_1 = Y_1H$), so inventories are being depleted and production expands to $0Y_e$. At income level $0Y_2$ above $0Y_e$, spending (= Y_2A) is less than production (= $0Y_2 = Y_2B$), so inventories are accumulating and production contracts to $0Y_e$.

unintended depletion of inventories. On the other hand, if production exceeds spending, there will be unintended inventory accumulation. This accumulation will be a signal to producers to reduce their output, and production will decline until it equals the level of demand. Thus, at income levels both above and below the equilibrium level, forces are at work to return the economy to the equilibrium income level.

The determination of the equilibrium level of income is shown graphically in Figure 5. The components C, I, G, and X have been added vertically, and imports have then been subtracted. The result is the $C + I + G + X - M$ line, which has an intercept of $(a + \bar{I} + \bar{G} + \bar{X} - \bar{M})$ and a slope of (MPC − MPC · t − MPM) or [MPC $(1 - t)$ − MPM].[2] Another important line in the diagram is the 45° line. Since a 45° line has the property that each point on it is equidistant from the vertical axis (spending) and the horizontal axis (production), it is clear that, for the economy to be in equilibrium, the economy must be located somewhere on this line. The equilibrium point q occurs where the $C + I + G + X - M$, or spending, line intersects the 45° line, and the equilibrium level of income associated with point q is income level $0Y_e$. Because $C + I + G + X - M$ shows desired spending and the 45° line illustrates points that are equidistant from both axes, the intersection of the E line with the 45° line gives us the single point where production equals spending.

To ascertain that $0Y_e$ is the equilibrium level, consider income level $0Y_1$. At $0Y_1$, spending is indicated by the height of the E line, distance Y_1F. However, production is $0Y_1$, which in turn because of the nature of the 45° line, is equal to distance Y_1H. Since Y_1F is greater than Y_1H, spending is greater than production (by HF) at income level $0Y_1$.

---

[2]Remember that the slope of a $C + I + G$ line by itself is MPC$(1 - t)$. When adding X and subtracting M, X is autonomous but $M = \bar{M} + $ MPM · Y. Thus MPM is subtracted from the MPC$(1 - t)$ slope of $C + I + G$ to give a slope of [MPC$(1 - t)$ − MPM].

With spending greater than production, inventories of firms will decline; as firms then step up their rate of production to eliminate the inventory depletion, income in the economy will rise until $0Y_e$ is reached. At $0Y_e$, there is no longer any unintended inventory depletion, and spending now equals production. A similar analysis applies to income level $0Y_2$ above the equilibrium level of income. At $0Y_2$, households and firms want to spend the amount Y_2A, but production is Y_2B (which equals distance $0Y_2$). Hence, production exceeds spending by AB, and unintended inventory accumulation will lead to cutbacks in production in order to avoid the inventory buildup. The cutbacks will continue until the income level reaches $0Y_e$.

The determination of the equilibrium level of income can also be derived algebraically. Our numerical example's equations are

$$C = 100 + 0.8Y_d \qquad G = 600$$
$$Y_d = Y - T \qquad\quad X = 140$$
$$T = 0.25Y \qquad\quad M = 20 + 0.1Y$$
$$I = 180$$

In equilibrium, the sum of the spending components, desired aggregate expenditures (E), equals production (or income, Y). In equilibrium,

$$Y = E = C + I + G + X - M$$
$$Y = 100 + 0.8(Y - T) + 180 + 600 + 140 - (20 + 0.1Y)$$
$$\quad = 100 + 0.8(Y - 0.25Y) + 180 + 600 + 140 - 20 - 0.1Y$$
$$Y = 1{,}000 + 0.5Y$$
$$Y - 0.5Y = 1{,}000$$
$$Y = 2{,}000$$

The equilibrium level of income is $2,000. This can be verified by using the Y of 2,000 to determine aggregate expenditures at this income level. With a Y of 2,000, $Y_d = 2,000 - (0.25)(2,000) = 1,500$, and therefore $C = 100 + (0.8)(1,500) = 1,300$, $I = 180$, $G = 600$, $X = 140$, and $M = 20 + 0.1(2,000) = 220$. Hence, $C + I + G + X - M = 1,300 + 180 + 600 + 140 - 220 = 2,000$.

At no other income level than 2,000 will E equal Y. For example, if Y is 2,100, then $Y_d = 2,100 - (0.25)(2,100) = 1,575$, and therefore $C = 100 + (0.8)(1,575) = 1360$, $I = 180$, $G = 600$, $X = 140$, and $M = 20 + (0.1)(2,100) = 230$. Hence, E is $1,360 + 180 + 600 + 140 - 230 = 2,050$. Since E of 2,050 is less than Y of 2,100, unintended inventory accumulation (of 50) occurs, and production is cut back until the equilibrium level of 2,000 is reached. You can verify that income levels below 2,000 will have $E > Y$, and pressures for expansion in output will exist.

Leakages and injections

An alternative method of determining the equilibrium level of income is to represent the equilibrium income level as that level that equates desired or planned saving, imports, and taxes with desired investment, government spending, and exports. In this approach, saving, imports, and taxes are thought of as **leakages** from the spending stream, in that they represent actions that reduce spending on domestic products. Investment, government spending, and exports are **injections** into the spending stream and therefore lead to home production. If the leakages exceed the injections, then there is downward pressure on spending and hence on income. If the injections exceed the leakages, there is pressure for expansion in the economy.

This approach is illustrated in Figure 6, panel (a), which shows the saving, tax, and import functions combined into an $S + T + M$ function [with a slope of MPS$(1 - t) + t +$

FIGURE 6   **Alternative Representations of the Equilibrium Level of Income**

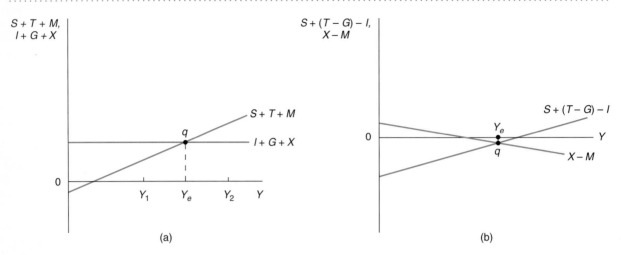

In panel (a), the equilibrium level of income $0Y_e$ occurs where the leakages from the domestic spending stream $(S + T + M)$ are equal to the injections into the spending stream $(I + G + X)$. At income levels below (above) $0Y_e$, injections are greater (less) than leakages, so there is pressure to expand (contract) income. Panel (b) shows an alternative representation using the relationship that, since $S + T + M = I + G + X$, then $S + (T - G) - I = X - M$. In this graph, equilibrium income level $0Y_e$ occurs simultaneously with a current account deficit (i.e., $X - M < 0$).

MPM][3] and the autonomous investment, government spending, and export schedules combined into an $I + G + X$ schedule. The equilibrium level of income is situated immediately below point q where the two schedules intersect, at income level $0Y_e$. This $0Y_e$ is the same $0Y_e$ as in Figure 5 because the two figures employ the same basic information but in a different form.[4] If the economy is at an income level below $0Y_e$, such as $0Y_1$, $(I + G + X)$ exceeds $(S + T + M)$. The economy will expand because the injections into the spending stream exceed the leakages or withdrawals from that stream. Inventories will decline and the economy will move upward to $0Y_e$. At income level $0Y_2$, the opposite is the case. Inventories will accumulate and income will fall back to $0Y_e$.

    For the algebraic determination of equilibrium in this leakages-injections approach, remember that the consumption function of $C = 100 + 0.8Y_d$ is associated with the saving

. . . .

[3]Remember that, in symbols, the saving function is $S = -a + sY_d$, with s = MPS. The tax function is $T = tY$, and the import function is $M = \overline{M} + mY$, with m = MPM. Hence,

$$S + T + M = -\underline{a} + s(Y - T) + tY + \overline{M} + mY \qquad [20]$$
$$= (-a + \overline{M}) + [s(1 - t) + t + m]Y$$

The $S + T + M$ line plotted against Y thus has an intercept of $(-a + \overline{M})$ and a slope of $s(1 - t) + t + m$.

[4]In the equilibrium expression $Y = C + I + G + X - M$, the right-hand side consists of expenditures that generate income, or it can be thought of as sources of income. Now consider the expression $Y = C + S + T$. The right-hand side of this equation indicates the uses of the income generated in the economy (for consumption, for saving, and for taxes). Since uses of income must equal sources of income,

$$C + S + T = C + I + G + X - M$$
$$S + T = I + G + X - M$$
$$S + T + M = I + G + X \qquad [21]$$

Expression [21] is another way of writing the equilibrium condition, and the intersection of the two schedules in panel (a) of Figure 6 thus also yields the equilibrium level of income.

function of $S = -100 + 0.2Y_d$. Using this function together with the tax ($T = 0.25Y$) and import ($M = 20 + 0.1Y$) functions and setting them equal to our numbers for investment, government spending, and exports, we have

$$S + T + M = I + G + X$$
$$-100 + 0.2Y_d + 0.25Y + 20 + 0.1Y = 180 + 600 + 140$$
$$-100 + 0.2(Y - 0.25Y) + 0.25Y + 20 + 0.1Y = 180 + 600 + 140$$
$$-80 + 0.15Y + 0.25Y + 0.1Y = 920$$
$$0.5Y = 1,000$$
$$Y = 2,000$$

Equilibrium income is again 2,000. You should be able to show that, at this income, $S = 200$, $T = 500$, and $M = 220$. Thus $(S + T + M) = (I + G + X) = 920$. At greater income levels $(S + T + M)$ will exceed $(I + G + X)$; at lower income levels, $(S + T + M)$ will be less than $(I + G + X)$.

Income equilibrium and the current account balance

A second alternative representation of equilibrium focuses on the current account balance for the economy. (In our model, $X - M$ embraces exports and imports of all goods and services; since we have no unilateral transfers in the model, $X - M$ is thus the current account balance.) In this approach, we take the equilibrium condition of

$$S + T + M = I + G + X$$

and rearrange it to obtain

$$S + (T - G) - I = X - M \qquad [22]$$

In expression [22], S is private saving and $(T - G)$ is government saving (which can be negative, as it has been in the United States for many years). Thus the expression makes the important point that, in an open economy, the difference between a country's total saving (private + government) and the country's investment equals the current account balance. If $X < M$, the country is saving less in total than it is investing domestically; if $X > M$, the country is saving more than it is investing domestically (and hence it can invest overseas via a capital outflow, with the capital account outflow being equal to the current account surplus).

Utilizing expression [22], we can then plot two new schedules as in Figure 6, panel (b). The upward-sloping $S + (T - G) - I$ line subtracts the *fixed* autonomous amount of investment and the *fixed* autonomous amount of government spending from private saving and taxes. Since S and T both depend positively on Y, the line is clearly upward-sloping. The $X - M$ line slopes downward because, at higher levels of Y, rising amounts of imports are being subtracted from a *fixed* amount of autonomous exports. As should be evident, the intersection of these two lines (at q) will also yield the equilibrium level of income $0Y_e$.

The virtue of this approach is that the state of the current account balance that exists at the equilibrium level of income can be observed. (In our numerical example, $X = 140$ and $M = 220$ at equilibrium, so the current account is in deficit by 80.) Further, an important point that emerges from this discussion is that, even though the economy is in income equilibrium, it is not necessary that the current account balance be zero. In Figure 6(b), the existence of the current account deficit when the economy is at its equilibrium income is reflected in the fact that the equilibrium position q is below the horizontal axis. If q occurs at a point above the horizontal axis, there would be a current account surplus; if q lies on the horizontal axis, $X = M$, which indicates balance in the current account.

CONCEPT CHECK

1. Explain why an income level below the equilibrium level of income cannot persist.
2. Suppose that imports are entirely induced, that is, that the import function is $M = mY$ (with m being the marginal propensity to import). What is the APM in this case? What is the value of the YEM?
3. If the economy is at its equilibrium level of income and has a current account deficit, what must be true of the total amount of saving (private plus government) in the economy relative to the amount of investment? How is the excess of investment over saving being financed?

The Autonomous Spending Multiplier

A familiar concept contained in Keynesian income models is the **autonomous spending multiplier.** The autonomous spending multiplier is used to answer the following question: If autonomous spending on $C, I, G,$ or X is changed, by how much will equilibrium income be changed? Graphically, as in Figure 5 earlier, this question is simply, if $(C + I + G + X - M)$ shifts in parallel fashion, what will be the ΔY as the economy responds to the change in autonomous spending?

Changes in autonomous consumption, investment, government spending, and exports

To answer this question, suppose that autonomous investment in our numerical example rises to $220 from its original level of $180. The best way to think of the multiplier concept is in terms of **rounds of spending in the multiplier process.** The autonomous increase of $40 in investment (assumed to be spent on domestic goods) generates production (and income) of $40 as firms produce the new machinery, for example, that is now in demand. The workers and owners of the firms producing the machinery receive $40 in income. But what happens to this $40 of new income? First, 25 percent of it (or $10, with $t = 0.25$) will be paid in income taxes, leaving an increase in disposable income of $30 (= 40 − 10). *Some* of this new disposable income will be spent as indicated by the MPC. So a second round of spending will occur; in our example with MPC = 0.8, $24 will be spent [= (0.8)(30)]. However, some of this new spending will be on imports and will not lead to increased domestic production. In addition, remember that in our model imports are a function of total income and not just disposable income because, besides consumption goods, some imports are also inputs for the new production being generated. With our MPM of 0.1, imports in total go up by the MPM times the change in *total* income, or MPM·ΔY (not ΔY_d), or (0.1)(40) = $4. This $4 amount must be subtracted from the $24 of second-round spending because the $4 does not generate domestic production and income, resulting in a net effect of $20 in this second round of the multiplier process. In sum, the $40 of production in the first round has led to $20 of new spending and income in the second round; 50 percent gets "respent."

The process continues into a third round. The $20 of spending from the second round leads to $20 of new income for the workers and firms producing the goods purchased in that round. Of the $20 new income thus generated, $5 [= (0.25)(20)] will be taken out of the spending stream via taxes. This leaves $15 of new disposable income; of this $15 new Y_d, $12 [= (0.8)(15)] will be spent. However, spending on imports will increase by the MPM times the $20 change in total income, and this $2 of imports [= (0.1)(20)], when subtracted from the $12 of spending, leaves a net increase in spending on domestic goods of $10. Thus, 50 percent of the second round amount of $20 has been "respent" in the third round. This $10 of spending leads to new income, and a fourth round is started. Theoretically, this process goes on through an infinite number of rounds.

What is the ultimate change in income occurring because of the original $40 of new investment? The total change in income after all the rounds have been completed equals the sum of the following geometric series:

$$\Delta Y = 40 + \quad 20 \quad + \quad 10 \quad + \quad 5 \quad + \ldots$$
$$\Delta Y = 40 + (0.5)(40) + (0.5)(20) + (0.5)(10) + \ldots$$
$$\Delta Y = 40 + (0.5)(40) + (0.5)^2(40) + (0.5)^3(40) + \ldots$$

which, mathematically, can be shown to be

$$\Delta Y = [1/(1 - \text{fraction respent in each round})](\text{initial } \Delta I)$$
$$= [1/(1 - 0.5)](40)$$
$$= (1/0.5)(40) = (2)(40) = 80$$

The 0.5 in the $(1 - 0.5)$ denominator term derives from the 50 percent respent in each round; in symbols, this 50 percent is $[\text{MPC}(1 - t) - \text{MPM}]$ or $[(0.8)(1 - 0.25) - 0.1] = [(0.8)(0.75) - 0.1] = (0.6 - 0.1) = 0.5$. Thus, the initial increase in autonomous investment spending of $40 has led to a total change in income of $80. An initial change in autonomous consumption spending[5] or in autonomous government or export spending of $40 would have had the same $80 impact on income as the $40 change in autonomous investment. The "multiplier" is simply the total change in income divided by the initial change in autonomous spending, or $80/$40 = 2.0. The formula for calculating the autonomous spending multiplier in the open economy (k_o) is

$$k_o = \frac{1}{1 - [\text{MPC}(1 - t) - \text{MPM}]}$$

or

$$k_o = \frac{1}{1 - \text{MPC}(1 - t) + \text{MPM}} \qquad [23]$$

Expression [23] is the basic **open-economy multiplier.**[6] If the economy were a closed economy, there would be no imports (or exports). Hence, the MPM would be zero and the closed economy multiplier would be $1/[1 - \text{MPC}(1 - t)]$. This multiplier would be larger than the open-economy multiplier (for any given MPC and t) because there is no leakage of spending out of the domestic economy into imports. In addition, if it is assumed that there is no government sector, then $t = 0$ and the multiplier becomes $1/(1 - \text{MPC})$ or, since MPC + MPS = 1.0, the multiplier is 1/MPS.

Changes in autonomous imports

A further multiplier exists in the open economy. We have dealt above with autonomous increases in consumption, investment, government spending on goods and services, and exports. But autonomous imports $\underline{M}$ constitute another type of autonomous spending in the open economy. What happens if $\underline{M}$ increases? This one is tricky. If the demand for imports increases autonomously, this is equivalent to an autonomous *decrease* in the demand for domestic goods. Therefore, in national income models, an autonomous increase in imports will lead to a *decrease* in the level of income. The autonomous increase in imports reflects

. . . .

[5]It is assumed that the first round of spending is entirely on domestic goods.

[6]If imports are made a function of *disposable* income rather than of total income, then the open-economy multiplier is

$$k'_o = \frac{1}{1 - \text{MPC}(1 - t) + \text{MPM}(1 - t)} \qquad [23']$$

For identical MPC, t, and MPM, this multiplier is slightly larger than the open-economy multiplier in [23].

a decrease in spending on domestic goods, which leads to lower income. Since the multiplier process for an autonomous increase in imports operates in a *downward* direction, the multiplier for a change in autonomous imports is equal to *minus* k_o; that is,

$$\Delta Y/\Delta M = -k_o$$
$$= -\frac{1}{1 - \text{MPC}(1 - t) + \text{MPM}}$$

[24]

There is no conflict between this negative impact of an increase in imports in macro models and the positive impact of imports on national well-being in international trade theory. Trade theory assumes that the country is always at full employment and on its production-possibilities frontier both before and after the change in imports. In the macro models, we are making no such assumption that the economy is always at its maximum output.

With this import multiplier in mind, what will happen if exports and imports both increase autonomously by the same amount? The net impact of an autonomous balanced change in the size of the foreign trade sector (that is, an equal autonomous change in exports and imports) is *zero*. This occurs because the export change has a multiplier of k_o while the autonomous import change has a multiplier of minus k_o. The two changes cancel each other out with respect to their impact on national income.

The Current Account and the Multiplier

Having examined the multiplier in the Keynesian income model, let us now look at relationships between national income, the current account balance, and the multiplier. First, recall the earlier point that national income equilibrium can coexist with a deficit in the current account. Suppose that, as a policy objective, we wish to eliminate the current account deficit by reducing imports, with the reduction in imports to be accomplished by reducing national income (through contractionary macroeconomic policy). *By how much would national income have to be reduced to eliminate the current account deficit?* The answer is easy to obtain. For instance, in our earlier numerical example, there was a deficit of $80 ($X$ was 140, M was 220); we must contract income enough so that imports fall by $80. Remembering the MPM, this means that income must fall enough so that the change in income multiplied by the MPM equals −80. Thus, if the ΔM target is −80,

$$\Delta M = \text{MPM} \cdot \Delta Y$$
$$-80 = 0.10 \cdot \Delta Y$$
$$\Delta Y = -800$$

The level of income must fall by $800 in order to reduce imports by an amount that will restore balance in the current account. If the economy is at less than full employment, this very large contraction in income will not be welcomed. There is a conflict between an "internal" target for the economy, such as full employment, and an "external" target, such as balance in the current account.

Second, suppose that we want to take policy measures to expand *exports* (e.g., by depreciating the value of our currency relative to other currencies and assuming that the Marshall-Lerner condition holds) as a way of eliminating the current account deficit. If exports increase by $80, will this eliminate the current account deficit? The answer is no. If exports increase by $80, then the open-economy multiplier of 2.0 is applied to this autonomous increase in exports. The level of Y will rise by (80)(2.0), or $160, to $2,160 from the original $2,000. But because Y has risen by $160, there will be induced imports of the MPM (= 0.10) times $160, or $16. The expansion of exports (by $80) has cut the deficit by $64 (= 80 − 16) but has not eliminated it.

By how much must exports increase in order to eliminate the current account deficit of $80 while still maintaining equilibrium in national income? To obtain the answer to this question, note that the objective is to increase X by \$80 more than any increase in induced imports. Hence, we want $\Delta X - \Delta M = 80$. The change in imports that will be induced by the increase in Y due to the export expansion is MPM $\times \Delta Y$. Thus, we want $\Delta X -$ MPM $\cdot \Delta Y = 80$. However, the ΔY is simply the ΔX times the multiplier. Thus,

$$\Delta X - \text{MPM} \cdot \Delta Y = 80$$

$$\Delta X - \text{MPM} \left[\frac{1}{1 - \text{MPC}(1 - t) + \text{MPM}} \right] \Delta X = 80$$

Using the numbers in our example,

$$\Delta X - (0.1) \left[\frac{1}{1 - 0.8(1 - 0.25) + 0.1} \right] \Delta X = 80$$

$$\Delta X - (0.1)[1/(1 - 0.5)] \, \Delta X = 80$$

$$\Delta X - (0.1)(2) \, \Delta X = 80$$

$$\Delta X - 0.2 \Delta X = 80$$

$$0.8 \Delta X = 80$$

$$\Delta X = 100$$

We know that this is the answer we are seeking because, with a multiplier of 2.0, an increase in autonomous exports of \$100 will yield an increase in income of \$200, thus inducing new imports of \$20. The current account deficit will have been eliminated because exports rose by \$80 more than induced imports. Note that this is a rather large increase in exports over the initial level of \$140. Whether this large an increase is feasible is a valid question, and the analysis has relevance to U.S. attempts to get other countries to open their markets to U.S. exports as a way of eliminating the large U.S. current account deficit.

The point that an autonomous increase in exports will improve the current account $(X - M)$ also relates to the general phenomenon of "adjustment" in the current account. Suppose that, in an initial income equilibrium position, it so happens that the current account is *balanced,* that is, $X = M$. Then suppose that there is an autonomous increase in exports. Will the current account ultimately be restored to balance again? Or, at the other extreme, will the current account improve by the full amount of the increase in exports? You should be able to recognize that the answer to both questions is no. In the Keynesian income model, if X increases by ΔX, Y rises (using expression [23]) by the multiplied amount:

$$\Delta Y = \left[\frac{1}{1 - \text{MPC}(1 - t) + \text{MPM}} \right] \Delta X$$

However, the rise in Y induces more imports by MPM $\times \Delta Y$. Thus, the current account will improve by

$$\Delta X - \Delta M = \Delta X - \text{MPM} \left[\frac{1}{1 - \text{MPC}(1 - t) + \text{MPM}} \right] \Delta X$$

$$\Delta X - \Delta M = \Delta X \left\{ 1 - \text{MPM} \left[\frac{1}{1 - \text{MPC}(1 - t) + \text{MPM}} \right] \right\} \qquad [25]$$

The expression inside the braces (i.e., the expression after ΔX on the right-hand-side of [25]) is less than 1, so ultimately the current account improves by less than the initial increase in X. (In our above examples, an X increase of \$80 led to an ultimate current account improvement of \$64, and an X increase of \$100 led to an ultimate current account improvement of \$80.) Hence, the current account *does* improve, but by less than the initial disturbance. (The same would be true for a decrease in autonomous imports.) Because the initial export increase is partly offset by induced imports, there is at least *some* adjustment to the initial disturbance, meaning that the repercussions in the economy reduce the imbalance first caused by the export increase. However, there is not full adjustment because the imbalance does not return to zero, and this is called a **partial current account adjustment** to any initial disturbance.

Foreign Repercussions and the Multiplier Process

A final matter to consider in our treatment of Keynesian income models is **foreign repercussions.** In the real world, when spending and income change in a home country, changes are transmitted to other countries through changes in imports of the home country. As reactions to the changes in trade occur in the other countries, there will be feedback upon the original home country. While full-scale econometric models of the world economy with hundreds of equations have been used to trace through foreign repercussions, we are less ambitious in this chapter. We give one limited example of how such repercussions can be taken account of in relatively simple macroeconomic models. This example concerns the multiplier process.

In the traditional (no repercussions) open-economy multiplier process, an autonomous investment increase in the United States, for example, will cause a rise in U.S. income by the change in investment times the standard open-economy multiplier. This multiplied change in income will generate an induced rise in imports (by the MPM times the change in income). Thus, in the following schematic diagram:

$$\uparrow I_{US} \longrightarrow \uparrow Y_{US} \longrightarrow \uparrow M_{US}$$

The process stops here in the model we have been using so far. However, when foreign repercussions are permitted in the model, the process continues. The rise in imports into the United States constitutes a rise in exports of the rest of the world (ROW). When exports in ROW increase, this initiates a multiplier process in ROW and a rise in ROW income. This rise in income causes ROW to import more goods based on its marginal propensity to import. Finally, at least some of the increased imports into ROW will be exports of the United States! These increased exports will then set in motion additional spending and income generation in the United States. Further, this additional U.S. income will cause more U.S. imports, and so on. The process continues in ever-diminishing amounts. The multiplier mechanism when foreign repercussions exist can be represented by the following flow diagram:

$$\uparrow I_{US} \to \uparrow Y_{US} \to \uparrow M_{US} \to \uparrow X_{ROW} \to \uparrow Y_{ROW} \to \uparrow M_{ROW} \to \uparrow X_{US}$$
$$\uparrow \qquad\qquad\qquad\qquad\qquad\qquad\qquad\qquad\qquad\qquad \downarrow$$
$$\leftarrow \leftarrow \leftarrow \leftarrow \leftarrow \leftarrow \leftarrow \leftarrow \leftarrow \leftarrow \leftarrow \leftarrow \leftarrow \leftarrow \leftarrow$$

As you can see, we continue going through the loop until the marginal changes in income approach zero.

When all of these repercussions have occurred, the total change in income in the United States that results from the initial increase in investment will be *larger* than was the case when repercussions were not considered because of the additional feedback on U.S. income from the rest of the world. The expression for this repercussions multiplier, the **open-economy multiplier with foreign repercussions,** is complicated and is explored further in the appendix at the end of this chapter.

The "foreign repercussions process" emphasizes that countries of the world are interdependent with respect to macroeconomic activity. When a boom (or recession) occurs in one country, it will be transmitted to other countries and will then feed back upon the originating country. We can therefore graph one country's income level as being

FIGURE 7   **Income Interdependence between Countries**

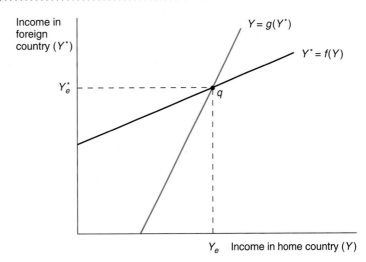

Because imports of one country are exports of the other country, a rise in income in one country will stimulate exports and therefore income in the other country. Thus, income in the foreign country (Y^*) is dependent on income in the home country (Y), and vice versa. There is simultaneous national income equilibrium in the two countries where the two lines intersect (i.e., at Y_e and Y^*_e).

positively related to other countries' income levels, and likewise can graph other countries' income levels as being positively related to the first country's income level, as in Figure 7. This graph demonstrates the simultaneous determination of equilibrium income in the two countries. Consequently, both levels of income are altered whenever autonomous spending in any one country changes (which would be a shift in one of the income lines). See Case Study 2 for examples of the impact of changes in one country's income upon other countries.

CONCEPT CHECK

1. What happens to the size of the open-economy multiplier (without foreign repercussions) if, other things being equal, the marginal propensity to import increases? Explain in economic terms, not just in algebraic terms.

2. Explain why an autonomous increase in investment spending in a country will lead to a greater increase in national income in that country if foreign repercussions are important than if foreign repercussions are unimportant.

AN OVERVIEW OF PRICE AND INCOME ADJUSTMENTS AND SIMULTANEOUS EXTERNAL AND INTERNAL BALANCE

This and the preceding chapter have been concerned with how the exchange rate and the state of the balance of payments lead to impacts on the current account and the internal sector of the economy. In the previous chapter, we examined the manner by which a change in the exchange rate affects export receipts and import outlays and the current account balance through altering the relative prices of home and foreign goods. In a context of fixed exchange rates, we discussed how a disequilibrium in the balance of payments (a deficit or surplus) sets into motion money supply changes and internal price

✸ CASE STUDY 2   INCOME INTERDEPENDENCE AMONG COUNTRIES

Several large-scale econometric studies have attempted to ascertain the impact of changes in one country's national income on the national incomes of other countries. Table 2 reports the results of one such study. For a given 1 percent autonomous income "shock" in the originating country, the table shows the consequent percentage change in income in other countries after one, two, and three years. For example, a 1 percent shock to U.S. GNP will raise Japan's GNP by 0.13 percent after one year, 0.20 percent at the end of two years, and 0.22 percent after three years.

Note from the table that the United States and the Federal Republic of Germany have larger impacts on the other two countries than the other countries have on the United States and Germany. However, even the Japanese impact on the United States of 0.04 percent is still about $3 billion. Note also that the 2.73 percent impact on the United States of a U.S. 1 percent income shock gives us an estimate of the U.S. open-economy multiplier with foreign repercussions, namely 2.73. Finally, the model was constructed under the assumption of fixed exchange rates, but all other prices were permitted to vary in response to the income shocks. Price effects could explain the seemingly paradoxical result that the impact of a shock originating in Canada on Canada itself is smaller after two and three years than after one year.

TABLE 2   Effects of 1 Percent Income Shock in Originating Country on Other Countries

Originating Country	Years	United States	Japan	Federal Republic of Germany	Canada
United States	1	1.60	0.13	0.13	0.53
	2	2.39	0.20	0.21	0.63
	3	2.73	0.22	0.33	0.63
Japan	1	0.01	1.08	0.03	0.02
	2	0.03	1.15	0.04	0.03
	3	0.04	1.22	0.06	0.04
Federal Republic of Germany	1	0.04	0.06	1.83	0.06
	2	0.10	0.11	1.87	0.09
	3	0.16	0.17	2.91	0.13
Canada	1	0.02	0.01	0.01	1.38
	2	0.04	0.01	0.02	1.36
	3	0.05	0.01	0.02	1.37

Source: V. B. Filatov, B. G. Hickman, and L. R. Klein, "Long-Term Simulations with the Project LINK System, 1978–1985," in B. G. Hickman, ed., *Global International Economic Models* (Amsterdam: North-Holland, 1983), as cited in John F. Helliwell and Tim Padmore, "Empirical Studies of Macroeconomic Interdependence," in Ronald W. Jones and Peter B. Kenen, eds., *Handbook of International Economics*, Vol. 2 (Amsterdam: North-Holland, 1985), pp. 1117–19.   ✸

changes so as to improve (deteriorate) the current account in the case of a BOP deficit (surplus). Finally, in the present chapter, we noted that a disturbance in the current account (such as an autonomous increase in exports) leads to national income changes, which in turn partly (but not completely) offset the initial current account disturbance through induced changes in imports.

An important feature of the interrelationships between the current account and the internal economy, and one which will be examined in more detail in subsequent chapters, is the possible conflict between the macroeconomic goals of "external balance" and "internal balance." **External balance** in this context refers to balance in the current account ($X = M$), while **internal balance** refers to the desirable state of the economy where there is a low level of unemployment together with reasonable price stability.

There are clearly four possible combinations of departures from external and internal balance:

Case I: Deficit in the current account; unacceptably high unemployment.

Case II: Deficit in the current account; unacceptably rapid inflation.

Case III: Surplus in the current account; unacceptably rapid inflation.

Case IV: Surplus in the current account; unacceptably high unemployment.[7]

If policymakers are confronted with any one of these four combinations in a situation of fixed exchange rates, what should the macroeconomic policy stance be? Cases II and IV are seemingly straightforward. In case II with a current account deficit and unacceptably rapid inflation, restrictive or contractionary aggregate demand–oriented monetary and fiscal policy (i.e., a reduction in the money supply, a decrease in government spending, an increase in taxes) is in order. With the adoption of such policies, the price level and the level of national income will fall. The falling prices—or at least prices that are rising less rapidly than prices in other countries—will expand exports and reduce imports, and the fall in income will also reduce imports via the MPM. Thus the restrictive policies will improve the current account and move the economy toward external balance, as well as dampen the inflation and move the economy toward internal balance. However, the degree of restriction needed to attain external balance may differ from the degree of restriction needed to attain internal balance, and thus policymakers may not be able to attain both targets simultaneously. Nevertheless, the direction of policy will be correct.

The same general conclusions hold in case IV where there is a current account surplus and unemployment. Of course, policy is moving in the opposite direction from case II. Expansionary monetary and fiscal policy—an increase in the money supply, an increase in government spending, a reduction in taxes—will stimulate national income and also induce more imports. In addition, any price pressures generated by the expansion will reduce exports and increase imports. Thus, again, the direction of policy works to reduce the current account surplus and to reduce the amount of unemployment, although of course the degree of necessary expansion may differ with respect to attainment of each particular goal.

Cases I and III present more intractable policy problems than cases II and IV. In case I, with a current account deficit and unacceptably high unemployment, even the *direction* of the appropriate policy stance is unclear. Expansionary monetary and fiscal policy to decrease unemployment will worsen the current account through induced imports by the MPM times the rise in income. In addition, if the price level rises due to the expansionary policy, exports will fall and imports will rise, thus worsening the already existing current account deficit. On the other hand, contractionary policy to reduce the current account deficit will drive national income downward and worsen the unemployment situation. Likewise, in case III, with a current account surplus and inflation, expansionary policy will reduce the current account surplus but worsen the inflation, while contractionary policy to alleviate the inflation will enlarge the current account surplus. Hence, the attainment of one "balance" in either of these cases will worsen the situation with respect

- -

[7]Of course, as the experience of the 1970s particularly indicated, it is also possible to have unacceptably high unemployment and unacceptably rapid inflation at the same time. We deal here only with the traditional macroeconomic analysis that treats the economy as having one of these internal problems but not the other simultaneously. The "stagflation" situation of high unemployment and rapid inflation at the same time is discussed more thoroughly in the chapter "Prices and Output in the Open Economy: Aggregate Supply and Demand."

to the other "balance." There is thus a conflict between the attainment of external balance and internal balance in these two cases. The policymakers may have to decide which goal is more important.

In these "conflict" cases, however, as well as in cases II and IV, where the degree of needed policy restriction or expansion was in doubt, it *is* possible to have the relative price effects and the income effects work together to attain both goals simultaneously. This can be accomplished by using a *change in the exchange rate* as an instrument of policy. This change in the exchange rate can be interpreted as a change in the official parity rate in a fixed-but-adjustable-rate system (e.g., the Bretton Woods system from 1947 to 1971, discussed in the last chapter of the book) or as government intervention to influence the exchange rate in a more flexible exchange rate system, such as the system that currently exists. A model that focuses on the use of exchange rate changes along with contractionary or expansionary macroeconomic policy to attain simultaneously the external goal and the internal goal has been developed by T. W. Swan (1963).

The Swan Model

In the Swan model, a basic diagram illustrates the policy options available in a pegged rate system where the exchange rate can be changed by government action (see Figure 8). The internal balance target is shown by the downward-sloping *IB* curve, whose position shows all combinations of domestic spending $(C + I + G)$ and the exchange rate e that will attain the target level of employment and price stability desired by policymakers. Why does the curve slope downward? Beginning at any point on *IB*, a fall in $(C + I + G)$ leads to less than the desired level of employment (a movement to the left of *IB*). This can

FIGURE 8   **External and Internal Balance—The Swan Diagram**

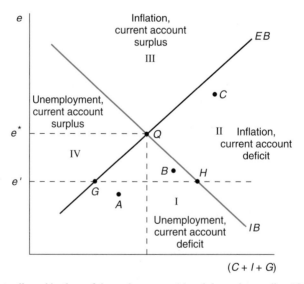

The *IB* curve reflects all combinations of the exchange rate (e) and domestic spending $(C + I + G)$ that generate the desired internal balance in the economy. Similarly, the *EB* curve shows all combinations of e and $(C + I + G)$ that produce external balance (balance in the current account). The area below the *IB* curve indicates unemployment, and the area above the curve reflects inflation. The area below the *EB* curve reflects current account deficits, and the area above the curve indicates current account surpluses. Simultaneous attainment of both internal and external balance targets occurs only at point Q. Areas I to IV indicate the possible combinations of current account surplus, current account deficit, unemployment, and inflation that will occur if Q does not obtain.

be offset by a depreciation of the home currency (a rise in e), which will increase exports, decrease imports, and move the economy vertically to the *IB* curve. Alternatively, from any starting point, the expansionary and inflationary stimulus of a rise in e requires a compression of $(C + I + G)$ through policy-induced reductions in expenditures. Any point lying above *IB* reflects a combination of e and $(C + I + G)$ that is inflationary since, for a given level of $(C + I + G)$, e is too high and will overstimulate exports and/or retard imports. Similarly, any point below the curve represents an exchange rate that is too low to generate the required exports and imports necessary to attain the level of target income. Consequently, the area below *IB* reflects combinations of e and $(C + I + G)$ that lead to unemployment.

The external balance goal is described by the upward-sloping *EB* curve, which shows all combinations of e and $(C + I + G)$ that maintain balance in the current account. From any starting point, a rise in $(C + I + G)$ worsens the current account through induced imports, requiring a rise in e (depreciation of the home currency) to restore current account balance. Alternatively, from the starting point, a rise in e leads to a current account surplus, which requires an increase in $(C + I + G)$ to eliminate the surplus. Points above (or to the left) of the *EB* curve show combinations of domestic spending and e leading to a current account surplus, while points below (to the right) of the curve reflect combinations of $(C + I + G)$ and e leading to a current account deficit.

Joint attainment of both policy targets in this simple open-economy model obviously lies at the levels of e and $(C + I + G)$ indicated by the intersection of the *IB* and *EB* curves, point Q. Any other point leads to one or both of the targets' not being realized. However, if both targets are not realized, *and* if we know the position of the economy in relation to point Q, policy *is* in a position to move the economy to Q. For example, if the economy is at point A with a current account deficit and unemployment, a depreciation of the home currency (a rise in e) and expansionary macro policy (e.g., a rise in G) can move the economy to Q. (Note also that if the economy is at point B, a depreciation of the home currency together with *contractionary* monetary and fiscal policy is called for, *even though B also has an unemployment-deficit situation.*) Alternatively, if the economy is at point C, an appreciation of the home currency (a fall in e) and contractionary macroeconomic policy are the prescription. Thus, from any point that does not have simultaneous external and internal balance, policy measures can be designed that will (at least theoretically) move the economy to point Q, with balance in both sectors. This Swan framework is an illustration of the general policy rule derived by Nobel Prize–winning economist Jan Tinbergen (1967) that the attainment of two targets requires two instruments—in this case the targets are external balance and internal balance, and the policy instruments are exchange rate changes and macroeconomic policy.

An important observation from this model is the realization that only one exchange rate permits the attainment of both targets. If the country incorrectly pegs the exchange rate at e' in Figure 8 (overvalues its own currency), then the country cannot reach its domestic target without experiencing a current account deficit (point H). On the other hand, external balance can be attained only by experiencing considerable unemployment (point G). A third possibility is a combination of unemployment and external deficit. If the country is unable (or unwilling) to correct the exchange rate, then no level of (policy-influenced) domestic spending will allow it to reach both of its targets.

Finally, a criticism of the Swan model is that it is difficult to know exactly where the *IB* and *EB* curves in Figure 8 are located and therefore where they intersect. The *actual* situation can be identified as it involves only knowledge of the current exchange rate and the state of $(C + I + G)$. Suppose we correctly identify point A as the existing situation, but the *IB* and *EB* curves in fact intersect above and *to the left* of point *A* (i.e., the real point *Q* is actually to the left of the hypothesized point *Q*). If the policymaker mistakenly thinks that *Q* is above and to the right of *A*, expansionary monetary and fiscal policy will be followed rather than the appropriate contractionary policy. Simultaneous external and internal balance will not be attained.

SUMMARY

This chapter considered the interrelationships between the current account and national income in the context of an open-economy Keynesian model. The equilibrium level of income occurs when desired aggregate expenditures equal production or, alternatively, when desired $S + T + M$ equals desired $I + G + X$ or $S + (T - G) - I$ equals the current account balance. In this model, increases in autonomous spending on consumption, investment, government spending, or exports lead to multiplied increases in national income through the multiplier of $1/[1 - \text{MPC}(1 - t) + \text{MPM}]$. The presence of "foreign repercussions" introduces additional features into the multiplier process, with these repercussions embodying the role of interdependence among economies in national income determination. In Keynesian income models in general, if the current account is in equilibrium, a disturbance to that equilibrium will set forces in motion to restore current account balance. However, only partial adjustment rather than a full restoration of current account balance will occur.

An important point emerging from the Keynesian income model is that, with a fixed exchange rate, equilibrium in national income need not occur with simultaneous equilibrium in the current account. Policymakers confront targets of both external and internal balance, and it may be difficult to attain both targets even if explicit changes in the exchange rate are permitted. Further policy considerations are explored in the next three chapters.

KEY TERMS

autonomous consumption spending
autonomous imports
autonomous spending multiplier
average propensity to import
  (APM)
consumption function
desired aggregate expenditures
equilibrium level of national
  income
external balance
foreign repercussions

import function
income elasticity of demand for
  imports (YEM)
induced consumption spending
induced imports
injections
internal balance
Keynesian income model
leakages
marginal propensity to consume
  (MPC)

marginal propensity to import
  (MPM)
marginal propensity to save
  (MPS)
open-economy multiplier
open-economy multiplier with
  foreign repercussions
partial current account adjustment
rounds of spending in the
  multiplier process
saving function

QUESTIONS AND PROBLEMS

1. Using the Keynesian model, explain the impact on national income of an autonomous increase in saving.

2. Given the following simple Keynesian model:

$$E = C + I + G + X - M \qquad I = 110$$
$$C = 50 + 0.85Y_d \qquad G = 208$$
$$Y_d = Y - T \qquad X = 82$$
$$T = 0.2Y \qquad M = 10 + 0.08Y$$
$$Y = E \text{ in equilibrium}$$

  (*a*) Determine the equilibrium level of income.
  (*b*) When the equilibrium income level is attained, is there a surplus or a deficit in the current account? Of how much?

  (*c*) What is the size of the autonomous spending multiplier?

3. (*a*) In the model of Question 2, by how much would income have to change in order to make $X = M$ (with no change in *X*)? How much change in autonomous investment would be necessary to generate this change in income?

  (*b*) In the model of Question 2, how much would autonomous exports have to change in order to produce an equilibrium income level at which the current account was in balance?

4. Explain why a country with a current account surplus (such as Japan) can be said to be saving more than it invests.

5. Germany has consistently pursued an anti-inflationary domestic policy that has resulted in sizable unemployment
   and a lower rate of economic growth than would otherwise
   have been the case. Why might Germany's trading partners
   have reacted adversely to such a German policy stance?

6. In the Swan diagram, suppose that the economy has a
   current account surplus and excessive inflation. Discuss the
   policy implications in this situation.

7. In trade negotiations with the Japanese over the large U.S.
   trade deficit with Japan, the Clinton administration urged
   the Japanese government to undertake a more expansionary
   fiscal policy. If the Japanese government did so, how might
   the U.S. trade deficit with Japan be reduced? Could U.S.
   imports from Japan rise because of the expansionary
   policy? Explain.

8. You are given the following four-sector Keynesian income
   model:

$$E = C + I + G + (X - M) \qquad I = 230$$
$$C = 120 + 0.75Y_d \qquad\qquad G = 560$$
$$Y_d = Y - T \qquad\qquad\quad X = 350$$
$$T = 40 + 0.20Y \qquad\qquad M = 30 + 0.10Y$$
$$Y = E \text{ in equilibrium}$$

(a) Calculate the equilibrium income level (Y_e). (Note that,
    in a slight difference from the models in this chapter,
    taxes have an autonomous component as well as the
    familiar component that depends upon income.)

(b) Calculate the amount of taxes collected when the
    economy is at Y_e. Then indicate whether the govern-
    ment has a surplus or deficit at Y_e and calculate the
    value of the surplus or deficit.

(c) Calculate the value of net exports when the economy is
    at Y_e.

9. Suppose that there are two countries in the world economy,
   countries I and II. The countries possess the following
   marginal propensities: $MPC_I = 0.7$; $MPM_I = 0.1$; $MPC_{II} = 0.8$; $MPM_{II} = 0.2$. There is no government sector. Using the
   formula for the open-economy multiplier with foreign
   repercussions, calculate the impact upon country I's income
   of a rise in autonomous investment in country I of $35
   billion. (Note: To answer this question, you need to read the
   appendix to this chapter.)

⬛ APPENDIX   DERIVATION OF THE MULTIPLIER WITH FOREIGN REPERCUSSIONS

This appendix derives the autonomous spending multiplier when foreign repercussions are taken
into account. To simplify to some extent the complicated algebra, we assume that there is no
government sector (in either country), and hence $G = 0$ and $t = 0$. Note that the standard
open-economy multiplier in this case is $1/(1 - MPC + MPM)$ or $1/(MPS + MPM)$.

   In the derivation, we designate foreign country variables with a *; unstarred variables refer to
the home country. Consumption contains the usual autonomous component and induced component
in both countries, as does the import function. Investment and exports are autonomous. The
equations for the two economies are thus

$$E = C + I + X - M \qquad E^* = C^* + I^* + X^* - M^*$$
$$C = a + bY \qquad\qquad C^* = a^* + b^*Y^*$$
$$I = \overline{I} \qquad\qquad\qquad I^* = \overline{I^*}$$
$$X = \overline{X} \qquad\qquad\quad X^* = \overline{X^*}$$
$$M = \overline{M} + mY \qquad\quad M^* = \overline{M^*} + m^*Y^*$$
$$Y = E \text{ and } Y^* = E^* \text{ in equilibrium}$$

   The equilibrium level of income for the home country is found by substitution into the $Y = C + I + X - M$ equilibrium expression:

$$Y = a + bY + \overline{I} + \overline{X} - (\overline{M} + mY)$$
$$Y - bY + mY = a + \overline{I} + \overline{X} - \overline{M}$$
$$Y = \frac{a + \overline{I} + \overline{X} - \overline{M}}{(1 - b + m)} \qquad\qquad [26]$$

However, in this two-country model, the exports of the home country are equal to the imports of the foreign country, so [26] can be written:

$$Y = \frac{a + \overline{I} + \overline{M}^* + m^*Y^* - \overline{M}}{(1 - b + m)}$$

For simplification, we substitute s (the marginal propensity to save in the home country) for $(1 - b)$, since b is the home country's marginal propensity to consume:

$$Y = \frac{a + \overline{I} + \overline{M}^* + m^*Y^* - \overline{M}}{s + m}. \qquad [27]$$

A similar procedure for obtaining equilibrium income in the foreign country yields the equation for Y^* as

$$Y^* = \frac{a^* + \overline{I}^* + \overline{M} + mY - \overline{M}^*}{s^* + m^*} \qquad [28]$$

where s^* is the foreign country's marginal propensity to save.

To obtain multipliers for the home country, expression [28] is substituted into expression [27].

$$Y = \frac{a + \overline{I} + \overline{M}^* - \overline{M} + m^*\left(\dfrac{a^* + \overline{I}^* + \overline{M} + mY - \overline{M}^*}{s^* + m^*}\right)}{s + m}$$

$$Y = \frac{(s^* + m^*)(a + \overline{I} + \overline{M}^* - \overline{M}) + m^*(a^* + \overline{I}^* + \overline{M} + mY - \overline{M}^*)}{(s^* + m^*) / (s + m)}$$

$$(s + m)Y = \frac{(s^* + m^*)(a + \overline{I} + \overline{M}^* - \overline{M}) + m^*(a^* + \overline{I}^* + \overline{M} - \overline{M}^*)}{s^* + m^*} + \frac{m^*mY}{s^* + m^*}$$

$$(s^* + m^*)(s + m)Y - m^*mY = (s^* + m^*)(a + \overline{I} + \overline{M}^* - \overline{M}) + m^*(a^* + \overline{I}^* + \overline{M} - \overline{M}^*)$$

Therefore equilibrium income Y can be expressed as:

$$Y = \left(\frac{s^* + m^*}{ss^* + ms^* + sm^*}\right)(a + \overline{I} + \overline{M}^* - \overline{M}) +$$

$$\left(\frac{m^*}{ss^* + ms^* + sm^*}\right)(a^* + \overline{I}^* + \overline{M} - \overline{M}^*) \qquad [29]$$

Expression [29] can be used to obtain a variety of multipliers. The autonomous investment multiplier in the home country simply involves looking at the ΔY associated with a ΔI:

$$\frac{\Delta Y}{\Delta I} = \frac{s^* + m^*}{ss^* + ms^* + sm^*}$$

or

$$= \frac{1 + \dfrac{m^*}{s^*}}{s + m + m^* \dfrac{s}{s^*}}. \qquad [30]$$

Inspection of this multiplier indicates that it is larger than it would be if there were no foreign repercussions. Without a government sector, or with $t = 0$, the standard no-repercussions open-economy multiplier (i.e., expression [23] in the chapter, with $t = 0$) is

$$\frac{1}{1 - \text{MPC} + \text{MPM}} = \frac{1}{\text{MPS} + \text{MPM}}$$

or, in the symbols of this appendix, $1/(s + m)$. Expression [30] is larger than this multiplier because the percentage change in the numerator in [30] from that in [23] is larger than the percentage change in the denominator.

The investment multiplier in [30] applies also to a change in autonomous consumption (i.e., to a change in "a"). However, note that, unlike the case where foreign repercussions are absent, the foreign repercussions multiplier for an autonomous change in *exports* of the home country will differ from the foreign repercussions multiplier for a change in autonomous investment (or consumption). Looking at expression [29], an autonomous change in exports for the home country is a change in autonomous *imports* ($\overline{M}$ *) for the foreign country. Thus,

$$\frac{\Delta Y}{\Delta X} = \frac{\Delta Y}{\Delta M^*} = \frac{s^* + m^*}{ss^* + ms^* + sm^*} - \frac{m^*}{ss^* + ms^* + sm^*}$$

$$= \frac{s^*}{ss^* + ms^* + sm^*}$$

$$= \frac{1}{s + m + m^*(s/s^*)} \tag{31}$$

The multiplier in [31] is smaller than the multiplier in [30] because of the absence of the m^*/s^* term in the numerator of [31]. Expression [31] is also *smaller than* the $[1/(s + m)]$ multiplier *when there are no foreign repercussions*. The economic reason is that an autonomous increase in home exports, while it stimulates home production and generates an expansion in home income, is also an autonomous increase in foreign country imports. The increase in autonomous foreign imports is at the expense of foreign consumption of goods produced in the foreign country, and it thus initiates a downward movement of income abroad. The decrease in foreign income in turn induces a decrease in purchases of home country exports through the operation of the marginal propensity to import in the foreign country, and it generates a downward movement in *home country* income that partly offsets the upward income effects of the original autonomous export increase in the home country.

Another multiplier of interest is the impact of a change in autonomous investment in the *foreign* country upon *home* country income. If I^* is changed in expression [29], the impact upon Y is

$$\frac{\Delta Y}{\Delta I^*} = \frac{m^*}{ss^* + ms^* + sm^*}$$

$$= \frac{\dfrac{m^*}{s^*}}{s + m + m^* \dfrac{s}{s^*}} \tag{32}$$

Obviously, the introduction of foreign repercussions makes multiplier analysis more complex!

PART II

MACROECONOMIC POLICY IN THE OPEN ECONOMY

The ultimate objectives of monetary and fiscal policy are economic growth and rising living standards, *not* exchange-rate stability or current account balance per se. Nonetheless, reasonably stable exchange rates and sustainable external balances are important aspects of a healthy economy. Particularly when these variables get far out of line, they should be of concern to policymakers.

Council of Economic Advisers, 1990

In the previous part, we examined how international transactions affect the overall economy and how the foreign exchange market functioned. In addition, we discussed how the impact of international transactions could be incorporated into macroeconomic theory for the purpose of policy analysis. It is obvious that the pursuit of domestic targets such as price stability, high employment, and economic growth through the use of monetary and fiscal policy is more complex in the open economy than in the closed economy. This is due in part to the fact that, as noted briefly in the previous chapter, macro policy now has to concern itself with external objectives as well as internal objectives. In addition, the fact that international transactions not only affect the impact of macro policy but are in turn affected by those policy actions means that the impacts of policy go beyond a country's borders, thus complicating the problem.

In this part, we expand our analysis of the problems associated with pursuing internal and external targets using monetary and fiscal policy in the open economy. The nature of the policy problem varies with the type of exchange rate arrangement in place and also with the ease with which financial capital moves between countries. Hence, we approach the problem by examining in detail the effects of policy under different institutional settings. The chapter "Economic Policy in the Open Economy: Fixed Exchange Rates" analyzes the effects of macro policy in the situation where a fixed exchange rate system is being used, taking note of how the degree to which capital moves between countries influences the results. This discussion is followed in the chapter "Economic Policy in the Open Economy: Flexible Exchange Rates" by an analysis of policy effects under a flexible exchange rate system, again focusing largely on the influence of different degrees of capital mobility. The final chapter in this part, "Prices and Output in the Open Economy: Aggregate Supply and Demand," then examines the effects of macroeconomic policy in the open economy when prices are allowed to change and looks as well at the effects of international shocks. ❋

In some cases, by not putting policy issues in an international perspective, we provide students with the "wrong" answers.

Joseph E. Stiglitz, 1993

ECONOMIC POLICY IN THE OPEN ECONOMY

Fixed Exchange Rates

INTRODUCTION

In this chapter, we examine how economic policy operates in the open economy when exchange rates are fixed. Since the effects of discretionary policy are different under a flexible exchange rate system compared to a fixed-rate system, we then consider economic policy under flexible exchange rates in the following chapter. Although the major industrial countries tend to have flexible rate systems today, many countries still peg their currencies and thus have to contend with the effects of fixed rates when carrying out monetary and fiscal policy. This is true even among the major industrial countries in the European Union, which have relatively fixed rates within the EU but have flexible rates against the rest of the world.

Prior to current monetary arrangements (discussed in detail in the last chapter in the book), the international monetary system was characterized by fixed exchange rates, and there is continual pressure on the part of a good many individuals to return to some sort of fixed standard. In our consideration of economic policy under fixed rates, we first examine a fixed-rate model that separates monetary policy from fiscal policy and that provides some guidance in the selection of appropriate policy instruments. We then introduce a macroeconomic framework that specifically incorporates the money markets, the real sector, and the foreign sector (the *IS/LM/BP* model), which we use to examine the effects of alternative policy actions under fixed exchange rates (in this chapter) and under flexible exchange rates (in the next chapter). Command of this material should help you understand both the impact of various policy actions within a broad and rigorous macroeconomic framework and the effects of the exchange rate system on macroeconomic policy actions. Consideration of possible price effects accompanying these policy actions will be discussed in the chapter "Prices and Output in the Open Economy: Aggregate Supply and Demand."

TARGETS, INSTRUMENTS, AND ECONOMIC POLICY IN A TWO-INSTRUMENT, TWO-TARGET MODEL

As an introduction to policy analysis in the open economy, we begin by developing a very basic framework that will allow us to examine the interaction between policies aimed at attaining external balance and those aimed at other domestic targets such as full employment and price stability. One of the early models that differentiated the effects of monetary and fiscal policy on the open economy was developed by Robert Mundell

(1962). The separation of monetary and fiscal policy was accomplished by extending the current account analysis of that time to include capital flows as well. "External balance," or "balance-of-payments equilibrium," was thus defined by Mundell to mean a zero balance in the official reserve transactions balance.[1] The attainment of the external balance target is influenced by both monetary policy and fiscal policy. For example, an increase in the money supply will reduce interest rates, leading to a reduction in short-term capital inflows or an increase in short-term capital outflows and to a BOP deficit. Expanding government spending will lead to increased income and an increase in imports and also to a BOP deficit.[2] Since expansionary monetary policy and fiscal policy are assumed to affect the balance of payments in a similar fashion, one concludes that maintaining balance-of-payments equilibrium for a given exchange rate requires an opposite use of monetary and fiscal policy in this model; that is, expansionary fiscal policy must be accompanied by contractionary monetary policy and vice versa.

There is a similar policy relationship with respect to the internal balance target. Increases in the money supply tend to lower the interest rate and thus to stimulate real investment. If this is not to be expansionary and/or inflationary, the increase in investment must be offset by a decrease in government spending or by an increase in taxes that will reduce consumption spending. Similarly, maintenance of a given domestic internal balance target indicates that any increase in government spending (or any increase in consumption spending via a decrease in taxes) must be offset by some decrease in domestic investment through monetary policy actions if inflationary pressures are not to ensue.

The policy problem in this instance is demonstrated graphically in Figure 1 using a **Mundell-Fleming diagram.** The effects of monetary policy are captured through the use of different rates of interest on the vertical axis. Fiscal policy is represented through the levels of net government spending $(G - T)$ plotted on the horizontal axis. The inverse relationship between the two policy instruments is shown by upward-sloping curves, since higher interest rates reflect, *ceteris paribus,* a smaller money supply. Internal balance is represented by the *IB* curve and external balance by the *EB* curve. In this case, each curve shows combinations of monetary and fiscal policy [i and $(G - T)$] that bring about internal and external balance, respectively.

Although both curves slope upward for the reasons given above, the *EB* curve is drawn flatter than the *IB* curve because changes in the money supply (and hence the interest rate) are assumed to have a greater relative effect on external balance than on internal balance. This is generally thought to be the case because changes in the interest rate affect the balance of payments through both the capital and the current accounts. A rise in the interest rate causes not only an increase in net short-term capital inflows but also reduced domestic real investment and income, which acts to reduce imports. Changes in the interest rate thus exert both a direct and an indirect impact on the balance of payments, whereas they affect the internal balance target only through the direct impact on real investment. This assumption allows us to reach a conclusion about the appropriate assignment of policy instruments to the *IB* and *EB* targets (i.e., effective policy classification).

In Figure 1 it is clear that only one combination of monetary policy and fiscal policy will allow the simultaneous attainment of both targets, that of i^* and $(G - T)^*$. Any other combination will lead to one or both of the targets not being met. All points to the left of

----

[1]Note that this definition of external balance differs from the definition in the Swan model in the preceding chapter, where the term referred to balance in the current account.

[2]In this Mundell model, it is assumed that expansionary fiscal policy worsens the balance of payments. As we see later, expansionary fiscal policy can improve the balance of payments under certain circumstances.

FIGURE 1   **Internal Balance, External Balance, and Policy Instrument Classification in a Mundell-Fleming Diagram**

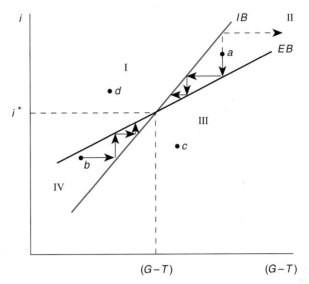

The *IB* curve reflects all combinations of interest rates *i* (monetary policy) and net government spending $(G - T)$ that lead to the attainment of domestic targets, that is, internal balance. Similarly, the flatter *EB* curve reflects all combinations of *i* and $(G - T)$ that generate equilibrium in the balance of payments for a given exchange rate. Points above the *IB* curve reflect unacceptably high unemployment, and points below reflect unacceptably rapid inflation. Similarly, points above the *EB* curve represent a surplus in the balance of payments, and points below represent a deficit. It is clear that internal balance and external balance are obtained simultaneously only at i^* and $(G - T)^*$. Finally, if the economy is not at i^* and $(G - T)^*$, monetary policy should be pursued to reach external balance and fiscal policy to reach internal balance.

or above the *IB* curve reflect combinations of the two instruments where the interest rate is too high given the fiscal policy stance, resulting in low income and in unemployment. Similarly, all points to the right of or below the *IB* curve lead to real investment levels that are too high, contributing to inflation. Points to the left of or above the *EB* curve reflect interest rates that are higher than necessary to bring the balance of payments into equilibrium at the given exchange rate, and hence generate a surplus in the balance of payments due to capital inflows. Points to the right of or below the *EB* curve reflect a balance-of-payments deficit. The policy space can thus be divided into four quadrants, each reflecting a different combination of missed targets:

   I. Unacceptably high unemployment; balance-of-payments surplus
   II. Unacceptably rapid inflation; balance-of-payments surplus
   III. Unacceptably rapid inflation; balance-of-payments deficit
   IV. Unacceptably high unemployment; balance-of-payments deficit

Again we see that the simultaneous attainment of the two targets can take place only by careful choice of the two instruments involved. For example, if the economy is at point *a,* altering one instrument will permit the attainment of one target but not both. To reach equilibrium, both instruments must be utilized.

    A further important point needs to be made relating to the assignment of instruments to targets. Given the nature of the *IB* and *EB* functions, it will be more efficient to assign the monetary policy instrument to pursue *EB* and fiscal policy instruments to pursue *IB* targets. This becomes obvious when one considers the possible sequence of policy decisions that could take place at point *a*. If monetary policy is directed toward the *IB* target, a decrease in the money supply (an increase in the interest rate) is required. If the fiscal policy instrument is then directed toward the *EB* target, expansionary fiscal action is required. These steps (shown by the dashed arrow in region II of Figure 1) would move the economy even farther away from *i** and $(G - T)*$, not closer. On the other hand, devoting monetary policy to the *EB* target and fiscal policy to the *IB* target[3] leads to a sequence of policy steps that drives the economy closer to the desired levels of *i** and $(G - T)*$ (indicated by the solid arrows in region II). A similar conclusion would be reached for points *b, c,* or *d*. This model thus suggests that effective policy classification of policy instruments and targets is an important element in the successful administration of economic policy in the open economy under fixed exchange rates.

CONCEPT CHECK

1. What is the difference between internal balance and external balance?
2. If the economy is operating at *c* in Figure 1, what policy actions should be carried out to reach the internal balance target? Why?
3. Which policy tool should be used to attain external balance in the Mundell-Fleming model? Why?

GENERAL EQUILIBRIUM IN THE OPEN ECONOMY: THE *IS/LM/BP* MODEL

Building on the introduction to policymaking in the open economy provided by the Mundell-Fleming model, we now turn to a broader general equilibrium construct that specifically incorporates the money market relationships developed in the chapter "The Monetary and Portfolio Balance Approaches to External Balance" and the real sector or income effects discussed in the chapter "National Income and the Current Account." In addition, the model specifically incorporates the effects of international trade and international capital flows on equilibrium in the open-economy model.

General Equilibrium in the Money Market: The *LM* Curve

Equilibrium in the money market occurs when the supply of money is equal to the demand for money. In the chapter "The Monetary and Portfolio Balance Approaches to External Balance," we covered both the supply of and the demand for money in considerable detail, and we presented the concept of money market equilibrium conceptually and algebraically in the following general manner:[4]

$$M_s = L$$

or

$$a(DR + IR) = a(BR + C) = f\,[\overset{+}{Y}, \overset{-}{i}, \overset{+}{P}, \overset{+}{W}, \overset{-}{E(\dot{p})}, \overset{?}{O}] \qquad [1]$$

[3]The reader may recall from other courses that fiscal policy has an effect on interest rates, since an expansionary policy, for example, will raise income, raise money demand, and therefore raise interest rates (given a fixed money supply). In the Mundell model, the monetary authorities are assumed to recognize this impact when implementing policy to meet any interest rate target.
[4]See expressions [1], [2], and [5] in that chapter.

where: M_s = money supply

L = money demand

a = money multiplier

DR = domestic reserves held by the central bank

IR = international reserves held by the central bank

BR = reserves of commercial banks and other depository institutions

C = currency held by the nonbank public

Y = level of real income in the economy

i = domestic interest rate

P = price level

W = level of real wealth

$E(\dot{p})$ = expected percentage change in the price level

O = all other variables that can influence the amount of money balances the country's citizens wish to hold (e.g., the foreign interest rate, expected changes in the exchange rate if the exchange rate is not fixed, risk premium for holding foreign assets)

The nature of the impact of changes in the principal independent variables on money demand is indicated above each demand variable in equation [1]. Since the income level and the interest rate are thought to be the two major influences on the demand for money, we focus our attention on these two variables with regard to money market equilibrium. Holding the variables other than Y and i constant, there will be a transactions demand for money fixed by a given level of income and an asset demand for money determined by the domestic interest rate (given the foreign interest rate, the foreign risk premium, and other financial considerations). Further, for any given income level, a graph of the demand for money can be portrayed as the downward-sloping L curve in Figure 2. This graph enables us to focus on the inverse relationship between the interest rate and the demand for money, holding other things constant. You will recall the various explanations for the inverse relationship; for example, a higher interest rate means an increase in the opportunity cost of holding non-interest-bearing money assets and reduces the amount of money that people wish to hold. If any of the "other things" besides the interest rate change, the L curve will shift (e.g., a rise in income shifts the L curve to the right since greater transactions demand for money would exist at each interest rate).

Having looked at the demand for money, let us comment briefly on the supply of money. For the time being, we assume that the supply of money at any given point in time is *fixed*. The money supply is presumed to be under the control of the monetary authorities (such as the Board of Governors of the Federal Reserve System in the United States). The specification of a fixed money supply (call it amount $\overline{M}_s$) is represented by the vertical line in Figure 2. Increases (decreases) in the supply of money shift this line to the right (left). The demand and supply of money jointly determine the **equilibrium interest rate,** at rate i_e.

Interest rate i_e is the equilibrium rate because, at any other rate, there is either an excess supply of or an excess demand for money. For example, at interest rate i_1, the amount of money demanded (represented by the horizontal distance i_1A) is less than the money supply (represented by the distance i_1B). The excess supply of money AB indicates that people hold more of their wealth in the form of money (distance i_1B) than they wish to hold (distance i_1A) at this relatively high interest rate. In response, the money holders will purchase other assets such as bonds with their excess cash balances. These asset purchases drive up the price of bonds and drive down the interest rate. (Remember the

FIGURE 2   **Equilibrium in the Money Market**

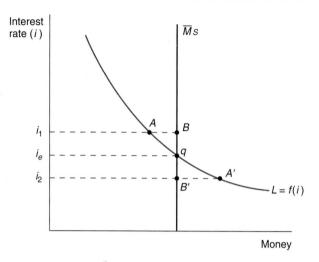

The fixed money supply is indicated by the vertical line $\overline{M}_s$. The demand for money is represented by the L curve, and the equilibrium interest rate is i_e. Above i_e at interest rate i_1, the demand for money is equal to horizontal distance i_1A, which is less than the supply of money i_1B. With an excess supply of money, people purchase bonds, which drives up bond prices and reduces the interest rate—a process that continues until i_e is reached. Below i_e, there is an excess demand for money. People sell bonds in order to obtain money, bond prices fall, and the interest rate rises until i_e is attained.

inverse relationship between bond prices and interest rates.) This process continues until the interest rate falls to the level at which the existing money supply is willingly held (at interest rate i_e). In the opposite situation, at low interest rate i_2, there is an excess demand for money of $B'A'$. People sell bonds and other assets to build up their money balances, and this action drives down the price of bonds and other assets and drives up the interest rate until the equilibrium rate is reached.

In light of Figure 2, consider what will happen when there are changes in the demand and supply of money. If the monetary authorities increase the supply of money, then line $\overline{M}_s$ shifts to the right (not shown). The resulting excess supply of money at old equilibrium interest rate i_e causes the interest rate to fall to the level corresponding to the intersection of demand curve L with the new money supply line. Going in the other direction from $\overline{M}_s$, a decrease in the supply of money shifts $\overline{M}_s$ to the left. Excess demand for money at old interest rate i_e causes the interest rate to rise to a new equilibrium level. Considering shifts in the demand curve, an increase (decrease) in the demand for money would shift the L curve to the right (left) and generate an excess demand for (supply of) money, given the money supply $\overline{M}_s$; the interest rate will rise (fall).

To this point, we have focused on the interest rate and equilibrium between the demand for and supply of money. But this is only a partial analysis because it has neglected the other main determinant of the demand for money—the level of income in the economy. We now introduce the role of income in money market equilibrium.

When we obtained the equilibrium interest rate in Figure 2, the interest rate was the only explicit determinant of the demand for money. Suppose that this is not so and that the level of Y in the economy goes up. Remembering expression [1], the level of income is positively associated with the demand for money. Consider Figure 3, panel (a). The L curve is the one we have been using, and we indicate by the parenthetical expression that this L curve is associated with income level Y_0. If income rises to Y_1, then we *generate a*

FIGURE 3   **Income and the Interest Rate: The *LM* Curve**

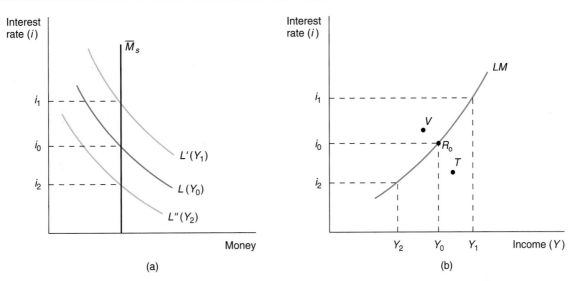

In panel (a), an increase in income from Y_0 to Y_1 increases the demand for money from L to L' and results in a rise in the interest rate from i_0 to i_1. A decrease in income from Y_0 to Y_2 decreases the demand for money from L to L'' and leads to a fall in the interest rate from i_0 to i_2. This positive relationship between Y and i is portrayed by the *LM* curve in panel (b), which shows the various combinations of income and the interest rate that yield equilibrium in the money market. To the right of the *LM* curve, such as at point *T*, there is an excess demand for money; to the left of the *LM* curve, such as at point *V*, there is an excess supply of money. In either case, movement will take place to the *LM* curve.

new L curve indicated by L' and by the Y_1 in parentheses. More money is demanded at this higher income level, and the equilibrium interest rate rises from i_0 to i_1. Similarly, a fall in income from Y_0 to Y_2 leads to a fall in the demand for money curve to L'', with the lower level of income Y_2 indicated in parentheses. The decrease in the income level has thus led to a lower equilibrium interest rate (i_2).

This discussion of the relationship between the income level, the interest rate, and money market equilibrium leads us to a graphical construct, the *LM* curve. The **LM curve** shows the various combinations of income and the interest rate that produce equilibrium in the money market.[5] Such a curve is illustrated in Figure 3, panel (b). At each point on this curve, for the particular income level on the horizontal axis, the associated interest rate on the vertical axis is the interest rate that makes the demand for money equal to the *fixed* supply of money. Thus, at point R_0, the income level Y_0 and the interest rate i_0 together give equilibrium in the money market when the money supply is $\overline{M}_s$.

Why does the *LM* curve slope upward? Suppose that the level of income rises from Y_0 to Y_1. As indicated above, the increase in income will generate an increase in the demand for money as L in Figure 3(a) shifts to L'; the interest rate thus rises from i_0 to i_1. Once the interest rate has risen to i_1, the excess demand for money has been eliminated and the money market is again in equilibrium. Similarly, if income falls from Y_0 to Y_2, the decrease in the demand for money to L'' lowers the equilibrium interest rate to i_2. From this discussion, we can see that any point to the right of the *LM* curve, such as point *T*, is

----

[5]Note that all variables (and especially the price level) influencing the demand for money other than the interest rate and income are being held constant along any given *LM* curve. The relationship of the price level to the *LM* curve is developed in detail in the chapter "Prices and Output in the Open Economy: Aggregate Supply and Demand."

associated with an excess demand for money. At point T, the interest rate is too low for the income level; equilibrium in the money market requires a higher i. (Alternatively, the income level is too high for the given interest rate; equilibrium requires a lower income and thus a lower demand for money in order to be at the interest rate associated with T.) Similarly, any point to the left of the LM curve, such as point V, involves an excess supply of money. For the income level associated with V, the interest rate needs to be lower in order to have equilibrium in the money market (or the income level needs to be higher for the interest rate associated with V).

A final point to make at this juncture is that increases in the demand for money (due to other things besides a rise in income) or decreases in the supply of money will shift the LM curve to the *left*. In either situation, the interest rate rises for any given income level, which is analogous to saying that the income level must fall in order to maintain the same interest rate. Thus, each interest rate is plotted against a lower income level than before the increase in the demand for money or the decrease in the supply of money. By reverse reasoning, decreases in the demand for money (due to other things besides a fall in income) and increases in the supply of money will shift the LM curve to the *right*.

CONCEPT CHECK

1. What impact will an increase in income have on the demand for money? The LM curve? Why?

2. Explain why the LM curve slopes upward.

3. If bank reserves increase, what happens to the supply of money ? The LM curve? Why?

General Equilibrium in the Real Sector: The *IS* Curve

In the preceding chapter we examined the goods and services markets, or the real sector of the economy. We indicated that, in income equilibrium, the "leakages" of saving, imports, and taxes were equal to the "injections" of investment, exports, and government spending on goods and services. However, a key feature was that the monetary sector was neglected in that real-sector analysis, meaning that we were assuming that the *interest rate was constant*. It is now time to relax that assumption! In Figure 4(a), the i_0 in parentheses indicates that the interest rate is held constant at some interest rate i_0 when we consider the $I(i_0) + X + G$ line. With this interest rate, the equilibrium level of income is Y_0. What if we reduce the interest rate from i_0 to i_1? Investors will want to undertake greater amounts of investment because borrowing costs have been lowered, and some investment projects that were previously unprofitable because their return was less than the borrowing costs are now profitable. (Remember that "investment" in the real sector refers to plant and equipment spending by firms, residential construction, and changes in inventories, *not* to the purchase of financial assets.) Empirical studies have indeed shown that residential construction spending is particularly sensitive to the rate of interest, but plant and equipment also responds to the interest rate (albeit to a smaller degree).[6]

Because of the responsiveness of investment to the interest rate, the lower interest rate i_1 is associated with an investment line (and therefore $I + X + G$ line) that is higher. The line $I(i_0) + X + G$ shifts upward to $I'(i_1) + X + G$, and the result is an intersection with the $S + M + T$ line at a *higher* equilibrium level of income Y_1. Similarly, a rise in the interest rate from i_0 to i_2 causes the $I(i_0) + X + G$ line to shift vertically downward to $I''(i_2) + X + G$. Thus i_2 is associated with a lower level of income Y_2.

This relationship between the interest rate (reflecting the importance of monetary variables), investment, and the resulting equilibrium level of income gives us the

----

[6]It is also possible that exports may increase with a lower interest rate if financing is thus easier.

FIGURE 4   **Income and the Interest Rate: The *IS* Curve**

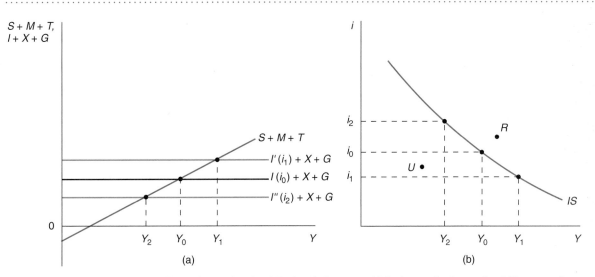

In panel (a), with interest rate i_0, equilibrium income is at level Y_0 since leakages equal injections at that income level. However, a lower interest rate i_1 will increase investment spending and shift $I(i_0) + X + G$ to $I'(i_1) + X + G$; income will rise from Y_0 to Y_1. Similarly, a higher interest rate i_2 will cause $I(i_0) + X + G$ to shift downward to $I''(i_2) + X + G$, resulting in a lower income level Y_2. The inverse relationship between the interest rate and income is plotted on the *IS* curve in panel (b), which shows the various combinations of i and Y that produce equilibrium in the real sector. To the right of the *IS* curve, such as at point R, $S + M + T > I + X + G$ and there is downward pressure on the income level. To the left of the *IS* curve, such as at point U, $I + X + G > S + M + T$ and there is upward pressure on the income level. Points off the *IS* curve thus generate movement to the *IS* curve.

information needed to generate the *IS* curve. The **IS curve** shows the various combinations of income and the interest rate that produce equilibrium in the real sector of the economy. In our model, this is equivalent to saying that the *IS* curve shows the combinations of income and the interest rate that make investment plus exports plus government spending equal to saving plus imports plus taxes. Thus, in Figure 4, panel (b), interest rate i_0 is plotted against income level Y_0, since this is one combination of the interest rate and income that generates equality between $(S + M + T)$ and $(I + X + G)$. The lower interest rate i_1 is plotted against the higher income level Y_1; in the opposite direction, the higher interest rate i_2 is associated with the lower income level Y_2.

If the economy is situated to the right of the *IS* curve, such as at point R in panel (b), then disequilibrium exists because saving plus imports plus taxes exceeds investment plus exports plus government spending. The income level is "too high" for the associated interest rate, and the high income level gives "too much" saving, taxes, and imports. (Alternatively, for the income level at R, the interest rate is "too high" and is thus choking off investment.) Income falls until the *IS* curve is reached through cutbacks of production because of unintended inventory accumulation at the higher levels of income. To the left of the *IS* curve, investment plus exports plus government spending exceeds saving plus imports plus taxes, and there is expansionary pressure due to unintended inventory depletion. For the given interest rate at point U, income is too low to generate enough saving, taxes, and imports to match investment, exports, and government spending. [Alternatively, for a given income level, the "too low" interest rate makes desired $(I + X + G)$ exceed desired $(S + M + T)$.]

What causes shifts in the *IS* curve? Clearly any change in autonomous investment, exports, government spending, saving, taxes, or imports will do so. An increase in

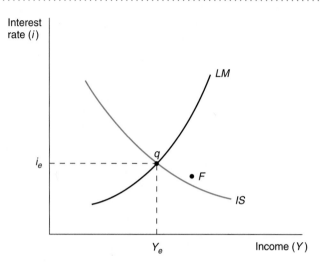

Only at point q is there equilibrium in both the real and monetary sectors of the economy. If the economy is situated away from q at point F, saving plus imports plus taxes exceeds investment plus exports plus government spending; in addition, there is an excess demand for money. Movement occurs (by any of a number of different paths) to point q. Any other point away from point q also sets forces in motion to move the economy to point q.

autonomous investment (due to something other than a fall in the interest rate), autonomous exports, and government spending or an autonomous *decrease* in saving, taxes, and imports will shift the *IS* curve to the right. On the other hand, an autonomous decrease in *I, X* or *G* or an autonomous increase in *S, M,* and *T* will shift the *IS* curve to the left.

Simultaneous Equilibrium in the Monetary and Real Sectors

The simultaneous determination of income and the interest rate when both sectors of the economy are considered involves plotting the *IS* curve and the *LM* curve on the same diagram, as in Figure 5. Equilibrium occurs where the two curves intersect at point q, giving the income level Y_e and the interest rate i_e. This is the only combination of income and the interest rate that simultaneously gives equilibrium in both sectors of the economy.

 If the economy has not settled at Y_e and i_e, forces are set in motion to move to this equilibrium position. For example, suppose that the economy is at point F. Since we are to the right of the *IS* curve, then $(S + M + T)$ is greater than $(I + X + G)$, so there is contractionary pressure on the level of income. But, since we are also to the right of the *LM* curve, the demand for money exceeds the supply of money and therefore the interest rate rises. These forces eventually move the economy to point q. However, various *paths* of adjustment might actually be taken, depending on the speed of adjustment in each sector. For example, from point F, the economy might first move vertically to a position on the *LM* curve; the monetary sector would then be in equilibrium but the real sector would not. We could then move horizontally to the *IS* curve where real sector equilibrium is attained, but then the economy would be to the left of the *LM* curve and would have an excess supply of money. This would drive interest rates downward and move us vertically to the *LM* curve. However, we would now be below the *IS* curve. The process of adjustment would continue.

Equilibrium in the Balance of Payments: The *BP* Curve

We need to introduce a further construct to describe the balance of payments in an open economy. This analytical device, the ***BP* curve,** shows the various combinations of income and the interest rate that produce equilibrium in the balance of payments. In this context, we are including both the current account and international financial capital flows in the balance of payments. In terms of the balance-of-payments accounting categories, not only category I (the current account) but also category II (long-term capital flows) and category III (short-term private capital flows) are considered (see the chapter "The Balance of Payments Accounts"). We are *not* dealing with category IV (official reserve short-term capital flows). The focus is on all items in the balance of payments besides government official reserve asset and liability changes. Balance-of-payments equilibrium in this sense means a zero balance in the official reserve transactions balance.

For the purpose of obtaining the *BP* curve, we consider how the income level and the interest rate affect a country's balance of payments. It is important to note that a given *BP* curve is constructed under the assumption of a *fixed* exchange rate. In addition, a number of other variables such as the foreign interest rate, foreign price level, expected exchange rate, and foreign wealth are assumed to be constant. Income in this analysis is presumed primarily to influence the current account through the impact of income on imports. Other things being equal, a rise in income induces more imports (by the marginal propensity to import times the change in income). With exports independent of income, this rise in imports means that the current account tends to deteriorate (move toward deficit) by the amount of the rise in imports. These changes would be reversed for a decline in income. On the other hand, the interest rate is assumed to have its primary influence on the capital account, and particularly on category III (short-term private capital flows). If the interest rate rises, liquid short-term financial capital from overseas comes into the home country in order to earn the higher interest rate, and some domestic short-term capital will "stay home" rather than be sent overseas. The inflow of foreign short-term capital and the reduced outflow of home capital move the capital account toward a surplus. If the interest rate declines, these responses are in the opposite direction.

With this background, examine the *BP* curve in Figure 6. Since the curve shows the various combinations of income and the interest rate that produce balance-of-payments (BOP) equilibrium, point Q_0 is one such point. The income level associated with this point is Y_0 and the interest rate is i_0. Why does the *BP* curve slope upward? Consider a starting point of Q_0 and introduce a rise in income. This rise in income (with no change in the interest rate) will move us horizontally to the right of Q_0, say, to point N. The balance of payments will move into deficit because the higher income level will have generated more imports. If the interest rate is then increased from i_0 to i_1, this will eliminate the BOP deficit. Why? Because the rise in the interest rate will generate net short-term capital inflows that will have a positive impact on the BOP and will completely offset the negative impact in the current account when we reach point Q_1. The current account deterioration is offset by the (private) capital account improvement, since Q_1 has a zero BOP deficit or surplus by definition. Thus point Q_1 illustrates that income level Y_1 and interest rate i_1 also combine to produce BOP equilibrium.

It is clear that point Q_2 with an income level (Y_2) lower than Y_0 and an interest rate (i_2) lower than i_0 shows another combination of Y and i that yields BOP equilibrium. If income falls from Y_0 to Y_2, this means reduced imports, a movement to point N', an improvement in the current account, and a BOP surplus. However, a reduction in the interest rate from i_0 to i_2 will cause the short-term private capital account to deteriorate by enough to offset the improvement in the current account. The capital account deteriorates because short-term funds seeking a higher rate of interest now leave the country and fewer foreign funds come into the country. With this reduction in the interest rate, movement takes place from point N' to point Q_2, another point on the *BP* schedule.

FIGURE 6   **Income and the Interest Rate: The *BP* Curve**

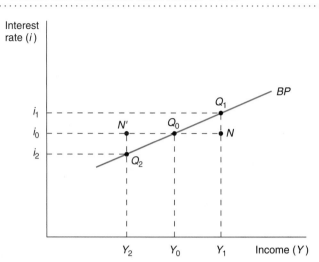

The *BP* curve shows the various combinations of income and the interest rate that yield equilibrium in the balance of payments. The curve slopes upward because a higher income level induces more imports and worsens the current account; a rise in the interest rate is then necessary in order to increase short-term capital inflows (and to reduce short-term capital outflows), which in turn improve the capital account and offset the worsening of the current account. A movement from point Q_0 to point N worsens the current account and must be offset by a rise in the interest rate from i_0 to i_1 in order to improve the capital account sufficiently to move the economy back to BOP equilibrium. Points to the right of the *BP* curve are associated with a BOP deficit; points to the left of the curve are associated with a BOP surplus.

If the economy is located to the right of the *BP* curve, then there is a BOP *deficit* because, for any given interest rate, the income level is leading to an "excessive" amount of imports, and the interest rate is "too low" to attract a capital inflow sufficient to match the current account's movement toward deficit. The result is that the balance of payments as a whole (official reserve transactions balance) is in deficit. For the reverse reasons, if the economy is located to the left of the *BP* curve, there is a BOP *surplus*. Later in the chapter we discuss the process by which an economy that is not located on its *BP* curve adjusts in order to attain balance-of-payments equilibrium (i.e., the process by which the economy reaches equilibrium on the *BP* curve).

An additional point about the *BP* schedule is that the precise value of the upward slope of the *BP* curve importantly depends on the degree of responsiveness of the short-term private capital account to changes in the interest rate. To demonstrate this point, consider the horizontal movement from point Q_0 to point N in Figure 6. This movement generated a movement toward current account deficit, and a return to BOP equilibrium required a rise in the interest rate. Other things being equal, if short-term capital flows are very responsive to changes in i, then a small rise from i_0 to i_1 will generate the requisite capital inflow. However, if capital flows are *not* very responsive to changes in the interest rate, a much larger rise in i_0 will be needed to return the economy to BOP equilibrium. The conclusion is that the less (more) responsive short-term capital flows are to the interest rate, the *steeper* (flatter) the *BP* curve will be.[7]

----

[7]The slope of the *BP* curve also depends on the extent to which changes in the interest rate affect real investment (plant and equipment, residential construction, changes in inventories) and, in turn, by the extent to which such real investment responses affect income and imports. However, the international short-term capital flow responses are the most crucial in practice.

FIGURE 7   **The *BP* Curve under Different Capital Mobility Assumptions**

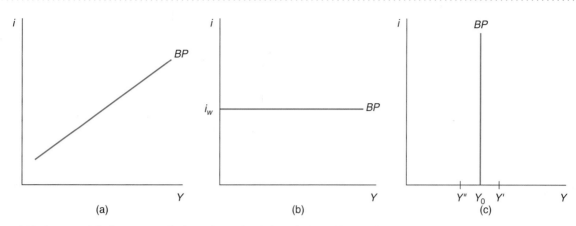

In panel (a), the upward-sloping *BP* curve indicates that capital is imperfectly mobile. In this case, capital moves between countries in response to changes in relative interest rates, but not so easily that domestic interest rates become identical to world interest rates. In panel (b), the horizontal *BP* curve reflects perfect capital mobility, and the domestic interest rate is always equal to the world interest rate. Any slight changes in the domestic interest rate will lead to sufficiently large movements of short-term capital so that the domestic rate will become equal again to the world rate. In panel (c), the *BP* curve is vertical, indicating that the barriers to capital movements are such that there is no short-term capital response to changes in the domestic interest rate; that is, there is perfect capital immobility. In this case, there is only one level of income (and imports) consistent with the level of exports and the controlled net capital inflows.

Although up to now it has been assumed that equilibrium in the foreign sector is described by an upward-sloping *BP* curve, this is not always the case. The upward-sloping relationship between *i* and *Y* in the open economy results whenever there are some impediments to the flow of short-term capital between countries (or the country is financially a "large country," able to influence the international level of interest rates; that is, the country is not a price taker with respect to the interest rate). Thus, the case where the *BP* curve slopes upward is referred to as the case of **imperfect capital mobility.** It is assumed that short-term capital is not completely restricted from moving between countries in response to changes in the interest rate but that the movement of short-term capital is not so complete as to remove all differences between the domestic interest rate and the international interest rate [see Figure 7, panel (a)]. This result also occurs in the context of a portfolio balance model, even with uncovered interest parity. As you will recall, the imperfect substitutability between foreign and domestic assets means that there is a risk premium associated with holding assets other than those of an investor's own country. Thus, in this case, the domestic interest rate will be above the foreign interest rate because the net capital inflow means that foreign investors' risk premium has increased since they are now holding relatively more domestic assets.

The upward-sloping *BP* curve can be contrasted with the case of **perfect capital mobility**, where the *BP* curve is fixed horizontally at the level of the world interest rate, i_w [panel (b) of Figure 7]. In this case, any slight deviation of the domestic interest rate away from the international rate leads to a movement of short-term capital sufficient to return the domestic rate to the level of the international rate. For example, suppose that an increase in the domestic money supply leads to a reduction in the domestic interest rate. This action causes financial investors to immediately move their short-term capital out of the country as they adjust their portfolios to include more foreign assets. This outward capital flight and resultant BOP deficit will reduce the holdings of international reserves (as such reserves are used to purchase domestic currency to maintain the fixed exchange rate) and hence the money supply, and it will continue until the domestic interest rate is once again at the international level. An increase in the domestic interest rate above the international level would trigger an inflow of short-term capital and a BOP surplus, which would increase the international reserves of the country and the money supply. This would take place until the domestic rate was once again at the level of the international rate. In this situation, there is perfect substitutability between foreign and domestic financial assets, and any interest rate differences are instantaneously removed by international capital flows.

Since the interest rate does not change with perfect capital mobility, what effect do changes in other economic variables have on the foreign sector? Remember that the BOP is influenced by variables such as the exchange rate, relative prices of traded goods, expected prices, and the expected profit rate in both countries as well as the level of Y and i. Suppose that there is an increase in the expected domestic profit rate that stimulates an inflow of long-term real investment (improvement in the capital account), which in turn stimulates income. To maintain the pegged exchange rate e, the central bank will purchase a sufficient quantity of foreign exchange with domestic currency, thereby increasing the domestic money supply and facilitating the expansion of income. The increase in domestic income will stimulate an increase in imports, causing a deterioration in the current account that exactly offsets the improvement in the capital account.

Changes in exogenous economic factors thus ultimately stimulate changes in the domestic money supply until the economy is once again in equilibrium. As this adjustment takes place, it can lead to a different composition in the balance of payments. More specifically, holding everything but domestic income constant, movements from left to right along the BP curve reflect a transition in the composition of the balance of payments from one of surplus in the current account (on the left) to one of deficit in the current account (on the right). In similar fashion, the capital account is changing from that of deficit (on the left) to a position of surplus (on the right) over the same income range. It must be emphasized that when there is perfect mobility in the capital markets in the open economy, the horizontal BP curve remains fixed at the level of the international interest rate. Changes in exogenous factors simply bring about movement in the domestic equilibrium along the BP curve concomitant with appropriate changes in the composition of the balance of payments. The country wishing to attain *current account* balance is thus forced to accept the level of income that is consistent with that particular composition in the balance of payments.

It is not uncommon to find countries with a pegged exchange rate strictly controlling the foreign sector both in the commodity markets and in the capital markets. This is often the result of having an overvalued exchange rate, which the governments ultimately maintain by strict foreign exchange control. (To get an idea of the prevalence of various exchange restrictions, see Case Study 1.) In this case, the BP relationship is characterized by **perfect capital immobility** [Figure 7(c)]. When short-term capital flows are strictly controlled and not permitted to respond to changes in the interest rate, the BP curve is *vertical* at the level of income that is consistent with the controlled use of foreign exchange (and the corresponding composition in the balance of payments) pursued by government policymakers. Given the control on the capital accounts, only one level of income (and hence imports) is consistent with the given exchange rate. Should income rise, for example, from Y_0 to Y', the level of induced imports would be too high and there would be a BOP deficit, putting upward pressure on the exchange rate (pressure toward depreciation of the domestic currency). To maintain the value of the domestic currency, the government would have to purchase it in the exchange market with foreign exchange reserves. In so doing, the domestic money supply would decline, raising domestic interest rates and reducing domestic investment and income until the domestic economy was once

✼ CASE STUDY 1   THE PRESENCE OF EXCHANGE CONTROLS IN THE
                 CURRENT FINANCIAL SYSTEM

Although few countries exercise complete exchange control, a surprising number of restrictions are in place around the world on access to foreign exchange and the uses to which it can be applied. Table 1 summarizes the degree to which various foreign exchange controls are in place within the membership of the International Monetary Fund. A cursory examination seems to suggest that capital is indeed somewhat, if not perfectly, immobile for many countries of the world. Relatively mobile capital conditions probably exist only for the major trading countries of the world whose financial markets have become increasingly integrated in recent years. Even in those cases, however, many different circumstances cause capital not to be perfectly mobile.

TABLE 1   **Foreign Exchange Restrictions in 179 IMF Member Countries, 1996***

Type of Restriction	Number of Countries	Percent of Countries
A. Multiple exchange rates		
1. For some or all capital transactions and/or some or all invisibles	28	15.6%
2. More than one rate for imports	22	12.3
3. More than one rate for exports	22	12.3
4. Import rates different from export rates	21	11.7
B. Payments restrictions		
1. For current transactions	59	33.0
2. For capital transactions	126	70.4
C. Cost-related import restrictions		
1. Import surcharges	43	24.0
2. Advance import deposits	10	5.6
D. Surrender or repatriation requirements for export proceeds	123	68.7
E. Country use intensity of the nine above-listed restrictions		
0–1 restrictions[†]	56	31.3
2–3 restrictions	85	47.5
4–5 restrictions	18	10.1
6–7 restrictions	14	7.8
8–9 restrictions	6	3.4

*Restrictions in place as of December 31, 1995.

†Thirty-eight countries, including the United States, Canada, and Germany, employ none of the above restrictions.

Source: International Monetary Fund, *Exchange Arrangements and Exchange Restrictions: Annual Report 1996* (Washington, DC: IMF, 1996), pp. 546–51.   ✼

again back in equilibrium on the *BP* curve. Similarly, a fall in income from Y_0 to Y'' would lead to downward pressure on the exchange rate and hence to an expansion of the money supply, until the economy was once again in equilibrium on the *BP* curve. The requisite changes in the money supply will thus automatically keep the economy on the *BP* curve.

In sum, the slope of the *BP* curve reflects the nature of capital mobility in the country under analysis. The more capital flows are restricted and short-term capital movements are not permitted to respond to changes in the domestic interest rate, the steeper the slope of the *BP* curve. Similarly, the less restricted are movements of capital and the more the country in question is financially a small country, the flatter the *BP* curve will be.

Finally, remember that the *BP* curve is drawn for a *specific exchange rate.* If the home country is the United States, for example, and if the exchange rate between the dollar and other currencies changes, then a different *BP* curve emerges. The simple rule is this: A depreciation of the home currency against foreign currencies shifts the *BP* curve to the right, and an appreciation of the home currency against foreign currencies shifts the *BP* curve to the left. To grasp this rule, consider an existing *BP* curve such as that shown in

Figure 6 earlier. If the home currency depreciates, then the home country's current account balance will improve, assuming that the Marshall-Lerner condition is met. For any given interest rate on the "old" *BP* curve, there is now a surplus in the balance of payments. Hence, a larger level of *Y* is needed for each *i* in order to have BOP equilibrium, since the larger *Y* will induce more imports and eliminate the BOP surplus. Each interest rate must now be plotted against a higher level of income in order to show the combinations of the interest rate and the income level that produce BOP equilibrium. This means that the "new" *BP* curve (not shown) will be to the right of the "old" *BP* curve.[8]

In addition, changes in a number of other variables will also shift the *BP* curve. Because changes in these factors can influence equilibrium in the open economy, it is useful to mention several of them before proceeding further with the general equilibrium analysis. For example, an autonomous increase in exports will cause the *BP* curve to shift to the right or downward since a lower rate of interest will now be sufficient to maintain BOP equilibrium with the stronger balance on current account. This would also be the case with an autonomous decrease in home country imports. Such a downward shift could also result from changes in monetary variables such as a fall in the foreign interest rate. Also, changes in expectations can influence equilibrium in the foreign sector and hence the *BP* curve. Further discussion of these and other factors and their impact on the *BP* curve is presented in the next chapter.

Equilibrium in the Open Economy: The Simultaneous Use of the *LM*, *IS*, and *BP* Curves

As a final step for preparing for the discussion of economic policy in the open economy, we bring together the *LM*, *IS*, and *BP* curves in Figure 8. There is simultaneous equilibrium in the money market, the real sector, and the balance of payments at point *E*, where all three schedules intersect. The income level associated with this three-way equilibrium is Y_E and the interest rate is i_E. However, this equilibrium position may not be optimal in terms of a country's economic objectives. In such cases, there is a role for macroeconomic policy in order to attain the objectives.

Having established general equilibrium in the *IS/LM/BP* framework, we now turn to a discussion of the nature of this equilibrium and the adjustment processes that move the system to that point.[9] To begin our analysis, we first examine the automatic BOP adjustment mechanism under a fixed-rate system. To do this, we begin with the economy in equilibrium at point *E* (*Y**, *i**) in Figure 9 and examine what happens when a shock to the system takes place. For example, suppose that there is an increase in foreign income, which increases the level of exports in the home economy. This exogenous change in exports shifts the *BP* curve to the right to *BP'* since any given level of the interest rate can now be associated with a higher income level and still have BOP equilibrium. A surplus in the balance of payments will now begin to occur as long as the domestic economy remains at the initial equilibrium at point *E*. However, the domestic equilibrium will no longer remain at *Y** and *i** since the expansion of exports also causes the *IS* curve to shift outward to *IS'*, raising the level of income and the interest rate to *E'* (*Y'*, *i'*).

Given the surplus that will occur in the balance of payments at *E'*, the economy will not remain at this point. Since the country is operating under a fixed-rate system, it has committed itself to keep constant the value of its currency. Under such a system, the central bank must stand ready to purchase the surplus foreign currency in the exchange market to prevent the appreciation of the domestic currency. Because the foreign exchange is purchased by the central bank with domestic currency, there is expansion of the domestic

---

[8]In the case of perfect capital mobility, changes in the exchange rate simply lead to movements along the *BP* curve, since the height of the horizontal *BP* curve is determined by the international rate of interest.

[9]Remember that the basic *IS/LM/BP* framework assumes that the price level remains fixed. This assumption will be dropped in the chapter "Prices and Output in the Open Economy: Aggregate Supply and Demand."

FIGURE 8   **Simultaneous Equilibrium in the Real and Monetary Sectors and in the Balance of Payments**

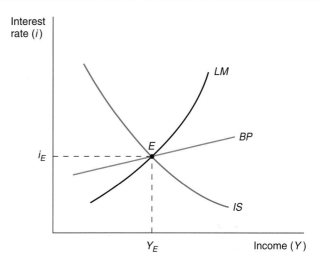

Only at point E is there equilibrium between saving plus imports plus taxes and investment plus exports plus government spending, between the demand and supply of money, and in the balance of payments. With the schedules as drawn, Y_E and i_E are thus the economywide equilibrium levels of income and the interest rate. Any other combination of Y and i is associated with disequilibrium in at least one part of the economy.

FIGURE 9   **Automatic Adjustment under Fixed Rates**

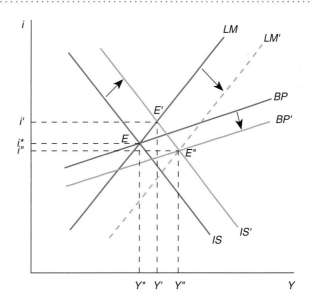

Starting with the economy in equilibrium at i^* and Y^*, an increase in foreign income leads to an autonomous increase in exports, causing the IS curve to shift to the right and the BP curve to shift to the right. A balance-of-payments surplus now occurs due to both the increase in exports (which improves the current account) and the higher domestic interest rate i' (which improves the capital account). Assuming that the government does not intervene to sterilize the effects on the money supply, the BOP surplus leads to an expansion in the money supply, causing the LM curve to shift to the right. The BOP surplus and the expansion of the money supply continue (the LM curve continues to shift to the right) until a new equilibrium is reached at Y'' and i''.

money supply. In our *IS/LM/BP* analysis, this has the effect of shifting the *LM* curve to the right. This **automatic monetary adjustment** will continue until there is no longer a surplus in the balance of payments. This will occur when the *IS, LM,* and *BP* curves again intersect at a common point E'' (Y'', i'') consistent with the new higher level of exports.

Under a fixed exchange rate, the automatic adjustment mechanism is the change in the domestic supply of money brought about by an underlying surplus or deficit in the balance of payments at the pegged exchange rate. (Any shock producing a deficit in the balance of payments leads to a reduction in the money supply as the domestic economy seeks out the new equilibrium.) Since the exchange rate cannot be changed under a pegged rate system, equilibrium combinations of i and Y (where *IS* and *LM* intersect) must necessarily lie on the *BP* curve dictated by underlying international economic considerations. As long as the exchange rate remains fixed, domestic policymakers may be faced with choosing between hitting a target interest rate (for example, to reach a particular growth target) and a target level of income (and hence employment). It should be emphasized, however, that the economy will automatically adjust to the new equilibrium levels as long as the central bank does nothing to interfere with the adjustment process by **sterilization,** or the offsetting of the effects of maintaining the fixed value of the currency in the foreign exchange market. Sterilization would be accomplished in Figure 9 by the central bank selling government securities in the open market (leading to a relative change in the composition of its portfolio away from domestic assets and toward foreign assets), causing a shift from *LM'* back to *LM.* Such sterilization, however, will perpetuate the balance-of-payments disequilibrium. Further, given the huge volume of capital flows across country borders in today's world, the question arises as to whether foreign central banks have enough international reserves to permit the continual acquisition of them by the domestic central bank for any length of time and in sufficient size to offset the intense exchange rate pressure.

Finally, it should be noted that nothing yet has been said about changes in prices. The above automatic adjustment process relies solely on monetary and income effects. The incorporation of price effects that might accompany this kind of adjustment are discussed in the chapter "Prices and Output in the Open Economy: Aggregate Supply and Demand."

CONCEPT CHECK

1. Ignoring the *LM* curve, suppose that the economy is located at a point to the left (right) of the *IS* curve. Why is there pressure for the economy to expand (contract)?
2. In Figure 5, suppose that the economy is located to the left of the *IS* curve and also to the left of the *LM* curve. Is $(S + M + T)$

greater or less than $(I + X + G)$? Is there an excess demand or excess supply of money? What will happen to income and why?
3. Explain the rationale for an upward-sloping *BP* curve.
4. Explain how the degree of capital mobility affects the degree of slope of the *BP* curve.

THE EFFECTS OF FISCAL POLICY UNDER FIXED RATES

The impact of expansionary fiscal policy under various international capital mobility assumptions is presented in Figure 10. First, consider the impact of fiscal policy under conditions of perfect capital immobility, as shown in panel (a). Beginning at Y_0 and i_0 an increase in government spending or a decrease in taxes shifts the *IS* curve to the right, putting upward pressure on domestic income and interest rates. As the economy begins to

FIGURE 10   **Fiscal Policy with Fixed Rates under Different Capital Mobility Assumptions**

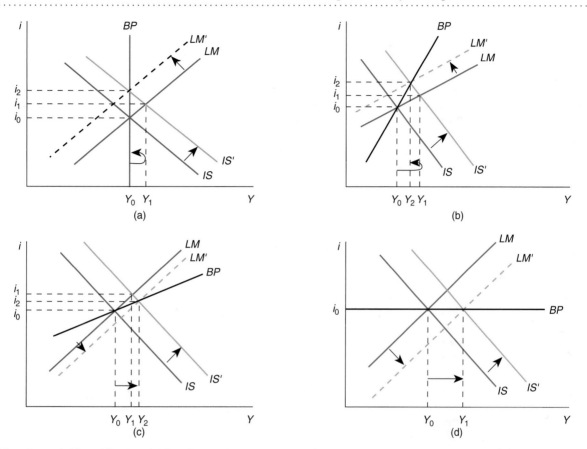

With perfect capital immobility [panel (a)], an increase in government spending (or a decrease in autonomous taxes) shifts the *IS* curve right, leading to increased income and imports. Since there is no short-term capital movement, a BOP deficit occurs. This leads to a fall in the domestic money supply, shifting the *LM* curve left and increasing *i* until there is once again equilibrium at Y_0. The increase in *G* has led to an equivalent crowding out of domestic investment. A similar result takes place in panel (b), with relative capital immobility, although the presence of some responsiveness of short-term capital to changes in the interest rate means that the crowding out of investment is not complete and there is a slight expansion of income. With relative capital mobility [panel (c)], the expansionary fiscal policy and the accompanying increase in domestic interest rates lead to a BOP surplus and an expansion of the money supply, causing income to increase even more to Y_2 since the crowding out of domestic investment is considerably reduced. Finally, with perfectly mobile capital there is no change in the interest rate with the expansionary policy, since there is a sufficient inflow of short-term capital (and increase in the domestic money supply) to finance the increase in net *G* without reducing domestic investment.

expand, there is an increase in desired imports and an increase in demand for foreign exchange. To maintain the exchange rate, the central bank sells foreign exchange for home currency, thus reducing the money supply. This leads to a leftward shift in the *LM* curve, which continues until the domestic interest rate has risen sufficiently to bring about a decrease in domestic investment, exactly offsetting the increase in government spending. The only impact of increased government spending under conditions of perfectly immobile capital is a **crowding out** of an equivalent amount of domestic investment; that is, the increased *G* has raised *i* and has decreased *I* by the same amount that *G* increased. Income and employment remain at their initial equilibrium levels. Fiscal policy is thus ineffective in stimulating income and employment in the case of perfectly immobile capital.

Figure 10, panel (b) reflects a situation with some degree of capital mobility, but where international capital flows are fairly unresponsive to changes in the interest rate so that the *BP* curve is steeper than the *LM* curve. We designate this situation as one of **relative capital immobility**. Starting from Y_0 and i_0, an increase in net government spending leads to a new domestic equilibrium at Y_1 and i_1. However, since this new equilibrium is below the *BP* curve, there is a deficit in the balance of payments. With the exchange rate fixed, the government must provide the necessary foreign exchange to meet the deficit and to maintain the value of the domestic currency. When this happens, the money supply declines and the *LM* curve shifts to the left until levels of income and the interest rate are reached that are consistent with BOP equilibrium. This new equilibrium is represented by Y_2 and i_2. We see that fiscal policy is somewhat effective in expanding income and employment in this case, although some of the expansionary effect has been offset by crowding out of domestic investment because of the new, higher equilibrium interest rate. Clearly, the less mobile capital is (and hence the steeper the *BP* curve), the less effective fiscal policy is in altering the level of income.

Figure 10, panel (c) demonstrates a case in which capital shows some degree of immobility because the *BP* curve is upward-sloping, but where the balance of payments is more responsive to changes in the interest rate than is the domestic money market (the *LM* curve). This is a situation of **relative capital mobility**. From Y_0 and i_0, an expansionary fiscal policy causes the domestic economy to seek a new equilibrium at Y_1 and i_1, which produces a surplus in the balance of payments. This comes about because the increase in the inflow of short-term capital more than offsets the increase in imports at the higher levels of Y and i. With a BOP surplus, the central bank is forced to purchase the surplus foreign exchange to maintain the exchange rate, which causes the money supply to expand and the *LM* curve to shift to the right. The expanding money supply causes a further expansion of the economy to Y_2 and i_2.[10] In this case, fiscal policy is complemented by the monetary effects associated with the automatic adjustments under a fixed exchange rate system.

We now turn to the final case, that of perfectly mobile capital, which is illustrated in Figure 10, panel (d). This case is similar to the previous case except for the fact that there is no crowding out of domestic investment because the interest rate remains fixed at the international level. This results from the fact that short-term capital movements instantaneously respond in large-scale fashion to the slightest movement of the interest rate on either side of the international rate since domestic and foreign financial assets are perfect substitutes. With an increase in net government spending, there is immediate upward pressure on the domestic interest rate, which stimulates an inflow of short-term capital and a surplus in the balance of payments. To keep the domestic currency at the pegged rate, the central bank purchases the surplus foreign currency in exchange for domestic currency. This expands the money supply, and this expansion continues until the interest rate effects due to the increase in government spending have been exactly offset by the inflow of short-term capital and the concomitant increase in the domestic money supply. This adjustment is shown by the rightward shift in the *LM* curve until it intersects the new *IS'* at a point on the horizontal *BP* curve. Expansionary fiscal policy is thus totally effective in the case of perfectly mobile capital, in that the economy suffers no offsetting crowding-out effects through increases in the interest rate. With perfectly mobile capital, the full expansion of income is facilitated by the inflow of short-term capital.

---

[10]Portfolio balance considerations would suggest that this may not be the final equilibrium. If the capital inflow was part of a portfolio stock adjustment shift, the capital flows would fall off after completion of the stock adjustment. This would shift the *BP* curve to the left, setting off further changes. See Willett and Forte (1969, pp. 242–62).

The above analysis of fiscal policy under fixed rates leads to the conclusion that, to varying degrees, fiscal policy is effective in influencing income under fixed exchange rates except when capital is perfectly immobile. The greater the mobility of capital, the greater the effectiveness of fiscal policy. Although the above discussion focused only on expansionary policy, the arguments are symmetric in nature; thus, a reduction in government spending or an increase in taxes will move the *IS* curve to the left and will generate the opposite effects in terms of ultimate changes of the money supply in response to capital flows resulting from the pressures on the interest rate.

THE EFFECTS OF MONETARY POLICY UNDER FIXED EXCHANGE RATES

The effects of expansionary monetary policy under the different assumptions of capital mobility are demonstrated in Figure 11. Beginning with the system in equilibrium at Y_0 and i_0, we examine the effects of rightward shifts in the *LM* curve brought about by increases in the money supply. Figure 11, panel (a), describes the situation with perfect capital immobility, with each successive graph demonstrating cases of greater and greater international capital mobility.

An increase in the money supply shifts the *LM* curve to the right. In every instance, there is a new intersection of the *IS* and *LM* curves at a combination of *i* and *Y* that lies below or to the right of the *BP* curve and thus is associated with a BOP deficit. The result of a deficit in the balance of payments is, of course, a loss of international reserves, as the central bank intervenes to provide the needed foreign currency. In the process of selling the desired foreign exchange, home currency is acquired by the central bank and the money supply falls. The effect is exactly analogous to that of selling short-term government bonds under open-market operations. The reduction in the money supply has the effect of shifting the *LM* curve back to the left. Since this will continue until *IS* and *LM* again intersect on the *BP* curve, one sees immediately that monetary policy is completely ineffective for influencing income under a system of fixed exchange rates, regardless of the degree of capital mobility. This is demonstrated in Figure 11 by the pair of arrows in each figure, which indicate that the *LM* curve first shifts to the right and then shifts back to the original position due to the automatic adjustment mechanism under fixed rates. It should be noted that the shift back to the original position can be delayed if the monetary authorities undertake open-market purchases of domestic securities, that is, sterilization operations (thus shifting the composition of the central bank's portfolio toward domestic assets and away from foreign assets). This postponement cannot be sustained indefinitely, however, because the country may soon decrease its stock of foreign exchange reserves below a target level. Thus, in the end under a fixed-rate system, a country loses the use of discretionary monetary policy to pursue economic targets. Alternatively, the country may weaken its commitment to the fixed-rate system. (See Case Study 2.)

THE IMPACT OF OFFICIAL CHANGES IN THE EXCHANGE RATE

Although changing the exchange rate cannot be an active tool of discretionary policy under a fixed-rate system, it is useful to examine briefly the macroeconomic effects of an official decision to change the pegged value of the home currency under the various capital mobility scenarios above. Since structural changes may at times require the devaluation/upward revaluation of a currency, it is important to understand how such changes would affect the economy. We proceed in the same manner as above. The four different market conditions are described in Figure 12.

FIGURE 11　　**Monetary Policy with Fixed Rates under Different Capital Mobility Assumptions**

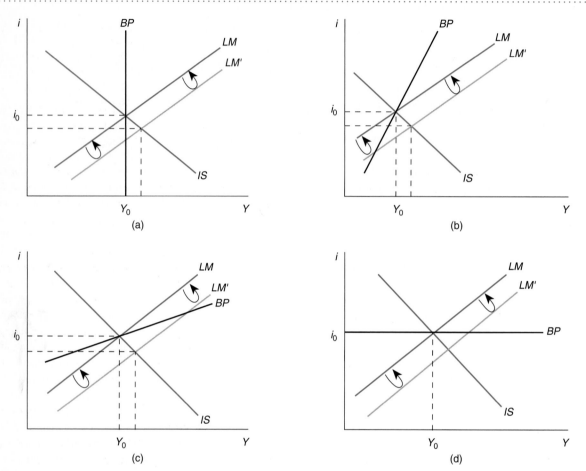

Starting with the economy in equilibrium at Y_0 and i_0, expansionary monetary policy leads to a rightward shift in the *LM* curve, lowering domestic interest rates and stimulating income. When capital is perfectly immobile [panel (a)], the increase in income stimulates imports and creates a deficit in the balance of payments. As the central bank sells foreign exchange to maintain the pegged rate, the money supply declines, causing the *LM* curve to shift leftward until the initial equilibrium point is again attained. When capital is imperfectly mobile [panels (b) and (c)], the increase in the money supply leads to a deficit in the BOP as imports increase *and* net short-term capital inflows decline or become negative. As before, attempts by the central bank to maintain the fixed exchange rate lead to a decline in the money supply, bringing the economy again to Y_0 and i_0. Finally, in the case of perfectly mobile capital [panel (d)], the slightest drop in domestic interest rate *i* instantaneously leads to a large-scale outflow of short-term capital. Again, the central bank must provide the desired foreign exchange to support the exchange rate, and the money supply declines. This continues until there is no further downward pressure on *i*, that is, at Y_0.

Changes in the exchange rate lead to expenditure switching between foreign and domestic goods and hence will affect both the *IS* curve and the *BP* curve. For example, as the currency is devalued or depreciates,[11] imports become more expensive to domestic residents and exports become cheaper to trading partners. Consequently, depreciation will generate an expansion of exports and a contraction of imports, leading to a rightward shift

. . . .

[11]Changes in an official pegged exchange rate are usually called devaluations (for a rise in *e*) or upward revaluations (for a fall in *e*). The terms *depreciation* or *appreciation* represent the actual market rate movements of the currency's value.

❋ CASE STUDY 2   INTERDEPENDENT MONETARY POLICIES UNDER FIXED EXCHANGE RATES: THE EUROPEAN COMMUNITY

The difficulties of implementing effective monetary policy with fixed exchange rates were illustrated in the early 1990s by experience in the European Community (which became the European Union in November 1993). The scenario began in 1990 when the German Democratic Republic (GDR, East Germany) merged with the Federal Republic of Germany (FRG, West Germany). The first order of business of the new country was to build up the economic strength of the former GDR. This part of the newly united Germany was considerably poorer than the former FRG. (For example, average household income in the East was only one-third of that in the West, and only 7 percent of East German households possessed a telephone while 98 percent of West German households did.)* To stimulate the East, fiscal authorities undertook large-scale expenditures but, fearful of the inflation that the resulting budget deficits might cause, the German Bundesbank (central bank) instituted tight money and high interest rates.

From the standpoint of this chapter, the most important point is that the restrictive monetary policy caused, in succeeding years, considerable consternation and resentment in other countries of the European Community (EC). Under the Exchange Rate Mechanism (ERM) of the European Monetary System at the time, most EC currencies were tied together with only 2.25 percent deviations permitted around their respective specified "central rates." With almost-fixed rates and highly mobile short-term capital among the countries, the other members of the ERM besides Germany were in a bind on monetary policy. If they tried to stimulate their economies by expansionary policy so as to recover from

the slow growth of the 1980s and the severe recession that began in 1990, they would lose short-term capital to Germany and suffer BOP deficits and large losses of international reserves. In terms of the *IS/LM/BP* diagram, a shift to the right of the *LM* curve would soon be followed by a shift back to the original position, with no impact on income. Fiscal stimulus, which might have been useful under the almost-fixed-rate system, was also difficult to implement because governments had large budget deficits that were thought necessary to keep under control to facilitate entry into the planned monetary union of the countries at the end of the decade. (This monetary union is discussed in the last chapter of this book.)

The consequence of the inability to undertake effective macro policy was that unemployment rates remained high. In July 1993, the unemployment rate was 9.5 percent in Belgium, 11.7 percent in France, 10.9 percent in Italy, and 22.3 percent in Spain.† When Germany resisted pressure to reduce its interest rates in that month, the non-German currencies fell in value and large-scale intervention was temporarily undertaken.‡ Finally, the finance ministers of the EC agreed that seven of the nine ERM members' currencies (all except the deutsche mark and the Dutch guilder against each other) could now be allowed to move ± 15 percent from the central rates.§ (Indeed, the United Kingdom had withdrawn entirely from the ERM a year earlier in order to stimulate its economy by letting the pound depreciate.) Thus, in the EC, the lack of ability of countries to conduct independent, effective monetary policy because of an almost-fixed-rate structure led to a significant modification of that structure.

---

*"The Spontaneous Union: A Survey of the New Germany," *The Economist,* June 30, 1990, pp. 6, 9, 11.

†*The Economist,* Sept. 11, 1993, p. 103.

‡"German Stance on Rates Sends ERM to Brink," *The Wall Street Journal,* July 30, 1993, pp. C1, C13.

§Michael R. Sesit, "EC to Allow Currencies to Fluctuate Widely," *The Wall Street Journal,* Aug. 2, 1993, pp. C1, C13.   ❋

---

in the *IS* curve.[12] An appreciation of the currency would do the opposite. The impact of changing the exchange rate on the *BP* curve will depend on the nature of international capital mobility.

Consider first the case of perfectly immobile capital in panel (a) of Figure 12. Beginning at Y_0 and i_0, depreciation of the currency shifts the *BP* curve to the right (*BP'*).

---

[12]Again we are assuming that the Marshall-Lerner condition is satisfied.

FIGURE 12   **Expenditure Switching with a Pegged-Rate Change under Different Capital Mobility Assumptions**

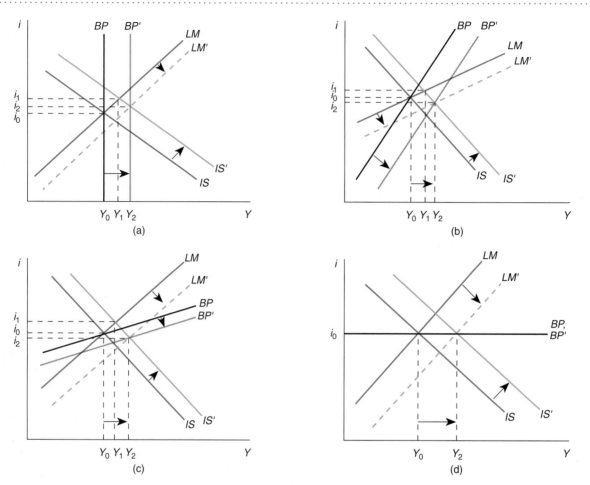

Starting at equilibrium at Y_0 and i_0, a depreciation of the currency leads to increased exports and decreased imports, shifting both the *IS* and the *BP* curves to the right and raising the level of income and the interest rate. With imperfect capital mobility [panels (b) and (c)], the improvement in the current account balance coupled with the higher relative domestic interest rate produces a surplus in the balance of payments. There is then an expansion in the money supply (rightward shift of the *LM* curve) as the central bank buys foreign exchange to maintain the pegged exchange rate, and a further increase in income to Y_2. A similar but less strong expansion in income occurs in panel (a) when capital is perfectly immobile, since there are no short-term capital movements taking place as the domestic interest rate rises. However, under perfect capital mobility [panel (d)], the upward pressure on the interest rate generates very large inflows of short-term capital. As the central bank purchases foreign exchange to maintain the new exchange rate, the money supply expands until there is no longer any upward pressure on the interest rate (at Y_2).

Exports increase and imports decrease because of the depreciation, causing the *IS* curve to shift to the right (*IS'*). Once the real expenditure changes have taken effect, any additional adjustment required will take place through automatic changes in the money supply (in the absence of sterilization). For example, if the *IS* shift moves the domestic economy to Y_1 and i_1, domestic equilibrium (the intersection of *LM* and *IS'*) is to the left of the *BP'* curve, indicating a surplus in the balance of payments. This surplus will cause the central bank to purchase the foreign exchange necessary to hold the new value of the currency, and, in the process, increase the money supply. The increase in the money

CHAPTER 8   ECONOMIC POLICY IN THE OPEN ECONOMY: FIXED EXCHANGE RATES   **217**

supply will show up as a rightward shift in the *LM* curve and continue until the *LM'* and *IS'* intersect at a point on the new *BP'* curve at Y_2. Under perfect capital immobility, expenditure switching does have an impact on income (and prices).

Under imperfect capital mobility [panels (b) and (c)], depreciation again leads to a rightward shift in both the *BP* and the *IS* curves. The expansionary effects associated with expenditure switching lead to higher levels of income and the interest rate and a surplus in the balance of payments. Central bank intervention to peg the new value of the currency leads to an expansion of central bank holdings of international reserves and, consequently, an expansion of the money supply. The increase in the money supply leads to a rightward shift in the *LM* curve, which continues until the economy is again in equilibrium at the level of Y_2 and i_2 where the three new curves intersect. Devaluation has altered the locus of points that produce equilibrium in the balance of payments, and the economy has found levels of income and the interest rate compatible with the new exchange rate. From a policy perspective, we again see that devaluation has had an expansionary effect on the economy. An upward revaluation of the domestic currency would have the opposite effect since it would stimulate imports and reduce exports, leading to a lower level of income.

The final case [panel (d)], that of perfect capital mobility, is slightly different in that altering the value of the currency does not change the position of the *BP* curve. With perfectly mobile capital, *BP* remains fixed at the level of the international interest rate. What does take place, as indicated earlier in this chapter, is that altering the value of the currency leads to a movement along the *BP* curve. For example, a devaluation (depreciation) of the currency again leads to a rightward shift in the *IS* curve due to the expansion of exports and the contraction of imports that will accompany it. As the economy expands in response to the increase in demand for domestic goods, the rise in the domestic interest rate will precipitate an inflow of short-term capital, putting upward pressure on the home currency. As the central bank purchases the excess foreign exchange (at the new pegged rate) the money supply increases, shifting *LM* to the right. The net short-term capital position will continue to improve (and the money supply to expand) until the *IS* and the *LM* curves again intersect on the *BP* line. This new equilibrium will necessarily be at a higher level of income.[13] Thus, we conclude that changing the exchange rate under a fixed-rate regime will influence the level of economic activity, regardless of the mobility of capital. As with fiscal policy, the effect will be the greatest under conditions of perfect capital mobility where there are no crowding-out effects to offset the expansion in demand for domestic goods and services brought about by the change in value of the currency.

CONCEPT CHECK

1. What will be the state of the balance of payments if the *IS-LM* intersection is below the *BP* curve? What then takes place in the economy under fixed exchange rates? Why?

2. Is monetary or fiscal policy more effective under fixed rates? Why?

[13]Remember that prices are held constant in this analysis and that income is not necessarily at the full employment level. We are also assuming that the foreign countries do not match the initial devaluation with devaluation of their own currencies.

SUMMARY

This chapter has examined macroeconomic policy under a system of fixed exchange rates. With prices and exchange rates fixed, it became evident very early that there was no guarantee that internal balance targets and external balance targets would necessarily be reached simultaneously. We then introduced a broad, general equilibrium model incorporating the monetary sector, real sector, and the balance of payments (the *IS/LM/BP* model). The effectiveness of domestic monetary and fiscal policy under fixed exchange rates was then analyzed under different international capital mobility assumptions. Monetary policy was generally ineffective in influencing income, whereas fiscal policy had varying degrees of effectiveness depending on the degree of capital mobility. Only when capital was perfectly immobile was fiscal policy totally ineffective in stimulating output and employment. Official changes in the exchange rate (to the extent permitted) were also effective in stimulating economic activity. However, since changing the exchange rate is often difficult under a pegged-rate system, countries may find themselves with an incorrectly valued exchange rate and therefore unable to meet their internal and external balance targets.

KEY TERMS

automatic monetary adjustment	imperfect capital mobility	perfect capital immobility
BP curve	*IS* curve	perfect capital mobility
crowding out	*LM* curve	relative capital immobility
equilibrium interest rate	Mundell-Fleming diagram	relative capital mobility
		sterilization

QUESTIONS AND PROBLEMS

1. Explain carefully why a country settles in equilibrium at the intersection of the *IS, LM,* and *BP* curves.

2. Why is domestic monetary policy ineffective in an open economy under a fixed exchange rate regime?

3. What will happen to the relative holdings of foreign and domestic assets by the home country if there is an increase in the money supply and capital is perfectly mobile? Why?

4. Explain why a developing country with a fixed exchange rate and foreign exchange controls in place (perfectly immobile capital) may find itself dependent on growth in exports, foreign investment, or foreign aid in order to attain economic growth.

5. Under what capital flow conditions is fiscal policy least effective in a fixed-rate regime? Most effective? Why?

6. Why does devaluing the domestic currency have an expansionary effect on the economy? Does this expansionary effect take place if capital is perfectly immobile? Why or why not?

7. Suppose you were instructed to construct a *BP* curve of one state in the United States with another, such as New York's *BP* curve with Illinois. What general slope would you expect for this curve and why?

8. Why must countries, especially those prone to balance-of-payments deficits, maintain relatively large holdings of foreign exchange reserves in a fixed exchange rate system?

9. Japan has been running huge current account surpluses in the last decade. Because of concern over this surplus (and over the associated U.S. current account deficit with Japan), U.S. government officials for several years urged the Japanese government to adopt a more expansionary fiscal policy stance. Using an *IS/LM/BP* diagram (assuming that the *BP* curve is flatter than the *LM* curve) and starting from a position of equilibrium, explain how the adoption of such a policy stance would affect Japan's national income, current account, capital account, and money supply. Would your conclusions be different if the *BP* curve were steeper than the *LM* curve? Why or why not? (Note: Assume throughout your answer that Japan does not allow the value of the yen to change.)

10. If financial capital is relatively mobile between countries (such as is the case in the European Union), what difficulties emerge if the various countries have different interest rate targets for attaining domestic inflation and/or growth objectives? (Assume fixed exchange rates.)

CHAPTER 9

ECONOMIC POLICY IN THE OPEN ECONOMY

Flexible Exchange Rates

INTRODUCTION

In the preceding chapter we examined how economic policy was affected by trade and capital flows in the open economy in a fixed-rate regime. It was determined that monetary policy was ineffective in altering the level of income but that fiscal policy was effective in all cases except when capital was perfectly immobile, and that specific adjustments in the exchange rate were effective in all instances. Since 1973, major trading countries of the world have no longer been pegging their currencies and have been letting them float. (See the last chapter in the book.) If the exchange rate continuously adjusts to maintain equilibrium in the foreign exchange market, there is no longer a need for central banks to intervene to remove any excess supplies or demands for foreign exchange. Consequently, the monetary authorities regain control over the money supply and can use it to pursue domestic targets. A system of flexible rates thus significantly alters the policy environment and the effects of policy actions. We now examine the effects of monetary policy and fiscal policy under a flexible-rate regime, comparing and contrasting the effects of policy actions under different capital mobility assumptions. It will again be assumed that the Marshall-Lerner condition is satisfied in the foreign exchange market. By the end of the chapter, you will have learned why both monetary policy and fiscal policy differ markedly in their ability to influence national income under flexible exchange rates, and why the impacts of each are different when compared to a fixed-rate system.

THE EFFECTS OF FISCAL AND MONETARY POLICY UNDER FLEXIBLE EXCHANGE RATES WITH DIFFERENT CAPITAL MOBILITY ASSUMPTIONS

In this section, we examine the effects of economic policy under flexible rates using the *IS/LM/BP* model employed in the last chapter. The only difference in the analysis is that domestic responses to combinations of income and interest rates that lie off the *BP* curve will produce disequilibrium situations in the foreign exchange market, which will lead to an adjustment in the exchange rate that brings the foreign exchange market back into equilibrium. As this happens, the *BP* curve will shift, reflecting the new equilibrium exchange rate. Consider, for example, the *BP* curves in Figure 1. Because the exchange rate is now subject to change, we denote a specific *BP* equilibrium by an exchange rate subscript, for example, BP_0 for initial exchange rate e_0. Suppose that the domestic economy moves to a point below the BP_0 curve. At this point, the domestic interest rate is too low

FIGURE 1   **The Effects of Changes in the Exchange Rate on the *BP* Curve**

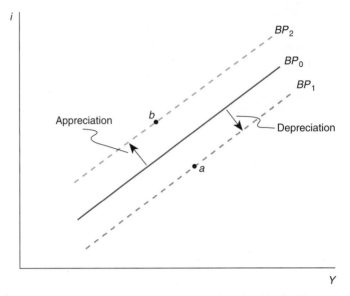

Initial balance-of-payments equilibrium at the exchange rate e_0 is depicted by the BP_0 curve. A depreciation of the currency leads to an expansion of exports and a contraction of imports. Thus, for any given level of income, a larger amount of net capital outflows, and thus a lower rate of interest, is required to balance the balance of payments. The *BP* curve thus shifts down (to the right) with currency depreciation to BP_1. In analogous fashion, an appreciation of the currency leads to greater imports and fewer exports, thus requiring a smaller amount of net capital outflows (or larger net capital inflows) to obtain external balance. A higher interest rate is therefore required at all levels of income, causing the *BP* curve to shift up (or leftward) to BP_2.

to attain equilibrium in the balance of payments for any level of income in question, and the economy begins experiencing a balance-of-payments deficit under the exchange rate e_0. However, since we have a flexible-rate system, as the economy begins to experience the deficit pressure, the home currency depreciates. Consequently, the country never experiences the deficit but, rather, observes a depreciation of the currency instead.

The initial disequilibrium in the foreign sector at point *a*, brought about by the new level of income and interest rate, is often referred to as an **incipient BOP deficit,** since it is not observed as a deficit per se but triggers a depreciation of the currency and a shift in the *BP* curve to BP_1. The lower *BP* curve reflects the fact that at the new, depreciated value of the home currency, any given income level (with its now more favorable current account position due to the enhanced exports and reduced imports caused by the depreciation) is associated with a lower interest rate (which worsens the capital account through additional net capital outflows that exactly offset the more favorable current account). Alternatively, any given interest rate is, in BOP equilibrium with the now-depreciated home currency, consistent with a higher level of income on BP_1 than on the original BP_0. Analogously, a combination of domestic income and the interest rate at point *b*, which lies above the initial *BP* curve, will trigger an **incipient BOP surplus** that causes the exchange rate to appreciate and shifts the *BP* curve to BP_2. It is important to emphasize the difference between the adjustment mechanisms under flexible and fixed rates. Under flexible rates, any disequilibrium leads to a change in the exchange rate and a shift in the *BP* curve. Under fixed rates, a disequilibrium in the foreign sector leads to a change in the money supply and a shift in the *LM* curve.

✽ BOX 1   REAL AND FINANCIAL FACTORS THAT INFLUENCE THE BP CURVE

A number of different factors influence the nature of the current account and the capital account in the balance of payments in addition to the domestic level of income, the domestic interest rate, and the current (spot) exchange rate. The level of exports is influenced by domestic and foreign price levels, the level of income in the rest of the world, and foreign tastes and preferences. Home country imports are also influenced by the level of foreign and domestic prices as well as by tastes and preferences. Capital flows depend on foreign interest rates, expected profit rates in both the home and foreign countries, expected future exchange rates, and the perceived risk associated with the investment alternatives.

All of these additional considerations are being held constant for a specific external balance *(BP)* curve. Should any of the factors change, the *BP* curve will shift to offset the effects of the changing condition and thus continue to reflect external balance. For example, an increase in foreign income will increase home country exports, thus permitting a higher level of domestic income to obtain balance-of-payments equilibrium for every interest rate. The *BP* curve will therefore shift to the right. A decrease in the foreign price level would have the opposite effect, leading to an increase in home country imports, a higher necessary rate of interest to balance the balance of payments, and hence a leftward shift in the *BP* curve.

Changes in financial variables will also shift the *BP* curve. For example, an increase in the foreign interest rate will stimulate an increase in short-term capital outflows from the home country. A higher domestic interest rate will therefore be required to balance the balance of payments for every given level of income, and the *BP* curve shifts to the left. A similar adjustment would take place for an increase in the expected profit rate abroad or a decrease in the expected profit rate at home. Finally, if investors' expectations regarding the future value of the exchange rate change—for example, there is an increase in the expected appreciation of the home currency—this would lead to a shift in the *BP* curve. An increase in the expected appreciation of the home currency leads to an inflow of short-term capital and hence to a rightward shift in the *BP* curve, since it now takes a lower rate of interest for each level of income to maintain external balance. These effects are summarized in Table 1.

TABLE 1   **Exogenous Factors and Shifts in the *BP* Curve**

Increase in foreign income	*BP* curve shifts right (down)
Increase in foreign prices	*BP* curve shifts right
Increase in domestic prices	*BP* curve shifts left (up)
Increase in the expected profit rate	
—foreign	*BP* curve shifts left
—domestic	*BP* curve shifts right
Increase in the foreign interest rate	*BP* curve shifts left
Increase in expected home currency appreciation	*BP* curve shifts right
(depreciation)	(left)

Finally, it must be noted that a number of different factors influence the position of the *BP* curve in addition to the exchange rate. These factors are assumed to be unchanged in our analysis, but they can, and often do, change. Changes in any one of these factors can cause the *BP* curve to shift, triggering a macroeconomic response. For a brief overview of several of the more important factors and the manner in which they affect the *BP* curve, see Box 1.

The Effects of Fiscal Policy under Different Capital Mobility Assumptions

Now we can turn to consideration of the effects of fiscal policy under the various international capital mobility assumptions. Expansionary fiscal policy is represented by a rightward shift in the *IS* curve, and its impacts are shown in Figure 2. Each of the four diagrams again reflects a different assumption about capital mobility. In each case, we

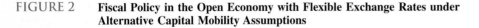

FIGURE 2   **Fiscal Policy in the Open Economy with Flexible Exchange Rates under Alternative Capital Mobility Assumptions**

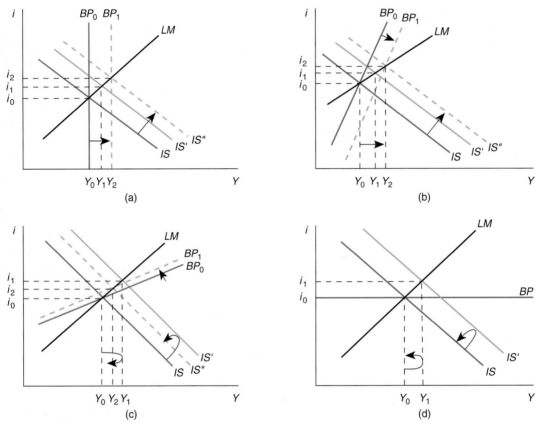

Starting at equilibrium Y_0 and i_0, an expansionary fiscal policy shifts the IS curve right (IS'). This causes income and imports to rise, leading to an incipient deficit when capital is perfectly immobile [panel (a)] or relatively immobile [panel (b)], and a depreciation of the currency. Currency depreciation shifts the BP curve right (BP_1), and increases exports and decreases imports, which generates an additional shift in the IS curve (IS''). A new, higher equilibrium, Y_2 and i_2, results. However, when capital is relatively mobile [panel (c)], the effectiveness of fiscal policy is reduced. In this case, expansionary fiscal policy (IS') produces an incipient surplus and currency appreciation. The BP curve thus shifts up and the IS curve shifts left as imports increase and exports decrease. The trade adjustment offsets some of the expansionary effect of the fiscal policy, and the expansionary effect on income is reduced, not enhanced as it was when capital was immobile or relatively immobile. Finally, note that with perfectly mobile capital [panel (d)], fiscal expansion sets in motion a currency appreciation that continues until the current account effect $(-\Delta X, +\Delta M)$ completely offsets the initial fiscal policy, leaving income at Y_0.

begin with the economy in equilibrium at Y_0 and i_0, and then examine the impact of an increase in government spending (or a decrease in taxes), which is captured by a shift in the IS curve to IS'.

Beginning with panel (a), an increase in government spending increases domestic demand for goods and services (IS'), leading to higher equilibrium income and a higher interest rate. Since capital is perfectly immobile, the increase in income creates an incipient deficit and causes the currency to depreciate. With depreciation of the currency, BP_0 shifts to the right to BP_1. At the same time, the depreciation of the currency causes exports to increase and imports to decrease, resulting in a further rightward shift of the IS curve to IS''. These adjustments stop when the IS, LM, and BP curves again intersect at a common point (Y_2, i_2). In the case of perfectly immobile capital, the adjustment in the foreign sector produces a secondary expansionary impulse through the increase in net exports. Note that, because the adjustment in the foreign sector is taking place through the exchange rate, there is no change in the money supply and hence no change in the *LM* curve.

Figure 2, panel (b) illustrates the situation of relative capital immobility, where international short-term capital movements are less responsive to changes in the interest rate than are the domestic financial markets. In this case, the *BP* curve is steeper than the *LM* curve. Increases in government spending again have an expansionary effect on the economy, leading to an incipient deficit in the balance of payments. The deficit pressure is less than it was when capital was perfectly immobile, since there is some degree of short-term capital response to changes in the domestic interest rate. An incipient deficit arises because induced imports from the higher *Y* outweigh the increased net capital inflow, and the resulting depreciation of the currency leads to a rightward shift of the *BP* curve to BP_1. An additional rightward shift of the *IS* curve to IS'' occurs as net exports increase with the depreciating currency. While the effects are smaller than those under perfect capital immobility, fiscal policy is still effective in expanding national income, and the adjustment of the foreign sector supplements the initial effect of the increase in government spending.

In panel (c), we have the case of relative mobility of international short-term capital, where the *BP* curve is flatter than the *LM* curve. While there is still imperfect mobility of capital in this instance, the foreign sector is seen to be more responsive to changes in the interest rate than the domestic money markets. An increase in government spending leads to an incipient *surplus* in the balance of payments due to net capital inflows more than offsetting the current account deficit and, hence, appreciation of the currency. With the currency appreciation, the *BP* curve moves to the left. The deterioration in the current account has an impact on aggregate demand as well, shifting the *IS* curve to the left. Consequently, the system comes to rest at a level of income Y_2 instead of Y_1. This takes place because part of the expansionary effects of the increase in government spending is offset by the deterioration in the current account that accompanies the appreciation of the currency. In this case, the foreign sector adjustment *dampens* the initial expansionary effect of the increase in government spending.

In the final scenario in panel (d), that of perfect capital mobility, we see that the shift in the *IS* curve to IS' due to the increase in government spending again causes an incipient surplus in the balance of payments (Y_1, i_1). This, of course, triggers an appreciation of the home currency (due to large-scale capital inflows), which continues until the current account balance deteriorates sufficiently to offset exactly the initial increase in government spending. When this occurs, the *IS* curve will be in the same position as before the increase in *G*. Thus, the principal real result of the increase in *G* is that it leads to a reduction in exports and an increase in imports, that is, to a change in the composition of GDP and the balance of payments. Since income has not expanded, the increase in government spending has essentially been facilitated by an increase in imports and a decrease in exports. Thus, exports have been "crowded out" and the imported goods have been "crowded in" by increased government spending. Note, however, that there has been no crowding out of real investment since, with perfectly mobile capital, the interest rate remains fixed at the international rate.

As you will have noted, in the circumstance where capital is neither perfectly mobile nor perfectly immobile, the effect of expansionary fiscal policy on the exchange rate is indeterminate without knowledge of the relative slopes of the *BP* and *LM* curves. If the *BP* curve is steeper than the *LM* curve (relative capital immobility), the home currency depreciates; if *BP* is flatter than *LM* (relative capital mobility), the home currency appreciates. Likewise, from a portfolio balance perspective, there is indeterminacy regarding the impact of the expansionary fiscal policy on the exchange rate. For example, if the expansionary policy involves a government budget deficit and the consequent issuance of new government bonds, then home country bonds may become more risky to foreign portfolio owners because there is now a greater supply of the home bonds. A depreciation of the domestic currency would then occur in order to induce foreign bondholders to buy the new bonds. This increase in riskiness is tantamount to making the *BP* curve steeper, approaching or becoming steeper than the *LM* curve (i.e., becoming the relative capital immobility case). On the other hand, if the expansionary fiscal policy did not involve issuing new bonds (i.e., there is no government budget deficit), the home currency would appreciate because of the short-term capital inflow response to the higher domestic interest rate. Finally, if deficit spending occurred but the deficit was financed by printing money rather than by issuing government bonds, the money supply increase would cause the home currency to depreciate. (As we see in the next section, increasing the money supply leads to depreciation.) Hence, portfolio balance considerations also yield uncertainty regarding the impact of the expansionary fiscal policy on the exchange rate.

An overview of the effects of fiscal policy under flexible rates thus indicates that the effectiveness of fiscal policy depends strongly on the degree of international mobility of capital. When capital is completely or relatively immobile, fiscal policy is effective in moving the economy to income and employment targets, and more so than under fixed exchange rates because of the extra income stimulus provided by the currency depreciation. On the other hand, as capital becomes more and more mobile, fiscal policy becomes less and less effective. In the case where capital is relatively mobile (*LM* steeper than *BP*), fiscal policy is less effective under flexible rates than under fixed rates because of the income-depressing effect of the currency appreciation. For the extreme case of perfect capital mobility, fiscal policy is totally ineffective. As financial capital becomes more and more mobile in our shrinking world, fiscal policy will become less and less effective for influencing the level of income and employment. While a flexible-rate system thus severely weakens the fiscal instrument in a world of mobile capital (since the adjustments in the foreign exchange markets can severely offset the effects of discretionary fiscal policy), it does free up the monetary policy instrument, as will be seen in the following section.

The Effects of Monetary Policy under Different Capital Mobility Assumptions

The economic response to increases in the money supply is straightforward and consistent across the different capital mobility scenarios (see Figure 3). Increases in the money supply shift the *LM* curve to the right and in all four cases expand domestic income from the initial Y_0, put downward pressure on the domestic interest rate from the initial i_0, and produce an incipient deficit in the balance of payments. Under a system of flexible rates, expansionary monetary policy leads to a depreciation of the domestic currency, accompanied by an increase in exports and a decrease in imports. With the depreciation, both the *BP* curve and the *IS* curve shift to the right. The end result is an increase in equilibrium income and a strengthening of the trade balance.

Looking more closely at each case, in the situation of perfectly immobile capital [panel (a)], the incipient deficit is caused by the increase in imports that accompanies the higher level of domestic income. Since capital flows are completely insensitive to changes in the interest rate, there is no capital-flow response to the monetary policy action. Consequently, the currency needs to depreciate only enough to offset the income effect on imports. As the currency depreciates, the *BP* curve shifts to the right from BP_0 to BP_1 and the increase

FIGURE 3   **Monetary Policy in the Open Economy with Flexible Exchange Rates under Alternative Capital Mobility Assumptions**

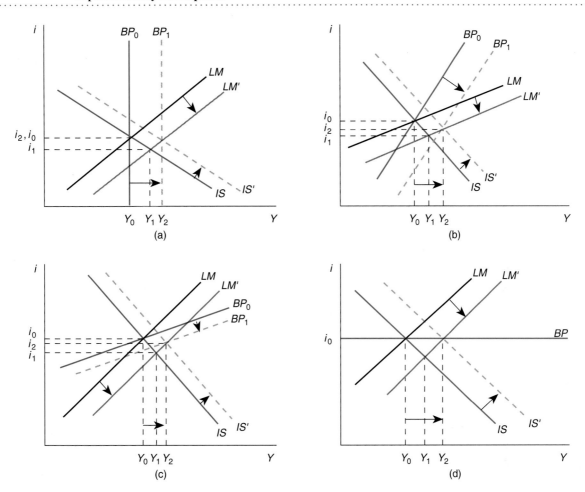

Starting at equilibrium at Y_0 and i_0, expansionary monetary policy shifts the *LM* curve to the right *(LM')*, lowering the interest rate and increasing income (Y_1, i_1). The lower interest rate reduces a net capital inflow or worsens a net capital outflow [except in case (a)], and the higher income level increases imports. Consequently, there is an incipient deficit in the balance of payments, resulting in a depreciation of the home currency and a rightward shift in the *BP* curve (BP_1). However, depreciation increases exports and decreases imports, causing a rightward shift of the *IS* curve *(IS')*. Depreciation (rightward shift of the *BP* curve) and improvements in the trade balance (rightward shift of the *IS* curve) continue until all three curves again intersect at a common point and equilibrium is obtained (Y_2 and i_2). In the case of perfect capital mobility [panel (d)], all the adjustments take place along the *BP* curve, since it remains horizontal at the world rate of interest. With flexible exchange rates, expansionary monetary policy is effective in influencing income regardless of the degree of capital mobility, and the current account effects complement the monetary policy in all cases.

in net exports also shifts the *IS* curve to the right to *IS'*. The system will eventually come to rest at a new equilibrium with a higher level of income Y_2, a depreciated currency, and a lower interest rate.[1] Note that the expenditure effects associated with the depreciation further enhance the initial effects of the monetary expansion.

The expansion of the money supply under imperfect capital mobility [panels (b) and (c)] leads to a fall in the domestic interest rate and in turn stimulates a short-term capital outflow, worsening the short-term capital account. Thus, both short-term capital movements and the increase in domestic income put downward pressure on the value of the home currency. The more responsive international capital flows are to changes in the domestic interest rate (the flatter the *BP* curve), the greater the additional pressure will be. Consequently, the more interest-elastic the *BP* curve is, the greater the depreciation that will take place to maintain equilibrium in the balance of payments. Since the expansion in net exports is greater with a greater depreciation, the overall expansionary effects of monetary policy are larger the more mobile international capital is. This is verified in the last case, panel (d), where capital is perfectly mobile and the *BP* curve is horizontal. Since capital is very responsive to the slightest change in the domestic interest rate, expansion of the money supply generates a very large capital outflow and a depreciation of the home currency. This depreciation leads to a large expansion of net exports (exactly offsetting the capital outflow), which in turn stimulates national income.

The more mobile international capital is, the more effective monetary policy is. However, the more mobile international capital is, the greater the degree to which expansionary monetary policy depends on the adjustment in the foreign trade sector to bring about the increase in income and employment. If the interest rate does not initially change, or changes very little with respect to changes in the money supply, then investment may not respond and the income expansion must come about through shifts in the *IS* function via changes in exports and imports. With all mobility assumptions, however, the subsequent adjustments in the foreign trade sector strengthen the initial impact of the growth in the money supply. One concludes, therefore, that, in general,

....

[1]The interest rate falls unambiguously because the *BP* curve shifts to the right to a greater extent than does the *IS* curve at any given interest rate. Remembering the autonomous spending multiplier from the chapter "National Income and the Current Account," the change in income at each interest rate is the depreciation-induced improvement in the trade balance (the net addition to spending in the economy at each interest rate) times the multiplier. This income change equals the size of the horizontal shift in the *IS* curve; that is,

$$\Delta Y_{IS} = \Delta (X - M) \cdot \{1/[1 - \text{MPC}(1 - t) + \text{MPM}]\} \qquad [1]$$

On the other hand, the *BP* curve shifts to the right at any given interest rate by the amount of increase in income needed to generate sufficient imports to restore balanced trade after the currency depreciation. In other words, imports must rise by the amount necessary to match the initial improvement in the trade balance; that is, imports must change by $\text{MPM} \cdot \Delta Y$. Hence,

$$\Delta M = \text{MPM} \cdot \Delta Y \qquad [2]$$

or the necessary rightward shift in the *BP* curve at each given interest rate is

$$\Delta Y_{BP} = \Delta M/\text{MPM} \qquad [3]$$

Since trade balance is restored after the *BP* shift, this means that ΔM associated with the *BP* shift is equal to $\Delta(X - M)$ associated with the *IS* shift. Letting $\Delta M = \Delta(X - M) = a$ in expressions [3] and [1], we see that $\Delta Y_{BP} = a/\text{MPM}$ and $\Delta Y_{IS} = a/[1 - \text{MPC}(1 - t) + \text{MPM}]$. Since $[1 - \text{MPC}(1 - t)]$ is a positive number, the denominator in the ΔY_{IS} expression is larger than the denominator in the ΔY_{BP} expression, and hence with an identical numerator, ΔY_{BP} is greater than ΔY_{IS}. In other words, the *BP* curve shifts farther to the right than does the *IS* curve at any given interest rate.

monetary policy is more effective under flexible exchange rates than under fixed exchange rates.

Policy Coordination under Flexible Exchange Rates

A general conclusion reached in the above analysis of fiscal and monetary policy is that monetary policy is consistently effective in influencing national income under flexible rates and that it is stronger the more mobile international short-term capital is. Fiscal policy is less effective under flexible rates than under fixed rates when capital is relatively or perfectly mobile. This results from the fact that the expenditure-switching effects can work against fiscal policy, whereas they complement monetary policy. It is not surprising, then, that policymakers may find it desirable to use both instruments in a coordinated fashion to achieve domestic targets. **Monetary policy–fiscal policy coordination** will permit policymakers to strive for other targets besides income, such as an interest rate target, stability of the foreign exchange rate, or a desired combination of government spending, export production/employment, and output/employment in the import-competing sector. Joint use of monetary and fiscal policies will allow the policymaker some control over the nature of the structural adjustment and over the distribution of the economic effects of the policies adopted.

This point can be seen in Figure 4. Let us start with the economy initially in equilibrium at Y_0 and i_0. Suppose that a target of Y^* and i^* is set, which would permit the expansion of the economy without affecting the exchange rate and hence relative prices. Turning first to panel (b), let us examine how attempts to reach that point using monetary policy alone will fare. Expanding the money supply alone (LM') leads to depreciation of the domestic currency (a rightward shift of BP) and an expansion of net trade in the foreign sector (a rightward shift of IS). Since the new equilibrium must lie on LM' with a depreciated currency (a lower BP), the equilibrium rate of interest will be less than i^*. Such an equilibrium interest rate is illustrated by i', occurring at the intersection of IS', LM' and BP_1. In this instance, both targets would be missed since Y' is less than Y^* and i' is less than i^*. In addition, exporters and import competitors would be rewarded and the nontraded sector would be harmed by the change in relative prices brought about by the change in the exchange rate.

If, on the other hand, government officials attempted to attain Y^* using only fiscal policy and they were successful, interest rates would be driven up to i_{y*}, as demonstrated in panel (a), clearly missing the target i^*. In all likelihood, it would prove difficult to attain Y^* with only fiscal policy, since expansionary fiscal policy (that is, a rightward shift in the IS curve to IS_{FP}) will create an incipient surplus, causing the currency to appreciate (a leftward shift of the BP curve). With the currency appreciating, exports decrease and imports increase, and the IS curve shifts back leftward to IS'_{FP}. The system thus moves to a new equilibrium on the LM curve, for example, the intersection of IS'_{FP} and BP_{FP}, which misses both targets. The use of fiscal policy alone will lead to an interest rate that is too high and in all likelihood a level of income below Y^*. Attempts to reach Y^* by additional government spending will simply drive the interest rate higher. Further, in this process, exporters and producers of import substitutes would be hurt and the nontraded sector would gain.

The only way to obtain the two targets in question without causing exchange rate changes and affecting relative prices—and therefore, the structure of the economy—is to rely on both of the instruments. In Figure 4 (c), Y^* and i^* are obtained by the joint use of monetary and fiscal policies $(IS'$ and $LM')$, which allows the economy to expand to Y^* without stimulating any expenditure-switching effects. For similar reasons, policymakers will likely find it effective to use both policy instruments to respond to exogenous shocks should they feel that a policy response is appropriate.

FIGURE 4   **Monetary-Fiscal Policy Coordination under Flexible Exchange Rates**

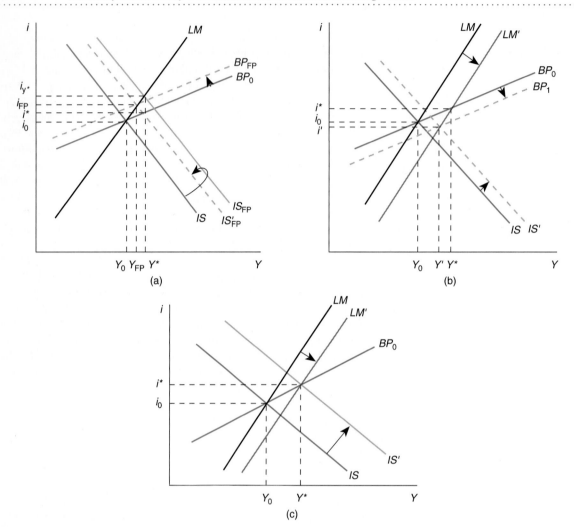

With the economy in equilibrium at Y_0 and i_0, policymakers decide that it would be desirable to be at Y^* and i^*. However, it is possible to reach this combination only by the coordinated use of monetary and fiscal policies as shown in panel (c). Turning to panel (a), attempts to use only fiscal policy (a rightward shift in the IS curve to IS_{FP}) will lead to an incipient surplus and appreciation of the home currency. Consequently, the BP curve starts shifting left, and at the same time exports decrease and imports increase, causing the IS curve to shift left. The new equilibrium that must be on the LM curve will either miss the interest rate target at Y^* (i.e., i_{y^*} will exist instead of i^*) or miss both targets such as at Y_{FP} and i_{FP} (IS'_{FP}, BP_{FP}, LM). Attempts to use only monetary policy (a rightward shift in the LM curve to LM'), as demonstrated in panel (b), will lead to an incipient deficit and depreciation of the currency. Consequently, the BP curve will start shifting right (toward BP_1) and, as exports increase and imports decrease, the IS curve will also start shifting to the right. The new equilibrium will occur on LM', but with a depreciated currency and hence with the IS' and BP_1 curves. Consequently, attempts to attain Y^* will lead to an interest rate less than i^*, or to a new equilibrium at i' and Y', which misses both targets. Hence, the only way to attain the two targets simultaneously is with coordinated use of the two instruments.

CONCEPT CHECK

1. Under what capital mobility conditions is fiscal policy effective in pursuing an income target in a flexible exchange rate system? When is it totally ineffective? Why?

2. Why is it said that the effectiveness of monetary policy in altering income is enhanced by induced changes in the foreign sector in a flexible exchange rate system?

THE EFFECTS OF EXOGENOUS SHOCKS IN THE *IS/LM/BP* MODEL WITH IMPERFECT MOBILITY OF CAPITAL

The analysis to this point has focused on the impact of monetary and fiscal policy, holding a number of important variables constant. These include such variables as the level of prices at home, the level of prices abroad, and the interest rate abroad, as well as the expected profit rates at home and abroad, the expected exchange rates, and the trade policies and economic institutions at home and abroad. Because these variables can, and often do, change abruptly or unexpectedly, it is useful to examine briefly the effects of changes in selected variables through comparative statics to get some idea of how economic "shocks" are transmitted in an interdependent world under flexible exchange rates.

Suppose that there is a sudden increase in the level of foreign prices, that is, a **foreign price shock** (see Figure 5). There will be an expansionary effect (a shift of the *IS* curve to the right) on the home economy as exports increase and imports decrease in response to the price change in question. In addition, there will be a rightward shift in the *BP* curve (from BP_0 to BP'_0) since the expenditure-switching effect of the increase in foreign prices means that a higher level of domestic income is consistent with BOP equilibrium for each given home interest rate. With the increased spending *(IS')* on the country's products, income and the interest rate begin to rise. The rise in the domestic interest rate generates upward pressure on the value of the home currency (appreciation) because of short-term capital inflows, as has the improvement in the current account, and the *BP* curve will begin to shift back up. As the currency continues to appreciate, exports fall and imports rise, shifting the *IS* curve back toward its initial position. The final result is a return to the original Y_0, i_0 equilibrium position. Thus, we see that under (completely) flexible rates the economy is insulated from price shocks originating outside the country. This case is

FIGURE 5   **Foreign Price Shocks and Macroeconomic Adjustment in the Open Economy**

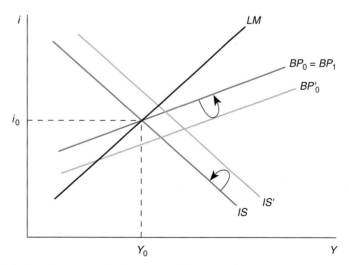

An increase in foreign prices causes the *BP* curve to shift out to BP'_0 and exports to rise and imports to fall. The improved current account shifts *IS* right to *IS'*, putting upward pressure on income and the interest rate. The improved current account and the higher domestic rate of interest produce an incipient balance-of-payments surplus, and the home currency begins to appreciate. With currency appreciation, the *BP* curve begins moving upward and the *IS* curve starts moving leftward. Equilibrium is again reached at Y_0 and i_0 as the appreciating currency offsets the foreign price shock.

✺ CASE STUDY 1   COMMODITY PRICES AND U.S. REAL GDP, 1973–1995

Price shocks can originate in a number of ways, for example, increases in the money supply, fiscal expansion, simultaneous expansion of several key industrial countries, sudden increases in wages, and changes in real commodity prices. Figure 6 focuses on commodity price changes and portrays the movement of world wholesale prices of food, agricultural raw materials, metals, and petroleum over the period 1973–1995. Oil prices almost quadrupled from 1973 to 1974 and then virtually tripled from 1978 to 1980, before falling about 60 percent from 1980 to 1986. There was clearly considerable price variability during this period in the other, broader commodity categories as well.

However, despite these major price shocks, real GDP in the United States demonstrated *relatively* steady growth over these years. Since major countries' exchange rates became more flexible in 1973, this relative stability of GDP is consistent with the notion that flexible rates tend to insulate an economy from external price shocks. Nevertheless, we do not wish to minimize the impact of the shocks, because unemployment and inflation in industrial countries were affected in particular by the OPEC price hikes in 1973–1974. The insulation from exogenous forces that was expected to accompany flexible exchange rates has not been complete (although exchange rates were and still are not completely flexible).

FIGURE 6   **Wholesale Prices and U.S. GDP, 1973–1995**

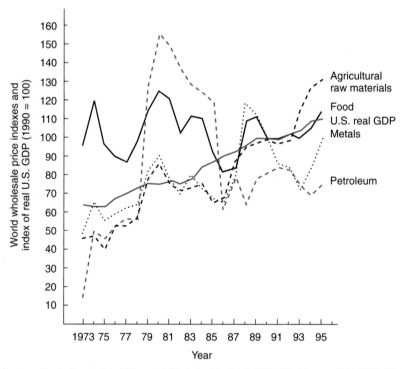

Sources: International Monetary Fund, *International Financial Statistics Yearbook 1996* (Washington, DC: IMF, 1996), pp. 108–9, 166–67; *Economic Report of the President,* February 1997 (Washington, DC: U.S. Government Printing Office, 1997), p. 302.   ✺

relevant to the period since 1973, when considerable price variability occurred in major commodity groups. (see Case Study 1).

Suppose on the other hand that there is a sudden increase in domestic prices, that is, a **domestic price shock** (see Figure 7). In this case, equilibrium in all three sectors will be affected. An increase in domestic prices will reduce the real money supply, shifting the *LM* curve to the left. At the same time, increased domestic prices will reduce the competitiveness of home exports and make imports more attractive to domestic consumers.

FIGURE 7   **Open-Economy Adjustment to Domestic Price Shocks in a Flexible-Rate Regime**

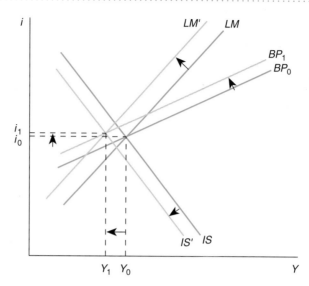

Assume that the economy is in equilibrium at Y_0 and i_0. An increase in the domestic price level will affect equilibrium in all three sectors. The LM curve will shift to the left to LM' as the real supply of money falls. The IS curve will shift to the left as exports fall and imports rise. Finally, the BP curve will shift upward as the deteriorating trade balance requires a higher rate of interest for every level of income to balance the balance of payments. Equilibrium will occur on LM' at a lower level of income (Y_1) and a new rate of interest (i_1).

Consequently, the IS curve will shift to the left. Finally, these same trade effects will lead to an upward shift of the BP curve, since it will now take a higher interest rate to attract sufficient short-term capital to bring the balance of payments into balance at every level of income. These adjustments are shown in Figure 7 by LM', IS', and BP_1. The new equilibrium will lie along LM' at a higher interest rate (i_1) and a lower level of income (Y_1) than the initial equilibrium (i_0, Y_0), although i_1 could be less than i_0. Should the initial shifts in the IS and BP curves not lead to a simultaneous equilibrium point with LM', an appropriate change in the exchange rate will occur, since an IS/LM equilibrium point that does not lie on the BP curve will bring about the requisite exchange rate adjustment.

Next, from an initial i_0, Y_0, suppose that there is an increase in the foreign interest rate, that is, a **foreign interest rate shock** (see Figure 8). Since this will make foreign short-term investments more attractive and cause portfolio adjustments, one would expect an increased outflow (or decreased inflow) of short-term capital. With the new, higher interest rate abroad and the same exchange rate, a higher domestic interest rate is now required to balance the balance of payments at all income levels. Consequently, there is an upward shift in the BP curve from BP_0, i_{f0} to BP_0, i_{f1}. With the new BP curve, the previous equilibrium level of interest (i_0) is too low for attaining domestic balance-of-payments equilibrium, and an incipient deficit appears. The domestic currency begins to depreciate (shifting BP_0, i_{f1} to BP_1, i_{f1}), and this depreciation stimulates exports and decreases imports. This current account impact (driven by the capital account developments) leads to a rightward shift in the IS curve to IS'. Eventually, a new equilibrium is reached on the LM curve with the new BP and IS curves. Both the interest rate (i_1) and the income level (Y_1) have increased. Thus, the initial rise in the foreign interest rate has led

FIGURE 8   **Foreign Interest Rate Shocks and Macroeconomic Adjustment in a Flexible-Rate Regime**

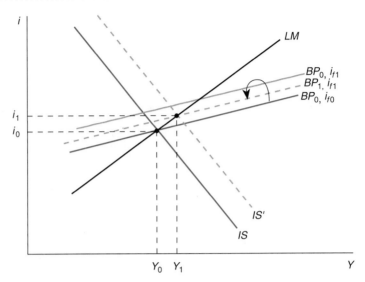

From the starting point of Y_0 and i_0, the increase in the foreign interest rate makes short-term foreign investments more attractive. It therefore takes a higher domestic rate of interest to maintain external balance for all levels of income, and the *BP* curve shifts up to BP_0, i_{f1}. As domestic investors increase their short-term financial investments abroad, there is an incipient deficit and the home currency begins to depreciate (the *BP* curve moves downward). Depreciation stimulates exports and discourages imports, causing the *IS* curve to shift to the right. A new equilibrium results at a higher level of income (Y_1) and interest rate (i_1) at the intersection of *LM*, *IS'*, and BP_1, i_{f1}. In addition, if the higher foreign interest rate reduces the home demand for money, *LM* will shift farther to the right and income will rise even further.

to an increase in the domestic interest rate as well as to a depreciation of the home currency.

An additional consideration relates to portfolio adjustments. Because the foreign interest rate has risen, home country asset holders will also reduce their demand for domestic *money* as they rearrange their portfolios to take advantage of the higher foreign interest rate. With a decrease in home money demand, the *LM* curve of Figure 8 will shift to the right. The initial incipient BOP deficit will be even larger than discussed in the previous paragraph, and the depreciation of the home currency will be even greater. The simultaneous intersection of the final *BP, LM,* and *IS* curves will, as before, be at a higher income level than Y_1. In the extreme case where home money demand is very responsive to the foreign interest rate, the *LM* curve could shift considerably to the right, and conceivably the new equilibrium interest rate could be lower than the original i_0. We think that this result is very unlikely. However, it cannot be determined a priori whether the final interest rate will be above, below, or the same as i_1. Finally, while there is no a priori way to discern whether the domestic adjustment to foreign interest rate shocks occurs relatively more via the exchange rate rather than via the domestic interest rate, some empirical evidence suggests that the exchange rate in practice carries the bulk of the adjustment between the United States and its major trading partners, with the possible exception of Canada (see the chapter "The Foreign Exchange Market").

As a last example of a shock, consider the case of a **shock to the expected exchange rate.** Suppose that, because of some exogenous event (such as the election of a foreign government that is expected to stabilize its country economically), there is now an expected greater appreciation of the foreign currency (or, alternatively, an expected greater depreciation of the home currency). Recall the uncovered interest parity (UIP) expression from earlier chapters (and ignore any risk premium):

$$i_d = i_f + xa$$

where i_d = the domestic interest rate, i_f = the foreign interest rate, and xa = the expected percentage appreciation of the foreign currency. From an initial UIP equilibrium, the rise in xa will now make the term $(i_f + xa)$ greater than i_d and there will thus be a short-term capital outflow from the home country to the foreign country. This change in the expected exchange rate has the same impacts in the *IS/LM/BP* diagram as did the foreign interest rate shock considered above, and Figure 8 can also be used to interpret this case. In terms of the figure, the rise in xa shifts the *BP* curve upward (to the left) since a higher domestic interest rate is now needed for home country BOP equilibrium at each income level. There is an incipient deficit at the old equilibrium income level Y_0, and depreciation of the domestic currency thus takes place, moving the *IS* curve to the right and also causing the *BP* curve to move back to the right. The end result (as at Y_1 and i_1) is a higher income level and, as the UIP expression also suggests, a higher domestic interest rate.[2]

In overview of external shocks, it is important to note that the greater the economic interdependence among countries, the greater the general likelihood that foreign shocks (other things equal) will have an impact on domestic interest rates and/or the exchange rate. Domestic policymakers are forced to make decisions that take into account both domestic variables and foreign economic variables, so policymaking becomes more difficult.

For example, in the foreign interest rate shock case, a rise in the foreign rate led to an increase in the domestic interest rate. However, the domestic economy may be in such a state that domestic authorities do not wish to have a higher domestic interest rate. To offset the rise in the domestic rate, suppose the monetary authorities increase the money supply. From i_1, Y_1 in Figure 8, this shifts *LM* to the right (not shown) and generates an incipient deficit. The *BP* curve shifts to the right, as will the *IS* curve due to the currency depreciation. The income level rises above Y_1 and the interest rate falls below i_1, perhaps all the way to i_0. The country has thus negated to at least some extent the original effects of the foreign interest rate increase, but it has also generated depreciation of the home currency. The foreign country in turn has now experienced an appreciation of its currency to a greater extent than it originally expected. Consequently, its income level may fall, and it may consider taking appropriate policy actions to counter these effects. Note, of course, that changes in the exchange rate are important actors in this scenario.

To reduce the degree of instability in exchange rates and domestic variables caused by this kind of sequence of policy reactions, a case can be made that there should be greater **international macroeconomic policy coordination** in a regime of flexible exchange rates. Such coordination of macro policy is currently being fostered (see Case Study 2). The most obvious examples of such joint consultations in practice consist of the annual economic summits held each summer by leaders of the Group of 7 or **G-7 countries** (Canada, France, Germany, Italy, Japan, the United Kingdom, and the United States).

....

[2]Again, were the *LM* curve in Figure 8 to shift to the right because of a reduced home country money demand, the conclusions would be that there would be a greater initial incipient BOP deficit, a greater depreciation of the home currency, a greater expansion in domestic income, and a likely final domestic interest rate above i_0.

❇ CASE STUDY 2   MACROECONOMIC POLICY COORDINATION, THE IMF, AND THE G-7

According to an IMF task force report, "Improving international coordination of national economic policies should be a major objective of industrial countries."[a] The director of the task force, Robert Solomon, pointed out that, because the world had become increasingly integrated both with respect to trade and capital mobility, policymakers must take into account that their policy actions have spillover effects in other countries:

> The failure to coordinate policies can be "dramatic," Solomon argued. He suggested that economic policy coordination among the major industrial countries could have averted at least some of the very sharp run up in inflation that followed the adoption of expansionary fiscal and monetary policies in 1972–73. Similarly, he observed, the 1981–82 downturn might have been less severe.
>
> Policy coordination among industrial countries, Solomon contended, should aim to harmonize targets. Industrial countries should also seek to maintain consistency in the goals and targets that they pursue and in the instruments that they utilize. The Group of 7 generally aims for high levels of employment and growth and for relative price stability. Its instruments are primarily monetary and fiscal policy.[b]

Because of the increased interdependency, the task force urged that governments become more flexible in their fiscal policy and that fiscal policy be focused more on medium-term targets instead of on short-term fine-tuning exercises.

In keeping with the greater focus on international coordination, the G-7 countries issued the following typical statement after their January meeting in New York in 1991:

> The finance ministers and central bank governors of Canada, France, Germany, Italy, Japan, the United Kingdom, and the United States met on January 20 and 21, 1991, in New York City for an exchange of views on current international economic and financial issues. The Managing Director of the IMF [Michel Camdessus] participated in the multilateral surveillance discussions.
>
> The ministers and governors reviewed their economic policies and prospects and reaffirmed their support for economic policy coordination at this critical time.

> They noted that although growth in all their economies had slowed, expansion of the world economy continues, and the pace of activity could be expected to pick up later this year.
>
> They noted that growth remains particularly strong in Germany and Japan.
>
> Implementation of sound fiscal policies, combined with stability-oriented monetary policies, should create conditions favorable to lower global interest rates and a stronger world economy. They also stressed the importance of a timely and successful conclusion of the Uruguay Round.
>
> The ministers and governors also discussed the situation in global financial markets in light of uncertainties arising from the gulf war and developments in the Soviet Union. They agreed to strengthen cooperation and to monitor developments in exchange markets.
>
> The ministers and governors are prepared to respond as appropriate to maintain stability in international financial markets.[c]

This emphasis on policy coordination has become a permanent feature of the world policymaking environment. For example, in July 1992, the G-7 leaders pledged to continue to promote monetary and fiscal policies that would support economic recovery without reigniting inflation and that would permit lower interest rates by reducing members' budget deficits and government spending.[d] In July 1993, the G-7 also demonstrated interest in specific country policies by encouraging Japan to implement macroeconomic policies that would reduce Japan's trade surplus and by praising President Bill Clinton for his efforts toward reducing the U.S. federal government budget deficit. Increasingly, other economic actions have also been agreed to by the G-7, such as the 1993 commitment of $3 billion of financial aid to Russia for assistance in the privatization of government enterprises.[e] Further, in June 1995, the G-7 countries introduced measures to reduce the likelihood of future crises similar to that of Mexico in late 1994 and early 1995,[f] when huge amounts of foreign capital exited the country and the value of the peso dropped precipitously in currency markets.

---

[a]"Task Force Backs Macroeconomic Policy Coordination," *IMF Survey,* Feb. 4, 1991, p. 33.

[b]Ibid., p. 41.

[c]Ibid.

[d]"G-7 Leaders Urge Strong IMF-Supported Policies in States of Former U.S.S.R.," *IMF Survey,* July 20, 1992, p. 226.

[e]David Wessel and Jeffrey Birnbaum, "U.S. Lines Up Aid for Russia at G-7 Meeting," *The Wall Street Journal,* July 9, 1993, pp. A3–A4.

[f]See "G-7 Offers Proposals to Strengthen Bretton Woods Institutions," *IMF Survey,* July 3, 1995, pp. 201–5.

⚹ CASE STUDY 2 (CONTINUED)

In a recent book, Bergsten and Henning[g] reviewed and assessed the record of the G-7. They indicated (p. 17) that there are five critical areas of international policy concern for the group: (1) world growth and stability, (2) exchange rates, (3) current account imbalances, (4) the stance of G-7 members toward other countries, and (5) the design of the international economic system. Bergsten and Henning pointed out, for example, the great success of the group in implementing the Plaza agreement in 1985 for correcting the overvaluation of the dollar (p. 21) and in devising arrangements for sharing the financial burden of the conduct of the Gulf war in 1991 (p. 24). On the other hand, the G-7 failed to work out a coordinated growth strategy for recovery from the high unemployment and slow growth of industrialized countries in the early 1990s (pp. 27, 29), and the group failed to design an acceptable set of currency arrangements in a world where, according to Bergsten and Henning (p. 39), "the polar extremes of both fixed and flexible exchange rates have been tried and found wanting."

[g]C. Fred Bergsten and C. Randall Henning, *Global Economic Leadership and the Group of Seven* (Washington, DC: Institute for International Economics, 1996).

⚹

CONCEPT CHECK

1. Explain the impact that a decrease in foreign prices has on the open economy under a flexible exchange rate system.
2. Using the *IS/LM/BP* framework, explain how an increase in the foreign interest rate influences the home country interest rate in the open economy under flexible exchange rates.

SUMMARY

This chapter has examined the automatic adjustment process under flexible exchange rates and the effects of discretionary economic policy under different capital mobility assumptions. It was found that monetary policy is effective in influencing income under flexible exchange rates, whereas it was ineffective under fixed rates. Further, the degree of effectiveness under flexible rates increases with the degree of capital mobility. Fiscal policy, on the other hand, was found to be much less effective under flexible rates than under fixed rates as capital becomes very mobile internationally, since expenditure-switching effects dampen initial expansionary effects. The impacts of fiscal policy on national income are the strongest when capital is immobile. The flexible-rate system does, however, give the country more policy options than a fixed-rate system since the external sector is always in balance. If a country wishes to attain several domestic targets, the coordinated use of monetary and fiscal policies can be helpful. The chapter concluded with a discussion of automatic adjustment to exogenous shocks under a flexible-rate system. The realization that a number of these shocks are often taking place simultaneously makes one keenly aware of the difficulties surrounding effective policymaking in a system of flexible rates.

KEY TERMS

domestic price shock	incipient BOP deficit	monetary policy–fiscal policy
foreign interest rate shock	incipient BOP surplus	coordination
foreign price shock	international macroeconomic	shock to the expected exchange
G-7 countries	policy coordination	rate

QUESTIONS AND PROBLEMS

1. What will happen under flexible rates if the intersection of the *IS* and *LM* curves is below (or to the right) of the *BP* curve? Why?

2. What exogenous real and financial factors influence the position of the *BP* curve?

3. Under what capital mobility conditions is fiscal policy totally ineffective in influencing income? Explain why this result occurs.

4. One strong argument for a flexible exchange rate system is that it frees up monetary policy for use in pursuing domestic targets. Explain why this is so.

5. Why does monetary policy get a boost from the external sector under a flexible-rate system?

6. Suppose that policymakers decide to expand the economy by increasing the money supply. Based on the trade effects, who do you expect to favor such a policy? Who is likely to be against this policy? Why?

7. If short-term capital is neither perfectly immobile nor perfectly mobile internationally, why is the predicted impact of expansionary fiscal policy on the exchange rate ambiguous?

8. Explain, using the *IS/LM/BP* model, how a rise in the expected appreciation of the foreign currency can lead to an increase in domestic interest rates.

9. Why might it be argued that recent changes in international prices of food and energy have had a smaller impact on the U.S. economy than would have been the case under the pre-1973 pegged rate system?

10. "A sudden increase in interest rates in the European Union would likely lead to both depreciation of the U.S. dollar and upward pressure on U.S. interest rates." Agree? Disagree? Why?

CHAPTER

10

PRICES AND OUTPUT IN THE OPEN ECONOMY

Aggregate Supply and Demand

INTRODUCTION

The analysis of trade and finance in the open economy up to this point has proceeded under the assumption that expansion and contraction of the macroeconomy would take place without affecting the level of prices. Although the comparative statics of a change in prices were examined in terms of the macroeconomic adjustment that would accompany such an exogenous shock in the previous chapter, no attempt was made to incorporate price changes endogenously into the analysis. Since changes in prices are a very important aspect of economic activity in the open economy, it is imperative to consider the interaction between the foreign sector and the domestic price level in the open macroeconomy. We will pursue this line of analysis using an aggregate demand and supply framework that incorporates the effects of trade and financial flows. The presentation begins by reviewing the concepts of aggregate demand and supply in the closed economy, taking into account differences between short-run and long-run effects. We will then open the economy and examine the effects of international transactions on the aggregate demand and supply curves under fixed exchange rates and flexible exchange rates. The chapter will conclude with a discussion of monetary and fiscal policy in the open-economy demand and supply framework and of the responsiveness of the economy to various shocks. This chapter should bring home to you the point that consideration of the price level complicates policy problems and, consequently, the design of effective macroeconomic policy. Also, you should note that, in the long run, measures that increase aggregate supply are paramount for increasing national income.

AGGREGATE DEMAND AND SUPPLY IN THE CLOSED ECONOMY

Aggregate Demand in the Closed Economy

We begin by reviewing the link between aggregate demand and prices in the closed macroeconomy. In the chapter "Economic Policy in the Open Economy: Fixed Exchange Rates," income and interest rate equilibrium was described using the *IS* and *LM* curves to portray equilibrium in the real sector and the money market, assuming that prices were constant. From the demand perspective, macroeconomic equilibrium takes place at the level of income and the interest rate determined by the intersection of the *IS* and *LM* curves. What happens to equilibrium in this model when prices change? Since equilibrium in the goods sector is measured in real terms, price changes do not directly affect the *IS* curve. Changes in price do, however, affect the size of the real money supply, M_s/P. As the price level rises, the real money supply declines; a decline in the real money supply

FIGURE 1   **Derivation of the Aggregate Demand Curve in the Closed Economy**

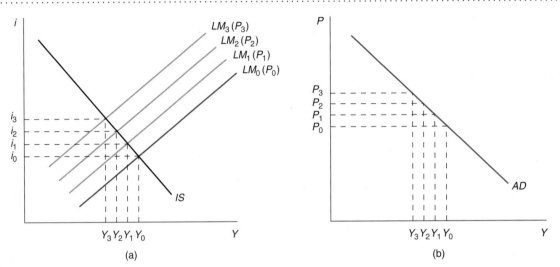

Starting at Y_0 and i_0 in panel (a), increases in the price level reduce the real money supply, shifting the *LM* curve to the left. Therefore, a particular *LM* curve is associated with each higher price level (e.g., LM_1 for P_1, LM_2 for P_2, etc.). With each new, higher price level, P_i, there is a new, lower equilibrium level of income Y_i determined by the intersection of the LM_i and the *IS* curve (e.g., for P_0, Y_0; for P_2, Y_2; etc.). These pairs of price levels and equilibrium income levels are now plotted on a different graph in panel (b), with price levels measured on the vertical axis and real income levels represented on the horizontal axis. Since successively lower equilibrium levels of income are associated with successively higher price levels, a normal downward-sloping aggregate demand curve results.

will have the impact of shifting the *LM* curve to the left. Such a shift is shown in Figure 1(a) by four *LM* curves (LM_0, LM_1, LM_2, LM_3) associated with four different price levels, where $P_0 < P_1 < P_2 < P_3$. Associated with each price level is an equilibrium level of income, Y_0, Y_1, Y_2, and Y_3. The higher the price level, the lower the equilibrium level of income.

The level of prices and the corresponding equilibrium level of income can be used to generate an aggregate demand curve in panel (b). Note that the vertical axis measures the price level and not the interest rate, while the level of real income is still measured on the horizontal axis. When the price level–equilibrium income coordinates are plotted, they produce a normal downward-sloping **aggregate demand curve** (*AD*) which shows the level of real output demanded at each price level. The slope of the *AD* curve is determined jointly by the slopes of the *IS* and the *LM* curves. The more elastic these curves are, the more elastic the *AD* curve is. Any change in the slope of either the *IS* or the *LM* curve will lead to a similar change in slope of the *AD* curve.

Similarly, the position of the *AD* curve is determined by the positions of the *IS* and *LM* curves. If the *IS* curve shifts to the right, it will lead to higher equilibrium levels of income for each respective price level. Consequently, a rightward (leftward) shift in the *IS* curve will lead to a rightward (leftward) shift in the *AD* curve. For example, an increase in government spending or domestic investment will lead to a rightward shift in the *IS* curve and hence in the *AD* curve. An increase in the tax *rate* would make the *IS* curve steeper and hence the *AD* curve steeper. Since it is changes in the nominal money supply (for given price levels) that shift the *LM* curve, an increase in the money supply shifts the *LM* curve to the right and, *ceteris paribus,* leads to higher equilibrium income and hence a rightward shift in the *AD* curve. Contractionary monetary policy would, on the other hand, lead to a leftward shift in the *AD* curve. Finally, any change in the transactions

FIGURE 2   **Aggregate Production and the Demand for Labor**

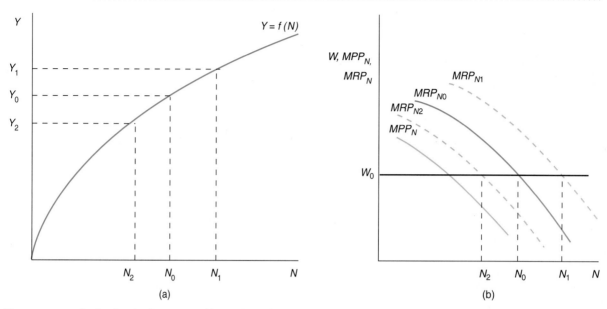

The aggregate production function is represented in panel (a). Given the level of technology and a fixed amount of other inputs, aggregate output is determined by the level of employment of labor, N. The decreasing slope of the production function indicates that the marginal product of each successive worker is getting smaller. The marginal physical product of labor (MPP_N) is then plotted against level of employment N in panel (b). If the MPP_N is multiplied by the price level P, the resulting marginal revenue product (MRP_N) indicates the value of using that particular unit of labor in production and is, therefore, the derived demand curve for labor. In order to maximize profits, producers should employ labor up to N_0, where the wage rate W_0 is equal to the MRP_{N0} when prices are P_0, N_1 when prices are P_1, etc. Note that an increase in the price level to P_1 (decrease to P_2) leads to a higher (lower) MRP of labor and hence to greater (less) employment and output.

demand for money or in the asset demand for money would lead to a change in slope and/or position of the *LM* curve and therefore a change in slope and/or position of the *AD* curve, the details of which are not critical for this chapter.

Aggregate Supply in the Closed Economy

Aggregate domestic supply is determined by the level of technology, the relative quantity of available resources, the level of employment of those resources, and the efficiency with which they are used. In the short run, factors such as the level of capital, natural resources, and technology are assumed to be fixed. This leaves labor as the principal variable input that firms hire in order to maximize expected profits. In this situation the representative firm will maximize profits where marginal cost equals marginal revenue. In the case of labor, this means hiring labor up to the point where the marginal factor cost (which equals the nominal wage rate with competitive labor markets) is equal (with competitive product markets) to the marginal product of labor times the price of the output (marginal revenue product). The nominal value of the additional worker is thus determined by the productivity of labor and the price level.

The relationship between labor and output can be represented by an **aggregate production function** such as that in panel (a) of Figure 2. Real output is shown to vary positively with labor employed, given the level of technology and the fixed availability of other inputs such as level of capital stock. The shape of the curve indicates that the marginal productivity of labor declines with additional employment of the labor input, since each successive unit of labor contributes less to output than the unit preceding it. The slope of the production function is the marginal physical productivity of labor (MPP_N), which is

FIGURE 3   **The Aggregate Supply Curve with a Fixed Wage**

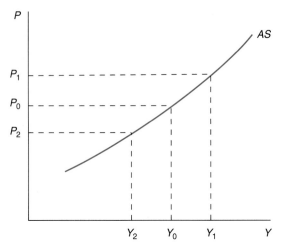

In panel (b) of Figure 2, higher price levels lead to increased demand for labor as producers hire labor so as to maximize profits for a given wage rate W_0. Higher levels of employment, such as N_1, lead to a higher level of output Y_1 [in Figure 2(a)]. If we now plot the level of prices against the resulting level of income at the level of employment that maximizes profits (e.g., Y_1, P_1; Y_0, P_0), an upward-sloping aggregate supply curve results.

plotted in panel (b). The decreasing productivity of labor causes the MPP_N schedule to have a downward slope. Multiplying MPP_N by different levels of prices produces different marginal revenue product curves of labor (MRP_{N0}, MRP_{N1}, MRP_{N2}). Inasmuch as these MRP_N curves show the value of labor to producers at different levels of employment and prices, they can each be viewed as an **aggregate demand curve for labor.**

Given a particular wage rate, one can immediately see the level of employment that will lead to a maximization of profits, *ceteris paribus*. For example, if the wage rate is W_0 and the price level is P_0, the desired level of employment is N_0. It is also apparent that if the price level changes, the MRP_N curve will change. An increase in prices will cause the MRP_N to shift to the right, and a decrease in prices will cause it to shift to the left. Thus for a fixed wage rate, W_0, an increase in the price level leads to a rightward shift in the MRP_N curve and hence to a higher level of employment and output. A reduction in the price level leads to a leftward shift in the MRP_N curve and to a reduction in the optimal level of employment and output. If we now plot these combinations of different price levels and equilibrium output at the wage W_0, we obtain the upward-sloping **short-run aggregate supply curve** (see Figure 3). It needs to be noted in passing that the marginal revenue product can also be altered by changes in the factors normally held constant, for example, changes in technology, changes in the level of capital stock, or changes in managerial efficiency. These changes are commonly viewed as long-run changes, as opposed to the short-run change brought about by the change in price level.

The aggregate supply curve in Figure 3 was derived assuming that firms could hire all the labor they wished, up to full employment, at the fixed wage W_0. However, microeconomic theory and practical experience indicate that while that assumption may hold in labor surplus economies, in industrialized economies with relatively high levels of employment, an increase in the quantity of labor supplied can be obtained in the short run only by increasing the wage rate. This line of thinking sees the labor supply curve as an upward-sloping curve, and not as a horizontal line as at W_0 in Figure 2(b). Its slope and

FIGURE 4   **Variable Wages and the Aggregate Supply Curve**

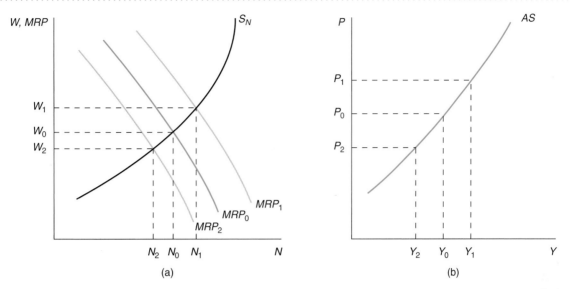

In panel (a), the labor market is characterized by a more typical upward-sloping supply curve of labor, instead of the infinitely elastic supply curve used in Figure 2(b). As a result, the increases in the MRP_N brought about by the increases in the price level lead to smaller increases in output compared to the previous case. Hence, the aggregate supply curve presented in panel (b) above will be steeper than the AS curve in Figure 3. The greater the wage increase required to increase the quantity supplied of labor, the steeper the AS curve.

position are influenced by such factors as the value of leisure, institutional factors, the characteristics of the labor force, and expectations regarding prices.

Labor market equilibrium with an upward-sloping aggregate supply curve of labor is shown in Figure 4(a), with an initial equilibrium at W_0 and N_0. If we again increase the price level, output increases, but not as greatly as it did when the labor supply curve was horizontal. Thus, we again get an upward-sloping aggregate supply curve of output [panel (b)], but it is now steeper than it was with the horizontal labor supply curve. In general, the greater the increase in wages necessary to attract the additional labor, the steeper the **short-run aggregate supply curve of labor** in Figure 4(a) will be.

It is generally accepted in the macroeconomics and labor economics literature that the quantity of labor supplied depends ultimately on the real wage received, and not on the money wage. Since the aggregate supply curve of labor is drawn under a given level of price expectations, changes in the price level that affect price expectations will cause the labor supply curve to shift—once workers *realize* that prices have changed. The realization that prices are higher than expected will lead labor to demand a higher nominal wage so that the same amount of labor is being provided at the same *real* wage. In other words, nominal wage increases eventually offset the increase in prices as workers adjust their wages to the new level of expected prices.

The worker adjustment to higher prices is shown in Figure 5. An increase in price leads to a new MRP'_N and a higher level of employment and income. However, once workers realize that prices are higher than expected, they increase their wage demands, shifting the short-run supply curve of labor to the left (S'_N) until it intersects MRP'_N at the original equilibrium level of employment. Thus, if labor is given sufficient time to respond, an increase in the price level simply leads to an offsetting increase in nominal wages and no real effect on employment and output. The longer labor takes to adjust its wage demands (the stickier wage movements are), the greater the short-run effect of price changes on output and employment. However, if wage demands change as quickly as

FIGURE 5   **Labor Market Adjustment to Higher Prices**

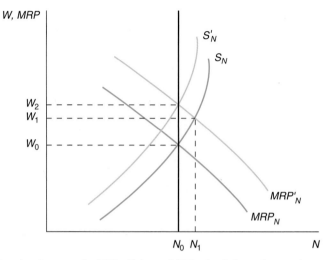

An initial increase in prices increases the *MRP* of labor to MRP'_N, stimulating a short-run increase in employment (from N_0 to N_1), income, and wages (from W_0 to W_1). However, since the labor supply is determined by the real wage and not the money wage, once workers realize that prices have risen, they alter their wage demands (shift the labor supply curve vertically upwards) until they again are offering the same amount of labor at the same real wage as previously, that is, N_0 at W_2 given the new price level. After sufficient time has passed for labor to adjust to the new price level, the labor market is again in equilibrium at the initial level of employment N_0.

prices (which takes place under the rational expectations assumption, where price changes are fully anticipated), then a price increase produces no change in real output or employment. The employment of labor is constant, and the aggregate supply curve is vertical both in the short run and in the long run at the initial equilibrium level— sometimes referred to as the **natural level of employment** (that is, the level of employment at which the actual price level equals the expected price level by workers). Note that the natural level of employment need not correspond with some society-defined level of full employment (for example, 95 percent employment or 5 percent unemployment). The equilibrium level of income associated with the natural level of employment is designated the **natural level of income.** (See Case Study 1 for estimates of recent natural and actual employment and income in the United States.)

There is considerable debate among macroeconomic theorists about whether wages are in fact sticky and about the length of the possible adjustment lag in the labor markets. Keynesians postulate a longer adjustment period due to various rigidities and market imperfections than do the Monetarists, and therefore a greater role for discretionary policy. The New Classical writers, a school of writers that emerged in the 1970s, generally adopt a rational expectations assumption, which leads to nominal wages rising as fast as prices. In this framework, workers immediately perceive the impact on real wages of any event that was anticipated and immediately act to maintain the same real wage. Consequently, a vertical short run–long run aggregate supply curve results. Hence, while most concur that the **long-run aggregate supply curve** of output is vertical at the natural level of income, there is a difference of opinion about the existence of a nonvertical short-run aggregate supply curve and the extent to which there is a short-run response of output to prices. Finally, increases in the natural level of employment and output are stimulated by changes in technology, increased quantities of capital, more efficient management, and growth in the supply and quality of the labor force.

✼ CASE STUDY 1   U.S. ACTUAL AND NATURAL INCOME, EMPLOYMENT,
                     AND UNEMPLOYMENT

Table 1 contains 1965–1996 figures for U.S. actual real GDP and employment, estimates of the natural levels of GDP and employment, and the actual and natural unemployment rates. The actual levels of income and employment tended to be above the natural levels in the late 1960s and in the early 1970s. However, the actual levels tended to be below the natural levels from the mid-1970s until the late 1980s and then rose above the natural levels in 1988–1990 and very recently.

TABLE 1   **Actual and Natural Income, Employment, and Unemployment in the United States, 1965–1996**

Year	Actual Real GDP*	Natural Real GDP*	Actual Employment[†]	Natural Employment[†]	Unemployment Rates	
					Actual	Natural
1965	2,874.8	2,788.7	71,088	70,286	4.5%	5.6%
1966	3,060.2	2,906.7	72,895	71,527	3.8	5.6
1967	3,140.2	3,013.2	74,372	73,016	3.8	5.6
1968	3,288.6	3,141.4	75,920	74,328	3.6	5.6
1969	3,388.0	3,266.9	77,902	76,213	3.5	5.6
1970	3,388.2	3,384.8	78,678	78,136	4.9	5.6
1971	3,500.1	3,515.5	79,367	79,488	5.9	5.8
1972	3,690.3	3,645.8	82,153	81,986	5.6	5.8
1973	3,902.3	3,789.0	85,064	84,242	4.9	5.8
1974	3,888.2	3,925.0	86,794	86,524	5.6	5.9
1975	3,865.1	4,050.9	85,846	88,149	8.5	6.0
1976	4,081.1	4,196.5	88,752	90,485	7.7	5.9
1977	4,279.3	4,334.8	92,017	93,068	7.1	6.0
1978	4,493.7	4,471.1	96,048	96,218	6.1	5.9
1979	4,624.0	4,618.4	98,824	98,769	5.8	5.9
1980	4,611.9	4,742.7	99,303	100,631	7.1	5.9
1981	4,724.9	4,883.1	100,397	102,150	7.6	6.0
1982	4,623.6	4,994.9	99,526	103,592	9.7	6.0
1983	4,810.0	5,115.6	100,834	104,857	9.6	6.0
1984	5,138.2	5,263.3	105,005	106,731	7.5	6.0
1985	5,329.5	5,412.3	107,150	108,533	7.2	6.0
1986	5,489.9	5,540.8	109,597	110,764	7.0	6.0
1987	5,648.4	5,655.9	112,440	112,673	6.2	6.0
1988	5,862.9	5,766.4	114,968	114,369	5.5	6.0
1989	6,060.4	5,932.5	117,342	116,437	5.3	6.0
1990	6,138.7	6,057.9	118,793	118,290	5.6	6.0
1991	6,079.0	6,185.1	117,718	118,765	6.8	6.0
1992	6,244.4	6,315.0	118,492	120,419	7.5	6.0
1993	6,386.4	6,481.9	120,259	122,094	6.9	5.5
1994	6,608.7	6,618.2	123,060	123,848	6.1	5.5
1995	6,742.9	6,756.9	124,900	125,027	5.6	5.5
1996	6,907.2	6,898.8	126,708	126,576	5.4	5.5

*Billions of 1992 chained dollars.
[†]Thousands of persons.

Sources and notes: Robert J. Gordon, *Macroeconomics,* 6th ed. (New York: HarperCollins, 1993), pp. A2, A3 (for natural real GDP and natural unemployment rates, 1965–1991); *Economic Report of the President,* February 1997 (Washington, DC: U.S. Government Printing Office, 1997), p. 338; U.S. Department of Commerce, *Survey of Current Business,* April 1997, p. D-34. Gordon's natural unemployment rate of 6 percent was assumed for 1992. This was arbitrarily reduced to 5.5 percent for 1993–1996 because lower unemployment rates were not accompanied by greater inflation during those years. Gordon's natural real GDP figures (in 1987 dollars) were converted to 1992 chained dollars, and his assumed growth rate of 2.1 percent in natural real GDP for the 1990s was applied for 1992–1996. However, the resulting natural real GDP figures for 1993–1996 were then adjusted upward utilizing the average product of labor in order to make them consistent with the assumed lower natural unemployment rate in those years.   ✼

FIGURE 6   **Equilibrium in the Closed Economy**

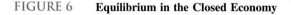

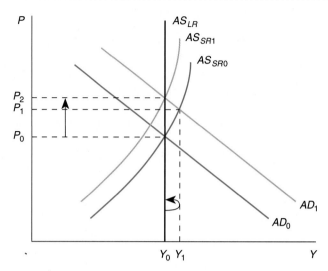

The initial equilibrium occurs at the point where AD_0, AS_{LR}, and AS_{SR0} intersect at Y_0, P_0. Expansionary forces in the economy shift the AD curve rightward to AD_1, increasing prices to P_1 and income to Y_1 (assuming that wage increases lag behind price increases). When workers realize that the price level has risen, altering their price expectations, wages begin to rise as the short-run aggregate supply curve shifts up. This will continue until the actual price level again equals the expected price level, which now occurs at P_2, Y_0 (the intersection between AS_{LR}, AS_{SR1}, and AD_1). The only way to increase income in the long run is to shift AS_{LR} to the right through accumulation of capital, changes in technology, and so on.

Equilibrium in the Closed Economy

Given the aggregate demand and the short-run and long-run aggregate supply curves, we can now examine equilibrium in the closed economy. **Aggregate supply-aggregate demand equilibrium** occurs where all three curves (AS_{LR}, AS_{SR0}, AD_0) intersect, for example, P_0 and Y_0 in Figure 6. Suppose that from this position there is an increase in aggregate demand due to an increase in government spending or an increase in the money supply. This will cause the aggregate demand curve to shift to the right. As this takes place, there will be an increase in the level of prices and a short-run increase in income as the economy moves to the new short-run equilibrium P_1, Y_1. This, of course, assumes that labor does not demand an instant adjustment in the nominal wage. Once labor alters its expectation about the level of prices, wages begin to rise as the short-run supply curve shifts vertically upward. This will continue until the new aggregate demand curve (AD_1), the long-run supply curve (AS_{LR}), and the new short-run supply curve (AS_{SR1}) again all intersect at a common point (P_2, Y_0). At that price level, actual prices are equal to the expected prices on which the short-run supply curve is based. Although this new aggregate supply–aggregate demand equilibrium will be at the same natural level of output Y_0 (and employment), the increase in demand will have generated a higher level of prices P_2 and will have had only a temporary effect on aggregate output. The adjustment of output from Y_0 to Y_1 and back to Y_0 is indicated by an arrow in Figure 6. The only way that a permanent change in the natural rate of output and employment can occur is if there is a change in basic underlying variables such as technology or the level of capital stock. For expansionary economic policy to have any permanent effect on income and output rather than only to increase prices, it must change one or more of these underlying variables.

1. Why does an increase in the price level lead to a lower equilibrium income in the *IS-LM* framework? What determines the slope of the resulting aggregate demand curve?
2. Why does an increase in the price level lead to both an increase in the demand for labor and a decrease (vertically upward shift) in the supply curve of labor? Do these shifts take place simultaneously?
3. What is meant by the natural level of income and employment?

AGGREGATE DEMAND AND SUPPLY IN THE OPEN ECONOMY

Opening the economy clearly affects the aggregate demand curve. Although there are possible long-run supply effects through international investment flows, technological innovations, and improved management techniques, from a policy standpoint the opening of the economy has considerably greater implications for short-term and medium-term aggregate demand. Consequently, we will focus on the nature of aggregate demand in the open economy under fixed and flexible exchange rates.[1] In this exercise, it will be assumed that capital is relatively mobile internationally (but not perfectly mobile) for the country in question; that is, the *BP* curve is upward sloping and flatter than the *LM* curve.

Aggregate Demand in the Open Economy under Fixed Rates

When the economy is opened, the discussion of aggregate demand must consider not only domestic equilibrium in the goods market (the *IS* curve) and the money market (the *LM* curve) but also equilibrium in the foreign sector (the *BP* curve). Such an initial equilibrium (i_0, Y_0) is shown in Figure 7(a). In order to obtain the domestic aggregate demand curve under fixed exchange rates [panel (b)], we increase prices. The increase in domestic prices reduces the real money supply and causes the *LM* curve to shift to the left. In addition, however, the increase in the domestic price level alters relative prices with trading partners since exports become more expensive and imports become relatively cheaper. The increase in the domestic price level thus leads to an expansion of imports and a contraction of exports. The change in relative prices causes the *BP* curve to shift to the left, since it now will take a higher level of the interest rate to generate the needed net short-term capital inflow to offset the deteriorating trade balance. The deterioration in the trade balance—that is, the expansion of imports and the contraction of exports—will also cause the *IS* curve to shift to the left. In sum, increasing the level of prices causes the *LM* curve to shift left (LM_{p1}), the *BP* curve to shift left (BP_{p1}), and the *IS* curve to shift left (IS_{p1}). Price increases thus lead not only to a decrease in the real money supply but also to changes in relative prices and hence in the demand for real domestic output.

With all three markets adjusting to the change in the level of prices, what will guarantee that a new equilibrium will result? How can one be certain that the three curves will again intersect at a common point? The change in relative prices will lead to new *IS* and *BP* curves, consistent with the new price level. If the intersection between the IS_{p1} and the LM_{p1} is not on the BP_{p1} curve, then there will be disequilibrium in the balance of payments (official reserve transactions balance). If they intersect above the BP_{p1} curve, then a balance-of-payments surplus will result. Under fixed rates, a surplus will lead to an

---

[1]When a country imports intermediate inputs, the aggregate supply curve in the open economy also depends on the exchange rate. A depreciation of the home currency would shift aggregate supply curves leftward due to the higher domestic prices of imported intermediate inputs, and an appreciation would shift them to the right for the opposite reason.

FIGURE 7   **Aggregate Demand in the Open Economy under Fixed Rates**

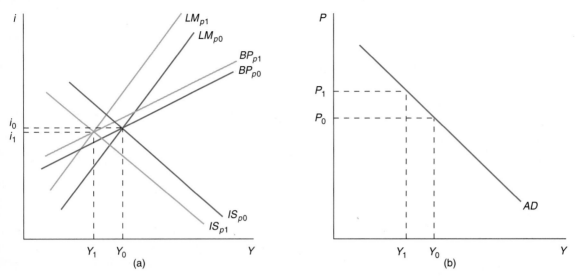

With the initial price level P_0, equilibrium occurs at i_0 and Y_0. An increase in the price level to P_1 causes (1) the *LM* curve to shift to LM_{p1} due to the decline in the real money supply; (2) the *BP* curve to shift up to BP_{p1}, as foreign goods become relatively cheaper and domestic exports become relatively more costly; and (3) the *IS* curve to shift left to IS_{p1}, as the current account deteriorates. The new equilibrium will occur at the intersection of IS_{p1}, LM_{p1}, and BP_{p1} at Y_1 and i_1. Should the intersection of IS_{p1} and LM_{p1} initially be above or below BP_{p1}, the balance of payments will not be in balance and pressure on the exchange rate occurs. As the central bank acts to maintain the exchange rate, the domestic money supply changes, shifting the *LM* curve into equilibrium at i_1 and Y_1. When the two price levels P_0 and P_1 are plotted against the two equilibrium levels of income Y_0 and Y_1 in panel (b), a downward-sloping aggregate demand curve *AD* results.

expansion in the money supply (assuming no sterilization) as the central bank purchases foreign exchange with domestic currency to maintain the pegged exchange rate. Consequently, the *LM* curve will shift right until there is no longer a surplus in the balance of payments and the economy is once again in equilibrium. Similarly, should IS_{p1} and LM_{p1} intersect at a point below the BP_{p1} curve, a balance-of-payments deficit will occur. As the central bank seeks to maintain the pegged value of the currency by selling foreign exchange for domestic currency, the money supply declines (with no sterilization), shifting the *LM* curve even further to the left. This continues until IS_{p1}, LM_{p1}, and BP_{p1} intersect at a common point. Thus, the nature of the adjustment in the open economy under fixed rates to price changes depends heavily on the degree to which price changes affect the demand for domestic goods and the balance of payments. Central bank intervention to maintain the value of the currency will automatically cause the *LM* curve to move to the new equilibrium point, which of course must lie on BP_{p1}.

Aggregate Demand in the Open Economy under Flexible Rates

The aggregate demand curve in the open economy under a flexible-rate system is obtained in the same manner. Increases in the domestic price level lead to leftward shifts in the *LM*, *IS,* and *BP* curves, just as in the case of fixed exchange rates.[2] The principal

. . . .

[2]The determination of the precise impact of price-level changes on the *LM* curve is considerably more complicated with flexible rates than with fixed rates. The reason is that, as the exchange rate changes, this will alter the domestic prices of imported goods, and these prices are part of the domestic price level. Thus changes in the exchange rate itself can affect the position of the *LM* curve. However, this factor does not alter the normal direction of shift of *LM* in response to price-level changes.

FIGURE 8   **Aggregate Demand in the Open Economy under Flexible Rates**

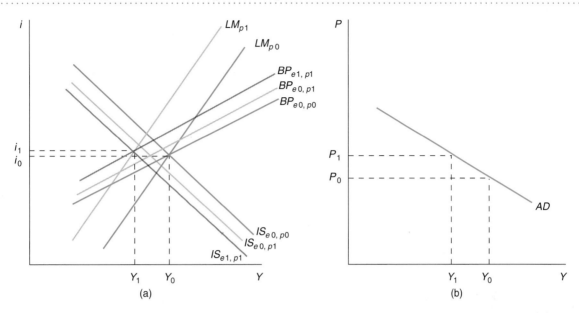

(a)

(b)

Starting from equilibrium at Y_0 and i_0 in panel (a), an increase in the price level from P_0 to P_1 reduces the real money supply, shifting the LM curve to LM_{p1}. It also raises the relative price of domestic products, leading to an upward shift in the $BP_{e0,p0}$ curve to $BP_{e0,p1}$ and a leftward shift in the $IS_{e0,p0}$ curve to $IS_{e0,p1}$ as the current account deteriorates. Should the new IS and LM curves not intersect on $BP_{e0,p1}$, there will be either an incipient surplus or an incipient deficit and the exchange rate will adjust (causing the IS and the BP curves to further adjust) until the system is in equilibrium at Y_1 and i_1 (in the above case of $IS_{e1,p1}$, LM_{p1}, and $BP_{e1,p1}$). When the old and the new levels of equilibrium income corresponding to the two price levels are plotted [panel (b)] against the two price levels, the downward-sloping aggregate demand curve AD is obtained.

difference between fixed and flexible rates lies in the adjustment process once the change in domestic prices has impacted upon the three markets. If the leftward shifts in the three curves do not initially produce a new equilibrium—that is, the intersection of IS_{p1} and LM_{p1} is not on the BP_{p1} curve—the balance of payments will not be in equilibrium. If this occurs, there will either be an incipient surplus (if the new IS-LM equilibrium is above the new BP curve) or an incipient deficit (if the IS-LM equilibrium is below the new BP curve). In the case of an incipient surplus, the exchange rate will appreciate, shifting both the BP curve and the IS curve even further left. This adjustment will continue until simultaneous equilibrium is once again attained in all three markets. This adjustment process and the resulting new equilibrium are shown in Figure 8(a). Note that under flexible rates, any needed adjustment to the LM shift takes place in the foreign sector and the goods markets. If the price increase had produced an incipient deficit instead, then the currency would have depreciated, leading to rightward shifts in the IS and BP curves until equilibrium is once again attained.

Regardless of the adjustment process, an increase in prices leads to a decline in equilibrium income, producing the normal downward-sloping aggregate demand curve [panel (b) of Figure 8]. Because of the nature of the further BP shift and its repercussions on IS after the initial shifts in these curves under flexible exchange rates (in contrast to the LM shifts under fixed rates), the aggregate demand curve in the open economy under flexible exchange rates might well have a different degree of negative slope than under a fixed-rate system.

THE NATURE OF ECONOMIC ADJUSTMENT AND MACROECONOMIC POLICY IN THE OPEN-ECONOMY AGGREGATE SUPPLY AND DEMAND FRAMEWORK

The Effect of Exogenous Shocks on the Aggregate Demand Curve under Fixed and Flexible Rates

In the open economy, any factor that affects the *IS* curve, the *LM* curve, or the *BP* curve can potentially influence the aggregate demand curve. The way it influences the *AD* curve depends, however, on whether there are fixed or flexible rates. For example, an increase in the foreign price level will stimulate domestic exports and reduce domestic imports. This has the effect of stimulating income as the *BP* curve and the *IS* curve both shift to the right due to the improvement in the current account. Under a fixed-rate system, this would produce a balance-of-payments surplus, which will lead to an expansion of the money supply and a further expansion in the economy. The end result, then, would be a rightward shift of the *AD* curve. Under flexible rates, however, the incipient surplus that accompanies the improvement in relative prices will lead to an appreciation of the home currency. Since the adjustment is taking place in the foreign sector, the change in the exchange rate neutralizes the initial increase in foreign prices. As the appreciation takes place, the *BP* and *IS* curves shift back to the initial equilibrium. There is thus no lasting effect of the initial change in relative prices under a flexible-rate system and no permanent change in the *AD* curve. One can generalize from this example and see that any shock originating in the foreign trade sector or current account will have an impact on the *AD* curve under fixed rates but not under completely flexible rates.

A shock originating in the foreign financial sector or capital account has a different effect in this model. Suppose there is an increase in the foreign interest rate. This will stimulate an outflow of short-term capital from the home country, producing either a deficit under fixed rates or an incipient deficit under flexible rates. In the fixed-rate case, the financial shock will cause the *BP* curve to shift to the left and the *LM* curve to shift to the left as the central bank responds to the new deficit pressure. Hence the *AD* curve will shift to the left. In the case of flexible rates, the shift in the *BP* curve will produce an incipient deficit, which will cause the home currency to depreciate. As the depreciation takes place, it will stimulate exports and reduce imports, leading to a rightward shift in both the *IS* function and the *BP* curve along the fixed *LM* curve. As a result, the *AD* curve will shift to the right. The *AD* curve shifts under either system, but in opposite directions due to the different nature of the adjustment in each case. Of course, remembering portfolio balance considerations, the increase in the foreign interest rate would also reduce the domestic demand for money, causing the *LM* curve to shift to the right. This would lead to an even greater rightward shift of the *AD* curve under flexible rates and an even greater leftward shift of the AD curve under fixed rates (as the BOP deficit to be adjusted to would be even greater).

Consider now the impact of domestic shocks originating in the real sector. A change in a variable that affects the real sector and the current account will cause a change in aggregate demand under fixed rates but will have little effect under flexible rates. For example, suppose that there is a shift in tastes and preferences away from foreign automobiles toward domestically produced automobiles. This change in the "state of nature" would cause the *IS* curve to shift out (due to the decline in autonomous imports) and cause the *BP* curve to shift to the right as well. Under fixed rates, this will create a surplus in the balance of payments, leading to an expansion in the money supply and a rightward shift in the *LM* curve. This adjustment will take place until all three sectors are again in equilibrium at a higher level of income, and will result in a rightward shift in the *AD* curve. Under flexible rates, however, the incipient surplus resulting from the change in tastes and preferences will lead to appreciation of the home currency. As the currency appreciates, the *BP* curve and the *IS* curve will both shift back to the left as the appreciation of the currency adjusts for the change in tastes and preferences. Consequently, there will be less overall change in aggregate demand once the expenditure-switching adjustment has taken place under flexible rates relative to fixed rates.

Changes in a domestic financial variable also generate different effects under the two systems. Suppose there is an exogenous shift of preferences in desired portfolio composition by domestic citizens toward domestic short-term investments and away from foreign short-term investments. The immediate effect of this change will be a rightward shift in the *BP* curve, due to the reduced outflow of short-term capital, creating a surplus in the balance of payments under fixed rates and an incipient surplus under flexible rates. This will prove to be expansionary under fixed rates, since the *LM* curve shifts out as the central bank responds to the surplus in the balance of payments. Under flexible rates, however, an appreciation of the currency results, leading to a worsening of the current account and a leftward shift in the *IS* curve and the new *BP* curve. The end result is a fall in income and hence in aggregate demand.

The Effect of Monetary and Fiscal Policy on the Aggregate Demand Curve under Fixed and Flexible Rates

As we learned in the preceding chapters, monetary policy and fiscal policy have different effects under the two different exchange rate regimes. Turning first to the case of fixed exchange rates, it was observed that monetary policy is ineffective for influencing income in a fixed exchange rate system under the various mobility assumptions. On the other hand, fiscal policy was found to be effective in all cases except when capital was perfectly immobile internationally. If we continue to restrict our analysis to the case of relatively mobile capital *(BP* curve flatter than *LM* curve) for ease of discussion, we can generalize and say that expansionary fiscal policy will shift the *AD* curve to the right and contractionary fiscal policy will shift it to the left. In contrast, altering the money supply will have no effect on the *AD* curve in a fixed-rate system unless the central bank continually sterilizes the balance-of-payments impact upon the money supply (that is, replaces the change in foreign exchange reserves by open market purchases or sales of domestic bonds).

Under a flexible-rate system, monetary policy was always shown to be effective regardless of the mobility assumption. The greater the mobility of capital, the more effective is discretionary monetary policy in influencing income. Fiscal policy, however, was less effective under flexible rates than under fixed rates when the *BP* curve was flatter than the *LM* curve, and more effective when the *BP* curve was steeper than the *LM* curve. The more mobile capital is, the less effective fiscal policy is, as short-term capital flows offset much of the effect of the discretionary policy. In the extreme case, when capital is perfectly mobile, fiscal policy is totally ineffective. Consequently, fiscal policy will have a weak effect on the *AD* curve under the relatively mobile capital assumption we have adopted for this discussion. Thus, fiscal policy under flexible rates will generally be relatively ineffective in shifting the *AD* curve compared to fixed rates, whereas expansionary (contractionary) monetary policy will shift the *AD* curve to the right (left) under a system of flexible exchange rates and monetary policy has no effect on *AD* under fixed rates (without sterilization).

Summary

Before moving on to an examination of how domestic and foreign policies and other selected economic variables affect prices and output in the open economy, let us take a moment to summarize how the *AD* curve is affected by changes in variables under fixed and flexible rates. We will continue to assume that the mobility of capital is such that the *BP* curve is upward sloping and flatter than the *LM* curve. These results are summarized in Table 2. Since the effects on the *AD* curve of changes in these variables are symmetrical, the results in Table 2 have been limited to one example per type of influence. Test your understanding of the adjustment process under fixed and flexible rates by examining both positive and negative changes in an important economic variable to verify the symmetry of the *AD* adjustment.

TABLE 2   **Influences on Aggregate Demand under Fixed and Flexible Exchange Rates**

	Fixed Rates	*Flexible Rates*
Change in partner country variable that increases home country exports	Shifts *AD* right	No effect on *AD*
Change in partner country variable that alters short-term capital flows in partner country favor	Shifts *AD* left	Shifts *AD* right
Change in home country variable that reduces home country exports	Shifts *AD* left	No effect on *AD*
Change in home country variable that stimulates short-term capital inflow	Shifts *AD* right	Shifts *AD* left
Expansionary monetary policy	No impact on *AD* (without sterilization)	Shifts *AD* right
Expansionary fiscal policy	Shifts *AD* right	Little effect on *AD* (slight rightward shift)

MONETARY AND FISCAL POLICY IN THE OPEN ECONOMY WITH FLEXIBLE PRICES

Having looked at the nature of aggregate supply and aggregate demand and the factors that influence them, we are now ready to examine the impact of discretionary economic policy in the open economy when prices are not fixed. Since the short-run–long-run distinction is important with regard to supply response, we will pay close attention to the time frame under consideration when discussing the likely economic effects of a policy action.

Monetary Policy

As you are now well aware, the impact of monetary policy on the domestic economy depends on the type of exchange system under consideration. Since monetary policy has a limited effect on aggregate demand under a fixed exchange rate system, we can ignore that case. However, we found that monetary policy was an effective policy instrument under flexible rates. In that case, expansionary monetary policy had the impact of shifting the *AD* curve to the right. The economic implications of that policy are examined in Figure 9. We begin with the economy in equilibrium at Y_0 and P_0 (point *E*), the intersection of the long-run supply curve (AS_{LR}), the short-run supply curve (AS_{SR0}), and the aggregate demand curve (AD_{M0}). *Remember, at that point, actual prices equal expected prices.* The expansion of the money supply leads to a rightward shift in the *AD* curve to AD_{M1}, creating a disequilibrium condition. Assuming that there is a lag between the change in the price level and workers' demands for higher wages, the economy will respond to the increase in demand. As output increases, prices begin to increase and the economy moves to a new short-run equilibrium at *F.*

However, once labor realizes that the actual price level is higher than the expected price level and has time to respond, workers will raise their wage demands commensurate with the increase in prices so that the same amount of labor is being supplied at the same real wage. This will cause the short-run aggregate supply curve to shift left until the expected price level is again equal to the actual price level, given the new larger supply of money. This equilibrium is, of course, point *G*, where AS_{SR1}, AS_{LR}, and AD_{M1} intersect

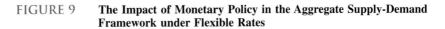

FIGURE 9   **The Impact of Monetary Policy in the Aggregate Supply-Demand Framework under Flexible Rates**

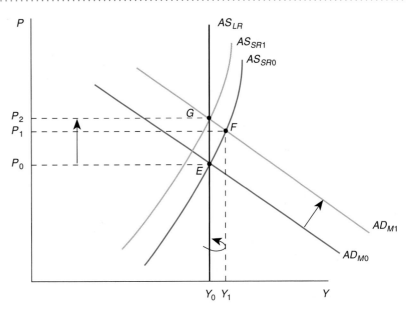

Beginning in equilibrium at point E, expanding the money supply causes the AD curve to shift right to AD_{M1}, putting upward pressure on income and prices in the short run. A new short-run equilibrium is established at F on the short-run supply curve AS_{SR0} at (Y_1, P_1). However, once workers realize that prices have risen and that their real wages have fallen, they will demand higher wages so that the same labor will be supplied at the same real wage as initially. The increase in nominal wages causes the short-run supply curve to shift upward along AD_{M1}, leading to a further increase in prices. A new equilibrium is reached at G, where AS_{LR}, AS_{SR1}, and AD_{M1} intersect. At this point, the actual price level P_2 equals the expected price level and the economy is again in equilibrium. The short-run expansionary effect on income is offset by the ultimate increase in the wage rate, leaving the economy again at Y_0 but at the higher price level P_2.

at (Y_0, P_2). After all adjustments have taken place, the economy is once again at the natural level of income Y_0 but at a higher price level P_2. Expansionary monetary policy can produce a short-run increase in income and employment, but it will last only until workers adjust their wage demands to the new higher level of prices.[3]

Given the change in the price level or rate of inflation as a result of the expansion in the money supply, what if anything can be said about the accompanying changes in the other key monetary variables, specifically the nominal rate of interest and the exchange rate? If one adopts the monetary approach perspective developed in the chapter "The Monetary and Portfolio Balance Approaches to External Balance," several clear conclusions can be reached. Following the relative purchasing power parity view, in the long run the exchange rate will rise (the home currency will depreciate) proportionally with the rise in the price level in the home country relative to that in the trading partner.

In addition, it is generally agreed that the real rate of interest is what concerns investors (i.e., the rate at which purchasing power is increased over the investment period

---

[3]Another factor involved is that, to the extent that there are intermediate goods imports, the depreciation of the home currency from the expansionary monetary policy will raise the costs of production of domestic firms. This also will shift the short-run aggregate supply curve (as well as the long-run aggregate supply curve) to the left. We generally ignore this repercussion but refer to it in occasional cases later in this chapter.

because of the sacrifice of current consumption). From this perspective, the nominal interest rate (what we have been calling the "interest rate" under the earlier fixed-price assumption) consists of two components: the real interest rate or rate of time preference, and a payment for expected inflation. Therefore, $i = i_r + E(\dot{p})$, [or $i_r = i - E(\dot{p})$], where i is the nominal rate of interest, i_r is the real interest rate, and $E(\dot{p})$ is the expected inflation rate. If real rates of interest are equalized (or differ by a more or less constant amount due to imperfect capital mobility) between any two countries through interest arbitrage, it follows that any difference in the nominal rates of interest must be attributable to differences in the expected inflation rate in the two countries.[4] This general relationship between relative nominal interest rates and relative inflation rates is referred to as the **Fisher effect** (after the early-twentieth-century American economist Irving Fisher). Therefore, an increase in the domestic inflation rate (with the expectation that it would continue), *ceteris paribus,* should lead to a comparable relative increase in the domestic nominal interest rate. For example, if the U.S. rate of inflation were to rise from 4 to 6 percent and the U.K. inflation rate and rate of interest remain constant, nominal interest rates in the United States should rise by 2 percentage points. Finally, since the change in relative prices is driving both a change in the nominal exchange rate and a change in the nominal interest rate, the **international Fisher effect** argues that the percentage change in the relative nominal interest rates between two countries should equal the expected percentage change in the exchange rate. This is, of course, another way of stating the uncovered interest parity condition discussed in previous chapters.[5] Basically, this can be thought of as extending the application of the law of one price to the financial markets (investors are receiving the same expected real rate of return in both countries when those rates are expressed in a single currency). In sum, after the long-run adjustments to the increased domestic money supply have been completed, there will be, in the domestic country, no change in income, an increase in the price level, an increase in the nominal interest rate, and an increase in the exchange rate (depreciation of the home currency).

Next, however, suppose that we begin with the economy in disequilibrium at a level of income Y_0 that is less than the natural level of income, Y_N (that is, point H in Figure 10). Is there perhaps a stronger rationale for using expansionary monetary policy in this instance? Expanding the money supply will cause the AD curve to shift up to a new long-run equilibrium, at P_1 and Y_N (point K). Domestic income will have increased, but again at the expense of an increase in the price level. On the other hand, since P_1 is consistent with the expected level of prices on AS_{SR0}, there will be no pressure on the part of labor to increase wages (and hence prices) further.

Suppose instead that there had been no policy reaction to the recession reflected by Y_0 and P_0. If wages and prices are flexible downward, once it is recognized that the actual level of prices, P_0, is less than the expected level of prices, P_1, the recession and unemployment should produce a fall in expected prices and consequently in the nominal wage rate. As expected prices decline, the short-run aggregate supply curve begins to shift downward to AS_{SR1} from AS_{SR0}. As actual prices begin to fall, movement occurs along

----

[4]In a U.S.-U.K. example, $i_{US} - i_{UK} = E(\dot{p})_{US} - E(\dot{p})_{UK}$, where i refers to the nominal interest rate and $E(\dot{p})$ to the expected inflation rate in each country as indicated by the subscript.

[5]Recall that the uncovered interest parity condition was, in an example case of the United States and the United Kingdom,

$$i_{US} = i_{UK} + xa \qquad \text{or} \qquad i_{US} - i_{UK} = xa$$

where xa was the expected rate of appreciation of the pound against the dollar, ignoring any risk premium. The term xa in turn is equal to $[E(e) - e]/e$, where $E(e)$ is the expected future exchange rate and e is the current spot rate (both in \$/£).

FIGURE 10   **The Role of Expansionary Monetary Policy When the Open Economy Is in Recession**

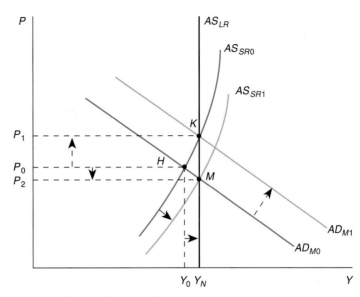

With the economy in equilibrium below Y_N at H, expanding the money supply causes the aggregate demand curve to shift right to AD_{M1}, and it then intersects AS_{LR} and AS_{SR0} at K. At that point, expected prices equal actual prices and aggregate demand equals both long- and short-run aggregate supply, so there will be no further adjustment. The economy is now at the natural level of income, but at a higher price level, P_1. If policymakers do nothing at H, and wages and prices are flexible downward, labor will eventually realize that the actual level of prices, P_0, is less than the expected level, P_1, and the wage rate will fall to increase the level of employment. This will cause the short-run aggregate supply curve to begin to drift down (along with prices) until long-run and short-run aggregate supply and aggregate demand are in equilibrium at M and the actual level of prices equals the expected level of prices, P_2.

AD_{M0}, exports increase, and imports decrease. These adjustments continue until the economy is once again in equilibrium at Y_N, but now at price level P_2 (point M).

In the situation where Y_0 is less than Y_N, there are thus two adjustment processes leading to long-run equilibrium at Y_N. One relies on discretionary monetary policy and the other on the natural market mechanism, assuming that wages and prices are flexible in both the upward and downward direction. Critics of the policy action point to the inflationary pressures stimulated by the expanding money supply, arguing that these pressures will contribute to further expectations regarding discretionary government policy and further price increases. Economists in favor of policy argue that, in reality, wages are not very flexible in the downward direction and that market adjustments take a long time to work themselves out. Thus, in this view, while the automatic adjustment may work to some degree, the adjustment cost of the recession in terms of lost output, unemployment, and social programs is far too high to leave to uncertain market forces.

In sum, monetary policy under flexible rates can cause short-run increases in income above the natural level of income as long as wage adjustments lag behind price increases. Eventually, however, the income gains will be lost as labor adjusts its wage demands to the new, higher level of prices. The increase in output and employment is thus temporary and ultimately leads only to higher prices and wages. Monetary policy can be effective in stimulating the economy when the economy is below the natural rate of employment, but again at the expense of higher prices. However, relying on the market mechanism and not on monetary policy may entail a long adjustment period and may be ineffective if wages are rigid downward.

Currency Adjustments under Fixed Rates

Aided by Figures 9 and 10, we can also briefly discuss another policy that is in the purview of the monetary authorities. Suppose that an economy is operating under a *pegged* exchange rate but that it now undertakes an official devaluation of its currency. In the context of an *IS/LM/BP* diagram, such a policy shifts *BP* to the right and also shifts *IS* to the right through the net export stimulus. There will be a BOP surplus and expansion of the money supply as the new exchange rate is pegged. The result is a shift of *AD* to the right as in Figure 9 (but for the reason that *BP, IS,* and *LM* have all shifted to the right). There is a temporary expansion of income as in Figure 9 until workers adjust their nominal wage, but the end result is then only inflation. Even worse, however, if intermediate imports are important as in many developing countries, AS_{SR1} and AS_{LR} will shift to the left because of the devaluation, leading to what has been called **contractionary devaluation** because output has fallen. This issue has been debated for developing countries, but for those countries it is possible that point *H* in Figure 10 is a more likely starting point and AS_{SR0} also may be flatter. In that case, no contraction of output (and some expansion) and only mild inflation may follow the devaluation.

Fiscal Policy

As noted in the previous chapter, fiscal policy is relatively ineffective in increasing the level of national income under flexible rates if short-term capital is relatively mobile (*BP* curve flatter than *LM*) or perfectly mobile (horizontal *BP* curve). To the extent that there is any effect on *AD,* the price and output effects are qualitatively similar to monetary policy, except that the home currency will *appreciate* due to the relatively higher domestic interest rate.[6] If capital is relatively immobile (*BP* curve steeper than the *LM* curve) or perfectly immobile (vertical *BP* curve), the price and output effects are larger as the *AD* curve shifts to a greater extent. In these situations, the home currency depreciates. In the fixed-rate case, expansionary fiscal policy will shift *AD* to the right, just as expansionary monetary policy did under flexible rates (see Figure 11). Assuming there is a lag between price increases and wage adjustments, the economy will expand in the short run from Y_0 and P_0 (point *E*) to Y_1 and P_1 (point *F*). At that point, the actual level of prices (P_1) will be higher than the initial expected level (P_0). Once the nominal wage of labor begins adjusting to the rising price level, the short-run supply curve will shift upward. This will continue until AS_{SR1}, AS_{LR}, and AD_{G1} intersect at a common point (Y_0, P_2). Expansionary fiscal policy can thus stimulate income and employment in the short run under fixed rates, but only temporarily. Once labor adjusts its wage demands, the economy returns to the natural level of income and employment. Should this happen very quickly, fiscal policy will only generate inflation, even in the short run.

The implications of the recession situation for fiscal policy under fixed rates are analogous to those of monetary policy under flexible rates. Recall that with the economy in recession as in Figure 10, there is greater unemployment than is the case when the natural rate is attained. The movement back to the natural level of income can take place through fiscal stimulus or through reliance on the market adjustment of wages and prices. Use of the fiscal instrument will lead to an increase in the price level, whereas the market adjustment will lead to lower wages and prices. The issues that once again emerge are the degree to which prices and wages are downwardly flexible and the length of time of the market adjustment process. Keynesian theorists tend to lean toward more policy intervention, whereas the Monetarists and the New Classical theorists place primary emphasis on the market solution.

. . . .

[6]If intermediate goods imports are significant, the short-run and long-run aggregate supply curves will also shift to the right because of the appreciation.

FIGURE 11   **The Impact of Fiscal Policy in the Aggregate Demand-Supply Framework
under Fixed Exchange Rates**

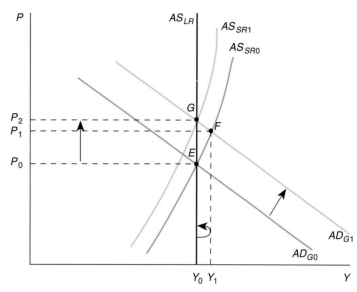

With the economy in equilibrium at Y_0 and P_0, expansionary fiscal policy shifts the aggregate demand curve
rightward from AD_{G0} to AD_{G1}. The expansion in demand causes the price level to rise to P_1 and output to
expand to Y_1, assuming that there is a lag in the wage adjustment to the increase in prices. Once workers
realize that the actual price level is now above the expected price level P_0, they demand higher wages,
shifting the short-run aggregate supply curve to the left. This will result in a decline in employment and
income that will continue until the economy is back in equilibrium, that is, where AS_{SR1}, AS_{LR}, and AD_{G1}
intersect at a common point. This occurs at P_2 and Y_0. Since supply now equals demand and actual prices P_2
equal expected prices P_2, no further adjustments will take place.

**Economic Policy
and Supply
Considerations**

The analysis up to now has focused entirely on the impact of monetary and fiscal policy
on aggregate demand. At this point, it is important to indicate that economic policy can
also have an effect on aggregate supply. If discretionary economic policy is to have any
lasting effect other than to increase prices, it must contribute to a growing production
capacity, that is, a rightward shift in the long-run aggregate supply curve. Monetary and
fiscal policies that encourage improvements in technology (either directly or indirectly
through programs such as a space program), improve the quality and mobility of the labor
force, stimulate private accumulation of capital, or provide needed social infrastructure
can have a lasting effect on income and employment. The effect of such policies is
demonstrated in Figure 12. Expansionary discretionary policy (for example, a tax cut)
again causes the AD curve to shift to the right to AD', producing some income and
employment gains in the short run along with the increase in prices. Suppose, however, it
also leads to a rightward shift in the long-run supply curve to AS'_{LR}. (This shift could
occur if the tax cut encouraged increased saving, investment, and/or work effort, as would
be stressed by supply-side economists.) After all the adjustments have taken place, the
economy now finds itself at a higher natural level of employment and income (Y_1), and
economic growth has occurred. The new price level could be higher, lower, or about the
same as the equilibrium price level prior to the policy undertaking, depending on the
relative shifts in all three curves. If tax policy stimulates a large supply response and little
AD response under flexible rates, the end result can be higher income and employment, a
lower price level, and an appreciated currency. What is critical here is that the ultimate

FIGURE 12 ·   **Economic Policy and Shifts in the Long-Run Aggregate Supply Curve**

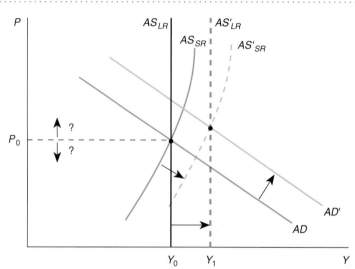

Starting with the economy in equilibrium at Y_0 and P_0, discretionary monetary and/or fiscal policy is undertaken that has an impact on domestic long-run supply conditions. The expansionary impact increases income and prices in the short run, but eventually shifts the long-run and short-run supply curves to the right. A new equilibrium will result at Y_1, where AS'_{LR}, AS'_{SR}, and AD' intersect. Because the new price level will depend on the relative movements of the curves, the exact position of the new equilibrium is uncertain.

impact on the level of income and employment depends on the degree to which there is a demand response and a long-run supply response. To be effective, government policy must be aware of the implications of its policy actions on long-run supply conditions.

This impact upon income and employment is particularly important if we recall from earlier in the chapter that some unemployment (the natural level) exists at the natural level of income Y_0. The implication of the preceding paragraph is that policy actions that shift AD to the right, as well as shift AS_{LR} to the right, are considerably more likely to result in a reduction of unemployment than are actions that affect AD only.

CONCEPT CHECK

1. Why could the AD curve in the open economy have a different degree of downward slope than the AD curve in the closed economy?
2. Under what conditions will expansionary policy increase income in the short run? In the long run?

3. What effect will an increase in exports have on the economy under flexible rates? Under fixed rates?

EXTERNAL SHOCKS AND THE OPEN ECONOMY

To conclude this chapter on the open economy with flexible prices, let us concentrate more specifically on the effects of some external shocks to the economy. Suppose that there is an increase in the world price of a critical imported intermediate input for which domestic demand is relatively inelastic. With a flexible-rate system, this causes depreciation of the home currency and an expansion of domestic aggregate demand in response to the expenditure-switching effects of the depreciation. At the same time, the higher world

FIGURE 13   **The Impact of a Price Shock of an Imported Input in the Open Economy**

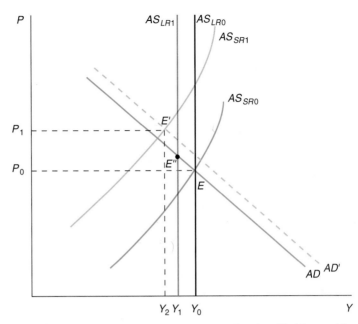

With the economy in equilibrium at E, a sudden increase in the price of a critical imported intermediate good for which demand is inelastic leads to depreciation of the currency and to a rightward shift in the aggregate demand curve to AD'. At the same time, it causes both the short-run and the long-run aggregate supply curves to shift left as production costs rise. The economy contracts to E', with a higher price level P_1 and a new short-run equilibrium income Y_2 (i.e., the economy is experiencing stagflation). Attempts on the part of labor to increase nominal wages would lead to more inflation and unemployment (not shown). Attempts to use expansionary monetary policy to increase income in this instance also would lead to further price increases (not shown). If wages were flexible downward, a fall in the nominal wage could move the economy into equilibrium at E'' and Y_1 (but not Y_0).

price of the critical intermediate good leads in Figure 13 to a leftward shift in both the short-run supply curve (from AS_{SR0} to AS_{SR1}) and the long-run supply curve (from AS_{LR0} to AS_{LR1}).

As you can see in the figure, both effects put upward pressure on the price level. If the price shock is sufficiently large, it could alter domestic supply conditions so much that the new equilibrium income is at Y_2 (that is, less than Y_1). Declining income coupled with rising inflation is often referred to as **stagflation.** The United States has, in fact, experienced two periods of stagflation in recent decades, both associated with sharp increases in petroleum prices (see Case Study 2). Attempts in the short run to ease the stagflation at point E' by expansionary monetary policy will lead to even higher prices. Attempts by labor to raise the nominal wage to offset the initial price shock would shift the short-run aggregate supply curve even further to the left, making the stagflation even worse. However, if wages were flexible downward at E', a fall in the nominal wage rate would shift the short-run aggregate supply curve to the right, increasing income and employment until it reached E'' and Y_1 (not, however, E and Y_0). Thus, external shocks that affect both supply and demand conditions create special problems for macro policy, for there may be little that can be done in the short run (absent effective and quick supply-side tax policies) to facilitate the needed structural adjustment without generating further inflation.

✦ CASE STUDY 2   INFLATION AND UNEMPLOYMENT IN THE UNITED STATES, 1970–1996

Figure 14 below indicates inflation (GDP deflator) and unemployment rates in the United States in recent decades. The two time series seem to move together rather consistently over most of the time period. However, two periods clearly stand out. During both the 1973–1975 period and the 1979–1981 period, the economy was experiencing high and increasing inflation rates and rising unemployment rates. Both of these periods followed upon the sizable increases in petroleum prices evident in Case Study 1, "Commodity Prices and U.S. Real GDP, 1973–1995," in the preceding chapter.

The increases in petroleum prices shifted the aggregate supply curves leftward, raising both the actual and natural unemployment rates as indicated in Case Study 1 in this current chapter. Note, however, that oil price increases due to the 1990 Iraqi invasion of Kuwait and the subsequent embargo on trade with Iraq were not associated with a rise in the U.S. inflation rate. Note further that in the early to mid-1980s and from 1992–1996 unemployment and inflation rates simultaneously fell. This suggests that there was important movement of the aggregate supply curves to the right in these years.

FIGURE 14   **U.S. Inflation and Unemployment Rates, 1970–1996**

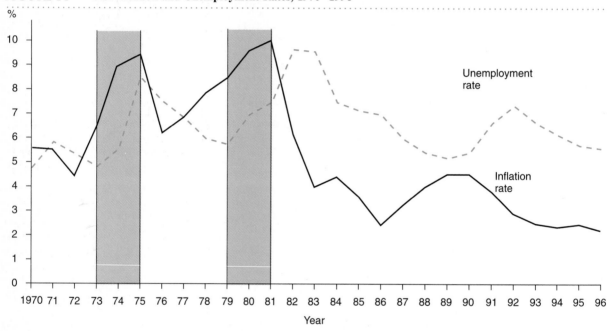

Sources: *Economic Report of the President,* February 1994 (Washington, DC: US Government Printing Office, 1994), pp. 273, 314; U.S. Department of Commerce, *Survey of Current Business,* April 1994, p. 25; *Economic Report of the President,* February 1997 (Washington, DC: U.S. Government Printing Office, 1997), pp. 306, 346.   ✦

Consider as a second external shock a foreign financial shock that triggers an inflow of short-term capital into the home country. Under flexible rates this will cause the *AD* curve to shift to the left as the home currency appreciates in value. As indicated in Figure 15, this will lead to lower income and prices in the short run as the expenditure-switching effects come into play (a movement from *E* to *E'*). In this case, expansionary monetary policy could be used to offset the initial short-term capital inflow, moving the economy back to the natural level of income and to the initial prices. This would, of course, then lead to a decline in the value of the home currency in the short run as the interest rate fell in response to the monetary action. The movement back to macro equilibrium could also take place through a downward or rightward shift in the short-run supply curve, once

FIGURE 15   **A Foreign Financial Shock and Adjustment in the Open Economy**

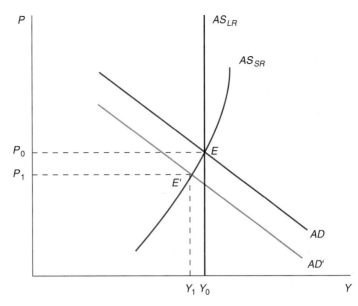

In this case, a foreign financial shock triggers an inflow of short-term capital into the home country, appreciating the currency and reducing aggregate demand to AD'. As a result, the economy will move to E', experiencing a lower level of income, employment, and prices in the short run. In this instance, expansionary monetary policy could increase aggregate demand and move the economy back to Y_0. The movement to Y_0 could also take place through a reduction in the nominal wage as labor realizes that the actual price level is below the expected price level P_0. This would cause AS_{SR} to shift to the right until equilibrium (not shown) is once again attained at Y_0.

labor adjusts its price expectations to the new, lower price level. In either case, the adjustment process is not complicated by an initial supply effect as it was in the previous example. The adjustments following this shock would also occur if the initial event were a change in expectations regarding the exchange rate such that the home currency was expected to rise in value.

As a final example (can you put up with one more example?!), let us examine the effect of an improvement in aggregate productivity, perhaps due to a change in technology. To see how productivity growth affects the open economy, consider an improvement in technology that shifts the supply curves AS_{LR0} and AS_{SR0} to the right (see Figure 16). If aggregate demand does not change from AD_{M0}, the new equilibrium level of income will lie to the left (at point E_1) of the new long-run supply curve (AS_{LR1}). For the economy to take further advantage of the new productivity gains, there must either be an increase in aggregate demand or a further downward shift in the short-run supply curve (by the labor market adjustment process). Proper growth in the money supply would lead to growth in aggregate demand that causes the economy to move to the new, higher level of income made possible by the productivity change without any major impact on prices from the original price level (point E_2).

On the other hand, the lower level of prices in place at Y_1 could eventually stimulate a fall in the expected level of prices on the part of labor, a consequent fall in wages from W_0 to W_1, and a rightward shift in the short-run supply curve. This adjustment continues to take place until the three curves intersect at the new level of income that reflects the new, higher level of technology (point E_3).

FIGURE 16   **Technological Change and Adjustment in the Open Economy**

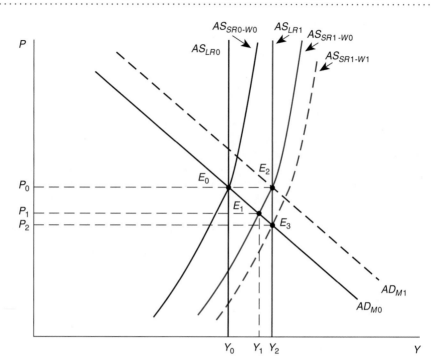

The improvement in technology shifts the aggregate supply curves to the right from AS_{LR0} to AS_{LR1}, and AS_{SR0-W0} to AS_{SR1-W0}. With no change in aggregate demand, equilibrium moves to E_1 at a higher level of income Y_1 and a lower level of prices P_1. Since $Y_1 < Y_2$, the economy is operating below the natural level of income and employment. In this instance, the economy can move to Y_2 (the natural level) through the use of expansionary monetary policy, which would shift the aggregate demand curve to the right (AD_{M1} at E_2), or wait for a fall in nominal wages, which would shift the short-run aggregate supply curve to the right until it reached Y_2 at E_3. Expansionary policy would cause the price level to drift back up from P_1, whereas the reduction in the nominal wage would lead to further deflation to P_2.

    This latter wage adjustment process relies on the assumption that prices and wages are downwardly flexible. On the other hand, the first situation of reliance on monetary policy requires that the monetary authorities correctly gauge the increase in the money supply necessary to move to the new natural level of income, and not beyond. Overestimating the growth in income capacity of course would lead to an overexpansion of the money supply and thus of aggregate demand, a response that would trigger an increase in the price level and expected prices and lead to continued inflation.

    Finally, with the productivity increase, if the price level does fall to a value such as P_2 in Figure 16, this can have an impact on the nominal interest rate and the expected exchange rate. If the lower price level reduces inflationary expectations, then the nominal interest rate in the country will fall. In addition, the international Fisher effect, in which the nominal interest rate in the home country minus the nominal rate in the foreign country equals the expected percentage depreciation of the home currency, would result in a lower expected percentage depreciation (or an expected appreciation) of the home currency.

SUMMARY

This chapter has focused on the open economy when prices are flexible. This was accomplished by deriving an aggregate demand curve for the open economy and combining it with aggregate supply curves. Both a short-run aggregate supply curve and a long-run aggregate supply curve were employed in the analysis. The aggregate demand–aggregate supply framework was then used to examine the effects of changes in policy variables and in exogenous variables. This was done for both a flexible-rate system and a fixed-rate system. The analysis demonstrated the automatic adjustment mechanism present when prices and wages are flexible. In addition, it pointed out the difference in the adjustment mechanism under fixed rates compared to that under flexible rates. Attempts to increase income and employment beyond the natural level by increasing aggregate demand ultimately lead only to increases in prices under either exchange rate regime. In the case when the economy was operating at a level below the natural level of employment, discretionary policy was seen to be effective in moving the economy back to the natural level, but only by increasing prices. Given sufficient time with actual employment below the natural level, the economy automatically would move back to the natural level through a fall in prices. The uncertainty surrounding the downward flexibility in prices and wages and the time required for such an adjustment underlie the view by many that the preferable adjustment mechanism is discretionary monetary policy under flexible-rate regimes and discretionary fiscal policy under fixed-rate regimes. The chapter concluded with a discussion of the impact of several exogenous shocks to the open economy operating under a flexible-rate system.

KEY TERMS

aggregate demand curve
aggregate demand curve for labor
aggregate production function
aggregate supply–aggregate
  demand equilibrium

contractionary devaluation
Fisher effect
international Fisher effect
long-run aggregate supply curve
natural level of employment

natural level of income
short-run aggregate supply curve
short-run aggregate supply curve
  of labor
stagflation

QUESTIONS AND PROBLEMS

1. What is meant by the natural level of income and employment? Why is the long-run aggregate supply curve vertical at the natural level?

2. What is the difference between the short-run aggregate supply curve and the long-run aggregate supply curve? Are they ever the same?

3. Is it possible that increased international economic transactions could affect the aggregate supply curves? Why or why not?

4. In the 1990s Germany attempted to control inflation through a restrictive monetary policy and high interest rates. Explain how this might have influenced income and prices in the United States.

5. Explain how appreciation of a country's currency could affect its aggregate supply curves when imported intermediate inputs are sizable.

6. If discretionary economic policy is to have more than a short-run effect on income and employment, what needs to take place?

7. If a country finds itself experiencing stagflation under a flexible-rate system, why is expansionary monetary policy unlikely to cure the problem? Why are technological improvements or general productivity improvements so critical in this situation?

8. Suppose that a home country's currency is expected to depreciate in a flexible-rate system. Trace through the impacts on home country *AD, AS,* prices, and income (output).

9. Suppose the economy is operating below its natural level of income (e.g., at point *H* in Figure 10). Would you recommend the use of expansionary policy in this instance? Why or why not?

ISSUES IN WORLD MONETARY ARRANGEMENTS

Flexible exchange rates are a means of combining interdependence among countries through trade with a maximum of internal monetary independence; they are a means of permitting each country to seek for monetary stability according to its own lights, without either imposing its mistakes on its neighbors or having their mistakes imposed on it.

Milton Friedman, 1953

Under floating exchange rates, the U.S. economy has suffered unprecedented financial instability for nearly 20 years.

Lewis E. Lehrman, 1990

In the last 30 years, the world has experienced considerable change in economic activity and in the nature of the world economy. Nations are becoming more closely linked through international trade and finance. The international monetary system has changed; a former large creditor country, the United States, has emerged as the world's largest debtor nation; and many of the developing countries find themselves with continuing development problems and relatively large amounts of foreign debt. In addition, the relatively fixed exchange rate system established at the end of World War II collapsed in the early 1970s. Since that time, individual countries and groups of countries have adopted a variety of different exchange rate arrangements, and greater variability in exchange rates has been a prominent feature of the international economy. Indeed, some observers think that the degree of exchange rate flexibility has been excessive, and they long for a more stable system of rates that might provide for greater economic stability worldwide.

This Part of the book is concerned with debates regarding the desirable nature of international monetary arrangements. The chapter "Fixed or Flexible Exchange Rates?" examines issues in the choice of floating versus fixed exchange rates, as well as exchange rate arrangements that feature compromises between completely flexible and completely fixed rates. The next chapter, "The International Monetary System: Past, Present, and Future," focuses on the current international monetary system, tracing its recent origins and evaluating its effectiveness. It also contains a discussion of possible alternatives to the current system and concludes with an examination of the developing-countries' debt problem, which has potential adverse implications for the international financial system.

Some have concluded that the foreign-exchange market is not working well. The conclusion is fed by recent developments in international financial markets, on the one hand, and by a number of academic findings on the other. . . .

. . . Having looked over the various proposals for radical reform, one is left wondering whether their drawbacks are not greater than those of the present system of (managed) floating, imperfect as it is.

Jeffrey A. Frankel, 1996

11

FIXED OR FLEXIBLE EXCHANGE RATES?

INTRODUCTION

A most prominent issue in any consideration of the effective use of economic policy in the open economy, as well as in discussions of the desirable nature of the international monetary system, is the degree of exchange rate flexibility that should be permitted. We have dealt with this issue in preceding chapters, and in the next chapter we deal with it again in the recent historical context. However, it is useful at this point to bring together a variety of relevant arguments. The first section of this chapter does so by examining the arguments for fixed or flexible rates in the context of major substantive issues. In this discussion the term *fixed exchange rates* refers to a system that permits only very small, if any, deviations from officially declared currency values. By *flexible exchange rates* we mean rates that are *completely* free to vary; that is, the foreign exchange market is cleared at all times by changes in the exchange rate and not by any buying and selling of currencies by the monetary authorities.

We then examine the controversy in the broader context of the theory of optimum currency areas. Finally, we look at cases of exchange rate flexibility located between the two extremes. The overall intent of the chapter is to acquaint you with the various economic implications of the choice regarding the exchange rate regime that a country should select. The choice is not an easy one, and "middle-ground" solutions are possible as well as the two extremes of fixed rates and completely flexible rates. It is our hope that, after you have completed the chapter, you will be better prepared to participate in and understand the debate on the exchange rate issue.

CENTRAL ISSUES IN THE FIXED–FLEXIBLE EXCHANGE RATE DEBATE

Do Fixed or Flexible Exchange Rates Provide for Greater "Discipline" on the Part of Policymakers?

A point made in favor of fixed exchange rates is that such a system provides for the "discipline" needed in economic policy to prevent continuing inflation. That is, in a fixed-rate system, there should be no tendency for greater inflation to occur in one country than in the world as a whole. Consider a country with a balance-of-payments (BOP) deficit. If the cause of the deficit is a more rapid inflation than that in trading partners, then the country's authorities will need to apply anti-inflationary policy to protect the country's international reserve position. The fixed-rate system virtually forces this type of policy action, since failure to do so will lead to an eventual elimination of the country's international reserves if the automatic adjustment mechanism takes considerable time.

What about the situation in a BOP surplus country? Given the objective of a fixed exchange rate, then forces working in the opposite direction from that for a deficit country are set into motion. Accumulation of foreign exchange reserves (which may be difficult to sterilize) will expand the money supply. This enhancement of the money supply will drive the interest rate downward, increase aggregate demand and prices, increase private purchases of goods and foreign financial assets, and thus eliminate the surplus.

Note that the result in the above discussion is a tendency for *deflation* in the deficit country and *inflation* in the surplus country. Therefore, if prices are flexible in both directions, it is likely that prices will be relatively stable in the world as a whole. In practice, the world could have some inflation if prices are less flexible downward than upward. However, the inflation will probably not be as rapid as it would be if the discipline of the fixed rates did not exist.

In addition to this emphasis on the discipline of fixed exchange rates, proponents of such a system stress that *flexible* rates could actually aggravate inflationary tendencies in a country. The point is made that, under flexible rates, inflation in a country becomes self-perpetuating; this argument is sometimes called the **vicious circle hypothesis.** Suppose that a country is undergoing rapid inflation because of an excess supply of money and excess demand in the economy. The inflation will cause the country's currency to depreciate in the exchange markets, which will add to aggregate demand in the economy and generate further inflationary pressure. In addition, the rise in prices will lead to correspondingly higher money wages, which also induces more inflation (see the preceding chapter). Thus, inflation will cause depreciation, but the depreciation itself will cause further inflation. This sequence of events continues until the monetary authorities put a stop to the monetary expansion.

Two major replies can be made to the above points. First, with respect to the vicious circle hypothesis, flexible-rate advocates think that the depreciation that was a response to the inflation and that is alleged to cause further inflation can actually be a clear signal to the authorities that monetary restraint is needed. This signal can therefore lead to the quick instigation of anti-inflationary policies. Thus, in this view, the danger of inflation is no greater under flexible than under fixed rates.

In response to the alleged "discipline" provided by the fixed-rate system, it can be questioned whether such discipline is necessarily always desirable. Countries also have other domestic goals besides maintenance of the fixed exchange rate and price stability, such as the generation of high levels of employment and of reasonably rapid economic growth. A BOP deficit implies that, whether the adjustment is accomplished through the automatic reduction of the money supply or through contractionary discretionary macroeconomic policies, the attainment of these other domestic goals may have to be sacrificed or at least pursued in a less determined fashion. If the deficit country is already in a state of high unemployment and slow economic growth, the contractionary tendencies will serve to worsen the internal situation. The United States faced this dilemma in a number of years in the 1960s.

On the other hand, if a country has a BOP surplus, there is upward pressure on the price level because of the expanding money supply. While this could potentially be helpful from the standpoint of employment and growth, it will aggravate internal performance with respect to the goal of price stability. For example, Germany has often had a BOP surplus but at the same time did not want its inflation rate to rise. Thus, whether a country is in BOP deficit or surplus, the attainment of some internal goal will be frustrated because of the fixed-rate system.

The resolution of the question of whether discipline and hence price stability is more prevalent with fixed rates than with flexible rates requires extensive empirical research. It can be noted that world inflation was more rapid in the floating-rate period of the 1970s than in the pegged rate period of the 1960s, but events occurring independently of the exchange rate system—such as the behavior of OPEC—undoubtedly played a role in generating this difference in world inflation.

Would Fixed or Flexible Exchange Rates Provide for Greater Growth in International Trade and Investment?

A long-standing point made by proponents of fixed rates is that flexible rates are less conducive to the expansion of world trade and foreign direct investment than are fixed rates. In particular, a flexible exchange rate system is judged to bring with it a considerable amount of risk and uncertainty. Suppose that a U.S. exporter is considering a sale of goods to a French buyer for future delivery in 30 days and that the exporter requires a price of $1,000 per unit to be willing to make the sale. If the French buyer is willing to pay 5,000 francs per unit *and* if the expected exchange rate in 30 days is 5 francs = $1, then there is a basis for a contract and the sale will be made. However, if the exchange rate changes to 5.25 francs = $1 by the end of the 30 days, then the U.S. firm will have made an unwise decision, since only $952.38 (= 5,000 francs ÷ 5.25 francs/$) rather than $1,000 will be received.

In the context of this example, the case for fixed rates is thus that current decisions can be more certain as to their prospective future outcomes because the risk of a change in the value of the foreign currency (a depreciation in this case) is relatively small. With a flexible rate instead of a fixed rate and with the natural characteristic of risk aversion of most firms and individuals, the exporting firm will require some insurance against the exchange rate change. This insurance can take the form of holding out for a slightly higher expected price than $1,000 or of hedging in the forward market (which incurs the transaction cost of hedging), although active forward markets exist only for major currencies. Further, it should be noted that the rapid increase in international financial derivatives (discussed in the chapter "International Financial Markets and Instruments; An Introduction") now provides a wide variety of instruments for hedging the risks associated with international financial transactions. In any event, there is a cost, which means that, other things equal, a smaller volume of trade will occur under flexible rates than under fixed rates. With a reduced volume of international trade, there is less international specialization and lower world welfare.

Aside from focusing on the potential reduction in the volume of trade, proponents of fixed rates also judge that the amount of long-term foreign direct investment will be less under flexible rates than under fixed rates. Any firm contemplating the building of a plant overseas, for example, will be concerned about the size of the return flow of repatriated profits in the future. If the exchange rate varies, then the real value of the return flow when converted into home currency may be less than anticipated when the original investment was made (if prices in the two countries have not moved proportionately with the exchange rate). In view of this prospect, firms will be more timid about investing overseas, and consequently capital may not flow to areas where the "true" rate of return is greatest. World resource allocation will hence be less efficient under flexible rates, and a fixed-rate system can prevent this reduced efficiency. The risk and uncertainty argument is thought to be stronger in the case of long-term investment than in the case of international trade because long-term forward currency contracts and other instruments for hedging are more difficult to acquire and more costly than short-term contracts to cover trade risk.

However, with respect to this alleged adverse impact of flexible rates on foreign investment, a directly opposite case can also be made. (See McCulloch 1983, pp. 9–10.) Given overseas profit and price volatility in terms of domestic currency due to a floating exchange rate, firms may decide to reduce risk and uncertainty by producing in the foreign country itself. The foreign market will then be supplied from the foreign plant. In this interpretation, the existence of floating rates in recent years might actually have *increased* the amount of foreign direct investment. Indeed, foreign direct investment, especially into the United States, grew during the recent floating-rate period, but of course we do not know what that investment would have been under fixed rates.

In further reply to the arguments concerning the volume of trade and investment, proponents of flexible rates note that governments under *fixed* rates have often been unwilling to undergo the internal macroeconomic adjustments necessary for dealing with BOP deficits. The deficit situation eventually requires contraction of national income, yet a country with unemployment and slow economic growth may seek to postpone such income adjustment by using expansionary policy to sterilize the impact of the BOP deficit on the domestic money supply. However, as reserves continue to decline, countries have resorted to import restrictions and controls on capital outflows as devices for reducing BOP deficits. It is debatable whether such trade and investment restrictions have been successful in accomplishing their BOP objective, but they clearly interfere with efficient resource allocation and reduce welfare.

In view of this behavior under fixed exchange rates, the argument is made that restrictions on trade and capital movements for BOP purposes are unnecessary in a flexible-rate system. Movements in the exchange rate will eliminate the BOP deficit, thus undermining the rationale for the restrictions. Trade can then take place in accordance with comparative advantage and capital can flow to locations where its marginal productivity is highest. Nevertheless, if the rationale for the restrictions under fixed rates is protectionism and the BOP objective is only being used as a cover for this rationale, the adoption of floating rates may not lead to a removal of the restrictions.

The question of whether or not flexible rates reduce the volume of international trade and investment in comparison with a fixed-rate system is difficult to answer, since the economist cannot take a country into a laboratory and conduct a test with all other conditions held constant. Nevertheless, the literature has tried to evaluate the argument, especially with respect to the volume of trade. For discussion of some results regarding exchange rate risk and the volume of trade, see Case Study 1.

Would Fixed or Flexible Exchange Rates Provide for Greater Efficiency in Resource Allocation?

Another argument put forward for fixed exchange rates is that the wasteful resource movements associated with flexible exchange rates are avoided. This argument states that, with a system where exchange rates can vary substantially, there can be constantly changing incentives for the tradeable goods sectors. If the country's currency depreciates in the exchange markets, then factors of production will be induced to move into the tradeable goods sectors and out of the nontradeable goods sectors because the production of exports and import substitutes is now more profitable. However, if the currency then appreciates, the incentives reverse themselves and resources move out of tradeables and into nontradeables. Therefore, if fluctuations in the exchange rate occur, there will be constant movement of factors between the sectors and this movement involves economic waste because factors are temporarily displaced, labor may need to be retrained, and so forth. Further, if resources are unwilling to undergo continuous movement, there is a more permanent misallocation and inefficiency. These various reductions in efficiency and welfare could be avoided if the exchange rate were not allowed to change in the first place.

However, in response, proponents of flexible rates attack a fixed-rate system because of its key characteristic that it fixes the most important price in any economy, the exchange rate. The main point is that, from microeconomic theory, the fixing of any price interferes with efficient resource allocation because optimum resource use is attained when prices are free to reflect true scarcity values. The absence of a flexible price for

❁ CASE STUDY 1   EXCHANGE RISK AND INTERNATIONAL TRADE

Economists disagree over whether fluctuations in exchange rates and their associated risks reduce the amount of international trade below what it would otherwise be. Peter Hooper and Steven Kohlhagen's frequently cited article (1978) indicated that exchange rate variability had no significant impacts on trade. More recent work in the late 1980s disputes this conclusion.

A paper by Jerry Thursby and Marie Thursby (1987) suggested that trade is inhibited by exchange rate volatility. This paper is of broad scope, focusing on the determinants of trade, including the role of exchange rate risk, of 17 industrialized countries over the period 1974–1982. The model tested was one of bilateral trade, where equations were developed for each country's trade with each of the other 16 countries. Income (total and per capita), distance between the trading partners, import and export prices, and home consumer prices were among the independent variables included. For consideration of exchange risk, the variability of the spot rate around a predicted trend was the independent variable, and variability in both the nominal and the real exchange rate was examined.

Of interest for this chapter, the Thursbys found that 15 of the 17 countries had negative relationships between size of trade and nominal rate variability, with the results for 10 of the 15 countries being statistically significant. The results using the real exchange rate were virtually identical to those using the nominal rate. Thursby and Thursby concluded that there was "strong support for the hypothesis that exchange risk affects the value of bilateral trade" (p. 494).

Another test of the impact of exchange risk on trade was conducted by David Cushman (1988). He examined

U.S. bilateral exports and imports with six trading partners (Canada, France, Federal Republic of Germany, Japan, the Netherlands, the United Kingdom) from 1974 to 1983. Five different measures of risk involving the real exchange rate were used, with each measure incorporating different assumptions about expectations patterns of traders (for example, expectations based on recent spot rate variability, forward rate behavior in relation to the spot rate) and time horizons. Allowance for the influence on trade of other factors such as real income, capacity utilization, and unit labor costs was made. Of the 12 U.S. bilateral flows, 10 showed negative effects of exchange rate risk on trade, with 7 of the 10 having statistical significance. Cushman concluded (p. 328) that "in the absence of risk, U.S. imports would have been about 9% higher, and U.S. exports about 3% higher on average during the period."

Nevertheless, debate has continued. For example, Joseph Gagnon (1993) argued from a theoretical model with numerical analysis that the recent variability in exchange rates of industrial countries could have had no significant effect on the volume of trade. However, a recent IMF study (Ito, Isard, Symanski, and Bayoumi 1996) examined exchange rate variability and trade among the 18 member countries of the Asia-Pacific Economic Cooperation Forum (APEC) and concluded that there was very strong evidence that medium-term exchange rate volatility does affect trade and can definitely cause complications for the economies of the countries. In addition, the volatility can affect the pattern of foreign direct investment by causing firms to diversify such investment on a geographic basis so as to reduce their exposure to risk.   ❁

foreign exchange in a fixed-rate system generates widespread price distortions and gives misleading signals and therefore inhibits efficient resource allocation. (Such a situation is common in developing countries, where fixed exchange rates have often been chosen over flexible rates.) The interference with efficiency can be best seen in the situation where a country's currency is overvalued but the fixed-rate system does not permit a devaluation. In this instance, export industries are penalized because of the arbitrary level of the exchange rate, and yet comparative advantage theory tells us that the export sector contains the relatively most efficient industries in the economy. This argument is given further strength by noting that comparative advantage is not a static phenomenon. Rather, any country's comparative advantage industries are changing over time as new resources, new technology, and new skills emerge. Such dynamic changes lead to and are caused by variations in relative prices. If the exchange rate is fixed, then the resource-allocating role of changing relative prices is prevented from generating its maximum benefits.

In addition, a second efficiency objection to a fixed-rate system is that resources need to be tied up in the form of international reserves. The successful operation of a fixed exchange rate system requires that countries maintain working balances of reserves in order to finance deficits in the balance of payments. Even if a deficit is temporary (perhaps because of seasonal factors in the trade pattern) and will reverse itself, reserve assets are needed to meet the temporary excess demand for foreign exchange so as to maintain the pegged exchange rate. In addition to these working balances, which reflect the **transactions demand for international reserves,** countries may also wish to hold extra reserves in order to guard against any unexpected negative developments in the balance of payments. Hence, there is also a **precautionary demand for international reserves.**

In this context, economic behavior by governments dictates that calculations be made of the costs versus benefits of holding reserves (the benefits being that macroeconomic adjustments such as a reduction in national income do not have to take place because temporary sterilization can be accomplished). The costs are the *opportunity costs* of holding part of the country's wealth in the form of reserves rather than in the form of productive capital stock. The forgone capital stock would have earned the marginal productivity of capital in the country, and this lost output is a measure of the cost of holding international reserves to defend a pegged exchange rate. Quantitative assessments can be made of these benefits and costs, and the country will be holding its **optimal size of international reserves** when the marginal benefit is equal to the marginal cost. The marginal cost will not be zero, however, so the fixed-rate system implies a burden in terms of forgone output.

In this framework, the argument in favor of flexible rates is that such a system eliminates the need for central banks to hold international reserves. If the exchange rate clears the market, resources are therefore freed to be used more productively elsewhere in the economy. Hence, the forgone capital stock and the forgone output which that capital would have produced do not have to be sacrificed. For a look at the relative size of holdings of international reserves in fixed-rate and flexible-rate periods in recent decades, see Case Study 2.

Is Macroeconomic Policy More Effective in Influencing National Income under Fixed or Flexible Exchange Rates?

Another argument made in favor of fixed rates is that fiscal policy is more effective in influencing the level of national income under fixed rates than under flexible rates. The basic point is that expansionary fiscal policy, for example, shifts the *IS* curve to the right in the *IS/LM/BP* diagram. With relatively mobile capital internationally (*BP* curve flatter than the *LM* curve), the policy generates a BOP surplus under fixed rates because of the rise in the interest rate and the subsequent net inflow of short-term capital, which expands the money supply and aids in the effort to expand national income. With a flexible exchange rate, the appreciation caused by the capital flow would work to return national income toward its original level. If international capital is relatively immobile, a BOP deficit occurs under fixed rates, weakening the income impact of the expansionary fiscal policy; with flexible rates, a depreciation of the home currency adds stimulus to income. Ultimately, of course, the outcome depends on the degree of mobility of short-term capital. At least among the industrialized countries, such capital is very mobile, and so the superior effectiveness of fiscal policy under fixed rates seems to be a valid argument.

However, whatever the degree of international capital mobility, monetary policy is more effective for influencing the level of national income in a flexible-rate system than in a fixed-rate system. This point was examined extensively in the previous two chapters. An expansion of the money supply to increase national income generates a depreciation of the home currency, and this will act to reinforce the income-increasing impact of the monetary expansion. A similar reinforcement mechanism applies in the case of contractionary monetary policy.

As noted in the text, the elimination of the need to hold international reserves and therefore of the opportunity costs of holding reserves is an advantage of a flexible-rate system over a fixed-rate system. It is therefore instructive to examine the comparative size of international reserves in a regime of fixed exchange rates and in a regime where exchange rates can vary considerably. Table 1, column (2), lists international reserves held by central banks during the 1960–1972 years of the Bretton Woods pegged exchange rate system in the world economy (see the next chapter) and since 1973, when currencies began floating subsequent to the breakdown of Bretton Woods. For relative comparison purposes, total world imports are also given in column (3), as is the ratio of reserves to imports in column (4). This reserves/imports ratio is often used as a rough indicator of the ability of countries to finance BOP deficits under a fixed-rate system.

With the advent of flexible rates in 1973, one would expect that the reserve ratios would have declined dramatically, since a flexible-rate system in theory requires no reserves. However, the table indicates that, in absolute size, reserves increased dramatically in the 1973–1996 period, rising from $184.2 billion at the end of 1973 to $1,610.3 billion at the end of 1996. Nevertheless, reserve holdings relative to imports have been lower in the floating-rate period (27.1 percent for the period as a whole) than in the 1960–1972 fixed-rate period (37.6 percent). The fall in the reserve/imports ratio suggests that at least the *relative* opportunity cost of holding reserves has declined. Of course, since countries still do intervene to influence exchange rates (that is, the system is not a complete flexible-rate system, especially with respect to developing countries), it would not be expected that reserve holdings would disappear.

TABLE 1   Absolute and Relative Reserves of Central Banks, 1960–1996

(1) Year	(2) World Reserves*	(3) World Imports†	(4) Ratio	(1) Year	(2) World Reserves*	(3) World Imports†	(4) Ratio
1960	$ 60.0	$125.9	47.7%	1973	$ 184.2	$ 559.7	32.9%
1961	62.0	130.6	47.5	1974	220.1	822.3	26.8
1962	62.9	137.4	45.8	1975	227.6	866.8	26.3
1963	66.8	149.4	44.7	1976	258.1	971.9	26.6
1964	69.1	167.0	41.4	1977	321.3	1,112.9	28.9
1965	71.2	181.7	39.2	1978	367.1	1,287.4	28.5
1966	72.8	203.8	35.7	1979	403.1	1,624.8	24.8
1967	74.6	213.1	35.0	1980	452.4	1,999.1	22.6
1968	77.8	236.3	32.9	1981	422.7	1,982.2	21.3
1969	78.7	268.6	29.3	1982	398.5	1,853.0	21.5
1970	93.2	313.5	29.7	1983	414.2	1,793.2	23.1
1971	134.2	344.8	38.9	1984	431.6	1,911.4	22.6
1972	159.2	405.6	39.3	1985	481.3	1,935.2	24.9
				1986	552.8	2,114.4	26.1
				1987	767.0	2,473.8	31.0
				1988	774.9	2,822.0	27.5
				1989	820.0	3,040.9	27.0
				1990	954.0	3,466.2	27.5
				1991	1,007.9	3,584.0	28.1
				1992	998.5	3,840.8	26.0
				1993	1,096.3	3,768.1	29.1
				1994	1,250.4	4,282.6	29.2
				1995	1,459.4	5,145.0	28.4
				1996	1,610.3	5,363.0	30.0
Average, 1960–1972	$ 83.3	$221.4	37.6%	Average, 1973–1996	$ 661.4	$2,442.5	27.1%

*In billions of dollars. Reserves consist of gold, foreign exchange holdings, reserve position in the International Monetary Fund (IMF), and holdings of special drawing rights (SDRs). The valuation of reserves is at the end of each year in SDRs, converted to dollars at the prevailing $/SDR rate. Gold is valued at 35 SDRs = 1 ounce of gold. The reserve components are explained in more detail in the next chapter.

†In billions of dollars, valued c.i.f.

Sources: International Monetary Fund publications: *International Financial Statistics Yearbook 1988* (Washington, DC: IMF, 1988), pp. 68, 124, 716–17; *International Financial Statistics Yearbook 1996* (Washington, DC: IMF, 1996), pp. 70–71, 118–19; *International Financial Statistics*, June 1997, pp. 4, 37, 75. ※

Hence, to an important extent, the comparative effectiveness of macro policy is a debatable issue only if fiscal policy is preferred to monetary policy as the instrument of choice. This decision on fiscal policy vis-à-vis monetary policy involves various other considerations with respect to direct versus indirect government influence on the economy and the proper role of government. The preference will vary from country to country.

Another argument that has been made for flexible rates is that such a system permits monetary and fiscal policies to be directed solely toward the attainment of internal economic goals. The point was made earlier that under fixed rates, policy authorities might have to sacrifice the attainment of internal objectives (for example, full employment) in order to satisfy the external objective of BOP equilibrium. On the other hand, if the exchange rate is flexible, the exchange rate itself will take care of any balance-of-payments problems: a deficit (surplus) situation will promptly set a depreciation (appreciation) of the home currency into operation, and this depreciation (appreciation) will remove the deficit (surplus). Hence, there is no need to use monetary and fiscal policies to deal with imbalances in the BOP, and these instruments can be directly used to deal with internal problems (that is, the "balance-of-payments constraint" on policy has been removed).

Proponents of this argument point to the fact that effective policymaking requires that the number of instruments match the number of targets (see the chapter "Economic Policy in the Open Economy: Fixed Exchange Rates"). The virtue of the floating-rate system is that an additional (automatic) instrument—the exchange rate—has been added. Thus, if the three targets are BOP equilibrium, full employment, and price stability, the three instruments are the exchange rate, fiscal policy, and monetary policy. Since the exchange rate is now handling BOP problems, fiscal policy can be directed toward raising the level of employment and monetary policy can be directed toward achieving price stability. Hence, the arsenal of instruments is enhanced under a floating-rate system.

In assessing this argument, note that a conflict will not necessarily arise between the policies needed for attaining BOP equilibrium and those needed for reaching internal targets. For example, a country with a BOP deficit *and* rapid inflation will require a contractionary policy stance for reaching both the external target and the internal target of price stability, although the degree of contraction necessary for reaching each respective target may differ. Similarly, a country with a BOP surplus and excessive unemployment will find that expansionary policies will work to remove the surplus as well as the unemployment, although again the extent of policy action may differ for each respective target. In the other cases—BOP deficit together with unemployment, BOP surplus together with inflation—the fixed-rate system imposes a constraint on the conduct of policy for the attainment of the internal target. Imaginative devices such as the use of monetary policy to attain the external target and of fiscal policy to attain the internal target (the Mundell prescription in the chapter "Economic Policy in the Open Economy: Fixed Exchange Rates") may be tried in these conflict situations, but they may also not be very successful.

CONCEPT CHECK

1. What is meant by "discipline" in the world economy, and how might fixed exchange rates work to promote such discipline?
2. Why might a fixed-rate system potentially enhance the growth of foreign trade and investment in the world economy?
3. How can the existence of the transactions and precautionary demands for international reserves reduce world output over what would otherwise be the case?
4. Explain why it can be uncertain whether fiscal policy is more effective for influencing national income under fixed exchange rates than under flexible exchange rates.

Will Destabilizing Speculation in Exchange Markets Be Greater under Fixed or Flexible Exchange Rates?

A major concern expressed by some economists is that a system of flexible exchange rates will be characterized by **destabilizing speculation.** This argument stresses that the normal fluctuations that occur with flexible rates are augmented by the behavior of speculators attempting to make profits on the basis of their anticipations of future exchange rates. If a currency depreciates (appreciates), speculators will project forward the depreciation (appreciation) and will conclude that their optimal strategy is to sell (buy) the currency. These sales (purchases) will worsen the depreciation (appreciation). The result of this speculative behavior is that cyclical fluctuations in exchange rates will have greater amplitude than otherwise would be the case.

This argument is illustrated in Figure 1. Line R shows regular (nonspeculative) fluctuations around the long-run equilibrium value of the exchange rate $\bar{e}$. Suppose that, from initial point A, the home currency begins to depreciate toward point B. With destabilizing speculation, speculators judge that, at a point like B, the currency will continue to depreciate. They sell the currency in anticipation of buying it back later at a lower price, driving e beyond the normal peak (point C). After the currency turns around and begins to appreciate, at point F the speculators will expect continued appreciation and will buy the home currency in anticipation of a future sale at a higher home currency price. This action will carry the exchange rate below the normal trough of e at point G. The cycle with destabilizing speculation is represented by R' (which need not have peaks and troughs at the same time as R or the same cycle lengths). Such behavior of the exchange rate, even without destabilizing speculation, is also characteristic of the

FIGURE 1   **Destabilizing and Stabilizing Speculation**

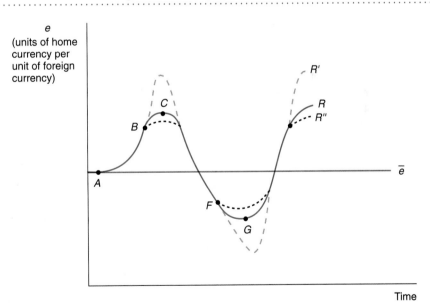

Normal fluctuations in the exchange rate around its equilibrium value $\bar{e}$ are pictured by line R. With destabilizing speculation, when a depreciation of the home currency occurs between point A and point B, speculators project a further depreciation and sell the home currency. This causes the home currency to depreciate to a level beyond that associated with the "normal" low value at point C. In the downswing of e, speculators project forward the appreciation of the home currency and purchase it at F. These purchases lead to a home currency value greater than its "normal" high value at point G. The resulting line R' has greater amplitude than R. If speculation were stabilizing, speculators would purchase the home currency at B and sell it at F, generating line R'' with a smaller amplitude than R.

overshooting phenomenon, discussed in the chapter "The Monetary and Portfolio Balance Approaches to External Balance."

However, a contrary case can also be made for **stabilizing speculation.** Suppose that, after the movement from *A* to *B,* speculators think that the currency has "depreciated enough" in view of the fundamentals of the economy and that it is now time to *buy* the currency. Speculative purchases of the home currency at *B* will cause the upswing of the cyclical movement to be diminished rather than enhanced. The sale of the currency on the downswing of the cyclical movement at point *F* will also dampen the cycle in that direction. With stabilizing speculation, the entire cycle is represented by dotted line *R″,* and greater stability exists than with the normal cycle *R.*

Debate on the nature of speculation has gone on for a number of years, and there is no unanimity of views. Milton Friedman, probably the best-known proponent of flexible rates (see Box 1) maintains that destabilizing speculation cannot persist indefinitely. Such speculation would imply that speculators are selling the home currency when its price is low (at point *B* in Figure 1) and buying the home currency when its price is high (at point *F*). Surely this is not the way to make a profit! Stabilizing speculation, on the other hand, involves the profitable activity of buying the currency at a low price and selling it at a high price. Thus, since speculation continues to exist in the real world, it must be profitable and therefore stabilizing. This conclusion on the profitability of speculation and its implication regarding stability have been disputed in more complex analyses. At issue is the nature of expectations. If a change in a variable leads to the expectation that the variable will return to (depart farther from) some "normal" level, the speculation will be of the stabilizing (destabilizing) sort. We do not know what circumstances will generate one or the other type of expectation.

Recent studies have explored the question of expectations in relation to policy actions. If speculators can figure out how the monetary authorities will react to an exchange rate change, then this knowledge can be profitable. For example, if a depreciation of the dollar causes the Federal Reserve to buy dollars and if speculators anticipate that action, the speculators will buy dollars ahead of the Federal Reserve to profit from the forthcoming rise in the dollar's price. The result is consistent with "stability." Other matters, such as the degree of confidence speculators place in the Federal Reserve, are also involved. Finally, much work has been done on how expectations are formed. Are expectations "adaptive" (based on recent past behavior) or are they "rational" and forward-looking (based on all available information on how the economy works and how policy authorities react)?

Since speculation may be destabilizing in a flexible-rate system, do we therefore conclude that it is stabilizing in a fixed-rate system? Some economists think that fixed rates do indeed invite stabilizing speculation, because the floor and ceiling for a rate suggest that the rate will never go outside those limits. Hence, when a currency falls to its floor value, speculators know that it will go no lower and could turn around, so they will likely buy it. This will turn the currency's value upward. This scenario in reverse would occur at the ceiling.

However, this argument rests on the assumption that central banks can indeed enforce the floor and ceiling limits. But this may not be the case. Suppose that, as in the Bretton Woods system, currencies are permitted to vary ±1 percent from their parity values. If the parity value of the British pound is $2.40 = £1, then the floor price of the pound is $2.376 and the ceiling is $2.424. In addition, suppose that because of greater inflation in Britain than in the United States, the pound starts to fall in value from parity toward the floor and that it eventually hits the floor. At this point, the British authorities will be using some of their international reserves to buy pounds in order to keep the pound from falling further.

BOX 1   MILTON FRIEDMAN (BORN 1912)

Milton Friedman was born in Brooklyn, New York, on July 31, 1912, the son of a poor immigrant family. He earned his A.B. at Rutgers in 1932, his master's degree at the University of Chicago in 1933, and his Ph.D. at Columbia in 1946. During the time between his master's and his Ph.D., he worked for the National Resources Committee in Washington, the National Bureau of Economic Research in New York, the U.S. Treasury Department, and the War Research division of Columbia University, as well as performing short-term teaching stints at the universities of Wisconsin and Minnesota. After finishing his Ph.D., he taught at the University of Chicago from 1948 to 1982 and was the Paul Russell Snowden Distinguished Service Professor of Economics from 1962 to 1982. He continues active work today as a Senior Research Fellow at the Hoover Institution at Stanford University.

Milton Friedman's contributions to economics are legendary and of extremely wide scope. His early work concentrated on statistical methods, but he then ventured into other areas. Still widely discussed is his 1953 book, *A Theory of the Consumption Function,* in which he developed the hypothesis that consumption spending by households depended not on current income but on the longer-term notion of permanent income, an expectation of income flows over many years. In this light, short-term transitory changes in current income would have virtually no impact on current consumption. Even more well known is Friedman's work on money and economic activity, and he is hailed as having been the driving force behind monetarism and its emphasis on monetary policy rather than on fiscal policy for influencing the macroeconomy. His work has been both historical [for example, Friedman and Anna J. Schwartz, *A Monetary History of the United States, 1867– 1960* (1963)] and theoretical (for example, "The Role of Monetary Policy," *American Economic Review,* March 1968). It led to such familiar doctrines as the modern quantity theory of money and the automatic "rule" for monetary growth. Friedman is also widely regarded as the father of the concept of the "natural" rate of unemployment, an attack on the notion of a downward-sloping Phillips curve reflecting a trade-off between inflation and unemployment. In addition, he has been the leading proponent of flexible exchange rates.

Throughout Professor Friedman's career, he has been vitally concerned that economics be "practical." His widely cited view is that theory should not be judged by its assumptions but by whether it can satisfactorily predict economic behavior in the real world. In addition, he has stressed continually the role of individuals, the market, and laissez-faire, even suggesting in his popular 1962 book, *Capitalism and Freedom,* that licensing of medical practitioners should be abolished since it is a barrier to entry and thus to efficient resource allocation. He is constantly suspicious of government intervention and regulation, and his public television series, *Free to Choose,* made his views known to millions worldwide. He is also known for the absolute clarity of expression that has helped to popularize his ideas. In the context of this chapter, for example, he makes the case that the adoption of flexible exchange rates is analogous to the adoption of daylight saving time. Instead of going through the confusion and inefficiency of having everyone move all their activities one hour earlier every summer, why not just change the clock?

For his many contributions, Milton Friedman was awarded the Nobel Prize in economics in 1976, and he was also elected president of the American Economic Association for 1967. In addition, he has received honorary doctorates from many colleges and universities. His awards have been virtually innumerable, and some of them are seldom given to ordinary academics—we note in particular such honors as "Chicagoan of the Year" and "Statesman of the Year." Not resting on his laurels, Milton Friedman continues his research, writing, lecturing, and debating.

Sources: Mark Blaug, ed., *Who's Who in Economics: A Biographical Dictionary of Major Economists 1700–1986,* 2nd ed. (Cambridge: MIT Press, 1986), pp. 291–93; John Burton, "Positively Milton Friedman," in J. R. Shackleton and Gareth Locksley, eds., *Twelve Contemporary Economists* (London: Macmillan, 1981), pp. 53–71; Alan Walters, "Milton Friedman," in John Eatwell, Murray Milgate, and Peter Newman, eds., *The New Palgrave: A Dictionary of Economics,* Vol. 2 (London: Macmillan, 1987), pp. 422–27; *Who's Who in America,* 46th edition 1990–91, Vol. 1 (Wilmette, IL: Marquis Who's Who, 1990), p. 1119; *Who's Who 1997* (New York: St. Martin's Press, 1997), p. 692.

However, if Britain does nothing to slow down its inflation rate, speculators will sell large volumes of pounds on the exchange markets because the speculators essentially have a *one-way bet*. The massive sales of pounds by speculators then will ensure that the prediction of a fall in the value of the pound is a self-fulfilling prophecy, since the continued sales will exhaust British reserves as the Bank of England futilely tries to purchase sufficient pounds. The speculators will have sold pounds at $2.376 and will later be able to buy them back at a lower price.

This speculative behavior against weak currencies thus makes it very difficult to keep the fixed exchange rates intact. And the Bretton Woods system did indeed have a number of instances of speculative attacks on currencies and changes in parity values. Further, speculation clearly played a role in upsetting the pegged rates among some members of the European Community in 1993. In practice, the applicability of this argument against the *viability* of a fixed-rate system depends in large part on the degree of confidence speculators place in governments. If government policymakers are able to implement effective measures for dealing with imbalances in the balance of payments, then speculators might behave in a stabilizing manner. Finally, the force of the argument also depends on the size of the speculative capital flows in relation to the size of the countries' international reserves. Most observers feel that the volume of potential speculative capital is currently large enough to cause difficulty for any central bank.

However, if the destabilizing speculation under fixed rates is an important phenomenon, it in a sense makes all previous points in the fixed-flexible debate rather moot, since the fixed-rate system may in fact not be viable with the existence of today's potentially huge volume of speculative capital. Indeed, many economists think that the structural and policy differences among countries make it highly unlikely that a fixed-rate system can operate successfully. An emphasis in this line of reasoning is that unemployment-inflation combinations differ across countries. In some countries (e.g., Sweden), the policy authorities aim for low levels of unemployment rather than toward the avoidance of inflation. In other countries (e.g., Germany), the preferences may be reversed. A physically small economy with a mobile labor force (e.g., Switzerland) may be able to attain a lower unemployment rate without incurring rapid inflation than can a physically large country with substantial structural unemployment (e.g., the United States). For these reasons and others (such as an ineffective tax collection system characteristic of many developing countries), some countries tend to have chronic higher inflation rates than other countries. The more rapidly inflating countries will find themselves with frequent BOP deficits, and countries with greater price stability will be running BOP surpluses. With limited international reserves, slow adjustment, and destabilizing speculation, deficit countries will ultimately have to devalue and the fixed-rate system will break down.

Will Countries Be Better Protected from External Shocks under a Fixed or a Flexible Exchange Rate System?

An important argument against a fixed exchange rate system is that, in such a system, business cycles will be transmitted from one country to other countries, meaning that no country is able to insulate itself from external real shocks. If a foreign country goes into a recession, it will buy less of the home country's exports. As a result, national income will fall in the home country. If "foreign repercussions" are important, the fall in income in the home country will then reduce the home country's purchases from the foreign country, which will in turn worsen the recession overseas and eventually feed back again upon the home country. The same scenario in an upward direction also occurs, resulting in the transmission of inflation from one country to another.

The fixed-rate system contributes to this transmission of business cycles because the exchange rate is a passive part of the process. In a *flexible*-rate situation, the exchange rate would take an active part in mitigating the transmission. For example, in the recession case above, the initial decline in the home country's exports (a leftward shift of its *IS* and *BP* curves) would cause a depreciation of the home currency and would stimulate the home country's production of exports and import substitutes. This would offset the downward thrust on income as the curves shifted back to their original positions. A similar offset would occur if an overseas boom had started the process. Thus, the flexible exchange rate serves to insulate the economy from external real sector shocks.

Note, however, that we have only discussed external *real* sector shocks so far in this section. Suppose instead that the external sector shock is a financial sector shock, such as a rise in interest rates abroad. As noted in the chapter "Economic Policy in the Open Economy: Flexible Exchange Rates," this causes the home country's *BP* curve to shift to the left, leading to an incipient deficit in the balance of payments as home country short-term funds move overseas. The home currency will then depreciate, shifting the *IS* curve to the right and shifting the *BP* curve rightward toward its original position. With the *LM* curve unchanged, the result is a higher level of home income. On the other hand, if the exchange rate had been fixed, the initial leftward shift in the *BP* curve and the resulting BOP deficit would have resulted in monetary contraction and a fall in home income. Thus, there is "insulation" in neither exchange rate system, but home national income moves in opposite directions depending on the system being used. Which result is more desirable will depend on the state of the domestic economy at the time of the foreign financial shock.

Finally, although this section has been concerned with external shocks, it can be noted that, under flexible rates, *internal* shocks to the economy can be more *destabilizing* to national income than under fixed rates. A domestic monetary or financial shock (a shift in the *LM* curve) produces a greater income response under flexible rates than under fixed rates. The same conclusion on income response applies for an internal real sector shock if the *BP* curve is steeper than the *LM* curve (relative capital immobility). However, the real sector shock yields less income response under flexible rates than under fixed rates if the *BP* curve is flatter than the *LM* curve (relative capital mobility). Hence, to determine whether flexible or fixed rates make for greater instability with respect to internal real sector shocks in practice, some determination must be made of the international responsiveness of short-term capital to changes in interest rates. (For empirical work on the effects of external versus internal shocks in the case of Japan, see Case Study 3.)

This concludes our discussion in this chapter of major issues in the fixed versus flexible exchange rate debate. In practice, the world has moved from a system of relatively fixed rates in the 1950s and 1960s to a system of considerably greater flexibility in exchange rates since 1973. As we shall see in the last section of this chapter, however, it is unnecessary to think only in terms of fixed rates versus completely flexible exchange rates. Some "hybrid" systems are possible, and these "hybrids" have also been important in practice in recent years.

OPTIMUM CURRENCY AREAS

A concept which lies under the surface in the previous discussion concerning fixed versus flexible exchange rates is that of the **optimum currency area.** An optimum currency area is an area that, for optimal balance-of-payments adjustment reasons as well as for reasons of effectiveness of domestic macroeconomic policy, has fixed exchange rates within the area but flexible exchange rates with trading partners outside the area. In other words, it may be best for the 50 states of the United States to have fixed rates among themselves (which they do to the extreme since a common currency is employed) but flexible rates

CASE STUDY 3   "INSULATION" WITH FLEXIBLE RATES: THE CASE OF JAPAN

A study to determine whether an economy is more insulated from outside shocks under flexible than under fixed exchange rates was carried out by Michael Hutchison and Carl E. Walsh (1992). Reacting to some 1980s literature that questioned whether flexible rates really "insulated" an economy (for example, Dornbusch 1983, Baxter and Stockman 1989), Hutchison and Walsh focused specifically on Japan. For the fixed-rate regime, they examined the period from the fourth quarter of 1957 through the fourth quarter of 1972; for the flexible-rate regime, they looked at the period from the fourth quarter of 1974 through the fourth quarter of 1986. While their work indicated that the proportion of variation in Japanese real GNP due to foreign shocks was considerably larger in the flexible-rate period than in the fixed-rate period, this variation could have occurred because there were more severe external shocks in the flexible-rate period (such as the oil shocks and the recessions in the industrialized countries in the 1970s and early 1980s). Thus, Hutchison and Walsh concerned themselves with the effects of shocks after controlling for the size of the shocks. Their statistical work estimated the impacts on Japan over time of a 1-unit shock

in oil prices (in real terms), a 1-unit shock in U.S. real GNP, and a 1-unit shock in the U.S. nominal money supply (M1).

What conclusions were reached? First, Hutchison and Walsh indicated that, after several quarters, a real oil price increase (by itself) caused a marked decline in the level of Japanese real GNP. However, the decline under fixed rates was significantly greater than under flexible rates. Similarly, a 1-unit change in U.S. GNP was long-lasting in its impact on Japan in both exchange rate systems, but the impact was greater under fixed rates. In the case of a U.S. money supply shock, the effect on Japan was the same for both exchange rate systems.

Thus, the overall conclusion of Hutchison and Walsh was that, in the case of Japan, flexible rates generally provided more "insulation" from external shocks than did fixed rates. Another interesting result from their model was that an initial 1-unit Japanese real GNP shock (an *internal* shock) also had less total impact on Japan itself under flexible rates than under fixed rates. This result logically follows if the *BP* curve for Japan is flatter than the *LM* curve.

vis-à-vis other countries. Similarly, most members of the European Union have more fixity in exchange rates among their own currencies than against the currencies of outside world countries. What determines the domain (or size) of an optimum currency area? An answer to this question may be helpful in resolving the fixed rate–flexible rate debate.

There have been two main analyses of the necessary characteristics of an optimum currency area. Robert Mundell (1961) focused on the degree of factor mobility between countries and on economic structure. Suppose that the only two countries in the world are the United States and Canada, that a flexible exchange rate exists between them, and that variations in the exchange rate smoothly handle any BOP problems. Suppose also, however, that the eastern part of each country specializes in manufactured goods (e.g., automobiles) while the western part of each country specializes in natural resource products (e.g., lumber products). In addition, assume that factors of production do not move easily between east and west in each country and between the two types of industries. Suppose now that there is a shift in the composition of demand by consumers from automobiles to lumber products. The effect of this demand shift can be to generate inflationary pressures in the western portion of each country and to cause unemployment in the eastern part. In this situation, the Federal Reserve could expand the U.S. money supply to alleviate the eastern U.S. unemployment, but this would aggravate the inflation in the western United States. Or the Federal Reserve could contract the money supply to alleviate the inflation in the west, but this would aggravate the unemployment in the east. The same dilemma would exist for the Bank of Canada with respect to the Canadian east and west. In this context, a smooth adjustment mechanism (the flexible exchange rate) exists between the *countries* but not between the *regions* in each country.

What is the way out of the dilemma? In Mundell's view, the problem is that the flexible exchange rate pertains to the national *political* units (the United States and Canada) while fixed rates exist (within the countries) between regions that are economically dissimilar and have little factor mobility between them. The situation would be much improved if the *economic* units of the eastern United States and eastern Canada adopted a fixed exchange rate between them, as should the western United States and western Canada. Further, the exchange rate between the East (comprising the eastern parts of both countries) and the West (comprising the western parts of both countries) should be flexible. Then, with the above shift of demand from automobiles to lumber products, the currency of the West would appreciate relative to the currency of the East. In addition, the monetary authorities in both countries could use contractionary policy in the West and expansionary policy in the East. The unemployment and inflation problems could both then be avoided.

The point of this discussion is that there is a role to play for both fixed and flexible rates. Countries that are similar in economic structure and have factor mobility between them should have fixed exchange rates among themselves, for they comprise an optimum currency area. They should also adopt flexible exchange rates relative to the rest of the world. Needless to say, an optimum currency area within which rates are fixed is not necessarily an individual country.

In later work extending his ideas on optimum currency areas, Mundell (1997) distinguishes between a "true" currency area and a "pseudo" currency area. In the former, the currency area adopts a monetary system such as a gold standard that contains an automatic adjustment mechanism. This mechanism, coupled with a commitment to stability, is "in times of peace" virtually absolute. A pseudo currency area, on the other hand, does not allow an automatic adjustment mechanism to function and a certain degree of country autonomy exists with regard to changes in parities. Consequently, interest rates can diverge in response to expected changes in exchange rates, and destabilizing speculation can occur. Since Mundell judges that modern currency areas tend to be pseudo in nature, he thinks that successful functioning of these agreements requires that the countries involved have sufficiently similar political and/or economic interests and a willingness to adapt when the situation demands it. In the absence of such political commitment, in Mundell's view, the member countries are unlikely to achieve the anticipated benefits of membership in the currency area.

Another noteworthy contribution regarding the characteristics of an optimum currency area is that of Ronald McKinnon (1963). McKinnon was concerned with the choice of a flexible exchange rate versus a fixed exchange rate in the contexts of BOP adjustment and of maintaining price-level stability. His analysis involved the distinction between a relatively open economy and a relatively closed economy. A relatively open (closed) economy is one which has a high (low) ratio of production of tradeable goods to production of nontradeable goods. Consider the open economy. If it has a flexible exchange rate, then a depreciation of its currency will raise the domestic price of imports and subsequently the price of domestic import-competing goods. Similarly, the depreciation increases the domestic price of exportable goods, because foreign demand for home exports increases with the depreciation. Since the prices of these tradeable goods are increasing, and since the tradeables comprise most of the country's production, the depreciation results in domestic inflation, which is roughly of the same percentage as the percentage by which the currency has depreciated. For the open economy, therefore, depreciation associated with the flexible exchange rate will do little to improve a BOP deficit and do much toward contributing to domestic inflation. This country might better be advised to maintain a fixed exchange rate.

In contrast, the relatively closed economy will find that a depreciation associated with a flexible exchange rate will have less effect on the domestic price level. Although the depreciation causes a rise in the price of tradeable goods, the price of these tradeables is not a very important component of the country's entire price level. But the rise in the price of tradeables relative to nontradeables will induce more production of tradeables, and the balance of payments will be easily improved by depreciation. Hence, for relatively closed economies, a flexible exchange rate can be very useful since it facilitates BOP adjustment without adding substantially to domestic inflation.

In the context of the fixed rate–flexible rate debate, McKinnon's analysis suggests that relatively open countries should consider fixed rates, while relatively closed economies should adopt floating rates with the outside world. This set of ideas can be married to Mundell's analysis by suggesting that open economies with factor mobility between them can, given sufficient political commitment, join together to form a currency area, while relatively closed countries can "go it on their own." In any event, these various considerations indicate that the optimum currency area is *not* the world as a whole. Obvious implications for the debate concerning fixed rates versus flexible rates are (*a*) to form blocs of similar countries, with fixed rates among the members of each bloc (such as perhaps within the European Union or within much of East Asia) and (*b*) to have exchange rate flexibility between the several blocs.

CONCEPT CHECK

1. Is the adoption of a fixed exchange rate system a guarantee that destabilizing speculation will not occur? Why or why not?
2. Explain how a sudden rise in the price level in foreign countries can be less inflationary

for the home country in a system of flexible exchange rates than in a system of fixed exchange rates.
3. Explain Mundell's point that a country may not be an optimum currency area.

"HYBRID" SYSTEMS COMBINING FIXED AND FLEXIBLE EXCHANGE RATES

Amid the continuing debate between proponents of fixed rates and proponents of flexible rates, several "compromise" or "hybrid" proposals have emerged. These proposals attempt to incorporate the attractive features while minimizing the unattractive features of each extreme system. We consider three such systems in this chapter; further discussion in the context of the current international monetary system is provided in the next chapter.

Wider Bands

This proposal takes as a point of comparison the Bretton Woods system, where exchange rates were permitted to vary by 1 percent on either side of parity values. The proposal for **wider bands** states that the permissible variations around parity should be set at some larger value, such as 10 percent around parity. Because a substantial amount of variation is permitted with this wider band, the exchange rate is able to carry out balance-of-payments adjustment. For example, if a country has a BOP deficit, the home currency could depreciate by up to 10 percent from its parity value, and this larger depreciation could be successful in altering exports and imports in the desired direction. Because the exchange rate is handling much of the BOP adjustment, there is less need for monetary and fiscal policies to be diverted from seeking the attainment of internal economic goals. In addition, because the variation from parity is limited to 10 percent, the wider band system still preserves some of the discipline of the fixed-rate system and also means that the problem of risk interfering with trade and investment is constrained, as is the problem of wasteful resource movements due to large and reversible movements in the exchange rate.

Nevertheless, because the proposal for wider bands maintains some limitations on exchange rate variability, it does not deal with some of the objections to fixed rates. For example, if countries consistently have different inflation rates, this system may break down, just as would a fixed-rate system. If Italy continually inflates more rapidly than does Germany because of a different unemployment-inflation preference, then sooner or later the Italian lira/deutsche mark rate will hit the ceiling. If no corrective steps or alterations in relative preferences by policymakers occur, a change in the lira/deutsche mark parity value will be required because Italy will deplete its international reserves. (The parity value of the lira in terms of deutsche marks in the European Monetary System was changed on several occasions, even though a 6 percent variation around parity was permitted. In addition, in August 1993, the ranges in general for the European Monetary System were enlarged to ± 15 percent around parity.) Further, when the rate first hits the ceiling, speculators will have a one-way bet against the lira, and thus speculative pressure against the lira is apt to ensure that a devaluation of the lira will occur.

Finally, other objections to the wider bands proposal can be raised. Because a total change in a currency's value of 20 percent is permitted (10 percent on either side of parity), there are still some additional risks introduced for international trade and investment, as well as some possibility of wasteful resource movements because of the rate changes. In addition, international reserves—with their associated opportunity costs—still need to be held, and business cycles will still be transmitted across country borders. A sophisticated extension of the wider bands proposal, known as the "target zone proposal," meets some of the objections to wider bands and is discussed in the next chapter.

Crawling Pegs

In the system known as the **crawling peg,** a country specifies a parity value for its currency and permits a small variation around that parity (such as ±1 percent from parity). However, the parity rate is adjusted regularly by small amounts as dictated by the behavior of such variables as the country's international reserve position and recent changes in the money supply or prices. (The adjustment can be accomplished by following a strict formula or by use of judgment by the policymakers.) When these variables indicate potential pressures for the country (such as when international reserves decline markedly), the currency's parity value is officially devalued by a small percentage. Of course, when the parity value is thus changed, the 1 percent band now applies to the *new* parity.

A stylized example of a crawling peg system is given in Figure 2. The solid lines indicate the ceiling and the floor associated with the peg, while the dotted line indicates the path of the actual exchange rate. Note that the actual rate is between the ceiling and floor until point *A* is reached. This ceiling rate after *A* can be maintained only by using up some international reserves; but continued use of the reserves eventually will trigger a change of the parity value, as reflected in the higher band (reflecting devaluation of the home currency) after point *B*. (For simplicity, we do not show a parity value line.) A continuation of this process occurs at points *C* and *D*. Then, if the currency reverses itself and hits the floor at point *F,* a buildup of reserves eventually will set off an increase in the parity value at point *G,* so the range shifts downward.

Advocates of the crawling peg concept point out that, at least in theory, the existence of the ceiling and floor can provide for some discipline on the part of the monetary authorities. In addition, the fact that the rate is periodically changed means that a role for the exchange rate in BOP adjustment is maintained. Finally, since each change is a small one, there is less danger of large-scale speculation against the currency.

An argument against the crawling peg is that a major change in the country's balance-of-payments position because of an internal or external shock may require a

FIGURE 2   **A Crawling Peg**

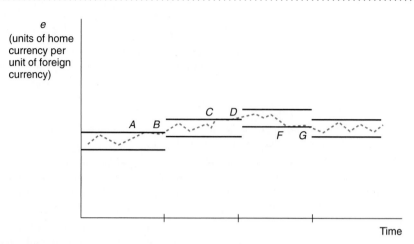

In this crawling peg example, the exchange rate fluctuates within its narrow band until point *A* is reached. The loss of reserves from *A* to *B* and any other indicators of currency weakness trigger a small devaluation of the parity value. When difficulties again occur from point *C* to point *D*, another small official devaluation takes place. This new parity value continues until a reserve buildup occurs from point *F* to point *G*, whereupon the parity value of the home currency is raised.

sizable change in the exchange rate to restore BOP equilibrium. If adherence to a strict crawling peg occurs, then a sacrifice of the pursuit of internal goals may be required since a large exchange rate change is not possible. Further, if the small parity changes are frequent (and unpredictable), there may still be some additional risks associated with international trade and investment. Finally, if experience is any guide, crawling pegs conducted in a context of unstable internal economic conditions (such as extremely rapid inflation) may amount virtually to a flexible exchange rate system. For an example of experience under a crawling peg system in the 1980s, see Case Study 4.

Managed Floating

The final hybrid arrangement of fixed and flexible exchange rates that we consider in this chapter is designated by the broad term **managed floating,** the term that is generally applied to the current international monetary system (see the next chapter). In general, a managed floating regime is characterized by *some* interference with exchange rate movements, but the intervention is discretionary on the part of the monetary authorities. In other words, there are no announced guidelines or rules for intervention, no parity exchange rates or announced target rates, and no announced limits for exchange rate variations. Rather, a country may intervene when it judges that it would be well served by doing so. For example, intervention to appreciate the home currency (or to keep it from depreciating so fast) might be desirable to fight domestic inflationary pressures, or intervention to prevent an appreciation might be desirable for assisting in reaching an employment target. Sometimes the intervention by a particular country takes the form of **coordinated intervention** with other countries, such as when several industrialized nations (the G-7 industrialized countries) agreed to drive the U.S. dollar down in value in 1985 and then agreed in 1987 that the dollar had fallen far enough. In general, a country tends to intervene in order to slow down a movement in the exchange rate in a particular direction, a type of intervention called **"leaning against the wind."** If the intervention is designed to intensify the movement of the currency in the direction in which it is already moving, the intervention is called **"leaning with the wind."**

✦ CASE STUDY 4 A CRAWLING PEG IN COLOMBIA

A country that employed a crawling peg system for a number of years is Colombia. In the Colombian case, the authorities followed "a policy of adjusting the peso in small amounts at relatively short intervals, taking into account (1) the movements of prices in Colombia relative to those in its major trading partners; (2) the level of Colombia's foreign exchange reserves; and (3) Colombia's overall balance of payments performance."* Despite small adjustments in each instance in a crawling peg system, however, the cumulative change in currency value can be rather large over a period of a few years. Table 2 presents relevant information for Colombia for the period 1980–1990. Following this experience, Colombia instituted, in mid-1991, a more directly market-oriented exchange rate system, although indicators are still taken into account and there is some government involvement. (It is noteworthy that other countries that previously had crawling pegs have also abandoned them.)

As can be seen from column (2) of the table, Colombia's peso/dollar exchange rate of 47.28 in 1980 rose to 502.26 in 1990. This was a 962 percent increase in the price of the dollar in terms of pesos or, when the exchange rate is expressed as dollars/peso [and put into indexes as in column (3)], a decline in the peso of more than 90 percent. A prime reason for this depreciation of the peso was the 736 percent rise in Colombia's CPI from 1980 to 1990 (not shown in the table). However, the fall in the peso relative to the dollar was unrepresentative of the size of the overall decline in its value. The nominal effective exchange rate [column (4)] of the peso against the trade-weighted average of all trading partners fell "only" from 148.7 to 52.0 from 1980 through 1990—a 65 percent decline. When adjusted for relative internal prices via the real effective exchange rate in column (5), the peso fell from an index of 107.0 to 54.5—a fall of "only" 49 percent. Nevertheless, Colombia's experience suggests that a crawling peg may indeed crawl rapidly!

TABLE 2   **Exchange Rate Behavior in Colombia, 1980–1990**

(1)	*(2)*	*(3)*	*(4)*	*(5)*
			Indexes of Value of Peso (1985 = 100)	
Year	*Pesos per U.S. $*	*Versus $*	*Nominal Effective Rate*	*Real Effective Rate*
1980	47.28	300.9	148.7	107.0
1981	54.49	261.0	145.8	118.1
1982	64.08	222.0	141.6	125.9
1983	78.85	180.4	134.2	125.3
1984	100.82	141.1	122.8	114.7
1985	142.31	100.0	100.0	100.0
1986	194.26	73.3	70.2	74.5
1987	242.61	58.6	58.2	66.4
1988	299.17	47.5	54.0	64.1
1989	382.57	37.1	53.8	61.7
1990	502.26	28.3	52.0	54.5

*International Monetary Fund, *Exchange Arrangements and Exchange Restrictions: Annual Report 1990* (Washington, DC: IMF, 1990), p. 105.
Source: International Monetary Fund, *International Financial Statistics Yearbook 1993* (Washington, DC: IMF, 1993), pp. 282–83. Column (3) calculated by the authors. ✦

An advantage cited for managed floating is that the country is not locked into some prearranged course of action by formal rules and announcements. This greater freedom to tailor policy to existing circumstances is thought to be superior to sticking to a set of rules devised in some prior period that is no longer relevant. In addition, in contrast to a fixed-rate system, the exchange rate under managed floating is allowed to play some role in external sector adjustment. Further, internal policy is not constrained to the extent that it is under a fixed-rate system. In comparison with a purely flexible-rate system, the country is able to moderate wide swings in the exchange rate that can have adverse price level risk and resource movement implications. Speculation is also more difficult since speculators do not know the timing of the intervention, the potential size of the intervention, or even necessarily the direction of the intervention.

Working against the concept of managed floating is the possibility that, without a set of rules and guidelines for each country, various nations may be working at cross-purposes. For example, Japan may want to moderate a rise in the value of the yen in terms of dollars at the same time that the United States wants to drive the dollar down in terms of the yen. A form of economic warfare can then ensue. In addition, because exchange rates can vary substantially with a managed float, there is still a possibility that traders may be wary of full participation in international trade because of the risks of exchange rate variation.

There is a danger of abuse to the free market allocation of resources according to comparative advantage if countries use intervention to engage in what is called **exchange rate protection.** A contrived comparative advantage can be gained from such protection, and world resources may not be used in their most efficient manner. For example, many observers thought that Japan was intervening in the early 1980s to keep the value of the yen down in exchange markets. The advantage to Japan of this undervaluation of the yen would be that Japan's enhanced exports and depressed imports would provide a boost to Japanese GNP. When countries tend to manipulate their managed floats in this fashion in order to pursue particular goals at the expense of other countries, the behavior is referred to as **dirty floating.**

Finally, some economists have questioned the ability of a single country to meaningfully influence its exchange rate in any event. (See Taylor 1995, pp. 34–37.) The size of any country's foreign exchange reserves is very small relative to the size of total foreign exchange market activity. The ability to convince foreign exchange market participants that the government is both willing and able to influence the exchange rate is critical for successful intervention.

CONCEPT CHECK

1. What alleged disadvantages of a fixed-rate system are still present in the proposal for wider bands around parity?

2. Why is destabilizing speculation considered conceptually rather unlikely in a crawling peg system?

SUMMARY

This chapter has surveyed issues in the debate over fixed versus flexible exchange rates. Those who prefer fixed rates to flexible rates stress the monetary discipline provided by the fixed-rate system and the conducive environment supplied for growth in international trade and investment—features alleged to be absent in a flexible-rate system. In addition, flexible rates are thought to generate various resource allocation inefficiencies and destabilizing speculation. Flexible rates may also aggravate the impacts of internal shocks on the economy. On the other hand, proponents of flexible rates point to the constraint on the attainment of internal goals inherent in a fixed-rate system, to the beneficial role of a free market in foreign exchange, and to the enhanced effectiveness of monetary policy for influencing

national income. Further, countries with flexible exchange rates are thought to be insulated from external shocks.

We examined compromise or hybrid systems, specifically the proposal for wider bands of permissible exchange rate variations, the crawling peg, and managed floating. These proposals satisfy to some extent the proponents of both fixed and flexible rates, but they also dissatisfy both sides in the debate because of other implications.

Given this background to exchange rate arrangements, we turn in the next chapter to a discussion of exchange rate arrangements and developments in the international monetary system since the end of World War II. In addition, proposals for "reform" of the system will be examined.

KEY TERMS

coordinated intervention
crawling peg
destabilizing speculation
dirty floating
exchange rate protection

"leaning against the wind"
"leaning with the wind"
managed floating
optimal size of international
    reserves
optimum currency area

precautionary demand for
    international reserves
stabilizing speculation
transactions demand for
    international reserves
vicious circle hypothesis
wider bands

QUESTIONS AND PROBLEMS

1. Why does the presence of different country preferences on possible inflation-unemployment trade-offs pose a problem for a system of fixed exchange rates?

2. What case can be made that flexible exchange rates reduce the flow of long-term foreign direct investment? What case can be made that flexible rates might actually lead to *more* foreign direct investment?

3. In what way might the relative susceptibility of a country to external shocks rather than internal shocks condition the choice between a fixed or flexible exchange rate for that country? Explain.

4. "If you believe that free markets maximize welfare, then you should also believe that a free exchange rate is an integral part of welfare maximization." Discuss.

5. Must the adoption of a flexible exchange rate mean that the rate will actually vary considerably over time? Why or why not?

6. Much discussion concerning floating rates stresses the risks to trade and investment involved with such a system. Is risk necessarily a bad thing? Why or why not?

7. Under what conditions would the world as a whole be an optimum currency area? Do you think that the industrialized countries should be one optimum currency area and the developing countries another? Explain.

8. "The 'hybrid' systems combining fixed and flexible exchange rates are merely ways of avoiding having to make a choice between a fixed rate and a flexible rate. These systems invariably involve the 'worst of both worlds.'" Discuss.

9. In the early 1990s, the foreign exchange reserves of Chile increased dramatically as foreign investment flows into the country increased substantially because of the favorable investment climate and impressive economic growth. At the same time, Chile began intervening in foreign exchange markets to stabilize the exchange value of its peso. How might these two events be related to each other?

10. Explain Mundell's distinction between a "true" currency area and a "pseudo" currency area. Why is this distinction important?

THE INTERNATIONAL MONETARY SYSTEM

Past, Present, and Future

INTRODUCTION

For countries to participate effectively in the exchange of goods, services, and assets, an international monetary system is needed to facilitate economic transactions. If the ability to import goods is limited because of a scarcity of foreign exchange reserves, for example, then countries will be tempted to impose tariffs, quotas, and other trade-restricting devices to conserve on their foreign exchange. In addition, controls on the outward movement of private funds from a reserve-scarce country may be imposed, or limitations on the ability of the country's citizens to travel overseas may be instituted.

To be effective in facilitating movement in goods, services, and assets, a monetary system most importantly requires an efficient **balance-of-payments adjustment mechanism** so that deficits and surpluses are not prolonged but are eliminated with relative ease in a reasonably short time period. Further, unless the system is characterized by completely flexible exchange rates, *(a)* there must be an adequate supply of **international liquidity,** that is, the system must provide adequate reserves so that payment can be made by BOP deficit countries to surplus countries, and *(b)* the supply of international liquidity must consist of **internationally acceptable reserve assets** that are expected to maintain their values.

Historically, international monetary systems have contained widely differing characteristics. Among those characteristics have been differences in the degree of exchange rate flexibility. About a hundred years ago, the prevailing international monetary system was the international gold standard (1880–1914). In this system (see the chapter "Price Adjustments and Balance-of-Payments Disequilibrium"), gold constituted the international reserve asset and gold's value was fixed by the declared par values that countries specified. This willingness to back currencies with an internationally acceptable reserve asset (gold) helped contribute to relatively free trade and payments. At the same time, balance-of-payments adjustment has been judged to have been relatively smooth during the 1880–1914 period. Little gold actually appears to have flowed from one country to another because central banks were willing to alter interest rates (raise them in the case of a deficit country, lower them in the case of a surplus country) in response to the external payments position. These changes in money market conditions meant that adjustments to balance-of-payments positions were greatly facilitated by the international flows of short-term capital. (For elaboration, see Bloomfield 1959, 1963, and Triffin 1964.)

The international gold standard broke down with the advent of World War I. In the 1920s, countries permitted a great deal of exchange rate flexibility, and there has been

✖ CASE STUDY 1   FLEXIBLE EXCHANGE RATES IN POST-WORLD WAR I EUROPE: THE UNITED KINGDOM, FRANCE, AND NORWAY

One strong argument against a flexible exchange rate system is that it results in considerable instability of the exchange rate and the rate consequently deviates significantly from the equilibrium rate as measured, for example, by purchasing power parity (PPP). In an interesting study in the late 1950s, S. C. Tsiang (1959) examined the flexible exchange rate experience of the United Kingdom, France, and Norway during the period following World War I. All three countries moved to flexible rates in 1919 and were floating their currencies through the mid- to late 1920s. The movements of each

country's dollar exchange rate, the relative PPP rate, and wholesale price levels are indicated in Figure 1.

All three graphs indicate that there was considerable volatility of the exchange rates during the initial phase of the system from 1919 to 1921. This, however, is not surprising, given the turbulent nature of the immediate postwar years, during which there were periods of scarcity, inflation, and recession. However, with the return of relative world stability in 1921, the floating exchange rates of the three countries appear to have followed PPP exchange rates very closely. What is critical here is not

FIGURE 1   **Wholesale Prices, Exchange Rate Movements, and PPP in the United Kingdom, France, and Norway in the 1920s**

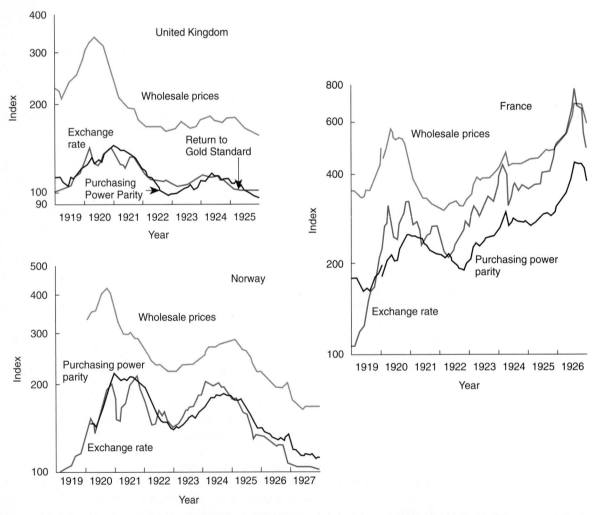

Source: S. C. Tsiang, "Fluctuating Exchange Rates in Countries with Relatively Stable Economies," *International Monetary Fund Staff Papers* 7, no. 2 (October 1959), pp. 250, 257, 260. Note that a logarithmic scale is used on each vertical axis.

that there was divergence between actual exchange rates and PPP rates but that the degree of divergence did not become increasingly large or sporadic.

The intriguing feature of this period is that the spot rates tended to move in a correlated fashion with PPP rates in all three countries even though monetary policy and domestic price experiences were different. The United Kingdom deliberately undertook contractionary monetary policy to reduce relative prices and increase the value of its currency, whereas Norway initially adopted a more expansionary policy, which increased relative prices, and then moved to a contractionary period with falling prices. France, on the other hand, chose a relatively easy money policy with greater increases in prices through the mid-1920s.

Tsiang's research suggests that the policy-induced inflationary environment in France not only contributed to greater divergences between the spot and PPP rates compared to those in the United Kingdom and Norway but also increased the speculative pressures on the exchange rate, adding increasingly to its volatility. However, there is no evidence that the franc fell into a vicious cycle of appreciation and depreciation inhibiting economic activity and seriously affecting France's foreign exchange reserves. The results in general suggest that foreign exchange instability in this period seems to have resulted from external factors and domestic policy actions, not the inherent instability of flexible rates. Such a conclusion is not inconsistent with experiences in the 1970s and 1980s, when external factors such as the oil-price shocks and the uncoordinated nature of monetary and fiscal policy in the world certainly contributed to the instability of the dollar.   ※

controversy over the extent to which this international monetary system was, in fact, efficient. Nevertheless, the extensive fluctuations in exchange rates did maintain a reasonably close relationship with purchasing power parity predictions (see Case Study 1). In the middle of the decade, however, Britain (then the financial center of the world) attempted to restore the gold standard, adopting the old prewar par value of the pound. That par value greatly overvalued the pound and caused payments difficulties for Britain. With the tremendous decline in economic activity in the 1930s, payments difficulties emerged for many countries. Extensive attempts to restore some fixity in countries' exchange rates soon gave way to a series of competitive depreciations of currencies. Although single-country depreciation alone can stimulate employment and output in that country, when many countries depreciate their currencies in retaliatory fashion, the expected beneficial results are short-lived or do not occur at all. Restrictive trade policies such as the infamous Tariff Act of 1930 (Smoot-Hawley) in the United States had also been instituted. These various actions led to great reductions in the volume and value of international trade. The measures also most likely worsened the Great Depression, and the low level of economic activity continued throughout most of the 1930s. Economic activity spurted upward with the advent of World War II, but involvement in the war prevented comprehensive consideration and adoption of a new system of international payments.

In this chapter, we begin at the end of World War II and describe the international monetary system set up at that time. We then discuss changes that occurred, and examine the current system and issues concerning the type of system needed for the future world economy. Particular attention at the end of the chapter is given to problems pertaining to the developing countries. With the material of this chapter in hand, you will be in a better position to evaluate policy issues pertaining to international monetary affairs.

THE BRETTON WOODS SYSTEM

As World War II was drawing to a close, the historic United Nations Monetary and Financial Conference was held in Bretton Woods, New Hampshire, in 1944. From this conference emerged two international institutions that are still extremely prominent in the world economy—the International Monetary Fund and the International Bank for

Reconstruction and Development (IBRD), now commonly known as the World Bank. The initial focus of the World Bank was to provide long-term loans for the rebuilding of Europe from the devastation of World War II, but since the 1950s it has been concerned with providing long-term loans for projects and programs in developing countries. This institution is more properly considered in courses on economic development, so we focus on the IMF in our discussion below.

The Goals of the IMF   The **International Monetary Fund (IMF)** was the key institution in the functioning of the post-World War II international monetary system known as the **Bretton Woods system.** In this context, the IMF had several objectives.

In broad terms one important goal of the IMF was to *seek stability in exchange rates.* When the institution was first set up and for three decades thereafter, the IMF charter called for a system of **pegged but adjustable exchange rates.** As the "linchpin" of the Bretton Woods system, the dollar was defined by the United States as having a value of $1/35$ of an ounce of gold. Other countries then defined their currency values in terms of the dollar. Thus, parity values were established by agreement, but variations of 1 percent above and below parity were permitted. These limits were to be maintained by central banks, which would buy dollars if the price of the dollar fell to the -1 percent floor or would sell dollars if the price of the dollar rose to the $+1$ percent ceiling. The word *adjustable* in the phrase "pegged but adjustable" refers to the fact that, if a country experienced prolonged BOP deficits or surpluses at the pegged exchange rate, an IMF-approved devaluation or upward revaluation of the currency's parity value could be undertaken. In fact, as the IMF evolved, there were few changes in parity values. The desire for stable and relatively fixed rates was a reaction to the wide fluctuations, the competitive depreciations, the shrinkage in trade, and the instability of the world economy in the interwar period of the 1920s and 1930s.

Another objective of the IMF was (and continues to be) the *reconciliation of country adjustments to payments imbalances with national autonomy in macroeconomic policy.* As you may remember, the conceptual gold standard adjustment mechanism involved, for deficit countries, a fall in wages and prices as gold flowed out. This mechanism, or the alternative mechanism of an increase in interest rates to attract foreign short-term capital, posed the difficulty that the resulting contraction of economic activity could cause a rise in unemployment and a fall in real income. In contrast, a surplus country experienced upward pressure on its wages and prices, downward adjustments in its interest rates, and the resulting threat of inflation. But, if the rules of the game were being followed, internal objectives were to be sacrificed to the objective of attaining balance-of-payments equilibrium. After the Great Depression of the 1930s, governments were unwilling to use their monetary and fiscal policy instruments solely for external balance. Conflicts arose between the external target and the internal targets of macroeconomic policy. The IMF sought to reduce this conflict.

Attempts were made to alleviate the conflict through the use of loans by the IMF to deficit countries. The rationale behind these short-term loans (three to five years) was that a country's BOP deficit might be temporary because of the stage of the business cycle in which the country was located. If a loan could provide finance to the borrower until the payments imbalance reversed itself, then there would be no need for alteration of the deficit nation's macro policies in the direction of sacrificing internal goals. In addition, an IMF loan might reduce the likelihood that the deficit country would impose tariffs and other restrictive instruments on imports in order to conserve its foreign exchange reserves. Along the same line, fewer exchange controls on capital movements might be introduced. Hence, the availability of IMF loans not only could serve the purpose of giving more autonomy to domestic macro policy instruments but also contributed to a third objective of the IMF: *to help preserve relatively free trade and payments in the world economy.*

What were the sources of the funds for the BOP loans? When a country joins the IMF (there are now 181 IMF member nations), it is assigned an **IMF quota.** This country quota is a sum of money to be paid to the IMF based on such factors as the national income of the country and the size of its foreign trade sector. Thus, for example, Kenya has a quota of $272.3 million, while the United States has a quota of $36.2 billion. (See Table 1 for the size of current IMF quotas for selected countries.) Under the original rules of the IMF, each country's quota was to be paid 25 percent in gold and 75 percent in the country's own currency.[1] When all countries subscribed their quotas, the IMF became a holder of gold and of a pool of member country currencies.

How do these quotas link up with balance-of-payments loans to member countries? Suppose that Kenya has a BOP deficit and that it needs, because of a foreign exchange shortage, to obtain German marks to pay for some of its imports. Kenya can "borrow" or "draw" marks from the IMF since the IMF has a quantity of marks on hand from the German quota. According to IMF rules, a country can potentially obtain loans of up to 125 percent of its quota. This figure of 125 percent is divided into five segments (or *tranches,* as they are officially called), with the first 25 percent called the **gold tranche** or **reserve tranche,** the next 25 percent called the first **credit tranche,** the next 25 percent the second credit tranche, and so on. The application for the first 25 percent is automatically approved by the IMF, but, as a country gets further and further into the credit tranches, the IMF will attach increasingly stringent conditions before approving the additional loans. These conditions are designed to ensure that the borrowing country is taking action to reduce its BOP deficit. For example, the IMF may prescribe that the country adopt certain monetary and fiscal policies or may even recommend a change in the value of the borrowing country's currency. These potential interferences by an international agency with the national policies of members have generated considerable ill will, since they are regarded by would-be borrowers as intrusions upon national sovereignty. Incidentally, the IMF levies a small service charge on these BOP loans; there is no interest charge on reserve tranche loans, but interest is assessed on credit tranche loans.

The Bretton Woods System in Retrospect

Most economists judge the Bretton Woods system to have performed well from its implementation at the end of World War II until the mid-1960s. World trade grew relatively rapidly during this period, and the major European countries removed most of their postwar exchange restrictions. In addition, Europe and Japan recovered from the World War II devastation, and growth in the world economy occurred with no major setbacks or recessions.

Despite this seeming success, some important problems emerged in the Bretton Woods system. Economists see these problems as falling broadly into three principal areas, and these areas correspond to the important functions of an international monetary system with which we began this chapter.[2]

The Bretton Woods international monetary system was thought to be facing an **adequacy of reserves problem** or **liquidity problem.** In general terms, this problem can be stated as follows: When world trade is growing rapidly, it is likely that the size of payments

---

[1]The 25 percent is now paid in internationally acceptable "hard" currencies rather than in gold.

[2]See, for more complete discussion, Fritz Machlup (1964); Machlup and Burton G. Malkiel (1964); Robert Triffin (1960).

TABLE 1   Selected IMF Country Quotas, April 30, 1997

	SDRs (millions)	U.S. Dollars (millions) ($1.36553/SDR)	Percent
All countries	145,318.8	$198,437.2	100.0
Industrial countries	88,425.2	120,747.3	60.8
Australia	2,333.2	3,186.1	1.6
Canada	4,320.3	5,899.5	3.0
France	7,414.6	10,124.9	5.1
Germany	8,241.5	11,254.0	5.7
Italy	4,590.7	6,268.7	3.2
Japan	8,241.5	11,254.0	5.7
Sweden	1,614.0	2,204.0	1.1
United Kingdom	7,414.6	10,124.9	5.1
United States	26,526.8	36,223.1	18.3
Developing countries	56,893.6	77,689.9	39.2
Africa	8,380.8	11,444.2	5.8
Algeria	914.4	1,248.6	0.6
Côte d'Ivoire	238.2	325.3	0.2
Kenya	199.4	272.3	0.1
Nigeria	1,281.6	1,750.1	0.9
South Africa	1,365.4	1,864.5	0.9
Zambia	363.5	496.4	0.3
Asia	13,679.8	18,680.2	9.4
China	3,385.2	4,622.6	2.3
Fiji	51.1	69.8	0.04
India	3,055.5	4,172.4	2.1
Indonesia	1,497.6	2,045.0	1.0
Pakistan	758.2	1,035.3	0.5
Philippines	633.4	864.9	0.4
Singapore	357.6	488.3	0.2
Thailand	573.9	783.7	0.4
Europe	12,074.3	16,487.8	8.3
Bulgaria	464.9	634.8	0.3
Croatia	261.6	357.2	0.2
Kazakstan	247.5	338.0	0.2
Poland	988.5	1,349.8	0.7
Russian Federation	4,313.1	5,889.7	3.0
Turkey	642.0	876.7	0.4
Ukraine	997.3	1,361.8	0.7
Middle East	11,309.4	15,443.3	7.8
Egypt	678.4	926.4	0.5
Iran	1,078.5	1,472.7	0.7
Iraq	504.0	688.2	0.3
Israel	666.2	909.7	0.5
Kuwait	995.2	1,359.0	0.7
Saudi Arabia	5,130.6	7,006.0	3.5
Western hemisphere	11,449.3	15,634.4	7.9
Argentina	1,537.1	2,099.0	1.1
Brazil	2,170.8	2,964.3	1.5
Chile	621.7	849.0	0.4
Colombia	561.3	766.5	0.4
Dominica	6.0	8.2	0.004
Mexico	1,753.3	2,394.2	1.2
Peru	466.1	636.5	0.3
Venezuela	1,951.3	2,664.6	1.3

Note: SDRs (special drawing rights) are an international reserve asset introduced in 1970 and discussed later in this chapter, and the IMF uses the SDR as its unit of account.

Source: International Monetary Fund, *International Financial Statistics,* June 1997, pp. 4, 10–12.

imbalances will grow in absolute terms. Hence, there is an increased need for reserves to finance BOP deficits. The framers of the Bretton Woods agreement envisioned that gold would be the primary international reserve asset, but the supply of gold in the world economy was growing at a rate of only 1 to 1.5 percent per year while trade in the 1960s was growing at a rate of close to 7 percent per year. Hence, the fear was that reserves in the form of gold were not increasing rapidly enough to deal with larger BOP deficits. If reserves do not grow roughly apace with BOP deficits, the danger exists that countries will use trade and payments restrictions to reduce their deficits, and these policies could reduce the gains from trade and the rate of world economic growth.

The second problem, the **confidence problem,** is related to the liquidity problem. Because the supply of gold held by central banks was growing relatively slowly, the growing international reserves consisted mostly of national currencies that were internationally acceptable and were thus being held by the central banks. The two national currencies held in largest volume were the U.S. dollar and the British pound. But, particularly with the dollar, this fact posed a danger to central banks. The dollar was the linchpin of the system because of the gold guarantee that the United States stood ready to buy and sell gold at $35 per ounce. However, the dollars held by non-U.S. central banks began to exceed by a substantial margin the size of the U.S. official gold stock. This gold stock itself was also being depleted by U.S. BOP deficits. If all foreign central banks attempted to convert their dollars into gold, the United States did not have enough gold to meet all demands. In addition, there were even larger amounts of dollar deposits located outside the United States in foreign private hands (Eurodollar deposits). These dollars could also be a claim on the U.S. gold stock. There was thus a loss of confidence in the dollar, that is, loss of confidence in what had become the principal reserve asset of the monetary system. Further, if the United States attempted to increase its ability to meet the conversion of dollars into gold by devaluing the dollar relative to gold (for example, by changing the price from $35 to $70 per ounce), then central banks that held dollars would suffer a reduction in the value of their reserves in terms of gold. Such a devaluation would surely have started a massive "run" on gold and would have brought the Bretton Woods system to a quick termination.

The third perceived problem of the Bretton Woods system was the **adjustment problem.** This refers to the fact that in the actual operation of the Bretton Woods system, individual countries had prolonged BOP deficits or surpluses. This was particularly true for the United States (deficits) and West Germany (surpluses). There did not seem to be an effective adjustment mechanism, since automatic forces were not removing the imbalances. Countries directed monetary and fiscal policies toward internal targets rather than external targets, and thus the contraction (expansion) in the money supply expected of a deficit (surplus) country did not occur (that is, sterilization was taking place). This was especially true with respect to the U.S. BOP deficit because of U.S. concern about slow economic growth and high unemployment. (In fact, the United States could sterilize without worrying excessively about a loss of reserves, since its own currency was being used as reserves.) In a similar vein, Germany's concern about inflation prevented it from adjusting to a BOP surplus by expanding its money supply.

GRADUAL EVOLUTION OF A NEW INTERNATIONAL MONETARY SYSTEM

Any attempt to recount the events associated with the gradual disintegration of the Bretton Woods system is bound to be arbitrary in its selection of events. With this caveat in mind, we summarize below the developments we regard as significant for the evolution of the current international monetary system.

Early Disruptions

In 1967, the British pound was officially devalued from its parity exchange rate of $2.80/£1 to $2.40/£1 (a 14 percent devaluation). This devaluation was a consequence of declining U.K. foreign exchange reserves in large part due to speculative short-term capital flows. The devaluation was significant because the pound and the dollar were **key currencies,** that is, the two national currencies most prominently held by central banks as official international reserves. The fact that the value of an international reserve asset had been changed suggested that the exchange rate pegs of Bretton Woods might not be sustainable.

A second important event was the decision by major central banks in 1968 that they would no longer engage in gold transactions with private individuals and firms. This decision meant that, henceforth, the central banks would no longer buy and sell gold in the private market but would continue to do so with each other. Transactions in gold between central banks would be made at the official gold price of $35 per ounce, but private individuals would buy and sell among themselves at whatever price cleared the private market (which at one time thereafter exceeded $800 per ounce). This new structure for gold was called the "two-tier gold market."

Some background is necessary in order to understand the significance of this event. Prior to 1968, since central banks had been willing to buy and sell gold with private individuals (although the U.S. government had not been willing to do so with its own citizens), there was only one price for gold. Central banks bought and sold at the $35 price, and, if the price in private markets tended to rise above (fall below) $35, dissatisfied buyers (sellers) could obtain (sell) gold from (to) the central banks at the $35 price. However, because of the uncertainties associated with the confidence problem in the 1960s, private speculators anticipated that the dollar might be devalued in terms of gold. They therefore were eager to buy gold at $35 per ounce for resale later at the expected higher price. This private demand for gold put upward pressure on its price, pressure which could be relieved only by sales of gold by central banks, reducing official reserves. To stem this outflow of gold to private buyers, the two-tier market was instituted.

The refusal of central banks to deal in gold with private individuals and firms was judged to be important symbolically because it represented a first step toward reducing the relative importance of gold in the international monetary system. Because the central banks were no longer dealing in gold with private citizens, gold holdings were frozen in size in the central banks' overall international reserve portfolios. As international reserves later grew through accumulation of more dollars in particular, gold constituted a declining fraction of total reserves.

Special Drawing Rights (SDRs)

A major development in the international monetary system occurred in 1970 when a new international asset appeared. This development was the introduction of **special drawing rights (SDRs)** by the IMF.[3] Unlike gold and other international reserve assets, the SDR is a paper asset (sometimes called "paper gold") created "out of thin air" by the IMF. On January 1, 1970, the IMF simply entered on the books of all participating members a total of $3.5 billion worth of SDRs. The SDR itself was defined as equal in value to $\frac{1}{35}$ of an ounce of gold and thus as equal in value to one U.S. dollar. The total of $3.5 billion was divided among member countries in proportion to the share of total IMF quotas of each member country. Additional SDRs have been created on several occasions since 1970.

The SDRs that a member country receives in an allocation add to international reserves and can be used to settle a BOP deficit in a fashion similar to any other type of international reserve asset. For example, if India needs to obtain Japanese yen to finance

---

[3]For extensive discussion of the SDR concept and agreement, see Machlup (1968).

a deficit, it can do so by swapping SDRs for yen held by some other country (e.g., France) that the IMF designates. Thus, the SDR could help to alleviate the liquidity problem discussed earlier. Further, since the SDR is not a national currency, and since it might eventually replace national currencies like the dollar in reserve portfolios, the new instrument could potentially alleviate the confidence problem.

In the India example above, where SDRs were exchanged for yen, a skeptic might question why France would be willing to part with some of its yen in exchange for a bookkeeping-entry paper asset. This question goes to the heart of a more basic question: "Why do some assets serve as money, while others do not?" The answer to this more basic question is that an asset serves as money if it is *generally acceptable in exchange;* one party to a transaction will accept the asset if that party knows that it too can use the asset to acquire other assets. SDRs have become "international money" because the recipient of the SDRs knows that it can use them to acquire other currencies from other countries later. Further, in the SDR scheme, each participant agreed to stand ready to accept SDRs to the extent of twice its accumulated SDR allocations.

Another feature of SDRs is that if a country is a net recipient of SDRs, meaning that it holds more than it has been allocated by the IMF, it receives interest on its excess holdings. Similarly, if a country holds less than its allocation of SDRs, that country pays interest on its shortfall. These rules help to encourage caution in the use of SDRs.

A final aspect of the SDR concerns its valuation. In the initial allocation of this new asset, the SDR equaled one U.S. dollar. With the later devaluations of the dollar (discussed below) and the advent of greater flexibility in exchange rates during the 1970s, the equality of the SDR and the dollar was discarded. The SDR is now valued as a weighted average of the values of five currencies: 39 percent for the U.S. dollar; 21 percent for the German mark; 18 percent for the Japanese yen; and 11 percent each for the British pound and the French franc. These weights are in effect until December 31, 2000.[4] By the end of April 1997, accumulated SDR holdings of central banks were 18.7 billion. With the SDR equal to $1.36553 at that time, the value of central bank holdings of SDRs when expressed in dollars was $25.5 billion.[5]

The Breaking of the Gold-Dollar Link and the Smithsonian Agreement

Chronologically, the next event of major significance occurred on August 15, 1971. At that time, because of continuing U.S. BOP deficits, escalating inflation, and lagging economic growth, the Nixon administration undertook several drastic steps. Most importantly, *the United States announced that it would no longer buy and sell gold with foreign central banks.* This action amounted to an abandonment of the Bretton Woods system, since the willingness of the United States to buy and sell gold at $35 per ounce had been the "linchpin" of that system. In addition, the administration temporarily froze wages and prices (to help in the anti-inflation effort), imposed a temporary 10 percent tariff surcharge on all imports (to help in reducing the BOP deficit), and instituted a tax credit for new productive investment (to stimulate economic growth), among other actions. From the standpoint of the exchange rate system, the cessation of the willingness to buy and sell gold was the key policy change because it altered the nature of the existing system. Without the "gold guarantee," there was no anchor to the value of the dollar. Foreign central banks were faced with the decision of whether or not to continue buying and selling dollars at the previously established parity values.

After this action, there was considerable turbulence in the international monetary system. To stem the speculation and uncertainty, the chief monetary officials of the

[4]*IMF Survey,* Apr. 1, 1996, p. 107.

[5]International Monetary Fund, *International Financial Statistics,* June 1997, pp. 4, 26.

leading industrial nations convened in Washington at the Smithsonian Institution in December 1971 to work out a new set of exchange rate arrangements. This meeting led to the **Smithsonian Agreement,** which established a new set of par values (called "central rates"). The deutsche mark and the Japanese yen were revalued upward by 13 percent and 17 percent, respectively. In addition, countries agreed to permit variations of 2.25 percent on either side of the central rates, thus introducing greater exchange rate flexibility than had been allowed under the ±1 percent variations of the Bretton Woods arrangements. Further, the United States changed the official price of gold from $35 to $38 per ounce. This devaluation of the dollar against gold was important symbolically rather than practically, since the United States was no longer buying and selling gold. The symbolism was that the United States, by devaluing its currency, was politically admitting that it was at least partly responsible for the troubles of the international monetary system (through the continual U.S. BOP deficits). The Smithsonian Agreement generated optimism for the future among participating governments, and President Nixon called it "the most significant monetary agreement in the history of the world" (quoted in Ellsworth and Leith 1984, pp. 508–9).

This judgment regarding the Smithsonian Agreement was premature, as continued speculation against the dollar resulted in further changes. Britain began floating the pound in June 1972. Early in 1972, the six countries of the European Community also began a joint float of their currencies, which meant that these countries (Belgium, France, Italy, Luxembourg, the Netherlands, West Germany) kept their own currencies tied closely together (±2.25 percent from specified values) but the currencies could vary by larger amounts against other currencies (although the 2.25 percent variation was also maintained against the dollar). In February 1973, the U.S. dollar was again devalued against gold (to $42.22 per ounce). Other currencies began floating either freely or in controlled fashion in 1973.

The Jamaica Accords   The next significant development occurred with the **Jamaica Accords** of January 1976. After consultation with officials of leading countries, the IMF made a series of changes that were incorporated into the IMF's Articles of Agreement.[6] The most important of these changes were the following:

1. Each member country was free to adopt its own preferred exchange rate arrangements. Thus, for example, a country might tie its currency's value to some particular currency, or it might let its currency float freely against all currencies, or it might peg its currency's value to some "basket" of currencies of countries with which it was most heavily involved in trade.

2. The role of gold was downgraded in the international monetary system. To this end, the official price of gold was eventually abolished and the IMF itself sold one-third of its gold holdings. Some of the proceeds were used to benefit developing countries.

3. The role of the SDR was to be enhanced. It was anticipated that SDRs would become very important in the reserve asset portfolios of central banks, although this objective has not been achieved.

4. The IMF was to maintain **surveillance** of exchange rate behavior. In general terms, this meant that the IMF intended that its members would seek to "avoid manipulating exchange rates . . . to prevent effective balance of payments adjustment" and would foster "orderly economic and financial conditions and a monetary system that does not tend to

[6]The changes officially went into effect on April 1, 1978. See *IMF Survey,* Apr. 3, 1978, pp. 97–107.

produce erratic disruptions."[7] These broad objectives essentially mean that the IMF advises its members, through regular consultations, on their exchange rate actions so that the international monetary system does not become subject to considerable uncertainty and instability.

The European Monetary System

A truly significant development in international monetary arrangements began in March 1979 with the inauguration of the **European Monetary System (EMS).**[8] This system was an outgrowth of the joint float (sometimes called the "European Snake" because of the wavelike movements of the six currencies as a unit against other currencies) that had begun in 1972. The first key feature of the EMS of the European Community members was the creation of a new monetary unit, the **European Currency Unit** or **ecu,** in terms of which central rates for the countries' currencies were defined. The value of the ecu was a weighted average of EMS member currencies and the ecu was used as the unit of account for recording transactions among EMS central banks.

A second key feature of the original EMS was that each currency was generally to be kept within 2.25 percent of the central rates against the other participating currencies, and a mechanism was put in place requiring central bank action as exchange rates approached the limits of divergence permitted from the central rates. There were also provisions for periodic realignments of the central rates. Third, the EMS participating currencies were to move as a unit in floating fashion against other currencies, including the U.S. dollar. This set of exchange rate rules is known as the **Exchange Rate Mechanism (ERM)** of the EMS. Finally, the **European Monetary Cooperation Fund (EMCF),** a "banker's bank" similar to the IMF, was established for receiving deposits of reserves from the EMS members and making loans to members with BOP difficulties.

The European Monetary System was conceived as a means of promoting greater exchange rate stability within Europe and, because of this stability and certainty, for generating more stable and soundly based economic growth. Since greater stability in exchange rates requires some degree of harmonization in macroeconomic policies, the EMS also promoted convergence of policies and inflation rates.

The Maastricht Treaty

In December 1991, the members of the European Community extended the EMS and took a dramatic step toward future monetary union. The **Maastricht Treaty** laid out a plan for the establishment of a common currency and a European central bank by, at the latest, January 1, 1999. Along with the implementation of various other changes to bring about closer trade and capital market integration, the participating European countries would have at that time a full **Economic and Monetary Union (EMU).** The transition to EMU was to take place in stages.[9] In stage 1, countries not yet participating in the ERM would begin to do so. Members of the EC were also to take steps toward convergence in their economic performance, as measured by inflation differentials, exchange rate stability, differences in interest rates, and fiscal deficits and government debt. In stage II (which began on January 1, 1994), the EC was to intensify its examination of whether the various criteria for convergence of economic performance were being met, and countries were expected to remove virtually all remaining restrictions on the flow of capital between them. In addition, the EMCF would be replaced by the European Monetary

---

[7]*IMF Survey,* Apr. 3, 1978, p. 98.

[8]For more complete discussion, see Commission of the European Communities (1986) and *The ECU* (1987).

[9]See *A Single Currency for Europe: Monetary and Real Impacts* (1992, pp. xi, 3).

Institute (EMI), consisting of the national central bank governors and a president, which would strengthen monetary cooperation. Finally, when stage III begins, members will irrevocably fix their exchange rates and form the monetary union with a common currency. The common currency to be used has been designated as the **euro.** The EMI will have been replaced by this time by the **European System of Central Banks (ESCB),** a Community-wide institution that will consist of the national central banks themselves working with a multinational component known as the *European Central Bank (ECB)*. The ESCB will be the *supranational monetary authority*—it will have control over monetary policy and exchange rate policy for the entire European Community.[10]

The ultimate establishment of EMU rests on the attainment of the convergence of the EC members' economic performance and policies. Why is this so? As we have noted earlier in this book, countries have difficulty in maintaining a system of fixed exchange rates if macroeconomic policies differ. For example, a country that seeks to stimulate its economy through low interest rates incurs reserve losses to another country that seeks to halt inflation through high interest rates, due to the short-term capital outflows from the first country to the second. Hence, there will be pressure for the country with the low interest rates to devalue its currency. To avoid such exchange rate pressures because of differing macro policies or performance among EC members, the Maastricht Treaty stipulated for stage I and stage II, as indicated above, some specific **convergence criteria.** In order to be permitted to join the EMU, (1) a country's inflation rate of consumer prices cannot be greater than 1.5 percentage points above the average of the three lowest-inflation EC countries; (2) the country's long-term government bond interest rate must not be more than 2 percentage points above that interest rate average in the three lowest-inflation countries; (3) the government budget deficit of the entering country cannot exceed 3 percent of GDP; (4) the ratio of total government debt to GDP of the country must be 60 percent or lower; and (5) for the last two years, the country's currency value must not have been changed within the EMS.[11]

The path to monetary union in Europe was thus charted by the framers of the Maastricht Treaty in some detail. However, actual experience has not been at all similar to what was planned. Concerns about recessions and unemployment in many EC countries because of the influence of high German interest rates, early uncertainties about ratification of the Maastricht Treaty in several countries (e.g., a Denmark referendum on the treaty was first defeated before later passage), and large speculative capital flows led to devaluations of several currencies and to the departure of Britain and Italy from the exchange rate mechanism in September 1992 (Eichengreen 1993, p. 1350). The old exchange rate variations of ±2.25 percent around the central rates were abandoned in August 1993, with ±15 percent now permitted (although Germany and the Netherlands agreed to keep the ±2.25 percent range between their two currencies).[12] Nevertheless, when the highest German court ruled in October 1993 against the charge that Maastricht violated the German constitution, the treaty had cleared all ratification and legal hurdles[13] and it finally came into effect on November 1, 1993. [The name "European Community" was then changed to "European Union" (EU).] Thus, even though no country was yet

[10]"European Leaders Agree to Treaty on Monetary Union," *IMF Survey,* Jan. 6, 1992, pp. 2–3.

[11]Ibid., p. 2; *Economic Report of the President,* January 1993, pp. 297–98. For useful discussion of the criteria, see Eichengreen (1993, pp. 1346–50).

[12]Michael R. Sesit, "EC to Allow Currencies to Fluctuate Widely," *The Wall Street Journal,* Aug. 2, 1993, p. C1.

[13]Mark M. Nelson and Charles Goldsmith, "Maastricht Treaty Doesn't Conflict with German Law, Court Says," *The Wall Street Journal,* Oct. 13, 1993, p. A19.

TABLE 2   **European Union Convergence Indicators (in percent) for 1995, 1996, and 1997 (projected)**

	Consumer Price Inflation			*Government Surplus (+) or Deficit (−)/GDP*			*Gross Government Debt/GDP[b]*			*Long-Term Interest Rates[c]*
	1995	*1996*	*1997*	*1995*	*1996*	*1997[a]*	*1995*	*1996*	*1997*	*March 1997*
Germany	1.8	1.5	1.8	−3.5	−3.8	−3.3	58.1	60.3	61.5	5.8
France	1.8	2.0	1.6	−5.0	−4.1	−3.3	52.9	56.3	57.8	5.7
Italy	5.4	3.9	2.4	−7.1	−6.8	−3.3	124.9	123.0	121.5	7.6
United Kingdom[d]	2.8	2.9	2.6	−5.6	−4.4	−3.1	47.3	49.3	49.4	7.5
Spain	4.7	3.5	2.5	−6.6	−4.4	−3.2	65.3	69.5	69.0	7.1
Netherlands	2.0	2.1	2.7	−4.0	−2.3	−2.2	79.7	78.8	76.1	5.7
Belgium	1.5	2.1	2.0	−4.1	−3.4	−2.9	133.5	130.0	127.1	5.9
Sweden	2.5	0.5	2.3	−7.9	−2.5	−0.8	78.2	78.6	76.6	7.1
Austria	2.2	1.9	1.9	−5.3	−3.9	−2.5	69.3	69.8	68.1	5.7
Denmark[e]	2.1	2.1	2.5	−1.9	−1.6	−0.1	72.2	69.9	67.3	6.5
Finland	1.0	0.6	1.3	−5.2	−2.6	−1.9	58.5	58.0	58.7	6.1
Greece[f]	9.3	8.5	6.9	−9.2	−7.6	−5.1	111.8	110.7	107.7	10.3
Portugal	4.1	3.1	2.5	−4.9	−4.0	−2.9	71.7	70.8	69.2	6.9
Ireland	2.5	1.6	2.2	−2.4	−1.0	−1.6	84.8	76.4	72.3	6.3
Luxembourg	1.9	1.8	2.0	+0.4	−0.1	−0.1	5.4	5.9	5.7	6.1
All EU[g]	3.0	2.5	2.2	−5.2	−4.4	−3.1	72.1	73.2	73.0	6.6
Reference value[h]	**2.9**	**2.4**	**3.1**	**−3.0**	**−3.0**	**−3.0**	**60.0**	**60.0**	**60.0**	**7.9**

[a]Based on information available up to the end of March 1997.

[b]Debt data refer to end of year. They relate to general government but may not be consistent with the definition agreed on at Maastricht.

[c]Ten-year government bond yield or nearest maturity.

[d]Retail price index excluding mortgage interest.

[e]Government deposits with the central bank, government holdings of nongovernment bonds, and government debt related to public enterprises amounted to some 20 percent of GDP in 1995.

[f]Long-term interest rate is 12-month Treasury-bill rate.

[g]Average weighted by GDP shares, based on the purchasing power parity (PPP) valuation of country GDPs for consumer price index, general government balances, and debt.

[h]The treaty is not specific as to what methodology should be used to calculate reference values for inflation and the interest rate beyond noting that they should be based on the three lowest-inflation countries. For illustrative purposes, a simple average for the three countries is used in calculating the reference values.

Source: International Monetary Fund, *World Economic Outlook, May 1997* (Washington, DC: IMF, 1997), p. 27.

meeting the convergence criteria and though Greece, Italy, and the United Kingdom were not in the ERM, the EU still planned to take this major monetary step.

Controversy regarding monetary union and the timetable set out in the Maastricht Treaty continued in the mid- and late 1990s, and the treaty's latest possible EMU starting date, January 1, 1999, was adopted. In early 1997, the election of a Labour government in Britain and a Socialist election victory in France signified the desire of the British and French public for expansionary policies to reduce unemployment even if the budget deficit and inflation criteria for EMU were thereby violated. This put these countries, particularly France, at odds with Germany, a strong advocate of relative price stability. Even Germany itself was facing difficulty in meeting the criteria, primarily because of its increasing government debt.

Table 2 indicates the 1995, 1996 and projected 1997 standing of EU members with respect to the EMU convergence criteria set out in the Maastricht Treaty. The initial EMU members were scheduled to be selected in early 1998 on the basis of actual 1997 data. The 1997 projections in the table (those available at the time of this writing) are those of the IMF. In these projections, (1) the target or reference value of 3.1 percent price inflation was satisfied by all countries except Greece; (2) the 3 percent ratio of government budget deficit to GDP was projected *not* to be met by Germany, France, Italy, the United Kingdom, Spain, and Greece; (3) the government debt to GDP ratio of 60 percent was projected to be met only by France, the United Kingdom, Finland, and Luxembourg; and (4) the reference value for the long-term interest rate was exceeded only by Greece. Thus, only Finland and Luxembourg were projected to meet these four criteria in 1997. Looking only at the inflation, deficit, and debt criteria, Finland and Luxembourg alone satisfied the requirements in 1996 as well. Finally, the exchange rate criterion is not shown in Table 2, but it has already been modified to the ±15 percent range for the two years prior to 1999 (when it becomes irrevocably fixed) in recognition of the fact that exchange rates have been changing.

The likelihood that most countries would not meet all the formal criteria (in particular the debt criterion) led to serious consideration of stretching the initial terms so that, for example, countries with budget deficits in excess of 3 percent of GDP might still be eligible if the deficit is close to the target and moving in the right direction or is perceived to be only "temporarily" high. Germany would like to maintain a strict interpretation of the rules by imposing sizable fines on members who do not hold to the criteria.[14] The key idea here is that, to avoid ever paying a fine, countries would be required to run budget surpluses during good or normal times in order to leave room for greater borrowing during economic slowdowns. The fine also reduces the probability of public-debt-based expenditures, which could be highly inflationary. However, many fear that such a debt rule (and accompanying fines) would actually work to intensify country recessions.

The Amsterdam Summit (June 18–19, 1997) led to the adoption of a "new Maastricht treaty," which for the most part sidestepped the critical EMU issues.[15] With regard to monetary union, the unemployment-versus-tight-money issues resulted in a resolution that talked vaguely, for example, of strengthening policy coordination between countries and establishing "guidelines to create jobs." In addition, little was said about how currencies would be locked in at the start of 1999. There was concern that if the rate fixing was left until the last minute, there might be considerable exchange rate turbulence brought on by speculators. Finally, many feel that the current (1997) plan to keep national currencies in circulation after exchange rates have been absolutely fixed until the currencies are replaced by the euro in 2002 is untenable because of likely runs toward strong currencies such as the deutsche mark. However, EU planners say this arrangement will work fine because by 2002 the ESCB and its component the ECB will be in total charge of monetary policy and national central banks will not be conducting operations on an independent basis.

So, heading into the final stretch at this time of writing, it appears that European monetary union is still on track, albeit a bit shaky at this point. Given the flexibility being shown by EU officials toward the attainment of convergence criteria, only Greece appears to currently be clearly in doubt of becoming a member when the list is drawn up in 1998

---

[14]The German formula, which was opposed by most other countries, would require countries which failed to keep their budget deficits below 3 percent of GDP to place a deposit with European authorities. Continued excess borrowing might result in a forfeit of those funds. Suggested fines were to be 0.2 percent of GDP plus another 0.1 percent for every percentage point by which the deficit exceeded 3 percent of GDP. A deficit of 6 percent of GDP would result in the maximum fine of 0.5 percent of GDP. Those against this strict interpretation argued that it was never envisaged that EMU members would be under a strict obligation always to stay below the 3 percent deficit ceiling or that violators would be automatically subjected to fines. See "EMU: And What Alice Found There" (1996, p. 23).

[15]For a summary of the results of the Amsterdam Summit, see "Europe: Mountains Still to Climb," *The Economist,* June 21, 1997, pp. 51–52.

TABLE 3   **Public Support for EMU in European Union Countries***

Italy	62%	France	25%
Spain	47	Germany	− 3
Ireland	46	Austria	− 6
Greece	44	Sweden	−23
Luxembourg	43	United Kingdom	−26
Netherlands	43	Finland	−27
Portugal	34	Denmark	−28
Belgium	32		
	15 EU countries	18%	

*Net percentage of population in favor of single currency = percentage in favor minus percentage against.
Source: "Towards EMU: Kicking and Screaming into 1999," *The Economist,* June 7, 1997, p. 21.

(as evidenced by the data in Table 2).[16] As stated in the treaty, early in 1998 the European Commission and the European Monetary Institute will report whether the Maastricht criteria have been met by EU members and the commission will then recommend countries for admission to EMU. Ultimately, heads of governments will make the final decision based on a qualified-majority vote.[17] This will undoubtedly make for interesting European politics.

The eventual success of EMU rests on both political and economic factors. The increased economic integration represented in this arrangement is a major step in uniting the countries of Europe and reducing even further the likelihood of another major conflict or country dominance of the continent. In addition, it will also enhance the European voice in world affairs. It certainly does, however, reduce the economic autonomy of the member countries. What is critical, of course, is public support of EMU. Unfortunately, public approval for the measure has been low, as evidenced in the figures from an October–November 1996 survey presented in *The Economist* and summarized in Table 3.[18] In addition, on the economic side, there remains concern that the gains in economic efficiency and increased investment in the EU will be more than offset by the inability of member country fiscal policy to substitute for the automatic adjustments associated with flexible exchange rates. There is also great concern that the members of the EU do not have sufficiently flexible wages and prices and/or labor mobility both within and between countries to adjust smoothly to changing economic structures and economic shocks.[19] Attaining this increased flexibility will entail reducing national government involvement in the economies in terms of market regulation and excessive borrowing to fund social programs. For monetary union to work well, every country needs to take on an EU perspective regarding inflation, growth, and unemployment, instead of focusing only on its own targets. Many believe that the lack of economic flexibility, particularly in the labor markets, and the lack of an EU perspective will ultimately cause EMU to fail.

---

[16]As evidence of "flexibility," the European Commission agreed to a plan whereby France Télé-com would pay the French government an amount roughly equal to 0.5 percent of GDP to take on its pension liabilities, thus supposedly reducing the French budget deficit in 1997. This action does nothing to improve French public finances, which is the thrust of the criterion on budget deficits. See "EMU: And What Alice Found There" (1996, p. 25).

[17]Ibid.

[18]For an excellent overview of the role of public attitudes on this issue, see Michael R. Sesit, "Europe's Economic Will Is Crucial to EMU Fate," *The Wall Street Journal,* June 16, 1997, p. A1.

[19]By locking their currencies into one, member countries lose the ability to devalue, which is a major shock absorber when a country is faced with inflation, slow growth, productivity growth differences compared to other countries, or external shocks.

Other, more optimistic views see EMU as the means for countries finally to break away from the ills brought on by overregulation and deficit spending by the public sector.[20]

Exchange Rate Variations

We conclude this survey of the evolution of the international monetary system by noting that, in general, exchange rate variations among major currencies have been very large since the breakdown of Bretton Woods. Fluctuations in nominal exchange rates have also been accompanied by large changes in *real* exchange rates (as noted, for example, by Richard Levich 1985 and Ronald McKinnon 1988) because national price levels have not varied as much as nominal exchange rates. Hence, there have been substantial variations in international competitiveness as well as dislocations in the export and import-competing sectors of countries. In addition, the most important variations in relative currency values have occurred with respect to the U.S. dollar, which rose dramatically from 1980 to 1985 and then fell dramatically after 1985 (especially from 1985 to 1987). As a consequence, in September 1985 the Plaza Agreement was reached in New York by central bankers from France, Japan, the United States, the United Kingdom, and West Germany. In this agreement, the five countries stated that the dollar needed to be lowered in value and that their central banks stood ready to intervene to accomplish this objective. The dollar did indeed fall in subsequent months, and the Louvre Accord was then announced in February 1987. In this accord, the G-7 countries declared that the dollar had fallen far enough (40 percent since 1985). The dollar was henceforth to be stabilized in a relatively narrow range (but unspecified as to the exact range) by cooperative central bank action. However, changes in the value of the dollar (as well as in the value of other currencies) have continued into the 1990s. For example, from September 1992 to September 1993, the dollar rose by 14 percent in terms of the German deutsche mark, 18 percent in terms of the British pound, 31 percent in terms of the Spanish peseta, and 50 percent in terms of the Swedish krona. Greater changes occurred against the currencies of some developing countries—for example, a 95 percent rise in terms of the Brazilian cruzeiro reàl. However, while rising against most currencies, the dollar *fell* in terms of the Japanese yen by 12.5 percent. (Indeed, the trade-weighted nominal value of the yen—the effective exchange rate—rose by 25 percent over that period.)[21] Further, in 1994 the dollar fell by over 10 percent against both the deutsche mark and the yen, and in early 1995 it dropped to post-Bretton-Woods lows against those two currencies. To put these changes in perspective, in 1973, at the beginning of the floating-rate period, 2.70 deutsche marks exchanged for one dollar; by March 1995 the figure was 1.38 marks per dollar. For Japan, the exchange rate was 280 yen per dollar in 1973, and it had fallen to 85 yen per dollar by June 1995. However, the dollar rebounded steadily against most currencies in 1996 and gained even faster momentum in early 1997, showing especially strong gains against the mark and the yen. The strengthening of the dollar against the yen took place as a lower Japanese discount rate and increased confidence in the U.S. economy revived Japanese capital flows to the United States. By March 1997, the dollar was over 30 percent above its 1995 average level in terms of yen. At the same time, increasing concern about the economic expansion in Europe (or lack thereof) led to a 20 percent increase in the value of the U.S. dollar relative to the deutsche mark. This recent overall strengthening of the dollar is evident in the strong movement of the dollar's effective exchange rate from November 1996 to April 1997. Although a very slight downward movement occurred in May 1997, the dollar appeared to stabilize in June and to maintain its relatively stronger position among the world's currencies.

[20]For an interesting array of views on the likely success of EMU, see "Whither the EMU," *The Wall Street Journal,* June 20, 1997, p. A18 and "Towards EMU: Kicking and Screaming into 1999," *The Economist,* June 17, 1997, pp. 19–21.

[21]*The Economist,* Oct. 2, 1993, p. 112.

CONCEPT CHECK
1. What were the key elements of the international monetary system devised at Bretton Woods?
2. What led to the breakdown of the Bretton Woods system?
3. What are the convergence criteria for EMU? Why are they necessary?

CURRENT EXCHANGE RATE ARRANGEMENTS

Since the breakdown of the Bretton Woods pegged rate system, and pursuant to the amended IMF Articles of Agreement of 1978, countries have chosen a variety of exchange rate arrangements. There is no longer a uniform system, and the current arrangements are often called a "nonsystem." The IMF classifies the arrangements chosen by its individual members into nine categories, as shown in Table 4. The first five categories involve "pegging" to a particular currency unit or group of currencies (a "basket" of currencies), and these countries are essentially still in a "relatively fixed-rate" category with respect to the particular currencies to which they are tied. The other four categories, which are "relatively flexible," are (1) limited flexibility in terms of a single currency; (2) "cooperative arrangements," which involve the countries participating in the Exchange Rate Mechanism of the European Monetary System; (3) "other managed floating," which indicates the absence of a peg to any currency or currencies but yet some intervention to prevent wide variations in the home currency value; and (4) the "independently floating" category, which includes large industrial countries as well as prominent developing countries.

It is clear that countries have chosen a wide variety of exchange rate arrangements.[22] The particular arrangement any given country chooses is conditioned by a number of factors, and no general rules or guidelines emerge from Table 4. Looking at the absolute number of countries opting for more "fixity" in their exchange rates, the table indicates that many countries have chosen to peg their currencies in some fashion. It should also be noted that there has been a shift of currencies in recent years away from "relatively fixed" categories (categories 1 to 5) to "relatively flexible" categories (categories 6 to 9). In Table 4, 21 currencies are tied to the U.S. dollar and there are 66 countries in total in the "relatively fixed" categories. This is 36 percent of the total 181 IMF members as of March 31, 1997. However, as recently as the end of 1987, 38 currencies had been tied to the dollar and 92 of the total 151 IMF member country currencies at the time were classified as "relative fixed" (61 percent). Even at the end of 1990, 85 currencies of 154 total (55 percent) had this degree of fixity. The category with the most flexible currencies, the "independently floating" category, had only 12 percent of the currencies in 1987 (18 of 151) and 16 percent in 1990 (25 of 154), but the figure in 1997 was 28 percent (51 of 181).

A generalization that emerges concerning present exchange rate arrangements is that large industrialized countries have tended to opt for flexibility in exchange rates while many (but certainly not all) developing countries have tended to choose fixity in their exchange rates. Some reasons for these selections can be gleaned from balance-of-payments theory and from characteristics of the two types of countries.[23]

---

[22]An interesting attempt to classify and interpret various exchange rate choices in the context of "rules versus discretion" and "cooperation versus noncooperation" among countries is "An Exchange-Rate Map," *The Economist,* May 21, 1988, p. 77 (part 1), and May 28, 1988, p. 65 (part 2).

[23]Another attempt to classify choices by country characteristics, with some overlap to this one, is in Robert J. Carbaugh, *International Economics* (Cambridge, MA: Winthrop Publications, 1980), pp. 346–47, 350.

TABLE 4   **Exchange Rate Arrangements as of March 31, 1997**

Category	Countries	Number of Countries
1. Pegged to U.S. dollar	Angola, Antigua and Barbuda, Argentina, the Bahamas, Barbados, Belize, Djibouti, Dominica, Grenada, Iraq, Liberia, Lithuania, Marshall Islands, Federated States of Micronesia, Nigeria, Oman, Panama, St. Kitts and Nevis, St. Lucia, St. Vincent and the Grenadines, Syria	21
2. Pegged to French franc	Benin, Burkina Faso, Cameroon, Central African Republic, Chad, Comoros, Congo, Côte d'Ivoire, Equatorial Guinea, Gabon, Mali, Niger, Senegal, Togo	14
3. Pegged to a single other currency	Bhutan (to the Indian rupee), Bosnia and Herzegovina (to the deutsche mark), Brunei (to the Singapore dollar), Estonia (to the deutsche mark), Kiribati (to the Australian dollar), Lesotho (to the South African rand), Namibia (to the South African rand), San Marino (to the Italian lira), Swaziland (to the South African rand)	9
4. Pegged to the SDR	Libya, Myanmar (Burma)	2
5. Pegged to other composite ("basket")	Bangladesh, Botswana, Burundi, Cape Verde, Cyprus, Czech Republic, Fiji, Iceland, Jordan, Kuwait, Malta, Morocco, Nepal, Seychelles, Slovak Republic, Solomon Islands, Thailand, Tonga, Vanuatu, Western Samoa	20
6. Flexibility limited in terms of a single currency (U.S. dollar)	Bahrain, Qatar, Saudi Arabia, United Arab Emirates	4
7. Cooperative arrangements (European Monetary System)	Austria, Belgium, Denmark, Finland, France, Germany, Ireland, Italy, Luxembourg, Netherlands, Portugal, Spain	12
8. Other managed floating	Algeria, Belarus, Brazil, Cambodia, Chile, China, Colombia, Costa Rica, Croatia, Dominican Republic, Ecuador, Egypt, El Salvador, Eritrea, Georgia, Greece, Guinea-Bissau, Honduras, Hungary, Indonesia, Iran, Israel, Republic of Korea, Kyrgyz Republic, Laos, Latvia, Former Yugoslav Republic of Macedonia, Malaysia, Maldives, Mauritius, Nicaragua, Norway, Pakistan, Poland, Russian Federation, Singapore, Slovenia, Sri Lanka, Sudan, Suriname, Tunisia, Turkmenistan, Turkey, Ukraine, Uruguay, Uzbekistan, Venezuela, Vietnam	48
9. Independently floating	Afghanistan, Albania, Armenia, Australia, Azerbaijan, Bolivia, Bulgaria, Canada, Ethiopia, The Gambia, Ghana, Guatemala, Guinea, Guyana, Haiti, India, Jamaica, Japan, Kazakstan, Kenya, Lebanon, Madagascar, Malawi, Mauritania, Mexico, Moldova, Mongolia, Mozambique, New Zealand, Papua New Guinea, Paraguay, Peru, the Philippines, Romania, Rwanda, São Tomé and Principe, Sierra Leone, Somalia, South Africa, Sweden, Switzerland, Tajikistan, Tanzania, Trinidad and Tobago, Uganda, United Kingdom, United States, Republic of Yemen, Zaïre (Democratic Republic of Congo), Zambia, Zimbabwe	51
		181

Source: International Monetary Fund, *International Financial Statistics,* June 1997, p. 8.

1. Many small developing countries, in contrast to large industrialized countries, concentrate their international trade and capital flows with one or a few trading partners. Examples are several Latin American and Caribbean countries with the United States and former French colonies in Africa with France. In this situation, a floating rate vis-à-vis the large trading partner could generate widespread instability in the small country's trade and payments, as well as instability internally whenever exchange rate changes produce significant variations in activity in domestic export and import-competing industries. Thus, greater stability is expected if the home currency is tied to the currency of the large trading partner.

2. Many developing countries have a significant amount of external debt to industrialized countries, and much of this debt is denominated in U.S. dollars. In this situation, variations in the exchange rate of the home currency with the dollar will alter the burden of the debt and its associated debt service payments. For example, suppose that the exchange rate for the Peruvian new sol is 2.7 new sol/$1. If Peru's annual interest payment on its debt is $1 billion, then Peru needs to generate 2.7 billion new soles in export earnings to meet this payment (without new loans). Suppose Peru now has a flexible exchange rate and that the rate changes to 3 new sol/$1. Now Peru must generate 3 billion new soles of exports to meet the same interest payment in dollar terms. This is a greater cost for Peru if the *real* exchange rate has depreciated as well as the nominal exchange rate, since more real resources must be devoted to exports. If the new sol had appreciated in real terms relative to the dollar, then the real resource cost would be lower. However, developing countries in general are more likely to have their currencies depreciate rather than appreciate relative to the dollar because of faster domestic inflation (especially in Latin America) than in the United States.

3. Balance-of-payments theory under fixed exchange rates also suggests the types of countries likely to prefer floating exchange rates. Consider an economy under fixed rates that is relatively closed in that it has a small marginal propensity to import. In the chapter "National Income and the Current Account," you learned that the open-economy multiplier (without foreign repercussions) was equal to $\{1/[1 - MPC(1 - t) + MPM]\}$. Any external shock will have a greater impact on national income if the country has a small MPM rather than a large MPM. Hence, other things equal, countries with small MPMs (that is, with limited reliance on foreign trade) will find fixed rates undesirable because of "large multiplier responsiveness" to any given external shock.

On the other hand, countries with large MPMs (and therefore small multipliers) will not find their national incomes as vulnerable to external events and will not on that account object to fixed rates. Since small developing countries tend to be considerably more open than large ones and large industrialized countries, we would expect small developing countries to opt more frequently for fixed exchange rates than do large developing countries and large industrialized countries. Such a pattern is evident in Table 4, where countries such as the Bahamas, Côte d'Ivoire, Nepal, Niger, and Senegal peg their rates while Brazil, India, Venezuela, China, Japan, Canada, and the United States have greater flexibility in their exchange rates.

4. A final observation on the choice of floating versus fixed exchange rates concerns international capital flows. As noted earlier in the text, the volume of international short-term portfolio capital movements has been increasing rapidly in recent years, and the size of these flows during any given year among the large industrialized countries dwarfs the size of their international flows of goods and services. In this context, a large developed country operating under fixed exchange rates would be subject to wide swings in its international reserve position. Sudden and large outflows (inflows) of capital producing BOP deficits (surpluses) would require substantial reserve transfers to (from)

other countries in order to maintain the fixed exchange rate. These potentially large swings in reserve positions can be dampened by letting the exchange rate vary. Hence, we would expect large industrialized countries with active capital markets to opt for floating rates rather than fixed rates. This expectation is consistent with observations in Table 4.

We will not pursue this matter of the choice of an exchange rate system by particular countries any further. Suffice it to say that there are many forces at work and many variables to be considered by a country's authorities when selecting the degree of exchange rate flexibility to be permitted. The type of exchange rate arrangement that is best for one country may not be the best for another country with differing features and institutions, and the best arrangement for a country at one point in time may not be the best at another point. For example, the increased liberalization in many developing countries in the 1990s has led to *relatively* greater adoption of more flexible exchange rate arrangements than was previously the case.

EXPERIENCE UNDER THE CURRENT INTERNATIONAL MONETARY SYSTEM

The historical record of the post-Bretton Woods international monetary system has been widely discussed and widely debated. A general consensus of economists regarding the operation of that system, often characterized by the general term "managed float" (especially for industrialized countries), is presented in this section. However, because the experience is relatively recent and because the system is still evolving, it is not certain that the views expressed will stand the test of time.

1. The post-Bretton Woods international monetary system has been characterized by substantial variability in exchange rates of the major industrial countries. This statement applies to nominal exchange rates and real exchange rates, and it is contrary to the expectations of many proponents of floating rates that the rates would move to an equilibrium level and then would show reasonable stability at that level. Even for countries with fixed nominal rates, there have been periodic official devaluations, and real exchange rates have varied in the presence of the fixed nominal rates.

Illustrations of the variability of exchange rates are commonplace, but a useful set of examples has been calculated by Ronald McKinnon (1988, pp. 84–85). McKinnon assembled monthly data on the yen/dollar and deutsche mark/dollar exchange rates from 1971 to March 1987 and calculated the mean rates for this period (252 ¥/$1 and 2.48 DM/$1). Next, he computed the percentage deviation from the mean for each month. He found that the yen/dollar price had ranged from 306 ¥/$1 (21 percent above the mean) to 151 ¥/$1 (40 percent below the mean). (The dollar went below 100 yen for a while after McKinnon's study.) This indicates that the price of the dollar in terms of yen was actually more than twice as high at one point (306 in 1975) than at another point (151 in 1987) during his examination period. Similarly, the DM/$ rate was at a peak of DM 3.31/$1 in early 1985 (33 percent above the mean) and at a trough of DM 1.72/$ in late 1979 (31 percent below its period mean). Again, the DM/$ price was about twice as high at one point as at another. This kind of variability clearly has potential implications for resource allocation, for uncertainty, and for international trade patterns.

2. Another feature of the international monetary system associated with this variability in exchange rates is that overshooting of exchange rates has occurred. Overshooting was discussed in the chapter "The Monetary and Portfolio Balance Approaches to External Balance."

3. A third characteristic of the post-Bretton Woods monetary system is that the variability in exchange rates has had *real economic effects*. This characteristic has occurred

because the variations in nominal exchange rates have not perfectly matched the variations in purchasing power parity (PPP) exchange rates, and thus real exchange rates have varied. If a country's currency undergoes a real depreciation, then the tradeable goods sectors of that country will attract resources since those sectors are now relatively more profitable than the nontradeable goods sectors. If the exchange rate then appreciates, the incentives will be shifted in the opposite direction, and resources will move out of the tradeable goods sectors and into the nontradeable goods sectors. However, such resource movements are not costless. Factors of production may have to move physically, retraining of workers may be needed, and unemployment occurs during the transition period. Thus, exchange rate movements may well lead to reduced real output in the world economy.

Another potential impact of movements in real exchange rates has been suggested by Robert Dunn (1983, p. 10). This impact concerns the capital gains and losses on long-term international debt that can occur because of variations in real exchange rates. Suppose that a Canadian firm borrows long-term funds from the U.S. capital market to finance real investment in Canada. The funds are borrowed in U.S. dollars and then are converted into Canadian dollars, but at repayment time, Canadian dollars will need to be converted into U.S. dollars. Obviously the C$/US$ rate at the two points in time is important. *If PPP holds,* however, meaning that the real exchange rate does not vary over the period, there is no impact on the investor from any variability in the nominal exchange rate.

For example, if the Canadian price level rises 10 percent relative to the U.S. price level, the Canadian dollar will depreciate by 10 percent relative to the U.S. dollar under PPP. Hence, the Canadian firm will have more Canadian dollars (because of the rise in price of its output) but will be using more Canadian dollars to repay the U.S. dollars, and the "true" amount being repaid is the same as the amount that was borrowed. (We abstract from interest payments in this example.) However, from 1976 to 1979, for example, the Canadian price level rose by 1 percent relative to the U.S. price level while the Canadian dollar depreciated by *15 percent* relative to the U.S. dollar. Therefore, Canadian inflation increased the value of the firm's output only slightly, but the firm needed considerably more Canadian dollars to repay the U.S. dollar loan. The Canadian borrower experienced a real capital loss in this example of roughly 14 percent of the value of the loan. Thus, Dunn concludes that real exchange rate variability can operate as a disincentive to long-term capital movements and can generate arbitrary losses (and gains) for investors. The resulting uncertainty can interfere with efficient resource allocation.

4. Another widely noted feature of the current international monetary system is that the system does not seem to have insulated countries from outside economic disturbances to the extent expected. Remember from earlier chapters that one of the alleged advantages of a floating-rate system is that insulation would occur, and hence that there would be little transmission of business cycles from one country to another. However, the conclusion of most observers is that business cycles have been transmitted across country lines in the floating-rate period for industrialized countries and that these countries have indeed had to worry about real external shocks.

What was the rationale for the earlier expectation that countries would be insulated from external shocks? Suppose that a country's exports suddenly decline because of a recession and reduced purchasing power abroad. Under fixed rates, this decline in export demand would have the ordinary open-economy multiplier process applied to it, and the home country's national income would fall. The recession abroad has thus been transmitted to the home country. However, under flexible exchange rates, this transmission would not occur, since the decline in exports would lead to a depreciation of the home country's currency. With this depreciation, production in the home country's export and import-competing sectors will increase. Hence, GDP will increase and will offset the original GDP decline. This process was discussed in more detail in the preceding chapter, "Fixed or Flexible Exchange Rates?" in the context of *IS/LM/BP* analysis.

Why do observers judge that the current system does not provide insulation? The most important reason is that central banks of the major industrial countries have been unwilling to allow complete flexibility in their exchange rates. The consequent official intervention in the exchange markets reflects the fact that the central banks may well have exchange rate targets in mind, as well as targets for national income. For example, authorities may wish to avoid a depreciation because it causes dislocations in the nontradeable goods sectors and worsens home inflation. In addition, they may also wish to limit the degree of appreciation, since appreciation can cause problems for the tradeable goods sectors and run into political opposition. The end result is that exchange rates have not been as flexible as in floating-rate theory, and therefore insulation from real external shocks has not occurred to the extent expected by proponents of flexible exchange rates.

5. Because exchange rates have not been fully flexible, another expectation of the proponents of flexible exchange rates has not been met: It was anticipated that, with floating rates, countries would not need to hold as large a volume of international reserves as under fixed rates, since reserve movements would not be needed in a major way to finance BOP deficits. However, in the post-Bretton Woods years, countries have added to their international reserves. Thus, the demand for international reserves has not decreased absolutely with floating rates, although reserves relative to imports have fallen. (See Case Study 2 in the preceding chapter.)

We have at least a partial explanation for the central banks' behavior from item 4 above, where we noted that intervention continues to take place. Because the United States had BOP deficits over much of the period, more dollars were supplied to the exchange markets than would otherwise have been the case. When foreign central banks purchased these dollars to mitigate the fall in the value of the dollar, the dollars were added to the international reserves of the foreign central banks. At the same time, since dollars are not counted as part of the reserves of the United States, there was no decline in the value of U.S. reserves. The result has been an increase in total world reserves.

To explore the increase in international reserves further, Table 5 presents recent information. As can be seen, the reserves of central banks are composed of four items:

Gold. The gold holdings of central banks constitute 2.7 percent of international reserves of central banks. However, the IMF values gold at the previous official price of 35 SDRs = 1 ounce of gold. At the time of the information in this table, the SDR was equal to $1.38689, so this gold valuation is at a price of $48.54 per ounce. This is hardly a realistic price, since private market gold has been selling for well over $300 per ounce for a number of years. If official gold holdings were valued at the market price, international reserves would be much larger, as would the share of gold in these reserves.

SDRs. Since SDRs make up only 1.6 percent of international reserves and are the smallest of the four components, it is clear that the IMF's objective of developing the SDR into a major international asset has not yet been achieved.

Reserve positions in the IMF. This element of international reserves roughly refers to the first 25 percent of countries' IMF quotas. A country can automatically obtain a loan of this size from the IMF when in BOP difficulties. This item is also a small fraction of world reserves (3.1 percent).

Foreign exchange. This currently accounts for over 92 percent of central bank reserves and is clearly the major international reserve asset central banks have at their disposal for settling BOP deficits. The U.S. dollar constitutes the major component of these foreign exchange holdings, but German marks and Japanese yen are becoming increasingly important.

TABLE 5   **Central Bank International Reserves as of March 31, 1997***

Reserve Asset[†]	Value ($, billions)	Percent of Total Reserves
1. Gold	$ 43.4	2.7%
2. SDRs	25.9	1.6
3. Reserve positions in the IMF	50.2	3.1
4. Foreign exchange	1,494.4	92.6
Total reserves	$1,614.0	100.0%

*The figures pertain only to IMF members.

[†]The IMF values the assets in terms of SDRs, with gold valued at a fixed 35 SDRs per 1 ounce of gold. SDR values have been converted to dollars at the rate prevailing on March 31, 1997 of 1 SDR = $1.38689.

Note: Details may not add to totals due to rounding.

Source: International Monetary Fund, *International Financial Statistics*, June 1997, pp. 4, 26, 27, 32, 36–37.

The point of this discussion of international reserves is that central banks continue to hold a sizable volume of reserves. (Indeed, reserves increased from $159.2 billion at the end of 1972—just prior to the advent of floating—to the March 1997 figure of $1,614.0 billion.) Such large reserves would not be needed in a truly flexible exchange rate system.

6. A further conclusion regarding the current international monetary system that commands fairly wide agreement is that there has not been an increase in inflation in the world economy because of the presence of greater floating of exchange rates. Recall that a fear concerning the adoption of flexible rates was that a "vicious circle" of inflation would develop. While the period from 1973–1974 until the early 1980s was indeed characterized by historically high inflation rates, it is not generally thought that this inflation was directly attributable to flexible exchange rates. Rather, the behavior of the Organization of Petroleum Exporting Countries (OPEC), of macroeconomic policymakers, and of price expectations played more crucial roles. Indeed, some observers doubt that the Bretton Woods system itself could have survived this inflationary episode. The floating-rate system permitted easier adjustment to the disturbances of this period than fixed rates would have done.

7. Finally, we note that many observers think that another fear concerning flexible rates—that the volume of world trade would shrink in the face of the risk associated with flexible rates—also does not seem to have been borne out. (However, see Case Study 1, "Exchange Risk and International Trade," in the preceding chapter.) World trade grew more rapidly than world production during the 1970s. In the early 1980s, trade growth dropped off sharply with stagflation from the second oil crisis and U.S. tight monetary policy, but trade continued to grow more rapidly than world production. Since that time, trade and production growth rates rose in the late 1980s, fell off with the recession of 1990–1991, and then recovered. However, trade still grew more rapidly than world output, although this might also have occurred under fixed rates.

CONCEPT CHECK

1. How would you describe the current international monetary system in terms of the nature of the exchange rate arrangements?

2. Why might large countries tend to opt for flexible rates whereas small countries might choose fixed rates?

3. What are two of the more serious problems that have surfaced with the current system?

SUGGESTIONS FOR REFORM OF THE INTERNATIONAL MONETARY SYSTEM

In view of the various performance characteristics of the current international monetary system, many observers have proposed changes in the system in order to make it work better. The principal objection to the present arrangements concerns the considerable exchange rate volatility in the currencies of the major industrialized countries (especially the United States, Germany, and Japan) and its potential adverse effects. Because these countries are so important in the world economy and because much of world trade and payments is denominated in their currencies, it is thought that some means must be found for reducing exchange rate variability. In this section we briefly review proposals currently being discussed.

A Return to the Gold Standard

Proponents of returning to a gold standard emphasize the need for an anchor for price levels within countries. The argument for a gold standard is that if currencies are defined in terms of gold *and national money supplies are tied to the size of countries' gold stocks,* then long-running BOP deficits and surpluses would not exist because of automatic adjustment, and the world would have less inflation because money supplies could not grow faster than the world's gold stock. There could also be reduced risks associated with holding currencies as international reserves because exchange rates would be fixed. Further, because gold would be the principal reserve asset in official reserve portfolios, stability would be introduced because foreign currencies would constitute a small portion of international reserves. Finally, if countries do indeed stick to their gold parities, the system eliminates the substantial volatility in exchange rates that has been of so much recent concern.

The principal disadvantage of this proposal is that it places the goal of external balance (that is, BOP equilibrium) above the internal goals of full employment and economic growth. Suppose that a country is running a BOP deficit; it is then expected to undergo a reduction of its gold stock and a contraction of its money supply. However, if the BOP deficit coincides with recession and slow growth internally, then contraction of the money supply will reduce economic activity even further. Since prices and wages in the modern economy tend to be inflexible in the downward direction, the result of monetary contraction will be a reduction of output and a rise in unemployment. The rise in interest rates expected of a deficit country would also deter long-term investment, which is necessary for sustained economic growth. This sacrifice of internal goals in the interests of BOP equilibrium is not a sacrifice many countries are politically prepared to make. Also, a surplus country will find inflationary pressures put upon it from the inflow of gold and international reserves, and a surplus country with a strong aversion to inflation (e.g., Germany) will be unlikely to sacrifice its internal goal of price stability. Another disadvantage of the gold standard is that exchange rate changes are not available for reallocating resources as comparative advantage changes, and sticky internal prices could not accomplish the reallocation easily. For a recent development that has similarities to the gold standard, see Case Study 2.

A proposal that has some similarities to the gold standard was put forward by Ronald McKinnon (1984, 1988); indeed, it has been dubbed the "gold standard without gold." McKinnon would have the central banks of the United States, Japan, and Germany jointly announce fixed nominal exchange rate targets among their currencies (with small actual deviations permitted). The rates would be set according to PPP at the time of announcement, and a constant price level for traded goods would be sought. Monetary policy would be directed toward preserving these rates and the constant price level. With exchange rates and policies thus "anchored," destabilizing short-term capital flows would become stabilizing. Again, however, sacrifice of national autonomy and unavailability of exchange rate changes to perform resource reallocations are present in this system, and unsterilized intervention would be used when necessary.

❈ CASE STUDY 2   ESTONIA'S CURRENCY BOARD

In June 1992, the Baltic country of Estonia (formerly a member republic of the Soviet Union, although never officially recognized as such by the United States) established a currency board arrangement that, while not a gold standard per se, generates results like the gold standard with respect to internal and external balance considerations. In this arrangement, the Estonian government pegs the Estonian currency to the German deutsche mark at the exchange rate of 8 krooni = 1 mark, a rate that can be changed only by vote of the Estonian parliament. The kroon in turn is backed 100 percent by foreign exchange reserves and gold. Prior to this time, Estonia had used the Russian ruble as its currency.

A major reason for the choice of this system was to slow down the inflation rate, which had been 210 percent in 1991. In addition, with 1991 = 100, the consumer price index had reached 910 in the second quarter of 1992. This hyperinflation had been caused by very rapid money creation in Russia and by the removal of price controls and distortions as Estonia undertook market-oriented reforms. In the currency board system, inflation can be drastically reduced since the money supply is tied to the currency board's foreign exchange and gold assets. Thus, increases (decreases) in the money supply can occur only as these reserves increase (decrease) with external sector trade and capital-flow performance. In other words, as with the gold standard, there is no independent monetary policy to be used for internal objectives. Of course, this also means that no money can be printed to cover government fiscal deficits either, since the money would not be appropriately backed. Indeed, Estonia's central bank is prohibited

from lending to the government. Estonia instituted tight fiscal policy along with the currency reform, and substantial increases in tax rates were put into place.

The early Estonian experience suggests that inflation indeed can be brought under control in such a system. The inflation rate dropped to "only" 90 percent in 1993, and it fell to 48 percent in 1994, 29 percent in 1995, and 23 percent in 1996. The increase in the money supply was reduced to an annual average rate of 27 percent for 1993–1996, an increase permitted by the fact that Estonia's holdings of foreign currency grew at an annual average rate of 25 percent during that period. In addition, the foreign exchange reserves were accumulating importantly because Estonia was attracting foreign capital due to the lack of exchange rate risk and the relatively low wages in the country. Foreign direct investment was especially interested in Estonia (an inflow of $800 million occurred from 1991 to 1996) because of a huge privatization program that aimed to have 90 percent of economic activity occurring in the private sector.

Nevertheless, there clearly have been difficulties, as real GDP fell by 26 percent in 1992, by 8.5 percent in 1993, and by 2.7 percent in 1994. Obviously some citizens have been injured by the new program; for example, there were cuts in government welfare expenditures, and people on pensions have been organizing to protect themselves. However, real GDP growth became positive in 1995 (2.9 percent), and, as noted above, foreign investors are very optimistic about the economy. Indeed, neighboring Lithuania, impressed by the Estonian program, introduced its own currency board in 1994 with a fixed exchange rate (tied to the U.S. dollar).

Sources: Matthew Brzezinski, "Estonia Sees Big Friends in Foreign Firms," *The Wall Street Journal,* Dec. 9, 1996, p. A8; Gail Buyske, "Estonia, Monetary Model for Russia," *The Wall Street Journal,* June 29, 1993, p. A18; "Currency Boards Circumscribe Discretionary Monetary Policy," *IMF Survey,* May 20, 1996, pp. 178–80; "Estonia Stablizes Economy through a Currency Reform," *IMF Survey,* Dec. 14, 1992, pp. 381–84; "Estonia's Currency Board Anchors Its Economy as Adjustment Proceeds," *IMF Survey,* Nov. 29, 1993, pp. 366–68; International Monetary Fund, *International Financial Statistics,* June 1997, pp. 274, 276; International Monetary Fund, *International Financial Statistics, Supplement on the Countries of the Former Soviet Union,* Supplement Series no. 16 (Washington, DC: IMF, 1993), p. 14.   ❈

A World
Central Bank

This proposal has been made in many different forms over several decades (e.g., by John Maynard Keynes in the early 1940s and by Robert Triffin in 1960) and recently by Richard Cooper (1986), although there has been less discussion of it in the past few years. The plans propose different degrees of control to be exercised by a new, centralized monetary institution, but all have some common elements. To set up the institution, at least part of the international reserves of the participating countries would be deposited in the new institution. This new bank would then have at its command billions of dollars of assets with which it could manage the world money supply. If faster (or slower) monetary growth were needed, the authority could purchase (or sell) government bonds in world financial markets (much as the Federal Reserve in the United States conducts its open-market operations). It could also make loans to countries in BOP difficulties, and variations in the authority's lending rate would influence the amount of borrowing (as the Federal Reserve in the United States does with its discount rate), which would in turn affect the size of the world money supply.

In an extreme form of the proposal, the new world central bank would issue a world currency as the means of controlling the world money supply. In this version (as well as in less extreme versions), countries have absolutely fixed exchange rates. If currencies are tied together permanently at fixed rates, then the next step toward a common currency is easy. The end result is a movement toward a worldwide currency area, and the instability associated with fluctuating exchange rates is eliminated.

The principal impetus behind a controlled world money supply is the view that today's fluctuations in exchange rates are due to the differing and uncoordinated macroeconomic policies (especially monetary policies) of the major industrialized countries. In the current system, if country A expands its money supply relative to that of country B, then the relatively lower interest rates in country A will cause an outflow of mobile short-term capital from A to B. This outflow will depress the country A currency value relative to that of B. Further, the depreciation of the A currency and the appreciation of the B currency will generate greater inflation in A relative to B, which can set in motion a further relative depreciation of A's currency. At the heart of the problem of the exchange rate changes is the differing monetary stance, which in turn can reflect differences in the desired inflation-unemployment trade-off in the two countries. By centralizing monetary policy in a new world institution, these destabilizing differences in monetary growth among countries can be avoided.

This plan in general could indeed work to reduce the amount of exchange rate instability and the effects of divergent monetary policies in the major industrialized countries. But the main criticism of proposals for a world central bank is that it is unrealistic to think that all countries would ever completely give up autonomy over their individual monetary policies. National sovereignty over economic policy is a cherished and firmly ingrained tradition. Proponents of such plans would argue that such autonomy is largely lost already in the current system because of the extremely high mobility of short-term capital across country borders. However, the lost autonomy is not as true for large countries as for small ones, and country officials *think* that they have considerable monetary control and thus will oppose such a plan.

The Target Zone Proposal

The leading proponent of the **target zone proposal** is John Williamson (1985, 1987, 1988). This plan attempts to reduce the element of conflict between internal goals and the external goal of BOP equilibrium. The major industrialized countries would first negotiate a set of mutually consistent targets for their *real effective* exchange rates. Absolute fixity of these rates is not envisaged, but rather each country would permit its real effective exchange rate to vary in, for example, a zone of 10 percent in either direction from the target rate. The target rate itself for each country would be chosen as the exchange rate that would be estimated to reconcile external and internal balance over a *medium-run* time period. If the exchange rate moved close to the ceiling or floor of the zone, this would be an indication that policy steps should be taken to moderate or reverse the movement, but there is no absolute requirement that the rates be kept between the ceiling and the floor. Rather the limits of the zone can be thought of as soft margins instead of hard boundaries.

Policy actions in the target zone system

What would be the policy actions necessary in the target zone system? The most important policy tool would be monetary policy rather than fiscal policy. Fiscal policy would play a key role in attaining the internal target (for example, reasonably full employment with reasonable price stability), but monetary policy is crucial because it can work to attain the internal goal as well as the external goal. In Williamson's framework, the immediate external goal is not balance-of-payments equilibrium per se but, rather, the existence of reasonable stability in the real effective exchange rate around the target rate. If the real effective exchange rate begins to move toward the ceiling price for foreign exchange (a real depreciation of the home currency), this would indicate that inflation is too high relative to that in foreign trading partners. A rise in interest rates would work to moderate the inflation but also would induce an inflow of short-term capital and thus moderate the home currency depreciation. Similarly, a downward movement of the real effective exchange rate (a real appreciation of the home currency) would indicate that the country's macroeconomic policy is too restrictive relative to that of other countries, so an easing of monetary policy is called for with respect to attaining both the internal and external targets. Monetary policy is supposed to be mainly directed toward internal goals, but because of capital mobility, it has the side benefit of assisting in stabilizing the exchange rate.

Two other aspects of this target zone proposal merit mention. First, an additional policy for attaining reasonable stability in exchange rates without sacrificing internal goals would be the use of coordinated intervention in exchange markets by central banks of the industrialized countries. Thus, if the dollar were falling and the mark were rising, the United States and Germany together might agree to buy dollars with marks in the exchange markets. Such concerted efforts would have the advantage that speculators would see a level of commitment of central banks to stable exchange rates and would be less likely to think that intervention would be unsuccessful; thus, greater confidence in the limits of the "zone" would be fostered. Second, the Williamson proposal permits some gradual changes in the zones if it is clear that fundamental changes in the participating economies are making the previously established zones inconsistent or obsolete.

Williamson's target zone proposal has desirable features in that it keeps internal goals at the forefront while also addressing exchange rate instability. In addition, the plan's focus is on real exchange rates rather than on nominal exchange rates, and the former are more influential for economic activity than the latter. However, real exchange rates are more difficult to manage than are nominal exchange rates, and it is also crucial that the target rate be chosen reasonably accurately. If the estimate of the target rate is incorrect, the operation of the proposal perpetuates a misalignment of exchange rates, which can interfere with efficient resource allocation in the world economy. Also, if a situation of "stagflation" occurs, in which unemployment and inflation may both be rising at the same time, it is not clear that the target zone plan would be useful without supplementation by additional policy instruments.

The Krugman version of the target zone

Another version of the target zone proposal has been put forward by Paul Krugman (1991). (See also Svensson 1992, pp. 121–25.) Unlike Williamson, Krugman would set upper and lower limits to the *nominal* effective exchange rate rather than to the real rate, and the limits would be *permanent* rather than "soft" limits. To build the case for the zone, Krugman develops a simple monetary/asset market model for the determination of the exchange rate. The exchange rate e (home currency price of 1 unit of spot foreign exchange) depends only on the home money supply, changes or shocks in the velocity of money, and the expected rate of depreciation of the home currency. In his equation, an increase in the home money supply will depreciate the home currency and its coefficient is therefore positive. An increase in the velocity of money (rate of usage or turnover of money) acts like an increase in the money supply and thus would also depreciate the currency. (Krugman postulates that changes in velocity are random.) Finally, Krugman employs uncovered interest parity (UIP) in asset markets, so that an increase in the expected rate of depreciation of the home currency (an increase in *xa* in the terminology of previous chapters) depreciates the home currency (a positive coefficient).

In the Krugman target zone model, the monetary authorities stand ready to decrease the money supply if *e* reaches the specified upper limit (that is, a depreciation of the home currency to its lower limit). Similarly, the authorities will increase the money supply if *e* falls to the floor (an appreciation of the home currency to its upper limit). A difference in the Krugman proposal from the Williamson proposal in this respect is that the monetary authorities basically act only *if* the exchange rate hits the limits—there is no change of behavior as the rate merely approaches the limits. In addition, Krugman postulates that the ceiling and floor may well *never be reached,* so the monetary authorities may not have to act at all (and if the ceiling and floor were actually reached, monetary action would only have to be minimal). Why is this so? First, the basic model postulates perfect credibility regarding the permanent ceiling and floor for *e,* thus assuming that any monetary actions will be effective if needed. This feature, along with the existence of UIP, would tend to keep the exchange rate within the limits as follows: Suppose *e* starts to rise toward its specified ceiling (that is, the home currency starts to depreciate in value). As *e* gets closer and closer to the ceiling, asset market participants, knowing that the monetary authorities will effectively intervene at the ceiling if it is hit, thus expect a fall in the rate of depreciation of the home currency near or at the ceiling as the authorities get ready to intervene. Given that there is a positive relationship between the expected rate of depreciation of *e* and *e* itself, this means that *e* itself will thus *fall.*[24] Hence, *e* will turn around and move in the direction away from the ceiling. Similarly, if, on other occasions, *e* approaches its lower specified limit (an appreciation of the home currency), market participants expect the monetary authorities to intervene soon to keep *e* from falling below the floor. This slowing down of the rate of expected appreciation of the home currency would raise *e* itself in the model. There is thus an automatic mechanism for keeping the exchange rate within the target zone and no actual variations in the money supply may be required.

The Krugman target zone proposal thus results in stability of exchange rates and offers a means of reducing the volatility of exchange rates in today's increasingly integrated financial world. Major criticisms of the plan concern the assumption of perfect credibility of the specified limits and the postulated confidence in and effectiveness of the monetary authorities. In addition, empirical tests of the relationship between the expected rate of change in the exchange rate and the exchange rate itself have not always yielded the Krugman relationship, and the actual existence of UIP has also been questioned. Further, other things influence the exchange rate besides the money supply, velocity, and the expected change in the exchange rate.[25] Little is also said about "internal balance" objectives. Nevertheless, given the desire of many observers to see more stability in exchange rates, this proposal as well as the Williamson proposal will continue to be debated, and they may suggest forthcoming modifications in the international monetary system.

....

[24]In the terminology of earlier chapters, when uncovered interest parity holds (ignoring a risk premium), $i_d = i_f + xa$, where i_d is the domestic interest rate, i_f is the foreign interest rate, and *xa* is the expected rate of depreciation of the home currency. A decrease in *xa* causes the right-hand side to be less than the left-hand side, leading to short-term capital flows into the home country and to a consequent appreciation of the home currency.

[25]Svensson (1992, pp. 125–39) discusses these and other objections to the Krugman proposal, as well as cases of imperfect credibility. Krugman regards the target zone proposal as less stabilizing when there is imperfect credibility, but it is still stabilizing (see Krugman 1991, p. 680).

Controls on
Capital Flows

This approach to the problem of exchange rate instability in the currencies of major countries states that the obvious major cause of the instability is the fact that short-term capital moves so freely between countries. Many of these flows of capital have nothing to do with "economic fundamentals" such as inflation rates, resource productivity, and general economic conditions. Rather, they reflect reactions to rumors, political events, and "bandwagon effects" and "herd instincts," where speculation against a currency in and of itself generates further speculation against that currency. Such volatile short-term capital flows cause considerable instability in exchange rates, and this instability is exacerbated by overshooting. Hence, so this approach specifies, a remedy is to impose limitations on the inflow and outflow of funds from major countries that are responding to such "uneconomic" motivations. (See Goldstein 1984, p. 5, for discussion.)

That substantial exchange rate changes can occur because of short-term capital flows is clear. A prominent example of this took place with respect to the Mexican peso in late 1994.[26] At that time, political instability (including the assassination of a leading presidential candidate, a revolt in the southern state of Chiapas, and kidnappings of businessmen) as well as lax bank regulation with consequent private borrowing beyond that permitted by prudent financial practice, led to a lack of confidence in the Mexican financial system. As a result, massive withdrawals from Mexico of short-term capital led to a dramatic decline in the international value of the peso. Speculative attacks also occurred because it was felt that the lower bound of the peso's value in its then relatively fixed-rate system would be breached. As a result of these events, the peso fell by 49 percent in four months as the Mexican authorities gave up pegging the peso and let it float. The loss of capital and internal economic disruption led to a fall in GDP of 7 percent in the first three quarters of 1995. In response to the crisis, the United States organized a $50 billion multilateral lending effort to assist Mexico, with the United States itself committing $20 billion. Mexico began strong recovery by late 1995 and had repaid the U.S. loan by early 1997. Nevertheless, the point here is that, because of the extremely mobile capital that exists in the current international monetary system, financial crises can emerge, exchange rate movements can be greatly amplified, and severe domestic consequences can occur. Hence, there is some support for controls on short-term capital.

Capital flows among countries could be restricted in a number of ways. A major proposal that has attracted attention for some time is that of James Tobin (1978), who suggests imposing an international tax on all spot transactions involving the conversion of one currency into another in securities markets. Such a tax would presumably discourage speculation by making currency trading more expensive, thereby reducing the volume of destabilizing short-term capital flows. [Tobin (1995) also hypothesizes that, by generating greater interest rate differentials across countries, the tax—say of 0.5 percent of transaction value—would create room for individual country monetary policies to be more effective in macroeconomic stabilization.] While the tax has the potential advantages of reducing some of the marginally based speculative transactions or market "noise" and of fostering international cooperation on tax policy, there are a number of problems with a transactions tax of this type.

Spahn (1996, p. 24) points out that there are four main problems with a Tobin tax that would inhibit its effectiveness. First, to limit the market distortions resulting from such a tax, the tax base would have to be as broad as possible and would have to exclude no category of market participants. However, a strong argument can be made that financial

----

[26]For further discussion, see Gil-Diaz and Carstens (1996); Calvo and Mendoza (1996); Hess and Ross (1997, pp. 471–72); "After the Storm," *The Economist,* June 29, 1996, pp. 75–76; and *Economic Report of the President,* February 1996 (Washington, DC: U.S. Government Printing Office, 1996), p. 240.

intermediaries or "market makers" who increase market liquidity should not be taxed. Unfortunately, the Tobin tax cannot distinguish between normal institutional trading which ensures market liquidity and efficiency and destabilizing financial activity. Second, there is the question of what type of transaction to tax. If the tax is applied only to spot transactions, it can easily be avoided by going into the derivatives market. Taxing the initial contractional value (or notional value) of derivatives, however, would likely severely injure the derivatives market. Applying a different tax rate to derivatives than to other instruments is a possibility, but a selective tax system would be arbitrary and extremely difficult to administer. Third, it can be argued that the tax should be applied only when markets are clearly in disequilibrium. Thus, the tax rate would be zero during conditions of stability and equilibrium and increase in accordance with the deviation from equilibrium. This, however, would again contradict Tobin's idea of a one-tax system and would also be incredibly complex to administer. Finally, there is the question of the distribution of revenues. Distribution of tax revenues is a controversial political question within countries, to say nothing of between countries. Significant costs could be incurred in simply trying to arrive at international consensus on this issue.

In response to these problems, Spahn (pp. 26–27) suggests a two-tiered Tobin tax which would consist of a minimal-rate transactions tax and an exchange rate surcharge that would be applied only during periods of great exchange market turbulence. Although it certainly would not deter sudden speculation based on fear of an event such as a payment default, the two-tier tax would be useful as a short-term monetary stabilization tool that could smooth market adjustment. It should not, however, be viewed as a means of dealing with underlying structural problems. In response to this idea, Stotsky (1996) argues strongly against employing such a tax. Like the Tobin tax, it may not work simply because there is little evidence that market volatility is reduced by these kinds of taxes. (For a different view, see Frankel 1996, p. 156.) Further, the increased transaction costs hinder market operations and efficiency. In addition, the use of variable tax rates can create uncertainty with respect to market prices and can be burdensome administratively. Finally, Stotsky questions the desirability of mixing monetary policy and tax policy, given the political and administrative differences in the way they are enacted. Thus, while discussion continues regarding the viability and/or desirability of using a Tobin-type tax to reduce exchange rate instability, the lack of any consensus on its overall effects suggests that it is unlikely that it will be adopted in the near future.

Another approach to controlling capital flows which has been utilized by a number of countries involves adopting a system of **dual exchange rates** or **multiple exchange rates.** In this situation, a different exchange rate is employed depending on the nature of the foreign transaction. If German deutsche marks are being purchased for normal trade transactions or for long-term overseas investment, the exchange rate might be specified as $0.60/DM 1; however, if the transaction involved a short-term capital flow, an exchange rate of $0.90/DM 1 might be used. The 50 percent higher price for the short-term capital transaction would presumably discourage such transactions. Or the central bank of the country could also restrict capital flows by exercising moral suasion or "jawboning" against capital outflows, as the United States did in the late 1960s through its "voluntary" restrictions on bank lending overseas. ("Guidelines" were published by the Federal Reserve.) Stronger measures such as outright prohibitions might also be adopted.

Capital movements between countries that are in the interests of economic efficiency are eminently desirable. If capital moves from a country where the marginal product of capital is low to a country where the marginal product of capital is high, there is an increase in world output and greater efficiency in resource allocation from the capital flow. However, proponents of capital controls contend that a large fraction of the capital flows in the recent floating-rate period is not of this type. Rather, the daily movements of speculative funds in and out of leading countries' financial markets may be hindering efficient resource allocation because traders and long-term investors are receiving misleading and uncertain signals. In addition, the fluctuations in real exchange rates that can result from these flows may be causing wasteful resource movements.

In general, economists dislike capital controls. The danger is that the controls will prevent the flow of capital that is moving in response to true marginal productivity differences. Further, there is no effective way to sort out which capital movements are "good" and which are "bad," and capital controls are easy to evade. For example, with dual exchange rates, a firm buying components from a foreign subsidiary could evade the capital controls by simply overstating the price of imported goods. Thus, capital is being moved out of the country to the foreign subsidiary. Nevertheless, there appears to be no time in the postwar period when at least some countries did not have capital controls (industrialized as well as developing countries). It is possible that such controls could become more widespread in the future if countries find no other solutions to the current problems with exchange rate instability.

Greater Stability and Coordination of Macroeconomic Policies across Countries

The proponents of this proposal attribute exchange rate instability among major industrialized countries primarily to two factors: *(a)* the macro policies of any given country tend to be unstable; and *(b)* macro policies across countries are often working in opposite directions. With respect to *(a),* evidence is provided by the proponents of stability and coordination that easy monetary policy, for example, is currently soon followed by an abrupt change to tight monetary policy. In this environment, short-term capital may leave the country because of low interest rates in the first period but then return in the next period when interest rates are higher. There will also be continuing reevaluation of expectations regarding the future stance of the monetary authorities, and these changes in expectations in and of themselves can induce capital flows. With respect to *(b),* if one country is pursuing an expansionary monetary policy while another is pursuing contractionary policy, then capital will flow toward the contractionary policy country; when both countries reverse their policies due to changing internal circumstances, capital will flow in the other direction. The result of these swings in the flow of short-term funds is a considerable amount of exchange rate variability.

A general view among economists (discussed in Goldstein 1984, pp. 5–6) is that floating exchange rates would be more stable if the private sector had firmer and less volatile expectations concerning future exchange rates. If countries adopted more stable macro policies, these policies not only would contribute to the attainment of domestic economic goals but would also stabilize expectations about exchange rates. If confident predictions can be made because of coordinated and stable policies, then minor shocks and rumors will not have sizable impacts upon exchange rates, and the rates will by and large be stable. Thus, the basic thrust of the policy coordination proposal is for greater stability and uniformity in macro policy, to be achieved by periodic conferences and constant communication among the policy authorities in the major industrialized countries. For example, the semiannual joint meetings of the members of the IMF and the World Bank have stressed policy coordination for achievement of various goals.

A major existing forum for discussing policy coordination, and one that receives wide coverage in the press, consists of the annual summit meetings held by leaders of the Group of Seven (Canada, France, Germany, Italy, Japan, the United Kingdom, and the United States). However, the actual effectiveness of the G-7 in coordinating and leading world response to international problems has been the subject of discussion as of late. In a recent book, Bergsten and Henning (1996) examine the past, present, and future of the

G-7 with regard to its ability to provide the world economic leadership that is critical to the success of the international monetary system. They regard the G-7 as having attained some notable successes in the late 1970s and in the 1980s. However, they argue that the leadership and the effectiveness of the group have declined in the 1990s and that there has been a loss of confidence in the group's ability to undertake successful collective strategies, even when it may wish to do so, due to major changes in global economic conditions. More specifically, the current huge volume of international flows of private capital almost certainly precludes the G-7 from effectively being able to influence the currency markets. In addition, the nearly universal presence of large government deficits interferes with the scope and flexibility of fiscal policy. Finally, with the primacy of monetary policy in the current international financial system, the major central banks that have become more important players in the world economy strongly defend their institutional independence from other governmental authorities in key countries such as the United States and Germany.

Bergsten and Henning offer a set of recommendations regarding the G-7. They argue for supporting and modifying ongoing initiatives to create an early warning system to head off Mexican-peso-type financial crises and to have available the necessary resources to deal with such crises when they do erupt. In addition, the G-7 should focus on the management of flexible rates, perhaps within a broad target zone system of rates, and not be concerned with coordination of G-7 members' own domestic macroeconomic policies directly. The G-7 should also undertake institutional reforms involving a greater participatory role for the central banks consistent with the management of exchange rates and stability of the rapidly expanding international financial markets. Finally, the G-7 should contemplate changes in its own membership, perhaps eventually including emerging economic powers to both enhance its own legitimacy and revitalize G-7 leadership.

The focus of the 1997 annual G-7 summit in Denver, Colorado, was certainly not inconsistent with several aspects of the Bergsten-Henning critique. Issues of concern were policies to head off or contain potential crises that emerge from the globalization of financial markets, definitions of financial health for banks in developing countries and greater IMF monitoring of the emerging financial markets, strategies for African development, and the integration of Russia into world financial and political institutions.[27] Because of the very visible inclusion of Boris Yeltsin, president of Russia, this summit was officially referred to as the "Summit of Eight."

Operationalizing any plan for greater stability and coordination in policies faces many difficulties. In addition to the institutional difficulties such as those of the G-7, the implementation of coordinated macro policies encounters variable and sometimes lengthy time lags in recognizing the current situation, devising and implementing the appropriate policy responses, and waiting for the policies to take effect. In addition, external shocks such as the oil crises and changes in expectations make accurate forecasting difficult. A major problem of policy coordination is also its feasibility. If business cycles do not hit all major countries at the same time (that is, the countries are "out of phase" with each other), it will be difficult to get the policy authorities to agree on the proper macroeconomic stance. Finally, coordinated policymaking involves some sacrifice of national autonomy, and countries tend to resist such an infringement on their sovereignty.

....

[27]According to Daniel Tarullo, international economics advisor to President Clinton, the G-7 countries "have agreed on the establishment of a network of supervisors for global markets ... and for a program to assist emerging economies in strengthening their own financial systems." (Quoted in Jacob M. Schlesinger, "G-7 Summit to Unveil Policies That Aim to Stave Off Global Financial Crises," *The Wall Street Journal,* June 17, 1997, p. A2.)

1. What obstacles does the G-7 face in implementing coordination of macro policy?
2. How does a target zone system differ from a world central bank system?
3. Why do economists in general not like the extensive use of capital controls?
4. How might the Tobin tax reduce exchange rate volatility?

THE INTERNATIONAL MONETARY SYSTEM AND THE DEVELOPING COUNTRIES

An additional broad topic regarding the international monetary system concerns the type of international monetary arrangements that seem most suitable for the developing countries, also called the less developed countries (LDCs). We have earlier discussed reasons as to why many developing countries prefer fixed exchange rates to flexible rates, and developing countries in general want to avoid the volatility in exchange rates that has occurred in recent years. To recap briefly, one reason for this preference is that many LDCs have a high ratio of trade to GDP, and thus they are vulnerable to exchange rate fluctuations. Another important reason is the sizable external debt of a number of LDCs. Since this debt is primarily denominated in dollars, any rise in the real exchange rate against the dollar means that the real burden of debt increases. While a depreciation of the dollar would have the opposite impact, risk-averse debtors prefer some certainty in the value of the debt and of debt service payments, and a real depreciation of the dollar against many developing country currencies is very unlikely.

However, a relatively fixed-rate framework also implies that participating countries must maintain adequate holdings of international reserve assets. But the developing countries have not been able to build up or even maintain their reserve stocks because of their needs for capital goods imports as well the capital flight from LDCs toward industrialized countries (ICs), where the real rate of return on capital may be higher and more stable. Hence, LDCs conclude that any reform of the international monetary system should include adequate provision for creation of new international reserves and liquidity. In their view, reform should be in large part based on new allocations of SDRs, and these allocations should be directed mainly toward the developing countries.

This emphasis on SDRs and their disproportionate provision to developing countries is often called the **link proposal.** This term refers to the fact that international monetary reform should be linked with additional foreign aid. SDRs allocated to the LDCs could provide both a long-term resource transfer for development purposes and a short-term means of finance for maintaining a fixed exchange rate system (perhaps through movement toward a world central bank). The industrialized countries, however, have been skeptical of the link proposal, for they view "aid" and "international monetary reform" as distinctly separate issues.

Another issue of concern to LDCs with respect to the current international monetary system is the issue of **IMF conditionality.**[28] This term refers to the fact that when a developing country draws resources or borrows from the IMF, the borrowing increasingly can have "strings" attached. The "strings" can include such items as IMF insistence that steps be taken to halt inflation, alter fiscal policies, remove price controls, adopt more market-oriented policies, allow the currency to float for a while, and so forth.[29] However, the LDCs may not judge such policy steps as necessary parts of their development strategy. Hence, the IMF is regarded as imposing a specific strategy for development upon the

[28]For elaboration, see Peera (1988, pp. 303–11).

[29]The conditionality issue also concerns loans from the World Bank.

developing country and as interfering with national sovereignty. In defense of the IMF position, the institution is desirous of having its loans repaid, and any lender can impose conditions that it thinks will help to ensure repayment. Although conditionality is a feature of virtually all IMF loans, the kind and size of loans available from the IMF now are much larger than the original balance-of-payments loans through the reserve tranche and the standard credit tranches that could provide up to 125 percent of a country's quota. A variety of "facilities" are now in existence beyond the original loan mechanism, namely, a Structural Adjustment Facility, an Extended Structural Adjustment Facility, a Compensatory and Contingency Financing Facility (to cover LDC export shortfalls, excessive spending on cereal imports, and other special occurrences), a Buffer Stock Facility (to cover instability in export earnings), and, as of 1993, a Systemic Transformation Facility (to assist with balance-of-payments problems associated with moving to a market economy). In total, a country can conceivably borrow over 500 percent of its quota. Therefore, though conditionality imposes unwanted restrictions on the developing countries and discussions ought to pursue the issue, the pool of resources available from the IMF is potentially quite sizable. Nevertheless, conditionality is a very heated issue, and the topic extends beyond economics with its implications for national sovereignty and political power.

Another developing-country view is that the international monetary system ought to generate more stability in the world economy. If business cycles occur frequently in the industrialized countries, these variations in economic activity will spill over to the LDCs because the purchases of their exports by the ICs will be unstable. Hence, economic fluctuations in the industrialized countries will be transmitted to the LDCs. From this point of view, the attainment of more stability and coordination of macro policies in the industrialized countries would be very desirable. Besides reducing the instability in developed-country exchange rates, it might provide greater macro stability for the LDCs if it succeeded in stabilizing conditions in the industrialized countries. The same kind of enhanced stability could also come from the adoption of an effective target zone system. However, these stability benefits would probably not come from a return to the gold standard. Economic activity within the ICs could become more variable under the BOP adjustment requirements of that system (even though exchange rates would be fixed).

In sum, the LDCs desire greater stability in exchange rates in the international monetary system, and they would like the system to play a greater role in enhancing their development prospects. This greater role could be played if the system generated greater stability in the world economy without the use of restrictions on trade and payments, and if the system provided an increase in international liquidity directed toward the developing countries.

THE EXTERNAL DEBT PROBLEM OF THE DEVELOPING COUNTRIES

A final topic of concern is the external debt problem of the LDCs. This problem is intimately bound up with the matter of access to finance in the world economy. If industrialized country banks that have outstanding loans to the developing countries experience difficulties because of this debt, the underpinning institutions in the world monetary system are placed in jeopardy. We thus conclude this chapter by examining in some detail the LDC debt "crisis." Table 6 provides an overview of the size of the external debt of LDCs, with data on the debt and its relationship to several key economic variables at the end of 1996, together with IMF projections (made in early 1997) of relative debt size for 1997 and 1998.

TABLE 6   **External Debt and Debt Ratios of the Developing Countries**

	(1) External Debt ($, billions)	(2) Debt as % of Gross Domestic Product			(3) Debt as % of Exports of Goods and Services			(4) Debt Service Ratio*		
	1996	1996	1997†	1998†	1996	1997†	1998†	1996	1997†	1998†
All developing countries	1,783.3	32.3%	30.2%	28.5%	159.0%	149.5%	145.4%	23.0%	19.8%	18.4%
Africa	286.8	62.3	66.2	62.0	226.5	212.3	202.1	23.7	25.6	25.4
Asia	563.7	26.3	24.9	24.1	117.7	112.6	109.6	16.2	14.9	13.7
Middle East and Europe	274.3	24.8	20.9	17.8	112.9	101.3	101.0	12.0	9.6	9.8
Western hemisphere	658.4	36.3	35.2	34.9	241.2	232.7	226.1	44.3	32.5	31.4

*Amortization payments on long-term debt plus interest payments on total debt as a percentage of exports of goods and services
†Projected.

Note: The IMF classifies 28 countries of Central and Eastern Europe, the former Soviet Union, and Mongolia as "transition economies," separate from developing countries. For these countries debt in 1996 was $271.8 billion, the debt/export ratio was 98.2 percent, and the debt service ratio was 11.0 percent. (The debt/GDP ratio is unavailable).

Source: International Monetary Fund, *World Economic Outlook, May 1997* (Washington, DC: IMF, 1997), pp. 190–91, 196.

Column (1) shows that Latin America and the Caribbean countries (Western hemisphere) and Asia have the largest dollar value of external debt. However, for a variety of reasons, including quicker adjustment policies to the debt problem, recent rapid GDP growth, and favorable export prospects, the Asian countries do not have as severe a debt problem as the Latin American and Caribbean countries and Africa. Column (2) is a measure of the LDCs' ability to carry the debt in relation to annual productive capacity, that is, the flow of annual output that conceptually could be available to repay the debt. The severity of the problem for Africa is evident in that not only is the debt/GDP ratio substantially higher than it is for any of the other regions but also the African ratio is projected to remain at this high level in 1997 and 1998 (whereas the ratios for the other groups are projected to decline).

Column (3) emphasizes the point that even though a country may produce the goods and services with which to repay debt, it still must convert these resources into foreign exchange (that is, hard, convertible currencies). Unless new external funds are forthcoming, this generation of foreign exchange has to occur through successful exporting. That is, in order to effectively transfer purchasing power back to the lenders as repayment, developing-country exports must be stimulated and imports reduced so that sufficient foreign exchange is available. This **transfer problem** of freeing up resources to accomplish repayment can be difficult indeed. Africa and Latin America have the highest debt/export ratios. Note, however, that the ratios are projected to decline for all regions in 1997 and 1998.

Finally, column (4) indicates the concept that many economists judge is the best measure of the severity of the debt problem facing LDCs. The **debt service ratio** is the percentage of annual export earnings that must be set aside for payment of interest on the debt and the scheduled repayment of the debt itself. When debt service ratios are of the order of Africa's 23.7 percent and Latin America's 44.3 percent, the countries must devote large portions of their foreign exchange earnings to debt service. These large fractions of foreign exchange earnings are therefore not available for the purchase of needed imports, and imports must be reduced dramatically if the country is to avoid drawing down its stock of international reserves or incurring even more debt. (In the 1980s, many Latin American countries compressed imports to such an extent that living standards fell drastically.) The IMF projections show that this ratio will rise for Africa through 1998 but will fall for the other three regions.

Causes of the
Developing Countries'
Debt Problem

Many factors have been suggested as having played a causal role in the LDC debt problem. However, the relative importance of the factors varies from country to country, and it is difficult to make generalizations.

1. A prominent element in discussions of the debt problem consists of the *oil price increases of 1973–1974 and 1979–1981.* The two "oil shocks" resulted in a huge increase in the oil import bills of many developing countries, and borrowing was necessary to finance the additional import expenditures. Much of the borrowing was from industrialized countries' commercial banks, which were recycling dollars deposited in them by members of OPEC (petrodollars).

2. Related to the oil price increases were the *recessions in the industrialized countries* in the 1970s and early to mid-1980s. The recessions resulted in large part from the oil shocks but also from anti-inflationary macroeconomic policies adopted in industrialized countries. From the standpoint of the LDCs, recessions in the ICs mean that purchases of LDC exports grow slowly or decline. With slower or negative export growth, LDCs must borrow more to continue a flow of imports.

3. *The behavior of real interest rates* was also important in generating and perpetuating the debt crisis. The real interest rate is equal to the nominal interest rate charged by lenders minus the expected rate of inflation. In the 1970s, this real rate was low and sometimes negative due to expectations of high inflation, and borrowers (the LDCs) were thus encouraged to undertake new loans. However, the rapid fall in inflation in the 1980s in the United States in particular—associated with tight monetary policy—caused the real rate to rise. This meant that any additional LDC borrowing to finance repayment of existing debt imposed extra burdens on the developing countries.

4. In addition, *primary-product prices declined dramatically in the 1980s.* Since primary products constitute a large fraction of the exports of developing countries, this decline necessitated additional borrowing in order to finance needed imports for development.

5. *Domestic policies within the developing countries* also played a role in generating the debt problem. If loans are used for consumption rather than for productive investment, or if the LDC inflates its price level rapidly by excessive monetary growth associated with government budget deficits, then repayment prospects are poor and new borrowing must be undertaken. The ability to finance development without resorting to external borrowing is also hindered if domestic price controls inhibit an efficient allocation of resources or if the LDC's currency is pegged at an overvalued rate. Such overvaluation makes exports "too expensive" to foreign buyers and imports "too cheap" to domestic buyers, leading to a trade deficit.

6. Another factor associated with increasing indebtedness was *capital flight from the developing countries.* This phenomenon is harder to document precisely than previous reasons, but that the phenomenon exists is unquestionable. With very rapid inflations taking place in Latin American countries and low real interest returns, many domestic citizens sent funds to IC banks. With these funds not available for domestic use, the LDCs had to borrow more capital on international markets. Indeed, the bank deposits in ICs of citizens of some LDCs at one point were estimated to be half the size of those countries' debts! (See Felix 1985, pp. 50–51.)

7. Finally, the hypothesis has emerged that a considerable portion of LDC indebtedness was due to *"loan-pushing" by banks in the developed countries* (Darity and Horn 1988). This view emphasizes that IC banks were awash in funds (importantly from the recycling of petrodollars) and, accompanied by the deregulation of financial institutions in the United States, were anxious to expand their loan portfolios. Hence, loans were often made that were not necessarily associated with sound economic analysis and did not adequately take risk factors into account. In many cases, the growing debt burden was

effectively ignored by banks as LDC officials were aggressively talked into taking on more debt than their countries could absorb. Indeed, in the middle of 1982, "the nine largest U.S. banks had loans outstanding to developing countries and Eastern Europe amounting to 280 percent of their capital, and most had over 100 percent of capital in loans to just Brazil and Mexico."[30] This large and concentrated amount of outstanding loans also led to fears of collapse of the financial systems in industrialized countries if defaults occurred.

Possible Solutions to the Debt Problem

In seeking solutions to the developing-country debt problem, it is important to distinguish between the liquidity problem and the solvency problem. The *liquidity problem* in this context refers to the fact that although a debtor country will eventually be able to repay its debts, there is a short-run problem of financing debt service payments because the country's assets are not immediately convertible into a form acceptable to creditors. Hence, policies should provide for temporary finance until longer-run adjustments can take place. The *solvency problem* refers to the fact that the country is in such poor condition and has such dismal economic prospects that it will never be able to generate the resources to repay its debt. If the problem is insolvency, then some form of debt forgiveness must be instituted or the country will have to default on its obligations. Until 1982, the LDC debt problem was generally regarded as one of liquidity, but the announcement by Mexico (the second-largest LDC debtor, after Brazil) that it would not be able to meet debt service obligations due at that time set in motion a concern that the problem in many LDCs was really one of insolvency.

Changing domestic policies

In general, there are several broad categories of solutions that can be suggested for dealing with the debt problem. First, *LDCs can change their domestic policies so as to increase their ability to service the debt.* (See Nowzad 1990, pp. 12–13.) This strategy is a long-term one that regards the debt problem as a matter of temporary illiquidity. The emphasis of the International Monetary Fund and the World Bank on **structural adjustment policies** falls into this category. When the IMF negotiates with a debtor country concerning new loans, it will often approve the loans (which extend beyond the BOP loans discussed earlier) only if the LDC undertakes various measures to strengthen its long-term repayment prospects. The conditionality measures usually include reduction of government budget deficits and the money supply (to reduce inflation and the accompanying balance-of-payments deficits) and the adoption of a realistic exchange rate—meaning a devaluation of the domestic currency.[31] These steps are often called "austerity policies." Devaluation undertaken along with contractionary monetary and fiscal policies can improve the trade balance and put the debtor country in a better position for servicing debt with hard foreign currency. Other recommended policies usually include the elimination of government production and/or consumption subsidies and of distortionary price controls. These measures allow the market rather than government policy to allocate resources, which the IMF argues will improve efficiency. The attachment of such conditions to new lending by the IMF, as noted earlier in this chapter, has generated considerable resentment among LDCs.

. . . .

[30]William R. Cline, "International Debt: From Crisis to Recovery," *American Economic Review* 75, no. 2 (May 1985), p. 185.

[31]One study of 24 LDCs indicated that failure to have an appropriate exchange rate had strongly negative implications for such performance characteristics as per capita income growth rate, export growth rate, and net investment rate. See Cottani, Cavallo, and Khan (1990).

Debt rescheduling

Another approach to the debt problem involves **debt rescheduling.** This approach also treats the debt problem as basically a liquidity rather than a solvency problem. In rescheduling operations, interest rates on the debt are often lowered, the time period of the loan is lengthened, or the grace period before repayments start is made longer. There have been a large number of reschedulings, particularly through the "Paris Club," a consortium of IC governments set up to deal with rescheduling of government (rather than commercial bank) loans. These reschedulings have been particularly relevant for Africa, where the debt is owed mostly to governments rather than to private banks. (Latin America's debt to banks is greater than to governments.)

Debt relief

Recently, attention has been focused on **debt relief** or **debt reduction** rather than on rescheduling. The most well-known initiative along this line has been the **Brady Plan,** proposed by U.S. Secretary of the Treasury Nicholas Brady early in 1989. Details vary from country to country, but in this general strategy, a pool of money from the United States or from the World Bank and the IMF is used to guarantee new bonds issued by developing-country governments. These new bonds are offered to existing lenders in such a fashion that the amount of debt outstanding is reduced. For example, $10 billion of new debt might be issued to retire $20 billion of old debt. The advantage to the LDC is that its debt is decreased, as well as its interest payments. For the lending bank, $20 billion of claims on the developing country have been swapped for only $10 billion of claims, but the smaller amount is now guaranteed. An alternative procedure might involve no reduction in the principal of the debt but a lower interest rate on the new debt than on the old debt. It is also anticipated that the developing country will carry out market- and growth-oriented reforms such as relaxation of price controls, elimination of distortions, and policies to stimulate domestic savings and investment.

An interesting hypothesis that has emerged in the context of debt relief is that a reduction in debt might in fact *enhance* an LDC's likelihood of repaying debt and that such a forgiveness of debt by lending banks might actually help those banks. (See Krugman 1989 and Kenen 1990.) The first part of the hypothesis that a reduction in debt can increase the chance of repaying debt is straightforward. Suppose that a developing-country government has a large debt to foreign banks or governments, and therefore has incurred large future debt service obligations. In this situation, domestic investors in enterprises in the LDC may come to expect future tax increases by the LDC government so as to pay the future interest and amortization. This expectation of future higher taxes would dampen current growth-creating investment since the expected after-tax rate of return to investors is lower because of the anticipated increased taxes. Or suppose that it is general opinion that the LDC's current debt level is so high that it can never be repaid. In this case, default may be likely by the LDC, and this default would confirm to any foreign private investor considering entering the country that the country is in trouble and is not a good place to invest. Hence, there could be a halt to any inflow of potential growth-creating foreign investment for at least some time in the future. Through scenarios such as these, a high level of LDC debt per se can interfere with the developing country's current economic performance. The implication of the scenarios is that reductions in debt can stimulate domestic investment (because of anticipated *lower* future tax burdens) as well as foreign private investment (because of less likelihood of default and more optimistic assessments by foreign investors of the country's prospects).

This line of thinking on debt reduction as a means of stimulating LDC growth has led to a useful graphical construct, and this construct also enables us to see the second part of the debt reduction hypothesis—that it can be in the interest of foreign lending banks to "forgive" some LDC debt. This graphical construct is the **debt-relief Laffer curve,**

FIGURE 2   **The Debt-Relief Laffer Curve**

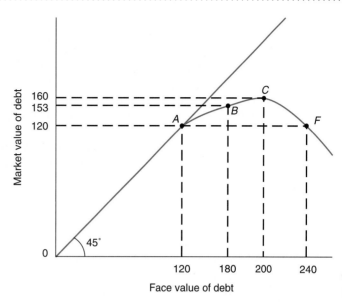

In the debt-relief Laffer diagram, in the range from the origin to point *A,* the outstanding debt of a less developed country is expected to be fully repaid. The value of the LDC's bonds in the secondary market is consequently equal to 100 percent of the face value of the bonds. From point *A* to point *C,* the market value of the debt increases with the face value but at a diminishing rate, being, for example, 85 percent at point *B* (= $153 million ÷ $180 million) and 80 percent at point *C* (= $160 million ÷ $200 million). Beyond point *C,* greater LDC debt is associated with a lower total market value. This reflects poorer growth and debt repayment prospects by the country as more debt is incurred since, for example, domestic firms may undertake less real investment because they expect taxes to be raised in order to service the very large debt.

brought to prominence by Paul Krugman (1989).[32] To understand this construct, consider the concepts of the face value of debt and the market value of debt. The *face value of debt* is simply the nominal monetary value of the bonds or debt instruments, say, a $100 million bond held by an industrialized country bank representing $100 million that the bank has lent to the developing country. The face value of LDC debt is what is represented by the dollar figures in Table 6. The *market value of debt* refers to the actual trading prices of the bonds or debt instruments. LDC debt instruments (and of course most kinds of debt instruments) are sold (and bought) in a **secondary debt market** after the initial issuance if a holder wants to exchange the bonds for other assets (or someone else wants to exchange other assets for these bonds). Prices in these secondary markets are thought to reflect the "true" value of the claims, and for LDC debt, prices have sometimes gone below 20 percent of face value.

A debt-relief Laffer curve is shown in Figure 2.[33] The face value of debt is measured on the horizontal axis, and the market value of debt (the value in the secondary market) is plotted on the vertical axis. If lenders expect the debt to be fully repaid (including

. . . .
[32]The analogy is to the "Laffer curve" (named after Arthur B. Laffer) used in consideration of fiscal policy, whereby a reduction in the marginal tax rate can increase tax revenues.

[33]For an excellent exposition of the debt-relief Laffer curve, see "Sisters in the Wood: A Survey of the IMF and the World Bank," *The Economist,* Oct. 12, 1991, pp. 24, 29–30, 33.

interest), the market value is equal to the face value, and the relationship is represented by a 45° line from the origin. This is the case from the origin to point *A* (where $120 million of debt has a market value of $120 million). However, after point *A*, lenders do not expect the debt to be fully repaid, and the LDC bonds sell at a discount in the secondary market. Thus, at point *B*, $180 million of debt sells for $153 million, for the market value is only 85 percent of the face value ($153 million ÷ $180 million = 0.85), a discount of 15 percent. At point *C*, $200 million of debt would sell for $160 million in the secondary market, or at a 20 percent discount. Finally, after point *C*, we get the situation where additional debt beyond $200 million actually *reduces* the market value; for example, at point *F*, $240 million of debt has a market value of only $120 million. This downward-sloping range after point *C* represents the situation of our earlier discussion that the level of debt so reduces domestic and foreign investment that the country's growth and debt repayment prospects become very poor. In this range, a reduction of the developing country's debt from $240 million to $200 million would actually *increase* the market value of the debt from $120 million to $160 million. Hence, if the LDC is located beyond point *C*, there is a clear case for voluntary debt reduction or write-offs by the lending banks. Such action would increase the country's growth prospects and ability to repay debt, and it would also help the banks by raising the market value of their loan portfolios.

In the range between points *A* and *C*, the situation is somewhat different, but there is still some incentive for debt reduction by both the LDC and the lenders. Starting at point *C* and going to point *A*, lending banks could forgive $80 million of debt (= $200 million − $120 million), and the cost of writing off $80 million would be only $40 million (the reduction in the market value from $160 million to $120 million). Alternatively, if the developing country could obtain $40 million of resources from some other source such as the IMF or the World Bank or by its own efforts, it could "buy back" or cancel $80 million of its outstanding debt to the banks by giving the banks this $40 million. In either event or in some combination of buybacks and forgiveness, the LDC benefits from having less debt and lower future interest and amortization payments, and it has reduced its debt at a cost of 50 cents for each dollar of debt reduction. The banks will have reduced their holdings of risky LDC debt by $80 million but at a maximum cost of only $40 million. The banks have also increased the quality of the LDC debt that they continue to hold, as its market value ($120 million) is now 100 percent of its face value.

Given the debt-relief Laffer curve analysis, why have we not seen a greater amount of debt reduction in practice? The reason is that, for the forgiveness or buyback actions such as in the *A* to *C* range of the curve to be undertaken, negotiations must be successfully concluded by the developing country with *all* the bank lenders as a *group*. If this is not done, no *individual* lender has an incentive to do the debt reduction on its own. Suppose that there are only four lending banks—banks I, II, III, and IV—and that each of the four banks holds an equal face value of LDC debt of $50 million at point *C*. Suppose now that bank I forgives $20 million of the $50 million debt owed to it, reducing the LDC's total debt from $200 million to $180 million and moving the LDC from point *C* to point *B*. Given the shape of the debt-relief Laffer curve, this forgiveness by bank I has reduced the market value of the LDC's total debt from $160 million to $153 million. What has happened? Bank I formerly held $50 million face value LDC bonds with a market value of $40 million (since the market value at point *C* was 80 percent of the face value). It now holds $30 million of bonds (its original $50 million minus the $20 million forgiven) with a market value of $25.5 million. (The $25.5 million results because, at point *B*, market value is 85 percent of face value and $30 million × 0.85 = $25.5 million.) Hence, this bank has forgiven $20 million of debt, but it has done so at a cost of $14.5 million. (The original market value of bank I's holdings was $40 million, which has now been reduced to $25.5 million.) If all four banks each had simultaneously undertaken $20 million forgiveness, we would have moved from point *C* to point *A* on the curve, and the cost to bank I would have been only $10 million for its $20 million of debt reduction. Hence, the individual negotiation has cost bank I $4.5 million more (= $14.5 million − $10 million) than if all banks had negotiated reductions simultaneously. (Alternatively, in the case of a buyback by the LDC from bank I, the LDC would have had to pay bank I $14.5 million for the $20 million debt reduction in a single negotiation and only $10 million in the multiple negotiation.)

But matters are even worse for bank I when it alone forgives the $20 million debt. Because of its unilateral debt reduction, its competitor banks II, III, and IV have actually *gained*. With bank I's debt forgiveness to the LDC and the consequent movement from point *C* to point *B,* the ratio of market value to face value has risen from 80 percent ($160 million ÷ $200 million) to 85 percent ($153 million ÷ $180 million). The $50 million face-value bonds that each of these other banks still hold previously had a market value of $40 million (= $50 million × 0.80) but now have a market value of $42.5 million (= $50 million × 0.85). Bank I's action has benefited each other bank by $2.5 million (= $42.5 million − $40 million); each other bank is getting a "free ride" while bank I imposes a cost on itself of $14.5 million. Therefore, any one bank would not undertake the debt relief on its own. In this framework, then, without joint negotiations embracing all lenders, no action can be expected by any one bank to reduce developing country debt.

Debt-equity swaps

A final broad type of strategy for dealing with LDC debt involves **debt-equity swaps.** In this arrangement, a holder of a debt claim on a developing country exchanges the claim for local LDC currency, which is then used to acquire shares of stock in a productive enterprise in the LDC. Thus, the LDC reduces its debt and its interest obligations. In turn, the creditor no longer holds a bond whose repayment is uncertain, but instead holds equity in an ongoing company in the developing country. Whether this is advantageous to the creditor depends on the future performance of the company involved.

We do not explore other plans in this book, but a large number of such plans for reducing the burden of debt on LDCs exists. That the burden has been great is reflected in the fact that, for much of the 1980s, living standards fell in the debtor countries (particularly in Latin America) as they compressed imports and undertook austerity programs. Trade surpluses were generated through such measures, and there was in fact a large net *outflow* of capital from Latin America as repayments and interest exceeded new inflows. Indeed, the chief economist for the World Bank, Stanley Fischer, in conjunction with Ishrat Husain has written that the LDC adjustments "were made at a high price. Investment and output levels have fallen, domestic consumption and wages have been compressed. . . . As a result, most of the countries in Latin America and Africa now look back at almost a decade of lost growth" (Fischer and Husain 1990, p. 24). Jeffrey Sachs of Harvard University (1988, p. 21) also noted that these worsening economic conditions were occurring as many of the debtor countries were newly experimenting with democracy and that the adverse reaction to the harsh conditions necessary for full repayment of debt threatened the continued existence of democracy.

In addition to the above specific measures, industrialized countries can undertake several general measures to lessen the severity of the developing-country debt problem. These measures can also be of benefit to the ICs as well. For example, a decrease in levels of tariff and nontariff protection against LDC export goods would increase the foreign exchange earnings of LDCs and hence their ability to repay debt, as well as improve welfare in the ICs via the standard arguments for freer trade. In addition, more rapid economic growth in the industrialized countries not only would increase well-being in the ICs but would stimulate LDC exports, foreign exchange earnings, and national income. Further, an increase in the amount of foreign aid given to the developing countries not only would be of use to them but, if such aid stimulates LDC growth, would also benefit the industrialized countries through increased exports sold to the LDCs. There is certainly scope for such an increase in aid as the United States, for example, in recent years has allocated two-tenths of 1 percent or less of its GDP to foreign aid. This aid can also be given indirectly if the IMF issues new SDRs and allocates proportionately more of them to developing countries. Such an allocation of SDRs could assist the LDCs in maintaining a flow of development imports, even when a large fraction of their current foreign exchange earnings is being used for debt service.

Finally, in the last few years, despite the size of LDC debt and the potential for disruptions in the international monetary system if large industrialized country banks should undergo difficulties because of their holdings of LDC debt, concern over the debt problem has lessened. The Brady Plan of voluntary debt reduction by the banks, together with IMF and World Bank offers to guarantee debt buyback plans as well as initiatives by various governments, has resulted in a number of negotiated agreements regarding the debt. Further, economic recovery and growth have been occurring in a number of debt-ridden countries, importantly because of market-oriented reforms. In addition private foreign capital inflows to Latin America have now resumed.[34] Debt service obligations are therefore now being met more easily. Industrialized country banks have written off some debt, and indeed, the positions of the banks now are much more secure than they were in the early and mid-1980s. In addition, as noted in Table 6, the various debt severity ratios are projected to decline in the future.

This progress has led many observers to conclude that the "debt crisis" is over. However, despite these recent developments, serious debt problems continue in the 1990s, especially among the poorest LDCs and in sub-Saharan Africa (see Ahmed and Summers 1992). Also, the 1996 total LDC debt figure of $1,783.3 billion in Table 6 is higher than that in any previous year, and the IMF projects that it will increase in 1997 and 1998. In addition, debt problems also exist for the countries of Central and Eastern Europe and the former Soviet Union that are undergoing transitions to market economies. In these countries, problems may be even greater than in the traditional developing countries, since whole new economic systems are being devised. In these "transition" economies as well as in the LDCs, much work remains to be done both internally and by the industrialized countries. It is important to continue to seek strategies by which debt-burdened countries can face better long-term economic growth prospects.

CONCEPT CHECK

1. Why do developing countries object to IMF conditionality?

2. Explain the concept of the debt-relief Laffer curve.

3. Explain the usefulness of the concept of the debt service ratio.

---

[34]See "The Debt Crisis R.I.P.," *The Economist,* Sept. 12, 1992, pp. 15–16.

SUMMARY

The choice of an international monetary system involves consideration of the adequacy of the volume of international reserve assets, the confidence countries place in those assets, the extent to which effective balance-of-payments adjustment occurs, the amount of national autonomy in economic policy that is desirable, and the degree to which variations in exchange rates cause instability in macroeconomic performance. The Bretton Woods system involved pegged but adjustable exchange rates built around parity rates defined in terms of the U.S. dollar, which in turn was defined in terms of gold. This system permitted substantial growth of trade and investment during its operation, but it broke down in the early 1970s under the strain of growing trade and the uncertainty regarding the value of the dollar. Since the breakdown, countries have adopted a wide variety of exchange rate arrangements, and the current international monetary system is often called a "non-system." Recent experience has been characterized by considerable volatility in nominal and real exchange rates of leading industrial countries and by continued transmission of economic fluctuations from country to country, although the volume of trade and payments has grown substantially.

A number of proposals have been made for change in the current arrangements, including a return to a gold standard, the establishment of a world central bank, and the implementation of target zones for exchange rates. To reduce current instability in exchange rates and in the world economy, the leading industrialized countries are attempting greater coordination of their macroeconomic policies, but other possibilities include the levying of a tax on exchange market transactions and the adoption of additional restrictions on short-term capital flows. Finally, the developing countries prefer an international monetary system with greater stability of exchange rates and allocation of international reserve assets in their direction. These two features could ease the burden of the LDC debt problem, as could the adoption of various other policy measures.

KEY TERMS

adequacy of reserves problem (liquidity problem)
adjustment problem
balance-of-payments adjustment mechanism
Brady Plan
Bretton Woods system
confidence problem
convergence criteria
credit tranche
debt-equity swaps
debt relief (debt reduction)
debt-relief Laffer curve
debt rescheduling
debt service ratio
dual exchange rates (multiple exchange rates)

Economic and Monetary Union (EMU)
euro
European Currency Unit (ecu)
European Monetary Cooperation Fund (EMCF)
European Monetary System (EMS)
European System of Central Banks (ESCB)
Exchange Rate Mechanism (ERM)
gold tranche (reserve tranche)
IMF conditionality
IMF quota
international liquidity
International Monetary Fund (IMF)

internationally acceptable reserve assets
Jamaica Accords
key currencies
link proposal
Maastricht Treaty
pegged but adjustable exchange rates
secondary debt market
Smithsonian Agreement
special drawing rights (SDRs)
structural adjustment policies
surveillance
target zone proposal
transfer problem

QUESTIONS AND PROBLEMS

1. What are the key characteristics of an effective international monetary system? Does the current system meet these requirements?

2. What were the main problems in the Bretton Woods system? Are such problems present in the current system?

3. Why are SDRs often referred to as "paper gold"? What role do they play in the current system?

4. What is the similarity, if any, between a gold standard and a world central bank? What is the difference?

5. What were the original purposes of the IMF? Have they changed since Bretton Woods? What is the justification for IMF surveillance?

6. Why might it be said that a target zone system contains both the best and the worst of flexible and fixed exchange rate systems?

7. "A target zone system will work only if there is coordination of economic policies among country participants. On the other hand, if this effective coordination of monetary and fiscal policy exists among the members, there is no need for a target zone system!" What is the logic behind this statement?

8. From the standpoint of any given EU member country, what are the potential advantages of joining EMU? What are the potential disadvantages?

9. "The developing countries got themselves into their debt problems, and it's up to them to get themselves out." Discuss.

10. How would you go about determining whether a developing country's external debt difficulties constituted a "liquidity" difficulty or a "solvency" difficulty?

REFERENCES FOR FURTHER READING

CHAPTER 2

Bernstein, Edward M. "The United States as an International Debtor Country." *The Brookings Review* 4, no. 1 (Fall 1985), pp. 28–36.

Board of Governors of the Federal Reserve System. *Federal Reserve Bulletin,* May issue annually. Reviews U.S. international transactions for previous year.

International Monetary Fund. *Balance of Payments Manual.* 4th ed. Washington, DC: IMF, 1977.

————. *Balance of Payments Statistics Yearbook.* Washington, DC: IMF, Annual.

Kemp, Donald S. "Balance-of-Payments Concepts—What Do They Really Mean?" Federal Reserve Bank of St. Louis, *Review* 57, no. 7 (July 1975), pp. 14–23.

Kvasnicka, Joseph G. "U.S. Balance-of-Payments Statistics: What They Are and What Do They Tell Us." In *Readings in International Finance.* 3rd ed. Edited by Joseph G. Kvasnicka. Chicago: Federal Reserve Bank of Chicago, 1986, pp. 1–12.

Nawaz, Shuja. "Why the World Current Account Does Not Balance." *Finance and Development* 24, no. 3 (September 1987), pp. 43–45.

Ott, Mack. "Have U.S. Exports Been Larger Than Reported?" Federal Reserve Bank of St. Louis, *Review* 70, no. 5 (September–October 1988), pp. 3–23.

Powelson, John P. *Economic Accounting.* New York: McGraw-Hill, 1955. Chapters 21–23.

"Schools Brief: In Defence of Deficits." *The Economist,* December 16, 1995, p. 68–69.

Stern, Robert M., et al. *The Presentation of the Balance of Payments: A Symposium.* Princeton Essays in International Finance No. 123. Princeton, NJ: International Finance Section, Princeton University, August 1977.

U.S. Department of Commerce, Bureau of Economic Analysis. *Survey of Current Business.* April, July, and September issues annually.

Walter, Bruce C. "Quality Issues Affecting the Compilation of the U.S. Merchandise Trade Statistics." In *International Economic Transactions: Issues in Measurement and Empirical Research.* Edited by Peter Hooper and J. David Richardson. Chicago and London: University of Chicago Press, 1991, pp. 89–103.

CHAPTER 3

Black, Stanley W. "Transactions Costs and Vehicle Currencies." *Journal of International Money and Finance* 10, no. 4 (December 1991), pp. 512–26.

Chalupa, Karel V. "Foreign Currency Futures: Reducing Foreign Exchange Risk." Federal Reserve Bank of Chicago *Economic Perspectives* 6, no. 3 (Winter 1982), pp. 3–11.

Chrystal, K. Alec. "A Guide to Foreign Exchange Markets." Federal Reserve Bank of St. Louis, *Review* 66, no. 3 (March 1984), pp. 5–18.

Einzig, Paul. *A Dynamic Theory of Forward Exchange.* London: Macmillan, 1961.

"Fear of Finance: A Survey of the World Economy." *The Economist,* September 19, 1992, following p. 66.

Fieleke, Norman S. "The Rise of the Foreign Currency Futures Market." Federal Reserve Bank of Boston *New England Economic Review* (March–April 1985), pp. 38–47.

Gendreau, Brian. "New Markets in Foreign Exchange." Federal Reserve Bank of Philadelphia *Business Review* (July/August 1984), pp. 3–12.

Hakkio, Craig S. "Is Purchasing Power Parity a Useful Guide to the Dollar?" Federal Reserve Bank of Kansas City *Economic Review* (3rd quarter 1992), pp. 37–51.

International Monetary Fund. *IMF Survey.* Washington, DC: IMF, Biweekly.

Jorion, Philippe. "Does Real Interest Parity Hold at Longer Maturities?" *Journal of International Economics* 40, nos. 1/2 (February 1996), pp. 105–26.

Kasman, Bruce, and Charles Pigott. "Interest Rate Divergences among the Major Industrial Nations." Federal Reserve Bank of New York, *Quarterly Review* 13, no. 3 (Autumn 1988), pp. 28–44.

Kubarych, Robert M. *Foreign Exchange Markets in the United States.* New York: Federal Reserve Bank of New York, 1978.

Machlup, Fritz. "The Theory of Foreign Exchanges." *Economica* 6, New Series (November 1939), pp. 375–97, and vol. 7 (February 1940), pp. 23–49. Reprinted in American Economic Association. *Readings in the Theory of International Trade.* Edited by Howard S. Ellis and Lloyd A. Metzler. Philadelphia: Blakiston, 1950, pp. 104–58.

McCormick, Frank. "Covered Interest Arbitrage: Unexploited Profits? Comment." *Journal of Political Economy* 87, no. 2 (April 1979), pp. 411–17.

Quirk, Peter, and Viktor Schoofs. "Forward Exchange Markets in LDCs." *Finance and Development* 25, no. 3 (September 1988), pp. 36–39.

Rivera-Batiz, Francisco L., and Luis A. Rivera-Batiz. *International Finance and Open Economy Macroeconomics.* 2d ed. New York: Macmillan, 1994. Chapters 1, 4–6.

Taylor, Mark P. "The Economics of Exchange Rates." *Journal of Economic Literature* 33, no. 1 (March 1995), pp. 13–47. (Pages 14–21 are particularly relevant for this chapter.)

Thornton, Daniel L. "Tests of Covered Interest Rate Parity." Federal Reserve Bank of St. Louis, *Review* 71, no. 4 (July–August 1989), pp. 55–66.

CHAPTER 4

Bank for International Settlements. *65th Annual Report.* Basle, Switzerland: BIS, June 12, 1995.

——. *66th Annual Report.* Basle, Switzerland: BIS, June 10, 1996.

——. *67th Annual Report.* Basle, Switzerland: BIS, June 9, 1997.

Bryan, Lowell, and Diana Farrell. *Market Unbound: Unleashing Global Capitalism.* New York: John Wiley and Sons, 1996.

Burghardt, Galen; Terry Belton; Morton Lane; Geoffrey Luce; and Rick McVey. *Eurodollar Futures and Options: Controlling Money Market Risk.* Chicago: Probus Publishing, 1991.

Dufey, Gunter, and Ian H. Giddy. *The International Money Market.* 2d ed. Englewood Cliffs, NJ: Prentice-Hall, 1994.

Eng, Maximo, and Francis A. Lees. "Eurocurrency Centers." In *International Finance Handbook.* Vol. 1. Edited by Abraham M. George and Ian H. Giddy. New York: John Wiley and Sons, 1983. Section 3.6.

Gibson, Heather D. *The Eurocurrency Markets, Domestic Financial Policy and International Instability.* New York: St. Martin's Press, 1989.

Johnston, R. B. *The Economics of the Euro-Market: History, Theory and Policy.* New York: St. Martin's Press, 1982.

Kambhu, John; Frank Keane; and Catherine Benadon. "Price Risk Intermediation in the Over-the-Counter Derivatives Markets: Interpretation of a Global Survey." Federal Reserve Bank of New York, *Economic Policy Review* 2, no. 1 (April 1996), pp. 1–15.

Kaufman, Herbert M. *Money and Banking.* Lexington, MA: D.C. Heath, 1992.

Kreicher, Lawrence L. "Eurodollar Arbitrage." Federal Reserve Bank of New York, *Quarterly Review* 7, no. 2 (Summer 1982), pp. 10–22.

Kvasnicka, Joseph G. "Eurodollars—An Important Source of Funds for American Banks." In *Readings in International Finance.* 3rd ed. Edited by Joseph G. Kvasnicka. Chicago: Federal Reserve Bank of Chicago, 1986, pp. 165–76.

Magraw, Daniel. "Legal Aspects of International Bonds." In *International Finance Handbook.* Vol. 1. Edited by Abraham M. George and Ian H. Giddy. New York: John Wiley and Sons, 1983. Section 5.3.

Mayo, Herbert B. *Investments: An Introduction.* 5th ed. Forth Worth, TX: Dryden Press, 1997.

Mendelsohn, M. S. *Money on the Move: The Modern International Capital Market.* New York: McGraw-Hill, 1980.

Mendelson, Morris. "The Eurobond and Foreign Bond Markets." In *International Finance Handbook.* Vol. 1. Edited by Abraham M. George and Ian H. Giddy. New York: John Wiley and Sons, 1983. Section 5.1.

Remolona, Eli M. "The Recent Growth of Financial Derivatives Markets." Federal Reserve Bank of New York *Quarterly Review* 17, no. 4 (Winter 1992–93), pp. 28–43.

Savona, Paolo, and George Sutija (eds.). *Eurodollars and International Banking.* New York: St. Martin's Press, 1985.

Shepherd, William F. *International Financial Integration: History, Theory and Applications in OECD Countries.* Aldershot, England: Averbury, 1994. Chapters 3–4.

CHAPTER 5

Black, Stanley W., and Michael K. Salemi. "FIML Estimation of the Dollar-Deutschemark Risk Premium in a Portfolio Model." *Journal of International Economics* 25, no. 3/4 (November 1988), pp. 205–24.

Blomberg, S. Brock, and Gregory D. Hess. "Politics and Exchange Rate Forecasts." *Journal of International Economics* 43, nos. 1/2 (August 1997), pp. 189–205.

Branson, William H.; Hannu Halttunen; and Paul Masson. "Exchange Rates in the Short Run: The Dollar-Deutschemark Rate." *European Economic Review* 10, no. 3 (December 1977), pp. 303–24.

Branson, William H., and Dale W. Henderson. "The Specification and Influence of Asset Markets." In *Handbook of International Economics,* Vol. II. Edited by Ronald W. Jones and Peter B. Kenen. Amsterdam: North-Holland, 1985. Chapter 15.

Cheung, Yin-Wong, and Kon S. Lai. "Long-Run Purchasing Power Parity during the Recent Float." *Journal of International Economics* 34, no. 1/2 (February 1993), pp. 181–92.

Crownover, Collin; John Pippenger; and Douglas G. Steigerwald. "Testing for Absolute Purchasing Power Parity." *Journal of International Money and Finance* 15, no. 5 (October 1996), pp. 783–96.

Dominguez, Kathryn M., and Jeffrey A. Frankel. "Does Foreign Exchange Intervention Matter? The Portfolio Effect." *American Economic Review* 83, no. 4 (December 1993), pp. 1356–59.

Dornbusch, Rudiger. "Exchange Rate Economics: Where Do We Stand?" *Brookings Papers on Economic Activity,* no. 1 (1980), pp. 143–85.

———. "Expectations and Exchange Rate Dynamics." *Journal of Political Economy* 84, no. 6 (December 1976), pp. 1161–76.

Frankel, Jeffrey A. "Monetary and Portfolio-Balance Models of the Determination of Exchange Rates." In Jeffrey A. Frankel, *On Exchange Rates.* Cambridge, MA: MIT Press, 1993, pp. 95–115.

———. "The Mystery of the Multiplying Marks: A Modification of the Monetary Model." *Review of Economics and Statistics* 64, no. 4 (August 1982), pp. 515–19.

———. "Tests of Monetary and Portfolio Balance Models of Exchange Rate Determination." In *Exchange Rate Theory and Practice.* Edited by John F. O. Bilson and Richard C. Marston. Chicago: University of Chicago Press, 1984. Chapter 7.

Frankel, Jeffrey A., and Andrew K. Rose. "A Panel Project on Purchasing Power Parity: Mean Reversion within and between Countries." *Journal of International Economics* 40, nos. 1/2 (February 1996), pp. 209–24.

Frenkel, Jacob A. "A Monetary Approach to the Exchange Rate: Doctrinal Aspects and Empirical Evidence." In *The Economics of Exchange Rates.* Edited by Jacob A. Frenkel and Harry G. Johnson. Reading, MA: Addison-Wesley, 1978. Chapter 1.

Frenkel, Jacob A. and Michael L. Mussa. "Asset Markets, Exchange Rates and the Balance of Payments." In *Handbook of International Economics.* Vol. II. Edited by Ronald W. Jones and Peter B. Kenen. Amsterdam: North-Holland, 1985. Chapter 14.

Friedman, Milton (ed.). *Studies in the Quantity Theory of Money.* Chicago: University of Chicago Press, 1956.

Froyen, Richard T. *Macroeconomics: Theories and Policies.* 5th ed. Upper Saddle River, NJ: Prentice-Hall, 1996. Chapters 6 and 15.

Graham, Frank D. *Exchange, Prices and Production in Hyper-Inflation: Germany, 1920–1923.* Princeton, NJ: Princeton University Press, 1930.

Harvey, John T. "Orthodox Approaches to Exchange Rate Determination: A Survey." *Journal of Post Keynesian Economics* 18, no. 4 (Summer 1996), pp. 567–83.

Isard, Peter. *Exchange Rate Economics: Surveys of Economic Literature.* Cambridge, England: Cambridge University Press, 1995.

Levich, Richard H. "Empirical Studies of Exchange Rates: Price Behavior, Rate Determination and Market Efficiency." In *Handbook of International Economics.* Vol. II. Edited by Ronald W. Jones and Peter B. Kenen. Amsterdam: North-Holland, 1985. Chapter 19.

MacDonald, Ronald, and Mark P. Taylor. "Exchange Rate Economics: A Survey." *International Monetary Fund Staff Papers* 39, no. 1 (March 1992), pp. 1–57.

Meese, Richard. "Currency Fluctuations in the Post-Bretton Woods Era." *Journal of Economic Perspectives* 4, no. 1 (Winter 1990), pp. 117–34.

Meese, Richard A., and Kenneth Rogoff. "Empirical Exchange Rate Models of the Seventies: Do They Fit Out of Sample?" *Journal of International Economics* 14, no. 1/2 (February 1983), pp. 3–24.

Melvin, Michael. *International Money and Finance.* 4th ed. New York: HarperCollins, 1995.

Mussa, Michael. "The Monetary Approach to the Balance of Payments." In *International Trade and Finance: Readings.* 2nd ed. Edited by Robert E. Baldwin and J. David Richardson. Boston: Little, Brown, 1981, pp. 368–73.

Niehans, Jürg. *International Monetary Economics.* Baltimore: Johns Hopkins University Press, 1984. Chapter 3.

Ott, Mack. "Post Bretton Woods Deviations from Purchasing Power Parities in G7 Exchange Rates—An Empirical Exploration." *Journal of International Money and Finance* 15, no. 6 (December 1996), pp. 899–924.

Rivera-Batiz, Francisco L., and Luis A. Rivera-Batiz. *International Finance and Open Economy Macroeconomics.* 2d ed. New York: Macmillan, 1994. Chapters 19–20.

Rogoff, Kenneth. "The Purchasing Power Parity Puzzle." *Journal of Economic Literature* 34, no. 2 (June 1996), pp. 647–68.

Stein, Jerome L.; Polly Reynolds Allen; and associates. *Fundamental Determinants of Exchange Rates.* New York and Oxford: Oxford University Press and Clarendon Press, 1995.

Taylor, Mark. "The Economics of Exchange Rates." *Journal of Economic Literature* 33, no. 1 (March 1995), pp. 13–47.

Ujiie, Junichi. "A Stock Adjustment Approach to Monetary Policy and the Balance of Payments." In *The Economics of Exchange Rates.* Edited by Jacob A. Frenkel and Harry G. Johnson. Reading, MA: Addison-Wesley, 1978. Chapter 10.

CHAPTER 6

Alexander, Sidney S. "Effects of a Devaluation: A Simplified Synthesis of Elasticities and Absorption Approaches." *American Economic Review* 49, no. 1 (March 1959), pp. 22–42.

———. "Effects of a Devaluation on a Trade Balance." *International Monetary Fund Staff Papers* 3, no. 1 (April 1952), pp. 263–78.

Appleyard, Dennis R., and Alfred J. Field, Jr. "A Note on Teaching the Marshall-Lerner Condition." *Journal of Economic Education* 17, no. 1 (Winter 1986), pp. 52–57.

Backus, David K.; Patrick J. Kehoe; and Finn E. Kydland. "Dynamics of the Trade Balance and the Terms of Trade: The J-Curve?" *American Economic Review* 84, no. 1 (March 1994), pp. 84–103.

Baldwin, Richard, and Paul Krugman. "Persistent Trade Effects of Large Exchange Rate Shocks." *Quarterly Journal of Economics* 104, no. 4 (November 1989), pp. 635–54.

Bloomfield, Arthur I. *Monetary Policy under the International Gold Standard: 1880–1914.* New York: Federal Reserve Bank of New York, 1959.

Dwyer, Jacqueline, and Ricky Lam. "The Two Stages of Exchange Rate Pass-Through: Implications for Inflation." *Australian Economic Papers* 34, no. 65 (December 1995), pp. 157–79.

Feenstra, Robert C. "Symmetric Pass-Through of Tariffs and Exchange Rates under Imperfect Competition: An Empirical Test." *Journal of International Economics* 27, no. 1/2 (August 1989), pp. 25–45.

Feenstra, Robert C.; Joseph E. Gagnon; and Michael M. Knetter. "Market Share and Exchange Rate Pass-Through in World Automobile Trade." *Journal of International Economics* 40, nos. 1/2 (February 1996), pp. 187–207.

Feldman, Robert A. "Dollar Appreciation, Foreign Trade, and the U.S. Economy." Federal Reserve Bank of New York *Quarterly Review* 7, no. 2 (Summer 1982), pp. 1–9.

Goldstein, Morris, and Mohsin S. Khan. "Income and Price Effects in Foreign Trade." In *Handbook of International Economics.* Vol. II. Edited by Ronald W. Jones and Peter B. Kenen. Amsterdam: North-Holland, 1985. Chapter 20.

Gron, Anne, and Deborah L. Swenson. "Incomplete Exchange-Rate Pass-Through and Imperfect Competition: The Effect of Local Production." *American Economic Review* 86, no. 2 (May 1996), pp. 71–76.

Houthakker, Hendrik S., and Stephen P. Magee. "Income and Price Elasticities in World Trade." *Review of Economics and Statistics* 51, no. 2 (May 1969), pp. 111–25.

Knetter, Michael M. "International Comparisons of Pricing-to-Market Behavior." *American Economic Review* 83, no. 3 (June 1993), pp. 473–86.

Krugman, Paul R., and Richard E. Baldwin. "The Persistence of the U.S. Trade Deficit." *Brookings Papers on Economic Activity,* no. 1 (1987), pp. 1–55.

Magee, Stephen P. "Currency Contracts, Pass-Through, and Devaluation." *Brookings Papers on Economic Activity,* no. 1 (1973), pp. 303–23, and "Discussion," pp. 323–25.

Marquez, Jaime. "Bilateral Trade Elasticities." *Review of Economics and Statistics* 72, no. 1 (February 1990), pp. 70–77.

Meade, Ellen E. "Exchange Rates, Adjustment, and the J-Curve." *Federal Reserve Bulletin* 74, no. 10 (October 1988), pp. 633–44.

Orcutt, Guy H. "Measurement of Price Elasticities in International Trade." *Review of Economics and Statistics* 32, no. 2 (May 1950), pp. 117–32.

Robinson, Joan. "The Foreign Exchanges." In Joan Robinson, *Essays in the Theory of Employment.* 2nd ed. Oxford: Basil Blackwell, 1947, pp. 134–55.

Stern, Robert M.; Jonathan Francis; and Bruce Schumacher. *Price Elasticities in International Trade: An Annotated Bibliography.* London: Macmillan, 1975.

Tsiang, S. C. "The Role of Money in Trade-Balance Stability: Synthesis of the Elasticity and Absorption Approaches." *American Economic Review* 51, no. 5 (December 1961), pp. 912–36.

Yang, Jiawen. "Exchange Rate Pass-Through in U.S. Manufacturing Industries." *Review of Economics and Statistics* 79, no. 1 (February 1997), pp. 95–104.

CHAPTER 7

Ammer, John, and Jianping Mei. "Measuring International Economic Linkages with Stock Market Data." *Journal of Finance* 51, no. 5 (December 1996), pp. 1743–63.

Bruce, Neil, and Douglas D. Purvis. "The Specification and Influence of Goods and Factor Markets in Open-Economy Macroeconomic Models." In *Handbook of International Economics.* Vol. II. Edited by Ronald W. Jones and Peter B. Kenen. Amsterdam: North-Holland, 1985. Chapter 16.

Dornbusch, Rudiger. *Open Economy Macroeconomics.* New York: Basic Books, 1980.

Filatov, V. B.; B. G. Hickman; and L. R. Klein. "Long-Term Simulations with the Project Link System, 1978–1985." In *Global International Economic Models.* Edited by B. G. Hickman. Amsterdam: North-Holland, 1983, pp. 29–51.

Froyen, Richard T. *Macroeconomics: Theories and Policies.* 5th ed. Upper Saddle River, NJ: Prentice-Hall, 1996. Chapter 5.

Harrod, R. F. *The Life of John Maynard Keynes.* New York: Harcourt, Brace, 1951.

Helliwell, John F., and Tim Padmore. "Empirical Studies of Macroeconomic Interdependence." In *Handbook of International Economics.* Vol. II. Edited by Ronald W. Jones and Peter B. Kenen. Amsterdam: North-Holland, 1985. Chapter 21.

Hess, Peter, and Clark Ross. *Economic Development: Theories, Evidence, and Policies.* Fort Worth, TX: Dryden Press, 1997. Chapter 24.

Kenen, Peter B. "Macroeconomic Theory and Policy: How the Closed Economy Was Opened." In *Handbook of International Economics.* Vol. II. Edited by Ronald W. Jones and Peter B. Kenen. Amsterdam: North-Holland, 1985. Chapter 13.

Keynes, John Maynard. *The General Theory of Employment, Interest and Money.* New York: Harcourt, Brace, 1936.

Kim, Yoonbai. "Income Effects on the Trade Balance." *Review of Economics and Statistics* 78, no. 3 (August 1996), pp. 464–69.

Machlup, Fritz. *International Trade and the National Income Multiplier.* Philadelphia: Blakiston, 1943.

Marquez, Jaime. "Bilateral Trade Elasticities." *Review of Economics and Statistics* 72, no. 1 (February 1990), pp. 70–77.

Meade, James E. *The Theory of International Economic Policy.* Vol. I. *The Balance of Payments.* London: Oxford University Press, 1951. Part III.

Niehans, Jürg. *International Monetary Economics.* Baltimore: Johns Hopkins University Press, 1984. Chapters 4–5.

Norton, Stefan C., and Don E. Schlagenhauf. "The Role of International Factors in the Business Cycle: A Multi-Country Study." *Journal of International Economics* 40, nos. 1/2 (February 1996), pp. 85–104.

Swan, T. W. "Longer-Run Problems of the Balance of Payments." In *The Australian Economy: A Volume of Readings.* Edited by H. W. Arndt and W. M. Corden. Melbourne: F. W. Cheshire Press, 1963, pp. 384–95.

Tinbergen, Jan. *Economic Policy: Principles and Design.* 4th rev. printing. Amsterdam: North-Holland, 1967.

Tsiang, S. C. "The Role of Money in Trade-Balance Stability: Synthesis of the Elasticity and Absorption Approaches." *American Economic Review* 51, no. 5 (December 1961), pp. 912–36.

CHAPTER 8

Black, Stanley W. "The Relationship between Exchange Rate Policy and Monetary Policy in Ten Industrial Countries." In *Exchange Rate Theory and Practice.* Edited by John F. O. Bilson and Richard Marston. Chicago: University of Chicago Press, 1984. Chapter 15.

Bonser-Neal, Catherine. "Does Central Bank Intervention Stabilize Foreign Exchange Rates?" Federal Reserve Bank of Kansas City, *Economic Review* 81, no. 1 (First Quarter 1996), pp. 43–57.

Crockett, Andrew. "Monetary Policy Implications of Increased Capital Flows." In *Changing Capital Markets: Implications for Monetary Policy.* Symposium sponsored by the Federal Reserve Bank of Kansas City, Jackson Hole, Wyoming, Aug. 19–21, 1993. Kansas City: Federal Reserve Bank of Kansas City, 1993, pp. 331–64.

Fender, John, and Chong K. Yip. "Open Economy Macroeconomics under Imperfect Competition: A Two-Country Model." *Journal of International Economics* 37, no. 1/2 (August 1994), pp. 49–63.

Fleming, J. Marcus. "Domestic Financial Policies under Fixed and under Floating Exchange Rates." *International Monetary Fund Staff Papers* 9, no. 3 (November 1962), pp. 369–79.

Frenkel, Jacob A., and Michael L. Mussa. "Asset Markets, Exchange Rates, and the Balance of Payments." In *Handbook of International Economics.* Vol. II. Edited by Ronald W. Jones and Peter B. Kenen. Amsterdam: North-Holland, 1985. Chapter 14.

Frenkel, Jacob A., and Assaf Razin. "The Mundell-Fleming Model a Quarter Century Later." *International*

Monetary Fund Staff Papers 34, no. 4 (December 1987), pp. 567–620.

Froyen, Richard T. *Macroeconomics: Theories and Policies.* 5th ed. Upper Saddle River, NJ: Prentice-Hall, 1996. Chapters 6–7, 21.

Gordon, Robert J. *Macroeconomics.* 6th ed. New York: HarperCollins, 1993. Chapters 3–5.

Kenen, Peter B. "Macroeconomic Theory and Policy: How the Closed Economy Was Opened." In *Handbook of International Economics.* Vol. II. Edited by Ronald W. Jones and Peter B. Kenen. Amsterdam: North-Holland, 1985. Chapter 13.

Machlup, Fritz. *International Payments, Debts, and Gold: Collected Essays of Fritz Machlup.* New York: Charles Scribner's Sons, 1964. Part 2.

Mundell, Robert. "The Appropriate Use of Monetary and Fiscal Policy for Internal and External Stability." *International Monetary Fund Staff Papers* 9, no. 1 (March 1962), pp. 70–77.

———. "Capital Mobility and Stabilization Policy under Fixed and Flexible Exchange Rates." *Canadian Journal of Economics and Political Science* 29, no. 4 (November 1963), pp. 475–85.

———. "The International Distribution of Money in a Growing World Economy." In *The Monetary Approach to the Balance of Payments.* Edited by Jacob A. Frenkel and Harry G. Johnson. Toronto: University of Toronto Press, 1980. Pp. 92–108.

Mussa, Michael. "Macroeconomic Interdependence and the Exchange Rate Regime." In *International Economic Policy: Theory and Evidence.* Edited by Rudiger Dornbusch and Jacob A. Frenkel. Baltimore: Johns Hopkins University Press, 1979. Pp. 160–204.

Tinbergen, Jan. *Economic Policy: Principles and Design.* 4th rev. printing. Amsterdam: North-Holland, 1967.

Willett, Thomas D., and Francisco Forte. "Interest Rate Policy and External Balance." *Quarterly Journal of Economics* 83, no. 2 (May 1969), pp. 242–62.

Williamson, John H. *The Exchange Rate System.* Washington, DC: Institute for International Economics, 1983.

CHAPTER 9

Argy, Victor, and Joanne Salop. "Price and Output Effects of Monetary and Fiscal Policy under Flexible Exchange Rates." *International Monetary Fund Staff Papers* 26, no. 2 (June 1979), pp. 224–56.

Black, Stanley W. "The Relationship between Exchange Rate Policy and Monetary Policy in Ten Industrial Countries." In *Exchange Rate Theory and Practice.* Edited by John F. O. Bilson and Richard C. Marston. Chicago: University of Chicago Press, 1984. Chapter 15.

Cooper, Richard N. "Economic Interdependence and Coordination of Economic Policies." In *Handbook of International Economics.* Vol. II. Edited by Ronald W. Jones and

Peter B. Kenen. Amsterdam: North-Holland, 1985. Chapter 23.

Currie, David. "International Cooperation in Monetary Policy: Has It a Future?" *Economic Journal* 103 (January 1993), pp. 178–87.

Dunn, Robert M., Jr. *The Many Disappointments of Flexible Exchange Rates.* Essays in International Finance No. 154. Princeton, NJ: International Finance Section, Princeton University, December 1983.

"Fear of Finance: A Survey of the World Economy." *The Economist,* September 19, 1992, following p. 66.

Fleming, J. Marcus. "Domestic Financial Policies under Fixed and under Floating Exchange Rates." *International Monetary Fund Staff Papers* 9, no. 3 (November 1962), pp. 369–79.

Friedman, Milton. "The Case for Flexible Exchange Rates." In Milton Friedman, *Essays in Positive Economics.* Chicago: University of Chicago Press, 1953, pp. 157–203.

Froyen, Richard T. *Macroeconomics: Theories and Policies.* 5th ed. Upper Saddle River, NJ: Prentice-Hall, 1996. Chapter 21.

Genberg, Hans, and Alexander K. Swoboda. "Policy and Current Account Determination under Floating Exchange Rates." *International Monetary Fund Staff Papers* 36, no. 1 (March 1989), pp. 1–30.

Glick, Reuven; Peter Kretzmer; and Clas Wihlborg. "Real Exchange Rate Effects of Monetary Disturbances under Different Degrees of Exchange Rate Flexibility: An Empirical Analysis." *Journal of International Economics* 38, no. 3/4 (May 1995), pp. 249–73.

Hutchison, Michael, and Carl E. Walsh. "Empirical Evidence on the Insulation Properties of Fixed and Flexible Exchange Rates: The Japanese Experience." *Journal of International Economics* 32, no. 3/4 (May 1992), pp. 241–63.

Kenen, Peter B. "Macroeconomic Theory and Policy: How the Closed Economy Was Opened." In *Handbook of International Economics.* Vol. II. Edited by Ronald W. Jones and Peter B. Kenen. Amsterdam: North-Holland, 1985. Chapter 13.

Krueger, Anne O. *Exchange-Rate Determination.* Cambridge: Cambridge University Press, 1983. Chapter 6.

Marston, Richard C. "Stabilization Policies in Open Economies." In *Handbook of International Economics.* Vol. II. Edited by Ronald W. Jones and Peter B. Kenen. Amsterdam: North-Holland, 1985. Chapter 17.

McCulloch, Rachel. "Macroeconomic Policy and Trade Performance: International Implications of U.S. Budget Deficits." In *Issues in U.S.-EC Trade Relations.* Edited by Robert E. Baldwin, Carl B. Hamilton, and André Sapir. Chicago: University of Chicago Press, 1988, pp. 349–68.

Mundell, Robert A. *International Economics.* New York: Macmillan, 1968. Chapters 17–18.

Quirk, Peter J., and Hernán Cortés-Douglas. "The Experience with Floating Rates." *Finance and Development* 30, no. 2 (June 1993), pp. 28–31.

Rivera-Batiz, Francisco L., and Luis A. Rivera-Batiz. *International Finance and Open Economy Macroeconomics.* 2d ed. New York: Macmillan, 1994. Chapter 17.

CHAPTER 10

Akerlof, George, and Janet Yellin. "Rational Models of Irrational Behavior." *American Economic Review* 77, no. 2 (May 1987), pp. 137–42.

Ball, Laurence; N. Gregory Mankiw; and David Romer. "The New Keynesian Economics and the Output-Inflation Trade-Off." *Brookings Papers on Economic Activity,* no. 1 (1988), pp. 1–66.

Black, Stanley W. (ed.). *Productivity Growth and the Competitiveness of the American Economy.* Boston: Kluwer Academic Publishers, 1989.

Blanchard, Olivier J., and Lawrence H. Summers. "Hysteresis and the European Unemployment Problem." In *NBER Macroeconomics Annual 1986.* Edited by Stanley Fischer. Cambridge, MA: MIT Press, 1986. Pp. 15–78.

Bruce, Neil, and Douglas D. Purvis. "The Specification and Influence of Goods and Factor Markets in Open-Economy Macroeconomic Models." In *Handbook of International Economics.* Vol. II. Edited by Ronald W. Jones and Peter B. Kenen. Amsterdam: North-Holland, 1985. Chapter 16.

Darity, William, Jr., and Arthur H. Goldsmith. "Social Psychology, Unemployment and Macroeconomics." *Journal of Economic Perspectives* 10, no. 1 (Winter 1996), pp. 121–40.

Economic Report of the President, January 1993. Washington, DC: U.S. Government Printing Office, 1993. Chapter 3.

Economic Report of the President, February 1997. Washington, DC: U.S. Government Printing Office, 1997. Chapter 2.

Froyen, Richard T. *Macroeconomics: Theories and Policies.* 5th ed. Upper Saddle River, NJ: Prentice-Hall, 1996. Chapters 8–13.

Gordon, Robert J. *Macroeconomics.* 6th ed. New York: HarperCollins, 1993. Chapters 6–8.

Greenwald, Bruce C., and Joseph E. Stiglitz. "Examining Alternative Macroeconomic Theories." *Brookings Papers on Economic Activity,* no. 1 (1988), pp. 207–60.

Hailstones, Thomas J. *Viewpoints on Supply Side Economics.* Englewood Cliffs, NJ: Prentice-Hall, 1983.

Maddock, Rodney, and Michael Carter. "A Child's Guide to Rational Expectations." *Journal of Economic Literature* 20, no. 1 (March 1982), pp. 39–51.

Mankiw, N. Gregory. "A Quick Refresher Course in Macroeconomics." *Journal of Economic Literature* 28, no. 4 (December 1990), pp. 1645–60.

Marston, Richard C. "Stabilization Policies in Open Economies." In *Handbook of International Economics.* Vol. II. Edited by Ronald W. Jones and Peter B. Kenen. Amsterdam: North-Holland, 1985. Chapter 17.

Sargent, Thomas, and Neil Wallace. "Rational Expectations and the Theory of Economic Policy." *Journal of Monetary Economics* 2, no. 2 (April 1976), pp. 169–83.

"Schools Brief: Keynes Rides Again." *The Economist,* November 17, 1990, pp. 97–98.

"Schools Brief: Tales of the Expected." *The Economist,* November 10, 1990, pp. 90–91.

Stiglitz, Joseph. "Reflections on the Natural Rate Hypothesis." *Journal of Economic Perspectives* 11, no. 1 (Winter 1997), pp. 3–10.

Weiner, Stuart E. "Challenges to the Natural Rate Framework." Federal Reserve Bank of Kansas City *Economic Review* 80, no. 2 (Second Quarter 1995), pp. 19–25.

CHAPTER 11

Artus, Jacques R., and Andrew D. Crockett. *Floating Exchange Rates and the Need for Surveillance.* Essays in International Finance No. 127. Princeton, NJ: International Finance Section, Princeton University, May 1978.

Baxter, Marianne, and Alan C. Stockman. "Business Cycles and the Exchange-Rate Regime: Some International Evidence." *Journal of Monetary Economics* 23, no. 3 (May 1989), pp. 377–400.

Bilson, John F. O., and Richard C. Marston (eds.). *Exchange Rate Theory and Practice.* Chicago: University of Chicago Press, 1984.

Cooper, Richard N. *Currency Devaluation in Developing Countries.* Essays in International Finance No. 86. Princeton, NJ: International Finance Section, Princeton University, June 1971.

Corden, W. M. *Inflation, Exchange Rates, and the World Economy: Lectures on International Monetary Economics.* 3rd ed. Chicago: University of Chicago Press, 1986.

Cushman, David O. "U.S. Bilateral Trade Flows and Exchange Risk during the Floating Period." *Journal of International Economics* 24, no. 3/4 (May 1988), pp. 317–30.

de Grauwe, Paul. *The Economics of Monetary Integration.* Oxford: Oxford University Press, 1992.

Dornbusch, Rudiger. "Flexible Exchange Rates and Interdependence." *International Monetary Fund Staff Papers* 30, no. 1 (March 1983), pp. 3–30.

Ethier, Wilfred, and Arthur I. Bloomfield. *Managing the Managed Float.* Essays in International Finance No. 112. Princeton, NJ: International Finance Section, Princeton University, October 1975.

Flanders, M. June. *The Demand for International Reserves.* Princeton Studies in International Finance No. 27. Princeton, NJ: International Finance Section, Princeton University, 1971.

Friedman, Milton. "The Case for Flexible Exchange Rates." In Milton Friedman, *Essays in Positive Economics.* Chicago: University of Chicago Press, 1953, pp. 157–203.

Friedman, Milton, with Rose D. Friedman. *Capitalism and Freedom.* Chicago: University of Chicago Press, 1962. Chapter IV.

Gagnon, Joseph E. "Exchange Rate Variability and the Level of International Trade." *Journal of International Economics* 34, no. 3/4 (May 1993), pp. 269–87.

Goldstein, Morris. "Whither the Exchange Rate System?" *Finance and Development* 21, no. 2 (June 1984), pp. 2–6.

Halm, George N. *The "Band" Proposal: The Limits of Permissible Exchange Rate Variations.* Special Papers in International Economics No. 6. Princeton, NJ: International Finance Section, Princeton University, 1965.

Heller, H. Robert. "Optimal International Reserves." *Economic Journal* 76, no. 302 (June 1966), pp. 296–311.

Hooper, Peter, and Steven W. Kohlhagen. "The Effect of Exchange Rate Uncertainty on the Prices and Volume of International Trade." *Journal of International Economics* 8, no. 4 (November 1978), pp. 483–511.

Hutchison, Michael, and Carl E. Walsh. "Empirical Evidence on the Insulation Properties of Fixed and Flexible Exchange Rates: The Japanese Experience." *Journal of International Economics* 32, no. 3/4 (May 1992), pp. 241–63.

Ito, Takatoshi; Peter Isard; Steven Symanski; and Tamim Bayoumi. *Exchange Rate Movements and Their Impact on Trade and Investment in the APEC Region.* IMF Occasional Paper 145. Washington, DC: IMF, 1996. (Summarized in "Study Examines Exchange Rate Changes and Impact on APEC Trade and Investment," *IMF Survey,* Feb. 10, 1997, pp. 37–38.)

McCulloch, Rachel. *Unexpected Real Consequences of Floating Exchange Rates.* Essays in International Finance No. 153. Princeton, NJ: International Finance Section, Princeton University, August 1983.

McKinnon, Ronald I. "Optimum Currency Areas." *American Economic Review* 53, no. 4 (September 1963), pp. 717–25.

Mundell, Robert A. "Currency Areas, Common Currencies, and EMU." *American Economic Review* 87, no. 2 (May 1997), pp. 214–16.

————. "A Theory of Optimum Currency Areas." *American Economic Review* 51, no. 4 (September 1961), pp. 657–65.

Niehans, Jürg. *International Monetary Economics.* Baltimore: Johns Hopkins University Press, 1984. Chapters 13–14.

Taylor, Mark P. "The Economics of Exchange Rates." *Journal of Economic Literature* 33, no. 1 (March 1995), pp. 13–47.

Thursby, Jerry G., and Marie C. Thursby. "Bilateral Trade Flows, the Linder Hypothesis, and Exchange Risk." *Review of Economics and Statistics* 69, no. 3 (August 1987), pp. 488–95.

Tower, Edward, and Thomas D. Willett. *The Theory of Optimum Currency Areas and Exchange-Rate Flexibility.*

Special Papers in International Economics No. 11. Princeton, NJ: International Finance Section, Princeton University, 1976.

CHAPTER 12

Ahmed, Masood, and Lawrence Summers. "A Tenth Anniversary Report on the Debt Crisis." *Finance and Development* 29, no. 3 (September 1992), pp. 2–5.

Baldwin, Robert E., and J. David Richardson. *International Trade and Finance: Readings.* 3rd ed. Boston: Little, Brown, 1986. [Contains the Cooper (1986), Dunn, Goldstein, and McCulloch readings listed below. All except Dunn are slightly abridged.]

Bergsten, C. Fred, and C. Randall Henning. *Global Economic Leadership and the Group of Seven.* Washington, DC: Institute for International Economics, 1996.

Black, Stanley W. *Exchange Policies for Less Developed Countries in a World of Floating Rates.* Essays in International Finance No. 119. Princeton, NJ: International Finance Section, Princeton University, December 1976.

———. "International Money and International Monetary Arrangements." In *Handbook of International Economics.* Vol. II. Edited by Ronald W. Jones and Peter B. Kenen. Amsterdam: North-Holland, 1985. Chapter 22.

Bloomfield, Arthur I. *Monetary Policy under the International Gold Standard: 1880–1914.* New York: Federal Reserve Bank of New York, 1959.

———. *Short-Term Capital Movements under the Pre-1914 Gold Standard.* Princeton Studies in International Finance No. 11. Princeton, NJ: International Finance Section, Princeton University, 1963.

Calvo, Guillermo A., and Enrique G. Mendoza. "Petty Crime and Cruel Punishment: Lessons from the Mexican Debacle." *American Economic Review* 86, no. 2 (May 1996), pp. 170–75.

Cline, William. "How One Big Battle Was Won." *The Economist,* February 18, 1995, pp. 17–19.

Commission of the European Communities. *The European Monetary System.* European File No. 15/86. Luxembourg: Office for Official Publications of the European Communities, 1986.

Cooper, Richard N. "Economic Interdependence and Coordination of Economic Policies." In *Handbook of International Economics.* Vol II. Edited by Ronald W. Jones and Peter B. Kenen. Amsterdam: North-Holland, 1985. Chapter 23.

———. "Is There a Need for Reform?" In *International Trade and Finance: Readings.* 3rd ed. Edited by Robert E. Baldwin and J. David Richardson. Boston: Little, Brown, 1986, pp. 337–55.

Cottani, Joaquin A.; Domingo F. Cavallo; and M. Shahbaz Khan. "Real Exchange Rate Behavior and Economic Performance in LDCs." *Economic Development and Cultural Change* 39, no. 1 (October 1990), pp. 61–76.

Darity, William A., and Bobbie L. Horn. *The Loan Pushers: The Role of Commercial Banks in the International Debt Crisis.* Cambridge, MA: Ballinger, 1988.

de Grauwe, Paul. *International Money: Postwar Trends and Theories.* 2d ed. Oxford and New York: Oxford University Press, 1996.

Dunn, Robert M., Jr. *The Many Disappointments of Flexible Exchange Rates.* Essays in International Finance No. 154. Princeton, NJ: International Finance Section, Princeton University, December 1983.

Economic Report of the President, January 1993. Washington, DC: U.S. Government Printing Office, 1993, pp. 279–310.

The ECU. 2d ed. Periodical 5/1987. Luxembourg: Office for Official Publications of the European Communities, 1987.

Eichengreen, Barry. "European Monetary Unification." *Journal of Economic Literature* 31, no. 3 (September 1993), pp. 1321–57.

Ellsworth, P. T., and J. Clark Leith. *The International Economy.* 6th ed. New York: Macmillan, 1984.

"EMU: And What Alice Found There." *The Economist,* December 14, 1996, pp. 23–25.

Feldstein, Martin S. "Distinguished Lecture on Economics in Government: Thinking about International Economic Coordination." *Journal of Economic Perspectives* 2, no. 2 (Spring 1988), pp. 3–13.

Felix, David. "How to Resolve Latin America's Debt Crisis." *Challenge: The Magazine of Economic Affairs* 28, no. 5 (November/December 1985), pp. 44–51.

Fischer, Stanley, and Ishrat Husain. "Managing the Debt Crisis in the 1990s." *Finance and Development* 27, no. 2 (June 1990), pp. 24–27.

Frankel, Jeffrey A. "Recent Exchange-Rate Experience and Proposals for Reform." *American Economic Review* 86, no. 2 (May 1996), pp. 153–58.

Frenkel, Jacob. "The International Monetary System: Should It Be Reformed?" *American Economic Review* 77, no. 2 (May 1987), pp. 205–11.

Gil-Díaz, Francisco, and Agustín Carstens. "One Year of Solitude: Some Pilgrim Tales about Mexico's 1994–1995 Crisis." *American Economic Review* 86, no. 2 (May 1996), pp. 164–69.

Goldstein, Morris. "Whither the Exchange Rate System?" *Finance and Development* 21, no. 2 (June 1984), pp. 2–6.

Gray, H. Peter, and Sandra C. Richard. *International Finance in the New World Order.* Tarrytown, NY: Elsevier Science, 1995.

Hess, Peter, and Clark Ross. *Economic Development: Theories, Evidence, and Policies.* Fort Worth, TX: Dryden Press, 1997. Chapter 15.

"The International Monetary System: Evolution Rather than Revolution." *IMF Survey,* Nov. 28, 1994, pp. 369–72.

Kenen, Peter B. (ed.). *Making EMU Happen. Problems and Proposals: A Symposium.* Essays in International Finance

No. 199. Princeton, NJ: International Finance Section, Princeton University, August 1996.

———. "Organizing Debt Relief: The Need for a New Institution." *Journal of Economic Perspectives* 4, no. 1 (Winter 1990), pp. 7–18.

———. *Ways to Reform Exchange-Rate Arrangements.* Reprints in International Finance No. 28. Princeton, NJ: International Finance Section, Princeton University, November 1994.

Krugman, Paul R. "Market-Based Debt Reduction Schemes." In *Analytical Issues in Debt.* Edited by Jacob A. Frenkel, Michael P. Dooley, and Peter Wickham. Washington, DC: International Monetary Fund, 1989, pp. 258–88.

———. "Target Zones and Exchange Rate Dynamics." *Quarterly Journal of Economics* 106, no. 3 (August 1991), pp. 669–82.

Levich, Richard H. "Empirical Studies of Exchange Rates: Price Behavior, Rate Determination and Market Efficiency." In *Handbook of International Economics.* Vol. II. Edited by Ronald W. Jones and Peter B. Kenen. Amsterdam: North-Holland, 1985. Chapter 19.

Machlup, Fritz. *Plans for Reform of the International Monetary System.* Special Papers in International Economics No. 3. Revised. Princeton, NJ: International Finance Section, Princeton University, 1964.

———. *Remaking the International Monetary System: The Rio Agreement and Beyond.* Baltimore: Johns Hopkins University Press, 1968.

Machlup, Fritz, and Burton G. Malkiel (eds.). *International Monetary Arrangements: The Problem of Choice. Report of the Deliberations of an International Study Group of 32 Economists.* Princeton, NJ: International Finance Section, Princeton University, 1964.

McCulloch, Rachel. *Unexpected Real Consequences of Floating Exchange Rates.* Essays in International Finance No. 153. Princeton, NJ: International Finance Section, Princeton University, August 1983.

McKinnon, Ronald I. "EMU as a Device for Collective Fiscal Retrenchment." *American Economic Review* 87, no. 2 (May 1997), pp. 227–29.

———. *An International Standard for Monetary Stabilization.* Washington, DC: Institute for International Economics, 1984.

———. "Monetary and Exchange Rate Policies for International Financial Stability: A Proposal." *Journal of Economic Perspectives* 2, no. 1 (Winter 1988), pp. 83–103.

Nowzad, Bahram. "Lessons of the Debt Decade." *Finance and Development* 27, no. 1 (March 1990), pp. 9–13.

Peera, Nural. "The International Monetary System and the Less Developed Countries." In George Zis et al., *International Economics.* London: Longman, 1988, pp. 263–319.

Sachs, Jeffrey D. "The Debt Crisis at a Turning Point." *Challenge: The Magazine of Economic Affairs* 31, no. 3 (May/June 1988), pp. 17–26.

Salvatore, Dominick. "The Common Unresolved Problem with the EMS and EMU." *American Economic Review* 87, no. 2 (May 1997), pp. 224–26.

A Single Currency for Europe: Monetary and Real Impacts. Report of a conference organized by the Banco de Portugal and the Centre for Economic Policy Research in Estoril on January 16–18, 1992. London: Centre for Economic Policy Research, 1992.

Spahn, Paul Bernd. "The Tobin Tax and Exchange Rate Stability." *Finance and Development* 33, no. 2 (June 1996), pp. 24–27.

Stotsky, Janet G. "Why a Two-Tier Tobin Tax Won't Work." *Finance and Development* 33, no. 2 (June 1996), pp. 28–29.

Svensson, Lars E. O. "An Interpretation of Recent Research on Exchange Rate Target Zones." *Journal of Economic Perspectives* 6, no. 4 (Fall 1992), pp. 119–44.

Tobin, James. "A Currency Transactions Tax. Why and How." Paper presented at Conference on Globalization of Markets, CIDEI Universita "La Sapienza," Rome, Oct. 27–28, 1994. Revised version, January 1995.

———. "A Proposal for International Monetary Reform." *The Eastern Economic Journal* 4, no. 3–4 (July–October 1978), pp. 153–59.

Todaro, Michael P. *Economic Development.* 6th ed. Reading, MA: Addison-Wesley, 1996. Chapter 14.

Triffin, Robert. *The Evolution of the International Monetary System: Historical Reappraisal and Future Perspectives.* Princeton Studies in International Finance No. 12. Princeton, NJ: International Finance Section, Princeton University, 1964.

———. *Gold and the Dollar Crisis: The Future of Convertibility.* New Haven: Yale University Press, 1960.

Tsiang, S. C. "Fluctuating Exchange Rates in Countries with Relatively Stable Economies." *International Monetary Fund Staff Papers* 7, no. 2 (October 1959), pp. 244–73.

Williamson, John. "The Case for Roughly Stabilizing the Real Value of the Dollar." *American Economic Review* 79, no. 2 (May 1989), pp. 41–45.

———. "Comment on McKinnon's Monetary Rule." *Journal of Economic Perspectives* 2, no. 1 (Winter 1988), pp. 113–19.

———. "Exchange Rate Management: The Role of Target Zones." *American Economic Review* 77, no. 2 (May 1987), pp. 200–4.

———. *The Exchange Rate System.* 2d ed. Washington, DC: Institute for International Economics, 1985.

INDEX

DATE DUE

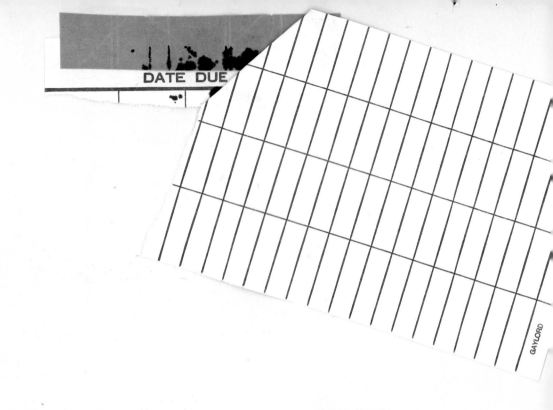

GAYLORD